INDIA AS A SECULAR STATE

INDIA
as a Secular State

By DONALD EUGENE SMITH

UNIVERSITY OF RHODE ISLAND

PRINCETON, NEW JERSEY

PRINCETON UNIVERSITY PRESS

1963

322.0954
S645i
98746

Printed in the United States of America
by Princeton University Press at Princeton, New Jersey

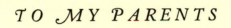

TO MY PARENTS

PREFACE

THE RELIGIOUS TEMPERAMENT and outlook of the Indian people may have been exaggerated by some writers, but it is nonetheless true that religion has been the most powerful single factor in the development of Indian civilization. Few would challenge Arnold Toynbee's characterization of that civilization as one displaying a "manifest tendency towards an outlook that is predominantly religious." In the light of this fact, the emergence of India as a secular state in the mid-twentieth century must be regarded as a significant political, social, and religious phenomenon.

That India is striving to be a secular state is remarkable not only in terms of the contrast with historic Indian civilization but also in contrast with the policies of neighboring countries. A quite different pattern has emerged in the now independent countries which were closely linked to India during the period of British rule. Pakistan, the new state which was created by the partition of India in 1947, later proclaimed itself an Islamic Republic. Its 1956 Constitution required that the head of state be a Muslim and forbade the enactment of laws "repugnant to the Holy Koran." Burma, which was a province of British India until 1937, after independence embarked on a course of extensive promotion of Buddhism through legislation and state patronage. The Constitution of Burma was amended in August 1961 to make Buddhism the state religion.

In both Pakistan and Burma these vital decisions, made by normal constitutional processes, were later reversed by military regimes with a more secularist orientation. But when functioning as free political societies, both the Pakistanis and the Burmese turned to the majority religion as expressive of the national identity and by constitutional recognition sought to make it a unifying and integrative force in the nation. Paradoxically, the majorities in these two countries profess international religions, Islam and Buddhism, while India has rejected an ethnic religion, Hinduism, as the basis for its national development.

Despite the very different policies of India's immediate neighbors, the significance of India as a secular state must also be gauged in terms of the very considerable prestige and influence of India among other Asian countries. While the idea of India's role as "leader of free Asia" must certainly be interpreted with important qualifications, there is a substantial core of hard fact which cannot be denied. As the largest and most populous non-communist country, and with stable government and democratic leadership, it would be surprising if India did not exert considerable influence in South and Southeast Asia. From this point of view, any major experiment undertaken in India, whether it be land reforms, five year plans, general elections with universal adult suffrage, or the development of a secular state, will have far-reaching implications for the rest of this region.

The secular state is important to the future of Indian democracy itself. It stands or falls as a basic and inseparable component of the modern liberal democratic state. The secular state is thus a fundamental aspect of India's democratic experiment, an experiment which might conceivably break down as much by establishing Hinduism as the state religion as by eliminating freedom of the press.

Despite the importance of this subject, no previous work gives a comprehensive picture of India as a secular state. Literally thousands of volumes have been written on church-state relations in the West, but none has dealt in any detail with the problem in the Indian context. Undoubtedly, it was necessary to allow some time to pass after independence so that the new pattern could emerge clearly. While it may well be questioned whether the pattern is yet completely clear, India's experience since 1947 has provided sufficient data to make the investigation both possible and useful. This book attempts to deal with the major developments through June 1962.

The problem of India as a secular state is a complex one. The rich diversity of religious life as well as the legacy of communalism and partition, the influence of ancient Hindu values as well as the impact of the West, the leadership of religious Gandhi and agnostic Nehru, the tendency of traditional religions to regulate virtually every aspect of life and the tendency of the modern state to do the same—all of these factors and many others are a part of the complex pattern. Problems frequently arise for which there is no clear parallel in western experience, which has contributed so greatly to India's political evolution in other respects. Indian solutions must be found for Indian problems.

As the table of contents indicates, I have sought to present a broad, comprehensive view of the entire subject, rather than to deal intensively with a segment of it. The chief emphasis is on the development of governmental policy in areas which require the interpretation and implementation of the principles of the secular state. In addition to providing the basic information on the subject, this study attempts to point out relationships, to define issues, to raise questions, to present an over-all picture of the implications of the secular state. It need hardly be added that the author does not have answers for all of the questions he raises. But most readers will probably be charitable enough to agree that asking the right questions is in itself a useful service.

I have not hesitated, however, to express my personal opinions on debatable issues, for that scholarship which ranges widely in the search for facts, but which then consciously draws back from a conclusion, does not fulfill its highest function. My point of view is that of one deeply committed to the principle of the secular state. My feeling is that this principle is so vital a part of modern liberal democracy that it is preferable by far to err on the side of a strict interpretation than to grow careless about it.

In a sense, the work on this book began in 1954 while I was in India doing research on Prime Minister Nehru's political ideas. The book which resulted from this research, *Nehru and Democracy: The Political Thought of an Asian Democrat*, published in 1958, contains one chapter on Nehru's ideas about the secular state. Since 1956 my spare time has been devoted to the present work. A year of intensive work in India, 1960-1961, enabled me to complete this book.

During this year, I benefited greatly from conversations with a large number of individuals. A few of those interviewed were Prime Minister Nehru, Dr. S. Radhakrishnan, Professor Humayun Kabir, Professor M. Mujeeb, Dr. Arcot Krishnaswami, Dr. B. C. Roy, Dr. C. P. Ramaswami Aiyer, Mr. Asoka Mehta, Dr. Tara Chand, Maulana Hifzur Rahman, Mr. Hayetullah Ansari, and Archbishop Thomas Pothacamury. In attempting to understand all points of view on the question of Indian secularism I was helped by conversations with members of the Indian National Congress, the Praja Socialist Party, the Hindu Mahasabha, the Jana Sangh, the Rashtriya Swayamsevak Sangh, the Bharat Sadhu Samaj, the Maha

Bodhi Society, the Muslim League, the Jamiat Ulama-e-Hind, the Jamaat-e-Islami, the Shiromani Akali Dal, the National Christian Council, and professors at the Banaras Hindu University, the Aligarh Muslim University, and the Jamia Millia Islamia. One of the most fascinating experiences was a day spent in the Gurdwara Sisganj in Delhi in November 1960 while the Punjabi Suba agitation was at its height.

I am grateful to Dr. Holden Furber, Dr. Katherine S. Van Eerde, Dr. Edward B. Hogan, Flight Lieutenant S. Krishnaswami, and Captain S. Ramanujam, all of whom read parts of the manuscript and offered valuable suggestions. For guidance and encouragement in other ways connected with this research project I am indebted to Dr. W. Norman Brown, Dr. Norman D. Palmer, and Dr. A. William Loos. A number of people helped me to obtain very useful material and in some cases translated it into English. Special mention must be made of the valuable assistance rendered in this connection by Mrs. Shanti Kacker, Mr. A. Venkataram, Mr. G. Channappa, Mr. N. S. Ramachandra, Dr. Earl R. Schmidt, Bishop N. C. Sargant, Rev. William Holder, Mr. A. Waheed Khan, and Mr. J. Balarajan. I greatly appreciate the helpful contributions of these friends to my research.

Grateful acknowledgment is made of the research grants-in-aid which I received from the University of Rhode Island during the summers of 1957, 1958, and 1959, and of the leave of absence granted for the year 1960-1961. The completion of this book in India was made possible by a Fulbright research grant, and I am deeply appreciative of the kindnesses shown by the United States Educational Foundation in India in helping me to carry out this project.

In 1960 the Carnegie Corporation of New York made a grant to the Council on Religion and International Affairs for a three-year research project under my direction on religion and the state in South and Southeast Asia. Arrangements were made to enable me to complete the present book during the year in India before actively embarking on the new research project. I am very grateful to the Carnegie Corporation of New York and the Council on Religion and International Affairs for making this special arrangement, and for making available funds for Mrs. Smith's travel with me to India and Southeast Asia. In a sense, the present book is the first installment of the broader study of the relationships between religion and the state in this part of the world.

Finally, a word of deep appreciation to my wife, Violet Ramanjulu Smith, who introduced me to the life of her native India and who has continued to lend encouragement and inspiration to my work.

D. E. S.

CONTENTS

xiii

CONTENTS

PART TWO

BASIS FOR THE SECULAR STATE IN INDIA

xiv

CONTENTS

PART FOUR

STATE VERSUS RELIGIOUS REGULATION OF SOCIETY

CONTENTS

PART FIVE

THE SECULAR STATE AND CULTURE

CONTENTS

PART SEVEN

PROBLEMS AND PROSPECTS

CHART

PART ONE
THE SECULAR STATE
IN PERSPECTIVE

CHAPTER 1

WHAT IS A SECULAR STATE?

An effective way of discouraging a hopeful reader is to subject him to a series of definitions in the first pages of a book. To devote the first half of a *chapter* to the matter of definition is even more deadly. Thus I am not unmindful of the risks involved when I do precisely that. One might wish that the definition of the secular state could be handled in a footnote, but the term is so little understood in its fullness that a more detailed treatment is demanded.

In this chapter I shall attempt to present, first, a definition of the secular state which will provide the theoretical framework necessary for the consideration of problems dealt with in later chapters. Second, in order to give depth and perspective to the discussion, the definition is followed by a broad historical survey of the development of the secular state in the West.

The Concept of the Secular State

The term "secular state" is commonly used in present-day India to describe the relationship which exists, or which ought to exist, between the state and religion. This in itself is sufficient reason for using the term in this book. In addition, the closest equivalent in Anglo-American usage, "separation of church and state," would be singularly inappropriate and misleading in discussing a country in which the majority religion is Hinduism.

The ideas which have contributed to the conception of the secular state were not produced in a vacuum, as will be shown in the historical survey later in the chapter. However, it may be well at the outset to indicate in general terms the historical orientation of the conception we are expounding. Three brief points will suffice to accomplish this.

First, our conception of the secular state is derived from the liberal democratic tradition of the West. It is thus to be distinguished from

3

the secularism of the Marxian communist tradition, which is motivated by an active hostility to religion as such. Second, while many aspects of our conception of the secular state are common to all the countries within the liberal democratic tradition, certain aspects constitute the particular contribution of the United States of America. Third, the conception here expounded is essentially that which can be derived from the Indian Constitution itself.

The working definition which I would suggest is as follows: The secular state is a state which guarantees individual and corporate freedom of religion, deals with the individual as a citizen irrespective of his religion, is not constitutionally connected to a particular religion nor does it seek either to promote or interfere with religion. Upon closer examination it will be seen that the conception of a secular state involves three distinct but interrelated sets of relationships concerning the state, religion, and the individual. The three sets of relations are:

1. religion and the individual (freedom of religion)
2. the state and the individual (citizenship)
3. the state and religion (separation of state and religion)

It may help to visualize a triangle in which the two angles at the base represent religion and the state; the apex represents the individual. The sides and base of the triangle represent the three sets of relationships mentioned above. We shall now proceed to examine these in some detail.

Freedom of Religion

This is the relationship between religion and the individual, a relationship from which the third factor (the state) is ideally excluded. Religion, as the word is used here, refers to organized religious groups and also to religious beliefs and practices which may or may not be associated with such groups. Freedom of religion means that the individual is free to consider and to discuss with others the relative claims of differing religions, and to come to his decision without any interference from the state. He is free to reject them all. If he decides to embrace one religion, he has freedom to follow its teachings, participate in its worship and other activities, propagate its doctrines, and hold office in its organizations. If the individual later decides to renounce his religion or to embrace another, he is at liberty to do so.

4

As noted above, the state is excluded from this relationship. The state cannot dictate religious beliefs to the individual or compel him to profess a particular religion or any religion. It cannot force him to contribute financially toward the support of a religion by taxation. However, there is a limited area in which the secular state can legitimately regulate the manifestation of religion, in the interest of public health, safety, or morals. Thus the prohibition of human sacrifices, to use an extreme example, would be upheld even though a religion might require such sacrifices.

I have thus far dealt with freedom of religion from the point of view of the individual. The collective aspect of this right is the freedom of two or more individuals to associate for religious purposes and to form permanent organizations to carry out these purposes. In the secular state, freedom of association for religious purposes is safeguarded as carefully as the individual's freedom of conscience. All religious groups have the right to organize, to manage their own affairs in religious matters, to own and acquire property, and to establish and administer educational and charitable institutions.

There are, of course, many other aspects of freedom of religion which could be considered, but the above paragraphs will serve our present purposes as a step toward the definition of the secular state.

Citizenship

This is the relationship between the state and the individual, and here again the exclusion of the third factor is essential. The secular state views the individual as a citizen, and not as a member of a particular religious group. Religion becomes entirely irrelevant in defining the terms of citizenship; its rights and duties are not affected by the individual's religious beliefs.

Many historical examples could be adduced to show how this principle has often been violated. In some cases citizenship itself and the right to vote have depended on adherence to the state religion. Dissenters were regarded as second-class citizens at best. In some cases discriminatory taxation penalized the religious nonconformists. The holding of public office and employment in government service has sometimes been legally dependent on religious affiliation. All such discrimination by the state on the basis of religion runs directly counter to the conception of the secular state.

We have now examined briefly two of the three component parts of the secular state. The first, freedom of religion, relates the individual to religion; the state is excluded from this relationship. The second, citizenship, relates the individual to the state; religion is excluded from this relationship. Thus the integrity of both of these relationships in which the individual is involved depends on the possibility of excluding the third factor in each case. And the only way this can be done is by maintaining a third relationship, separation of state and religion. For the closer the connection between the state and a particular religion, the greater the danger that (1) religious qualifications will distort the principle of democratic citizenship, and that (2) the state will interfere with freedom of religion, both individual and corporate. If we return to our graphic representation of the problem this becomes immediately clear. The two sides of the triangle maintain their integrity only by virtue of the third which separates them.

Separation of state and religion

The underlying assumption of this concept is simply that religion and the state function in two basically different areas of human activity, each with its own objectives and methods. It is not the function of the state to promote, regulate, direct, or otherwise interfere in religion. Similarly, political power is outside the scope of religion's legitimate aims. The democratic state derives its authority from a secular source ("the consent of the governed") and is not subordinate to ecclesiastical power.

Separation of state and religion is the constitutional arrangement which attempts to give effect to these convictions. Separation involves the rejection of the historical pattern of state churches. Some of the characteristics of the state church system are: an ecclesiastical department within the government, the requirement that the head of state be an adherent of the official religion, the appointment of bishops by the government, the use of public funds to pay the salaries of the clergy, etc. Aspects of the system which characterized earlier periods were the legal enforcement of religious conformity and the distortion of the rights of citizenship by religious tests.

A state religion may be merely a branch of the government and completely dominated by the state, a useful instrument of state policy. In other cases the state religion may wield the dominant power, and the state may be reduced to the position of being the executive arm of the church. In still other cases a fairly equal partnership may link the two. In any of these three forms the relationship is opposed to the principle of the secular state.

In a secular state all religions are, in one limited respect, subordinate to as well as separate from the state. As voluntary associations of individual citizens, religious groups are under the general laws of the state and responsible for the proper discharge of civil responsibilities (payment of taxes, maintenance of public order, etc.). In this respect religions are viewed by the state in much the same way that it views other voluntary associations based on common social, cultural, or economic interests. However, this minor qualification does not affect the essential principle of separation of state and religion.

Under the principle of separation, both religion and the state have freedom to develop without interfering with each other. Religious groups can organize, frame their own creeds and regulations, choose their own ecclesiastical officers, found their own educational institutions, and finance their own activities, all without interference from the state. Such organized religious groups function as autonomous entities, subject only to the general regulations mentioned in the preceding paragraph.

The state, on the other hand, is free from the financial responsibility of supporting an official religion, from the troublesome problem of deciding religious questions, and from the political meddling of vested ecclesiastical interests. The state is free to devote itself to the temporal concerns which fall within its proper area of concern, and with which it is equipped to deal. Separation of state and religion thus seeks to fulfill the ideal formulated by Cavour, "a free church in a free state."

The definition of the secular state in terms of three interrelated components—freedom of religion, citizenship, and separation of state and religion—makes explicit the essential elements which are only implied in other definitions. The problem is usually approached simply in terms of "church and state," with little clear recognition of the other relationships involved. But the secular state in the liberal democratic tradition surely means far more than the legal separation of state and religion.

The conception of the secular state outlined in this chapter is an ideal which is perfectly achieved in no country. The United States comes close, but there are still obvious anomalies as well as important issues yet to be decided. Any modern state within the liberal democratic tradition will have many of the characteristics of a secular state. The United Kingdom, for example, can be regarded as a secular state in many respects, although the existence of a state church goes contrary to one important part of our definition. Basically, what has happened is that the pressure of religious minorities and the growth of liberal and democratic ideas have combined to overthrow the more illiberal aspects of the state church system. In the United Kingdom there is today a very vital religious liberty and democratic conception of citizenship. The state church and the monarchy itself have continued to be venerated as forms which link modern England with the past, even though these forms are at variance with the liberal democratic ideas on which the modern state is built.

In stressing the total pattern of relationships as necessary to an understanding of the secular state, there is no desire to minimize the importance of separation of state and religion. It is definitely not a matter of indifference. The history of the past hundred years has clearly indicated a trend in the direction of church-state separation, and for good reasons. Separation of state and religion is especially important in the newly independent states of Asia. For while liberal democratic traditions have saved modern western states from the more dangerous historical implications of the state church system, these traditions have been but recently transplanted in Asia and in general have not yet taken firm root. The Asian state which adopts an official religion may thus be more easily lured into these dangerous implications.[1]

THE SECULAR STATE IN HISTORY

Having defined the secular state in broad outline, we may now turn our attention to its development in history. Our broad survey

---

[1] This point is well illustrated by the 1953 agitation against the Ahmadis, a dissident Muslim sect in Pakistan. The Ahmadis were hunted down as heretics by other Muslims. The inability of the government to deal effectively with the disturbances was in part attributable to a basic confusion over what it meant for Pakistan to be an Islamic Republic. See *Report of the Court of Inquiry constituted under Punjab Act II of 1954 to inquire into the Punjab Disturbances of 1953,* Superintendent, Government Printing, Lahore, 1954.

will attempt to point out the most significant events and ideas which have shaped the secular state in the West.

Church and state through the Middle Ages

The rise of Christianity produced a new set of relationships unknown to the ancient world, and led to the problem of church and state. From its inception Christianity recognized and taught a basic duality—the spiritual and the temporal, each with its appropriate loyalties. "Render therefore unto Caesar the things that are Caesar's; and unto God the things that are God's." The distinction between church and state in early Christian thought has no clear parallel in Hinduism, and certainly none in Islam. The early church, a small but increasingly well-organized religious institution in a vast and frequently hostile empire, could not be other than separate from the state.

Inevitably, the Christians' loyalty to the state came into conflict with their loyalty to God. They could not readily adjust their consciences to such mandatory practices as emperor-worship, and persecution by the state was the consequence of their disobedience. Under the Edict of Milan (A.D. 312 or 313) a great step toward freedom of religion was taken, with the provision that "liberty of worship shall not be denied to any, but that the mind and will of every individual shall be free to manage divine affairs according to his own choice."

With the conversion of Constantine, and under successive Christian emperors, the old relationships were completely reversed. Christianity became established as the state religion, and the faith which had once been persecuted, then tolerated, then granted equality, finally emerged triumphant and began to persecute its rivals. So in the year 346 the state, closely linked to the church, ordered all non-Christian temples to be closed and imposed the death penalty for the crime of offering sacrifices to the gods. But the emperors not only struck out at paganism and heresy they also convened and dismissed church councils. State interference in religious affairs was the high price paid for imperial favors to the church.

The partnership between pope and emperor, church and state, was at some points a mutually advantageous one. But at other points conflict was inevitable. The most important theory which sought to define the jurisdiction of each was that expounded by Pope

Gelasius I in the fifth century. His doctrine of the two swords implied the dual organization of human society—the church to conserve spiritual interests and to mediate eternal salvation, and the state to maintain peace, order, and justice in temporal affairs. Nevertheless, this arrangement could not be one of absolute equality. In his letter to the emperor, Gelasius I wrote: "There are indeed, most august Emperor, two powers by which this world is chiefly ruled: the sacred authority of the Popes and the royal power. Of these the priestly power is much more important, because it has to render account for the kings of men themselves at the divine tribunal. "[2]

Modifying the original idea of the two swords, the papalists later insisted that all authority, spiritual and temporal, was originally given to the church; retaining the spiritual power, the church handed down the temporal authority to be exercised by the state. But the original and ultimate title to all temporal power belonged to the church. The imperialist, or antipapalist, position was simply that both powers were handed down directly from God to church and state.

The discussion was far more than a theological debate; it was a manifestation of conflicting vital interests and claims to power. In 800 Charlemagne was crowned by the pope as the first head of the Holy Roman Empire; but in order to reject the inference of subordination arising from this act, he himself crowned his son as his successor. In the eleventh century the investiture controversy arose over the role of secular rulers in the choice of bishops. Emperor Henry IV, like his predecessors, did not hesitate to sell high ecclesiastical appointments to the highest bidder. Pope Gregory VII, on the other hand, claimed great authority for the clergy on the ground that the spiritual order was higher than the temporal; the pope therefore had power not only to excommunicate but to depose an unworthy Christian ruler. The first clash between Pope Gregory VII and Emperor Henry IV resulted in a humiliating defeat for the latter. Three years later, however, Henry marched on Rome, deposed Gregory VII, and set up a rival pope. The investiture controversy was temporarily settled by their successors, who agreed that the

[2] Sidney Z. Ehler and John B. Morrall, *Church and State through the Centuries: A Collection of Historic Documents with Commentaries,* Newman Press, Westminster, Maryland, 1954, p. 11.

pope should appoint bishops but that they should be invested in office by the touch of the emperor's scepter.

It must be remembered that throughout most of the medieval period there prevailed a conception of a universal Christian society. The church was viewed as something much more than the voluntary association of Christian believers it had been in the first century. The church was universal in the same sense that the empire (theoretically) was, for both included all men. The conception was that of two governments, each with its own hierarchy, laws, and jurisdiction, both ruling the Christian society.

At the end of the thirteenth century, the struggle between spiritual and temporal rulers took a somewhat new turn when Pope Boniface VIII clashed with Philip the Fair, king of France. The papacy was now confronted not by a theoretically universal emperor but by an independent king. Philip succeeded in imposing taxes on the French clergy despite the pope's objections, and went so far as to call a session of the States-General at which Boniface was arraigned as a criminal and heretic. This dramatic incident marked a decisive and permanent victory of state over church in the contest for temporal supremacy.[3] The rise of independent sovereign states produced a politically fragmented Europe which successfully challenged the papacy's temporal claims. The Reformation was later to intensify this fragmentation by the introduction of religious diversity.

One of the most influential thinkers to contribute to the idea of the secular state was Marsiglio of Padua. Living in the fourteenth century, Marsiglio defended the independence of secular rule as good and necessary in itself apart from its sanction by Christianity. He developed a theory of secular government based upon the conceptions of the Italian city-states. He conceived of the state as a self-sufficient and omnipotent community, with power to regulate the temporal concerns of the church much in the same way as it controlled agriculture or trade. Marsiglio, in his great work *Defensor Pacis* (1324) made a sharp distinction between divine and human law. Divine law is enforced only by the rewards and punishments which God will mete out in the next world. Hence no temporal compulsion can be used to enforce conformity in religious beliefs. Marsiglio clearly grasped two of the components of the

[3] John B. Noss, *Man's Religions,* Macmillan Company, New York, 1949, pp. 652-658.

secular state when he declared: "The rights of citizens are independent of the faith they profess; and no man may be punished for his religion."[4]

Marsiglio's plea for the abandonment of compulsion in religion was completely ignored. The spirit of the times endorsed rather the ideas of Augustine and Aquinas, who regarded heresy as the worst possible sin and crime, for which the death penalty alone was adequate. The papal bull *Ad Extirpanda* (1252) prescribed torture and the death penalty as the proper methods to be used in combating heresy. The standard procedure of the Inquisition was for members of the Dominican order to travel from place to place, trying and condemning heretics and Jews. The victims were then turned over to the secular authorities who carried out the sentences.

The Reformation: religious diversity and its problems

The Protestant Reformation of the sixteenth century, under the leadership of Luther, Calvin, Zwingli, and others, did not immediately introduce any new principle in the church-state problem. The church continued to be viewed as the guardian of the only revealed truth, but the center of authority was transferred from the pope to the Bible, as interpreted by each reformer. No new notion of religious liberty was expounded by the principal leaders. Luther indeed argued for freedom of conscience as long as he was on the defensive. But when he had made firm alliances with some of the princes, he did his utmost to persuade them that a government which tolerated heresy was responsible for the eternal perdition of souls.

The Protestant leaders assumed, as did the Catholics, that civic cohesion could not exist without religious unity within a state. This principle was translated into concrete policy by the Peace of Augsburg (1555), which produced a compromise between Lutherans and Catholics in the German states. The formula was simply *cujus regio, ejus religio*—whatever the religion of the ruler, that would be the religion of the state. Religious minorities were encouraged or compelled to emigrate to states professing their own religion.

The Lutherans and the Zwinglians thus tended to regard religion as basically an aspect of state policy. The state churches were clearly subordinate to the governments. This pattern (called Erastianism)

[4] Leo Pfeffer, *Church, State and Freedom,* Beacon Press, Boston, 1953, p. 18.

pervaded Europe after the Protestant revolt. Only in Calvin's Geneva did the theocratic pattern emerge, in which the state was undeniably subservient to the church.

The doctrinal and ecclesiastical unity of the Christian church had become a thing of the past. The territorialism of the Peace of Augsburg was one solution to the problem created by religious diversity. In France and England, however, the Reformation produced the phenomenon of sizable religious minorities which continued to live in these countries. This fact set the stage for the development of a conception of citizenship not dependent on a common religious faith. As Sabine describes the process, "Only slowly and under the compulsion of circumstances that permitted no other solution did a policy of religious toleration emerge, as it was discovered that a common political loyalty was possible to people of different religions."[5] This kind of solution to the problem, however, was generally repugnant to Calvinist and Jesuit alike. During the religious wars in France (1562-1598), this solution was advocated by a party called the Politiques, which was anxious to strengthen the monarchy and French nationalism.

The establishment in England of a church with royal headship was an attempt to continue the medieval conception of a church-state, but on national lines. In terms of the secular state, some of the more creative ideas which came out of the Reformation were the contribution of English dissident sects, Independents or Congregationalists, Baptists and Quakers. One of these ideas was a new conception of the nature of the church. The church, according to this view, was a voluntary association of like-minded believers grouped in autonomous congregations.[6] There was thus no attempt at all to identify the membership of the church with that of the state, as the Anglicans sought to do. Religion was essentially a matter of inward spiritual faith and experience, and freedom of conscience was sacred. The self-governing congregations managed their own affairs in every respect; their ministers were appointed by neither state nor bishop, but selected democratically by the members of the fellowship.

Closely related to this idea was another, namely, the essential separateness of the church, based on voluntary faith, from the state,

[5] George H. Sabine, *A History of Political Theory*, Henry Holt and Company, New York, 1950, p. 357.
[6] M. Searle Bates, *Religious Liberty: An Inquiry*, International Missionary Council, New York, 1945, p. 151.

based on coercive power. A petition presented by a Baptist to James I in 1614 stressed this point. "Kings and magistrates are to rule temporal affairs by the swords of their temporal kingdoms, and bishops and ministers are to rule spiritual affairs by the Word and Spirit of God, the sword of Christ's spiritual kingdom, and not to intermeddle one with another's authority, office, and function."[7] These ideas were later to be largely implemented in the New World.

The progress of religious liberty in England during the sixteenth and seventeenth centuries was frequently uncertain. Elizabeth's usual policy was nonenforcement of the laws against Catholics, but an act of 1605 not only compelled them to attend the Anglican service but to partake of the communion. Cromwell's constitution of 1647 granted full liberty to all Protestant sects but denied even toleration to Catholics. The great Act of Toleration of 1689 also excluded Catholics from its provisions, and their legal disabilities were not finally removed until 1829.

Significant contributions to the arguments for religious liberty and church-state separation were also made by individuals outside of the dissident Protestant sects. In John Locke's first *Letter Concerning Toleration*, he clearly expressed the idea that religion is outside the jurisdiction of civil government. But his toleration did not extend to Catholics or atheists. Locke's *Two Treatises of Government*, which became the Bible of modern liberalism, laid great stress on the individual's "life, liberty and property" upon which a legitimate government would not dare to encroach. Religious liberty was thus interpreted in terms of a broader theory of the state and society.

Many other factors contributed to the development of religious tolerance by the end of the seventeenth century: the essential stupidity of fratricidal religious conflict began to impress thinking people. A spirit of relativism was engendered by the very multiplicity of sects, each heralding its own version of absolute truth. The material destructiveness of religious strife in France was contrasted with the commercial prosperity of tolerant Holland. Toynbee writes of "the seventeenth-century secularization of western life," by which science replaced religion as "the paramount interest and pursuit of

[7] Quoted in Anson Phelps Stokes, *Church and State in the United States*, Harper & Brothers, New York, 1950, vol. i, p. 113.

the leading spirits in the western society."[8] All of these were contributing factors. But for the most significant events in the development of the secular state, we must now turn our attention to the
western hemisphere.

The American experiment of church-state separation

For the most part, the pattern of church-state relations which
evolved in the British colonies in America was one which had been
transplanted from Europe. This pattern was twofold: a close union
of church and state within a colony with but limited tolerance for
dissenters, combined with considerable religious diversity from one
colony to another. Calvinist Congregationalism was the established
religion of four New England colonies. The Church of England was
established in three of the southern colonies. In New York, New
Jersey, Maryland, and Georgia the established state-churches were
changed one or more times. Finally, and very important for our
discussion, in Rhode Island, Pennsylvania, and Delaware no single
church was ever established as the official religion.

The Calvinist Congregationalists (Puritans) who came to Massachusetts Bay in 1628 established a theocratic type of polity not
dissimilar to Calvin's Geneva. Although they came to the New World
seeking religious liberty for themselves, they were not prepared to
extend it to others. Both Quakers and Catholics were forbidden to
enter the colony; banishment was decreed for the first offense, and
death for the second. Four Quakers were actually executed. A new
charter granted in 1691 proclaimed liberty of conscience to all
Christians "except Papists."[9] In Virginia and other southern colonies
the established Church of England was largely controlled by the
state. Here too Quakers and other Protestant dissenters were subject
to varying degrees of legal disabilities. As in New England, the
Act of Toleration of 1689 improved their situation, but not that
of Catholics.

The colony of Rhode Island was founded by Roger Williams after
he had been banished in 1636 from Massachusetts for teaching
"divers new and dangerous opinions." Among these opinions was one
relating to the separation of church and state, and this principle was

[8] Arnold Toynbee, *An Historian's Approach to Religion,* Oxford University Press,
New York, 1956, p. 184.
[9] Pfeffer, *op. cit.,* p. 68.

made the foundation on which the new state was built.[10] The 1663 charter of Rhode Island decreed that no person "shall be in any wise molested, punished, disquieted or called in question, for any differences in opinion in matters of religion." Williams rejected as totally unjust the policy of taxation for religious purposes. In his famous pamphlet, *The Bloody Tenet of Persecution for Cause of Conscience*, Williams declared that "an enforced uniformity of religion throughout a nation or civil state, confounds the civil and religious, denies the principles of Christianity and civility."

Roger Williams was a Baptist at the time of the founding of his colony; he later became a Seeker. Another great exponent of religious liberty was a Quaker, William Penn, who founded the colony of Pennsylvania. The colony was a business venture as well as a religious experiment, and its success depended on attracting large numbers of settlers. Penn therefore advertised widely the promise of religious toleration, and many persecuted dissenters responded. By the time of the American Revolution the churches in Pennsylvania included German Reformed, Presbyterian, Lutheran, Quaker, Episcopalian, Baptist, Moravian, Mennonite, Dunker, Catholic, and Dutch Reformed.

The principle of separation of church and state received widespread acceptance during the last quarter of the eighteenth century. Numerous factors contributed to this acceptance. The multiplicity of sects scattered throughout the thirteen states was one of them. For if there was to be one official church for the new American nation, which was it to be? The success of the Rhode Island and Pennsylvania experiments in religious freedom clearly indicated an alternative solution to the church-state problem. Baptists, Presbyterians, and others regarded church-state separation as an article of faith, and agitated for it constantly in New England and Virginia. Deists and Unitarians opposed the "spiritual tyranny" of those churches which promoted their respective orthodoxies with the aid of the coercive arm of the state. Locke's ideas were very influential during the period of the Revolution, as well as the rationalism and skepticism of the eighteenth-century Enlightenment which came to America primarily from France. All of these factors worked together to reduce the dogmatism and fanaticism of religious groups and to

[10] Evarts B. Greene, *Religion and the State: The Making and Testing of an American Tradition*, New York University Press, New York, 1941, pp. 48-51.

stress freedom of conscience, which could only be guaranteed by church-state separation.[11] James Madison and Thomas Jefferson were prominent leaders in the agitation for separation of church and state in Virginia, and their efforts met with full success by 1786. Separation was achieved in the states, one by one, with Massachusetts the last to disestablish its church, in 1833.

But more important was the pattern outlined for the national government in the Constitution of the United States. The Constitution, ratified in 1789, contains no reference to God. Article VI specifies that "no religious test shall ever be required as a qualification to any office or public trust under the United States." In order to make the secularity of the state more explicit, the first amendment, introduced in the House of Representatives by Madison, was adopted in 1791. "Congress shall make no law respecting an establishment of religion, or prohibiting the free exercise thereof." In this pithy statement the principles of church-state separation and freedom of religion are linked together. In 1802 President Jefferson, in a letter to the Danbury Baptists Association, referred to the first amendment in the following words: "I contemplate with sovereign reverence that act of the American people which declared that their legislature should make no law 'respecting an establishment of religion or prohibiting the free exercise thereof' thus building a wall of separation between the church and the state."

Jefferson's "wall of separation"—a strict interpretation of church-state separation—was not acceptable to all Americans then, nor is it now. The appointment of Protestant, Catholic, and Jewish chaplains in the armed services, the tax exemption granted to churches and synagogues, the opening of state and national legislative sessions with prayer—all attest to the fact that the separation is not absolute.

Nevertheless, with relatively few exceptions the basic principles of religious freedom and church-state separation have been faithfully adhered to throughout 170 years of American history. It would be difficult to exaggerate either the inherent significance or the influence of this great experiment.

Church and state in modern Europe

Let us now redirect our attention to Europe and note some of

[11] For an exhaustive discussion of these and other factors, see Stokes, *op. cit.,* pp. 65-357.

the events and ideas which have contributed to the secular state from the early eighteenth century to the present. In England, both Roman Catholics and Protestant dissenters were excluded from public office, and Catholics were subject to a double land tax. Successive indemnity acts, beginning in 1727, removed the former disability from Protestants, but the granting of equal citizenship rights to Catholics did not come until 1829. Throughout the nineteenth century liberal and democratic currents of thought contributed greatly to the strengthening of religious liberty and democratic citizenship. Jeremy Bentham's reforms envisaged an equality in citizenship rights and before the law based on his utilitarianism and individualism. John Stuart Mill's great essay *On Liberty* became a classic statement of the liberal creed and buttressed freedom of religion.

The Church of England, however, has remained to the present time the established church. The bishops and archbishops, appointed by the prime minister, sit as voting members of the House of Lords. Some sentences of the ecclesiastical courts are still enforced by the state, and the church enjoys extensive properties and endowments protected by the state over the years.[12] The church was disestablished in Wales, however, in 1920.

Developments in France, on the other hand, led to a clearer conception of the secular state through separation of church and state. The Protestant minority, the Huguenots, were an important factor in this development. But strong secular influences were also at work. The eighteenth-century philosopher Montesquieu, in his famous work *The Spirit of the Laws*, forcefully attacked the notion that there ought to be religious uniformity in a state. Voltaire protested vehemently against the religious prejudice and bigotry of his day, and Rousseau rejected the exclusive, domineering type of religion which hampered the development of social cohesion based solely on citizenship. Despite these voices of protest, it was not until 1745 that Protestants were permitted to worship freely, and the death penalty for religious dissent was not removed from the books until 1762.[13]

The French Revolution overthrew the established Catholic Church along with the hated monarchy. In the Assembly of 1789 the revolutionary leader Mirabeau made the classic distinction between liberty

[12] Cyril Garbett, *Church and State in England*, Hodder and Stoughton, London, 1950, pp. 123-127, 148-149.
[13] Bates, *op. cit.*, pp. 193-194; James H. Nichols, *History of Christianity 1650-1950: Secularization of the West*, Ronald Press Company, New York, 1956, pp. 32-33, 38.

and tolerance: "I do not come to preach tolerance. The most bound-less liberty of religion is in my eyes a right so sacred that the word tolerance which tries to express it seems to me in some manner tyrannical in itself, since the existence of the authority which has the power to tolerate strikes at the liberty of thought by the very fact that it tolerates and that, therefore, it would be able not to tolerate." But the later excesses of the Revolution resulted in a bitter persecu-tion of Catholicism, in which thirty to forty thousand priests were sent into exile. Public Catholic worship was suppressed, and for a time a new cult of rationalism, with the worship of a goddess of Reason, was established by the revolutionary state.

The Restoration of 1815 returned to power the Bourbon monarchy united with the Catholic Church under the official device of "Union of the Throne with the Altar." Not many years later, however, a number of Roman Catholic laymen became deeply convinced that the union of church and state, so essential in the eyes of the French clergy, was in fact undermining not only individual liberty but the spiritual vitality of the church itself. Montalembert, Lamennais, and Lacordaire, distinguished leaders in the public life of France, declared in 1830: "Religion has need of only one thing, liberty. Its strength is in the conscience of peoples and not in the support of government. It fears from the side of the latter only their dangerous protection, for the arm which is extended to defend it is employed almost always to enslave it. Catholicism, by calling compulsion to the aid of the faith, would arouse against it the noblest sentiments of the human heart, which, especially in the matter of religion, is irritated by everything that resembles force."[14] Montalembert later epitomized one of the objectives of his thirty years of public life in these words: "Religious liberty, sincere and equal for all, without privilege for or against Catholicism, in a word the free church in a free nation."

After 1870 anticlericalism played a powerful role in French politics. Widespread resentment of the church's control over educa-tion was one of the important issues which eventually led to the separation of church and state in 1905. All state subsidies to the church were withdrawn, and the public schools were completely secularized. The reaction of the papacy to this decision was expressed in the encyclical *Vehementer* (1906): "In virtue of the supreme authority which God has conferred upon Us, we disapprove and

14 Quoted in Bates, *op. cit.*, p. 316.

condemn the law passed in France separating Church and State . . . because it is profoundly insulting to God, whom it officially repudiates by laying down the principle that the Republic acknowledges no form of worship." Although the Republic was forced to retreat from its original position regarding control of places of worship, the separation of church and state was for all practical purposes complete.

The separation in France had an immediate effect elsewhere in western Europe, and Geneva and several other Swiss states soon adopted similar policies.[15] From the unification of Italy in 1870 until Mussolini's Lateran Treaty with the Vatican in 1929, that country experienced a *de facto* separation of church and state. Although the present constitution grants to all religions equality before the law, it also ratifies the Lateran Treaty which recognizes Catholicism as "the sole religion of the state." The German Weimar Republic of the 1920's adopted the principle of the separation of church and state, although the states maintained their own religious establishments, and continue to do so.

The Netherlands, with its strong tradition of religious liberty, provides a constitutional guarantee of equality before the law and public aid to all religions, as does Belgium. Ireland in its constitution recognizes the special position of the Catholic Church, yet has successfully combined this recognition with its grant of freedom and equality to other religions. Canada, Australia, New Zealand, and South Africa have no established churches, and half of the twenty Latin American countries provide for church-state separation.

From the above survey it is obvious that, while the principle of separation has made impressive gains, there are still many countries where the state-church system prevails. We must remember that the secular state, as we have defined it, is not to be equated with church-state separation. For the secular state, it will be recalled, is a complex of three vital relationships, of which church-state separation is but one.

Church-state separation can exist simultaneously with flagrant denials of freedom of religion, as in Soviet Russia; this is *not* a secular state. On the other hand, a state-church system can exist simultaneously with broad freedom of religion and a democratic con-

---

[15] Adolf Keller, *Church and State on the European Continent*, Epworth Press, London, 1936, pp. 260-263.

ception of citizenship, as in England; this is in many respects a secular state. This is not to suggest that separation of church and state is unimportant. Church-state separation in the context of a liberal democratic state is the arrangement which most clearly, logically, and effectively preserves the values of individual and corporate freedom of religion and equal citizenship. Church-state separation is "the last consequence of the principle of religious liberty and of the neutrality of the state in religious matters."[16]

As we have seen, the secular state in the West has evolved out of many different kinds of historical situations; many different and even conflicting motives lie behind its development. In France the secular state emerged from centuries of struggle between church and state and was a victory for the tradition of anticlericalism. In the United States, on the other hand, the secular state was achieved with no hostility toward religion as such, and it has continued to evolve on a basis of mutual good feeling between church and state.[17] As we turn now to the problem in the Asian setting, we will find similar differences. The Turkish Republic secularized the state in a manner not unlike that employed by France; the secular state in India, on the other hand, is more reminiscent of the American experience.

[16] *Ibid.*, p. 243.
[17] Jacques Maritain, *Man and the State*, University of Chicago Press, Chicago, 1951, pp. 182-183.

CHAPTER 2

THE PROBLEM IN THE ASIAN SETTING

AS WE HAVE SEEN, the secular state is a principle which has developed over a period of several centuries of western political experience. In Europe and America it has emerged as an important aspect of the liberal democratic tradition. The secular state is, in origin, a western and not an Asian conception. This is not to deny the obvious fact that certain *elements* of the secular state, as we have defined it, have a long tradition in Asia. Individual freedom of religion, for example, has strong roots in the Hindu and Buddhist countries. But other elements of the conception have been totally lacking. For example, the idea that government should not extend financial aid and other forms of patronage to religion finds no support in Hindu, Buddhist, or Islamic traditions. Village self-government has a long history throughout South and Southeast Asia, but this fact certainly is not sufficient to refute the assertion that the parliamentary democracy which is now being experimented with in countries of this region is based on western conceptions and practices. Similarly, individual elements of the secular state can be found in South and Southeast Asian traditions, but the development of the whole integrated conception has been a western phenomenon.

The traditional pattern of relationship between religion and political authority in the countries of this area was one of interdependence. It was the duty of the king to promote religion—to build places of worship, to contribute to the maintenance of the clerical class, to use his power to enforce religious regulations relating to doctrine, ritual, or social observances. Religious functionaries were expected to advise, support, and help the king. Through coronation ceremonies and other religious rites in the royal court, the divine legitimation of his temporal power was effected, which provided the essential basis for the willing obedience of his subjects.

There were, of course, important differences in the religion-state

22

relationship depending on whether a particular kingdom was Hindu, Buddhist, or Muslim. There were indeed significant differences between one Hindu (or Buddhist, or Muslim) state and another. But the general pattern described above was common to the entire area. In some cases western imperial rule completely obliterated the traditional religion-state relationship. In other cases the absence of western domination (Thailand, Nepal) or the imperial device of indirect rule (the Hindu and Muslim princely states in India, the Malay states, and the Buddhist kingdoms of Laos and Cambodia) permitted the ancient system to continue relatively undisturbed.

As shall be seen in the next chapter, the Hindu ruler built temples and endowed them with vast wealth in the form of money, jewels, and lands. The management of the financial affairs of the temples was a normal part of the administration of the state, and in some cases the raja controlled the form of the ceremonies performed in temple worship. The king was the "protector of cows and Brahmans," imposing severe penalties on those who would dare kill a cow and according Brahmans reverence and preferential treatment in every respect. He was the final arbiter in all matters concerning caste regulations, carrying out the sanctions prescribed by the ancient texts where violations occurred. A Brahman royal chaplain advised the king and performed the sacred ceremonies deemed essential for the success of his rule.

The Buddhist king built and endowed pagodas and shrines, and was the chief patron of the monastic order. The protection of the purity of the Teaching was one of the important functions of the monarch, and the suppression of heresy was sometimes found necessary. When the monastic order became corrupt, it was the function of the king to discipline and reform it. In some cases new sects resulted from the monastic reforms implemented by the royal power. The Buddhist monastic order generally supported the authority of the king and instructed the people to obey him. In Burma, royal patronage of Buddhism was the most important basis for the loyalty of the diverse ethnic groups to the king.

Muslim rulers in South and Southeast Asia recognized their obligation to promote Islam through building and administering mosques, giving grants to individuals and institutions devoted to the study of theology and Islamic law, suppressing heretical teaching, and at times directing campaigns of proselytization. A special tax was sometimes imposed on non-Muslims, and Muslims were compelled by the state to fulfill certain religious obligations such as the giving of alms and attendance at the mosque. Doctors of Islamic law (in some cases headed by a Chief Theologian) had an established place in the court as advisers to the king, and during certain periods they exercised great influence over him.

The conception of the secular state, then, is western in origin and contains important elements which are opposed to traditional Asian conceptions and practices. The question which concerns us in this chapter is: What factors are involved in determining the relevance of this western conception to the countries of South and Southeast Asia? Can this conception be successfully transplanted to the countries of this region? We shall seek to identify the religious, historical, political, and social factors which help to explain why the people of a given Asian country are likely to accept, modify, or reject the principle of the secular state. Placing the question in this broader perspective will illuminate the problems of India's experiment with the secular state.

THE NATURE OF THE MAJOR RELIGIONS

Hinduism, Buddhism, and Islam are the major religions of this region. Although Roman Catholicism is professed by about 16 million people in the Philippine Islands (83 per cent of the total population), it will not be considered in this analysis. There are five aspects of religion which are particularly relevant to our inquiry; the first two aspects concern doctrine, the other three relate to organization.

First, the view of history taken by a religion, that is, whether human history is regarded as real and important, is a vital point. A religion which regards history as unreal, or if real, ultimately unimportant, may be assumed to be unconcerned with securing or maintaining temporal power. This should be favorable to the secular state. On the other hand, a religion which regards the proper course of history as crucial and central to its task in the world, is more likely to rely upon political power in order to influence history. The challenge to the secular state would be correspondingly greater.

Second, we must consider the attitude of a religion toward other religions. Since the peaceful coexistence of diverse faiths is basic to the secular state, the degree of tolerance shown by the majority religion to other religions will obviously be important. Widespread intolerance would make the secular principle practically impossible of realization.

Third, it will be important to note what capacity a given religion has demonstrated for effective ecclesiastical organization. A highly organized religious institution, like the Roman Catholic Church in the West, is in a position to confront the state and to make demands upon it. In general, the more highly organized the majority religion, the greater the difficulties which will be encountered in making or keeping the state secular.

Fourth, we must consider the historical traditions of separation or fusion of political and religious functions. It is obvious that if the traditional conceptions and practices of a religion support the idea of separation, there will be some basis for the building of a secular state.

Fifth, the extent to which a religion has tended to regulate social life will be significant. All religions prescribe rituals, ceremonies, and festivals which are important to the social life of their peoples, but some go far beyond this to regulate virtually every aspect of society, as in the caste system or Muslim law. The greater the degree of such social regulation by a religion, the more difficult it will be to implement the principles of secularism.[1]

We shall now examine the major religions of South and Southeast Asia in the light of these five points. It will be necessary to deal in broad generalizations in attempting to discern the principal implications of each religion for our subject. There are exceptions to practically every generalization which will be made in the following pages. However, they are generalizations in which many scholars concur, and are presented as rough guides for the exploration of this field of inquiry.

Hinduism: metaphysical tolerance and social rigidity

THE HINDU VIEW OF HISTORY. Hinduism provides a theory of cycles or recurring periods of creation and destruction. Each world system makes one complete cycle of creation and destruction, and this process has been repeating itself eternally. The present natural world

---

[1] Here, and in the rest of the book, the term "secularism" is used interchangeably with "secular state," except where the context clearly indicates that the reference is to philosophies or attitudes which reject religion in all areas of life, individual as well as social and political.

of human experience was created out of the combination of matter and spirit by means of the action of *maya,* the illusory cosmic energy of Brahma the Creator. The universal dissolution and destruction comes about when Brahma vanishes into himself. As S. J. Samartha puts it, "In the classical Hindu view history is not significant because it is swallowed up in the vastness of the cosmic process."[2]

Hindu thought holds that the essential self in man (*atman,* sometimes translated as soul) and the ultimate Reality are one. This doctrine, according to a Hindu writer, "emphasizes the fact that neither the empirical self nor the tangible phenomenal world, with which the empirical self seems to come into contact, possess any reality from the ultimate point of view."[3] Through original ignorance the essential self assumes individuality, and the permanence of the essential self is the basis for rebirth upon death. The law of cause and effect, *karma,* operates in such a way that one's lot in the succeeding life will be the moral consequence of deeds performed in this life. Liberation from the cycle of rebirths is reached by man's attaining complete realization of the nature of the self, namely, identity with the Supreme Being. The highest spiritual goal of the Hindu is escape from the cycle of history.

Hinduism regards human history as a lower level of experience, for the essential self of man is never involved in the affairs of this world of phenomena. How does Hinduism reconcile this metaphysical position with its extremely detailed regulation of individual and social life? Chiefly by its teaching regarding the four ends of man. The expression of man's natural instincts (*kama*), material prosperity (*artha*), and the ethical life (*dharma*), all pertain to the lower, empirical life. Spiritual liberation (*moksha*) pertains to the higher level of reality, man's essential self.

Hinduism's concern with political institutions and the course of human history is thus a secondary concern at most. This view of history is conducive to the development of a secular state. That is,

[2] S. J. Samartha, *The Hindu View of History: Classical and Modern,* Christian Institute for the Study of Religion and Society, Bangalore, 1959, p. 7.

[3] R. N. Dandekar, "The Role of Man in Hinduism," *The Religion of the Hindus,* ed. Kenneth W. Morgan, Ronald Press Company, New York, 1953, p. 121. This is not the only Hindu view on the subject. Some modern Hindu philosophers, most notably Dr. S. Radhakrishnan, are consciously reinterpreting the Hindu doctrines of *maya* and *karma* in order to give real meaning to the world and human history. This process of reinterpretation is well summarized in Samartha's pamphlet.

the ultimate philosophical and religious values of Hinduism do not require a Hindu state, or any particular kind of a state, for that matter. At this point the contrast with Islam is quite marked.

THE BASIS OF HINDU TOLERANCE. The remarkable tolerance of Hinduism derives basically from the belief that Ultimate Reality or the Supreme Spirit is without name, form, personality, or qualities. The particular name and attributes of any deity are regarded as limitations imposed on the Supreme Spirit by the weakness of man, who hungers for a god of love and mercy. The Vedic seer proclaimed, "Reality is one; sages speak of it in different ways." The doctrine of the chosen deity (*ishta-devata*) invites the worshipper to choose, from among all the gods conceived by man in the past, the one which best satisfies his spiritual longing. While this doctrine was originally applied to the numerous deities mentioned in the Hindu scriptures, there is no logical stopping-place, and the same tolerant attitude is taken toward other religions.

Hinduism thus holds that there are many ways, many paths which lead toward spiritual liberation. Historically it has convincingly demonstrated this belief. In addition to Jains and Buddhists, communities of Jews, Syrian Christians, and Zoroastrians settled in India and lived there unmolested. Muslims lived peacefully in India for three hundred years before Islam came as a military force in the eleventh century A.D.

Hinduism, unlike Buddhism and Islam, is not a missionary religion, and the rejection of proselytism on principle is regarded by many Hindus as an important part of tolerance. While Hinduism's tolerance is a strong point in support of the secular state, other aspects are not so favorable. Hinduism is an ethnic religion, the faith of one particular people, rather than an international missionary religion. India is the only home of the Hindus. As has been illustrated by Judaism in modern Israel, an ethnic religion may easily become closely identified with nationalism and national culture. The promotion of national ideals by the state thus tends to become the promotion of religion. This poses a more subtle challenge to the secular state.

HINDU ECCLESIASTICAL ORGANIZATION. What capacity for organization has Hinduism demonstrated? Has it succeeded in developing effective institutional means by which it can confront the state and make demands on it? The answer to these questions is an almost unqualified negative. In the first place, there is no congregational worship in Hinduism such as is found in Christianity and Islam. In Christianity the parish church is a center of organized religious activity and the basic unit of ecclesiastical organization. The lack of a clearly defined and trained Hindu clergy subject to the discipline of superiors is another point. The hereditary priesthood of the Brahman caste has not functioned effectively, and relatively few Brahmans today are priests by actual occupation. The clerical functions in Hinduism are performed by a wide variety of temple priests, pandits, astrologers, *sadhus* (holy men), swamis, *gurus,* and so forth.

The Hindu "clergy" is thus not organized for an effective political role, nor do the *sadhus* and temple priests enjoy the general prestige which would make for success in politics. Many people in India, not only among the educated, regard them as ignorant men of questionable morals. They are tolerated but hardly revered. This is in marked contrast to the veneration shown the members of the monastic order in the Theravada Buddhist countries by all levels of society.

While members of the monastic order (Sangha) in Burma and Ceylon have made their political influence felt, and similarly the Muslim clerical class (*ulama*) in Pakistan, the political expression of Hindu religion has only been through organizations of laymen. The Hindu Mahasabha and other communal political parties are the only groups which profess to speak for Hinduism on the Indian political scene.

Hinduism is divided into a vast variety of sects and subsects, although most of them could be classified as Vaishnava, Saiva, or Sakta groups. A reformist group founded in the nineteenth century, the Arya Samaj, is controlled through a central authority with power to enforce discipline. The Radhaswami sect has a pontiff. The Ramakrishna Mission is organized along the same lines as an efficient religious denomination in the West. Certain Lingayat subsects have "an ecclesiastical organization comparable in thoroughness to that of Catholic Rome."[4] But most of the sects do not have such well-knit organizations, to say nothing of Hinduism as a whole.

Commenting on this lack of ecclesiastical organization a British scholar wrote: "Hence Hinduism has never prepared a body of canonical Scriptures or a Common Prayer Book; it has never held

[4] *Mysore Gazeteer*, Government Press, Bangalore, 1927, vol. I, p. 143.

a General Council or Convention; never defined the relations of the laity and clergy; never regulated the canonization of saints or their worship; never established a single center of religious life, like Rome or Canterbury; never prescribed a course of training for its priests."[5] Furthermore, the writer added, Hinduism's failure to develop such institutions cannot be attributed to war, foreign domination, or any other external circumstance, but simply to the fact that "all such action is essentially opposed to its spirit and traditions." But Hinduism's failure at this point might well be a significant factor in the future success of the secular state in India.

There is, however, a negative consideration also. Hinduism's lack of organization renders it largely incapable of effecting internal reforms, however badly they are needed. The state has thus been pressed into service as the agency of religious reform, and its efforts to legislate various reforms of Hindu religious practice have to some extent compromised the principle of separation of state and religion. The same characteristic which precludes a major political role for Hinduism in the state, also encourages state interference in religion. On balance, however, this characteristic is much more an asset than a liability for the secular state.

RELIGIOUS AND POLITICAL FUNCTIONS. Hindu traditions give strong support to the idea that the functions of priest and king are not to be fused. According to the divinely ordained caste system, the priestly function belonged to the Brahmans, and rulership to the Kshatriyas. The Brahman was expected to advise the king, but could not himself rule without violating his caste *dharma*.

THE REGULATION OF HINDU SOCIETY. In contrast with its total lack of centralized ecclesiastical institutions, Hinduism has demonstrated a powerful capacity for the detailed ordering of social life through caste and Hindu law. Some reformist writers, such as K. M. Panikkar, have argued that Hindu social institutions have resulted from certain historical factors and "are in no way concerned with religion."[6] It is undoubtedly true that many Hindu social practices were non-religious in origin but were absorbed into the religious complex, rationalized by religious theories, and enforced by religious sanctions.

---

[5] W. Crooke, "Hinduism," *Encyclopedia of Religion and Ethics*, ed. James Hastings, 1925, vol. 6, p. 712.
[6] K. M. Panikkar, *Hindu Society at Cross Roads*, Asia Publishing House, Bombay, 1955, p. 49.

But the question of origin is of academic significance only. If for a thousand years Hindus have regarded a particular social practice as part of their religion, it *is* a part of their religion.

Panikkar chose to deny recognition to the traditional Hindu understanding of the close relationship between religion and social institutions because his real concern is not with the past but the future. His deliberate attempt to separate the two aspects of Hindu life is intended to strengthen the cause of radical social reform. But the fact remains that many Hindus still accept the scriptural analogy that the four original castes proceeded from the parts of the Creator's body, and that birth in a particular caste is governed by the inexorable law of *karma*.

We shall deal with this problem of the relationship between Hindu religion and Hindu social institutions in later chapters. For our present purposes, however, it is sufficient to make the general statement that Hinduism has included detailed regulations which have in large measure determined the pattern of society. Caste is not a "system" in any coordinated sense, but is rather the all-pervasive principle on which social life has developed. The social regulations of Hinduism have not emanated from a single central authority (as we have seen, there is no such authority), but they have nonetheless been effective in providing a pattern of social organization.

Buddhism: social freedom and ecclesiastical power

Our brief discussion here will deal with Theravada Buddhism, the principal religion of Ceylon, Burma, Thailand, Cambodia, and Laos. Buddhism as practiced in China, Korea, and Japan is of the Mahayana school and differs significantly from the Theravada in several points of doctrine and practice.

THEORY OF HISTORY. The Theravada Buddhist view of history must be examined from both the metaphysical and the practical points of view. As regards metaphysics, the Buddha insisted that all existence is impermanent, substanceless, and suffering. This fact is clear to the man of wisdom, even though others may regard the phenomenal world as permanent reality. All existence is in constant flux. All of life is a cycle of rebirths, and upon a man's death his consciousness flows on into another life. The law of *kamma*, cause and effect, operates inexorably to ensure that his rebirth will be the moral consequence of actions in the past life. The doctrine of *kamma* thus gives a moral significance to history, but the whole process perpetuates man's bondage. Freedom from the bondage of this cycle of birth, death, and rebirth comes only by insight into the impermanent and substanceless nature of existence. This insight has the effect of uprooting attachment or desire. Being freed from desire and passion, one's actions no longer accumulate the potentiality of *kamma* which perpetuates the cycle of rebirth.

As in the case of Hinduism, the metaphysics of Buddhism seems to assert that the course of human history is ultimately unreal, based as it is on impermanent and substanceless existence. There is no particular goal toward which history is moving, and the most important thing that the individual can do is to extricate himself from history.

The Buddhist's practical view of history, however, is in marked contrast with that of the Hindu. Although history may ultimately be unreal, it is not without importance. Unlike Hinduism, Buddhism has a founder, a historical figure. It is important to the Buddhist that the Buddha lived in the sixth century B.C., that he is more than a shadowy mythological figure like Rama. Theravada countries use a calendar based on the Buddhist era, beginning with the death of the Buddha (544 B.C.).

The Sangha, the monastic order founded by the Buddha, has maintained a historical continuity for twenty-five centuries. This historical awareness is well expressed in the words of a Buddhist scholar: "If there had not been the Sangha, the Dhamma (doctrine) would have been a mere legend and tradition after the demise of the Buddha —it is the Sangha which has preserved not only the word of the Master, but also the unique spirit of the Noble Teaching since the Master's passing away."[7] Six Great Councils have been convened throughout the history of Buddhism, the first shortly after the Buddha's death and the sixth in 1954-1956 in Rangoon.

Buddhism came into existence at a time when India had a highly organized society. Primarily a new individualistic doctrine of salvation, early Buddhism had no political or social philosophy. Under the Buddhist emperor Ashoka, however, the whole context was transformed. As the "established church" of the vast empire,

[7] Maha Thera U Thittila, "The Fundamental Principles of Theravada Buddhism," *The Path of the Buddha*, ed. Kenneth W. Morgan, Ronald Press Company, New York, 1956, p. 75.

Buddhism suddenly had a definite stake in worldly concerns such as politics. All of this seems to indicate that, metaphysics notwithstanding, Theravada Buddhism is capable of developing an impressive concern for the course of human history.

ATTITUDE TOWARD OTHER FAITHS. What degree of tolerance has Buddhism demonstrated throughout its long history? The attitude toward other religions is largely determined by the limited claims which the Buddhist makes for his own faith. Theravada Buddhism rejects the idea of revelation—it does not claim "to present through any form of divine revelation the whole truth of the absolute beginning and end of mankind's spiritual pilgrimage."[8] The Buddha himself *searched* and *discovered* the nature of the universe, and he invited others to engage in this search for truth by rational inquiry. The searcher is instructed not to believe anything on the basis of tradition or authority, even the authority of the Master himself. He is invited to doubt the teaching until he is convinced of its truth through his own reflection and experience. This experimental approach to religious and philosophical truth has predisposed the Buddhist to assume an attitude of broad tolerance toward those who seek the truth by other paths.

While Buddhism is nondogmatic and not based on any revelation of absolute truth, its adherents have nevertheless been extremely conscious of the uniqueness of their message. Buddhism has been a missionary religion ever since the Buddha sent out his followers to spread the *Dhamma*, a universal teaching which would bring enlightenment to all men. Buddhism differs significantly from Hinduism in this conviction that there is, after all, one known path to perfect enlightenment, and that the Buddha has discovered it. Within the Buddhist monastic order there has been a strong emphasis on the preservation of doctrinal purity, and rulers have from time to time intervened in order to suppress heretical elements in the Sangha, sometimes resorting to violent means. Buddhism is not as tolerant as Hinduism with the latter's constant emphasis on many ways, many paths.

Buddhism, nevertheless, has demonstrated a great practical tolerance of other faiths. From India it gradually spread over most of Southeast Asia and the Far East, but conversions took place only by

[8] *Ibid.*, p. 71.

persuasion. There is no record that force was ever used to obtain converts to Buddhism.[9] Furthermore, a liberal attitude was evidenced by the inclusion of many Hindu gods and goddesses in Buddhist ceremonies in the Theravada countries. In the Mahayana countries many indigenous deities have been accorded a place of honor within the system. Tolerance in Buddhism is not based on Hinduism's essential relativism as to the means of attaining salvation, but the path of the Buddha has never led to rigid exclusivism.

BUDDHIST ECCLESIASTICAL ORGANIZATION. The Sangha, or order of monks, is the institution founded by the Buddha to propagate the teaching. In most of the Theravada countries of the present day the Sangha is divided into two or three sects, but sectarian differences are very slight, reflecting historical origins and minor variations in practices. The Buddha promulgated detailed rules governing life in the Sangha—the internal government of the order, admission to the order, ordination, the duties of the monks, etc. A senior monk is selected by the members of each monastery to head their organization and attend to the details of monastic life.

In pre-colonial Burma, the king appointed one of the senior abbots as a kind of archbishop of the Sangha, and he was assisted by district "bishops." "This system did not constitute a genuine ecclesiastical hierarchy, however, for the clergy over whom it presided was an aggregation of individual ascetics rather than an organized church community."[10] While the corporate life of the Sangha in modern Theravada countries is most impressive, the ecclesiastical organization is not one based on a hierarchy of authority by which decisions made at the top could be immediately passed down a chain of command. In some cases, however, the personality and informal spiritual authority of the leading elders of the Sangha is sufficient to achieve the same ends.

The most highly centralized organization of the Sangha is found

[9] Hajime Nakamura, "Unity and Diversity in Buddhism," *The Path of the Buddha*, ed. Kenneth W. Morgan, p. 367.

[10] John F. Cady, *A History of Modern Burma*, Cornell University Press, Ithaca, N. Y., 1958, p. 54. For a discussion of Sangha organization in Thailand, see Luang Suryabongse, "Buddhism in Thailand," *2500 Buddha Jayanti Souvenir*, eds. Ananda W. P. Guruge and K. G. Amaradasa, The Buddhist Council of Ceylon, Ministry of Local Government and Cultural Affairs, Colombo, 1956, p. 64. See also Prince Dhaninivat, Kromamun Bidyalabh, *A History of Buddhism in Siam*, The Asia Foundation, Bangkok, 1960, p. 40; Kenneth E. Wells, *Thai Buddhism*, Christian Bookstore, Bangkok, 1960, pp. 7-11.

in Thailand. There are two sects in Thailand, the Maha Nikaya (Great Sect) and the Dhammayuttika Nikaya (Sect of the Followers of the Dhamma). Approximately 200,000 monks and novices belong to the former and 4,000 to the latter sect. The highest Buddhist dignitary of the kingdom is the Sangharaja (Ruler of the Sangha, or Supreme Patriarch), who is chosen by the heads of the two sects, approved by the ministry of education, and appointed by the king. The Sangharaja appoints a ten-man Council of Ecclesiastical Ministers headed by the Sangha Nayaka (corresponding to a cabinet and prime minister). Under the Sangha Nayaka there are four boards: the board of ecclesiastical administration, the board of education, the board of propaganda, and the board of public works.

It might be thought a weakness that the basic unit of Buddhism's ecclesiastical organization is a monastic institution. However, the Buddhist *vihara* has traditionally been a center of social life, especially in the villages. It is not the secluded and inaccessible dwelling usually suggested by the word "monastery" in the West. Furthermore, in all of the Theravada countries except Ceylon, laymen frequently spend some time in the monasteries receiving instruction in the teaching, and then return to their secular occupations.

The Sangha, then, not only commands the reverence of the laity but is organized in such a way that it can effectively mobilize public opinion. If the leadership should desire a political role for the Sangha, there is no doubt of its ability to fulfill it, despite the Vinaya rules of monastic discipline which forbid a monk's involvement in mundane political affairs. The political potential of the Sangha in Ceylon and Burma has already been impressively demonstrated.[11] The Theravada Buddhist countries will encounter special problems in attempting to secure or maintain the principle of the secular state,

[11] Organized associations of Buddhist monks, although not the Sangha as a whole, played a significant role in supporting S. W. R. D. Bandaranaike's Sri Lanka Freedom Party in the 1956 elections in Ceylon. The political power of the Buddhist clergy would still be considerable had not the assassination of Prime Minister Bandaranaike by a monk in 1959 discredited the whole trend toward political involvement. See W. Howard Wriggins, *Ceylon: Dilemmas of a New Nation*, Princeton University Press, Princeton, 1960, pp. 198, 342-348. Buddhist monks played an important role in the 1960 election campaign in Burma, giving powerful support to U Nu, who had promised to make Buddhism the state religion. See Kingsley Martin, "Nu's Victory," *New Statesman*, March 12, 1960. In Thailand the Sangha hierarchy is heavily dependent on government support, and government regulations have effectively kept the monks out of politics.

for the Sangha can easily become a vigorous pressure group demanding for Buddhism the place traditionally accorded it by the state. Organizations of Buddhist laymen can also play an important role. The All Ceylon Buddhist Congress, for example, with the support of prominent leaders of the Sangha, has had considerable influence in promoting the role of Buddhism in national life and in urging the government to do the same.

RELIGIOUS AND POLITICAL FUNCTIONS. There has been relatively little fusion of religious and political functions in Theravada Buddhism, although the separation is not as clear-cut as in Hinduism, where priest and king belonged to different castes. In a few cases, members of the royal families in Burma and Thailand gave up the yellow robe after many years in the Sangha in order to ascend to the throne. While the same person could be monk and king, the two roles could never be accepted simultaneously. The renunciation of the world required of the monk was incompatible with the temporal wealth and power of kingship.

BUDDHISM AND SOCIETY. Our last consideration is the extent to which Theravada Buddhism has tended to regulate the general social life of its adherents. At this point an interesting comparison can be drawn between Hinduism and Buddhism. In Hinduism there has been very little over-all ecclesiastical organization, but extremely detailed regulation of ordinary social life through the caste system and Hindu law. In Buddhism the reverse is true—ecclesiastical organization is relatively well developed, but the regulation of ordinary social life is minimal. In this respect the Theravada Buddhist countries may bear some resemblance to modern western countries, where religion is highly organized institutionally but has relatively little connection with the pattern of social life.

Buddhism originated partly as a protest against the caste system, and it has continued to pride itself on the absence of caste in the Theravada countries with the exception of Ceylon. There is no Buddhist law comparable to Hindu or Islamic law. The moral code to be followed by the Buddhist layman is a relatively simple one, centering in the Five Precepts—refraining from killing, stealing, unlawful sexual indulgence, wrong speech, and drinking liquor. As regards the prescription of ritual, "Indian Buddhism did not establish a system of ceremonies for family life comparable to those in Hinduism, nor have such ceremonies grown up in Theravada or

Mahayana Buddhism."[12] Marriage ceremonies are performed by the elder men of the family and are not regarded as religious ceremonies. Funerals and the tonsure ceremony performed upon male children, however, are religious ceremonies conducted by the monks.

Islam: decisiveness of history and all-pervasive law

ISLAM'S APPROACH TO HISTORY. Wilfred Cantwell Smith, in comparing the theories of history held by representatives of various faiths, arranges them in the following graded series: "the Hindu, for whom ultimately history is not significant; the Christian, for whom it is significant but not decisive; the Muslim, for whom it is decisive but not final; the Marxist, for whom it is all in all."[13] Hindu philosophy, as we have seen, relegates history to a lower metaphysical level and ultimately regards it as unreal or at least not significant. Christianity regards itself as rooted in history and as having as part of its mission the redemption of society as well as of individuals. But Christianity's consciousness of the failures and sinfulness of all human institutions prevents it from becoming totally absorbed in the present scene, and it looks beyond history for final redemption.

Islam cannot go as far as Marxism, for the Muslim (like the Christian) looks ultimately to God, and his endeavor to redeem history is derived from his faith in One beyond history. But it would be difficult to exaggerate the intensity with which Islam approaches its mission of establishing on earth a divinely revealed social order. Among the profoundest convictions held by the world of Islam are "that there is inherent in the structure of this world and its development a proper course, a right social shape; that the meaning of history lies in the degree to which these become actualized; and finally that they who understand the essential laws for these, and accept the responsibility involved, are entrusted with the task of executing that actualization, of guiding history to its inevitable and resplendent fulfillment."[14] In these vital respects, Islam approaches history with almost the total commitment of Marxism.

ATTITUDE TOWARD OTHER FAITHS. Islam is a religion of revelation in the broad tradition of Judaism and Christianity. The Islamic teaching, in the words of H. A. R. Gibb, is that "in Mohammed the

---

[12] Nakamura, op. cit., p. 398.

[13] Wilfred Cantwell Smith, Islam in Modern History, Princeton University Press, Princeton, 1957, p. 21.

[14] Ibid., p. 26.

series of Apostles reached its culmination and that the Koran revealed through him is the final and unchangeable revelation of the Divine Will, abrogating all previous records of revelation."[15] The exclusivist claims of Islam have thus largely determined its attitude toward other faiths. These claims have made Islam an aggressively missionary religion.

The Koran deals with the question of religious toleration rather unevenly, with statements ranging from expressions of broad tolerance to extreme fanaticism. In one text (V, 73), Jews, Christians, and Sabians are included as inheritors of Paradise along with Muslims, provided they believe in Allah and the last judgment and do good works.[16] In other passages they are classified together with pagans, and friendship with them is forbidden. In still other texts, Muslims are instructed to fight relentlessly against all other communities until they accept Islam or pay tribute. The system which was ultimately adopted was to tolerate the above three communities as "people of the book" (believers in a revealed scripture), but to disarm them and make them tributary. Strictly speaking, the very existence of other communities was forbidden.

The contacts of the West with Islam, from the time of the Crusades, have unfortunately resulted in the stereotype of the Muslim as bigoted and fanatical. There is much evidence to the contrary. Nevertheless, as we think of Islam in relation to our subject, we cannot avoid the conclusion that its general attitude toward other religions will continue to constitute a serious obstacle to the realization of the secular state. The same is true of several Christian churches and goes far toward explaining the resistance to the secular state principle in many countries of the West, despite the tremendous impact of secularizing forces.

ORGANIZATION; RELIGIOUS AND POLITICAL FUNCTIONS. When Mohammed and his followers moved to Medina in A.D. 622 he established an autonomous society, and it soon became clear that Islam was far more than a body of private religious beliefs. The Islamic community had most of the characteristics of a state, with its own system of government, laws, and institutions. This autonomous community was

[15] H. A. R. Gibb, *Mohammedanism: An Historical Survey*, New American Library, New York, 1955, p. 12.
[16] D. S. Margoliouth, "Muhammad," *Encyclopedia of Religion and Ethics*, ed. James Hastings, 1925, vol. 8, p. 877.

central in the very concept of Islam—its institutions were not mere appendages. Furthermore, it was a unitary society in which ecclesiastical and political functions merged together—in which, indeed, there was no significant distinction between religious and secular. "Mohammed ruled over his people as a divinely inspired and guided prophet. He led the public prayers; he acted as judge; he controlled the army."[17]

Upon his death a "successor" (khalifah, caliph) was chosen, who exercised similar authority. Successive caliphs delegated many of their powers to the vizier (prime minister), *diwans* (heads of administrative departments), the *imam* (leader of public prayers), and the corps of judges (*kadis*). But the power and prestige of the caliphate declined rapidly, and within the first century after Mohammed there was a growing cleavage between the religious and secular institutions of the Muslim community. The doctors of the Islamic law (*ulama*) refused to concede any spiritual authority to the caliphs. With the expansion of Islam and the inclusion of independent rulers within the faith, the state diverged more and more from the classical pattern. The Mongol invasions of the thirteenth century put an end to the historic caliphate of Baghdad. The Ottoman Empire later revived the institution (although in an unorthodox manner), and it continued until the Turkish Republic finally abolished the caliphate in 1924.

The *ulama* are in no sense priests; rather, they correspond to the "scribes" in Judaism. Strictly speaking, Islam has no clergy, as any Muslim may lead a congregation in prayer. Nevertheless, the *ulama* early took on the characteristics of a clerical class, and "acquired precisely the same kind of social and religious authority and prestige as the clergy in the Christian communities."[18] The *ulama* continue to function in present-day Islam as legal and theological interpreters of the Koran and Tradition. However the *ulama* are in general poorly organized and frequently disagree among themselves.

As we come to evaluate the organizational effectiveness of Islam, the evidence is mixed. In the past, tremendous concern for the organization of the community produced the caliphate of the classical period, which was truly theocratic in intent. The final elimination of

[17] Duncan B. MacDonald, "Islamic Institutions," *Encyclopaedia Britannica*, 1956, vol. 12, p. 712.
[18] Gibb, *op. cit.*, p. 77.

this institution left the *ulama* as the sole authoritative spokesmen for Islam, unorganized as they were and are. One writer commented: "The complete absence of Muslim religious organization has (to non-Muslim observers) always appeared to be the missing backbone for all Muslim activity."[19] Islam has yet to develop institutions which can function in a coordinated way within a modern society.

The argument which has been advanced in these pages is that the lack of effective ecclesiastical organization is generally favorable to the development of a secular state. It seems clear, as one looks at the contemporary scene, that the religion of Islam, if it were well organized, could be a much more significant political force in Pakistan, Malaya, or Indonesia than it actually is. It is arguable, however, that had Islam, in the course of its history, developed a hierarchical ecclesiastical structure, the possibility of separation of state and religion along western lines might have been enhanced.[20]

REGULATION OF MUSLIM SOCIETY. The minute regulation of ordinary social life has been accomplished by the Islamic law (*shari'ah*). This law is a total system of duties which fails to distinguish what modern jurisprudence would classify as religious, ethical, and legal considerations. It includes all branches of civil and criminal law. The *shari'ah* was developed on the bases of the Koran, tradition, analogy, and consensus.

As Islam spread beyond the Arabian Peninsula, it had to come to terms with the customary law of the new countries, which sometimes differed from the *shari'ah* in important respects. In modern times, statute law emanating from the sovereign introduced a further complication, so that two systems of courts have developed in almost every Muslim country, the one administering the *shari'ah* in private, religious and family affairs, and the other administering statute law. Despite these limitations, the *shari'ah* continues to exercise an extremely influential role in regulating the daily life of the Muslim.

In summing up this discussion of Hinduism, Buddhism, and Islam, it will be helpful to indicate our findings on the chart found on

[19] C. A. O. Van Nieuwenhuijze, "Religious Freedom in Indonesia," *International Review of Missions*, 1951, vol. 40, p. 97.

[20] As Professor Joachim Wach pointed out: "Conflicts analogous to those between church and state in medieval Christianity could not arise in Islam because there never was anything like a distinct ecclesiastical body, to say nothing of a hierarchical constitution." Joachim Wach, *Sociology of Religion*, Kegan Paul, Trench, Trubner and Company, Ltd., London, 1947, p. 310. It was *partly* the very conflicts between church and state in the West which led to the solution of separation.

ASIAN RELIGIONS AND THE SECULAR STATE

	HINDUISM	BUDDHISM	ISLAM
1. *Theory of history.* Indifference to history would make political arrangements like the secular state more acceptable.	History is metaphysically at a lower level of reality, and is ultimately not significant. +	Metaphysically, similar to Hinduism. In practice, history is taken more seriously. +	History is decisive. A certain pattern of life must be established on earth. —
2. *Attitude toward other religions.* An attitude of tolerance is important in developing a secular state.	Extremely tolerant philosophically, and generally so in practice. +	Missionary religion, but tolerant. +	Theologically intolerant, and often so in practice. —
3. *Capacity for ecclesiastical organization.* The more highly organized a religion, the more difficult to establish a secular state.	Practically no ecclesiastical organization. +	Relatively well organized monastic order, the Sangha. —	*Ulama* (doctors of the law) not effectively organized. +
4. *Political and religious functions.* Tradition of separation of these two functions supports the secular state.	Two functions performed by separate castes. +	Principle of renunciation of world—monks cannot rule. +	Tradition of Mohammed and caliphs—fusion of temporal and spiritual authority. —
5. *Tendency to regulate society.* The stronger this tendency, the more difficult to establish a secular state.	Caste system, Hindu law. —	No attempt to regulate society. +	Islamic law—detailed regulation of society. —

+ = favorable to secular state   — = unfavorable to secular state

page 40. The plus signs indicate factors which are favorable to the secular state; the minus signs indicate factors which militate against it.

We must emphasize again that these generalizations merely represent rough guides as to what can be expected. In some cases local influences have modified considerably the character of these religions. Indonesian Islam, for example, is different from Islam in any other part of the world. About 90 per cent of the population professes the faith, but the actual Islamic culture "forms only a top layer of Indonesian culture, of which the older lower layers—Hinduism, Buddhism, and Javanese mysticism—are often just as deep and important."[21] In recent years considerable anthropological work has been done which reveals the great importance of animistic beliefs and practices in the daily life of the Thai or Burmese Buddhist. Nevertheless, when due allowances are made for these factors, the generalizations are still useful in evaluating the prospects for the principle of the secular state in this region.

The Role of Religious Minorities

Almost as important as the question of the major religion of a country is the question of what religious minorities exist and their relative strength. For, as we have seen in chapter 1, religious minorities in the West have played a creative role in the development of the secular state. Until the Reformation, the church-state problem was largely a power struggle between Roman pontiff and national monarch (or Holy Roman Emperor, in the earlier period). The Protestant Reformation introduced the phenomenon of religious diversity, and the possibility of religious minorities within a state. While the Catholic minority in seventeenth-century England sought to secure religious *toleration,* the Baptist minority in New England insisted that the real solution had to go beyond this. Only by separation of church and state could differing religious persuasions coexist on a basis of equality, in a state built upon a secular concept of citizenship. Minorities have thus acted as catalytic agents in the

[21] George McT. Kahin, "Indonesian Politics and Nationalism," *Asian Nationalism and the West*, ed. William L. Holland, Macmillan Company, New York, 1953, p. 67. See also Clifford Geertz, *The Religion of Java*, The Free Press, Glencoe, Ill., 1960.

process of separating the respective jurisdictions of religion and the state.

The question of minorities is important in considering the prospects for the secular state in South and Southeast Asia. The presence of sizable religious minorities, sufficiently well organized and articulate, ought to make a difference. Self-preservation will require that they resist pressures emanating from the majority to give the dominant religion a special place in the structure and administration of the state.

Throughout Southeast Asia, the Chinese and Indians constitute the largest racial minority groups. Religiously, the Chinese frequently adhere to an ill-defined synthesis of Confucianism, Taoism, and Mahayana Buddhism. Of the total 165-170 million population of Southeast Asia, the Chinese represent about 11 million; roughly 1¼ per cent of the population in Burma, 2½ per cent in Indonesia, 20 per cent in Thailand, and 43 per cent in Malaya and Singapore. The majority of the Indians are Hindus, but there are also Muslims, Sikhs, and a few Parsis among them. In 1954 there were about 1¼ million Indians in Southeast Asia, mostly in Burma and Malaya.[22]

Several factors militate against the usefulness of these particular minorities in strengthening secular political life. For the most part they are unassimilated immigrant groups maintaining strong cultural ties with their countries of origin. Significant racial differences, in the case of the Indians, separate them from the peoples among whom they live. In Malaya there are sizable numbers of Chinese and Indian "Malayan citizens," but elsewhere most members of these communities are aliens. Furthermore, neither the Hindu nor the Mahayana Buddhist would be likely to have any strong convictions about the subject under discussion.[23]

Indigenous Muslim minorities in countries having Christian, Buddhist, or Hindu majorities (Moros in the Philippines, Malays in Thailand, or Muslims in India) might conceivably reenact the role described above. The Moros represent only 4 per cent of the popula-

[22] These estimates are taken from an article by Victor Purcell, "The Influence of Racial Minorities," *Nationalism and Progress in Free Asia*, ed. Philip W. Thayer, Johns Hopkins University Press, Baltimore, 1956, pp. 234-235.

[23] Hindu Tamils in Ceylon became concerned about the agitation to make Buddhism the state religion only because it was closely linked to Sinhalese linguistic and racial extremism ("One language, one race, one religion"), which directly threatened their interests.

tion of the Philippines, and their concentration in the southern portion of the islands in some respects increases, and in others limits their potential influence on national life.[24] Similarly, Muslim Malays predominate in the four southern, peninsular provinces of Thailand, and constitute approximately 3.8 per cent of the total population. The Muslim minority in India is of impressive size—45 million, or roughly 10 per cent of the total population. Psychologically, the Indian Muslim community has had to make many adjustments in the decade since partition. Despite traditional theology with its conception of the Islamic state, Indian Muslims have quickly realized that their future welfare depends squarely on the secularity of the state. Furthermore, there are Muslim organizations seeking to interpret and reinforce the secular state in India.

Christians are small but important minorities everywhere in South and Southeast Asia, except in the Philippines, where Roman Catholicism predominates. The largest Christian minority (in proportion to total population) is found in Ceylon, where Christians represent 8.8 per cent of the population. Christian minorities can potentially play an especially significant role for two reasons. First, as a result of greater familiarity with western thought on the problems of church and state, Christian nationals may well have a better grasp of the meaning of secularism in state and politics than their Hindu, Buddhist, or Muslim neighbors. Secondly, the Asian Christian churches are in general sufficiently well organized and skilled in the techinques of communication that they can make their influence felt. The great handicap under which the Christian communities labor is their former identification, in the minds of many, with western colonial rule.[25]

In August 1961 Prime Minister U Nu introduced in Parliament two bills, one amending the Constitution to make Buddhism the state religion of Burma, and the other (the State Religion Promotion Bill) seeking to implement this decision by providing for Buddhist instruction in state schools, strict observance of Buddhist Sabbath days, etc.[26] The minorities protested vigorously, although there was

[24] Chester L. Hunt, "Moslem and Christian in the Philippines," *Pacific Affairs*, 1955, vol. 28, pp. 331-349.
[25] See chapter 5, "Christian Minorities," in Virginia Thompson and Richard Adloff, *Minority Problems in Southeast Asia*, Stanford University Press, Stanford, 1955.
[26] For the text of the two bills, see the *Guardian*, Rangoon, August 1, 1961.

not the slightest chance of the bills being rejected by Parliament. Muslims, Protestant Christians, and Animists alike feared that the further identification of the state with the majority religion would adversely affect their interests. The National Religious Minorities Association was formed to oppose the state religion amendment; Muslim and Christian organizations staged demonstrations to protest the government's move. While the opposition was unsuccessful in this case, the attempt illustrates the natural role of minorities as guardians of the neutrality of the state.

To sum up, the presence of fairly large religious minorities of the same ethnic stock as the majority, effectively organized and articulate, will be an important factor in the development of the secular state. We may note in passing that India, with her numerous and sizable minorities (Muslims, Christians, Sikhs, Jains, etc.), compares favorably with other countries of the region in this regard.

THE COLONIAL BACKGROUND

In this section our concern is with the religious policies evolved by the western colonial powers in South and Southeast Asia. With the exception of Thailand and Nepal, all of the countries of this region were colonial areas until the present postwar period. The prospects for the secular state in independent Asia cannot be judged without reference to the patterns of religion-state relations which were evolved during the colonial period. We shall now survey briefly the religious policies of American, British, French, and Dutch colonial administrations in this region.

American separation of church and state in the Philippines

The colonial record of the United States in the Philippines (1899-1946) provides the clearest example of an imperial power deliberately undertaking to establish a secular state. The American administration succeeded three centuries of Spanish rule, in which the connection between the government and the Roman Catholic Church was apparently even more intimate than in Spain. Spanish friars—Augustinians, Franciscans, Jesuits, Dominicans, and others—"watched over the meetings of municipal councils, gave decisions on questions of public works, supervised the police, the prisons, and charities, and censored the theater."[27] The public schools were completely under

[27] Paul H. Clyde, *The Far East: A History of the Impact of the West on Eastern Asia*, Prentice-Hall, New York, 1952, p. 280.

ecclesiastical control, and the real political power of the archbishop of Manila was said to be equal to that of the governor-general.

Nationalist Filipino revolts in the years preceding the Spanish-American War were aimed as much at the domination of the friars, who owned 400,000 acres of the best farm lands, as at the civil government. Public opinion was thus well prepared for the establishment of the American principle of separation of church and state. The policy of the new government was clearly indicated in the instructions given by President McKinley to the second Philippine Commission: "the separation between state and church shall be real, entire and absolute."[28]

The Organic Act of the Philippine Islands of 1902 included the following section: "That no law shall be made respecting an establishment of religion or prohibiting the free exercise thereof, and that the free exercise and enjoyment of religious profession and worship, without discrimination or preference, shall forever be allowed." The wording of the first half of this section is almost identical with that found in the First Amendment of the American Constitution. The Organic Act of 1916 (sec. 3) repeated the above provision and went on to specify that no religious test should be required for the exercise of civil or political rights, and that no public funds should be used for any religious institution. The Constitution of the Philippines, drafted by the Filipinos in 1934, incorporated all of the above-mentioned provisions.[29]

The public school system established early in the twentieth century by American administrators was secular. Teachers were strictly forbidden to deal in any way with religion in the classroom, although arrangements were permitted whereby priests or ministers could give religious instruction for one-half hour three times a week. Essentially, American colonial policy regarding religion involved a rather simple transference of principles already well established in the homeland.

British religious neutrality in India

This subject is considered in some detail in the next chapter, so that only a few sentences need be devoted to it here for comparative purposes. The basic policy which the British evolved in the eighteenth and nineteenth centuries was that of "religious neutrality." However,

[28] Joseph R. Hayden, *The Philippines: A Study in National Development*, Macmillan Company, New York, 1942, p. 562.
[29] *Ibid.*, p. 932.

there were various kinds of involvements in religious affairs which produced a somewhat confused interpretation of this simple phrase.

During certain periods in the eighteenth and nineteenth centuries, grants of money were given by the British government for the support of Hindu temples and Muslim mosques, and Christian missionaries were actively discouraged. Under other officials, missionary work was vigorously promoted, and in 1813 Parliament established a legal connection between the government of India and the Church of England. The administration was in general fair, impartial, and secular. By the end of the nineteenth century most educated Indians would have been willing to concede that, despite its partial denial in outward forms, the vital aspect of the principle of religious neutrality was being faithfully adhered to.

French secularism and anticlericalism in Indo-China

French interest in Indo-China began in the seventeenth century with the formation, under Jesuit leadership, of the Society of Foreign Missions. Missionary work prospered despite outbursts of persecution by native rulers. Almost all of the Roman Catholic missionaries were French citizens, and this fact constituted the ground for military intervention by the French government when the persecution became intense during the 1850's.[30] Conquest followed intervention, and by the end of the nineteenth century France had created a centralized administration for the colony of Cochin-China and the protectorates of Tongkin, Annam, Cambodia, and Laos.

During the earlier period of French rule, many of the military and civil officers were of the nobility, the traditional ally of the church, and official policy favored the missionaries. The mission acquired great tracts of agricultural land and built its churches, schools, and hospitals. Its tremendous economic power as landowner, together with its closeness to and influence over native Christians, later brought the mission into open rivalry with the civil government. During the Third Republic, which came into existence in 1875, French anticlericalism often asserted itself in the colonial administration with an active hostility toward the church.

The mission at times applied pressure on the government to favor

[30] D. G. E. Hall, *A History of Southeast Asia,* St Martin's Press, New York, 1955, pp. 556-560.

native Christians in making appointments and to exempt Christian villages from taxation. Showing no reluctance to engage in direct political activity, the mission "took active steps to get the Emperor of Annam deposed in 1891, and to substitute for him a prince, one of their converts, who would exercise pressure on his compatriots to turn Catholic."[31] However, this political interference was vehemently resisted by the more anticlerical governors-general. Under one of them, Bert, the policy of taxing church property on an equal basis with other private property was initiated. Many of the highest colonial officials were Freemasons, and they waged intensive press campaigns against the mission. Under Governor-General Beau the schools were laicized and nursing nuns removed from the hospitals.

The separation of church and state in France in 1905 confirmed secular colonial policies. By the time of the First World War, however, the bitterness in church-state relations had largely disappeared, although the same secular policies were continued by the administration. In the 1930's the government dealt heavy blows to mission prestige by becoming the patron of Theravada Buddhism in Cambodia and Laos. As a part of the French policy to revive the cultural heritage of these peoples, a Buddhist Institute was founded in Luang-Prabang for the training of monks.[32] French policy in Indo-China in general reflected the church-state relations of the homeland, and evolved a secular, religiously neutral administration.

The Dutch established church in Indonesia

The policy of the Dutch was based upon their historic preference for the established church. The official Protestant Church in the Netherlands East Indies was subsidized to the extent of five-sixths of its total church budget, and its ministers were for many years classified as civil servants. It was not until 1934 that the Protestant Church received its entire administrative freedom from governmental control.[33] The Roman Catholic Church also received generous stipends from public funds for the support of its clergy. The government did not subsidize the evangelizing activities of missionaries, however. The close connection between church and state was periodically de-

[31] Virginia Thompson, *French Indo-China*, Macmillan Company, New York, 1937, p. 272.
[32] *Ibid.*, pp. 356, 379.
[33] M. Searle Bates, *Religious Liberty: An Inquiry*, International Missionary Council, New York, 1945, pp. 122-123.

cried by religious leaders as well as by secularists. Attempts to separate the church and state dated back as far as 1864, but were unsuccessful because of the tremendous financial dependence of the state church.[34]

The Dutch policy was one of impartiality and non-interference as far as Islam was concerned. There was no general financial aid extended, although occasionally grants were made for the construction of mosques. All private educational institutions, Muslim as well as Protestant or Catholic, were eligible to receive generous grants-in-aid from the government provided they met certain educational standards. All religious groups were permitted to provide religious instruction for an hour or two a week for pupils of their respective faiths in the public schools.

We have sketched here in bare outline the religious policies evolved by four imperial powers—the United States, Great Britain, France, and the Netherlands. Let us now evaluate these respective colonial administrations in terms of the degree to which they strengthened the principle of the secular state. United States policy in the Philippines involved a relatively simple transplanting of the clear-cut American doctrine of separation of church and state, and was highly successful from this point of view. Dutch policy in Indonesia must be ranked last, for it included regular and heavy subsidies to the state church (and also to the Roman Catholic Church) and very little to the faith professed by 90 per cent of the population. Somewhere between the American and Dutch policies, we would rank the British and the French. The British administration was in general religiously neutral, but this was to some degree offset by the institutional connection between the government of India and the Church of England. French policy in Indo-China was complicated by the fact that the Catholic mission antedated the civil government, and had built up great temporal power. The secular nature of the French administration was occasionally marked by bitter anticlericalism, which was also a departure from the ideal of religious neutrality.

THE PATTERN OF NATIONALISM

In order to evaluate the prospects for secularism in South and Southeast Asia, we must consider not only the legacy of colonial

[34] J. S. Furnivall, *Netherlands India: A Study of Plural Economy*, Macmillan Company, New York, 1944, p. 380.

policies but also the patterns of nationalism which evolved in opposition to western imperialism. What was the role of religion in the development of the various nationalist movements? A nationalism imbued with the spirit of militant religious revivalism is not likely to lead to a secular independent state.

A study of Asian nationalist movements indicates that the degree of religious orientation varied greatly from country to country. It is not possible to go into a detailed discussion of the religious aspect of each nationalist movement, but a few paragraphs may serve to illustrate the point.

Buddhism in Burmese and Ceylonese nationalism

As we approach the study of Buddhist involvement in nationalist movements, we recognize immediately the considerable departure from the implications of its view of history discussed above. (The same is true of Hindu nationalism.) Shortly after the first Anglo-Burmese War a very matter-of-fact British officer concluded that Buddhism was definitely not a fighting religion, and would be of little use as a focal point of resistance to western aggression.[35] Proceeding logically from the philosophical tenets of Buddhism, his analysis was sound, but the course of subsequent history has proved him at least partly wrong. Despite the fact that, as D. T. Niles put it, "race, nation and history are outside the Buddhist circle of explanation," resurgent Buddhism has demonstrated its ability to serve as a powerful ally of various political movements.[36]

Burma's Buddhist monks (*pongyis*) were responsible for the first stirring of nationalist sentiment in the early years of this century. Concerned originally with Burma's cultural and religious revival, the monks founded numerous Young Men's Buddhist Associations, which soon developed definite political interests. After the First World War the associations were welded into the General Council of Buddhist Associations (GCBA), which made home rule its minimum demand. A rallying point of Buddhist nationalism was the fact that British policy tended to push the village monastic schools into the background by establishing secular government schools and by granting financial assistance to missionary institu-

[35] U Ba Nyunt, "Commentary," *Nationalism and Progress in Free Asia*, p. 49.
[36] Quoted in S. Kulandran, *Resurgent Religions*, Lutterworth Press, London, 1957, p. 25.

tions. Aggressive *pongyis* of the GCBA were active in the Saya San rebellion of 1930-1931 which was directed primarily at the Indian Chettyar money-lenders, but also at the British power. The political influence of the monks was strong right up to the Second World War. They were not prominent, however, in the decisive final struggles against the Japanese and then the British.[37]

In Ceylon the pattern of nationalism was quite different, and followed a much more moderate course. Buddhist revival was indeed one lesser aspect of the nationalist movement, but it was the politicians, not the monks, who provided the leadership. Furthermore, among the significant contributors to Ceylonese nationalism were Hindu Tamils, such as Sir Ponnambalam Arunachalam and Sir Ponnambalam Ramanathan. Ceylonese nationalism never became a mass movement as in India under Gandhi's leadership; its course was directed by the westernized elite whose ideology and values were rooted in nineteenth-century liberalism.

Islam in Indonesian nationalism

In Indonesia, religion provided the same initial impetus to nationalism, and at about the same time, as in Burma. "The Mohammedan religion provided the earliest channel of development of modern, mature Indonesian nationalism."[38] Indonesian students at Cairo during the first decades of this century were profoundly influenced by the modernist teachings of Mohammed Abduh, who called for a purified Islam willing to face the challenges of modern science and the West.

In 1912 the *Sarekat Islam* (Islamic Association) was founded, and seven years later its membership reached almost 2,500,000. It later became the Indonesian Islamic Association Party and engaged in an intense struggle with the Indonesian Communist Party for domination of the nationalist movement. In the late 1920's and the early 1930's its influence declined, and secular non-communist nationalists like Sukarno and Hatta assumed a dominant role in the move-

[37] Maung Maung, *Burma in the Family of Nations*, Djambatan, Amsterdam, 1956, pp. 80-82; William L. Holland, *op. cit.*, pp. 33-34; John F. Cady, "Religion and Politics in Modern Burma," *Far Eastern Quarterly*, 1953, vol. 12, pp. 149-162.

[38] George McT. Kahin, "Indonesian Politics and Nationalism," *Asian Nationalism and the West*, p. 73. See also Amry Vandenbosch, "Nationalism and Religion in Indonesia," *Far Eastern Survey*, December 17, 1952.

ment. With the proclamation of Indonesian independence in 1945, Islamic ideology again assumed an important political role, chiefly through the *Masjumi* (Council of Indonesia Muslim Associations) and offshoot parties. In addition, the Darul Islam movement in western Java set up a theocratic Islamic state in 1948, enjoyed several years of effective terrorist power, and has still not been brought under complete control by the Indonesian army.

Religion in Indian nationalism and the Pakistan movement

The role of Hinduism in the Indian nationalist movement will be considered in some detail in the next chapter. The Indian National Congress, founded in 1885, reflected principally the values of Victorian liberalism, but for a few years early in this century it came under the control of the Extremists with their Hindu revivalist emphasis. In 1920 leadership of the nationalist movement was assumed by Gandhi. While his personal philosophy and techniques of political action were unmistakably Hindu, he strove unceasingly to promote Hindu-Muslim unity. Jawaharlal Nehru and others influenced by socialist ideology gave powerful support to the ideal of secular nationalism. Despite occasional lapses in practice, this ideal was the dominant one in the Congress movement, and it continues to be an important foundation stone of the secular state in India.

The demand for Pakistan, on the other hand, was explicitly based on M. A. Jinnah's "two-nation theory," according to which Hindus and Muslims in India represented two distinct and incompatible civilizations. It was to enable the adherents of Islam to forge their own political destiny that the subcontinent was partitioned in 1947, and this basic fact continues to obstruct the path of those Pakistanis who would like to see the development of their country along modern secular lines. The involvement of Islam in the creation of Pakistan, in one way or another, is a historical fact which made almost inevitable the attempt to establish an Islamic state, however this term might be defined.

The pattern of nationalism, then, varied greatly among the countries of South and Southeast Asia. It ranged from Ceylonese nationalism, in which religion played a relatively small part, to the demand for Pakistan, in which religion provided the essential *raison d'être* of the movement.

These, then, are the four key factors which have a bearing upon the future of secularism in politics in South and Southeast Asia: the nature of the major religion, the role of religious minorities, the colonial background, and the pattern of nationalism. India's prospects for maintaining and strengthening her position as a secular state would appear to be relatively good, on the basis of this analysis. As we have seen, the majority religion, Hinduism, has characteristics which are in general conducive to the secular state. The large Muslim minority, the much smaller but well organized and articulate Christian minority, and others, may well be powerful deterrents to any departure from the principle of secularism. The British colonial policy of religious neutrality, although not without ambiguities, provided an essentially secular foundation for government. The last years of the Indian nationalist movement, which culminated in independence, saw the emergence of strong secularist leadership in the person of Jawaharlal Nehru, although Gandhian nonexclusivist Hindu philosophy also played a major role.

But a discussion of the problems of applying the idea of secularism in Asia would be very incomplete without at least a brief treatment of the first conscious endeavor of a free Asian country to become a secular state. For, a full twenty-five years before the secular Indian Constitution was adopted, the Turkish Republic made such an attempt, and largely succeeded.

Turkey as a Secular State

The emergence of Turkey in the 1920's as a secular state was remarkable in every respect. Three of the four factors relating to the applicability of secularism, in the analysis above, were unfavorable in the case of Turkey. The last factor, however, was of such tremendous power that it swept the field. The major religion was and is Islam, the most difficult faith to adjust to a secular state. The non-Muslim minorities were composed of ethnically distinct Jews, Armenians, and Greeks, many of whom supported the European enemies of the Turkish Republic and had no part in the movement to secularize the state. Turkey never came under western colonial rule, and hence did not receive whatever benefits could have been derived from British or French tutelage in religious neutrality.

The pattern of nationalism, however, was clearly one which looked to the West. Turkey's geographical proximity to Europe, and, indeed, the European dominions of the Ottoman Empire, facilitated the western impact. Western-trained military and naval officers, exiled Turks living in Paris, London, and Geneva, as well as European cultural influences within Turkey, were all part of the background. Turkey's disastrous defeat in the First World War, and the break-up of her once-glorious empire, set the scene for a resentful rejection of the decadent institutions which had allowed all this to happen. Bitter dissatisfaction with the Islamic heritage was heightened by the revolts of Arab coreligionists during the war, but climaxed by Caliph Vahid-ud-Din's collusion with Allied invaders in 1919.[39]

At this critical juncture Mustafa Kemal was able to mobilize the Turkish people in a mighty effort to drive out the invaders. His military successes led to final victory in 1922, and he became the heroic idol of Turkey. Mustafa Kemal's desire was to transform Turkey into a modern, westernized, secular state, and the task could be accomplished only by sweeping reforms. The intelligentsia, as we have noted, were fairly well prepared for moves in this direction. Mustafa Kemal's executive ability and, above all, his immense popularity were utilized to make these steps acceptable to the more conservative peasantry.

It is not possible here to do more than sketch an outline of the steps by which the state was secularized. In 1924 the Grand National Assembly at Ankara abolished the caliphate and banished members of the imperial family from the country. The following year was marked by an act abolishing all Muslim religious orders. In 1926 a momentous step was taken when the *shari'ah* (Islamic law) was replaced by western legal codes—a civil code from Switzerland, a penal code from Italy, and a commercial code from Germany.

The 1924 Constitution of the Republic of Turkey had provided that "the religion of the Turkish state is Islam," but this clause was deleted by an amendment of 1928. The original Constitution provided that the deputies of the Assembly and the president take an oath of office swearing on the Koran; this was changed to an oath on their word of honor. A constitutional amendment also established

[39] Henry E. Allen, *The Turkish Transformation: A Study in Social and Religious Development*, University of Chicago Press, Chicago, 1935, pp. 10-43. See also Niyazi Berkes, "Historical Background of Turkish Secularism," *Islam and the West*, ed. Richard N. Frye, Mouton and Company, The Hague, 1957, pp. 41-68.

"laicism" as one of the six cardinal principles of the Turkish Republic. The reforms were effected largely in a spirit of hostility toward the religious authorities. But many Turks interpret these steps also as a much-needed reformation of Islam as a religion. As Professor Smith explained their position, even if the reforms were originally motivated by political considerations, Turkey "had at the same time liberated and rediscovered true Islam."[40]

Turkey's experiment in secularism is of particular relevance in view of its influence upon Indian nationalist leaders. Jawaharlal Nehru's first mention of the secular state in his writings (1933) was in connection with the Turkish Republic.[41] In a later work, Nehru mentioned that Mustafa Kemal's building up of a secular state gradually produced a silent resentment among the more orthodox of the Indian Muslims. "This very policy, however, made him more popular among the younger generation of both Hindus and Muslims."[42]

[40] Smith, *op. cit.*, p. 176.
[41] Jawaharlal Nehru, *Glimpses of World History*, John Day Company, New York, 1942, p. 706.
[42] Jawaharlal Nehru, *The Discovery of India*, John Day Company, New York, 1946, p. 352.

PART TWO

BASIS FOR THE SECULAR

STATE IN INDIA

CHAPTER 3

THE HISTORICAL FOUNDATION

K. M. PANIKKAR rightly rejected the notion that the ancient past can adequately explain modern Indian secularism. He wrote: "Clearly, our new democratic, egalitarian and secular state is not built upon the foundations of ancient India, or of Hindu thought."[1] Panikker went on to assert unequivocally that the roots of modern India are to be found primarily in the European traditions of the past century and a half. Nevertheless, there were significant factors in the ancient past which to some extent looked toward a secular political order.

ANCIENT AND MEDIEVAL INDIA

Dharma and the Hindu state

In ancient India the promotion of *dharma* (law, duty, morality, religion) was regarded as the foremost aim of the state. The king was expected to encourage piety and virtue and to aid religious institutions. Government was not based on dogma, and considerable impartiality was evidenced in the treatment accorded the various sects. Nevertheless, the religious orientation was very pronounced. The conception of *dharma* in relation to the state indicated that the latter was ultimately tied up with the final goal of existence.[2]

In promoting *dharma* the Hindu kings built temples, granted them large endowments, and exercised strict supervision over their affairs. The state was tolerant of all creeds and frequently aided them all. The religiously tolerant Hindu state which patronized all sects impartially provided one of the historical bases of secularism. However, the traditional Hindu state cannot be *equated* with the modern secular state. As Dr. E. C. Bhatty well pointed out, "the essential

[1] K. M. Panikkar, *The State and the Citizen*, Asia Publishing House, Bombay, 1956, p. 28.
[2] J. J. Anjaria, *The Nature and Grounds of Political Obligation in the Hindu State*, Longmans, Green and Company, Calcutta, 1935, p. 280.

basis of a modern secular state is the institutional separation of state and religion."[3] The state limits itself to the promotion of the secular welfare of the people, leaving the religious aspects of life to the private individual. In this respect the Hindu state was decidedly not secular, for one of its chief functions was the active promotion and patronage of religion.

A clear-cut distinction was made in ancient Indian polity between the functions of priest and king. The Vedic king discharged no priestly functions; he performed no sacrifices on behalf of the nation, as was done in ancient Egypt and Greece.[4] A conception of the two powers—the temporal and the spiritual—existed from earliest times, and was supported by a divinely ordained social order. The Brahman embodied the spiritual authority, and he alone could perform the sacrifices and utter the sacred incantations. The Kshatriya caste provided the rulers and the warriors, although in course of time a few non-Kshatriya dynasties were founded. While the Brahman stood at the top of the caste system, spiritually superior to the Kshatriya, his valid function was the priestly office only; his superior position gave him no direct authority in matters of government. This tradition supports one aspect of secularism.

The Brahman *purohita,* or royal chaplain, occupied a prominent place among the king's councilors during the Vedic age. His chief task was to counteract the magic of the enemy through the performance of the necessary rituals. The royal chaplain consecrated and blessed the war elephants and horses of the army before battle. Accompanying the king to the battlefield, he sought to ensure a victorious outcome by his prayers, sacrifices, and incantations. The *purohita* also wielded considerable influence in some cases through his role as the king's *guru,* or spiritual preceptor.

The struggle between church and state, which occupies such a prominent place in early medieval European history, had a rather pale counterpart in ancient India. In the *Gautama Dharmasutra* (c. 500 B.C.) it is stated that the king's authority cannot touch the priests, since his prosperity depends on their support. Other texts warn that the gods will spurn the king's oblations if he fails to employ a qualified Brahman priest. By bowing three times before the

[3] E. C. Bhatty, "Religious Minorities and the Secular State," *Religious Freedom,* Committee for Literature on Social Concerns, Bangalore, 1956, p. 74.

[4] A. S. Altekar, *State and Government in Ancient India,* Motilal Banarsidass, Banaras, 1949, p. 48.

Brahman at his coronation, the king accepts his subordinate position, and his success depends on continued recognition of this fact. Bitter curses are pronounced against rulers who confiscate the cows (i.e., wealth) of Brahmans.[5]

As most of the texts were written by priests, only one side of the case was generally presented, and the Brahman's claims were greatly exaggerated. According to some texts the Brahmans were to be exempt from capital punishment and also from taxation; these claims were sometimes based on the divinity of the Brahmans. But practice varied on both points. Other passages admit that the king could dominate the Brahmans and expel the royal chaplain at will. Some works stressed the independence of the spiritual from the temporal power; others emphasized the interdependence of the two powers.[6]

The *purohita's* influence was greatest during the period when there was widespread faith in the Vedic sacrifices. These fell into disuse around the fourth century B.C., partly under the impact of Upanishadic, Jain, and Buddhist thought. The available evidence does not point to a strong theocratic tendency in the polity of ancient India, despite the extreme claims made by the priests in the literature. There is little to suggest that the religious authority ever seriously attempted in practice to usurp the powers of the king.

The Brahmanical order never developed the kind of tight-knit organization which would enable it to enjoy an effective political role comparable to that of the church in medieval Europe. Furthermore, the divinely ordained social system had clearly given the function of governance to the Kshatriyas. U. N. Ghoshal referred to "the striking fact that this class (the Brahmans) throughout our history failed to assert (except in theory and in legend) its claim to control kings and emperors."[7] The absence of an effective ecclesiastical organization within Hinduism even today is a significant factor in the development of a modern secular state in India.

The Brahmans' pretensions were also kept in check by somewhat similar royal pretensions, such as the theory of the king's divinity. When the king was crowned, the gods Agni, Savitri, and Brihaspati

---

[5] *Ibid.*, pp. 31-35. See also D. Mackenzie Brown, *The White Umbrella: Indian Political Thought from Manu to Gandhi*, University of California Press, Berkeley, 1953, pp. 17-18.

[6] U. N. Ghoshal, *A History of Indian Political Ideas*, Oxford University Press, Bombay, 1959, pp. 32-33.

[7] *Ibid.*, p. 7.

were believed to enter his person. Sacrifices performed on behalf of the king before engaging in wars of conquest were thought to make him equal with the gods. Manu even held that the king "is verily a great divinity in human form; his very body is formed by the Creator by taking particles from the bodies of the divine guardians of the eight quarters." In course of time the divinity of the king became a generally accepted belief, and many of the medieval dynasties traced their origin to the gods Brahma, Rama, or Lakshman.

If the king was a god, the Hindu state might be regarded as a theocracy in the most literal sense. However, it is necessary to see this claim in proper perspective. Professor A. L. Basham made the point well: "Divinity was cheap in ancient India. Every Brahman was in a sense a god, as were ascetics with a reputation for sanctity. . . . If the king was a god on earth he was only one god among many, and so his divinity might not always weigh heavily upon his subjects."[8]

The early theory of the two powers clearly distinguished between temporal and spiritual authority, as we have noted. But this theory was itself based on religious assumptions and expounded in religious texts. It was derived from the idea of the divinely created social order in which each caste had its particular function to perform in the furtherance of *dharma*. The supremacy of *dharma* was the central conception in early Hindu political thought. In the *Arthashastra* of Kautilya and others (fourth century B.C.), we find a radically different approach to the problems of government.

Dr. U. N. Ghoshal asserted: "To the early *Arthashastra* thinkers belongs the credit of separating politics from theology and raising it to the dignity of an independent science."[9] Kautilya classified the sciences as follows: Philosophy, the Vedas, economics, and the science of polity. One of Kautilya's predecessors, however, had gone so far as to exclude the Vedas entirely from the class of sciences, on the ground of their being superfluous to men of the world. The *Arthashastra* writers severed the connection between *dharma* and political science and concerned themselves with the central problem of statecraft—how to acquire and preserve power. While Kautilya apparently believed in the efficacy of supernatural rituals and recog-

[8] A. L. Basham, *The Wonder that was India*, Sidgwick and Jackson, London, 1954, p. 86.
[9] Ghoshal, *op. cit.*, p. 102.

nized the work of the royal chaplain, he did not hesitate to recommend the exploitation of religion for political purposes. His amoral approach to the problem of interstate relations anticipated the thought of Machiavelli by many centuries.

The *Arthashastra* tradition represented, according to Panikkar, "a purely secular theory of state of which the sole basis is power."[10] Kautilya's secularism did not envisage the institutional separation of state and religion; the patronage and regulation of temples was simply another area of state administration. However, the *Arthashastra* did undermine the theoretical basis for the promotion of religion by the state. It is difficult to assess the influence of the *Arthashastra* on the conduct of government in the Hindu state, but it is quite clear that it never succeeded in replacing the old ideas of *rajadharma*.

The system of justice in ancient India was based on a principle of radical inequality. The *Smritis* prescribed lighter punishments for Brahmans than for others guilty of the same offense. In fact all penalties were graded according to the respective castes of the offender and the person against whom the offense was committed. According to the law of Manu, a Brahman who slandered a Kshatriya would be fined fifty *panas*, but for slandering a Vaishya or a Shudra his fine would be only twenty-five and twelve *panas*, respectively. And the penalties were much more severe for slandering one's superiors. The principle of the equality of all before the law finds no support in ancient Indian thought and practice.[11] This part of the Hindu tradition is a complete negation of secular principles.

The religious liberty which prevailed in ancient India, however, does represent one essential aspect of the secular state. Government never sought to impose a particular creed upon the people. Various schools of thought propounded the doctrines of agnosticism, atheism, and materialism. Jainism, Buddhism, and later Judaism, Christianity, Zoroastrianism, and Islam were permitted to propagate their teachings, build their places of worship, and establish their respective ways of life. The struggle for freedom of conscience in Europe and America, stretching over many centuries, has no counterpart in Indian history. From the earliest days this right seems never to have been denied. As Max Weber put it: "It is an undoubted fact that in India, religious and philosophical thinkers were able to enjoy

[10] Panikkar, *op. cit.*, p. 116.
[11] Basham, *op. cit.*, p. 120.

perfect, nearly absolute freedom for a long period. The freedom of thought in ancient India was so considerable as to find no parallel in the West before the most recent age."[12]

Islam and the Muslim State

The society established by Mohammed in the seventh century A.D. was an integrated religio-political community. It gave no recognition either in theory or in practice to the distinction between spiritual and temporal. Religious devotion and political allegiance were merged, for Mohammed was both the Messenger of God and the divinely appointed Governor and Commander.

This unitary tradition was continued by the early caliphs, but by the ninth century the *ulama* (doctors of Islamic Law) succeeded in arrogating to themselves the exclusive authority to define orthodox dogma. Furthermore, the rapid territorial expansion of Islam made effective control by the caliph impossible, and large parts of the Muslim world were governed by independent rulers whose recognition of the caliph's headship was little more than a convenient legal fiction. Their independence became complete when in 1258 the caliphate of Baghdad came to a violent end at the hands of the Mongol invaders.

Thus the caliphate, the historical link with classical Islamic polity, did not exist throughout most of the important period of Muslim rule in India, the Delhi sultanate (1211-1504) and the Mughal Empire (1526-1757). Indian Muslim thought was called upon to define the relationship between Islam and the Muslim ruler, in the context of a situation never envisaged by the Prophet. In the words of Professor P. Hardy, "Indo-Muslim theory met the situation by stressing the divine ordination of the function of temporal government, the duty of obedience, and the desirability of the sultanate in India acting as caliph *de facto* for its own dominions—that is by ascribing to it those functions, including the defense and maintenance of true religion and the Holy Law, of dispensing justice and of appointing the god-fearing to office, which Sunni jurists had earlier ascribed to the caliphate."[13] In carrying out this role, the Muslim ruler was

[12] This remarkable freedom of thought, however, was not accompanied by a comparable freedom of *action* in the many areas of social life which were dominated by Hindu religious conceptions, for example, caste regulations.
[13] *Sources of Indian Tradition*, ed. William Theodore de Bary, Columbia University Press, New York, 1958, p. 465.

necessarily dependent on the religious guidance of the *ulama*, for unlike the caliph he could claim no past tradition of independent spiritual authority.

The *sadr-us-sadur* was the chief theologian of the state, the most learned doctor of the law, and it was his responsibility to guide the ruler in the interpretation and application of the law and traditions of Islam. He also controlled vast patronage in the form of state grants which he dispensed to scholars, theologians, schools, and mosques. Sultan Salim Shah brought the state under almost complete subjection to the *ulama* by his reverential obedience to the *sadr-us-sadur*. The Mughal emperor Akbar, on the other hand, greatly reduced the powers of that official, especially in matters of patronage. Akbar also arranged to have a declaration made by certain of the *ulama* at his court to the effect that if they should disagree on a point of law, the emperor would have full authority to give a legally binding interpretation.

The religious policies of the Indian Muslim rulers ranged from the tolerance and syncretism of Akbar to the bigotry and fanaticism of Aurangzib. During the period of the Delhi Sultanate, heretical Shi'a sects such as the Ismaili and Qarmatians were subjected to severe persecution by the orthodox Sunni government, and many Muslims belonging to these sects were imprisoned and executed. The public worship of Hindu idols was generally forbidden, and Hindus were not allowed to build new temples or repair old ones. Sometimes rulers like Feroz Shah Tughlaq would desecrate temples upon the conquest of new territory as a symbol of the victory of Islam. On some occasions "a particularly pious Muslim king, like Sikander Lodi, would have a fit of religiosity and desecrate or destroy even existing temples in peaceful times."[14] In 1669 Aurangzib issued a general order for the destruction of all Hindu temples and schools.

During the sultanate and later under Aurangzib, many thousands were forcibly converted to Islam. Shah Jahan appointed a superintendent of converts charged with special responsibility for making converts. The sentences of criminals and prisoners of war were readily remitted and the individuals were granted daily allowances upon embracing Islam. The conversion of Muslims to Hinduism, on

[14] Sri Ram Sharma, *The Religious Policy of the Mughal Emperors*, Oxford University Press, Calcutta, 1940, pp. 4-5.

the other hand, constituted the crime of apostasy and was punished by death. The *jizya*, a special tax levied on all non-Muslims, was both a heavy financial burden and a badge of inferiority worn by the Hindu; it also stimulated conversions to Islam. The attempt was made by Aurangzib to exclude all Hindus from government posts, although this was only partially successful due to the lack of qualified Muslim personnel. Hindus were forbidden to wear rich clothing, ride horses, or drive in carriages; they were to be constantly reminded of their inferior status in an Islamic state.

In marked contrast, Akbar followed a policy of broad religious tolerance and equality of treatment for all his subjects. He forbade forcible conversions to Islam and permitted Hindus, Christians, and Shi'as to make converts also. If Akbar permitted his Hindu wives to conduct idol worship in the palace, how could he reasonably prohibit it outside? He removed all restrictions on the building of temples, and soon many new ones were under construction. Man Singh, one of Akbar's Hindu provincial governors built two temples, the one at Brindaban costing half a million rupees.[15] The emperor abolished the hated *jizya* in 1564, and also the laws regarding the clothing and outward way of life of non-Muslims. He threw open high public offices to Hindus; Todar Mall became his finance minister, and among the provincial governors at various times were Man Singh, Bhagwan Das, and Rai Singh. In 1594-1595 Akbar appointed twelve provincial finance ministers; eight of them were Hindus.

Akbar gave official encouragement to the spirit of tolerance by the religious discussion which he sponsored in his "Hall of Worship." Muslim theologians and scholars, as well as Sufi mystics, came and expounded their teachings. But Akbar's spirit of inquisitiveness reached beyond the fold of Islam. Hindu and Jain scholars of all shades of opinion explained their views to the emperor; three Portuguese Jesuits expounded the Christian doctrine; and Parsis were also brought to present the Zoroastrian teachings. Akbar and his successor further encouraged freedom of thought by ordering the preparation of Persian translations of such Hindu religious books as the *Atharvaveda,* the *Mahabharata,* the *Ramayana* and others. Out of Akbar's own religious quest came his syncretistic Divine

[15] *Ibid.,* p. 24.

Faith, which incorporated elements of Sufi, Shi'a, Zoroastrian, and Hindu doctrine.

It is clear that whatever historical antecedent of the secular state there may be in the Muslim period will be found in the policies of Akbar. His contribution to religious tolerance is indeed impressive. Dr. Sri Ram Sharma, after reminding us that in sixteenth-century Europe, Roman Catholics and Protestants were busily engaged in killing each other, pointed out that Akbar brought peace not only to warring sects but to completely different religions. "In the modern age, he was the first and almost the greatest experimenter in the field of religious toleration if the scope of his toleration, the races to which it was applied, and the contemporary conditions be taken into account."[16]

Dr. S. Abid Husain wrote that the new Indian nation which Akbar forged was based "not on the community of religion but on the citizenship of the same state."[17] It is certainly true that the emperor did much to create what we would now call a common citizenship with equal rights for all irrespective of religious differences. In this respect Akbar's state came much nearer to the modern conception than the Hindu state, which was religiously tolerant but which dealt with people in legal and administrative matters according to caste status. Religious liberty and a common citizenship are two of the three components of the secular state, and these are probably what Professor Humayun Kabir had in mind when he referred to Akbar's as "perhaps the first conscious attempt to formulate the conception of a secular state."[18] However, the third component, the institutional separation of religion and the state, would probably have appeared as strange to Akbar as to a sixteenth-century Hindu monarch in South India.

THE BRITISH PERIOD

The religious policy of the British government in India was complex, for it was the result of an attempt to combine three conflicting roles. One religious policy was dictated by the commercial-imperial objectives of the British government, a second by its status as an In-

[16] *Ibid.*, p. 60.
[17] S. Abid Husain, *The National Culture of India*, Jaico Publishing House, Bombay, 1956, p. 67.
[18] Humayun Kabir, *The Indian Heritage*, Asia Publishing House, Bombay, 1955, p. 21.

dian ruler, and a third by its official profession of Christianity. During much of the first half of the nineteenth century, all three of these roles were being carried out simultaneously. Debate on questions of religious policy was frequently inconclusive, for there were three basic assumptions to choose from, each leading to a different conclusion on many issues.

The policy of religious neutrality

The British East India Company began as a commercial enterprise, but in time became a vast colonial power exercising all the functions of government. What was to be the religious policy of this European trader-government ruling over millions of Hindus and Muslims? Common sense dictated its policy of non-interference in the religious life of the country, for any other policy would be unlikely to produce either sound business relations or loyal subjects. Hence, the policy of religious neutrality, clearly formulated by the eighteenth century, was in perfect consonance with this commercial-imperial role.

The East India Company in the seventeenth century had indeed entertained some ideas of mixing religion with business. One of the directors' requests for a chaplain from Oxford or Cambridge contained the explanation that the company had resolved to attempt the spreading of the gospel in India. Twenty years later, in 1698, the charter granted by Parliament directed that the company's chaplains should learn the languages of the country in order to instruct the Indian servants or agents of the company in the Protestant religion.[19] But these intentions and instructions remained a dead letter.

Far more significant, in terms of the evolution of British policy, was the order given in Bombay in 1662: "There shall be no compulsory conversion, no interference with native habits, and no cow-killing in Hindu quarters." As Arthur Mayhew pointed out, the principle of toleration embodied in this statement was unprecedented in the history of earlier European powers in India. The government of Portuguese India in the sixteenth century had not hesitated to resort to coercion in order to secure conversions to Catholicism. Inducements such as government posts and free rice were held out to those who would embrace the official faith. The Inquisition was exported to Goa in 1546, and all practice of "pagan" ceremonies

[19] Arthur Mayhew, *Christianity and the Government of India*, Faber and Gwyer Ltd., London, 1929, pp. 30-38.

was made liable to severe punishment. Similarly the Dutch, a Protestant power, openly used the machinery of the state to propagate their religion in Ceylon in the seventeenth century. The government forbade the erection of Buddhist temples and reserved the best appointments for Christian converts.[20] With such precedents, the development of the British policy of religious neutrality could not have been expected.

Protestant missionary work in India began in 1705, and for a century and a half the relationship between the government and Christian missions was to be one of the most crucial questions of religious policy. As this subject is considered in some detail in a later chapter, we shall here limit ourselves to a few generalizations.[21] The policy toward missionaries varied greatly, depending on the particular presidency, set of officials, and period of time. In some cases officials actively aided the missionaries, considering their work to be good in itself, and useful in promoting indirectly the interests of the company. They regarded the freedom and even encouragement given to private missionary agencies to be entirely consistent with the pledge of official non-interference in the Indians' religious beliefs and practices.

In other cases non-interference was interpreted to mean a positive duty on the part of government to restrict and if possible exclude any influences which might disturb the religious status quo. Official attitudes toward Christian missionary work ranged from open and enthusiastic approval to stern condemnation of such meddling with "native habits." While both opinions could be found among company officials in India, there can be no doubt that the court of directors in London took a generally dim view of all missionary efforts throughout most of the eighteenth and early nineteenth centuries.

In 1793 an unsuccessful attempt was made in Parliament to commit the government of India to a policy of direct and official missionary work. When the question of renewal of the company's charter was being discussed, William Wilberforce sought the inclusion of a provision which would in effect have created a government missionary establishment. Under his plan, the court of directors would have been required to send out persons approved by the ecclesiastical authorities of the Church of England and paid by the company

[20] *Ibid.*, pp. 39-40.
[21] See chapter 7, "The Question of Foreign Missionaries."

for "the religious and moral improvement" of the native inhabitants of India. Parliament rejected this clause, after the directors in a vigorous representation asserted that the Hindus had "as good a system of faith and morals as most people and it would be madness to attempt their conversion."[22]

It should be noted that many missionaries, especially those of the nonconformist persuasions, held strong convictions against any efforts by the state to promote conversions to Christianity. Having struggled against officially imposed religious uniformity at home, they were consistent enough to reject it in India. "Let not government touch my work," declared Baptist William Carey. "It can only succeed in making them hypocrites; I wish to make them Christians."

It was not until the next charter renewal, in 1813, that the legal right of missionaries to enter British India, under a new system of licensing, was established by Parliament. The procedure of licensing would provide a measure of official control over the missionaries; Parliament was concerned that "the principles of the British government on which the natives of India have hitherto relied for the free exercise of their religion be inviolably maintained."

As has already been stated, the policy of religious neutrality was bound up with the primary objective of the East India Company which was trade. The directors "felt themselves under no obligation to risk their dividends or position by any steps that might lead to tumult or uprising, or to any radical changes in the habits and attitude of the people from whom their wealth was derived."[23] Their policy was not based on any abstract theories of religious tolerance, and certainly not on any ideas of the separation of church and state. It was a rather obvious pragmatic solution to a concrete problem. As Britain's Indian empire expanded the conviction deepened that religious neutrality was sound imperial policy as well as good business.

[22] Frank Penny, *The Church in Madras*, Smith, Elder and Co., London, 1912, vol. 2, pp. 2-4, and Mayhew, *op. cit.*, p. 26.

[23] Mayhew, *op. cit.*, p. 44. Note also the statement of A. C. Lyall: "Moreover, toleration, meaning complete non-interference with the religions of the natives, was of such plain and profitable expediency with the East India Company in its earlier days, that not to have practiced it would have been downright insanity in an association whose object was to do business with Indians; wherefore the merchants who enforced a strict monopoly of material commerce were always careful to encourage free trade and unlimited speculation in religion." "Our Religious Policy in India," *Fortnightly Review*, April 1872, pp. 388-389.

The neutrality was certainly never perfect. Governor-General Wellesley, for example, did much to identify the government with Christianity, both in external symbols and by official patronage of missionary projects (e.g., translations of the Bible). And many later government officials gave open encouragement to Christian work, occasioning periodic admonitions from nervous directors against "indiscreet" and "tactless" support of the missionaries. The establishment of the Church of England in India, and the royal appointment of the "Governor-General's Guru" (the bishop of Calcutta) were hardly in keeping with the profession of neutrality.

On the other hand, the government went to such lengths to demonstrate that Christianity was not being favored, that Indian Christians were by law debarred from appointment to various judicial and military posts. This discrimination was written into government regulations, continuing a policy which had prevailed under certain of the Indian rulers whom the company had displaced. After several representations were made, the directors in 1831 ordered the governor-general to remove these injustices, explaining that the "neutrality which we think it our duty to observe does not require that converts to Christianity should be placed by law in a less advantageous situation than other persons."[24]

Perplexities and inconsistencies abounded in the government's attempts to define and implement its religious policy. In his minute on the suppression of *sati* (1829), Lord William Bentinck struggled with the problem of the religious sanction given to the practice. He agreed with the reformer Rammohan Roy that the Hindu reaction to the abolition of *sati* might be as follows: "While the English were contending for power they deemed it politic to allow universal toleration and to respect our religion, but having obtained the supremacy their first act is a violation of their profession, and the next will probably be, like the Mohammedan conquerors, to force upon us their own religion."[25] Despite such misgivings, Bentinck enacted the measure chiefly on humanitarian grounds.

One of the great contributions made by the British raj was the establishment of the principle of equality before the law. Hindu

[24] Penny, *op. cit.*, p. 348.
[25] *Sati* was the burning of a widow on the funeral pyre of her husband. The practice is discussed in greater detail in chapter 8. Bentinck's minute is reproduced in Ramsay Muir, *The Making of British India 1756-1858*, The University Press, Manchester, 1917, pp. 293-296.

criminal law had scaled punishments according to the caste of the offender, and Muslim law had discriminated against infidels. The introduction of a uniform criminal law was an indispensable foundation for the development of a secular state.

But problems arose in certain areas of civil law. The British government as early as 1772 pledged itself to a strict application in its courts of the Hindu and Muslim laws regarding marriage, inheritance, and other matters of personal law. In the case of Hindus, the "law of the Shastras" was to be applied, and with respect to Muslims the "law of the Koran."[26] Under both Hindu and Muslim law, apostasy was penalized by the loss of inheritance rights. The law thus inflicted an economic loss on those who abandoned their ancestral religion, and this fact operated as a significant deterrent to conversion. A Bengal regulation of 1832 removed this legal disability, and Christian spokesmen called for a law that would apply to all British India. In 1850 the government of India enacted the Caste Disabilities Removal Act which declared that any law or usage which "inflicts on any person forfeiture of rights or property, or may be held in any way to impair or affect any right of inheritance, by reason of his or her renouncing or having been excluded from the communion of any religion, or being deprived of caste, shall cease to be enforced as law."[27]

There were definitely two points of view regarding this legislation. On one hand it was hailed as the "Freedom of Religion Act," a measure which established the great principle that a person could not be deprived of his civil rights because of his profession of any religion. Orthodox Hindus, however, protested that the law interfered most grievously with their religious usages, for the right to inherit property was accompanied by religious obligations which only a Hindu could fulfill. "The right of succession," one of their petitions stated, "depends exclusively upon the right to present the funeral oblations. It is by virtue of such last act, which can only be performed by a Hindu, that sons and near kinsmen take the property, because, according to the belief of the Hindus, it is by such acts his father's spiritual bliss, and that of his ancestors to the remotest degree,

[26] See chapter 10, "Religion, Law, and Secularism."
[27] Courtenay Ilbert, *The Government of India*, Clarendon Press, London, 1898, p. 392.

is secured."[28] Governor-General Dalhousie, however, overruled this argument by distinguishing between ceremonial and legal responsibility, and by asserting that "it is the duty of the state to keep in its own hands the right of regulating succession to property." The act also protected the convert's right of guardianship of children. Previously, Hindu and Muslim law deprived the apostate of the custody of his own children.

The act of 1850 applied to all cases of religious conversion. Its main result, however, was the protection of converts to Christianity. Similarly, the system of grants-in-aid to educational institutions managed by private agencies, established in 1854, was of general application. The principle was that the neutral government would aid all institutions alike solely on the basis of their teaching of secular subjects, and irrespective of their religious objectives. In practice, missionary schools were the chief beneficiaries of the new policy. This was inevitable in view of the enormous headstart in the educational field which the missionaries had over Hindu and Muslim agencies. Nevertheless, it provided an unprecedented opportunity for the extension of the system of mission schools and of Christian influence generally. Regarding government schools, the 1854 despatch declared that as these "were founded for the benefit of the whole population of India . . . the education conveyed in them should be exclusively secular." All references to Christianity in the classroom were specifically forbidden.[29]

The cry of "religion in danger" was one significant factor in the situation leading up to the mutiny of 1857. It was of course not true that the government was deliberately seeking to undermine the Indian creeds with the object of proselytism, but the charge was widely believed throughout northern India. The following year brought Queen Victoria's momentous proclamation of the crown's assumption of the governance of India. This document combined a forthright witness to the sovereign's Christian faith with a strong commitment to religious neutrality in the state's relations with its Indian subjects. "Firmly relying ourselves on the truth of Christianity, and acknowledging with gratitude the solace of religion, we disclaim alike the right and desire to impose our convictions on any

[28] John William Kaye, *Christianity in India: An Historical Narrative*, Smith, Elder and Company, London, 1859, p. 461.
[29] See chapter 12, "Education and Religion."

of our subjects. We declare it to be our royal will and pleasure that none be in any wise favored, none molested or disquieted, by reason of their religious faith or observances, but that all shall alike enjoy the equal and impartial protection of the law; and we do strictly charge and enjoin all those who may be in authority under us that they abstain from all interference with the religious belief or worship of any of our subjects on pain of our highest displeasure."[30] The proclamation, while not adding anything new to the government's religious policy, did restate it in clear and emphatic language. Memories of the mutiny made it unlikely that the neutrality of the state would henceforth be tampered with. And despite all the ambiguities mentioned above, the British policy of religious neutrality represents one of the important historical bases of modern India's secular state.

Patron and protector of Indian religions

The East India Company had to act not only in its primary role as a commercial-imperial enterprise but also in the role of the Indian rulers whom it displaced. The British government, anxious to reassure its subjects as each new territory was annexed, invariably pledged itself to the continuation of all the rights, privileges, and immunities which had been enjoyed under the former Hindu or Muslim ruler. As the Indian prince had given grants and endowments for religious purposes, supervised the arrangements for festivals and pilgrimages, and administered the affairs of temples and mosques, these functions became the responsibility of the European government.[31]

Public opinion in India was quite clear that the British were under obligation to undertake these tasks. The fact that the new rulers were of a different faith would not justify their neglecting the traditional role of patron and protector of religion. For both Hindu and Muslim princes had, during certain periods, patronized and administered the institutions of the other religion with considerable impartiality. In 1790 Tippu Sultan, Muslim ruler of Mysore, issued a circular order to his local administrators: "The temples are under your management; you are therefore to see that the offerings to the gods and the

[30] Muir, *op. cit.*, pp. 382-383.
[31] *The Madras Hindu Religious and Charitable Endowments Act (1951)*, Madras Law Journal Press, Madras, 1952, p. 3.

temple illumination are duly regulated, as directed, out of the government grants." The order then went on to direct in detail the method of financial supervision of the Hindu temples.[32] In assuming this administrative responsibility, Tippu Sultan followed a pattern imposed by centuries of history.

The British were in a very similar situation. The first instance of their active assumption of this role came in 1796 when Lionel Place, a collector in the Madras presidency, was put in charge of the famous temples at Conjeeveram. Place himself had requested that the government undertake their management, on the ground that it would promote the happiness of the Indian subjects. In the absence of an efficient authority, maladministration of temple funds and neglect of the religious ceremonies were inevitable. Place established an effective administration, carefully disbursing the "church funds," as he called them, and assigning proper duties to the "church-wardens" (Brahman keepers of the shrines). To crown all his good works, the collector presented to the god jewels reputedly worth a thousand pounds![33]

Regulations were passed in Bengal in 1810 and in Madras in 1817 providing for the regular administration of temple endowments by the government. The Madras measure referred to the endowments for temples, mosques, and "other pious and beneficial purposes" (a phrase which greatly disturbed the missionaries), and the government's responsibility to ensure that these endowments were applied according to the intent and will of the grantor. Within a short time government servants were involved not only in the strict financial aspects of temple administration but in virtually everything concerned with the institutions. As Mayhew put it, "Whether it was the appointment of temple staff, or regulations for dancing girls, temple fees, or pilgrims' certificates, or the collection of local dues, everything was done decently and in order, with a lavish expenditure of government paper and time."[34]

By 1833 the Madras government could report that no less than 7,600 Hindu temples were being administered by government officials. The same report quoted the collector of North Arcot as fol-

[32] *The Mysore Muzrai Manual*, Government of Mysore Press, Bangalore, 1934, p. 2.
[33] Kaye, *op. cit.*, pp. 380-381. Many British officials, from district collectors to governors, made sizable gifts to Hindu temples. See "Orion," "Sahebs and Shrines," *The Hindu*, March 5, 1961.
[34] Mayhew, *op. cit.*, p. 148.

lows: "Our interference has extended over every detail of management; we regulate their funds, superintend the repairs of their temples, keep in order their cars and images, appoint the servants of the pagodas, purchase and keep in store the various commodities required for their use, investigate and adjust all disputes, and at times, even those of a religious nature."[35] The British collector was highly esteemed by the Hindus as the "friendly guardian of their religion." And Hindu institutions flourished under European superintendence; the temples were kept in good repair, their finances were on a solid footing, and the religious ceremonies were regularly performed.

The British government was the direct patron as well as the administrator of Hindu and Muslim religious institutions. Sizable sums of public money were paid toward their support. In some cases these payments were made in lieu of the revenue of lands assigned to temples or mosques by former rulers, but resumed by the British. In other cases the payments were annual grants made by the government in continuance of similar contributions from the rajas who were displaced. By the middle of the nineteenth century, the total annual payments made to temples and mosques in Madras presidency alone amounted to about £100,000.[36]

Another important aspect of the government's relation to Hindu institutions was the question of the pilgrim tax, also inherited from the Indian rulers who preceded the British. There were various interpretations of this tax. It could be regarded as an oppressive measure intended to exploit and at the same time to discourage Hindu pilgrimages, as it indeed had been when imposed by the Muslim rulers of northern India. If the British were to continue the tax, it might well be interpreted as undue interference in the religious affairs of the people, quite opposed to the pledge of toleration and neutrality. On the other hand, to abolish it would be to open government to the charge that it had deliberately removed a customary fee in order to encourage "Hindu idolatry," contrary to its principle of neutrality.

But the British resolved the dilemma on altogether different grounds when the case of the great Jaganath temple in Orissa was considered. The temple had been maintained at great expense by the former Hindu government in Cuttack, and this responsibility de-

[35] Quoted in Kaye, *op. cit.*, pp. 391-392.
[36] A. C. Lyall, *op. cit.*, p. 402.

volved upon the British. The governor-general, Lord Wellesley, decided to continue the pilgrim tax imposed by the raja, as the Brahmans and general Hindu public regarded it as a permanent security that the temple expenses would be defrayed by the government. "There can be no objection," wrote Wellesley, "to the British government availing itself of these opinions for the purpose of relieving itself from a heavy annual expense, and of providing funds to answer the contingent charges of the religious institutions of the Hindu faith maintained by the British government."[37] In point of fact, proceeds from the pilgrim tax more than covered expenses, and the surplus was swept into the government's own treasury! "The religious institutions of the Hindu faith maintained by the British government"—the bluntness of this wording disturbed many Christian consciences—frequently became financial assets under careful administration.

The British participated in religious festivals much as tradition dictated. Government officials were present to inaugurate annual festivals; troops and artillery were used to make each occasion as splendid as possible. In the military salute which ushered in Ramzan, in the official breaking of coconuts at the commencement of the monsoon, and in the employment of Brahmans to invoke propitious weather, the government was careful to enact its time-honored role to perfection.

It was inevitable that there would be an adverse reaction to all of these evidences of "government connection with idolatry." Some officials objected to their compulsory participation in what they regarded as the encouragement and promotion of false religions. Bishops and missionaries added their protests; memorials were drawn up, and as the facts became known the agitation for official withdrawal from such activities gathered force in England. Some of the representations contained bitter accusations that the company had willingly become the "dry nurse to Vishnu" and the "church-warden of Jaganath." Others, more temperately worded, suggested that the government had in all good faith assumed certain general responsibilities for temple administration, but that the very thoroughness of its superintendence had been interpreted by the native population as evidence of positive approval and support. In any case, the net result was that a Christian government, by restoring public confidence in

[37] Kaye, *op. cit.*, p. 385.

the administration of the institutions, had greatly promoted the standing and prestige of Hinduism and Islam.

As a result of the pressures built up by this agitation, the court of directors issued a despatch in 1833 which directed the withdrawal of the government from involvement in the religious institutions of the country. The despatch asserted that the government appeared before the people of India "in such intimate connection with their unhappy and debasing superstitions, as almost necessarily to inspire them with the belief either that we admit the divine origin of those superstitions, or at least that we ascribe to them some peculiar and venerable authority."[38] It went on to forbid the interference of British officials in the internal management of temples and to abolish the pilgrim tax and fines formerly considered as sources of revenue by the government.

The despatch was epitomized in the statement "That in all matters relating to their temples, their worship, their festivals, their religious practices, their ceremonial observances, our native subjects be left entirely to themselves." The directors were anxious that the Indians not misinterpret their action; it was to be explained to them that "so far from abandoning the principles of a just toleration, the British government is resolved to apply them with more scrupulous accuracy than ever; and that this proceeding is, in truth, no more than a recurrence to that state of real neutrality from which we ought never to have departed."

For five years the despatch was virtually ignored in India while "further information" was being gathered. In 1838 another letter from the directors reaffirmed the previous orders, and shortly thereafter the effective withdrawal from temple management began. The religious institutions were entrusted to prominent individuals or committees, and, despite certain real difficulties, the severance of government from their management proceeded. In 1841 the attendance of troops or military bands at religious festivals and the firing of salutes was discontinued by order, "with the object of separating the government and its officers, as far as possible, from all connection with the ceremonies of the Hindu and Mohammedan religion."[39]

The direct money payments by government to temples and

[38] *Ibid.*, p. 417.   [39] *Ibid.*, p. 437.

mosques continued, since the British had pledged themselves to the continuance of grants made by the former rulers. As a matter of fact, in the Madras presidency the government promised at the time of withdrawal from temple management that this step would not affect the customary grants and allowances. While in some Christian circles this decision was very unpopular, John W. Kaye wrote in 1859, "If the religion of the few is to be supported from the revenues of the country, why, on any conceivable principle of neutrality, is not the religion of the many?"[40] If the Church of England, why not the temple of Jaganath?

The withdrawal of the government from temple management was bitterly criticized by many Indians. Despite the government's protestations of a more perfect religious freedom for the Indians in the administration of their own institutions, the move was interpreted as a blow to Hinduism and Islam. The government, it was charged, had abdicated one of its most essential functions, had cast off the immemorial duty of Indian rulers, had left the institutions at the mercy of inefficient and dishonest trustees. The decision was also criticized by British administrators who saw in the successful European management of temples and mosques a source of great prestige for the government, a relationship which strengthened the Indian's loyalty to the empire. These advantages, it was argued, had been thrown away for no urgent motive.

One such administrator, A. C. Lyall, wrote discerningly in 1872 that religious neutrality had different meanings in England and in India, and that the government's interpretation or misinterpretation of it would never satisfy the Indian. "In England the phrase might be understood as an assurance that the government had determined to have nothing whatever to do with the affairs, temporal or spiritual, of any sect or creed; in India it is taken, I believe, to convey a welcome guarantee that the Queen will not favor one religion more than another. But I suspect that the Indians no more supposed that perfect neutrality meant the complete renunciation by their governors of all direct authority or leadership over the management of the temporal interests of their religions, than they imagined that neutrality in civil administration means that the government will disband the police."[41] To complete the process of severing itself from

[40] *Ibid.*, p. 439. [41] A. C. Lyall, *op. cit.*, p. 407.

the affairs of temples and mosques, the government passed an act in 1863 by which their properties were made over absolutely to local trustees or committees. The government appointed these trustees once and for all and thereafter ceased to have any control over them or to nominate any new trustees. There was no change in this policy until 1920, when the Imperial Legislature, now representative of Indian opinion, passed the Charitable and Religious Trusts Act.[42]

The Church of England in India

The third role which the British government had to assume was that of a Christian government. The East India Company, beginning in 1644, sent Anglican chaplains to attend to the religious needs of its employees stationed in India. The early chaplains ministered to isolated congregations of British merchants and soldiers, with little thought of propagating their faith among the Indians. Toward the end of the eighteenth century, however, a group of "evangelical chaplains" began missionary work in addition to their ministry to Europeans and Anglo-Indians.[43] At first the company did not take the initiative in the building of churches for its civil and military servants, but it was willing to make contributions in support of private efforts. By the early nineteenth century, however, the policy in all three presidencies (Calcutta, Bombay, and Madras) was for the government to pay for the entire cost of chapels in all of the permanent garrisons to which chaplains were assigned.[44] With the annexation of vast new territories, the number of chaplains increased slowly. But the growing ecclesiastical establishment lacked direct supervision, as the chaplains were under the jurisdiction of the bishop of London.

In 1813 the company's charter was renewed. Along with the clauses permitting the entry of missionaries, Parliament provided for the appointment of a bishop and three archdeacons of the Church of England, who were to superintend ecclesiastical matters in India. The see of the bishop of Calcutta included not only all of India but Ceylon and Australia as well. Parliament particularly directed that all payments for ecclesiastical purposes were to be made from the

[42] The more recent legislation regarding the administration of religious endowments is discussed in chapter 9, "The Reform of Hindu Temples."

[43] Eyre Chatterton, *History of the Church of England in India*, Society for Promoting Christian Knowledge, London, 1924, p. 108.

[44] Penny, *op. cit.*, pp. 52-54.

territorial revenues of India, not from the company's trade profits. This clause satisfied the stockholders who had opposed the creation of the bishopric on financial grounds.

The legislation had also been opposed by some who feared that the open identification of Christianity with the government of India would antagonize the Indians and perhaps even lead to an uprising. Thomas F. Middleton, the first bishop of Calcutta, reached India in 1814. His landing, he wrote, "was without any éclat, for fear of alarming the prejudices of the natives."[45] But the bishop's arrival and subsequent activities produced no commotion; he was greeted everywhere by the Indians with respectful curiosity, and the "Lord Padre Sahib" comported himself with the utmost dignity.

The first bishop refused to license missionaries or ordain Indians because, as he interpreted his letters patent from the crown, he had no authority to do so. Parliament had not created an ecclesiastical establishment in order to promote missionary work among the Indians; this idea had been decisively rejected in 1793.[46] The state was not "interfering in the religious beliefs of the natives" but was simply providing spiritual ministrations to its own employees of the Christian faith.

Middleton's successor, Bishop Heber, had no such scruples; he "put the evangelization of India in the forefront of the Church's duty."[47] He ordained Indians to the ministry; he became president of the Church Missionary Society Committee and openly referred to himself as the first missionary of the society. But even apart from the efforts of such missionary-minded men as Heber, the position of the bishop of Calcutta was anomalous. India was a diocese, and the bishop had spiritual and ecclesiastical jurisdiction over all Anglican ministers, including missionaries, within his diocese. He was bound to exercise this jurisdiction according to the ecclesiastical laws of England. Thus, as Whitehead put it, "the company through the bishops became officially connected with the missionaries and their Indian congregations."[48]

[45] Quoted in Kaye, *op. cit.*, p. 290.
[46] A reference to Wilberforce's proposal for a government missionary establishment.
[47] *Other Men Labored: Centenary of the Diocese of Madras*, Diocesan Press, Madras, 1935, p. 27.
[48] Henry Whitehead, *Indian Problems in Religion, Education, Politics*, Constable and Company, London, 1924, p. 97.

In 1833 Parliament divided the vast diocese of the bishopric of Calcutta, and the bishoprics of Madras and Bombay were created. At the same time the bishop of Calcutta was designated metropolitan of all India. The East India Company had opposed the move on the usual grounds—three bishops would be too expensive—but all objections were brushed aside.

Presbyterian chaplains of the Church of Scotland were appointed to minister to company servants of that persuasion after 1813. In 1840 the first grant was made by the Madras government toward the cost of building a Roman Catholic chapel, and, in the years following, Roman Catholic missionaries and bishops began to receive allowances for their ministrations to British soldiers of their faith. During this period the building of Anglican churches, now mostly for British and Anglo-Indian civilians, greatly increased. The presidency governments customarily paid for one-half the cost of construction, and the churches remained the property of the government.[49]

The ecclesiastical organization of the Church of England in India around the middle of the nineteenth century was relatively simple. The bishops were appointed by the crown and paid from the public revenues of India. Later developments, however, justified Bishop Whitehead's statement in 1924 that "the position of the Church of England in India for the last hundred years has been more complex and anomalous than that of any other church in Christendom." At the time of his writing, "Of the thirteen bishops in the province, seven are appointed by the crown under letters patent, and paid either entirely by government or partly by government and partly by endowments; the bishop of Travancore and Cochin is appointed by the archbishop of Canterbury under what is known as the Jerusalem Act and is entirely paid by the Church Missionary Society. The bishop of Chota Nagpur is appointed by the metropolitan and entirely paid by the Society for the Propagation of the Gospel. The bishop of Tinnevelly and Madura is appointed by the bishop of Madras with the approval of the metropolitan and is paid partly by endowments and partly by grants from the two societies, the S.P.G. and C.M.S."[50]

Quite apart from the complexity of the system, it is interesting to note the way in which state, church, and missionary society

[49] Penny, *op. cit.*, pp. 58-63.　　　　[50] Whitehead, *op. cit.*, p. 90.

became linked together in the course of time. Before the bishopric of Calcutta was created by the historic decision of Parliament in 1813, William Wilberforce made it clear that the bishop "was to be in no way responsible for mission work, and that his appointment would suggest no association of government with that work."[51] A century later, half of the bishops were being paid by the government and half by missionary societies!

Bishop Whitehead himself recognized the difficulty (others would have said impossibility) of reconciling the position of state-appointed bishops with the principle of religious neutrality. With great candor he explained the difficulty: "It is quite true that they are appointed and paid by the state to minister to the Christian servants of the government, but at the same time, by virtue of their position as bishops they are the heads of a church of which the government servants form only a small minority; and as every Christian church, so far as it is faithful to its commission, is bound to be a missionary body, the bishops cannot do their duty as bishops of the church of Christ unless they take an active interest and an active part in the missionary work of the dioceses over which they rule."[52] Stated more bluntly, a government which professed religious neutrality appointed and paid bishops whose duty it was to convert Hindus and Muslims to Christianity.

The whole position of the established church in India was subjected to serious questioning from the beginning of the twentieth century. As a matter of fact, critics usually echoed the point made in a letter to the *Times* back in 1871: "Starting from our own standpoint of strict religious neutrality, both Hindus and Mohammedans might reasonably object to a considerable sum out of revenues raised by the sweat of their brows being devoted annually to the maintenance of an established church for the benefit of Christians, be they government servants or not, while no annual grant at all is made for the support of Hindu and Mohammedan places of worship, or for their clergy."[53] The objection that an annual grant to an established church is not consistent with the profession of religious neutrality certainly carries much weight. The writer of the letter, however, like most of the other critics, European, Hindu, and Muslim, over-

[51] Mayhew, *op. cit.*, p 102. [52] Whitehead, *op. cit.*, p. 103.
[53] Letter of Colonel Nassau Lees to the *London Times*, October 20, 1871. Quoted in A. C. Lyall, *op. cit.*, pp. 401-402.

looked the sizable payments made annually by the British government to temples and mosques. As we have explained above, these were customary allowances granted in perpetuity by the rajas and continued by the British.

But criticisms of the church-state connection came more frequently from within the church, especially during the early 1920's. Writing on "The Case for the Severance of Church and State in India," J. E. C. Welldon pointed out that the church had been tightly bound by acts of Parliament, that it was dangerously dependent on the good will of the secretary of state and viceroy. The church needed freedom to carry out its missionary task, but as the government by its professed neutrality was prevented from encouraging this, their legal connection had become an anomaly. As Indians year by year assumed a larger role in the legislative and executive functions, the prospects of a government controlled by Hindus and Muslims together with an established Christian church became all the more anomalous. Lastly, the church was gravely hampered in its outreach because of the suspicion lurking in many Indian minds that it was a branch of the government, a serious handicap in a day of rising nationalism and antigovernment sentiment. Disestablishment and disendowment would mean a considerable financial loss to the church, but this was the price it would have to pay for its freedom.[54]

Non-Anglican Protestants and secularists in the British Parliament had from time to time criticized the imposition of the established church on India. The serious proposal for disestablishment, however, came from the church itself, and was effected by the Indian Church Measure passed by Parliament in 1927. This act dissolved the legal union between the Church of England and the Church of England in India and removed the metropolitan bishop of the Indian church from the jurisdiction of the archbishop of Canterbury. Bishops of the Indian church were no longer to be appointed by the crown, and the royal mandate was no longer necessary for their consecration.[56]

Although the legal ties with the Church of England were indeed dissolved, the Indian church continued to have a close relationship with the government of India. This was chiefly due to the system of

[54] J. E. C. Welldon, "The Case for the Severance of Church and State in India," *The Church Missionary Review*, 1922, vol. 73, pp. 197-203.
[55] *The Constitution, Canons and Rules of the Church of India, Burma and Ceylon*, D. S. McKenzie, for the Metropolitan of India, Calcutta, 1930, pp. 260-264.

chaplains and "maintained churches," which had a long history. Chaplains continued to be paid by the government, although the attempt was made to distinguish their work sharply from that of other ministers. In the Indian Church Statutory Rules of 1929 is the following regulation: "No chaplain shall undertake any work other than that of ministering to His Majesty's troops and the servants of the crown and their families if either the bishop or the governor-general in council objects to his undertaking such work."[56] Bishops were no longer appointed and paid by the government. However, if the government recognized the bishop who had been elected to a diocese as superintendent of its chaplains, it paid a sum about equal to two-thirds of his former pay. Churches which had been built wholly or in part at government expense, continued to receive substantial allowances for maintenance and repair.

As a matter of fact, all Christian denominations were on an equal footing, legally, after 1927. Anglican chaplains enjoyed no privileges that were not equally accorded Presbyterian, Wesleyan, and Roman Catholic chaplains. Nevertheless, the legal fact of disestablishment made little impact on the popular mind in India. The distinction between chaplain and missionary was not always clear. To the casual observer, the important fact was simply that the government was spending substantial sums of money to pay the salaries of Christian clergy and to maintain churches, and that most of this went to the clergy and churches of the "Church of England."[57]

With the attainment of independence and the withdrawal of British soldiers and administrators, the long era of the government chaplain came to an end. Terminal block grants were given, and government-maintained churches were formally handed over to the proper ecclesiastical authorities. The Indian Ecclesiastical Establishment was abolished on March 31, 1948.

[56] *Ibid.*, p. 282. While the Indian Church Measure of 1927 separated church and state in India, the Indian Church Act of the same year gave the governor-general of India power to regulate the licensing, posting, discipline, duties, and supervision of chaplains, to make provision for episcopal ministrations, to make grants out of the revenues of India for these purposes, etc. Dr. N. C. Sen Gupta asserted that the Indian Church Act of 1927 is *ultra vires* the Constitution and should be repealed. See *Law Commission of India*: Fifth Report, Government of India Press, 1958, pp. 88-89. It was announced in Parliament that this step was being considered by the ministry of law. *The Hindu*, March 14, 1960.

[57] After disestablishment, the Church of England in India adopted as its official name the "Church of India, Burma and Ceylon."

The great debates on the government's religious policy in the nineteenth century revolved around the three roles which have been discussed. In the attempt to implement the principle of religious neutrality, patronize and regulate the Indian religions, and promote its own Christian religion, the government time and again found itself in a hopelessly inconsistent position. As has been suggested, the principle of religious neutrality did emerge as the predominant factor. By the end of the nineteenth century there was rather wide agreement that the religious neutrality of the British government was genuine, despite its formal denial in the existence of an established church.

In the nineteenth century, then, the British were faced with the problem of defining and implementing their policy of religious neutrality as a Christian government vis-à-vis the "native religions." The government had to deal with questions of religious freedom and of the proper scope of state regulation and promotion of religious beliefs and practices. In the twentieth century the nature of the problem changed radically. In chapter 1 the secular state was defined in terms of three components: freedom of religion, separation of state and religion, and common citizenship. Broadly speaking, one might say that British policy was fairly successful in constructing the first two components in the nineteenth century, but was much less successful in producing the third, a common citizenship unrelated to religious creed, in the twentieth century.

Constitutional reforms and separate electorates

In the principle of equality before the law, the foundation for a common citizenship had already been well laid. Opportunities for further building on this foundation presented themselves when, toward the end of the nineteenth century, the first small concessions were made by the British to Indian participation in the legislative process. Elections were introduced early in the twentieth century, and in successive measures of constitutional reform the electorate was greatly enlarged. The forces of politically conscious India divided, however, as Hindu-Muslim communalism complicated the nationalist struggle against the British raj. Group antagonisms were extended from the socio-religious sphere into that of politics. Against a background of mutual distrust between the two communities, the demand was made by the Muslim minority for separate electorates.[58]

In 1906 the Agha Khan headed a Muslim deputation which presented its demand for separate representation to Lord Minto, the governor-general. The latter, in replying to the delegation, summed up their case as follows: "the pith of your address, as I understand it, is a claim that under any system of representation . . . the Mohammedan community should be represented as a community. You point out that in many cases electoral bodies as now constituted cannot be expected to return a Mohammedan candidate, and that if by chance they did so, it could only be at the sacrifice of such a candidate's views to those of a majority opposed to his community, whom he would in no way represent." Lord Minto expressed his approval of the proposed principle of communal representation.

Lord Morley, the secretary of state for India, resisted the idea but ultimately agreed under pressure from Minto. The Indian Councils Act of 1909 provided for separate Muslim electorates in most of the major provinces. Muslim seats were reserved in the Indian Legislative Council and the provincial councils, and only Muslims could vote for candidates for these seats. In addition, Muslims retained the right to vote in the general electorates.

The new system was opposed by many professional organizations, partly on communal grounds, no doubt, as most of these groups were predominantly Hindu in membership, but also on grounds of the principle involved. The Madras Landholders' Association objected that separate electorates were calculated to accentuate differences which were rapidly losing their importance in public life, and would impede the development of a sense of national unity so necessary to India's progress. Some writers have interpreted the introduction of separate electorates as part of a deliberate British policy to divide India still more sharply in order to perpetuate foreign rule. The Muslims were set as a counterpoise to the rising nationalism led by Hindus; it was the old device of "divide and rule." There is indeed some evidence to support this view. The charge against the British

---

[58] The problem of communal representation has been dealt with in many works. See especially: *Report on Indian Constitutional Reforms*, His Majesty's Stationery Office, London, 1918; Reginald Coupland, *The Indian Problem: Report on the Constitutional Problem in India*, London, 1944; K. B. Krishna, *The Problem of Minorities: or Communal Representation in India*, George Allen and Unwin, Ltd., 1939; Sadiq Ali, ed., *Congress and the Problem of Minorities*, Allahabad Law Journal Press, Allahabad, 1947; Dhirendranath Sen, *The Problem of Minorities*, Calcutta University Press, Calcutta, 1940.

has frequently been overstated, however. The British obviously did not create the Hindu-Muslim communal problem; they did exploit it for their own purposes from time to time.

In 1916 the Indian National Congress and the Muslim League, enjoying a brief period of harmonious relations, concluded an agreement regarding the representation of Muslims in the various legislative councils. It also provided that one-third of the elected Indian members of the Imperial Legislative Council should be Muslims. The agreement, known as the Lucknow Pact, confirmed the principle of separate electorates. This was a momentous decision which was later effectively used by the League to overpower Congress objections to the extension of the principle.

The Montagu-Chelmsford Report of 1918 deprecated communal electorates as incompatible with modern political institutions: "Division by creeds and classes means the creation of political camps organized against each other, and teaches men to think as partisans and not as citizens. . . . We regard any system of communal electorates, therefore, as a very serious hindrance to the development of the self-governing principle." Nevertheless, the report tended to accept the view that a pledge had been made by the British government to provide separate Muslim electorates when the Morley-Minto reforms were adopted. Only the Muslims could release the government from this pledge, and they obviously did not wish to do so. And, of course, by the Lucknow Pact the Congress had also agreed to separate electorates. The report therefore reluctantly recommended that the system be maintained, "even at the price of slower progress toward the realization of a common citizenship."

The Government of India Act which finally emerged in 1919 accorded communal representation not only to Muslims (on the basis of the pact), but to the Sikhs in the Punjab and to Europeans, Anglo-Indians, and Indian Christians. In addition, a definite proportion of seats was reserved for non-Brahmans in Madras and for Mahrattas in Bombay.

The 1930 report of the Indian Statutory Commission quoted with approval the Montagu-Chelmsford evaluation of separate electorates; they were theoretically wrong, harmful in practice, but politically necessary in view of the Muslim attitude. The Round Table Conferences in London (1930-1932) failed to resolve the question of the number of seats for each community. The Muslims wanted the continuation of separate electorates but with greatly increased representation; the Congress, although opposed to communal representation in principle, urged joint electorates with reservation of seats as a compromise. This failure led to Prime Minister Ramsay MacDonald's Communal Award, which provided for separate electorates with a specified number of reserved seats for Muslims, Europeans, Sikhs, Indian Christians, Anglo-Indians, and the Depressed Classes, and was made the basis for representation under the Government of India Act of 1935.

The system of separate representation undoubtedly stimulated the further growth of communalism. It encouraged the very defect it sought to remedy. The system encouraged the most vociferous and aggressive Muslim politicians; there was no need for the moderation which is inevitably developed when a candidate has to appeal to all groups. The minorities tended to lean on the artificial prop of separate electorates instead of strengthening their educational and economic position. The various religious communities became political units and functioned increasingly as such with each successive constitutional reform—1909, 1919, and 1935. The ultimate conclusion of this process—for a religious community to constitute itself a separate state—was reached with the partition of India and the creation of Pakistan as a separate Muslim state.

Hinduism and Indian nationalism

Thus far in the discussion of the British period, our concern has been with the development of government policy. We have sought to identify those policies of the British government which provide some of the historical roots of modern India's secular state. We have also noted the policies which militated against the development of secularism.

We must at this point discuss the religious policy of a non-governmental institution—the Indian National Congress—which with the attainment of independence became the ruling political party in the central government and in all the state governments. The roots of Indian secularism must be sought as much in the history of the Congress as in the pronouncements and policies of British governors-general. To what extent did the Congress espouse and implement the ideal of a secular, non-communal nationalist organization? And to what extent was its nationalism associated with Hindu revivalism, communal and exclusivist in its tendencies?

In a general way the Indian nationalist movement received considerable initial impetus from the reformist Hindu sects of the latter half of the nineteenth century. Leaders of the Hindu renascence such as Swami Dayananda and Swami Vivekananda abandoned the earlier defensiveness, and in different ways confidently proclaimed the superiority of Hindu religion and culture over the Christian West. The Indian National Congress, however, received no direct inspiration from this source at the time of its founding in 1885. A retired British civil servant, Allan Hume, was prominently associated with its formation, and four of the early presidents of the Congress were Englishmen. The leading members of the organization were western-educated Indians who subscribed to the ideals of British liberalism. Most of them had a sincere appreciation of the beneficial results of western rule in India, and the government for its part was generally sympathetic to the Congress in the early years.

Every effort was made to place the Congress on a solidly non-communal basis, despite the fact that the first meetings were predominantly Hindu gatherings. The report of the second Congress (1886) made it clear that religious community was irrelevant to membership in the nationalist organization. "The Congress is a community of temporal interests and not of spiritual convictions that qualify men to represent each other in the discussion of political questions; we hold their general interests in this country being identical, Hindus, Christians, Muslims and Parsis may fitly as members of their respective communities represent each other in the discussion of public secular affairs."[59] Differences of opinion were inevitable, it was recognized, but these would hinge "not on differences of creed, but on differences in social position, profession, occupation and the like." In the early Congress sessions there were Europeans, Eurasians, Hindus of many castes and sects, Shi'a and Sunni Muslims, Jains, Jews, Parsis, and Sikhs.

In 1887 Badruddin Tyabji, a Muslim, was elected president of the Congress, and nine years later Rahmatullah Muhammad Sayani occupied the same position. In 1888 the attendance at the Congress session was divided as follows: Hindus 965, Muslims 221, and

[59] *Report and Proceedings of the Second Indian National Congress.*

others 62.[60] In that same year the Congress adopted a resolution which stated that any subject introduced for discussion would be dropped if the Muslim or the Hindu delegates objected as a body. There was no unwillingness to reassure the minority group. The Muslim community as a whole, however, remained aloof from the Congress, following the lead of Syed Ahmed Khan. And by 1905, the militant Hinduism of the Extremists had reduced the number of Muslim delegates to a handful.

The late nineteenth and early twentieth centuries witnessed a mighty struggle for control of the Congress. The two factions, the Moderates and the Extremists, held radically different views as to the proper ends and means of the nationalist movement. The Moderates, represented by such men as M. G. Ranade and G. K. Gokhale, continued the liberal tradition. Convinced of the "blessings of British rule," they sought to promote the gradual political evolution of India along parliamentary lines and to press for social reforms which they deemed essential to the building of an enlightened modern state. "Although they were not men devoid of religious faith," wrote Stephen Hay, "they accepted the divorce of religion from government and maintained a secular view of politics which contrasted markedly with the religious outlook of the Extremists."[61] The Extremists, led by such men as Bal Gangadhar Tilak and Aurobindo Ghose, combined the western ideas of patriotism and nationalism with the religious symbolism of Hinduism. Rejecting the slow methods of the moderates, who submitted cautiously worded petitions to the government, the Extremists urged a program of action, immediate and even violent if necessary. Nationalism, identified with religion, became an absolute; India became the Mother, the goddess to whom fervent and undivided devotion must be given.

In Maharashtra, Tilak promoted the celebration of two festivals which became the vehicles of nationalist expression. One, dedicated to the Hindu god Ganesh, was a ten-day festival which provided a good occasion for both anti-British propaganda and the building up of a sense of Hindu solidarity.[62] The Shivaji festival honoring the

[60] M. V. Krishna Rao, *The Growth of Indian Liberalism in the Nineteenth Century*, H. Venkataramiah and Sons, Mysore, 1951, p. 304.
[61] *Sources of Indian Tradition*, p. 662. The religio-political thought and program of the Extremists is discussed in Maganlal Amritlal Buch, *Rise and Growth of Indian Militant Nationalism*, Baroda, Atmaram Press, 1940.
[62] Victor Barnouw, "The Changing Character of a Hindu Festival," *American Anthropologist*, 1954, vol. 56, pp. 74-86.

Maratha hero who had successfully fought against the Mughal empire, had a distinctly anti-Muslim tone. Swami Dayananda, mentioned above, had founded the Cow Protection Association in 1882, and Tilak continued the anti-cow killing agitation. His scholarly commentary on the *Bhagavad Gita* propounded the thesis that the *Gita*'s call to action in this world included political as well as religious deeds. At both the popular and the more sophisticated levels, Tilak effectively invoked the spirit of a resurgent Hinduism to fight the nationalist cause, but at the inevitable cost of alienating the Muslims.

After the mutiny, the Muslims had been considered the most dangerous opponents of British rule, but in the early twentieth century the government's policy began to favor them. The partition of Bengal in 1905 created a Muslim-majority area, widened the breach between the two communities, and gave further stimulus to Extremist activities. The religious symbols which Tilak used with such effectiveness in Maharashtra had no appeal in Bengal, but others of even greater potency were at hand. The land of Bengal, and by extension all of India, became identified with the female aspect of Hindu deity, and the result was a concept of divine Motherland. Bankim Chandra Chatterjee's poem *Bande Mataram* ("Hail to the Mother") soon became the great Congress nationalist song throughout India. The country was the Mother, but not a defenseless female: "Thou art Durga (the Goddess Mother), Lady and Queen, with her hands that strike and her swords of sheen."[63]

Some of the most passionate statements of the Extremist creed came from the pen of Aurobindo Ghose. "Liberty is the fruit we seek from the sacrifice and the Motherland the goddess to whom we offer it," he wrote in 1907. "Into the seven leaping tongues of the fire of the yajna (ritual sacrifice) we must offer all that we are and all that we have, feeding the fire even with our blood and lives and happiness of our nearest and dearest; for the Motherland is a goddess who loves not a maimed and imperfect sacrifice, and freedom was never won from the gods by a grudging giver."[64] Aurobindo's religious symbolism was much more than vivid imagery; he identified the country with its ancient faith so completely that patriotism and worship became indistinguishable. "Nationalism is not a mere

[63] *Sources of Indian Tradition*, p. 711.
[64] *Ibid.*, p. 727.

political program; nationalism is a religion that has come from God."

The cult of Durga or Kali, with its tantric ritual and animal sacrifices, quickly became associated with revolutionary terrorism in Bengal. A pamphlet printed at a secret press called upon the sons of India to rise up, arm themselves with bombs, and invoke the Mother Kali. "What does the Mother want? A coconut? No! A fowl or a sheep or a buffalo? No! . . . The Mother is thirsting after the blood of Feringhis (foreigners) who have bled her profusely."[65] While most of the Congress leaders condemned the terrorism in Bengal, Tilak gave veiled approval by his silence.

Bepin Chandra Pal, another Extremist leader, wrote in *The Soul of India* that the traditional gods and goddesses who had lost their hold upon the modern Hindu mind were now being reinstated with a new nationalist interpretation. Hundreds of thousands of people had now begun to hail their motherland as Durga or Kali. "These are no longer mere mythological conceptions or legendary persons or even poetic symbols. They are different manifestations of the Mother. This Mother is the spirit of India. This geographical habitat of ours is only the outer body of the Mother. . . . Behind this physical and geographical body, there is a Being, a Personality—the Personality of the Mother."

Failing to win control of the Congress in 1907, the Extremists split off from that body, and for various reasons their influence waned during the next decade.[66] Despite the intensity of the Extremists' efforts and the fervent religious appeal of their message, the main body of Indian nationalism preferred the slower path of progress through constitutional reforms. However, the Extremists made it doubly difficult for the Congress to attract the already suspicious Muslim minority, and the founding of the Muslim League (1906) coincided with the peak of Extremist influence.

In 1920 the Congress came under the control of Mohandas K. Gandhi, whose nationalism had deep roots in religious faith. In his autobiography Gandhi asserted that "those who say that religion has nothing to do with politics do not know what religion means." There can be no doubt that much of Gandhi's power as a political leader was based upon the Hindu reverence for a saint, for the ascetic who

[65] Quoted in Percival Griffiths, *The British Impact on India*, Macdonald and Company, London, 1952, p. 296.
[66] They were reunited with the Congress in 1916.

renounces personal comfort in order to attain a higher end. Further-more, Gandhi used religious terminology to explain the objectives of the nationalist movement. In the future, India would become *Ram rajya*, the kingdom of Rama, a golden age of peace and prosperity.

Gandhi's religious faith, however, was utterly different from that of the Extremists. He declared that his Hinduism included all that he knew to be best in Islam, Christianity, Buddhism, and Zoro-astrianism. Gandhi strove unceasingly for Hindu-Muslim unity, con-vinced that ultimately both religions were true and valid.[67] His deepest conviction was that God, Truth and *Ahimsa* (non-violence) were all one and the same. *Satyagraha* (truth-force, non-violent re-sistance) was thus based on Gandhi's personal religious faith, but as a political device it was employed by many thousands who did not share that faith. Gandhi's leadership of the Indian National Congress gave it a somewhat Hinduized appearance, but his constant emphasis on the religious, social, and political unity of the various communities helped to lay the foundation of the secular state.

There were other elements in the Congress which strengthened the non-communal approach during this period. Lawyers steeped in the principles of the British constitution had little in common with the representatives of Hindu revivalism; they continued the nineteenth-century liberal tradition through the entire inde-pendence movement. Muslim leaders of the Congress, especially Abul Kalam Azad, and members of other minorities by their very presence helped to maintain the non-communal nationalism of the movement. Men such as Jawaharlal Nehru and Subhas C. Bose subscribed to a secularist view of life and helped to produce a growing temper of mind which relegated religious matters entirely to the individual's conscience. The growth within the Congress of a socialist organization added the teachings of Marx and Laski to the other forces promoting secular nationalism.

In 1931 the Congress session at Karachi adopted a resolution on the fundamental rights which were to be incorporated in the future constitution of India. Along with the statements concerning religious liberty and the protection of the rights of minorities, we find this explicit commitment: "The state shall observe neutrality in regard

[67] See M. K. Gandhi, *Communal Unity*, Navajivan, Ahmedabad, 1949.

to all religions."[68] The secularism of the Constitution of 1950 was thus the fulfillment of a pledge made by the Indian National Congress nearly two decades before.

Paradoxically, the Muslim League also contributed to the secularism of the Indian National Congress. In the late 1930's and early 1940's, M. A. Jinnah repeatedly claimed that the League represented all the Muslims of India and furthermore insisted that the Congress publicly acknowledge itself as a purely Hindu organization. This challenge made it imperative that the Congress emphasize all the more its non-communal character. The League's demand for Pakistan in 1940 reinforced Congressmen's thinking about the nature of the independent Indian state of the future. If the proposal for the partition of India and the creation of a Muslim state was unsound, what was the Congress' alternative plan? The alternative could only be in terms approximating the secular state—a united India in which government would be kept separate from religion, and in which all citizens would have equal rights.

Anyone who is convinced that the basic idea of the secular state represents the only sound democratic solution to the problem of religious diversity must regard the partition of India as unfortunate, even tragic. British policy was undoubtedly partly responsible, and Indian writers frequently point to the initial decision to introduce separate electorates. Dr. S. Radhakrishnan saw a very clear cause-and-effect relationship: "Separate electorates intensified communal consciousness and created such an atmosphere of mistrust and hostility as to arouse the demand for Pakistan."[69]

British writers, on the other hand, tend to find that Congress inflexibility was the chief cause. Sir Percival Griffiths asserted that "it is undoubtedly true that the real creators of the demand for Pakistan were the Congress High Command. If they had been prepared to abate their claims to be the sole spokesmen for India and had tried to allay Muslim fears even slightly, Pakistan might never have come to birth."[70] While agreeing in part with Griffiths' statement, Pakistani writers interpret the founding of their country as a great positive achievement, the credit for which must go to

[68] See appendix in Jawaharlal Nehru, *The Unity Of India*, John Day Company, New York, 1948, p. 406.
[69] S. Radhakrishnan, *Religion and Society*, George Allen and Unwin Ltd., London, 1948, p. 242.
[70] Percival Griffiths, *op. cit.*, p. 342.

M. A. Jinnah and the Muslim League. We shall leave the precise evaluation of the innumerable factors which operated in this complex situation to the clearer perspective of future historians.

Religious policies of the princely states

Our discussion of the British period has thus far dealt exclusively with British India, that is, the territory governed directly by the foreign power. One-third of the country, however, never came under direct British rule; these 562 Indian states continued to be governed by rajas, maharajas, and nizams, in some cases with a minimum of British interference. Since the Indian states constituted such a sizable segment of the country, a word must be said about their religious policies.

Most of the states were ruled by Hindu dynasties, and in general they carried on the traditions of the ancient and medieval Hindu state. The raja was advised by his *purohita* or court chaplain, usually a Brahman, and the chief official functions were performed with elaborate religious ritual. Around the middle of the eighteenth century the maharaja of Travancore officially dedicated his kingdom to the god Padmanabhaswamy. The maharaja ruled the state as the deputy or agent of the god, assuming the title of Sri Padmanabha Dasa (servant of Lord Padmanabha).[71] The Hindu princes gave large grants and endowments to temples and *maths* and sometimes to mosques as well. In many cases the temples of the state were directly administered by the government.

In the Hindu state of Mysore, the detailed supervision of religious and charitable institutions was one of the regular administrative duties of government officers at the district and taluq (subdivision of a district) levels. These officials had power to inspect and control all religious institutions in their jurisdiction, settle questions of hereditary succession of temple priests, manage the personnel of religious institutions (appoint, fine, suspend, dismiss, transfer, and grant leave to hereditary servants), fix the scale of expenditures for each institution, sanction additional expenditures up to certain amounts, maintain a register of temple jewels and inspect them periodically, etc. The minuteness of detail in which official supervision of temples was exercised is illustrated by a Mysore government

[71] V. Nagam Aiya, *The Travancore State Manual*, Travancore Government Press, Trivandrum, 1906, vol. 2, p. 377.

order in 1922 which requested the chief administrative officers of the districts, whenever locks were required for the use of religious institutions, to send indents for them to the Muzrai superintendent. This official would then arrange to send as many as were required from his stock of locks of an approved pattern, with their serial number engraved thereon.[72]

In Mysore, the Hindu and Muslim institutions which received grants from and were managed by the government were known as Muzrai institutions and were so closely linked with the government as to raise the question whether they had a separate legal identity. A government order in 1906 sought to clarify this point. "The Muzrai institutions are legal persons capable of holding property and are distinct from government. The mere fact that some land or money grants have been made by government towards the object of the institutions or that the institutions themselves and their properties are in the management of government, cannot make any difference in their character as legal persons enjoying an existence separate from government. In the management of these institutions, therefore, the government should be considered to be acting as agents or trustees."[73] The close identification of government with the religious institutions gave rise to various questions. Some years before, the deputy accountant-general had found it necessary to issue a formal opinion explaining that persons serving in Muzrai institutions were not eligible to receive the pensions paid to government servants.

Almost invariably the construction of new places of worship was made possible by building grants sanctioned by the government. Grants of agricultural land enabled the temple or mosque to have a source of steady income, and in addition there were many cash grants sanctioned by the government in perpetuity. In 1856-1857 the government of Mysore disbursed over 376,000 rupees for the support of religious institutions, 212,000 in money and 164,000 in land. Because the Hindu population and number of religious institutions was much greater than that of the Muslims, and also no doubt because Mysore was a Hindu state, over 365,000 rupees went to temples and *maths* and only 11,000 to mosques and Muslim tombs.[74]

It would be quite inaccurate to say that government control ex-

[72] *The Mysore Muzrai Manual,* Superintendent, Government Press, Bangalore, 1934, pp. 399-400.
[73] *Ibid.,* p. 398.   [74] *Ibid.,* p. 6.

tended only to the financial and administrative work of the institutions. Government officers were frequently called upon to settle religious controversies which threatened the peaceful conduct of worship. In 1919 the Mysore Muzrai superintendent examined the question whether a temple priest of a particular non-Brahman caste should be permitted to wear the sacred thread. Finding that "there is no express Shastric prohibition against wearing such threads though they may not be consecrated *Yagnopavitams* according to Vedic ritual," the superintendent ordered the practice to be permitted. Other government orders dealt with: the presenting to a Brahman of the *prasadam* (a sweet liquid drunk by the worshipper) in plates when the temple priest was a non-Brahman, the proper caste or sect marks to be placed on the foreheads of temple images, and the placing of an image of Ramanuja along with that of the principal temple deity in a car festival.[75]

In 1949 the rulers of Travancore and Cochin entered into a covenant for the merger of the two states. The covenant, made with the concurrence and guarantee of the government of India, also dealt in detail with the future management of the temples then under the control of the respective maharajas. While the general arrangement was that such management would vest in boards, there was an interesting proviso that "the regulation and control of all rituals and ceremonies in the temple of Sri Poornathrayeesa . . . shall continue to be exercised as hitherto by the Ruler of Cochin."[76] Similar arrangements for the patronage and supervision of religious institutions existed in the states ruled by Muslim dynasties. In Hyderabad, a full-fledged Ecclesiastical Department supervised religious and charitable endowments and made grants of money to religious institutions. It was not until 1950 that the decision was made to abolish this department.[77]

The special rights and privileges of the Brahmans were considerable in some of the Indian states. More closely analogous to the prerogatives of the clergy in certain periods of European history, however, were the considerations shown the heads of *maths* (Hindu monastic institutions) by some of the maharajas. In Mysore, for example, a number of these *swamis* were exempted from personal ap-

---

[75] *Ibid.*, pp. 336-340, 393-395.
[76] *White Paper on Indian States*, Government of India Press, Delhi, 1950, p. 288.
[77] *Times of India*, September 9, 1950.

pearance in the civil courts of the state and from the payment of tolls when their carriages passed through state toll-gates.[78] The head of an important *math* received the "first day's bhiksha" from the government on the occasion of his visit to Bangalore. This was a sum of money, usually 50 or 70 rupees, granted as a token of hospitality and reverence to those of high spiritual status. However, the government of the maharaja of Mysore was careful to nip in the bud any pretensions to independent power. In 1892 a government order noted that in a few cases the established custom of obtaining the maharaja's previous consent to the nomination of successors to the headship of *maths* had been ignored. The order went on to state in no uncertain terms that every such nomination for succession should be submitted for the approval of the maharaja, and "non-recognition of a successor by His Highness will involve the resumption of all state grants in land or money." A government order passed in 1930 gave strict instructions to all subordinate officers neither to use nor recognize the title of "Diwan" (prime minister) assumed by the chief agents of some of the most influential heads of *maths*.[79]

In many of the Hindu states the government exercised final authority over caste matters, including the penalty of excommunication, until well into the twentieth century. Following the ancient law of Manu, punishment for crime varied with the caste of the offender long after equality before the law had been firmly established in British India. Untouchability was legally enforced in a number of the states, especially in Rajasthan, right up to the day of independence.[80] On the other hand, some of the states were ruled by enlightened rajas who took the lead in various measures of religious and social reform. In 1936 the maharaja of Travancore issued a proclamation which secured for untouchables the right of entry into Hindu temples throughout the state. In 1907 the Mysore government upheld an order of excommunication passed by the head of a Jain *math,* which among other things disqualified the individual from entering the public Jain temples. The government order stated: "It is an order (of excommunication) passed purely in the exercise of the ecclesiastical jurisdiction of the Swami and government cannot interfere therewith." In other cases, however, the government did

[78] *The Mysore Muzrai Manual*, pp. 501-502, 509.
[79] *Ibid.*, pp. 497-498, 509.
[80] See chapter 11, "Caste and the Secular State."

not hesitate to overrule the excommunication orders of ecclesiastical authorities, asserting that the question of admission to public temples had to be decided on "principles more catholic" than those recognized by certain religious leaders.[81]

Some of the princely states enforced the ancient Hindu law by which one who renounced his ancestral faith was deprived of the right to inherit property and of his rights over his infant children. Such disabilities were removed throughout British India in 1850, but continued in some of the Indian states through the early decades of this century.[82] This was true even in the progressive states of Travancore and Mysore. In 1894 the Chief Court of Mysore in the case of *Dasappa* v. *Chikkamma* held that a convert to Christianity, in consequence of his change of faith was *ipso facto* deprived of the right of guardianship over his children. The judgment stated: "It does not seem necessary to quote from *Smritis* and Digests of Hindu law to prove that an apostate from Hindu religion who is expelled from caste loses his civil rights." Various measures to remove these disabilities were rejected by the state legislature, and it was not until 1938 that the Caste Disabilities and Religious Change Act came into force.

In some of the small kingdoms the rajas ruled in the most autocratic fashion, and freedom of religion suffered along with other liberties. In a number of states religious conversion was made practically impossible. Just two years before independence the Surguja Apostasy Act was promulgated. This measure provided that conversions from "the Hindu religion" to "an alien faith" could not take place without the sanction of the government authorities.[83]

The religious policies of the Indian states were a part of the heritage which India received with her independence in 1947. With few exceptions these policies were not nearly as conducive to the realization of a secular democracy as those evolved in British India.

The legacy of history

In concluding this chapter it will be useful to summarize briefly the aspects of Indian history which provide the foundation for the

---

[81] *The Mysore Muzrai Manual*, pp. 505-506.

[82] William Lee-Warner, *The Native States of India*, Macmillan and Company, London, 1910, pp. 200, 307-308.

[83] See chapter 6, "The Propagation of Religion."

modern secular state. First, the long tradition of Hindu religious tolerance enabled the most diverse creeds to coexist peacefully. Freedom of religion, a basic component of the secular state, has strong roots in India's past. The embryo of a common secular citizenship (another basic component) can be seen in the practice of both Hindu and Muslim rulers in appointing high officials of state from the other community.

Secondly, the British policy of religious neutrality provided the direct antecedent of the secular state in India. This policy was reinforced by an equalitarian legal structure, a secular educational system, and the traditions of a modern administrative state. Thirdly, the Indian National Congress from its inception defined its aims in terms of secular political objectives, and, with the exception of a short period of Extremist dominance, generally remained faithful to the ideal of non-communal nationalism. In addition to this question of principle, the presence in India of large religious minorities made it politically inexpedient for the Congress to permit a closer association of Hindu religion (with its undeniable mass appeal) and Indian nationalism.

While these three points go far in explaining the secular constitution of India, it should be noted that other aspects of Indian history militate against the ideal. The Hindu state in both ancient and modern times enforced caste inequality by law, promoted Hindu religion as its first duty, and generally maintained a close institutional connection with religion. Despite the principle of religious neutrality, the British government gave substantial aid to Christian missionaries during certain periods, established the Church of England as its official religion, and by separate electorates hindered the evolution of a common Indian citizenship. Despite its secular ideals, the Indian National Congress must be held partly responsible for the alienation of the Muslims which led to the demand for partition.

On balance, however, the positive factors outweigh the negative ones. It is clear that the emergence of India as a secular state in the mid-twentieth century did not represent an abrupt break with the past, as in the case of Turkey in 1928. It was rather the result of attitudes, policies, and forces which had taken shape over hundreds of years, thousands of years if one considers the tradition of Hindu religious tolerance.

CHAPTER 4

THE CONSTITUTIONAL FRAMEWORK

Dr. B. R. Ambedkar, chairman of the drafting committee, observed in the Constituent Assembly that it would be impossible to frame an absolutely new or original constitution at this point in history. The only innovations possible in a constitution framed so late in the day, he declared, would be the variations needed to adapt it to the peculiar conditions prevailing in India. The Government of India Act of 1935 provided a large part of the basic framework, but important principles were borrowed from the constitutional systems of Great Britain, the United States, Canada, Eire, and Australia.

Part III of the Indian Constitution deals with fundamental rights, and here the framers drew heavily upon the principles of the United States Constitution, including the historic statement of religious liberty and church-state separation contained in the first amendment. The influence of the American constitutional system has been extensive not only in the formulation of fundamental rights but in their interpretation by the courts. The first chief justice of the Supreme Court of India in his inaugural address in 1950 attached great importance to the example of the United States Supreme Court, predicting that "the jurisprudence of that country and the principles of law laid down by that Court will be perhaps more relied upon for our decisions." This has indeed proved to be the case, and Indian judges have frequently been guided by American court decisions in dealing with questions of the individual, religion, and the state.[1]

[1] "Indian judges interpreting the provisions of their own Constitution often look to the decisions of the American Supreme Court which invariably provide guidance in deciding matters of religious freedom." C. H. Alexandrowicz, "The Secular State in India and in the United States," *Journal of the Indian Law Institute*, 1960, vol. 2, p. 273. Professor Alexandrowicz accepted the basic constitutional principles of the United States as the criteria for evaluating the claim that India is a secular state. A similar position was taken in another constitutional study, by Dr. Ved Prakash Luthera. See "The Concept of the Secular State and India," unpublished Ph.D. dissertation, University of Delhi, 1958. For the exact wording of the constitutional provisions regarding the secular state, see the Appendix to this chapter, p. 135.

A reading of a few of the leading cases, or even a glance at the exposition of articles 25-28 of the Indian Constitution in any commentary, is sufficient to indicate that the influence of United States constitutional law has been substantial.

In discussing the historical foundations of the Indian secular state, attention was naturally focused on the political history of India, especially the British period. In a very real sense, however, the century and a half of experience under the United States Constitution, including hundreds of judicial decisions on freedom of religion and church-state separation, form a vital part of the historical background of Indian secularism. American constitutional law had little relevance to India before 1947, but was deliberately appropriated as the framers of the Constitution and later the courts found in it certain valid answers to some of India's problems. Parts of the American constitutional tradition were grafted on to the British Indian stock and are now bearing fruit.

This chapter will examine the basic constitutional provisions which give shape to the concept of the secular state, and their interpretation by the Indian High Courts and Supreme Court. The term "secular state," it should be noted, does not appear in the Constitution itself. The late Professor K. T. Shah, a member of the Constituent Assembly, attempted on two occasions to secure the inclusion of the word "secular" in the fundamental law, but without success. His second attempt took the form of a proposed new article which read in part: "The state in India being secular shall have no concern with any religion, creed or profession of faith."[2] Shah argued that in view of the tragic results of communalism in India, it would be well to emphasize the secularity of the state in the most explicit terms. His amendment did not receive the support of the law minister, however, and was rejected by the Assembly. The inclusion of such an article in the Constitution, however laudable the intention behind it, would certainly have produced a conflict with article 25 which, as we shall see, permits extensive state intervention in matters connected with religion in the interest of social reform.

As was pointed out in chapter 1, it is helpful to think of the secular state as an interconnected set of relationships involving the individual, religion, and the state. We shall now examine the Indian Constitu-

[2] *Constituent Assembly Debates*, vol. 7, p. 815.

tion in terms of the three components of this conception—freedom of religion, citizenship, and separation of state and religion.

FREEDOM OF RELIGION

The Indian Constitution provides for the religious liberty of both the individual and associations of individuals united by common beliefs, practices, and discipline. The individual and collective aspects of religious liberty shall be discussed in this order.

Individual freedom of religion

The basic guarantee of this right is found in article 25(1):

Subject to public order, morality and health and to the other provisions of this Part, all persons are equally entitled to freedom of conscience and the right freely to profess, practice and propagate religion.

In discussions of the origin of this article, attention is frequently drawn to its similarity to the following provision of the 1937 Constitution of Eire: "Freedom of conscience and the free profession and practice of religion are, subject to public order and morality, guaranteed to every citizen."[3] There were, however, other sources nearer at hand. The language of the Indian Constitution is very similar to that of the resolution on fundamental rights adopted at the Karachi Congress in 1931. "Every citizen shall enjoy freedom of conscience and the right freely to profess and practice his religion, subject to public order and morality."[4]

The original draft of the article presented to the Constituent Assembly was even closer to the wording of the Karachi resolution than the final form, for it contained no mention of the right to propagate religion. Some members of the Assembly asserted that the right to propagate was contained in the right to practice religion, and that it was therefore unnecessary to specify it. Other members, however, were clearly motivated by the Hindu objection to the kind of propagation which leads to conversions from one religion to another. In this connection it is interesting to note the relevant provision (article 5) in the 1959 Constitution of the Kingdom of

[3] Article 44(2).
[4] Sadiq Ali, ed., *Congress and the Problem of Minorities*, Law Journal Press, Allahabad, 1947, pp. 119, 129.

Nepal. In this Hindu kingdom (the monarch must be an "adherent of Aryan Culture and Hindu Religion"), freedom of religion is guaranteed as follows: "Every citizen, subject to the current traditions, shall practice and profess his own religion as handed down from ancient times. Provided that no person shall be entitled to convert another person to his religion." In the Constituent Assembly of India, however, the demand of the small Christian minority for an explicit recognition of the right to propagate religion was agreed to.[5]

The freedom of religion guaranteed by the Indian Constitution is not confined to citizens but extends to "all persons," including aliens. This point, underlined by the Supreme Court in *Ratilal Panchand* v. *State of Bombay*, is of special interest because of the substantial number of foreign Christian missionaries in India, some of whom are exclusively engaged in propagating their faith among the adherents of other religions.[6]

The Constitution thus declares that every person has a fundamental right not only to hold whatever religious beliefs commend themselves to his judgment (freedom of conscience) but also to manifest his beliefs in such overt acts as are prescribed by his religion and to propagate its tenets among others (right to profess, practice, and propagate religion). The exercise of this right, however, is "subject to public order, morality and health." Here the Constitution succinctly expresses the limitations on religious liberty which have been evolved by judicial pronouncements in the United States and Australia. In a long series of cases the courts of the United States have held that: polygamy may be prohibited by legislation although it is sanctioned by a religious body, a person claiming supernatural healing powers many not use the postal services in order to procure money, religious propaganda on the streets is subject to regulation, etc. Strictly speaking, the language of the Indian Constitution makes freedom of conscience as well as the right freely to profess, practice, and propagate religion subject to state control in the interest of public order, morality, and health. This, however, is simply a case of inaccurate drafting, and the courts have made it clear that the

[5] This development is discussed in some detail in chapter 6, "The Propagation of Religion."

[6] 1954 Supreme Court Appeals, p. 546. See chapter 7, "The Question of Foreign Missionaries."

state can have no power over the conscience of the individual—this right is absolute.

The necessity of the state's power to preserve public order was pointedly enunciated when the United States Supreme Court asked: "Suppose that one believed that human sacrifices were a necessary part of religious worship, would it be seriously contended that the civil government under which he lived could not interfere to prevent a sacrifice?"[7] The Indian Penal Code (sections 295-298) makes it a crime to injure or defile a place of worship or to disturb a religious assembly, etc., even though these actions might be sanctioned by the offender's own religion. Practices like *sati*, or *devadasi* dedication which frequently led to temple prostitution, may have some basis in Hindu religion, but the state still has constitutional power to ban them.

The right to freedom of religion is subject not only to public order, morality, and health but to the other provisions of Part III. Therefore, the practice of untouchability (forbidden in article 17) could not be protected under article 25. Land can be compulsorily acquired by the state with compensation under article 31, despite the fact that it is part of a religious endowment.

The Indian courts have sketched out other areas in which freedom of religion is not absolute. It was held that article 25(1) did not give a Hindu student the right to perform the ceremonies of his religion in the compound of a Christian college.[8] In another case the Supreme Court held that an optional religious practice need not be protected by the constitutional guarantee of freedom of religion. Thus, a Muslim accustomed to sacrifice a cow at *Bakr-Id* would be compelled to obey a law prohibiting cow slaughter, for Islam recognizes as equally valid the sacrifice of a goat.[9]

Who defines religion?

It is obvious that the definition of "religion" becomes the crucial point in the application of article 25(1) to particular cases. And who is to give the authoritative definition—the individual, the religious body, or the state? The United States Supreme Court found

[7] *Reynolds* v. *United States*, 1878, 98 U.S., p. 145.

[8] *Sanjib Kumar* v. *St. Paul's College*, All India Reporter 1957 Calcutta, p. 524.

[9] *M. H. Quareshi* v. *State of Bihar*, A. I. R. 1958 Supreme Court, p. 731. A detailed discussion of this case is found in chapter 15, "The Challenge of Hindu Communalism."

it difficult to decide in an interesting case involving a compulsory salute to the American flag by school children. Children whose parents belonged to the religious group called Jehovah's Witnesses disobeyed the state law, refusing to salute the flag on the ground that, according to their religion, this act constituted idolatry, which was a sin. In a case in 1940 the court upheld the requirement of the flag salute; in effect it said that the state will determine what is religion, and that the state had rightly decided that the compulsory flag salute did not violate religious liberty. Three years later the court reversed itself and struck down the legislation requiring the flag salute. The court now said that if a religious body and the individual adherent seriously regarded this particular requirement as a violation of religious liberty, the state would respect such conscientious objections.[10]

It would obviously be impossible to accept the approach embodied in the latter decision in India, unless one were prepared to abandon all plans of social progress and modernization. As Dr. B. R. Ambedkar remarked concerning the relationship of personal law (Hindu, Muslim, Parsi, etc.) to religion: "The religious conceptions in this country are so vast that they cover every aspect of life from birth to death. There is nothing which is not religion and if personal law is to be saved I am sure about it that in social matters we will come to a standstill. . . . There is nothing extraordinary in saying that we ought to strive hereafter to limit the definition of religion in such a manner that we shall not extend it beyond beliefs and such rituals as may be connected with ceremonials which are essentially religious. It is not necessary that the sort of laws, for instance, laws relating to tenancy or laws relating to succession, should be governed by religion . . . I personally do not understand why religion should be given this vast expansive jurisdiction so as to cover the whole of life and to prevent the legislature from encroaching upon that field."[11]

The Bombay High Court has in several decisions given a very narrow interpretation of religion and the freedom of religion guaranteed by article 25(1). In *Ratilal* v. *State of Bombay*, the definition of religion did not even include the rituals and ceremonials referred to

[10] *Minersville School District* v. *Gobitis*, 1940, 310 U.S. p. 586, and *West Virginia State Board of Education* v. *Barnette*, 1943, 319 U.S. p. 624.
[11] *Constituent Assembly Debates*, vol. 7, p. 781.

by Dr. Ambedkar, but was restricted to ethical and moral precepts. "Therefore, whatever binds a man to his own conscience and whatever moral and ethical principles regulate the lives of men, that alone can constitute religion as understood in the Constitution. A religion may have many secular activities, it may have secular aspects, but these secular activities and aspects do not constitute religion as understood by the Constitution."[12] Similarly, in another case religion was interpreted solely in terms of faith and belief, and the authority of a religious body in relation to its members was held to have nothing to do with religion.[13]

The Supreme Court, however, has been unwilling to accept this extraordinarily narrow definition of religion. While unable to go as far as the United States Supreme Court in granting recognition to what are claimed to be religious beliefs and practices, there is nonetheless a vast difference between its interpretation and that cited in the previous paragraph. "A religion may not only lay down a code of ethical rules for its followers to accept, it might prescribe rituals and observances, ceremonies and modes of worship which are regarded as integral parts of religion, and these forms and observances might extend even to matters of food and dress." (This interpretation, incidentally, is strengthened by the rather curious Explanation 1 to article 25, which states that the wearing and carrying of *kirpans* shall be included in the profession of the Sikh religion. The *kirpan* is a sword, one of the five emblems which an orthodox Sikh must wear.) In this same Supreme Court judgment, the definition of religion was broadened to include still more. "What constitutes the essential part of a religion is primarily to be ascertained with reference to the doctrines of that religion itself. If the tenets of any religious sect of the Hindus prescribe that offerings of food should be given to the idol at particular hours of the day, that periodical ceremonies should be performed in a certain way at certain periods of the year or that there should be daily recital of sacred texts or oblations to the sacred fire, all these would be regarded as parts of religion and the mere fact that they involve expenditure of money, or employment of priests and servants or the use of marketable commodities

[12] A.I.R. 1953 Bombay, p. 242.
[13] *Taher Saifuddin* v. *Tyebbhai Moosaji*, A.I.R. 1953 Bombay, p. 183.

would not make them secular activities partaking of a commercial or economic character."[14]

The Supreme Court's statement that "what constitutes the essential part of a religion is primarily to be ascertained with reference to the doctrines of that religion itself" should not be taken too seriously, however. Much textual and historical evidence could be adduced to show that the caste system constitutes an essential part of Hinduism. But caste practices will certainly not be protected by the Constitution; as a matter of fact they are indirectly and directly attacked by the Constitution itself. Article 25(2) grants to the state broad, sweeping powers of interference in religious matters.

Limitations imposed by Indian conditions

The restrictions on freedom of religion based on considerations of public order, morality, and health are obvious ones and have many parallels in the constitutional law of the West. Article 25(2), however, imposes drastic limitations on the rights just guaranteed in 25(1) and reflects the peculiar needs of Indian society.

> Nothing in this article shall affect the operation of any existing law or prevent the state from making any law—
> (a) regulating or restricting any economic, financial, political or other secular activity which may be associated with religious practice;
> (b) providing for social welfare and reform or the throwing open of Hindu religious institutions of a public character to all classes and sections of Hindus.

Laws providing for the very extensive supervision by the state of temple administration (Hindu religious endowment acts) have been enacted by virtue of this provision. These are considered briefly in the discussion of the next article, and in considerable detail in chapter 9, "The Reform of Hindu Temples."

The extensive modification of Hindu personal law (marriage, divorce, adoption, succession, etc.) has been effected by legislation based on the provision which permits measures of social welfare and reform.[15] In an interesting case the validity of the Bombay Prevention

[14] *Commissioner, Hindu Religious Endowments* v. *Lakshmindra*, 1954 Supreme Court Appeals, pp. 431-432.
[15] See chapter 10, "Religion, Law, and Secularism."

of Hindu Bigamous Marriages Act of 1946 was upheld by the Bombay High Court. Chief Justice Chagla (a Muslim, later appointed as the Indian ambassador to the United States) delivered the judgment of the court and of necessity dealt with the religious question raised by the case. "It is only with very considerable hesitation that I would like to speak about Hindu religion, but it is rather difficult to accept the proposition that polygamy is an integral part of Hindu religion. It is perfectly true that Hindu religion recognizes the necessity of a son for religious efficacy and spiritual salvation. That same religion also recognizes the institution of adoption. Therefore, the Hindu religion provides for the continuation of the line of a Hindu male within the framework of monogamy." The learned judge went on to argue that, even assuming that polygamy is a recognized institution according to Hindu religious practice, the right of the state to enact this legislation could not be disputed. The enforcement of monogamy among Hindus is a measure of social reform which the state is empowered to legislate by article 25(2)(b) "notwithstanding the fact that it may interfere with the right of a citizen freely to profess, practice and propagate religion."[16]

The same constitutional provision permits legislation opening Hindu religious institutions of a public character to all classes and sections of India. Harijan temple entry laws have been enacted by many of the state legislatures. The central Untouchability (Offenses) Act of 1955 provides *inter alia* that any attempt to prevent Harijans from exercising their right of temple entry is punishable with imprisonment, fine or both.[17]

Article 25(2) thus authorizes the state to regulate any secular activity associated with religion, to legislate social reforms, and to force open the doors of Hindu temples to Harijans. C. H. Alexandrowicz wrote: "The above clause constitutes in itself a revolution in the traditional conception of religion in India." The revolution is that the state is engaged in "an extensive program of disentanglement of religious and secular activities."[18] This is indeed one aspect of the revolution, best illustrated by the standardization of Hindu personal law as one big step toward a uniform civil code. A secular civil law

[16] *State of Bombay* v. *Narasu Appa*, A.I.R. 1952 Bombay, p. 84.
[17] See chapter 9, "The Reform of Hindu Temples."
[18] Alexandrowicz, *op. cit.*, pp. 284-285.

equally applicable to all Indian citizens will be a notable achievement in this process of disentanglement by the secular state.

Another aspect of the revolution envisaged by this clause, however, is the assumption by the state of vast powers of control over the financial administration of Hindu religious institutions. In many respects this development moves in the opposite direction from the process of disentanglement of the religious and the secular. This development is revolutionary in that it constitutes a marked departure from the policies of the last seventy-five years of British rule. But essentially it represents a return to the pattern of extensive state control of religious institutions found in the ancient and medieval Hindu states and continued by some of the Indian states (Mysore, Travancore, and others) right up to 1947 and after.

Individual freedom of religion, basically guaranteed in article 25, is further strengthened by article 27, which declares that no person shall be compelled to pay taxes for the support of any particular religion. The interpretation of this provision is considered in another section of the chapter. The protection of the individual's freedom of conscience is also the object of article 28(3), which forbids compulsory religious instruction or worship in educational institutions recognized or aided by the state.

Collective freedom of religion

Religious denominations as well as individuals have certain important rights; collective freedom of religion is spelled out in article 26.

Subject to public order, morality and health, every religious denomination or any section thereof shall have the right—
(a) to establish and maintain institutions for religious and charitable purposes;
(b) to manage its own affairs in matters of religion;
(c) to own and acquire movable and immovable property; and
(d) to administer such property in accordance with law.

In the West, it is possible to speak of collective freedom of religion with greater precision than in India. The Christian churches are generally well organized, each with its own creedal statements, hierarchy of clergy, canon law or constitution, organs of church government, etc. To a large extent, the conception of separation of church and state presupposes this kind of ecclesiastical organization which is fully capable of internal autonomy. Hinduism and Islam do not fit into this pattern.[19] Although western analogies cannot be discarded if India is to continue to progress toward the ideal of the secular state, at the same time their limitations must be noted.

The conflict between the internal autonomy of a religious denomination and the role of the state in social reform was most dramatically manifested in the case of *Taher Saifuddin* v. *Tyebbhai Moosaji*.[20] The Bombay Prevention of Excommunication Act of 1949 prohibits the expulsion of a person from any community of which he is a member thus depriving him of his rights and privileges. The rights and privileges referred to are those which are legally enforceable by a civil suit and include the right to office or property or to worship in any religious place, and the right of burial or cremation. The head priest of the Dawoodi Bohra community passed two orders of excommunication against a member of the community which were later declared to be void, illegal, and of no effect by virtue of the Prevention of Excommunication Act. The Bombay High Court in this case upheld the constitutionality of the act which, according to the head priest, deprived his religious denomination of the right "to manage its own affairs in matters of religion."

The court reiterated its narrow definition of religion: religion is a matter of a man's faith and belief, and is to be sharply distinguished from *religious practice*. "Further, it does not seem to us that when a religious denomination claims a right to expel or excommunicate a member, it is managing its own affairs in matters of religion. Religion has nothing whatever to do with the right of excommunication or expulsion." Excommunication deprives a member of his legal rights and privileges, and a religious denomination which exercises this power is doing much more than managing its own affairs;

---

[19] This point is forcibly made in Ved Prakash Luthera, *op. cit.*, pp. 18-20. Because of the organizational deficiencies of religion in India, the state is called upon to perform many of the regulatory functions which are exercised internally in well-organized religions. Luthera concluded that India is not and cannot be a secular state. I disagree with this conclusion (1) because it proceeds from too narrow a definition of the secular state (Luthera equates it with separation of state and religion, which is only one of the three components in my definition), and (2) because it takes too static a view of Hindu religion which, as I have argued in chapter 9, has the potentiality for much greater organizational development.

[20] A.I.R. 1953 Bombay, p. 183.

it is interfering with the rights of its members, and such acts cannot be protected by article 26 of the Constitution.

Undoubtedly this decision is diametrically opposed to the basic idea of the freedom of the church in the West. There, the power of spiritual discipline, even to the extent of excommunication, has always been recognized as a prerogative of ecclesiastical authority, whether vested in the clerical hierarchy or in the collective membership of the church. In India, interference by the state in the internal affairs of religious groups, such as the Bombay legislation provides for, is definitely undesirable. At the same time, it should be noted that membership in a "community" in India is not strictly comparable to membership in a church in the West. The definition of a community in the Prevention of Excommunication Act is very broad; a community is a group of people who by birth, conversion, or the performance of any religious rite are regarded as belonging to the same religion or religious creed, *and it includes a caste or subcaste*. While excommunication in the West is mainly a religious matter, in India the social aspects of the act are likely to be more significant than the religious. The Bombay legislature, desirous of protecting the rights and privileges of the individual, prohibited excommunication as a measure of social reform.

It is not in the interest of the secular state to strengthen the social role of "communities" as such. Far from it. As a matter of fact, the present proliferation of highly organized caste associations is a trend which to some degree undermines the secular state. To the extent that the Bombay act discourages the arbitrary power of such organizations over its members it will serve a useful function. But how to achieve this without interfering with the spiritual discipline which an individual accepts as a condition of membership in a religious denomination? Will the Bombay Prevention of Excommunication Act shield the Anglican or the Roman Catholic from the discipline of his ecclesiastical authorities in the same way that this law has operated in relation to the Dawoodi Bohra community?

Another important case which involved the right of a religious denomination to manage its own affairs in matters of religion was *Venkataramana Devaru* v. *State of Mysore*, which is considered in detail in a later chapter.[21] Briefly, the case concerned the Venkatara-

---

[21] A.I.R. 1958 S.C., p. 255. See pp. 242-243.

mana temple belonging to the Gowda Saraswath Brahman community. The Madras Temple Entry Authorization Act, supported by article 25(2)(b) of the Constitution, threw open all Hindu public temples in the state to Harijans. The trustees of this denominational temple refused admission to Harijans on the ground that the caste of the prospective worshipper was a relevant matter of religion according to scriptural authority, and that under article 26(b) of the Constitution they had the right to manage their own affairs in matters of religion. The Supreme Court admitted that this was a matter of religion, but, faced with the conflict between articles 25(2)(b) and 26(b) of the Constitution, it approved a compromise arrangement heavily weighted in favor of the rights of Harijans and with but token concessions to the right of a religious denomination to exercise internal autonomy.

It is in the interest of the secular state to strengthen the internal autonomy of religious denominations, although this fact is little realized by the various legislatures. The demand for social reform and (as we shall see in chapters 8 and 9) *religious reform* is so pressing that little attention is paid to the principle of separation of state and religion. At the same time, it must again be emphasized that the Gowda Saraswath Brahman community only partly resembles a "religious denomination" in the western usage of the word. Probably a *math* (Hindu monastic institution) comes closer to the meaning of this term. A *math* propagates a particular set of doctrines, has a definite number of disciples, and is presided over by a single *guru* or *swami* in whom are vested complete powers over both the spiritual and the temporal affairs of the institution.[22]

Article 26(c) and (d) recognize the right of a religious denomination to own, acquire, and administer movable and immovable property in accordance with law. It was held, however, that this guarantee did not imply that such property was not liable to compulsory acquisition under the Uttar Pradesh Abolition of Zamindari Act. In a case in Orissa, land reforms resulted in the expropriation of a village and surrounding agricultural land dedicated to the maintenance of a Hindu deity. Since compensation was paid, the High

[22] Some of the modern reformist Hindu movements, of course, are organized very much like religious groups in the West. The Ramakrishna Mission is an outstanding example of this highly developed kind of ecclesiastical organization.

Court held that there was only a change in the form of the property.[23]

It should be emphasized that the right of a religious denomination is to administer its property "in accordance with law." In Bombay, Madras, and Orissa, religious endowments legislation granted to state officials vast powers of control over the financial affairs of Hindu temples and *maths*. This legislation presupposed a sharp distinction between the "administration of property" and "matters of religion" which is simply untenable. The Madras High Court found it difficult to separate the two, since the temporal affairs are managed in order to promote the religious affairs for which the institution exists; they are "inextricably mixed up."[24]

The Supreme Court, however, drew the distinction in clear-cut terms. "Under article 26(b), therefore, a religious denomination or organization enjoys complete autonomy in the matter of deciding as to what rites and ceremonies are essential according to the tenets of the religion they hold and no outside authority has any jurisdiction to interfere with their decision in such matters." So much for the management of religious affairs; the court then immediately turned to the financial question. "Of course, the scale of expenses to be incurred in connection with these religious observances would be a matter of administration of property belonging to the religious denomination and can be controlled by secular authorities in accordance with any law laid down by a competent legislature; for it could not be the injunction of any religion to destroy the institution and its endowments by incurring wasteful expenditure on rites and ceremonies."[25] This crushing blow to the concept of internal autonomy was mitigated only by the court's observation that a law which would take the right of administration from the hands of a religious denomination altogether and vest it formally and legally in any other authority would constitute a violation of article 26(d).

Thus, the right of collective freedom of religion guaranteed by article 26 does not provide the kind of protection from state interference which is found in a secular state in the West, the United

[23] *Suryapal Singh* v. *State of U.P.,* A.I.R. 1951 Allahabad, p. 674, and *Chintamoni* v. *State of Orissa*, A.I.R. 1958 Orissa, p. 18.
[24] *Lakshmindra Theertha Swamiar* v. *Commissioner of Hindu Religious Endowments*, A.I.R. 1952 Madras, p. 613.
[25] *Commissioner, Hindu Religious Endowments* v. *Lakshmindra Theertha Swamiar*, A.I.R. 1954 S.C., p. 291.

States, for example. Article 30 deals with another aspect of collective freedom of religion:

(1) All minorities, whether based on religion or language, shall have the right to establish and administer educational institutions of their choice.

(2) The state shall not, in granting aid to educational institutions, discriminate against any educational institution on the ground that it is under the management of a minority, whether based on religion or language.

In its advisory opinion on the Kerala Education Bill of 1957, the Supreme Court considered the scope of this special fundamental right guaranteed to linguistic and religious minorities. Out of the total population of 14,200,000 in Kerala there were 3,400,000 Christians and 2,500,000 Muslims. The Roman Catholics especially felt their educational institutions threatened by the provisions of this legislation drafted by the Communist government of the state.

The Supreme Court made it clear that, with the exception of certain Anglo-Indian institutions provided for under article 337, private educational institutions had no constitutional right to receive any grant from the state. Nevertheless, the situation was such that without state aid practically none of these institutions could operate (for example, every Christian school in the state was heavily dependent on government grants). The court declared: "No educational institution can in actual practice be carried on without aid from the state and if they will not get it unless they surrender their rights they will, by compulsion of financial necessities, be compelled to give up their rights under article 30(1)."[26]

Clauses 14 and 15 of the Kerala Education Bill enabled the government under certain circumstances to take over the entire management of aided institutions, and the institutions were made subject to this possibility as a condition for the grant of aid. The Supreme Court declared these clauses unconstitutional. However, it upheld drastic regulations providing for rigid state control over the appointment of teachers, the collection of fees, and the payment of teachers' salaries by the government, etc. The court observed only that these were "serious inroads on the right of administration and appear perilously near violating that right."

[26] *In re Kerala Education Bill*, 1957, A.I.R. 1958 S.C., p. 983.

CITIZENSHIP

The second component of the secular state, the concept of citizenship, is based on the idea that the individual, not the group, is the basic unit. The individual is confronted by the state which imposes duties and responsibilities upon him; in return the state guarantees rights and grants privileges to the individual. The sum total of these individual-state relationships constitutes the meaning of citizenship.

No state discrimination on grounds of religion

In the Indian Constitution there are many provisions dealing with the citizen's relations with the state. Here we shall concern ourselves only with those articles which specifically rule out any religious considerations in defining the rights and duties of the citizen. After guaranteeing in article 14 the right to equality before the law and the equal protection of the laws, the Constitution goes on in article 15(1) to provide: "The state shall not discriminate against any citizen on grounds only of religion, race, caste, sex, place of birth or any of them."

We have already discussed the effect on freedom of religion of legislation prohibiting Hindu polygamy, since it was contended by some that the practice of polygamy was a part of Hindu religion. Also involved, however, is the question whether such legislation does not discriminate against Hindus contrary to article 15(1). This was raised in the case referred to previously, *State of Bombay* v. *Narasu Appa*.[27] It was alleged that the Bombay Prevention of Hindu Bigamous Marriages Act discriminated between Hindus and Muslims on the ground of religion and applied a measure of social reform to Hindus, restricting them to monogamy while allowing Muslims to continue the practice of polygamy. Furthermore, Hindus were discriminated against also in relation to Christians and Parsis, since severer penalties were provided in the impugned act than in the Penal Code applicable to the other two communities for whom monogamy was also the law.

The Bombay High Court upheld the severer penalties on the ground that they were necessary to make the law socially effective. Laying emphasis on the word *only* in article 15(1), it held that the legislation did not single out the Hindus on the ground of religion

---

[27] *State of Bombay* v. *Narasu Appa*, A.I.R. 1952 Bombay, p. 84.

only. The legislature had to take into account the social customs and beliefs of the Hindus and other relevant considerations before deciding whether it was necessary to provide special legislation making bigamous marriages illegal. The state was entitled to consider, for example, the relative educational development of the Hindus and the Muslims. "One community might be prepared to accept and work social reform; another may not yet be prepared for it. . . . The state may rightly decide to bring about social reform by stages and the stages may be territorial or they may be community-wise."

In a similar case arising under the Madras Hindu Bigamy Prevention and Divorce Act of 1949, it was held that the act did not discriminate between Hindus and Muslims on the ground of religion.[28] While only Hindus were affected by the legislation, "the essence of that classification is not their religion but that they have all along been preserving their personal law peculiar to themselves which was derived from the *Smritis*, commentaries, custom and usage." According to this interpretation, the act did not discriminate on the ground of religion since it applied not to those who professed Hindu religion but to those who were governed by Hindu law! The Madras High Court here indulged in a bit of pure sophistry.

The strained interpretations of the courts notwithstanding, there is absolutely no doubt that such legislation is discriminatory and contrary to article 15(1). This is not to suggest that the courts should have declared these laws unconstitutional. During this transitional period when India is struggling to become a modern state, it is precisely the function of the courts to concoct such ingenious interpretations in order to harmonize the permanently valid principle, article 15(1) in this case, with the dynamic urge for social reform which still has to find expression within the antiquated framework of religious civil laws. Not only the Hindu Bigamous Marriages Act, but the whole system of Hindu and Muslim personal law is contrary to article 15(1)! It is only when there is a uniform civil code that the courts will be able to afford the luxury of a natural and straightforward interpretation of this fundamental constitutional principle of the secular state.[29]

While the existence of different personal laws contradicts the principle of non-discrimination by the state contained in article 15(1),

[28] *Srinivasa Aiyar* v. *Saraswati Ammal*, A.I.R. 1952 Madras, p. 193.
[29] See chapter 10, "Religion, Law, and Secularism."

the Constitution itself contradicts this principle in dealing with the problems connected with the caste system. In its special provisions for the Scheduled Castes, Scheduled Tribes, and other backward classes, the Constitution "introduced what may be called *protective discrimination* in favor of those sections of the community which require urgent support, for, if the principle of equality were applied without any exception, the reorganization of Indian society and the uplift of its hitherto neglected strata would be difficult if not impossible."[30] While the motive behind such protective discrimination is laudable, the problems which it has created are enormous.

One of the problems was the constitutional one, namely, how to reconcile the principles of protective discrimination and non-discrimination by the state. In certain specific areas this adjustment had already been made in the Constitution as adopted in 1950, but there was no qualification of the non-discrimination principle contained in article 15(1). Adverse court decisions (described later in the chapter) necessitated the First Amendment Act, 1951, which *inter alia* inserted article 15(4): "Nothing in this article or in clause (2) of article 29 shall prevent the state from making any special provisions for the advancement of any socially and educationally backward classes of citizens or for the Scheduled Castes and the Scheduled Tribes." The state is thus permitted to discriminate among citizens on grounds of religion, caste, etc., when providing for the advancement of certain sections of the population.

In 1950 the president promulgated the Constitution (Scheduled Castes) Order which specified the castes which were to be deemed Scheduled Castes for the purpose of the Constitution. Paragraph 3 of the order provided that "no person who professes a religion different from Hinduism shall be deemed to be a member of a Scheduled Caste."[31] There was only one exception made: in the case of the Punjab, the members of four of the castes listed were deemed to be members of the Scheduled Castes whether they professed the Hindu or Sikh religion. A Sikh member of the Bawaria caste (which was not one of the four excepted castes) challenged the president's order, since he was denied the special privileges accorded to Hindu

[30] Alexandrowicz, *op. cit.*, p. 289.

[31] This provision of the order was no innovation, but generally followed paragraph 3 of the Government of India (Scheduled Castes) Order, 1936, which excluded Indian Christians, Buddhists, and the adherents of tribal religions from the definition of membership in a Scheduled Caste.

members of the same caste. He contended that the order was un-constitutional because under article 15(1) no discrimination was to be made against any individual on the ground of religion.

The Punjab High Court, however, upheld the order, relying chiefly on article 15(4). "So in the Constitution," the court declared, "exceptions have been made to the general rule of clause (1) of article 15, and that being so, the state can legitimately (and without doing violence to the rights of any citizen under the Constitution) choose for special treatment the members of a certain caste or some members of that caste."[32] As far as the Sikhs are concerned, this discrimination was removed by an act of Parliament in 1956 which amended the president's order. The new paragraph 3 provides that "no person who professes a religion different from the Hindu or the Sikh religion shall be deemed to be a member of a Scheduled Caste."

The chief purpose served by the Constitution (Scheduled Castes) Order was to provide the authoritative list of castes for whom the reservation of seats in the legislatures could be made. A number of the state governments, however, used the same or similar lists as the basis for the granting of educational fee concessions and economic assistance. Christian, Muslim, or Buddhist converts of Scheduled Caste origin were denied these benefits, even though their economic position was the same as before conversion. Upon reconversion to Hinduism they once more became eligible for the special aid. While practice varied greatly from state to state, there was widespread dis-crimination on this basis.

In Madras the school fee concession to Harijan children was ex-tended to those who were converted to Christianity or whose parents were converts, but not to children whose grandfathers or other an-cestors were converted. The Madras High Court upheld this rule as non-discriminatory. Harijan converts could not claim the fee concession as a matter of right; the state was granting an indulgence and it was for the state alone to decide how far the indulgence should extend.[33] In 1956 B. R. Ambedkar led a mass conversion movement of his Scheduled Caste followers into the Buddhist re-ligion. The Bombay government thereupon withdrew the special concessions which the converts had previously enjoyed as Hindu

[32] *Gurmukh Singh* v. *Union of India*, A.I.R. 1952 Punjab, p. 143.
[33] *In re M. Thomas*, A.I.R. 1953 Madras, p. 21.

Harijans. After a vigorous agitation, these concessions were restored to the neo-Buddhists, but they are still not available to Christian converts. In some states converts of Scheduled Caste origin receive similar concessions under the classification of Backward Classes, but many anomalous and inequitable situations still remain.[34]

In 1953 the Backward Classes Commission was appointed to determine the criteria for classifying any sections of the population as socially and educationally backward classes. These, of course, would be in addition to the Scheduled Castes and Scheduled Tribes. The report of the commission suggested the classification of these groups mostly on the basis of caste and subcaste.[35] The government of India found the commission's caste criterion for determining backwardness unacceptable, since its adoption would tend to perpetuate the very evil of casteism which should be eradicated. The state governments, however, have drawn up their own lists of Backward Classes.

Applying the non-discrimination principle

It seems clear that the fundamental conception of citizenship as a relationship between the individual and the state is being seriously undermined by the attempt to deal with the problem of the underprivileged on the basis of the group, especially the caste. Article 15(1) lays down the basic democratic principle that the state shall not discriminate against any citizen on grounds only of religion, caste, etc. This general principle is then applied to three specific areas: (1) public employment or office, (2) admission to state educational institutions, and (3) voting and representation in legislatures. However, just as article 15(1) is qualified by a major exception, there are similar exceptions to the principle of non-discrimination in each of these specific areas.

In regard to public employment the guarantee is stated both positively and negatively. Article 16(1) asserts the principle of equality of opportunity for all citizens in matters relating to employment or appointment to any office under the state. Negatively, according to article 16(2): "No citizen shall, on grounds only of religion, race, caste, sex, descent, place of birth, residence or any of them, be in-

[34] For a detailed discussion of this problem see chapter 11, "Caste and the Secular State."

[35] *Report of the Backward Classes Commission,* Government of India Press, Delhi, 1956, vol. 1, p. 46.

eligible for, or discriminated against in respect of, any employment or office under the state."[36]

The Constitution provides for one exception to the principle of no *religious* qualifications for public office. Article 16(5) permits laws requiring that the incumbent of an office connected with the affairs of a religious institution be an adherent of that religion. Thus the commissioner and all of his subordinates in the Madras Hindu Religious Endowments Department must be Hindus. Although these are all officers of the secular state, the religious qualification is allowed by this clause.

Another exception to the general principle of non-discrimination is found in article 16(4):

> Nothing in this article shall prevent the state from making any provision for the reservation of appointments or posts in favor of any backward class of citizens which, in the opinion of the state, is not adequately represented in the services under the state.

Article 335 of the Constitution states that the claims of the members of the Scheduled Castes and Scheduled Tribes shall be taken into consideration in the making of appointments to government posts and services. Such special consideration must be made "consistently with the maintenance of efficiency of administration." Article 16(4) refers to "any backward class of citizens," which includes the Scheduled Castes and Tribes as well as others. Furthermore, it goes beyond the vague provisions of article 335 by permitting the state to reserve certain posts and appointments for these sections of the population.

An important test case turning on this provision of the Constitution was *Venkataramana* v. *State of Madras.*[37] The Madras government had issued a Communal G. O. (government order) making reservation of posts for Harijans, backward Hindus, non-Brahmans, Brahmans, Muslims, and Christians. As a result of this setup a Brahman was refused a particular appointment without regard to his personal qualifications, simply because he was a Brahman and the number of posts reserved for his community had already been filled. The Supreme

---

[36] Similarly, the Government of India Act, 1935, provided that "no subject of His Majesty domiciled in India shall on grounds of religion, place of birth, descent, color or any of them be ineligible for office under the Crown in India."

[37] A.I.R. 1951 S.C., p. 229.

Court declared the Communal G. O. to be repugnant to article 16(1) and (2), and therefore null and void. The point of unconstitutionality was that the order had gone beyond the reservation of posts for *backward classes* envisaged in clause (4). It had established a distribution of posts among all communities according to fixed ratios, and this infringed on the petitioner's fundamental rights.

However, it is possible to define backward classes in such a way as to rob this decision of all its significance. The Mysore government, in an order dated 1921, had classified "all communities other than Brahmans who are not adequately represented in the services" as backward communities. In the 1956 case of *Kesava Iyengar* v. *State of Mysore,* the High Court upheld this order, under which seven of ten posts were reserved for the backward classes.[38] Commenting on this decision, A. T. Markose asserted: "It is common knowledge in India that there are many groups or castes in the class 'Brahmans' who are very much backward educationally, and unrepresented in government employment. A classification on such naked communal nomenclature is approved by the High Court. The battle for social integration of the nation could be lost before it was scarcely begun."[39]

When the scope for equality of opportunity is reduced to three posts out of ten, the modern conception of the individual as the basic unit within the state is in grave peril. This kind of arrangement produces a state composed of castes and communities, not individuals. It may effect a static kind of justice, but it does not lead to a dynamic society or a truly secular state.

The second area to which the principle of non-discrimination is applied is that of admission to state educational institutions. Article 29(2) provides that "no citizen shall be denied admission into any educational institution maintained by the state or receiving aid out of state funds on grounds only of religion, race, caste, language or any of them."

The Communal G. O. issued by the Madras government, mentioned above, also established a policy of admission to the engineering and medical colleges of the state. It provided that admissions should

[38] A.I.R. 1956 Mysore, p. 20.
[39] A. T. Markose, "The First Decade of the Indian Constitution," *Journal of the Indian Law Institute,* 1960, vol. 2, p. 160xv.

be granted by the selection committee strictly on a communal basis. Out of every fourteen seats, six were to be allotted to non-Brahman Hindus, two to backward Hindus, two to Harijans, two to Brahmans, one to Anglo-Indians and Indian Christians, and one to Muslims.

A lady candidate complained that she was denied admission to the medical college on the ground that she belonged to the Brahman community. The Madras High Court gave judgment in her favor, and the government appealed the case to the Supreme Court. In *State of Madras* v. *Sm. Champakam Dorairajan*, 1951, the Supreme Court declared the G. O. unconstitutional inasmuch as it distributed seats among communities according to a fixed ratio.[40] The court found that the classification made in the order constituted a clear violation of the fundamental right guaranteed to citizens under article 29(2). This right is a right conferred on a citizen as an *individual* and not as a member of a class. The denial of admission to a qualified Brahman cannot be defended under the Constitution on the plea that there is no exclusion of Brahmans as a class. The article is not concerned with the rights of classes but of individual citizens.

This decision produced a constitutional problem for the state and central governments. How could reservation of seats be made in state educational institutions for the Scheduled Castes and Tribes and other backward classes (protective discrimination) in the light of the non-discrimination principle of article 29(2)? In the area of public employment the Constitution had already provided an exception to this principle in favor of the backward classes of the population, but there was no exception to article 29(2). This lacuna was filled by the first amendment, discussed above, which inserted article 15(4). The new clause stated that nothing in articles 15 or 29(2) would prevent the state from making any special provision for the advancement of any socially and educationally backward classes of citizens or for the Scheduled Castes and Tribes. It is important to note that the amendment does not validate the distribution of seats on communal lines (as was done in the Madras G. O.), but only validates reservation of seats for these weaker sections of the population.

[40] A.I.R. 1951 S.C., p. 226.

Non-discrimination in political functions

The third application of the principle of non-discrimination among citizens is in the area of voting and representation in the legislatures. Article 325 states:

> There shall be one general electoral roll for every territorial constituency for election to either House of Parliament or to the House or either House of the Legislature of a state and no person shall be ineligible for inclusion in any such roll or claim to be included in any special electoral roll for any such constituency on grounds only of religion, race, sex or any of them.

The first important provision to be noted here is that there can be no religious or caste requirements for voting. Article 326 states the principle positively and simply by declaring that elections "shall be on the basis of adult suffrage."

The second aspect to be noted is that the system of separate communal electorates, first established in 1909, was abolished. "There shall be one general electoral roll for every territorial constituency. . . ." Under the old system each of the larger minority communities (Muslims, Christians, Sikhs, etc.) had its electoral roll and a number of reserved seats in the legislatures. Thus, only Muslim voters could vote for Muslim candidates standing for election to seats specifically reserved for Muslims in the legislatures.

While the system of separate electorates was abolished, the Constitution does provide for the reservation of seats for the Scheduled Castes and Scheduled Tribes[41] in the central and state legislatures (articles 330 and 332). According to the original article 334, the reservation of seats was to cease after a period of ten years from the commencement of the Constitution, or in 1960. The eighth amendment, however, extended this reservation for another ten years.

[41] As has been noted above, the Constitution (Scheduled Castes) Order provides that no person who professes a religion different from the Hindu or Sikh religion shall be deemed a member of a Scheduled Caste. In *S. Michael* v. *S. Venkateswaran,* the Madras High Court upheld this order under which a Christian convert from a Scheduled Caste was denied the right to stand for election to a reserved seat in the legislature. A.I.R. 1952 Madras, p. 474. The Constitution also makes provision for the special representation of the Anglo-Indian community in the central and state legislatures by nomination (articles 331 and 333).

Difficult constitutional problems have arisen over this arrangement, especially under the system of double-member constituencies (one reserved and one general seat). In *V. V. Giri* v. *D. S. Dora* the Supreme Court upheld the election of Scheduled Tribes candidates to both the reserved and the general seats.[42] In 1961 Parliament enacted legislation providing for the division of two-member constituencies. While this will eliminate certain problems, it will undoubtedly create others. Thus a non-Scheduled Classes person residing in a constituency for which there is a reserved seat will be unable to stand for election to that seat. If he is a person of limited financial resources it will be very difficult for him to conduct an effective election campaign in another constituency where he is less well known.

The provision for joint electorates in article 325 refers specifically to elections to the central and state legislatures only. The question arose whether a state law could provide for separate electorates for the members of the various religious communities, in elections to local legislative bodies. The Supreme Court in *Nainsukh Das* v. *State of U. P.* held that such a law went counter to the non-discrimination principle of article 15(1). The court observed: "Now it cannot be seriously disputed that any law providing for elections on the basis of separate electorates for members of different religious communities offends against article 15(1). . . . The constitutional mandate to the state not to discriminate on the ground, *inter alia,* of religion extends to political as well as to other rights."[43]

In concluding this section on the constitutional basis for the concept of citizenship in the Indian secular state, a few generalizations may be made. It is obvious that the fundamental principle of equality and non-discrimination in the state's relationships with the individual citizen is seriously compromised in several areas. Almost all of the difficulties have their roots in the state's commendable recognition of its special responsibilities toward those sections of the population which in the past have been the victims of exploitation. However, the approach to the problem has too often identified special need with a caste designation, and there is no doubt that caste consciousness has thereby been strengthened.

[42] A.I.R. 1959 S.C., p. 1318. See S. S. Nigam, "Equality and the Representation of the Scheduled Classes in Parliament," *Journal of the Indian Law Institute*, 1960, vol. 2, pp. 297-320.

[43] A.I.R. 1953 S.C., p. 385.

The assumption of the framers of the Constitution, of course, was that the special provisions based on protective discrimination would be of a temporary nature. With the expected rise of mass education and the general standard of living in India over the next twenty years, there should be more of equality and fewer special provisions in the state's dealings with its citizens. Individuals coming from groups which in the past have been underprivileged will be able to compete with others on a basis of relative equality. As India becomes a welfare state in reality, many of the special provisions will be extended to all citizens; this is already happening in the field of elementary education. So one can be hopeful about future developments. However, the present approach to the problem is creating a large number of people who are far more interested in perpetuating and augmenting the privileges extended to them on a caste basis than they are in securing equality of opportunity. Having created these vested interests, the state will not find it a simple matter to dissolve them.

SEPARATION OF STATE AND RELIGION

We now come to the third component of the secular state. Separation of state and religion is the principle which preserves the integrity of the other two relationships, freedom of religion and citizenship. Once the principle of separation of state and religion is abandoned, the way is open for state interference in the individual's religious liberty, and for state discrimination against him if he happens to dissent from the official creed. Even today in some of the democratic states of western Europe, the state-church system retains vestiges of these consequences. The individual may be compelled by taxation to support the official religion, or may be disqualified from the highest office in the state by virtue of his profession of another religion.

In 1947 the United States Supreme Court defined separation of church and state as follows: "Neither a state nor the federal government can set up a church. Neither can pass laws which aid one religion, aid all religions, or prefer one religion over another. . . . No tax in any amount, large or small, can be levied to support any religious activities or institutions, whatever they may be called, or whatever form they may adopt to teach or practice religion. Neither a state nor the federal government can, openly or secretly, participate in the affairs of any religious organizations or groups and vice versa. In the words of Jefferson, the clause against establishment of religion by law was intended to erect 'a wall of separation between church and state.' "[44]

In actual practice the separation is not absolute, as is shown by the fact that each house of Congress has a chaplain who daily invokes divine guidance for the proceedings of the legislature. But the statement helps to clarify the meaning of separation of church and state. It is a conception of two separate and mutually non-interfering organizations, each operating within its own sphere of activity.

It is clear that such a thorough-going separation of state and religion does not exist in India. We have already discussed the important areas in which state interference in religious matters is permitted by the Constitution: the financial administration of temples and *maths*, the admission of Harijans into Hindu temples, the practice of excommunication from religious communities, the modification of religious personal laws, etc. The chief reason for such state interference is that Hinduism lacks the kind of ecclesiastical organization necessary to set its own house in order; the tremendous urge for effective social and religious reform which characterizes present-day India can only be satisfied by state action.[45] The organizational deficiency of Hinduism is indeed a serious problem. How can there be separation of church and state where there is no church?

The firmly established principle in the United States that the courts will not decide controversies over matters of religious doctrine or ritual has a pale reflection in Indian judicial decisions of some years ago. In 1935 the Bombay High Court held that a civil court is not competent to decide whether a particular cult is within Vedic religion or not. In a 1939 case in Madras, it was held that the question whether a particular *namam* or mark should be placed on an idol's forehead was one pertaining to religious ritual and as such was excluded from the cognizance of a civil court.[46] Since 1950, however, the courts have frequently had to deal with doctrinal questions in

[44] *Everson* v. *Board of Education*, 330 U.S. 1 (1947).

[45] In chapter 2 it was argued that Hinduism's lack of organization is a factor which is favorable to the development of a secular state. While this is basically true, the greater opportunity for state intervention in religious affairs constitutes the negative aspect of the situation.

[46] *Devchand Totaram* v. *Ghanasham*, A.I.R. 1935 Bombay, p. 361; *Aiyanchariar* v. *Sadagopachariar*, A.I.R. 1939 Madras, p. 757.

defining the scope of freedom of religion guaranteed in articles 25 and 26. For example, the courts have had to determine the correct interpretation of scriptures which forbid the entry of untouchables in temples, the doctrinal basis for the practice of polygamy in Hinduism, and similar matters. These cases, of course, have not involved religious controversies between individuals, but between individuals and the legislating state.

There are, however, other aspects of the principle of separation of state and religion which are supported by the Indian Constitution: (1) there is no provision regarding an official state religion, (2) there can be no religious instruction in state schools, (3) there can be no taxes to support any particular religion.

What the Constitution does not say is just as significant as what it does say. There is no mention made of any official state religion. There is no explicit prohibition of the adoption of a state religion, as in the American Constitution, but it is inconceivable that such a radical step would be attempted without a constitutional amendment. Not only is there no state religion in India but no official recognition is given to the religion of the majority. By way of contrast, the Constitution of Burma before 1961 declared: "The state recognizes the special position of Buddhism as the faith professed by the great majority of the citizens of the Union."[47] Similarly, the Constitution of Eire, which considerably influenced the framers of the Indian Constitution in other matters, recognizes the special position of the Roman Catholic Church. The 1959 Constitution of the Kingdom of Nepal links the state with Hinduism through its description of the monarch as an "adherent of Aryan Culture and Hindu Religion" (preamble and article 1).

The sharpest contrast with the Indian Constitution, however, is the 1956 Constitution of "the Islamic Republic of Pakistan." The preamble begins: "In the name of Allah, the Beneficent, the Merciful; whereas sovereignty over the entire universe belongs to Allah Almighty alone, and the authority to be exercised by the people of Pakistan within the limits prescribed by Him is a sacred trust. . . ."[48] Article 25, one of the Directive Principles of State Policy, is as follows:

[47] Constitution of Burma, article 21(1). In August 1961 this was amended to read as follows: "Buddhism being the religion professed by the great majority of the citizens of the Union shall be the State Religion."

[48] The Indian Constitution makes no reference to God except in the forms of oaths or affirmations contained in the third schedule. Ministers of the Union, members

(1) Steps shall be taken to enable the Muslims of Pakistan individually and collectively to order their lives in accordance with the Holy Koran and Sunnah.

(2) The state shall endeavor, as respects the Muslims of Pakistan—

(a) to provide facilities whereby they may be enabled to understand the meaning of life according to the Holy Koran and Sunnah;

(b) to make the teaching of the Holy Koran compulsory;

(c) to promote unity and the observance of Islamic moral standards; and

(d) to secure the proper organization of zakat, wakfs and mosques.

Article 32(2) makes an exception to the provisions for equality and non-discrimination among citizens by stating that a person shall not be qualified for election as president unless he is a Muslim. Article 198(1) asserts: "No law shall be enacted which is repugnant to the Injunctions of Islam as laid down in the Holy Koran and Sunnah . . . and existing law shall be brought into conformity with such Injunctions."[49] The Constitution of 1956 was abrogated two years later, however, when a military regime headed by General Iskander Mirza was established by a bloodless *coup*.

India has no state religion, nor does it give any constitutional recognition to Hinduism as the religion of the majority of citizens. It is also important to note that there is no Ecclesiastical Department in the central government, such as existed during the British period. Before 1927 the bishops of the established Church of England in India were appointed by the crown. Right up to 1948, however, the Ecclesiastical Department continued to pay a large number of Christian chaplains and maintain Christian churches out of the public revenues of the country. The unstated principle embodied in the Indian Constitution is that found in the 1931 Karachi resolution of

of Parliament, judges, etc., may either "swear in the name of God" or "solemnly affirm" that they will faithfully perform the duties of their respective offices.

[49] The draft Constitution of 1952 contained a provision by which legislation suspected of being un-Islamic would be referred to a board of canon lawyers. If the board unanimously found this to be the case, the legislation could be sent back to the legislature with suggested amendments which could only be rejected by a majority of the Muslim members. The Constitution as adopted, however, left the question of repugnancy to the Injunctions of Islam to be determined by Parliament.

the Indian National Congress. "The state shall observe neutrality in regard to all religions."

Taxation and religious education

Article 27 of the Constitution states: "No person shall be compelled to pay any taxes, the proceeds of which are specifically appropriated in payment of expenses for the promotion or maintenance of any particular religion or religious denomination."[50] Several writers have very erroneously equated this provision with the principle laid down in such rigid terms by the United States Supreme Court in the Everson case: "No tax in any amount, large or small, can be levied to support any religious activities or institutions, whatever they may be called, or whatever form they may adopt to teach or practice religion." The differences of constitutional position on this point between the United States and India are considerable.

First, the Indian Constitution forbids only taxation for the benefit of any *particular* religion. Non-discriminatory taxes for the benefit of *all* religions would be perfectly constitutional. Such an arrangement would in fact be in accord with the general traditions of the Hindu state. However, it would seriously undermine the fundamental principle of separation of state and religion as it has here been defined. Separation means that it is not the function of the state to aid one religion or to aid all religions.[51] The secular state will not coerce any individual (by taxation or any other means) to support any religion.

Second, Indian and American law vary greatly in their treatment of educational institutions managed by religious bodies. While in the United States public funds may be used to support parochial schools only in very limited ways (bus transportation, free lunches, textbooks for the pupils), in India the system of government grants to privately managed schools has over a century of history behind it and is still very important.

[50] Article 21 of the 1956 Constitution of Pakistan presents an interesting contrast: "No person shall be compelled to pay any special tax the proceeds of which are to be spent on the propagation or maintenance of any religion *other than his own*" (italics added).

[51] This sentence, and my general approach throughout the book, represent the "wall of separation" approach to the problem. American constitutional law is by no means settled on this fundamental question, and court decisions fluctuate between this and the "no-preference" doctrine, which envisages limited state aid to all religions on an equal basis.

Third, in the United States no government grants of money may be made to religious institutions.[52] The Indian Constitution explicitly provides for state contributions to Hindu temples and shrines! This surprising provision is found in article 290 A:

A sum of forty-six lakhs and fifty thousand rupees (4,650,000 rupees) shall be charged on, and paid out of, the Consolidated Fund of the state of Kerala every year to the Travancore Devaswom Fund; and a sum of thirteen lakhs and fifty thousand rupees (1,350,000 rupees) shall be charged on, and paid out of, the Consolidated Fund of the state of Madras every year to the Devaswom Fund established in that state for the maintenance of Hindu temples and shrines in the territories transferred to that state on the first day of November, 1956, from the state of Travancore-Cochin.

Briefly, the background of this article is as follows. Before 1949 Travancore and Cochin were contiguous Indian States ruled by Hindu maharajas. The rulers had sanctioned large annual grants of money to the Hindu temples and shrines in their respective states, and the management of these institutions was directly controlled by them. The two states were merged in 1949. As the grants made to the temples had been sanctioned in perpetuity, these obligations passed over to the united state of Travancore-Cochin and were detailed in the covenant signed by the two rulers and the government of India.[53] The states reorganization of 1956 created the state of Kerala to which most of their financial obligations were passed on, although part of it also went to Madras.

There are other examples of this continuation of the old system of state patronage of religious institutions. The Mysore government's budget for the year 1960-1961 contains some interesting illustrations of this fact. Under "Endowments and Charitable Allowances" there

[52] Protestant, Catholic, and Jewish chaplains, however, serve in the armed forces of the United States as commissioned officers. Similarly, in the larger defense service establishments in India, qualified "Religious Teachers" of the Hindu, Muslim, Sikh, and Christian (Protestant and Catholic) faiths are either engaged as civilians or hold a rank corresponding to that of junior commissioned officers. They conduct religious services and rites and assist at attestation parades when the oath of obedience and discipline is administered to trained recruits.

[53] See "The Covenant entered into by the Rulers of Travancore and Cochin for the Formation of the United State of Travancore and Cochin," *White Paper on Indian States*, Government of India Press, Delhi, 1950, p. 288.

are budget estimates for the following: temples (160,000 rupees), *maths* (78,000 rupees), Mohammedan institutions (33,300 rupees).[54] Recurring grants sanctioned in perpetuity were made years ago by the government of the maharaja of Mysore to most of the temples, *maths*, and mosques which now receive these annual allowances. However, some such grants from state revenues have been made in recent years, and it was not until 1958 that a Mysore government order stated: "No recurring grants either in perpetuity or for a specified period will be sanctioned to religious institutions such as temples, *maths*, etc., in future, merely to augment their income."[55]

There are other items of expenditures for religious institutions provided for in the 1960-1961 budget which are clearly *not* in fulfillment of obligations assumed by previous governments of Mysore. One hundred and fifty thousand rupees is the budget estimate for "Construction and Repairs" of religious institutions and their equipment. In other years similar amounts have been spent for the repair or renovation of temples, temple cars, guest houses for pilgrims, etc., and for the construction of new temples.[56] It was not until 1958 that the use of public funds for the last-mentioned purpose was stopped. The same government order referred to in the last paragraph also stated: "No building grants will be sanctioned by government for the construction of new places of worship."

The use of public funds for sectarian religious purposes is clearly opposed to the principle of separation of state and religion. In India, however, such a practice would stand a very good chance of being held constitutional by the courts. Article 27 represents a very feeble defense against it. The freedom of a person from compulsion to pay a special religious tax may reinforce the armor of individual rights, but it sidesteps the basic question of public policy. What if there is no special tax, "the proceeds of which are specifically appropriated in payment of expenses for the promotion or maintenance of any

[54] *Budget Estimates for the year 1960-1961: Expenditures,* Mysore Government Press, Bangalore, 1960, p. 396.

[55] Government order No. RDC 10 DHR 57, dated July 9, 1958. One of the last fresh cash grants was made by government order No. RD 10 DHR 57, dated May 21, 1957, in which government "were pleased to sanction a cash grant of 300 rupees per mensem to Sri Degila Math at Kanakapura, the cost being met from '47 Miscellaneous Departments.'" (A budget sub-heading under "Expenditure met from Revenue"). See *Administration Report of the Muzrai Department for the Year 1956-1957,* Government Branch Press, Mysore, 1959, p. 21.

[56] *Ibid.,* pp. 17-18.

particular religion or religious denomination"? What if, instead, the legislature simply appropriates funds for the promotion of religion out of the general revenue of the state? This is what is happening in Mysore state, and in all probability it is perfectly constitutional.

Article 28 deals with the question of religious instruction in three different types of educational institutions.[57] The first provision refers to institutions which are of a completely public nature. Clause (1) lays down: "No religious instruction shall be provided in any educational institution wholly maintained out of state funds."[58] The prohibition here is absolute; neither the state nor any private agency may provide religious instruction in state educational institutions.[59] Here we have a stricter adherence to the principle of separation of state and religion than in the previous article examined. Article 27 would permit taxation for the benefit of all religions but not for "any particular religion." The logical counterpart in the field of education would be a provision enabling the state to provide instruction in all religions but not in one particular religion alone. But such is not the case; there is to be "no religious instruction" in state educational institutions.

Article 28(2) deals with a second, special type of educational institution in which the state functions in the role of trustee. "Nothing in clause (1) shall apply to an educational institution which is administered by the state but has been established under any endowment or trust which requires that religious instruction shall be imparted in such institution." The Banaras Hindu University and the Aligarh Muslim University were established under endowments which require that instruction be imparted in Hinduism and Islam, respectively. Although administered by the central government, religious instruction in these universities is permitted by clause (2).

The third type of educational institution is the state-aided denominational school. As we have seen, every religious group has the right

[57] See chapter 12, "Education and Religion."
[58] The 1956 Constitution of Pakistan would permit religious instruction in state schools, and such instructions could be made compulsory for those who profess the religion or religions taught. Article 13(1): "No person attending any educational institution shall be required to receive religious instruction, or take part in any religious ceremony, or attend religious worship, if such instruction, ceremony or worship relates to a religion *other than his own.*" (italics added).
[59] *Constituent Assembly Debates*, vol. 7, p. 871.

to establish and administer its own educational institutions. Furthermore, in granting aid to educational institutions, the state may not discriminate against those managed by minority groups. The principle involved in article 28(3) is that the state cannot become a party to the active propagation of religion in state-aided institutions by permitting compulsory religious instruction. "No person attending any educational institution recognized by the state or receiving aid out of state funds shall be required to take part in any religious instruction that may be imparted in such institution or to attend any religious worship that may be conducted in such institution or in any premises attached thereto unless such person or, if such person is a minor, his guardian has given his consent thereto." Any other policy would involve the state in aiding the coercion of its citizens to receive instruction in a particular religion.

An evaluation of the Constitution

The constitutional framework of the secular state in India has been discussed in terms of its three basic components: freedom of religion, citizenship, and separation of state and religion. There are undoubtedly serious problems in each of these areas. Freedom of religion, especially collective freedom of religion, is compromised by constitutional sanction for extensive state interference in religious affairs. Citizenship based on equality and non-discrimination by the state is weakened by the numerous special provisions made for the underprivileged classes on the basis of caste. Separation of state and religion includes two distinct principles: (1) the non-interference of the state and religious organizations in each other's affairs; (2) the absence of a legal connection between the state and a particular religion. The Indian Constitution, as already noted, does not subscribe to the first principle; it does, however, uphold the second.

If one evaluates the Constitution solely in terms of abstract legalistic principles, there will indeed be considerable to criticize. This is especially true if one compares the constitutional basis for secularism in India with that in the United States. However, to do this is to ignore the dynamics of the Indian situation. All aspects of contemporary Indian life—political, economic, social, and religious—are in a process of rapid change, and the Indian Constitution is rightly geared to these changes.

Three interrelated developments have a direct bearing on the secular state. First, in order to become a modern state, the state in India is seeking to enlarge its jurisdiction at the expense of religion. The religious regulation of Indian society by caste and Hindu law must give way to regulation by the state. By this process religion is being restricted to an area of life roughly corresponding to its role in the West. Second, the sphere of activity which is left to religion is also the object of extensive reform by the state. This is especially clear in the case of the extremely close supervision of temple administration by the state. The state's role, we have suggested, is closely related to Hinduism's organizational deficiencies. Third, the powerful impulse for social reform demands that the deprived castes, which never enjoyed equality of opportunity, now be given not equality, but privileged treatment by the state, so that their educational, social, and economic status may be rapidly raised.

There is a good chance that twenty years from now, many of India's constitutional anomalies regarding the secular state will have disappeared. It is reasonable to expect that by that time there will be a uniform civil code and that Hindu and Muslim law, as such, will have ceased to exist. Legislation having already dealt with the most serious abuses in Hindu religion there will be little need for further interference by the state. Bureaucracy being what it is, however, there will likely be more and not less official supervision of temple administration. In twenty years the need for special class privileges, which now distort the principle of equal citizenship, should be very much less. In any case such privileges should be abandoned by that time. Thus, if one is willing to incorporate this dimension of *time* into his evaluation, the conclusion is that the Constitution of India provides a relatively sound basis for the building of a secular state.

APPENDIX TO CHAPTER 4

CONSTITUTIONAL PROVISIONS
REGARDING THE SECULAR STATE

I. FREEDOM OF RELIGION

Individual freedom of religion

Art. 25(1) Subject to public order, morality and health and to the other provisions of this Part, all persons are equally entitled to freedom of conscience and the right freely to profess, practice and propagate religion.

(2) Nothing in this article shall affect the operation of any existing law or prevent the state from making any law—

(a) regulating or restricting any economic, financial, political or other secular activity which may be associated with religious practice;

(b) providing for social welfare and reform or the throwing open of Hindu religious institutions of a public character to all classes and sections of Hindus.

Explanation I.—The wearing and carrying of *kirpans* shall be deemed to be included in the profession of the Sikh religion.

Explanation II.—In sub-clause (b) of clause (2), the reference to Hindus shall be construed as including a reference to persons professing the Sikh, Jaina or Buddhist religion, and the reference to Hindu religious institutions shall be construed accordingly.

Collective freedom of religion

Art. 26 Subject to public order, morality and health, every religious denomination or any section thereof shall have the right—

(a) to establish and maintain institutions for religious and charitable purposes;

(b) to manage its own affairs in matters of religion;

(c) to own and acquire movable and immovable property; and

(d) to administer such property in accordance with law.

Art. 30(1) All minorities, whether based on religion or language, shall have the right to establish and administer educational institutions of their choice.

(2) The state shall not, in granting aid to educational institutions, discriminate against any educational institution on the ground that it is under the management of a minority, whether based on religion or language.

II. CITIZENSHIP

No state discrimination on grounds of religion

Art. 15(1) The state shall not discriminate against any citizen on grounds only of religion, race, caste, sex, place of birth or any of them.

(4) Nothing in this article or in clause (2) of article 29 shall prevent the state from making any special provision for the advancement of any socially and educationally backward classes of citizens or for the Scheduled Castes and the Scheduled Tribes.

Equality of opportunity in public employment

Art. 16(1) There shall be equality of opportunity for all citizens in matters relating to employment or appointment to any office under the state.

(2) No citizen shall, on grounds only of religion, race, caste, sex, descent, place of birth, residence or any of them, be ineligible for, or discriminated against in respect of, any employment or office under the state.

(4) Nothing in this article shall prevent the state from making any provision for the reservation of appointments or posts in favor of any backward class of citizens which, in the opinion of the state, is not adequately represented in the services under the state.

(5) Nothing in this article shall affect the operation of any law which provides that the incumbent of an office in connection with the affairs of any religious or denominational institution or any members of the governing body thereof shall be a person professing a particular religion or belonging to a particular denomination.

No discrimination in educational institutions

Art. 29(2) No citizen shall be denied admission into any educational institution maintained by the state or receiving aid out of state funds on grounds only of religion, race, caste, language or any of them.

No communal electorates

Art. 325   There shall be one general electoral roll for every territorial constituency for election to either House of Parliament or to the House or either House of the Legislature of a state and no person shall be ineligible for inclusion in any such roll or claim to be included in any special electoral roll for any such constituency on grounds only of religion, race, caste, sex or any of them.

Art. 330(1) Seats shall be reserved in the House of the People for—
            (a) the Scheduled Castes;
            (b) the Scheduled Tribes . . .

Art. 332(1) Seats shall be reserved for the Scheduled Castes and the Scheduled Tribes . . . in the Legislative Assembly of every state.

III. SEPARATION OF STATE AND RELIGION

No special taxes for promotion of religion

Art. 27   No person shall be compelled to pay any taxes, the proceeds of which are specifically appropriated in payment of expenses for the promotion or maintenance of any particular religion or religious denomination.

Art. 290A   A sum of forty-six lakhs and fifty thousand rupees shall be charged on, and paid out of, the Consolidated Fund of the state of Kerala every year to the Travancore Devaswom Fund; and a sum of thirteen lakhs and fifty thousand rupees shall be charged on, and paid out of, the Consolidated Fund of the state of Madras every year to the Devaswom Fund established in that state for the maintenance of Hindu temples and shrines in the territories transferred to that state on the first day of November, 1956, from the state of Travancore-Cochin.

No religious instruction in state educational institutions

Art. 28(1) No religious instruction shall be provided in any educational institution wholly maintained out of state funds.

     (2)   Nothing in clause (1) shall apply to an educational institution which is administered by the state but has been established under any endowment or trust which requires that religious instruction shall be imparted in such institution.

(3)   No person attending any educational institution recognized by the state or receiving aid out of state funds shall be required to take part in any religious instruction that may be imparted in such institution or to attend any religious worship that may be conducted in such institution or in any premises attached thereto unless such person or, if such person is a minor, his guardian has given his consent thereto.

CHAPTER 5

THE THEORETICAL UNDERGIRDING

UNDERGIRDING the secular constitutional structure are both practical and theoretical considerations. The secular state may be interpreted as a pragmatic solution to the problem of religious pluralism. Political expediency alone would dictate such a policy, and expression has frequently been given to this practical consideration. In 1950 Nehru declared: "The government of a country like India, with many religions that have secured great and devoted followings for generations, can never function satisfactorily in the modern age except on a secular basis."[1] From the standpoint of national unity and stability, the principle of the secular state represents a sound practical approach. Any other approach would tend to alienate the religious minorities and impede the processes of national integration.

There are also important theoretical supports, ideas which influenced political developments in the years immediately preceding independence, and which are appealed to by the present-day Indian leadership in attempting to secure broader support for secularism. This chapter is devoted to a consideration of the three most significant theories upon which the secular state is based: Indian nationalism, Hindu tolerance, and western secularism.

THE THEORY OF INDIAN NATIONALISM

The present writer asked an Indian professor in 1961 why he supported the principle of the secular state. The reply, "Because I have always been a nationalist," emphasized an important but not too obvious relationship. The concept of Indian nationalism to which he referred was based squarely on the geographical fact of a territory known as India; the nation was composed of all who claimed India as their homeland. In 1932 a prominent Muslim leader, Maulana Syed Husain Ahmed Madani, propounded the thesis: "Nations

[1] *The Hindu*, September 13, 1950.

are formed from countries."[2] Therefore, Hindus, Muslims, Christians, Sikhs, and others formed one Indian nation. The term "nationalism" signified the freedom movement of the whole Indian people, opposed not only to the foreign ruler but to all separatist political tendencies based on loyalty to religious communities.

"Communalism" is the term used in India to describe the political functioning of individuals or groups for the selfish interests of particular religious communities or castes. Today the antithesis of communalism is secularism, the principle of the secular state and the kind of political life which is in consonance with it. Before 1947 the term "secularism" was rarely used in this context; the antithesis of communalism was "nationalism."

The assertions of Indian nationalism were that India was one country, despite the existence of hundreds of separate states on the subcontinent, and that the Indians constituted one nation, despite all racial, religious, and cultural differences. Garibaldi and Mazzini provided much of the early inspiration for the Indian nationalist movement, for they had done two things which needed to be done in India: they had driven out the foreign rulers and had united their nation under one flag.

British officials regarded the assertion that India was a nation as the product of the wildest imaginings of political agitators. Quite willing to overlook for the moment their own substantial contribution to the unification of India (efficient systems of transportation and communication, the English language, and modern political, administrative, and legal institutions), the British vehemently rejected the notion that a people speaking hundreds of different languages and divided into thousands of distinct castes and sects could ever be regarded as a nation. Much of the nationalist's time and energy was devoted to the defense of his thesis that an Indian nationality did already exist or was at least rapidly evolving. R. K. Mookerjee's *The Fundamental Unity of India*, published in 1914, provided the basic theme for much of the later nationalist writing.

The Indian nationalist felt compelled to assert that India was a nation, even though there were some embarrassing facts which had to be glossed over. In the modern world, nationality and nationalism

[2] Maulana Mohammed Mian, *A Brief History of Jamiat Ulema Hind,* All India Jamiat Ulema Hind, Delhi, n.d., p. 4.

were the basic premises of political life, and it seemed absolutely *improper* for India to be without a nationality. Furthermore, part of the heritage of the nineteenth century was the principle that any people who constituted a nation were thereby entitled to self-government. If India was to gain its freedom from British rule, it was therefore necessary to assert that it was indeed a nation.

Unity in diversity had been the age-old pattern of Indian civilization. While the nationalist movement emphasized a greater degree of unity in certain areas of culture—the development of a national language, for example—religious differences were assumed to be permanently valid. The main current of Indian nationalism assumed the separation of religion and politics; there was no conflict between India's religious pluralism and the goal of independence with political unity.

In the decade which preceded independence there were three frontal attacks *by Indian parties* on this basic concept of Indian nationalism. Despite the intensity of their hostility to each other, the Hindu Mahasabha, the Muslim League, and the Communist Party could all agree on one point: India could not be regarded as one nation because of its religio-cultural heterogeneity.

In the 1920's the Hindu Mahasabha absorbed many of the Congressmen who were sympathetic to the earlier Extremist leadership and gradually became aggessively communalist. V. D. Savarkar formulated the basic ideology of Hindu communalism in his book *Hindutva,* published in 1923. He asserted that the Hindus, as a people united by a common country, blood, history, religion, culture, and language, were a *nation.* In his presidential address to the Hindu Mahasabha in 1937, Savarkar recognized the Muslims also as a nation, thus intensifying the separatist implications of his ideology. "India cannot be assumed today to be a unitarian and homogeneous nation, but on the contrary there are two nations in the main; the Hindus and the Muslims." Two years later, in another presidential address to the Mahasabha, he repeated more emphatically his views on the existence of these "two antagonistic nations living side by side."[3]

The Hindu Mahasabha never commanded much popular support,

[3] V. D. Savarkar, *Hindu Rashtra Darshan,* L. G. Khare, Bombay, 1949, p. 26. A detailed analysis of Savarkar's *Hindutva* is found in chapter 15, "The Challenge of Hindu Communalism."

and the Congress could afford to ignore it most of the time. But it could not ignore the Muslim League. In his 1940 presidential address to the League, M. A. Jinnah propounded his two-nation theory which became the basis for the Pakistan demand. Islam and Hinduism, Jinnah declared, were far more than religions in the strict sense of the word; they were two distinct social orders, two different civilizations "based mainly on conflicting ideas and conceptions." Each had its own religious philosophies, social customs, legal system, literature, and sources of history. It was "a dream" that the Hindus and Muslims could ever evolve a common nationality, and to yoke together two such nations under a single state could only lead to disaster.

Jinnah declared that the misconception of one Indian nation resulted from a flagrant disregard of the past history of the Indian subcontinent. "Notwithstanding a thousand years of close contact, nationalities, which are as divergent today as ever, cannot at any time be expected to transform themselves into one nation merely by means of subjecting them to a democratic constitution and holding them forcibly together by unnatural and artificial methods of British parliamentary statute." Muslim India could not accept any constitution which would necessarily result in a Hindu majority government; this could only mean Hindu raj. The Muslims, Jinnah declared, were not a minority in the usual sense of the word. "Mussalmans are a nation according to any definition of a nation, and they must have their homelands, their territory, and their state."[4]

---

[4] William Theodore de Bary, ed., *Sources of Indian Tradition*, Columbia University Press, New York, 1958, pp. 835-838. Jinnah attached the greatest importance to the assertion that the Indian Muslims were a nation, and in his September 1944 correspondence with Gandhi insisted that the Congress accept this "fundamental principle" as a basis for further negotiations. Jinnah was unmoved by Gandhi's argument that acceptance of this and other principles of the Lahore resolution was unnecessary since Gandhi had "accepted the concrete consequences that should follow from such acceptance." Jamil-ud-din Ahmad, ed., *Some Recent Speeches and Writings of Mr. Jinnah*, Muhammad Ashraf, Lahore, 1947, vol. 2, pp. 196-199. Jinnah's two-nation theory was essentially an elaboration of ideas which had long been held by certain sections of the Indian Muslim leadership. As early as 1888 Sir Syed Ahmed Khan attacked the Indian National Congress on this basis. "I do not understand what the words 'National Congress' mean. Is it supposed that the different castes and creeds living in India belong to one nation, or can become a nation, and their aims and aspirations be one and the same? . . . I object to every Congress in any shape or form whatever which regards India as one nation." Sir Syed also referred explicitly to the two nations, Mohammedan and Hindu. *Source Material for a History of the Freedom Movement in India*, vol. 2, 1885-1920, New Delhi, 1958, p. 71.

The Communist Party of India, for reasons of its own, supported the Pakistan demand by its theory that India was multinational. A Communist writer disclosed that as late as 1938, "we were yet wrapped up in the theory, like the rest of the nationalists, that India was one nation and that the Muslims were just a religious cultural minority."[5] But by 1941 an important tactical shift was discernible. In 1942 the CPI adopted a resolution which, on the basis of Stalin's definition of the concept of nationality, listed sixteen Indian "nations." While the classification was based primarily on language, religion was also important: the Sikhs, Western Punjabis (dominantly Muslims), and Bengali Muslims were held to be nations entitled to separate states. By 1945, CPI nationality policy definitely supported the partition of India and the creation of a Muslim state.

Rajendra Prasad, Asoka Mehta, and many others wrote books attempting to refute Jinnah's two-nation theory. This in itself was not a difficult task. Nehru posed the question why, if nationality was based on religion, there were only two nations. In India there would be many nations, if the theory were followed logically. Nationality might well cut through family units, for if one man was a Hindu and his brother had been converted to Islam, they would belong to two different nations. Geographically the theory presented problems because the two nations were interlocked in most of the villages of India. Culturally the demarcation was difficult to defend, for "a Bengali Muslim and a Bengali Hindu, living together, speaking the same language and having much the same traditions and customs, belonged to different nations."[6]

Nehru asserted that there was hardly any satisfactory definition of a nation. The definition could be attempted from historical, cultural, racial, or many other points of view. Essentially it was a question of consciousness of unity. If a number of nations wanted to pull together and consider themselves one nation (as in the multinational USSR), they were one nation. On the other hand, if a particular community or group did not want to work along with the rest of

[5] G. Adhikari, *Pakistan and Indian National Unity*, People's Publishing House, Bombay, 1944, p. 29, quoted in Selig S. Harrison, *India: The Most Dangerous Decades*, Princeton University Press, Princeton, 1960, p. 150. See also Gene D. Overstreet and Marshal Windmiller, *Communism in India*, University of California Press, Berkeley, 1959, pp. 492-497.

[6] Jawaharlal Nehru, *The Discovery of India*, John Day Company, New York, 1946, pp. 396-397.

the country, then it did not matter whether it was one nation or two nations. But the basic assumption of the Indian nationalist movement was that all who lived in the territorial unit known as India, and acknowledged it as their homeland, belonged to the one Indian nation.

Muslim support for this concept of territorial and secular nationalism came from Maulana Abul Kalam Azad and the small group of nationalist Muslims which supported the Congress. Azad's own views had changed radically over the years. Before 1920 his position was that, while the Hindus could revive their national identity on the basis of secular nationalism, this was not possible for the Muslims, who could define their collective identity only in terms of Islam. But from 1920 onward Azad was powerfully influenced by the phenomenon of Hindu-Muslim political cooperation under Gandhi's leadership, and by the emergence of secular Turkish and Arab nationalism. He was impressed by the fact that in Syria the Muslims, Christians, and Druzes had united for the liberation of their country under the slogan "Religion is for God and the homeland is for everyone." Azad decided to strive for the development of a similar nationalism in India.

The Maulana sought to construct an Islamic theoretical basis for the evolution of a joint Hindu-Muslim nation in India.[7] He turned to the covenant which in the seventh century A.D. was drawn up between the followers of the Prophet and the Jews of Medina. Essentially an alliance for the common defense against the hostile Quraish tribe, the covenant declared that the Believers (i.e. Muslims) and the Jews were "one people." Azad translated the Arabic phrase as "one nation," and interpreted this covenant as a historical precedent (an Islamically valid precedent) for the formation by the Muslims and the Hindus of a common Indian nationality. Whatever the textual and historical objections to the theory, Azad was con-

[7] The material in this paragraph and the preceding one is drawn from Professor Hafeez Malik's excellent paper, "Abul Kalam Azad's Theory of Nationalism," presented at the meeting of the Association for Asian Studies, Boston, April 3, 1962. Azad's theory of the covenant is found in *Khutbat-i-Abul Kalam Azad*, al-Minara Academy, Lahore, n.d., p. 42. Since Independence the leaders of the Jamiat Ulama-e-Hind have used this concept of the covenant in a slightly different way. According to their theory, the Muslims and non-Muslims of India have entered into a covenant to establish a secular state, and the covenant is embodied in the Constitution. See W. C. Smith, *Islam in Modern History*, Princeton University Press, Princeton, 1957, pp. 284-285.

vinced of the soundness of his conclusion. In his presidential address to the Indian National Congress in 1940, Maulana Azad declared proudly: "I am part of the indivisible unity that is Indian nationality."

Jinnah's two-nation theory revived the medieval concept of a religious group constituting a political community, the idea of a state based on a creed. Implicit in the nationalist refutation of Jinnah's theory was the idea of a secular state, although the term itself was not generally used. But it was frequently stated that the objective of the nationalist movement was not a Hindu raj, but an independent India in which all citizens would have equal rights, privileges, and obligations irrespective of religion. As early as 1931 the Congress had committed itself formally to the principle of the religious neutrality of the state in the free India of the future.

Debate over the two-nation theory and the demand for partition did serve to clarify thinking concerning the proper relationship between religion and the state. This debate, which lasted right up to 1947, reinforced the Congress leadership's commitment to secularism. The alternative to Pakistan was a united secular state; after Pakistan was created, any other policy for India would have constituted a complete repudiation of principles which Indian nationalism had always claimed as basic convictions. The strength of the nationalist idea is indicated by the fact that the concept of a secular state was not seriously challenged in the years immediately following independence, despite the unprecedented communal violence of 1947, and despite the fact that the partition had removed the pressure of the largest religious minority. Indian rejection of the secular state and the official recognition of Hinduism after independence would also have tended to prove the rightness and the necessity of the creation of Pakistan as the only sure protection for the Muslims of the subcontinent.

The ideology and the political movement which produced Pakistan made inevitable the proclamation of the new state as an Islamic Republic, however difficult it might be to give meaningful content to this term in the modern context. Similarly, although not so obviously, the basic theory of Indian nationalism firmly committed the leaders of independent India to the establishment of a secular state. Preindependence nationalism and postindependence secularism are segments of the same continuous tradition. In nineteenth-century Europe, nationalism was intimately associated with the idea of democracy; in twentieth-century India, nationalism is also closely linked to secularism. And the theory of Indian nationalism continues to lend powerful support to the secular state.

THE THEORY OF HINDU TOLERANCE

Paradoxically, a number of contemporary Indian thinkers derive their concept of the secular state from religious premises. These religious premises are an integral part of Hindu thought, and may be traced back through three thousand years of philosophical tradition. Dr. S. Radhakrishnan, the president of India, wrote that in the Roman Empire diverse religious beliefs and practices were generally tolerated as long as they did not become politically dangerous. In the history of the West, religious toleration was well established in certain periods, but it was based to some extent on intellectual curiosity and, more often, on political expediency. That is, religious diversity made toleration necessary if peace were to be maintained within the state. The British government in India likewise sought to offend no creed and give no special advantage to its own official religion, insofar as that was possible. But the Hindu conviction stood in marked contrast to the western approach. "The Hindu view is not motivated by any considerations of political expediency. It is bound up with its religion and not its policy."[8]

Radhakrishnan noted that the Hindu attitude assumes that religion is a matter of personal realization. The creeds, dogmas, and rituals which characterize outwardly the different religions are mere symbols. The symbols are necessary, but their value is only instrumental; that is, they may be used to help lead men to the apprehension of the Absolute, by which the creature surrenders to the uncreated spirit. An idol or fetish is a symbol; so also an abstract thought about God; the difference between the two is quantitative and not qualitative. "The highest symbols are only symbols, signs of an enduring reality which is larger than man's conception or picture of it." The Absolute is the one reality. The Absolute or God may be known by different names, but is one. So also men may seek by different paths, but all paths if pursued sincerely will lead to the Supreme. The path one chooses depends on his environment, heredity,

[8] S. Radhakrishnan, *Eastern Religions and Western Thought*, Oxford University Press, London, 1940, p. 316.

and other factors. But all religions are true, for all can be instruments of personal realization.

The basis for this conception of the relative nature of religious differences is first found in the Rig Veda, the most ancient of the Sanskrit scriptures. "The real is one, the learned call it by various names, Agni, Yama, Matarisvan." "Priests and poets with words make into many the hidden reality which is but one." The Upanishads develop the conception further. In the paraphrase of Dr. Radhakrishnan: "In the boundless being of Brahman are all the living powers that men have worshipped as gods, not as if they were standing side by side in space, but each a facet mirroring the whole. The different deities are symbols of the fathomless."[9] Vedanta philosophy carries on this tradition with its insistence upon one absolute Truth expressed through manifold manifestations. This conception accounts in large part for the freedom of thought and conscience and the absence of religious persecution throughout most of Hindu history.

This philosophic and religious tradition, so ancient in its origin, continues to provide the framework for much of modern Hindu thought. The political implications of these conceptions are not difficult to deduce. If all religions are equally true, the state must allow all religions to function freely. If all religions are equally true, the granting by the state of a special status to one particular religion is without meaning or justification; all must be accorded equal treatment.

Radhakrishnan explicitly related the Hindu view of reality to the conception of a secular state. "It may appear somewhat strange," he wrote in 1955, "that our government should be a secular one while our culture is rooted in spiritual values. Secularism here does not mean irreligion or atheism or even stress on material comforts. It proclaims that it lays stress on the universality of spiritual values which may be attained by a variety of ways." Emphasizing the unity of the religious experience despite all doctrinal differences, he declared: "This is the meaning of a secular conception of the state though it is not generally understood."[10]

[9] *Ibid.*, p. 308. Hindu tolerance stems not only from this conception of the relative nature of religious differences, but also from the doctrine that men are *born* different because of their *karma*, and that therefore the same attitudes, capacities and behavior cannot be expected of all men.

[10] S. Radhakrishnan, "Foreword," in S. Abid Hussain, *The National Culture of*

Discussing the tradition of Hindu tolerance in more general terms, Dr. Radhakrishnan pointed out that from Rig Vedic times to the present the Indian genius adopted a policy of live and let live toward different religions. According to his interpretation, this same genius found expression in a resolution adopted by the Indian National Congress in 1951: "It has been the aim and declared policy of the Congress since its inception to establish a secular democratic state which, while honoring every faith, does not discriminate against any religion or community and gives equal rights and freedom of opportunity to all communities and individuals who form the nation."[11] Radhakrishnan saw an organic relationship between the Rig Vedic text and the Congress resolution.

Gandhian universalism and the secular state

This approach to the secular state is clearly revealed in Gandhi's statements on the proposal to partition India and create a Muslim state. Gandhi's religious convictions were of course in line with the Hindu tradition. In 1928 he declared: "After long study and experience I have come to these conclusions, that: (1) all religions are true, (2) all religions have some error in them, (3) all religions are almost as dear to me as my own Hinduism. My veneration for other faiths is the same as for my own faith."[12] Because all religions are true, Gandhi was convinced that a state based primarily on adherence to a particular religion was worse than undemocratic. It was a negation of truth.

In 1940 Gandhi readily admitted that if eighty million Muslims insisted on the partition of India, nothing could prevent it. This was the political aspect of the problem, and it had to be recognized. But the more important religious aspect was that "at the bottom of the cry for partition is the belief that Islam is an exclusive brotherhood, and anti-Hindu." Gandhi thus opposed the partition proposal on religious grounds and called it "an untruth." "Partition means a patent untruth. My whole soul rebels against the idea that Hinduism

---

India, Jaico Publishing House, Bombay, 1956, pp. vii-viii. A number of sentences from this passage were reproduced verbatim (with no reference to the eminent author, however) in Mr. Sanjiva Reddy's presidential address to the Indian National Congress at Bhavnagar in January 1961.

[11] S. Radhakrishnan, *East and West: Some Reflections*, George Allen and Unwin Ltd., London, 1955, p. 40.

[12] Quoted in Nehru, *op. cit.*, p. 365.

and Islam represent two antagonistic cultures and doctrines. To assent to such a doctrine is for me denial of God. For I believe with my whole soul that the God of the Koran is also the God of the Gita, and that we are all, no matter by what name designated, children of the same God."[13] The proposal for the creation of a Muslim state, Pakistan, was the logical culmination of religious exclusivism, and ran directly counter to Gandhi's deepest convictions.

Furthermore, Gandhi's conception of the spiritual nature of true religion made him reject any form of state support for religion. "We have suffered enough from state-aided religion and a state church," he wrote in 1948. "A society or a group which depends partly or wholly on state aid for the existence of its religion does not deserve, or better still, does not have any religion worth the name."[14]

The state must be so organized that all religions can peacefully coexist. In order to ensure this, the functions of the state must be non-religious, and the state must deal with people as individuals and not as members of religious communities. Gandhi raised the question: "What conflict of interest can there be between Hindus and Muslims in the matter of revenue, sanitation, police, justice, or the use of public conveniences? The difference can only be in religious usage and observances with which a secular state has no concern." The capacity of the state for serving the people "stops short of the service of the different faiths, and the services it can render apply to all irrespective of their faiths."[15]

Hindu tolerance is far more than an intellectual abstraction expounded by Radhakrishnan and Gandhi. It is indeed a living tradition which has contributed vitally to the establishment of a secular democratic state in India. There is the doctrinal assertion of the essential oneness of all religions, to which many educated Indians (and not only Hindus) subscribe as a self-evident truth. More important, however, is the general attitude of "live and let live" toward all manifestations of religious diversity. When questioned about the theoretical basis of India's secular state, a large majority of the Indian leaders of all persuasions will immediately relate it to the Hindu tradition of tolerance.

[13] M. K. Gandhi, *To the Hindus and Muslims,* ed. Anand T. Hingorani, Law Journal Press, Allahabad, 1942, pp. 415-416, 428.
[14] *Harijan,* March 23, 1948.
[15] *To the Hindus and Muslims,* pp. 442-443.

This ancient tradition, Hindu in its origin, is an integral part of the Indian way of life which is shared by all communities. Maulana Abul Kalam Azad could speak with a sense of complete identification with this tradition. "It is possible that other nations may have to learn new lessons for broadening their outlook and for cultivating a spirit of tolerance. But so far as India is concerned we can say with pride and glory that it is the main trait of our ancient civilization, and that we have been steeped in it for thousands of years. In other countries differences of thought and action led to mutual warfare and bloodshed but in India they were resolved in a spirit of compromise and toleration. Here every kind of faith, every kind of culture, every mode of living was allowed to flourish and find its own salvation."[16] More important than a theory to support the secular state, this tradition provides a social value of considerable effectiveness in influencing day-to-day life.

While the social attitude of tolerance is an unmixed asset, the proposition that all religions are equally true and ultimately the same has significant limitations as a theoretical foundation for the secular state. First, the theory will not be acceptable to those Muslims, Christians, and others who believe that there are elements of ultimate uniqueness in their respective faiths. Any theory which cannot be broadly shared by the members of the minority communities is of limited usefulness.

Second, the theory is itself an unverifiable religious dogma, and any attempt on the part of the state to propagate it would come into sharp conflict with the basic principles of the secular state. This, incidentally, is what was recommended by the University Education Commission of which Dr. Radhakrishnan was the chairman. "The absolute religious neutrality of the state," the report concluded, "can be preserved in state institutions, if what is good and great in every religion is presented, and what is more essential, the unity of all religion."[17] The assertion of the unity of all religions is as much a dogma as the assertion that one religion is infinitely superior to all others. The propagation of religious dogmas is simply not a proper function of the secular state, despite the fact that some of them

[16] *Speeches of Maulana Azad, 1947-1955*, Publications Division, Government of India, Delhi, 1956, pp. 20-21.
[17] *Report of the University Education Commission*, Government of India Press, Simla, 1950, p. 302.

(such as the theory under consideration) might be quite useful in strengthening the same secular state.

Third, the assertion that all creeds are equally true can lead, paradoxically, to a kind of religious intolerance. A group of Christians made the following observation: "The assumption that all religions are true in different ways leading to the same goal is claimed to be the true basis of tolerance. But actually this belief (which, of course, anyone is free to hold) has given rise to an attitude of intolerance towards those who are convinced of the uniqueness of their faith and feel impelled to preach and propagate it."[18] As we shall see in the next chapter, vigorous attempts have been made in India to restrict the right of religious conversion.

Last, the proposed basis for the secular state which we are considering here places no limitation on the religious functions of the state except that of equal treatment to all religions. A system in which a state Department of Religious Affairs distributed large grants to *all* religions and exercised vast powers of control over their internal affairs would also be in perfect accordance with this principle. This is essentially what C. Rajagopalachari proposed, and he based it explicitly on Gandhian doctrine. His argument was as follows: The Mahatma taught that all religions are equally worthy of reverence; this teaching was not an invention of his for political ends, but was derived from common sense and Hindu religious texts of the highest authority. India today dare not forget religion in its quest for material prosperity. "And if India's *government* is to be an institution integrated with her people's lives, if it is to be a true democracy and not a superimposed western institution staged in Indian dress, religion must have an important and recognized place in it, with impartiality and equal reverence for all the creeds and denominations prevailing in India. This alone would be historically consistent with the peaceful revolution brought about by our Nation's Father."[19] Yet this could not be done in a secular state as we have defined it. There is need for a political theory which limits the scope of state activities to secular functions.

While the theory of Hindu tolerance has these weaknesses as a

[18] *The Secular State in India: A Christian Point of View*, Y.M.C.A. Publishing House, Calcutta, 1954, p. 6.
[19] C. Rajagopalachari, "The Place of Religion in Future India," *Message of India*, 1959, vol. 1, p. 83. (Italics added.)

theoretical basis, its great significance should not be underestimated. A theory which has strong roots in the indigenous thought and culture of India, as this one has, is an invaluable asset in creating a deep sense of acceptance of the secular state. Intellectually, psychologically, and religiously, the theory is a powerful one in developing the broad-based conviction that secularism *belongs* in India.

The Theory of Western Secularism

K. M. Panikkar categorically declared that the roots of India's democratic, egalitarian, and secular state were in the West, not in ancient Hindu thought. The valid experience of any country becomes the common inheritance of civilized humanity, Panikkar asserted, and India has assimilated much of western thought.[20]

In chapter 1, the historical development of the conception of the secular state in the West was examined. Many theoretical strands, both religious and secular, have been woven into this conception. Some of the most ardent advocates of separation of church and state were found among the Protestant minorities in seventeenth- and eighteenth-century America. Their characteristic emphasis was that religion is purely a matter of the individual conscience, that its spiritual nature is such that civil authority based on coercive power has no rightful jurisdiction over it. New scientific interests and theories, the rationalism and scepticism of the Enlightenment, anticlericalism, the industrial revolution, humanist liberalism, Marxism and democratic socialist theories, and pragmatism have all helped to produce an outlook on life that is fundamentally non-religious, and this secularism has led to a much diminished role for religion in government and public affairs as in private life.

How has western secularism influenced contemporary Indians in their thinking about the secular state? A substantial number of intellectuals have been profoundly influenced by western rationalism and humanism, and are secularists in their personal philosophies of life. They see religion, especially in India, as associated with social backwardness, gross superstition, and fanaticism. The scientific, economic, and social progress of the country, they assert, will vary inversely with the prevalence of the religious outlook. Other mem-

[20] K. M. Panikkar, *The State and the Citizen*, Asia Publishing House, Bombay, 1956, p. 28.

bers of the westernized minority, however, take a more kindly view of religion. Recognizing in their ancestral faiths certain values worth keeping, they would like to see religion stripped of its unwholesome accretions and brought more into line with the requirements of modern life. A third group, and one that is growing rapidly under the secularizing influences of modern life, is profoundly indifferent to religion. The defects of religion elicit neither hostility nor the desire for reform.

Intellectual leaders representing all of these views see the secular state as one of the West's valuable contributions to India. The secular state is fundamental to the *modern* approach to political life; it is part of the liberal democratic tradition which India has inherited. The secular state is also the only fair and democratic solution to the problem of religious minorities.

The proposal for the partition of India and the creation of a Muslim state provided the political background for Gandhi's definition of the secular state. During the period 1940-1946 much was written on the controversial question of partition including a small book entitled *A Secular State for India* by Dr. Lanka Sundaram. The writer referred to himself as one who had "drunk deep at the fountain of western democratic ideas." In this book is presented a conception of the secular state derived from western sources. The approach of the writer is political and historical rather than religious, and religion is viewed purely as a sociological phenomenon. "If the history of the world yields any lesson of a lasting character, it is that religion cannot be mixed up with politics, if religion is to survive and if politics is to preserve unto any people their just rights and to make them strong and self-representing." Sundaram pointed out that despite ritualistic forms, ceremonies, and institutions which still bind the Church of England to the state, "British polity today is secular in the extreme, and has nothing to do with religion as such being the foundation and motive force of politics."[21] The writer argued the feasibility of a secular constitution for India under which all religions would enjoy equal status and rights and by which the unity of India could be preserved.

Prime Minister Jawaharlal Nehru has undoubtedly been the outstanding champion of the secular state in India since independence.

[21] Lanka Sundaram, *A Secular State for India*, Rajkamal Publications, Delhi, 1944, pp. 2, 4-5.

His personal philosophy of life is completely secular. On occasion he has severely criticized the superstitious practices and dogmatism sometimes associated with religion. Writing in 1944 Nehru claimed to have no interest whatsoever in the question of a future life, and regarded the idea of a personal God as completely foreign to his way of thinking. His closest approximation to a religious feeling was a sense of awe when he contemplated the mysteries of the universe. Nevertheless, as to the question of what the mysterious was Nehru could only say, "I do not know." He revealed much of his own mind when he wrote: "We have therefore to function in line with the highest ideals of the age we live in. . . . Those ideals may be classed under two heads; humanism and the scientific spirit."[22]

It has been pointed out, however, that Nehru has been more tolerant of Buddhist superstition than of the Hindu variety. Nehru participated in Buddhist ceremonies in Calcutta in 1949 when he received the sacred relics of the two disciples of the Buddha, Sariputta and Mogallana, from the British government. The relics, object of intense veneration and worship, were transferred by Nehru to a Buddhist monastery and, in 1952, were finally restored to the great *stupa* at Sanchi. Hindus have frequently complained of Nehru's lack of a corresponding reverence for their religious traditions; since Hindu religion, unlike Buddhism, has no international political implications, the Prime Minister does not hesitate to denounce its superstitions. On several occasions Nehru has referred to the huge hydro-electric dams as the "temples of the new India" from which people can draw inspiration to press on in the task of building a modern nation.

A few references will illustrate the western orientation of Nehru's conception of the secular state. Because his view is not dependent on religious presuppositions, the divergence from Gandhi's approach was basic. It has been noted elsewhere that "Gandhi's starting point was that of a religious man who, believing all religions to be true, accepted a theory of the state which fit in with this belief; hence the secular state. Nehru's starting point was that of a practical political thinker and leader who, while personally believing all religions to be mostly untrue, had to provide for their freedom to function peace-

[22] Nehru, *op. cit.*, pp. 16, 571.

fully without prejudicing the democratic system; hence the secular state."[23] Gandhi and Nehru very well typify two of the diverse currents of thought presented in this chapter.

Nehru defined the secular state as a state which protects all religions but does not favor one at the expense of others, and does not establish any religion as the official creed. The secular state meant the "cardinal doctrine of modern democratic practice, that is, the separation of the state from religion."[24] The idea of the secular state as the *modern* form of polity is often found in Nehru's statements and reflects the western orientation of his thinking. "Do we believe in a national state which includes people of all religions and shades of opinion and is essentially secular as a state, or do we believe in the religious, theocratic conception of a state which considers people of other faiths as something beyond the pale? That is an odd question to ask, for the idea of a religious or theocratic state was given up by the world some centuries ago and has no place in the mind of the modern man. And yet the question has to be put in India today, for many of us have tried to jump back to a past age."[25] For Nehru, the secular state is the *sine qua non* of modern democratic practice.

Materialist and Christian interpretations

While Nehru is an agnostic humanist and highly critical of certain unenlightened forms of religious practice, he is not motivated by a spirit of hostility toward religion as such. The secular state is part of the democratic tradition, an arrangement which permits agnostics and believers alike to function according to their respective convictions. There is a school of thought, however, which insists that a secular state cannot function in a religious society, that secularism in government can only be built upon a broad-based philosophy of rationalism and materialism. According to this view, the Gandhian idea that all religions are equally true may lead to a non-communal state but never to a truly *secular* state.

Marxian materialism, which regards all religion as a reactionary element in society, contributed much to the development of this view

[23] Donald E. Smith, *Nehru and Democracy: The Political Thought of an Asian Democrat*, Orient Longmans, Calcutta, 1958, p. 156.
[24] *The Hindu*, July 17, 1951, and April 11, 1950.
[25] Jawaharlal Nehru, *Independence and After*, John Day Company, New York, 1950, p. 122.

of secularism in India.[26] M. N. Roy was a prominent Communist leader until his expulsion from the Comintern in 1929. Thereafter, Roy launched out on an intellectual quest which ultimately led him to his own synthesis of materialism and liberal humanism. Until his death in 1954, Roy was the most noted exponent of the view that the essential reform which Indian society must undergo is the elimination of the religious outlook.

A prolific writer, Roy concluded his two-volume historical survey of western thought with the affirmation that only a restated materialism could provide the metaphysical foundation for the view of life which was needed—"a secular humanist ethics and a revolutionary social philosophy." Man could be made spiritually free only by abolishing the supernatural. "The desire for freedom in social and political life, being an expression of the basic human urge for spiritual freedom, can be satisfied only by . . . a world view which does away with the necessity of assuming a supernatural power or metaphysical sanction."[27] According to this approach, a constitutional setup which excludes religion from the functions of the state is necessary, but this only touches the fringe of the real problem. What is required is something far more fundamental, the secularization of both individual and social life. True spiritual freedom means not the freedom to choose from among various religious doctrines, but the freedom of the human spirit from the tyranny of all of them.

Ancient India produced several schools of political and philosophical thought which were in some sense secular. In chapter 3 mention was made of the *Arthashastra* thinkers, who severed the connection between theology and politics. Reason was placed over sacred authority, and religion was not permitted to encroach upon the domain of political science or economics. Various schools of philosophy rejected some of the basic tenets of Hindu orthodoxy. Thus the *Lokayatas* and the *Carvakas* denied the existence of the soul, and the classical *Samkhya* school was originally atheistic. But these schools of thought have not maintained a continuous living tradition down to modern times. They are intellectual museum-pieces, interesting but not influential. While logically they might have

[26] The contribution was not made by the Communist Party of India, however. As we have noted, the Indian Communists followed the opportunistic policy of supporting Muslim separatism in 1942-1947.

[27] M. N. Roy, *Reason, Romanticism, and Revolution*, Renaissance Publishers, Ltd., Calcutta, 1955, vol. 2, p. 298.

contributed something to the theoretical undergirding of the modern secular state, in terms of recent history their influence has been practically nil. However, secularists whose thinking has been largely molded through contact with western thought often attempt to strengthen their case by appealing to these ancient Indian traditions.

In a biting critique of Radhakrishnan's interpretation of the Hindu view of life, M. N. Roy pointed out that, like ancient Greece, India also had produced naturalist, secular, and rationalist currents of philosophical thought. "More than two thousand years before Radhakrishnan, the founder of the *Samkhya* system of philosophy, Kapila, denied the existence of God because there was no evidence. And Kapila's agnostic naturalism was preceded by the materialist (atomist) rationalism of the *Nyaya-Vaisesika* system expounded by Kanada and Gautama."[28] Roy complained that Radhakrishnan expounded the post-Buddhist Vedanta system as though it were the only Hindu view of life.

M. N. Roy's "Radical Humanism" has won a small but devoted following of Indian intellectuals, but has made very little impact on the thinking of the masses. The same is true of such organizations as the Indian Rationalist Association. Only among the Tamils of South India has a frontal attack on Hindu religion developed into a popular movement. E. V. Ramaswamy Naicker's Self-Respect Movement, founded in 1925, derived much of its attitude toward religion from the writings of Robert Ingersoll. Ingersoll's attacks on the Bible and Christianity inspired similar arguments against the *Puranas* and Hinduism.

The emotional appeal of this movement and the later Dravida Kazhagam, however, was provided by its anti-Brahmanism. Opposition to priestcraft and superstition became closely associated with the struggle against the alleged domination of the Brahman, the Aryan, Sanskrit, and North India. Idealized values were associated with the non-Brahman, the Dravidian, and the Tamil language. Whatever the effect of the rationalism of the Dravida Kazhagam and its offshoot, the Dravida Munnetra Kazhagam (founded in 1949), the blatant racialism and communalism of the

[28] M. N. Roy, "Radhakrishnan in the Perspective of Indian Philosophy," *The Philosophy of Sarvepalli Radhakrishnan*, ed. Paul Arthur Schilpp, Tudor Publishing Company, New York, 1952, p. 548. See Dale Riepe, *The Naturalistic Tradition in Indian Thought*, University of Washington Press, Seattle, 1961.

movement must be regarded as extremely deleterious to the development of the secular state.[29]

We have noted that many diverse currents of thought, both secular and religious, have contributed to the concept of the secular state in the West. Nehru and M. N. Roy drew heavily upon the rationalist and humanist traditions. Other Indians, however, and especially the intellectual leaders of the Christian community, have stressed the theory of the secular state derived from religious sources in the West.

A group of Protestant Christian leaders met at Nagpur in 1953 to discuss the secular state, and the initial fruit of their discussion was a pamphlet entitled *The Secular State in India: A Christian Point of View.* The theoretical basis presented in this report can be summed up briefly. The secular state is necessary, since partiality to any one religion would tend to create group disharmony and militate against national unity. But, "apart from this consideration of practical politics, the secular state is desirable also from the viewpoint of religion." The state exists in order to establish justice and promote the social and economic well-being of its citizens, in accordance with the higher moral law. The Christian faith claims that the primary concern of religion is with man's spiritual life, with salvation, and thus "concerns an area of human need which is outside the scope of the state."

Religion and the state must thus be viewed from the point of view of their differing aims and purposes. "In fulfilling their varied functions, the church and the state adopt different methods. While the state by its very nature exercises coercive authority in order to secure order and justice in human relations, the church in its witness to God's redemptive action seeks the free response of man through persuasive understanding and loving fellowship."[30] Because of the inherently different functions and methods of religion and the state, any official relationship between them tends to damage the true nature of both. As can be seen from this brief summary, the principles

---

[29] See P. D. Devanandan, *The Dravida Kazhagam: A Revolt against Brahmanism,* Christian Institute for the Study of Religion and Society, Bangalore, 1960. In the 1962 elections the Dravida Munnetra Kazhagam won 50 out of 206 seats to become the chief opposition party in the Madras state assembly. The DMK demands the creation of Dravidanad, a separate sovereign state composed of the present states of Madras, Andhra Pradesh, Mysore, and Kerala.

[30] *The Secular State in India,* pp. 2-3.

of Roger Williams are still being expounded, and in words not very different from those used in the seventeenth century.

There are obvious differences between the Hindu and Christian approaches to the theoretical basis of the secular state. The development of the secular state in the western Christian tradition never proceeded on the assumption that all religions were equally true and valid, and ultimately one and the same. As between Catholic and Protestant, or even among various Protestant denominations, there was usually far more consciousness of differences than of similarities, despite the fact that all were Christians. It was the frank recognition of these differences which led to the conclusion that the state, which governs and protects all the people, must therefore be divorced from religion. Accordingly, matters of religious belief were left strictly to the conscience of the individual citizen.

A western conception: relevant to India?

The western origin of the conception of the secular state has given rise to some serious questions. Hindu leaders object that the secular state in the West was the result of the failure to solve the religious problem. Since the religious problem had been solved successfully in India, the secular state today is a western importation with no real relevance to India's needs.[31] The secular state in the West was the answer to a twofold problem. First, separation of church and state in Europe was in part an arrangement to curtail the political power of the ecclesiastical hierarchy. But religious authority in India never attempted to usurp the powers of the secular authority; there is no Indian parallel to the struggle between pope and emperor, church and state, which occupies such a large part of the history of Europe. Second, the secular state in the West was found to be the best guarantee of the preservation of religious liberty. By the separation of church and state the coercive power of the latter could not be used to enforce religious conformity. By denying to government the right to interfere in religious matters, the freedom of religion of the individual and the dissenting church could be assured. At this point also, the secular state in India is the solution to a nonexistent problem. The Hindu state was always tolerant of religious differences,

[31] This thesis was propounded in an interesting lecture by Professor M. A. Venkata Rao, president of the Mysore state Jana Sangh, in Bangalore in May 1961. Parts of this argument have frequently been used by Hindus of other political persuasions who regard the secular state in India as a regrettable necessity at best.

and there was never any attempt to enforce uniformity in religion. The freedom of religion of the individual in the traditional Hindu state was practically unlimited.

With respect to the first objection, the desire to restrict the political power of the church was a factor in the separation of church and state in France, but had little to do with this development in the United States. It can be readily admitted that this objective has no relevance to the Indian situation. As far as freedom of religion is concerned, however, the secular state is of undoubted importance, in India as in any other country. Even under the present Constitution, the powers of state interference in the internal affairs of religious institutions are considerable. Corporate freedom of religion would certainly suffer if the state were legally connected with Hinduism, in which case one could expect the creation of a state Ecclesiastical Department with vast powers of control over Hindu temples and *maths*, and probably over Muslim, Christian, and Sikh institutions as well.

These objections to the secular state are based on the broad sweep of Indian history starting with Vedic times, but they conveniently overlook the last thirty years of the Hindu-Muslim communal problem. This too, unfortunately, is a part of Indian history, and the secular state is surely an important part of the solution to this problem. In view of the bitter communal suspicion and hostility which led to the partition of the country, and the continued existence of large minorities, it is impossible seriously to claim that the secular state has no relevance to India's real problems. By refusing to identify the state with any particular religion, the equality of the individual citizen and the equal protection of all faiths are secured and confirmed.

PART THREE
RELIGIOUS LIBERTY AND STATE REGULATION

CHAPTER 6

THE PROPAGATION OF RELIGION

The Indian Constitution guarantees to all persons not only freedom of conscience but the right to profess, practice, and *propagate* religion. The liberal tradition has insisted that liberty of thought and liberty of expression are intimate and inseparable. John Stuart Mill defined the former right in sweeping language—"absolute freedom of opinion and sentiment on all subjects, practical or speculative, scientific, moral or theological." The liberty to express and publish such opinions, Mill continued, might at first appear to fall in a different category, "but, being almost of as much importance as the liberty of thought itself, and resting in great part on the same reasons, is practically inseparable from it." This chapter will deal with the numerous problems which have arisen in India in applying this principle to the propagation of religion.

Conflicting Views of Propagation

Despite the clarity of the constitutional provision, there is in India a continuing debate on whether the propagation of religion should be permitted, and, if so, on what terms. Very much involved in the debate are some of the basic assumptions and affirmations of Hindu religion. As an ethnic religion, Hinduism has never sought to bring converts into its fold. Hindu doctrine contains little which would support the missionary motive as religiously valid, and much that would condemn it. The fact that the proselytizing faiths which came to India, Islam and Christianity, were also associated with foreign conquerors, further complicates the problem. In the continuing debate on the propagation of religion there are five important points of view, which we shall now consider.

The general Hindu attitude

"The preaching of religion" is a phrase which is out of place in the context of Hinduism. From the days of the Upanishadic sages to the present, the Hindu emphasis has been on *teaching*—the explication of abstruse religious doctrine. The *guru* or swami attempts to enlighten the understanding of his disciples by the patient exposition of certain scriptures and by practical guidance drawn from his own religious experience. The purpose of such teaching is to bring the small group of disciples through a course of self-discipline toward the goal of mystic union with the Absolute.[1]

In recent years there has been a new emphasis within Hinduism on the systematic propagation of religious teaching among the masses. Itinerant swamis expounding the Bhagavad Gita or other scriptures attract vast audiences. Concerned over the growth of secularist and materialist influences in Hindu society, religious leaders sense the need for more coordinated efforts to teach the principles of Hindu *dharma*.

Part of the difficulty is that, on the whole, Hinduism has lacked effective institutional means to propagate its teachings. There are now signs of a trend toward a congregational form of worship which would provide such means. In a few of the temples in cities and towns there are weekly discourses on doctrinal subjects. The Dharma Prachara Sangam presented a memorandum in 1956 to the commissioner of Hindu religious endowments in Madras, requesting that temples set aside funds to provide lectures explaining the fundamentals of Hinduism. "It is absolutely necessary that temple funds be used for religious instruction as part of congregational worship in the temples," the Sangam asserted. "It is an essential duty of temple trustees to devote part of the funds to propagating the Hindu religion."[2]

Mr. M. Patanjali Sastri, former chief justice of the Supreme Court of India, emphasized similar ideas when addressing a Hindu religious and cultural conference in Kerala in 1955. Expressing alarm that in these days "God is dismissed as a superstition and religion is regarded as a mode of exploitation," Mr. Patanjali Sastri called for a positive program to propagate the truths of religion. He felt that the *maths* (or mutts) should take the lead. "When that religion is being attacked and its deities are exposed to vilification and insult in public, is it not the obvious duty of the mutts to come forward and organize

[1] Paul David Devanandan, "Hindus and Christian Evangelism," *Christian Century,* 1957, vol. 74, p. 740.
[2] *Christian Century,* 1956, vol. 73, p. 1456. See also *The Hindu,* August 2, 1955.

a counter-movement on missionary lines, not for proselytizing, for that is foreign to the spirit and tradition of the Hindu faith, but for refuting and repelling these onslaughts by spreading knowledge of the fundamentals of that faith. Properly trained and equipped *pracharaks* (preachers) can be employed as evangelists of the Hindu faith. Religious literature could also be published and distributed summarizing in easily intelligible form the teachings of the Vedas, the Upanishads and the Bhagavad Gita."[3]

There is thus a new emphasis on the propagation of religious teaching within Hinduism. The constitutional guarantee of the right to propagate religion will perhaps have greater significance for the Hindu in the future than it has in the past. The general Hindu attitude toward propagation which results in conversion from one religion to another, however, is a decidedly negative one. Several basic objections to conversions are put forth.

First, conversions have tended to disrupt the established patterns of family, caste, and village social life.[4] The conversion of a Hindu to Christianity or Islam has invariably led to excommunication from his caste and frequently to expulsion from the joint family to which he belonged. Hinduism allows the greatest latitude in religious and philosophical beliefs, but actions which threaten its social solidarity by transferring the individual to a different religious community will be vigorously resisted. The general Hindu attitude places the value of social cohesion far above that of individual freedom.

Second, it has frequently been stated that conversion, especially to Christianity, leads to the virtual abandonment of Indian culture. Gandhi once wrote: "In Hindu households the advent of a missionary has meant the disruption of the family, coming in the wake of change of dress, manners, language, food and drink."[5] Christian converts, he asserted, tended to become denationalized and westernized—they not only gave up their ancestral faith but also their national culture.

[3] *The Hindu*, May 19, 1955.

[4] See C. Rajagopalachari's letter to Dr. Blaise Levai, quoted in full in Blaise Levai, ed., *Revolution in Missions*, The Popular Press, Vellore, 1957, pp. 5-6.

[5] *Harijan*, May 11, 1935. Two very useful collections of excerpts from Gandhi's writings on this and related topics are: *Christian Missions: Their Place in India*, Navajivan Press, Ahmedabad, 1941, and Clifford Manshardt, ed., *The Mahatma and the Missionary*, Henry Regnery Company, Chicago, 1949. Most of the excerpts are from *Harijan* and *Young India*.

A third criticism of conversions, voiced frequently in the pre-independence period, was that they were often motivated by political considerations. Under the system of separate electorates, the various religious communities received representation in the legislatures roughly in proportion to their numerical strength, but with weightage for the Muslim minority. As political consciousness developed through the 1930's with the approach of self-government, the Hindu-Muslim power struggle became more intense. In the light of separate electorates, defections from Hinduism or accessions to the Muslim fold had obvious political implications. B. R. Ambedkar, spokesman for the Depressed Classes, in 1935 urged the Harijans to renounce Hinduism and embrace any other religion which would afford "equality of status and treatment." Thus the prospect of mass conversions to Christianity or Islam became a distinct political threat to the majority community. With the abandonment of separate electorates under the present Constitution, this argument has lost much of its force. The Niyogi report, however, found new political motives connected with the cold war.[6]

Another criticism of religious conversions is that they are frequently promoted by unethical or at least questionable methods. It has been contended that the foreign missionaries' medical, social, and educational work is conducted not out of humanitarian considerations but with ulterior motives, namely, the desire for conversions. Gandhi frequently expressed the idea that true humanitarian service could never be lowered to anything less than an end in itself. "Service, which has not the slightest touch of self in it, is itself the highest religion. . . . Conversion and service go ill together."[7]

Mass conversions to Christianity or Islam have drawn the heaviest criticism. This method of propagating a new religion accepted the fact of the solidarity of the Indian family or village and made use of it, thus avoiding the problems which were created when individual converts were uprooted from their social milieu. The Hindu criticism, of course, was that this method frequently resulted in the formal conversion of many people who had very little understanding of their new faith.

---

[6] The charge was that American missionaries were creating Christian enclaves in India to further United States objectives in the struggle against the Soviet Union. The report is discussed in detail in the next chapter.

[7] *Harijan*, May 25, 1935; *Young India*, January 19, 1928; *The Mahatma and the Missionary*, p. 125.

Recent developments in India have included conversions, even mass conversions, in a form which the Hindu finds it difficult or embarrassing to criticize. In recent years great stress has been laid on the Hindu origins of Buddhism, and the close relationship between the two faiths. Commenting on the renaissance of Hinduism, S. Radhakrishnan stated: "The re-affiliation of Buddhism to Hinduism is one of the achievements of the present renaissance."[8] Mass conversions of Hindus to Buddhism have thus posed a special problem for those who reject on principle the propagation of religion with the object of conversions.

The conversion to Buddhism of 20,000 Hindus of the Koliya Kshatriya caste in Ajmer, northern India, produced a considerable stir throughout the country. But this was not to be an isolated phenomenon. In 1955 Ambedkar, who twenty years before had urged the Harijans to abandon Hinduism, announced his decision to embrace Buddhism, a religion which does not recognize caste. As president of the Scheduled Castes Federation, he made an all-out bid to lead *en masse* his followers into the new faith, on the occasion of the 2,500th anniversary of the Buddha's death.

At a special ceremony in Nagpur in October 1956, Dr. Ambedkar took what he called the "most important step" of his life, when he along with 300,000 followers entered the Buddhist fold. The ceremony was conducted by Mahathevar Chandramani, the oldest Buddhist monk in India. The converts took the threefold Buddhist vow: "I take refuge in the Buddha; I take refuge in the Dhamma (law); I take refuge in the Sangha (Buddhist order)."

Addressing a mass meeting the day after the ceremony, Ambedkar stated: "The Hindu religion offered no opportunity for the untouchables to improve their lot, for it is based on inequality. . . . On the other hand, Buddhism . . . is based on equality and justice."[9] Dr. Ambedkar expressed his determination to spread the gospel of Buddhism. "I would like to see all India become Buddhist," he declared. Ambedkar died, however, within two months of his conversion.

Interestingly enough, among the converts was M. B. Niyogi, a Brahman and former chief justice of the state of Madhya Pradesh.

[8] Quoted in S. Kulandran, *Resurgent Religions*, Lutterworth Press, London, 1957, p. 22. The relationship between Hinduism and Buddhism is discussed in another context in chapter 13, "Hinduism and Indian Culture."
[9] *Christian Century*, 1956, vol. 73, p. 1494.

A few months before, Mr. Niyogi had submitted the report of his committee's inquiry into Christian missionary activity in the state. The report, considered below, condemns in harsh terms the practice of encouraging mass conversions to Christianity.[10]

The Hindu universalist approach

In the last chapter the concept of Hindu tolerance as part of the theoretical undergirding of the secular state was discussed. Gandhi and Radhakrishnan contributed much to this school of thought which emphasized the conviction that all religions are equally valid and equally partial paths to truth. The authority for this belief is found in the ancient Hindu scriptures, such as the Upanishad which declares: "As the different streams having their sources in different places all mingle their water in the sea, so, O Lord, the different paths which men take through different tendencies, various though they appear, crooked or straight, all lead to thee." This belief in the essential unity of all religions can, as we have seen, be used as the foundation for a state which does not grant a special status to any one religion. But it can also be used as the basis for significant restrictions on the right to propagate religion. For if all religions are equally true, what justification can there be for the propagation of one religion among the adherents of another? Any attempt to proselytize is resented as a profoundly unspiritual act.

Gandhi once wrote that the different religions were branches of the same majestic tree; all faiths were "equally true, though being received and interpreted through human instruments equally imperfect."[11] This great truth should preclude even the thought that another individual embrace one's own faith. "Accepting this position, we can only pray, if we are Hindus, not that a Christian should become a Hindu, or if we are Mussalmans, not that a Hindu or a Christian should become a Mussalman, nor should we even secretly pray that any one should be converted, but our inmost prayer should be that a Hindu should be a better Hindu, a Muslim a better Muslim and a Christian a better Christian."[12] Gandhi felt so strongly about this question that on another occasion he wrote: "If I had power and could legislate, I should stop all proselytizing."[13] Gandhi did

[10] See chapter 7, "The Question of Foreign Missionaries."
[11] *Harijan*, January 30, 1937.
[12] *Young India*, January 19, 1928; *The Mahatma and the Missionary*, p. 73.
[13] *Harijan*, May 11, 1935; *The Mahatma and the Missionary*, p. 69.

agree, however, that if an individual found that he could realize God better through embracing a different religion, he should have complete freedom to do so.

A bishop of the Church of South India analyzed the Hindu's metaphysical and religious objections to conversion in forceful language: "The absolute monism of the Vedanta destroys in advance all claims on behalf of any religion for the allegiance of all men. To those who are under the influence of the Vedanta, Christian evangelism is an intolerable assertion of ultimate truth on behalf of one among the many forms of illusion."[14] Bishop Newbigin went on to state that, for most well-educated Hindus, "the attempt to persuade a man to change his faith is something that arouses the deepest hostility and disgust." There is some exaggeration in this statement, but not much.

Does the Hindu universalist approach entirely preclude the propagation of spiritual teaching across religious boundaries? Not at all, for once the conversion motive is eliminated, there is wide scope for the sharing of religious insights among the various world faiths. Professor P. J. Mehta expressed this view in his remarks to Christian missionaries: "By all means discuss your faith with us, share your views and your experiences with us, but . . . India would like to suggest that the true missionary is one who . . . helps the other to live his own faith more perfectly and not to forsake to the missionary's faith."[15]

The Hindu communalist position

The tradition of militant Hinduism can be traced from the Arya Samaj, founded in 1875, through Tilak and the Extremists, to the Hindu Mahasabha and present-day Jana Sangh. Abandoning the earlier defensiveness, Swami Dayananda Saraswati, founder of the Arya Samaj, confidently proclaimed the superiority of Hinduism over Islam and Christianity. In the 1920's an important expression of this tradition was the *shuddhi* ("cleansing" or "purification") movement, which sought to reconvert to Hinduism those who had formerly been won to Islam or Christianity.[16] The stated objective

---

[14] J. E. Leslie Newbigin, *A South India Diary*, SCM Press, London, 1951, p. 59.
[15] Quoted in P. D. Devanandan, *loc. cit.*
[16] William Roy Smith, *Nationalism and Reform in India*, Yale University Press, New Haven, 1938, pp. 332-333, 350-351.

of the movement was "to realize the ideal of unifying India nationally, socially and religiously."[17]

The *shuddhi* movement never defined the sphere of its operations too clearly. Recent converts to Islam or Christianity were surely regarded as potential proselytes. But the vast majority of the Indian Muslims and Christians were the descendants of converts from Hinduism, although the conversions had taken place generations or even centuries ago. There seemed to be no necessity to exclude these groups from the scope of *shuddhi* activities.

The movement gained impetus because of the "political implications" of conversions mentioned above. V. D. Savarkar, a leader of the Hindu Mahasabha, declared: "Political power in democracies hinges more and more on the population strength of a community which in the case of the Hindus must depend in the main on the proportion in which the Hindus succeed in stopping the dreadful conversion activities of alien faiths and in accelerating the reclamation of the alienated numbers back to the Hindu fold. In a country like India where a religious unit tends inevitably to grow into a cultural and national unit, the *shuddhi* [reconversion to Hinduism] movement ceases to be merely theological or dogmatic, but assumes the wider significance of a political and national movement. If the Muslims increase in population, the center of political power is bound to be shifted in their favor."[18] The All India Hindu Mahasabha began to gather strength in the 1920's, and a number of outstanding Arya Samaj leaders became associated with this more politically-oriented organization. The *shuddhi* movement became an important aspect of the party's program. It was claimed that 450,000 Muslim Rajputs were reconverted to Hinduism in 1922-1923.[19]

The *shuddhi* movement gave rise to a counter-movement, called *tanzim*, in which the Muslims organized their efforts to win adherents from other religions and to resist the reconversion of Muslims to Hinduism.[20] In its election manifesto of 1951 the Hindu Mahasabha pointed with pride to its part in the *shuddhi* movement over

[17] R. C. Majumdar, H. C. Raychaudhuri, and K. Datta, *An Advanced History of India,* Macmillan Company, London, 1950, p. 883.
[18] "The Hindu Mahasabha," *The Indian Year Book 1942-1943,* Times of India Press, Bombay, p. 826.
[19] *Ibid.,* p. 827.
[20] W. R. Smith, *op. cit.,* p. 351.

the past thirty years.[21] Hindu missionary preachers have gone out to propagate their faith vigorously and have not lacked success. In 1949 a *shuddhi* ceremony was held at a famous temple near Tiruvalla, in the then state of Travancore, at which 1,500 Christian converts were formally readmitted to Hinduism.[22]

As will be recognized immediately, a vast gulf separates the thought of Gandhian Hinduism from that of communalist Hinduism. The Gandhian universalist holds to the equal validity of all religions; the legitimate propagation of religion means the sharing of spiritual experience with no desire for conversions. The Hindu communalist regards his as the oldest and highest of the living religions of the world; the propagation of religion means aggressive and determined efforts to bring Muslims and Christians back into the Hindu fold. Because of the way in which Hinduism, Indian culture, and nationalism are all linked together in his mind, he tends to regard the conversion of Muslims and Christians to Hinduism as something akin to naturalization.

Gandhi deprecated the *shuddhi* movement on numerous occasions. Although glorying in the broad tolerance which had traditionally permitted all kinds of doctrines and practices to find lodgment within Hinduism, he could not see a place there for this movement. "In my opinion there is no such thing as proselytism in Hinduism as it is understood in Christianity or to a lesser extent in Islam. The Arya Samaj has, I think, copied the Christians in planning its propaganda. The modern method does not appeal to me. It has done more harm than good. Though regarded as a matter of the heart purely and one between the Maker and oneself, it has degenerated into an appeal to the selfish instinct. The Arya Samaj preacher is never so happy as when he is reviling other religions. My Hindu instinct tells me that all religions are more or less true."[23] It was Gandhi's conviction that "the real *shuddhi* movement should consist in each one trying to arrive at perfection in his or her own faith."

In concluding this discussion of the Hindu communalist position on the question of the propagation of religion, it is important to note one further point. The fact that certain Hindu groups are zealous in their efforts to convert non-Hindus does *not* mean that they are

[21] *Election Manifesto of the Akhil Bharat Hindu Mahasabha*, New Delhi, 1951, p. 2.
[22] *Christian Century*, 1949, vol. 66, p. 1546.
[23] *Young India*, May 29, 1924; *The Mahatma and the Missionary*, p. 67.

prepared to grant equal rights to other religions to propagate their respective faiths. The militant Hindu position is built not upon the *principle* of full freedom to propagate religion, but upon the *fact* that deep inroads have been made on the Hindu community by conversions to other religions. The *shuddhi* movement was a defensive reaction to this particular historical situation. Hinduism has been the victim of aggression, and hence has rights which cannot legitimately be claimed by the aggressor faiths. Furthermore, according to the communalist, conversion to Hinduism is necessary to make Indian nationals out of Muslims and Christians. As one RSS worker told the author, "Hinduism *is* Indian nationalism."[24]

The Indian Christian stand

All shades of theological opinion are represented in the leadership of the Christian churches in India. In general, however, Protestants as well as Roman Catholics stress the absolute uniqueness of Christianity. One Indian Christian acknowledged the truths embedded in the older religions of India, but went on to assert: "We dare not offer Christianity to the Indian people if we do not believe with all our soul and with all our strength that Christianity is not only nearer the truth than any other religion but is the Truth."[25] There are indeed theologically liberal Christians in India who repudiate these exclusivist claims, such as Rajkumari Amrit Kaur, formerly minister for health in Nehru's cabinet, but they are in a minority. As might be expected, such claims of Christianity's uniqueness render understanding with the exponents of universalist Gandhian Hinduism difficult.

The National Christian Council, which represents most of the Protestant churches, addressed itself to this and other points in its 1955 statement on "The Church's Freedom for Its Missionary Task." The council declared that everyone should have freedom to believe that all religions are basically the same, but that the same freedom should be enjoyed by those who think differently. "It can be said that religions are both like and unlike each other, and that their differences are as important as their similarities." But the council

[24] The Rashtriya Swayamsevak Sangh is a Hindu communalist youth organization. See chapter 15, "The Challenge of Hindu Communalism."
[25] Rajaiah D. Paul, "Missionary Activity in Present-Day India," *Revolution in Missions*, p. 10.

noted a certain tendency in India "to compel all to accept what some believe about the nature of the religions."[26] One Christian leader expressed appreciation of the fact that the Gandhian view provided a philosophical basis for religious tolerance in present-day India, which was all to the good. However, he claimed that the view that "all religions are the same" was being constantly imposed upon people, and was not less dogmatic than the Christian claim.[27]

Not only do Indian Christians regard their faith as possessing elements of uniqueness but they also regard the propagation of it as an essential part of Christianity. The missionary impulse of the church in any nation is not a historical accident; rather, it derives from the essential nature of Christianity and could not be eliminated without "mutilating" the faith.[28] Rejecting the view that the emphasis on propagation was an unnecessary and unhealthy accretion to Christianity, one Christian member of Parliament wrote that anyone could hold the opinion that Christianity should have developed along different lines, "but that will be to say that the Christianity of their preference or imagination is different from the actual historical Christianity."[29]

We have noted that some Hindus make a sharp distinction between propagating religion and making converts. Some leaders have declared unequivocally that the right to make converts ("proselytize") is not included in the right to propagate religion guaranteed in the Constitution.[30] The Indian Christian rejects this distinction as artificial. The Rev. R. C. Das wrote: "The statements that one may preach but not convert, or that in serving one should not be actuated by motives of conversion, show confusion of thought and a lack of knowledge of psychology and of normal human behavior. Why is something preached? Is it not to convince others? And when convinced, are they not inwardly converted? The word 'conversion' simply means 'change.' . . . The Hindu does not object to conversion in politics, in a new attitude to science, history, or philosophy. How then is objection to religious conversion valid where a man's happi-

[26] *National Christian Council Review*, 1955, vol. 75, p. 206.
[27] A. E. Inbanathan, "The Christian Message in the Indian Setting," *Revolution in Missions*, p. 42.
[28] *N.C.C. Review*, 1955, vol. 75, p. 200.
[29] C. P. Mathew, "Religious Freedom from the Christian Point of View," *Revolution in Missions*, p. 29.
[30] *Christian Century*, 1957, vol. 74, p. 31.

ness and welfare are even more at stake?"[31] In the Indian Christian view, effective propagation will lead to inward conversion manifested in an outward change of religious affiliation.

Thus rejecting a distinction made by the Hindus, the Indian Christians emphasize another distinction which the Hindus usually overlook or reject, namely, the distinction between conversion and proselytism. Proselytism, in this usage, means the social transfer of large numbers from one religion to another without a corresponding inward change (conversion).[32] This practice is repudiated by responsible Christian leaders, as well as the use of inducements which have sometimes been associated with proselytism.[33]

With respect to the Hindu complaint that Christianity is a foreign religion and that conversion to this faith involves the virtual abandonment of Indian culture, the Indian Christian's answer is twofold. First, he points to the ancient Syrian Christian churches of Kerala and reminds the critics of Nehru's remarks in Parliament: "Christianity is as old in India as Christianity itself. Christianity found its roots in India before it went to countries like England, Portugal and Spain. Christianity is as much a religion of the Indian soil as any other religion in India."[34] Second, there is a frank recognition that the Christian churches established by the missionary movements which began in the eighteenth century do reflect the cultural forms of the West, and efforts are being made to express Christianity through elements of indigenous Indian culture.[35]

The Indian Christian position is that communal harmony is not endangered by Christian evangelization. Every person has the right to preach his religion; if others are convinced by this preaching, they have the right to change their faith. There is no threat to communal harmony in these actions. If the legitimate exercise of these rights

[31] R. C. Das, "The Christian Enterprise and the Government," *N.C.C. Review*, 1954, vol. 74, p. 381.

[32] Note the statement of the National Christian Council: "Conversion has been confused with proselytism, but there is a difference. The proselyte may have no inner change of life, hence he has no conversion. He is one who has passed from one religion to another, changing some external features of his life, manners and customs. But these may not correspond to any spiritual illumination, reconciliation and peace." *Ibid.*, 1955, vol. 75, p. 205. See also E. Stanley Jones, "Evangelism and Independent India," *The Guardian*, Madras, 1947, vol. 25, pp. 347-349.

[33] *N.C.C. Review*, 1955, vol. 75, p. 206.

[34] Speech in the Lok Sabha, December 3, 1955. Quoted in *Revolution in Missions*, p. 274.

[35] *N.C.C. Review*, 1955, vol. 75, p. 210.

evokes unreasonable hostility on the part of some people, the law must prevent *them* from creating public disturbances. C. P. Mathew used the analogy of an election campaign in which rival political parties put forth their propaganda. Nobody would suggest that the legitimate expression of political views by any party should be prohibited simply because other political parties disliked these views. Regarding the assumption that conversion from one religion to another is undesirable, Mathew's comment was: "This is a matter of individual religious or philosophical opinion. A secular state like ours can have no view on it, without ceasing to be secular."[36]

The humanist liberal position

This position, exemplified most clearly by Prime Minister Nehru, is characterized by a secular and scientific view of the universe, combined with a commitment to human values stressed by nineteenth-century liberalism. Those who represent this position are thus members of the westernized elite, and have largely cut themselves off from the religious outlook of traditional India.

The humanist liberal thinker, unlike spokesmen for the other positions we have discussed, approaches the question of religious propagation without strong emotional involvement in the fortunes of any particular religion. He tends to view religion as a social phenomenon, possibly undesirable, but one which must be dealt with in such a way that the order and harmony of society are not disrupted. First and foremost his concern is for the individual's freedom of belief and expression, for only through such freedom can human values be realized. In 1949 Nehru declared: "Nothing can be worse for the world, I think, than a deprivation of human freedom of the individual."[37]

From this detached position with respect to the various religions, the humanist liberal thinker throws his weight on the side of unrestricted freedom to propagate religious as well as other ideas, subject only to general regulations in the interest of public safety and order. The humanist liberal view rejects the Hindu distinction between propagation and conversion and is prepared to see changes in religious affiliation as a result of preaching. With no desire either to promote

[36] C. P. Mathew, *op. cit.*, p. 38.
[37] Jawaharlal Nehru, *Visit to America*, John Day Company, New York, 1950, p. 136.

or to prevent them, there is the recognition that where individual freedom is exercised, religious conversions are not unlikely.

In an interview with the *London Catholic Herald* in 1946, Nehru asserted: "It stands to reason that any faith whose roots are strong and healthy should spread; and to interfere with that right to spread seems to me to be a blow at the roots themselves. . . . Unless a given faith proves a menace to public order, or its teachers attempt to thrust it down unwilling throats of men owning other persuasions, there can be no justification for measures which deprive any community of its rights."[38] In this statement can be seen the liberal tradition of John Stuart Mill, which values freedom of expression for its own sake without attempting to judge the content of what is expressed. Nehru declared in 1954 that he personally did not appreciate attempts at proselytization, but that this was a personal opinion of his own and he had no business to thrust it on others.[39] In the open "marketplace of ideas," there must be full freedom to offer and accept different beliefs on all subjects.

STATE REGULATION OF PROPAGATION

The debates in the Constituent Assembly ultimately led to the inclusion in the Indian Constitution of the propagation of religion as a fundamental right. The full significance of this decision, however, can only be grasped against the background of the regulations which were in effect in various parts of India before the Constitution came into force.

Regulation before 1950

One factor which operated as a significant deterrent to religious conversion during the early British period was that, under both Hindu and Muslim law, apostates were deprived of their right to inherit property and even of the right of guardianship over their children. We have already discussed the Caste Disabilities Removal Act of 1850, which provided that any law or usage which inflicted on any person forfeiture of such rights by reason of conversion or being deprived of caste would cease to be enforced as law. This act, of course, applied only to British India, and in the princely states the Hindu and Muslim law continued in force. Even in the progressive

[38] Quoted in *N.C.C. Review*, 1946, vol. 66, pp. 335-336.
[39] Jawaharlal Nehru, *Circular to the Pradesh Congress Committees*, August 1954.

state of Mysore, it was not until 1938 that legislation similar to the act of 1850 was adopted, and in many of the states this step was never taken.

Another aspect of the propagation of religion, considered in detail in a later chapter, concerns religious instruction in state-aided schools operated by religious denominations.[40] In 1920 the United Provinces introduced what was known as the "conscience clause," which forbade making religious instruction compulsory in such schools (mainly Christian missionary institutions). The regulation gave to each student the right to be excused from the classes in religion on the request of his parent or guardian. After 1920, similar "conscience clauses" were introduced in the educational regulations in many parts of India.[41]

Another kind of regulation dealt with the question of conversions, and laws which were intended to discourage conversions were enacted by the maharajas of a number of the Indian states. When independence was attained in 1947, approximately seventeen Indian states had such legislation in effect, including Kotah, Bikanir, Jodhpur, Raigarh, Patna, Surguja, Udaipur, and Kalahandi.[42] Even after the integration of the Indian states in the Indian Union, these laws were enforced in some cases until 1950.

The Raigarh State Conversion Act was promulgated in 1936 because some Roman Catholic priests had entered the state without permission and had gained some converts. The raja had expressed to the British agent his strong objections to the conversion of his people to Christianity and had inquired whether there would be any objection to his introducing a law to regulate proselytism. Upon being assured that such power lay within his legal competence, the raja enacted the law.[43]

According to the Raigarh State Conversion Act, an individual wishing to change his religion had to submit an application in a prescribed form to a designated government officer. The officer then investigated the application and, if satisfied that the conversion was

[40] See chapter 12, "Education and Religion."
[41] N.C.C. Review, 1947, vol. 67, p. 474.
[42] E. Stanley Jones, "Evangelism in Independent India," N.C.C. Review, 1947, vol. 67, p. 351.
[43] Letter dated April 20, 1936, from Lt. Col. A. S. Meek to the Political Secretary to the Government of India, New Delhi. Quoted in Report of the Christian Missionary Activities Inquiry Committee, Madhya Pradesh Government Press, Nagpur, 1956, vol. 2, part B, p. 326.

genuine, granted a certificate of conversion. The act made liable to punishment any person found guilty of misrepresentation, fraud, intimidation, coercion, or undue influence in connection with any case of conversion. It further declared that general preaching for purposes of conversion was unauthorized.[44]

Similar legislation was promulgated in Patna state in 1942 under the euphemism "Freedom of Religions Act." Its purpose was defined in the following terms: "to provide freedom of conscience in religious matters," and "that religious freedom and toleration hitherto enjoyed by the subjects of the state should be properly safeguarded from undue interference." This law required a person wishing to change his religion to file an affidavit before the registrar of conversions, and then an inquiry could be ordered to determine whether the individual was acting of his free will and accord. A person below the age of 21 years was not permitted to file an affidavit. An Indian Christian leader complained: "These acts aim at preserving the status quo and make it almost impossible for anyone to change his religion."[45]

The Patna act was most severe in its provisions regarding the custody of children in a family in which changes of religion had taken place. If one parent only were converted, the minor would be left in the custody of the unconverted parent. If both parents changed their religion, the father's kinsmen (and failing that, the mother's kinsmen) would be given the opportunity of taking the children into their custody. The act went so far as to provide that if a widow were converted, and neither her deceased husband's kinsmen nor her own desired custody of the children, the state had the right to assign the minor to an orphanage until he attained his majority. As K. F. Weller pointed out: "The standpoint of the act is that the religion of any person shall be presumed to be that in which he was born and officially he cannot change his religion until he attains the age of twenty-one years."[46]

The Surguja State Apostasy Act (no euphemism here!) of 1945 required a person to notify the government of his intended conversion three months in advance, and the formal change of religion

[44] K. F. Weller, "Religious Liberty in Some Indian States," *N.C.C. Review*, 1946, vol. 66, p. 80.
[45] Rajah B. Manikam, "The Effect of the War on the Missionary Task of the Church in India," *International Review of Missions*, 1947, vol. 36, p. 180.
[46] K. F. Weller, *op. cit.*, p. 81.

could not take place until sanctioned by the authorities. The act made no pretense of being a general regulation covering all conceivable changes of religion. It specifically dealt with conversions from "the Hindu religion" to "an alien faith."[47]

An interesting correspondence developed in 1936 regarding the policies of the British agent, Lt. Col. A. S. Meek, toward Jesuit missionary activity in Udaipur state.[48] At that time the raja was a minor, and so the direct supervision of the administration of the state became a responsibility of the agent. It was charged that the Jesuit fathers granted loans of money and other material inducements to potential converts. Most of the converts came as the result of mass movements among the illiterate tribal peoples of the state.

The most important factor which determined the British policy, however, apparently was the desire to maintain the status quo with regard to religion. As the father of the young raja had strongly opposed conversions to Christianity, it was incumbent upon the British administrators to do the same. The agent's policy was: "The Udaipur state should remain in so far as the religion, habits and customs of its population are concerned in the same general condition as it was on the death of the late ruler . . . all teaching designed to secure any change in the mode of religion being prohibited."[49]

The Roman Catholic bishop of Ranchi contended that the converts could not be morally prevented from following the religion of their choice, although this was the net result of the agent's "repressive measures." The bishop charged that the agent, "in his anxiety to safeguard the rights and privileges of the ruler, has never consented at any stage to give a thought to the rights of the state's subjects."[50] The bishop noted that although the principle of religious toleration contained in Queen Victoria's proclamation was not strictly applicable outside of British India, the spirit of the principle at least should be reflected in the agent's policies in a state under his guardianship. On the contrary, however, the agent had apparently endorsed the sixteenth-century formula, *cujus regio, ejus religio.*

In the course of the extensive correspondence, a secretary in the Foreign and Political Department, New Delhi, suggested that the

[47] *Hitvada*, Nagpur, January 17, 1946.
[48] *Report of the Christian Missionary Activities Inquiry Committee*, vol. 2, part B, pp. 325-374.
[49] *Ibid.*, p. 339.
[50] *Ibid.*, p. 344.

best solution to the problem was the enactment of legislation similar to that of other states. Mr. F. V. Wylie wrote: "Personally I feel inclined to suggest that a conversion law be introduced in Udaipur on the lines of that recently promulgated in Raigarh."[51] However, the political secretary, Mr. B. J. Glancy, rejected this proposal. Referring to the Raigarh enactment, he commented: "The kernel of this legislation is that a change of religion, in the absence of official sanction, constitutes a penal offense. We should, I think, expose ourselves to severe criticism in certain quarters if we proceed on these lines."[52] The governor-general of India concurred in this decision, and the proposal was dropped.

Early in 1941 the British agent issued regulations relating to the propagation of religion in Udaipur state. No lay preachers were to be permitted to enter the state. Ordained clergymen, with the prior permission of the superintendent of the state, could enter once every quarter in order to administer the sacraments to Christians. Their stay was limited to forty-eight hours, and could be extended to ninety-six hours only by special permission. The clergymen were forbidden to conduct any religious propaganda other than among the members of their own church. These regulations were superseded by the Udaipur State Anti-Conversion Act of 1946, enacted about a year and a half after the raja of the state was installed.[53]

Attempts to regulate conversions were not entirely limited to the Indian states, for the Central Provinces and Berar Public Safety Act of 1947 also dealt with this question. One clause of the act stated: "No person shall convert another person from that person's religious faith to his own except before a District Magistrate."[54] Indian Christian groups, both Roman Catholic and Protestant, made representations to the authorities, claiming that the clause would obstruct the freedom of those who from genuine conviction desired to embrace a different religion.

In reply the home minister explained that the clause was intended to stop the forcible mass conversions which were being carried out by Muslims in those parts of the provinces near Hyderabad.[55] The government insisted that it did not prohibit bona fide conversions.

[51] Ibid., p. 356.
[52] Ibid., p. 358.
[53] Report of the Christian Missionary Activities Inquiry Committee, vol. 1, p. 12.
[54] N.C.C. Review, 1948, vol. 68, p. 459.
[55] Christian Century, 1948, vol. 65, p. 1283.

However, when the Safety Act came before the assembly for re-enactment one year later, the home minister proposed that the clause be deleted on the ground that it was no longer necessary. The assembly then unanimously passed the Public Safety Act without the conversion clause.[56]

Provisions in the Indian Constitution

The explicit recognition of the right to propagate religion in the Constitution of India came about largely through the initiative of the Christian minority. The 1931 Karachi Congress resolution on fundamental rights included the following article on religious liberty: "Every citizen shall enjoy freedom of conscience and the right freely to profess and practice his religion, subject to public order and morality." The Karachi resolution made no mention of the propagation of religion, and the first draft of the article on religious liberty by a committee of the Constituent Assembly did not refer to it either. The wording of the draft article (the work of the Advisory Committee on Minorities, Fundamental Rights, etc.) followed that of the Karachi statement very closely indeed.

The Indian Christian community, however, had frequently expressed its conviction that freedom of religion included the right to propagate one's faith and to win converts to it. Thus, as early as October 1945 the joint committee of the Catholic Union of India and the All India Council of Indian Christians passed a resolution declaring: "In the future constitution of India, the free profession, practice and propagation of religion should be guaranteed, and the change of religion should not involve any civil or political disability."[57] The Christian members of the Constituent Assembly and of the Advisory Committee on Minorities and Fundamental Rights began to press for the inclusion of the word "propagate" in the draft article. They were ably led in this endeavor by the late Dr. H. C. Mookerjee, a Christian of great prestige among Congressmen of all ranks and the vice-president of the Constituent Assembly.

There was some opposition to the inclusion of the word "propagate" on the ground that this was amply provided for in the draft article guaranteeing freedom of speech and expression. More vehement opposition came from Hindu members who flatly denied that

[56] *N.C.C. Review*, 1948, vol. 68, p. 459.
[57] *Ibid.*, 1946, vol. 66, p. 3.

181

the propagation of religion and the winning of converts should be considered a legitimate aspect of religious freedom. Despite such objections by a few, there was a general willingness on the part of many Hindus to make some concessions to the Christian viewpoint. The Christian community, after all, had refused to support the Muslim League demand for partition, and had indicated its confidence in the majority by being willing to relinquish communal reservation of seats in the legislative bodies.

A key figure in the ultimate settlement of this issue was Sardar Vallabhbhai Patel, chairman of the advisory committee. Although generally conservative and "Hindu-minded," Patel sought to understand the minority's point of view and exerted his great prestige in support of recognizing the right to propagate religion.[58] The advisory committee presented its "Interim Report on Fundamental Rights" to the Constituent Assembly in April 1947. The draft article on freedom of religion (clause 13) included the key word *propagate*. It was not, however, a clear-cut victory for those who had urged recognition of the right to propagate religion. Clause 17 of the same report stated: "Conversion from one religion to another brought about by coercion or undue influence shall not be recognized by law."[59] Christian reaction to this clause was that while freedom of religion was classed as a fundamental right, no one had ever claimed the same for coercion or undue influence. The introduction of this clause in a constitution was therefore inappropriate; such acts could be prohibited by ordinary legislation.

When clause 17 was debated on the floor of the Constituent Assembly, a number of amendments were offered; one added the word "fraud." Mr. K. M. Munshi's amendment added an entirely new element: "Any conversion from one religion to another of any person brought about by fraud, coercion or undue influence or of a minor under the age of eighteen shall not be recognized by law."[60] This amendment was immediately attacked on several grounds. One Christian member asserted that spiritual awakening and inward conversion can very well take place in the experience of a person under eighteen years of age. This provision would prohibit him from giving outward expression to deep religious convictions.

[58] *Ibid.*, 1951, vol. 71, p. 60.
[59] *Constituent Assembly Debates*, 1947, vol. 3, pp. 427-428.
[60] *Ibid.*, p. 480.

Mr. Purushottam Das Tandon, who later became president of the Indian National Congress, gave expression to his orthodox Hindu ideas: "Mr. President, I am greatly surprised at the speeches delivered here by our Christian brethren. Some have said that in this Assembly we have admitted the right of every one to propagate his religion and to convert from one religion to another. We Congressmen deem it very improper to convert from one to another religion or to take part in such activities." Tandon declared that it was only in order to enlist the support of the Christian minority in the great task facing the nation that they had agreed to the right of propagation. But to convert a child under eighteen was going too far. "If a boy of eighteen executes a transfer deed in favor of a man for his hut worth only 100 rupees, the transaction is considered unlawful. But our brethren come forward and say that the boy has enough sense to change his religion. That the value of religion is even less than that of a hut worth 100 rupees."[61]

The crucial problem, however, centered in the dilemma which would be faced by parents who embraced another religion without being able (according to the amendment) to bring up their children in the new faith. Mr. Frank Anthony stated: "By this clause you will say, although the parents may be converted to Christianity, the children shall not be brought up by these parents in the faith of the parents. You will be cutting at the root of family life. I say it is contrary to the ordinary concepts of natural law and justice." Christian opinion saw the clause as an attempt to nullify in large measure the freedom of religion guaranteed in the main clause (13). The *National Christian Council Review* commented editorially: "If parents who are convinced of the need for a change of faith are prevented from doing so for strong reasons of affection and attachment to their children, then the freedom of conversion becomes a mockery."[62]

B. R. Ambedkar, the law minister, strongly opposed the Munshi amendment. The Constituent Assembly thereupon voted to refer the clause back to the advisory committee. The Christian members of the Assembly, under the leadership of H. C. Mookerjee, then drew up a memorandum addressed to Sardar Patel, explaining in some detail their objections to clause 17. When the Advisory Committee met,

[61] *Ibid.*, p. 484.
[62] *N.C.C. Review*, 1947, vol. 67, p. 278.

Patel himself proposed that the entire clause be omitted; this decision was made by the committee and later, through Patel's careful handling of the issue, approved by the full Constituent Assembly.[63]

The Constitution as finally adopted, then, contains only the positive statement of the right of religious liberty. Article 25 is as follows: "Subject to public order, morality and health and to the other provisions of this part, all persons are equally entitled to freedom of conscience and the right freely to profess, practice and propagate religion."

Legislation relating to conversions

In December 1954 a private member's bill dealing with conversions was introduced in the Lok Sabha (House of the People) by Mr. Jethalal Joshi, a member of the Congress Party. It was entitled the Indian Converts (Regulation and Registration) Bill. The basic provisions of the bill were: persons or institutions engaged in converting people would have to secure a license from the district magistrate; a register of conversions would be maintained; a prospective convert would have to make a declaration of his intentions to the district magistrate one month prior to the actual date of conversion; the license-holder and the convert would be required to give particulars regarding the conversion within three months after it took place.

In an unusual move, the bill was opposed at the initial stage of introduction by a Muslim member, Mr. Pocker Saheb, who declared that the bill clearly contravened article 25 of the Constitution. "When such conditions are put, then it means that the conversion of a man from one religion to another is dependent upon the discretion of the district magistrate, which, I submit, is a virtual denial of the right."[64] Over Pocker Saheb's objections, the house adopted the motion granting leave to introduce the bill.

Debate on the bill did not begin until September 1955. In attempting to show the necessity for legislation such as he had introduced, Mr. Jethalal Joshi bitterly attacked foreign missionaries, accusing them of having resorted to bribery, coercion, vicious propaganda, and even the destruction of village temples. He quoted with some effect the words of Rajkumari Amrit Kaur, a member of the central

[63] Father J. D'Souza, "The Constituent Assembly and the Question of Conversions," *The Guardian*, Madras, October 2, 1947.

[64] *Lok Sabha Debates*, 1954, part 2, vol. 9, col. 4078-4079.

cabinet and a Christian: "Conversion or the desire to impel other persons to change their faith has always savored of an arrogance which must surely be against the doctrine of life for which Christ lived and died."

As the debate continued it became very clear that, although the provisions of the bill were avowedly of general application and would cover conversions to any religion, they were aimed primarily at Christian evangelism. Mr. G. H. Deshpande, also of the Congress, saw sinister motives behind such activities. "There is a political motive behind this conversion. It is not merely religious, there is a political motive behind it. What we suspect is that there are some imperialist powers who are not free even today from their dreams of imperialism. They probably think there was a Pakistan, why should there not be in India a Christianstan even?"[65]

In December 1955 the bill received further consideration in the Lok Sabha, and was opposed by the government. In a notable speech Prime Minister Nehru declared that the proposed legislation would create more evils than it would remedy. "I am anxious, many other members of this house must be anxious, to avoid giving the police too much power of interference everywhere." Such legislation would likely inflict considerable harassment on a large number of people. "Personally, I would not pass such a measure unless it has the fullest support from the principal parties who are likely to be affected by it. If this measure apparently is meant to apply to Christian missionaries carrying on this conversion, I would like the real decision to lie with the Christian members of this house. Let them decide. In principle there is no difference. Nobody wants deception; nobody wants coercion. In practice this attempt to prevent that may well give rise to other forms of coercion."[66] Nehru also urged the Lok Sabha to bear in mind the effect its decisions would have on the minorities: "We must not do anything which gives rise to any feeling of oppression or suppression in the minds of our Christian friends and fellow-countrymen in this country." At the conclusion of the debate the bill was rejected by the house by an overwhelming vote.

In March 1960 the Lok Sabha rejected the Backward Communities

[65] *Ibid.*, 1955, part 2, vol. 8, col. 16001.
[66] The text of this speech of December 2, 1955 is reproduced in full in *N.C.C. Review*, 1956, vol. 76, pp. 19-21.

(Religious Protection) Bill moved by Prakash Vir Shastri of the Swatantra Party. This non-official bill sought "to provide for more effective protection of the Scheduled Castes, Scheduled Tribes and other backward communities from change of religion forced on them on grounds other than religious conviction." The bill sought to regulate conversions among these classes from Hinduism to "non-Indian religions," defined in the measure as Christianity, Islam, Judaism, and Zoroastrianism. Mr. Shastri asserted that the object was to stop the forced mass conversions being perpetrated by the foreign missionaries. He warned that if the government did not take note of it now the country might have to face a serious situation and there might be a demand for another partition. However, B. N. Datar, minister of state for home affairs, declared that there had been no mass conversions as alleged by Mr. Shastri. Furthermore, the bill was unconstitutional as it discriminated among the various religions. Datar asserted that Islam, Christianity, Judaism, and Zoroastrianism were as much Indian religions as Hinduism. The bill was rejected by a voice vote.[67]

Thus far, attempts to secure legislation regulating or restricting religious conversions have failed. Central legislation has touched the question of conversion only indirectly, in several of the acts dealing with Hindu personal law. The Hindu Marriage Act of 1955 lists as one of the nine grounds for divorce the other party's ceasing to be a Hindu by conversion to another religion. S. Natarajan commented that this provision is understandable from the viewpoint of Hindu marriage as a religious sacrament, but added: "It is rather strange that a secular state should not insist on further proof to establish that the conversion interferes with the religious life and practices of the other party."[68]

Under the Hindu Adoptions and Maintenance Act of 1956, a Hindu wife is entitled to live separately from her husband without forfeiting her claim to maintenance if he has been converted from Hinduism to another religion. This provision would certainly constitute a serious obstacle to a husband contemplating conversion if his wife were unsympathetic to his new religious convictions. Note, however, the next clause of the act: "A Hindu wife shall not be

[67] *The Hindu*, March 6, 1960.
[68] S. Natarajan, *A Century of Social Reform in India*, Asia Publishing House, Bombay, 1959, p. 194.

entitled to separate residence and maintenance from her husband if she is unchaste or ceases to be Hindu by conversion to another religion."[69] Unchastity and conversion must be penalized! Thus, even if the husband treated her with cruelty, were a leper, or kept a concubine in the same house in which the wife was living (all grounds for separate maintenance under the act), she would still not be entitled to separate maintenance if she ceased to be a Hindu. The principle is broadened further; the act gives an elaborate definition of the relatives deemed to be dependents but then states (section 24) that no person shall be entitled to claim maintenance under these provisions upon conversion to another religion.

It will be recalled that legislation enacted in 1850 protected a convert from the loss of his civil rights, especially the right to inherit property. This provision is still in force. However, the Hindu Succession Act of 1956 made sure that none of the convert's children or their descendants would similarly benefit. "Where before or after the commencement of this act, a Hindu has ceased or ceases to be a Hindu by conversion to another religion, children born to him or her after such conversion and their descendants shall be disqualified from inheriting the property of any of their Hindu relatives, unless such children or descendants are Hindus at the time when the succession opens."[70] Intentionally or unintentionally, this provision could in some cases constitute a powerful financial inducement for the children or descendants to be converted to Hinduism.

There can be no doubt but that the net effect of these provisions is to discourage conversions from Hinduism and to reinforce the religious status quo. However progressive, even radical, these acts are in terms of the Hindu social system (the introduction of divorce, inheritance by daughters, etc.), they actively discourage change in religious affiliation. There are definite penalties to be borne if the exercise of freedom of conscience leads the Hindu outside the fold.

Another area in which, intentionally or unintentionally, government policy has tended to perpetuate the solidarity of the Hindu community and to prevent defections to other religions is in the matter of educational and economic aid to the Scheduled Castes. For example, in 1947 the Bombay government issued an order which stated: "Scheduled Caste converts to Christianity should not be held

[69] Section 18(3).
[70] Section 26.

eligible, even on individual certification basis, for the educational concessions provided by government for the Scheduled Castes." Seven months later another government order stated: "Scheduled Caste persons on reconversion to Hinduism should be held eligible for educational concessions intended for these castes."[71] Adjustments have been made since 1948, and in most states aid is now extended to the converts from these castes under the category of "other backward classes." However, there are still very few states in which it is as advantageous economically to be a Christian or Buddhist of Harijan background as it is to be a Hindu Harijan. The discouragement of full religious liberty implicit in such a situation is obvious; in a number of cases converts have renounced their new faith and returned to Hinduism, succumbing to "economic inducements" in a new form. This important problem is discussed in detail in chapter 11.

Problems of public order

The problem is to balance a broad freedom to propagate negative or unpopular views of religion with the maintenance of public order. Religious beliefs being frequently cherished with intense devotion, virulent public attacks upon such beliefs may well lead to the breakdown of law and order. India's delicate communal situation, especially the tension between Hindu and Muslim, underlines the importance of this fact. However, subjecting the religious beliefs of one's own community to ridicule or vilification may be equally disruptive. Article 25 of the Constitution grants freedom to propagate religion "subject to public order."

In the Indian Law Commissioners' second report (1847) on the Penal Code, they made some interesting comments on what later became section 298 of the code. This section punishes the uttering of words with the deliberate intention of wounding the religious feelings of any person. However, the commissioners did not wish this provision to become an obstacle to efforts to propagate Christianity. They pointed out that in England the attempt to convert anyone from the religion of the country even by the most gentle persuasion was by law an offense. Conversion was not recognized as a legitimate object since the law assumed the truth of Christianity. But it was

[71] The two government orders were dated July 17, 1947, and February 28, 1948. Quoted in *Catholic Bishops' Conference of India, Report of the Working and Standing Committees,* Good Shepherd Convent Press, Bangalore, 1951, p. 21.

obvious that in India the law could not assume the truth of any religion. "And, as free discussion, or, in other words, attempts at conversion, is the best criterion of the truth of anything the truth or falsehood of which is not already assumed by law to be beyond controversy, it seems to follow that a bona fide attempt to convert ought not in this country to be treated as a crime, even though the intention to convert be an intention to do so by wounding the religious feelings of the persons addressed."[72] This is a remarkable argument indeed; the best way to find out religious truth is by free discussion, unless, of course, a law has already settled the matter! The commissioners were very anxious to promote free religious discussion *in India*. They added that it was almost impossible to convert a sincere votary of any faith without wounding his religious feelings in the early stages of the process.

In 1924 a Hindu bookseller of Lahore published a pamphlet entitled *Rangila Rasul*—"The Gay Prophet"—a scurrilous and grossly abusive attack upon the prophet Mohammed. The bookseller, Rajpal, was prosecuted under section 153A of the Indian Penal Code, which penalized attempts to promote enmity between different classes of His Majesty's subjects. Numerous delays held up the progress of the case, but after two years Rajpal was convicted and sentenced to prison for eighteen months. An appeal to the High Court of the Punjab, however, resulted in his acquittal, on the technical grounds that section 153A was not intended to prevent criticism of deceased religious leaders. The High Court judge held that the attack was undoubtedly malicious but that it could not be punished under existing law.[73]

A few days after this decision was handed down, another attack on the prophet appeared in the *Risala Vartman*, a monthly journal published by several members of the Arya Samaj in Amritsar. This time, however, the defendant was convicted, fined, and imprisoned under section 153A of the Penal Code. As this decision was in direct conflict with that in the *Rangila Rasul* case and the law was consequently in doubt, the government of India introduced a bill which provided for the insertion of section 295A.

This bill was passed by the legislative assembly in 1927, and in its present form section 295A is as follows: "Whoever, with deliberate

[72] *Second Report on the Penal Code by the Indian Law Commissioners,* 1847, p. 255.
[73] W. R. Smith, *op. cit.,* pp. 353-355.

and malicious intention of outraging the religious feelings of any class of citizens of India, by words, either spoken or written, or by visible representations, insults or attempts to insult the religion or the religious beliefs of that class, shall be punished with imprisonment of either description for a term which may extend to two years, or with fine, or with both." In the case of, *Ramji Lal Modi* v. *State of U. P.,* 1957, the validity of this section was challenged on the ground that it interferes with a citizen's right to freedom of speech guaranteed under article 19(1)(a) of the Constitution. It was contended that this right could be restricted only "in the interest of public order" and that insulting remarks about a religion do not lead to breaches of public order in all cases although they may do so in some. The Supreme Court upheld the constitutionality of section 295A on the ground that it punishes only those aggravated forms of insult to religious beliefs which are perpetrated with malicious intentions and have a calculated tendency to disrupt public order. However, the language of the section itself and much of the earlier case law do not support this interpretation. The malicious outrage of religious sentiment, not necessarily leading to public disturbances, has been the basic offense.[74]

There can be absolutely no doubt, however, about the general tendency of spoken or written attacks on religion to engender violence in present-day India. A casual reading of any daily newspaper over a period of time will produce ample evidence of this tendency. To cite one example: in 1953 a Muslim poet of Lucknow, Yas Changezi, whose religious views were described as atheistic, wrote some verses derogatory to the prophet Mohammed. The verses were published in an Urdu weekly, and shortly thereafter the writer's house was attacked with brickbats. The following day a crowd seized the seventy-five-year-old poet, blackened his face with tar, hung a garland of shoes around his neck, and took him out in procession in a rickshaw drawn by a donkey.[75] Had the verses been written by a Hindu, it is most likely that bloodshed would have resulted. In 1954 riots took place in Madura over the staging of a drama which ridiculed Rama and other Hindu *avatars* and gods. Those responsible for presenting

[74] A.I.R. 1957 S.C., p. 620. See D. C. Pande, "Offenses against Religion: A Critical Review of *Ramji Lal Modi* v. *State of U.P.*,"S.C.J. 958, pp. 93-98.
[75] *Times of India*, April 3, 1953.

the drama were Hindus convinced of the necessity of attacking what they regarded as superstitious beliefs.

In the light of this tendency to violence, both central and state governments have frequently resorted to preventive action. In 1956 the governments of Bihar and West Bengal banned the distribution of the book, *Living Biographies of Religious Leaders*, which was held to contain material likely to wound the religious feelings of the Muslim community.[76] Aubrey Menen's work entitled *Rama Retold* dealt with the characters of Rama and Sita in a satirical manner hardly calculated to please the orthodox Hindu. The government of India, mindful of Hindu susceptibilities, prohibited the importation of copies from England. K. M. Panikkar argued that this restriction on the right to propagate unpopular ideas should have been challenged in a liberal democratic society. "It may be that the home ministry was justified in the action it took on the grounds of public security and the maintenance of law and order. But the point here is that the action of the government passed practically unnoticed and was not subjected to any criticism in India itself."[77]

In 1954 the Madras legislative assembly passed the Dramatic Performances Bill. This legislation gave the state government the authority to prohibit objectionable performances, one of the categories of which was a play "deliberately intended to outrage the religious feelings of any class of the citizens of India by insulting or blaspheming or profaning the religion or the religious beliefs of that class." During the debate on this bill, the members of the Dravida Kazhagam, the Communists, and the Socialists accused the government of attempting to perpetuate the status quo with respect to religious belief. They declared that the real motive behind the measure was to suppress the propagation of all rationalist, atheist, antireligious, or progressive ideas. "Vested interests" could always curb the expression of such ideas by protesting that their religious feelings were being wounded.[78]

One member later moved an amendment to exclude from the scope of the clause performances which sought to "prove or condemn any

[76] *Notes on Islam*, 1956, vol. 9, p. 134.
[77] K. M. Panikkar, *The State and the Citizen*, Asia Publishing House, Bombay, 1956, p. 7.
[78] *The Hindu*, December 21, 1954.

religious belief as irrational or unscientific and/or detrimental to the interests of the people."[79] The rejection of this and other amendments by the assembly led some opposition members to contend that the measure would surely be used to hinder social reform and the development of a more scientific outlook among the people. It seems probable, however, that the government's true concern was with the prevention of breaches of the peace, as stated.

It cannot be denied that in India freedom of expression is rather consistently subordinated to the requirements of maintaining public order. By way of contrast we may note the words of the United States Supreme Court in 1940: "In the realm of religious faith and in that of political belief, sharp differences arise. In both fields, the tenets of one man may seem the rankest error to his neighbor. To persuade others to his own point of view, the pleader, as we know, at times resorts to exaggeration, to vilification of men who have been, or are, prominent in church or state, and even to false statement. But the people of this nation have ordained in the light of history, that, in spite of the probability of excesses and abuses, these liberties are, in the long view, essential to enlightened opinion and right conduct on the part of the citizens of a democracy."[80] Such an approach is at present clearly impossible for a country like India, with its memories of recent religious and communal violence. But one may hope that the various aspects of modernization—especially increased educational opportunities and industrialization—will gradually produce a situation in which the problems of public order will become less acute and freedom of expression enlarged.

[79] *The Hindu,* December 23, 1954.
[80] *Cantwell* v. *Connecticut,* 310 U.S. 296 (1940).

CHAPTER 7

THE QUESTION OF FOREIGN MISSIONARIES

WE NOW COME to an aspect of the propagation of religion which is considerably more complex than the problems discussed in the last chapter. Even if the right to propagate religion, including the seeking of conversions, is established as a fundamental right, the admission of foreigners into a country to carry on such activities raises many additional questions.

POLICIES PAST AND PRESENT

It is interesting to note that in its earliest recorded connection with organized missionary effort, India was the sending and not the receiving country. In the third century B.C., the emperor Ashoka embraced the message of the Buddha and renounced his policy of military conquest in favor of *dharma-vijaya* ("conquest by piety"). He instituted royal tours in which he instructed his subjects in the fundamentals of morality and piety. He later appointed *dharma-mahamatras*, high officers in charge of the promotion of religion. But Ashoka did not attempt to impose the Buddhist faith on his subjects.[1] The moral instruction which was offered his people was based on broad, almost universal, ethical principles.[2]

The emperor also emphasized the importance of religious tolerance. In one edict he wrote: "All sects deserve reverence for one reason or another. By thus acting a man exalts his own sect and at the same time does service to the sects of other people." Ashoka found this tolerant attitude to be completely compatible with his deep devotion to Buddhism. For he was an ardent Buddhist, "convinced of the truth of Buddha's teaching, of the efficacy of worship at the Buddhist holy places, of the necessity of making a confession

[1] R. C. Majumdar, H. C. Raychaudhuri, and K. Datta, *An Advanced History of India*, Macmillan Company, London, 1950, pp. 104-109.
[2] M. Searle Bates, *Religious Liberty: An Inquiry*, International Missionary Council, New York, 1945, p. 268.

of faith in the Buddhist trinity, of keeping in close touch with the Buddhist Sangha and maintaining its solidarity."[3] Only occasionally did his Buddhist convictions bring him into conflict with the popular religious practices of the day, as when he prohibited the sacrificial slaughter of animals, ceremonies which were essential to Brahmanic religion.[4]

Ashoka's zeal for Buddhism caused him to send missionaries beyond the limits of his empire. His envoys achieved little success in spreading the message of the Buddha in Syria, Egypt, or Greece, but in central Asia, Burma, and Siam the progress of Buddhism was marked. The most spectacular success was achieved in Ceylon, where Mahendra and Sanghamitra (according to tradition, Ashoka's son and daughter) were able to convert the king and many of his subjects.

This great missionary effort proceeded by peaceful methods, by patient exposition of the *Dhamma*, without recourse to any form of coercion.[5] Ashoka's missionary approach thus contained three basic elements: (1) a broad tolerance for all faiths; (2) the conviction that Buddhism was the path of enlightenment for all men; and (3) an organized effort to preach Buddhism at home and abroad in such a way that voluntary converts were won.

The problem with which we are primarily concerned, of course, is the place of the foreign Christian missionary in the independent secular Indian state. This necessitates a quick look backward to the policies regarding missionaries evolved during the British period.

Religious neutrality under the British

Prior to 1813, the East India Company to some extent actively discouraged the spreading of Christianity in India.[6] This position reflected both the personal indifference of some of the directors to religion (although others were very devout), and their fear that meddling with the Indians' religion would endanger the company's

---

[3] Majumdar, *op. cit.*, p. 108.

[4] William Theodore de Bary, ed., *Sources of Indian Traditions*, Columbia University Press, New York, 1958, p. 148.

[5] Jawaharlal Nehru, *The Discovery of India*, John Day Company, New York, 1946, p. 125.

[6] Arthur J. Mayhew, *Christianity and the Government of India*, Faber and Gwyer Ltd., London, 1929, pp. 26-38.

lucrative commercial interests.[7] No missionary was allowed to land in British India without a license from the directors, and these were not easily obtained. One of the most notable missionaries, William Carey, was refused a license but found refuge in the Danish territory of Serampore, in Bengal, where he established his work. A few chaplains were sent out by the company to look after the religious needs of the European employees, but even this was sporadic; not one chaplain was added to the establishment between 1760 and 1800.[8]

On the other hand, in some cases company officials were extremely friendly toward missionaries, and the latter proved their usefulness to the company in many ways. In general, missionaries were well received by officials in Madras, while in Bengal they were usually regarded with coolness if not animosity. In 1715 the Madras authorities actually invited the Danish mission, aided financially by the Society for the Propagation of Christian Knowledge, to open up work in their territories, promising every assistance and encouragement.

The missionaries cooperated with the company in the capacity of translators, interpreters, experts in Indian customs, and even as political agents, for some had developed friendly relations with the Indian princes. The Madras officials prevailed on the directors to give free passage on company ships to some missionaries who had been of service.[9] Grants of land were often made for the establishment of mission stations.

Lord William Bentinck, while governor of Madras, gave every encouragement to the missionaries to carry on their work of converting Hindus. But the Vellore Mutiny of 1806, widely attributed to resentment of the government's attempts to promote Christianity, produced an immediate reaction. All public preaching by missionaries in British territory was forbidden except by the express permission of the court of directors. Indian Christians could preach only if they dissociated themselves from the missions. Lord Minto, who became governor-general in 1807, established rigid control over the publications of the mission press at Serampore.

A flurry of pamphlets published in England attacked the past policy of encouraging Christian missions, although the company officials who had favored this policy were not without their defenders.

[7] W. H. Moreland and A. C. Chatterjee, *A Short History of India*, Longmans, Green and Company, London, 1957, p. 341.
[8] Mayhew, *op. cit.*, p. 47.   [9] *Ibid.*, p. 36.

A retired servant of the company published in 1807 *A Letter to the Chairman of the East India Company, on the Danger of interfering in the Religious Opinions of the Natives of India.*[10] An author who identified himself solely as "a late resident at Bhagulpore" wrote a small volume entitled *The Dangers of British India, from French Invasion and Missionary Establishments.* The writer asked: "Shall we, for the precarious benefit of converting a few Hindus, plunge Hindustan in rebellion, and occasion the massacre of every Englishman who resides there?"[11] His opinions were shared by the governor-general, who wrote: "The only successful engine of sedition in any part of India must be that of persuading the people that our government entertains hostile and systematic designs against their religion."[12]

A few years later, however, persistent campaigning by evangelical leaders in England resulted in new recognition of the legitimate place of Christian missions in India. Despite the objections of some directors of the company, the Charter Renewal Act passed by Parliament in 1813 included a clause admitting the principle of missionary activity in India.[13] Their right of entry was now firmly established.

The attitudes and actions of the British government in India toward missionaries never followed a clear-cut, simple, or consistent pattern. The policies varied during different periods, in different regions, and under different governors-general and other officials. According to Mayhew, the British policy was one which "oscillated between covert acceptance, or even carefully veiled approval, of evangelists, who were spreading what was presumably their own religion, and nervous disavowal of them and all their work."[14]

However, from approximately 1840 to 1865 a succession of British officials publicly expressed their approval and support of the Chris-

---

[10] Thomas Twining, *A Letter to the Chairman of the East India Company, on the Danger of interfering in the Religious Opinions of the Natives of India,* London, 1807.

[11] "A late resident at Bhagulpore," *The Dangers of British India, from French Invasions and Missionary Establishments,* Black, Parry and Kingsbury, London, 1808, p. 23.

[12] Letter written by Lord Minto in 1807. The Countess of Minto, ed., *Lord Minto in India,* Longmans, Green and Company, London, 1880, p. 62. For references to the defense of missionary activity and its relationship to the Vellore Mutiny, see Kenneth Ingham, *Reformers in India 1793-1833: An Account of the Work of Christian Missionaries on Behalf of Social Reform,* Cambridge University Press, Cambridge, 1956, p. 7.

[13] *Ibid.,* p. 11.   [14] Mayhew, *op. cit.,* p. 87.

tian missionary enterprise in no uncertain terms. Governor-General Dalhousie brushed aside the misgivings of his subordinates when the decision was made in 1854 to extend grants-in-aid to mission schools. "Even from the political point of view," he declared, "we err in ignoring so completely as we do the agency of ministers of our own true faith in extending education among the people."[15] During these years a governor of a province stated in a public ceremony that he looked forward to the Christianization of all India, and the commissioner of Sind signed a memorial urging the extension of mission work.[16]

The overt support extended to missions by government officials was one of the contributing factors in the situation which led to the Mutiny of 1857. Hilton Brown wrote: "With the best will in the world one cannot, I think, overlook as a cause of ruin the wave of militant Christianity on which the British in India were at that time riding."[17] In the following year the administration of the country was taken over by the crown, and the British East India Company ceased to function as the government of India. Thereafter, government officials practiced a much stricter adherence to the principle of religious neutrality, and it became generally accepted by Indians that the rulers did not intend to impose Christianity upon them.[18]

Religious liberty and religious neutrality were also interpreted to mean that there should be no unreasonable restrictions on the propagation of religion. Accordingly, in increasing numbers European and American missionary societies established work in India during the late nineteenth and early twentieth centuries. But the unrestricted entry of missionaries was found undesirable, and so a system was set up in 1920 for granting recognition to responsible missionary societies which desired to work in India.

This system of recognition, which was in effect until 1947, may be briefly described. The entire procedure was carried out in London by the secretary of state for India. Political reliability and financial stability were the key criteria in determining whether a missionary

[15] Arthur I. Mayhew, "The Christian Ethic and India," *Modern India and the West*, ed. L. S. S. O'Malley, Oxford University Press, London, 1941, p. 319.

[16] *Ibid.*, p. 320.

[17] Hilton Brown, "Racial Incompatibility in the British Raj," *The Hindu Weekly Review*, July 7, 1958.

[18] For an interpretation of the British period which stresses the religious identity and motivation of the rulers, see B. D. Basu, *Rise of the Christian Power in India*, Prabasi Press, Calcutta, 1931.

society should be recognized. Missionaries were debarred from any participation in politics and were required to pledge their support of lawfully constituted government.[19] This requirement created difficulties for those few missionaries who sympathized with the Indian nationalist movement.

The secretary of state for India ordinarily acted in accordance with the recommendation of three sponsoring authorities: the Conference of Missionary Societies in the United Kingdom, the Foreign Missions Conference of North America, and the Archbishop of Westminster (for Roman Catholic missions).[20] The whole procedure of recognition was weakened, however, by the practice of allowing missionary societies not on the "recognized lists" to work in India. The attainment of independence in 1947 brought with it certain inevitable procedural changes in the relations between the government of India and Christian missionary organizations. But of far greater importance has been the search for a policy which would take into account the numerous facets of national life which impinge upon the problem.

The first years of independence

After independence, the home ministry of the government of India was authorized to regulate the entry and activities of foreign missionaries. Parallel with this transfer of regulating power from the United Kingdom to India, the ministry of home affairs began to deal exclusively with missionary organizations in India. The National Christian Council and the Catholic Bishops' Conference thus became the sponsoring authorities. In the early years of independence eleven new missionary societies recommended by the National Christian Council were accorded recognition. At present this organization represents about fifty recognized missionary societies, and the Catholic Bishops' Conference about sixty-five recognized Roman Catholic societies.[21] As in the period of British administration, however, missionary societies have been permitted to start work in the country without securing recognition through these sponsoring authorities.

[19] Korula Jacob, "The Government of India and the Entry of Missionaries," *International Review of Missions,* 1958, vol. 47, pp. 410-411.

[20] Roland W. Scott, "Christian Missionary Decline in India," *Pacific Affairs,* 1957, vol. 30, pp. 366-367.

[21] *Ibid.,* p. 367.

In 1949 a slightly revised pledge required of foreign missionaries was published by the home ministry.[22]

Numerous tributes were paid to the work of Christian missionaries during this period. Dr. P. Sitaramayya, then president of the Indian National Congress, commented publicly that the last British soldiers and many civilians had left the shores of India, "but the missionary lingers, and I hope he will stay for he is a desirable commodity." Dr. Sitaramayya commended particularly the "magnificent social service" which had been rendered.[23] The work done in Christian missionary hospitals, schools, and colleges has always been highly esteemed by the general Hindu public. Many prominent Indian leaders have received part of their education in missionary institutions, and there has been no reluctance to acknowledge their great contribution to India.

The number of Christian missionaries in the country increased considerably after independence, reaching a total of 4,683 in 1952. Many of the new missionaries were replacements for those who had retired or died during the war. But reports of a large influx of western missionaries were alarming to those who interpreted their presence as a form of continued foreign influence and control. The historical link between western imperialism and the missionary movement had left a legacy of doubt in the minds of Indian nationalists, and some Hindus saw continued missionary activity as a vestige of western rule.

While missionary institutions have been greatly appreciated, the popular image of the foreign missionary in India has never been a wholly favorable one. The sense of racial superiority which some missionaries have displayed in their relations with Indians, both Hindus and Christians, has not been forgotten. The nineteenth-century conception, far from unknown in the twentieth century, of messengers bearing the light of western Christian civilization to benighted "natives" was profoundly insulting to those who were struggling to reawaken pride in their own cultural heritage. As we

---

[22] "I . . . hereby undertake to give all due obedience and respect to the lawfully constituted government of India and while carefully abstaining from participating in political affairs, it is my desire and purpose that my influence in so far as may be peacefully exerted in such matters, shall be so exerted in loyal cooperation with the government." *National Christian Council Review*, 1949, vol. 69, p. 162.

[23] *Ibid.*, p. 151.

have seen, Gandhi and many others decried the "denationalization" of the convert by the Christian missionary.

To these psychological factors must be added the Hindus' religious objections to activities aimed at securing conversions. Some of these objections are based on spiritual principles, others simply on the instinct of group self-preservation, since the conversions were made mostly from Hinduism. Christian missionary work constituted a challenge to the status quo, and hence had to be resisted. It is also true that the Hindu's instinctive distrust of highly organized religion has led him to regard the modern missionary movement with its committees, councils, secretaries, and sizable financial resources as extremely unspiritual.

The generally friendly attitude toward Christian missions which prevailed during the first few years of independence gradually gave way to expressions of doubtful questioning and in some cases hostility. Although government reports concerning the number of missionaries in the country were not always accurate, the fact was that the number had increased greatly since 1947, and many Hindus found this fact alarming. The changed climate of opinion was reflected in government policy. In 1952 an unprecedented number of applications for visas for new missionaries of recognized societies was refused. Christian organizations which requested clarification and reconsideration by the home ministry were informed that there had been no change of policy. It seemed clear, however, that the ministry felt that there was need for a reduction in the number of missionaries coming to India.[24] It was suggested that the time had come for the transfer of both routine jobs and positions of leadership from missionary to Indian Christian hands to develop self-sufficiency of personnel in all aspects of the work of the church.[25]

A missionary pointed out that the philosophy of Christian missions developed over the past fifty years has stressed precisely this objective. He noted: "It seems strange that to make it really effective, it will take the action of a secular government. Still that action would be more welcome, or at least less disturbing, if the motive behind it were as pristine as some of us would like to believe, and if the statements of religious extremists of other communities seemed less intended 'to

[24] Jacob, *op. cit.*, p. 412.
[25] E. C. Bhatty, "Visas for Missionaries," *National Christian Council Review*, 1952, vol. 72, p. 552.

smite the shepherds and scatter the sheep.' "[26] Recent developments have compelled the missionaries to work toward the goal of an independent, self-sufficient Indian church with a new sense of realism.

Factors in the formulation of a new policy

The heated public discussion of the problem which ensued clearly revealed that the antipathy toward religious conversions felt by many Hindus was an influential factor in official circles. Dr. K. N. Katju, the home minister at that time, spoke approvingly of the work carried on by missionary educational, medical, and social service institutions. But he also deprecated the "proselytization or propagation of religion" as a harmful aspect of missions as it involved a "comparison between different faiths."[27] A member of the upper house of Parliament made the statement that missionary societies could not exist in India unless they did evangelistic work. In reply, Dr. Katju was reported as saying, "I think if they come here for evangelistic work, then the sooner they stop it the better." Bishop R. B. Manikam interpreted the anti-missionary sentiment as based more on the Hindu opposition to conversions than on anti-foreign nationalism.[28]

Anti-missionary agitations flared up in different parts of India. Many newspapers and magazines printed special reports on the problem, and Hindu communal groups organized demonstrations against missionary institutions. The Hindu Mahasabha, for example, conducted a public procession led by a former mayor of Poona to protest the presence of a Christian mission in Nasik, an important Hindu religious center. In 1954 the government of Madhya Pradesh appointed a Christian Missionary Activities Inquiry Committee (frequently referred to as the Niyogi committee). The work and report of this committee occasioned still wider discussion of the missionary question, and are of such importance that the subject is considered separately in a later section of this chapter. The radical recommendations of the Niyogi report were never implemented, but this official document is significant as an expression of the extremist Hindu sentiment which is sometimes found where it would not be expected.

A point repeatedly made in the debate was the charge that mission-

[26] R. M. Bennett, "The Church and Foreign Personnel," *Revolution in Missions*, ed. Blaise Levai, The Popular Press, Vellore, India, 1957, pp. 67-68.
[27] *The Mail*, Madras, May 1, 1953.   [28] *N.C.C. Review*, 1953, vol. 73, p. 195.

aries were involved in the political movement among the tribal peoples in Madhya Pradesh and Bihar (the Jharkand movement), and in the movement of the Naga tribesmen of Assam for an independent state. In both of these cases Christian tribal leaders participated with others, but there was apparently little evidence to indicate any general missionary involvement in the instigation or encouragement of these movements. Investigations by the government of India led to the expulsion of only three out of about 300 missionaries in Assam. The National Christian Council denied that even these three missionaries were engaged in political activities.[29]

The council made it clear, however, that real violations of a missionary's pledge to abstain from political activity should be dealt with sternly. "If there is a missionary who does not faithfully observe his pledge he should be sent out of the country. No responsible Christian, whether Indian citizen or foreigner, will protest against the government doing so for political reasons."[30]

It is unlikely that foreign missionaries in the Naga Hills of Assam have played any direct role in the separatist political movement there. The possible motives which might have led intelligent men to encourage the fantastic demand for a sovereign Naga state are difficult to imagine. It is undeniable, however, that the very success of Christian missionary work among the Naga tribesmen has led to a considerable degree of western cultural influence and has accentuated the Nagas' sense of separateness from Hinduism and Indian culture. The hill peoples have always been suspicious of the Indians living on the plains and have sometimes been exploited by them. Conversion to Christianity has intensified differences with the majority of other Indians, and the differences tend to be perpetuated by the near-inaccessibility of the tribal areas. This cultural and religious background undoubtedly has had some indirect bearing on the separatist political movement.[31]

Another significant factor in the complex question of foreign missionaries has been the theological orientation of some of the missionary societies which have entered India in recent years. In 1957 Prime Minister Nehru stated that since independence the number of missionaries sent to India by "regular" churches had

[29] Jacob, *op. cit.*, p. 412.
[30] "The Church's Freedom for its Missionary Task," *N.C.C. Review*, 1955, vol. 75, p. 208.
[31] *New York Times*, December 27, 1960.

decreased while those from "irregular" churches had increased.[32] As has been pointed out, both before and after independence missionary societies not recognized through the sponsoring authorities have been permitted to work in India. The failure on the part of the government to make full use of the experience of these sponsoring authorities has led to some real problems.

Some of the new missions represent what could be described as Protestant fringe groups, and others are nondenominational fundamentalist groups. Many are characterized by a strong disinclination to become involved in ecumenical cooperation (such as is represented by the National Christian Council) and by a tremendous zeal for evangelism, with considerably less emphasis, sometimes none, on medical and educational work. One Indian Christian leader, Dr. Eddy Asirvatham, was distressed over the situation created by certain "extreme sects." "By their type of theology and methods of work they have created some problems for Christian missions in general. Many a non-Christian fails to make a distinction between the well-established churches of India and the new sects which have come into the country recently."[33]

A significant constitutional point was raised when Dr. Katju, then minister of home affairs, declared in 1953 that the right to propagate religion guaranteed in the Constitution applied only to Indian nationals, not foreigners.[34] Justice Mukherjee of the Constitution bench of the Supreme Court of India, however, simply used the language of the Constitution to refute this view. In his March 1954 judgment on an appeal against the Bombay Public Trusts Act, Justice Mukherjee declared: "Article 25 of the Constitution guarantees to every person and not merely to the citizens of India, the freedom of conscience and the right freely to profess, practice and propagate religion."[35]

An Indian Lutheran bishop felt that the question of foreign missionaries did indeed involve a vital constitutional point, but his interpretation was quite different from Dr. Katju's. Rev. R. B. Manikam wrote: "The crux of the whole matter is this: today a church in India invites a foreign missionary and shows cause why;

[32] *Religious News Service,* October 1, 1957.
[33] Eddy Asirvatham, "The Missionary in Present-Day India," *Revolution in Missions,* p. 20.
[34] *The Mail,* May 1, 1953.
[35] *Ratilal Panchand* v. *State of Bombay,* 1954 Supreme Court Appeals, p. 546.

then if its reasonable request is turned down by the state on the ground that the foreigner is only an addition to the existing missionary personnel and not a substitute, or that his work is not 'of value to India,' then to that extent the state does interfere with the work of the church and the religious freedom which has been guaranteed in the Constitution of India is being denied to it."[36] The National Christian Council pointed out that increasingly, missionaries were going to India at the invitation of the Indian churches, to carry on their work "in association with, and very frequently under, the direction of Indian Christian leaders."[37] The new relationship meant that the denial of entry visas to missionaries hampered primarily the work of the Indian church rather than an enterprise directed from London or New York.

Indian Christian statements made in defense of the missionaries' continued presence also stressed the idea of reciprocity in the international exchange of diverse religious and cultural influences. It was pointed out that Hindu and Muslim missionaries from India are now going abroad to propagate their respective faiths and are permitted to do so by the governments of western countries.[38] While this is true, it is unrealistic to compare seriously the Vedanta Society, which maintains approximately fourteen "missionaries" in centers in the United States, with American Christian missionary societies whose representatives in India now number several thousands. However, Indian Christians were on firmer ground when they pointed out that within the Christian church the sending of fraternal workers from one country to another is being practiced on an increasingly reciprocal basis. Indian Christian leaders are now going to the West in order to make their contribution there, especially in the field of church union, in which the Church of South India has pioneered.[39]

Indian Christian spokesmen have emphasized their desire to have fraternal workers from abroad continue their work in the Indian church. Until very recently the missionary was very far from being a "fraternal worker"; he was frequently the boss, the lord of the mission compound, the holder of the all-important purse-strings, and the Indian Christian was well aware of his financial and adminis-

[36] R. B. Manikam, "Some Living Issues before the Church in India," *Revolution in Missions*, p. 210.
[37] "The Church's Freedom for its Missionary Task," *N.C.C. Review*, 1955, vol. 75, p. 209.
[38] *Ibid.*, p. 210.   [39] E. C. Bhatty, *op. cit.*, p. 553.

trative powers. Such relationships are fast disappearing in the light of Indian independence, and most missionaries today regard themselves and are regarded as fraternal workers in a sense which upholds the dignity and the equality of the Indian church. Dependence on western financial support, however, is still so considerable as to make this "the weakest link in the freedom and self-determination of the church."[40]

An important aspect of this problem involves the transfer of mission property to the Indian churches. During the last twenty years the attitude of the western missionary boards has changed radically with regard to the ownership of such property, so that now "the major missionary societies have frankly accepted the principle that the church in India is the *ultimate heir to all their property in the country*."[41] Strenuous efforts were made to effect such transfers, but certain practical difficulties arose, chiefly the great expense involved in the payment of stamp duty and registration charges. It was estimated, for example, that in the city of Madras alone it would cost the Church of South India about $100,000 just to accept the property given by related missionary societies. The National Christian Council in 1955 appealed to the government to make special provisions, as the duties and charges were beyond the resources of the churches to meet.[42] Since then, special government provisions have permitted the transfer of large mission holdings in land and buildings to the Indian churches, and the process continues.

The 1955 policy statement

As noted above, the refusal of visas to many missionaries in 1952 was followed by an assurance that the ministry of home affairs had not adopted any change in policy. Nevertheless, the number of rejected visa applications continued to be high. In 1955 the government announced its new policy regarding the admission of foreign missionaries. The key provision was that missionaries "coming for the first time in augmentation of the existing strength of a mission or in replacement will be admitted into India, if they possess outstanding qualifications or specialized experience in their lines."[43]

[40] Scott, *op. cit.*, p. 376.
[41] "Mission Property" (editorial), *N.C.C. Review*, 1954, vol. 74, p. 409. (Italics in source.)
[42] "The Church's Freedom for its Missionary Task." *N.C.C. Review*, 1955, vol. 75, p. 209.
[43] Jacob, *op. cit.*, p. 413.

Other features of the policy are: missionaries returning from leave after five or more years' service in India will ordinarily be eligible for admission; new missionaries will not be admitted for work in border and tribal areas; missions must obtain the approval of the government before opening new centers or institutions; and, missionaries from Commonwealth countries will be dealt with on the same basis as other missionaries. The last provision introduced a system of visas for Commonwealth missionaries, who previously had needed none. A short time later, however, this was amended so that such missionaries are now required to obtain only a special endorsement in their passports, which has usually been granted without delay.

However, the part of the policy which bears the most far-reaching implications is that which limits the admission of new missionaries, even replacements, to those who possess "outstanding qualifications or specialized experience." The government's position is that, where qualified Indians are available to fill a post, they should ordinarily be preferred. The consideration of providing employment for citizens of the country is undoubtedly a factor in official thinking; similar restrictions are placed on the personnel policies of western industrial and commercial concerns which establish plants or offices in India.[44]

How will the ministry of home affairs interpret "outstanding qualifications"? The government has made it clear that it should not be necessary to bring missionaries from other countries to become secondary school teachers or superintendents of hostels. It was reported that one minister of government interpreted "outstanding qualifications" by declaring that no man under thirty could be considered an expert in his field. An N.C.C. secretary wrote that the new policy could be administered in such a way that the present missionary situation would not be greatly altered. "But it should be recognized," he added, "that the new policy can be used for a gradual closure of missionary work."[45]

The number of foreign missionaries in India has decreased somewhat in the past few years. At the beginning of 1955 the figure was over 5,700; early in 1959 it was around 4,800.[46] However, the National Christian Council reported in November 1960 that since January of that year forty-five applications for missionary visas had been sub-

---

[44] Scott, *op. cit.*, p. 375.   [45] Jacob, *op. cit.*, p. 414.
[46] *Times of India Directory and Yearbook*, Times of India, Bombay, 1960, p. 323, and *Hindustan Times*, October 11, 1959.

mitted and that only three had been refused (eleven were still pending), indicating that the visa situation was "quite satisfactory."[47]

THE NIYOGI COMMITTEE

In 1954 the governments of two states, Madhya Pradesh and Madhya Bharat (an area which was later incorporated in the former state), appointed official committees to investigate the activities of Christian foreign missionaries. The reports of both committees were published in 1956, but it was the Madhya Pradesh inquiry which attracted nation-wide attention and which merits consideration here.

The Christian Missionary Activities Inquiry Committee (the Niyogi Committee) was appointed by the government of Madhya Pradesh to investigate the numerous charges and countercharges made concerning missionary work. On one hand, representations were made to the government that missionaries were converting the illiterate aboriginals and other backward people through the use of fraud, coercion, or monetary inducements, and that this was creating widespread resentment among the Hindus. The missionaries denied these allegations and charged that local officials and others were harassing the Christian communities in the tribal areas.[48]

Dr. M. B. Niyogi, retired chief justice of the High Court, Nagpur, was named chairman of the six-man committee. The composition of the Niyogi committee became a matter of controversy as soon as it was announced. Five of the members were Hindus, and the one Christian member was S. K. George, who belonged to the Syrian Christian Church. The Roman Catholic archbishop of Bangalore wrote that the only Christian member of the committee did not believe in the divinity of Christ and had no representative status in the Christian community.[49] Answering such criticisms in a press note, however, the government stated that the members had been chosen as "men of unbiased and impartial outlook, who would function more as judges than as advocates of one side or the other."[50]

[47] National Christian Council of India, minutes of Executive Committee, November 1960.

[48] *Report of the Christian Missionary Activities Inquiry Committee*, Government Printing, Madhya Pradesh, Nagpur, 1956, vol. 1, p. 1. Hereafter referred to as the *Niyogi Committee Report*.

[49] Thomas Pothacamury, *The Church in Independent India*, Maryknoll Publications, Maryknoll, N.Y., n.d. [1958?], p. 18. This was one of the points made in a memorandum (June 15, 1954) from the standing committee of the Catholic Bishops' Conference of India to the chief minister of Madhya Pradesh.

[50] Press note of May 3, 1954.

The committee was authorized to frame its own procedure, and it decided to tour the key districts of the state in order to ascertain the nature of the complaints on both sides. Having devoted six months to extensive tours, the committee then issued a lengthy questionnaire which any member of the public could answer. Indian Christians protested that the questionnaire revealed that the original scope of the inquiry had been greatly widened without authorization; "starting as an inquiry into the activities of Christian missionaries, presumably in relation to those outside the Christian community, it has become in some respects an inquiry into the activities of the Christian church and community as a whole."[51] The Christians pointed to question 11 as an illustration of the tendentious nature of the questionnaire: "Do you think that conversion to Christianity adversely affects the national loyalty and outlook of converts? Give instances and state reasons." The Indian Christian reaction was: "It would appear that the whole community is on trial."[52]

Findings of the Niyogi committee

The committee's report was submitted to the government of Madhya Pradesh on April 18, 1956. The report contained a number of findings, some of which were simple statements of fact. For example, it was found that since 1950 there had been an appreciable increase in the American missionary personnel working in India and that large sums of foreign money were being spent in connection with educational, medical, and evangelistic work. Other findings, however, were unsubstantiated generalizations. For example: "Conversions are mostly brought about by undue influence, misrepresentations, etc., or in other words not by conviction but by various inducements offered for proselytization in various forms."[53] The report reflected no awareness at all of the complex methodological problems involved in such an inquiry.

Another finding was that, despite assurances that missionaries would not engage in political activities, "missions are in some places used to serve extra-religious ends."[54] But the committee's understanding of "extra-religious activities" apparently embraced even agricultural and village development projects. "The (Indian) Roman Catholics support the Congress government mainly because they are

[51] *N.C.C. Review*, 1955, vol. 75, p. 3.   [52] *Loc. cit.*
[53] *Niyogi Committee Report*, vol. 1, p. 131.   [54] *Loc. cit.*

anti-communist. There seems to be an unholy alliance between Roman Catholics and American money to save India from communism. The West must realize that this is none of their business and that Independent India needs no foreign help in solving its economic and social problems. For Christian missions to interest themselves in such economic and social problems and help in finding solutions for them would be regarded as extra-religious activity and as highly undesirable."[55] The committee resented the fact that large sums of foreign money were being spent on these projects "without the cooperation and advice of non-Christian leaders."

The next finding, which drew an immediate and outraged protest from Indian Christian leaders, was: "As conversion muddles the convert's sense of unity and solidarity with his society, there is a danger of his loyalty to his country and state being undermined."[56] As an example of the "denationalization" of the Christian convert, it was pointed out that in some cases after conversion the common salutation "Jai Rama" (Hail Rama) is dropped in favor of "Jai Yeshu" (Hail Jesus).[57] "Jai Rama" has never been used by Indian Muslims or Christians, and the criticism made in the report reflected its characteristic failure to distinguish between Indian culture and Hindu culture.

The report declared that the Christian idea of a supranational loyalty to Christ had definite political implications smacking of extraterritoriality. Referring to Roman Catholicism it stated: "We have shown how supranationalism is propagated among Christians in India. It really means allegiance to a Theocratic State, styled the Universal Church."[58] The report concluded that the missionary strategy was "to detach the Christian Indian from his nation" and that in times of crisis Christians might be used to promote foreign interests.

Closely related was another finding which interpreted present-day missionary activities in terms of western imperialism. "Evangelization in India appears to be a part of the uniform world policy to revive Christendom for reestablishing western supremacy and is not prompted by spiritual motives. The objective is apparently to create Christian minority pockets with a view to disrupt the solidarity of the non-Christian societies."[59] According to the committee's interpretation, missions play a definite part in the West's cold-war strategy.

[55] *Ibid.*, p. 158.
[57] *Ibid.*, p. 125.
[59] *Ibid.*, p. 132.
[56] *Ibid.*, p. 131.
[58] *Ibid.*, pp. 144, 150.

As the United States has lost military bases in Asia through the attainment of independence by several countries, "the drive for proselytization in India is an attempt to acquire an additional base which of course would be psychological."[60]

The report mentioned the American secretary of state, the late John Foster Dulles, a most unpopular figure in India, as one of the delegates to the World Council of Churches Assembly at Amsterdam in 1948. His name is repeated several times (pages 45, 52, 100, 141) in such a way as to suggest a mysterious link between American foreign policy and the strategy of foreign missions in India. The committee felt that it could "safely conclude" that one of the major aims of accelerating conversions to Christianity was to disrupt the progress of national unity in the newly independent countries.[61] Another objective was "to create a Christian party in the Indian democracy on the lines of the Muslim League ultimately to make out a claim for a separate state, or at least to create a 'militant minority.' "[62]

A statement issued by the National Christian Council of India recorded the "sorrow and indignation" felt throughout the Indian Christian community over the committee's report. The council attacked the procedure of the inquiry; the committee had permitted witnesses to make sweeping charges without adequate cross-examination, and had then included these unproved assertions in its report.[63] The council repudiated the assertion that the Indian Christian community was a "foreign pocket" in the nation. "The publication of this slander against a whole community in an official report is a grievous offense."[64] Acknowledging that errors may have been made by certain missionaries and other Christians, the council asserted that on the whole the record of missionary work had been a worthy one. The Christian group absolutely repudiated the charge that missionary work in India is a political instrumentality of any foreign power.[65]

Indian Christian statements also attacked the committee's lack of fairness in its treatment of the case of J. C. Christie, a British missionary who was sentenced to imprisonment. Detailed references to this fact were made in the report (pages 18-22). But, as an editorial

[60] *Ibid.*, p. 58.   [61] *Ibid.*, p. 59.
[62] *Ibid.*, p. 60.
[63] Statement on the *Niyogi Committee Report* adopted by the National Christian Council at its 13th Triennial Sessions at Allahabad, October 27, 1956, *Revolution in Missions*, p. 288.
[64] *Ibid.*, p. 289.   [65] *Loc. cit.*

pointed out, no mention was made of his appeal to a higher court nor of "the judgment delivered by that court before the submission of the report, acquitting Mr. Christie of all the charges against him."[66]

Recommendations and reactions

Of the principal recommendations made in the Niyogi report, the first point is: "Those missionaries whose primary object is proselytization should be asked to withdraw. The large influx of foreign missionaries is undesirable and should be checked."[67] A related recommendation calls for an amendment to the Constitution specifying that the right to propagate religion applies only to citizens of India.

Another recommendation is that a law very similar to one in force in Greece be enacted. The effect of such legislation would be to eliminate the propagation of religion entirely. The report states that "any attempt or effort (whether successful or not), directly or indirectly to penetrate into the religious conscience of persons (whether of age or under age) of another faith, for the purpose of consciously altering their religious conscience or faith, so as to agree with the ideas or convictions of the proselytizing party should be absolutely prohibited."[68] The report makes no mention of a constitutional amendment at this point, but it is quite clear that article 25 would have to undergo vital changes if such legislation were to be enacted. It is very doubtful whether any of Gandhi's discussions with Christians or Muslims, for example, would have been accounted legal had such a law been in force.

Another recommendation urges a piece of advice on the Indian Christians: "The best course for the Indian churches to follow is to establish a United Independent Christian Church in India without being dependent on foreign support."[69] The *National Christian Council Review* asserted that it was well known that the churches were seeking a greater unity with less dependence on foreign assistance. "But in this they are not prompted by the reasons which actuate the committee, namely to free them from some imagined foreign domination."[70]

[66] *N.C.C. Review*, 1956, vol. 76, p. 320.
[67] *Niyogi Committee Report*, vol. 1, p. 163.
[68] *Loc. cit.*
[69] *Loc. cit.*
[70] *N.C.C. Review*, 1956, vol. 76, p. 367.

The report recommends the creation of a department of cultural and religious affairs in the state government, with powers of censorship. "Circulation of literature meant for religious propaganda without approval of the state government should be prohibited."[71] An Indian Christian writer saw in these proposals the beginning of the end of the cherished ideal of the secular state. According to M. M. Thomas, such steps would initiate the process of making the state "the final arbiter of the religious and cultural life of the citizens."[72] With the censorship of religious literature, he also wondered what would become of freedom of expression in other fields.

Other recommendations are that the state government be solely responsible for maintaining orphanages and for providing education, health, and other services for members of the Scheduled Castes and Tribes. It is also specified that nonofficial organizations should be permitted to operate institutions only for members of their own faith, and only with the prior approval of the state.[73] Christians pointed out, however, that the schools and colleges run by Christian agencies are open to all people. In view of the fact that there are constant requests from the public to enlarge the services of these institutions, "we can easily imagine the reaction that a policy of exclusion would evoke among the people in general."[74]

In considering these recommendations—the banning of conversions, rigid control of religious literature by a department of cultural and religious affairs, the total absorption of social services by the state—M. M. Thomas asserted that the implications of the Niyogi report go far beyond the question of foreign missionaries or the Indian Christian community. "The philosophy of state and its relation to religion, culture and society underlying the report and advocated by it is unashamedly totalitarian. . . . In fact, the writer of these comments is frankly more afraid of the political idea it represents and its effect on the future of the state in India than about the effect of the report on Christianity. Christianity is an anvil that has survived many hammers. It will outlive one more. But the infant secular democratic state of India has yet to find roots in the indigenous

[71] *Niyogi Committee Report*, vol. 1, p. 164.
[72] M. M. Thomas, "State and Other Spheres of Life," *N.C.C. Review*, 1956, vol. 76, p. 395.
[73] *Niyogi Committee Report*, vol. 1, pp. 164-165.
[74] *N.C.C. Review*, 1956, vol. 76, p. 366.

cultural soil and is imperiled by totalitarian ideas finding their place in government committees."[75] The clear trend of the committee's thinking was that the state is everything and should bring virtually every aspect of society under its detailed regulation.[76]

Thomas also challenged the committee's assumption that Indian citizens should have no supranational loyalties and declared that the idea of democracy itself was threatened by this assumption. Only under fascism is the state made a law unto itself; democratic states always recognize supranational loyalties, whether they be to God, natural law, or humanity. Without such supranational loyalties there is no criterion for judging national policies.[77] Thomas wrote that by attacking the Christian's supranationalism as a form of extraterritoriality, the Niyogi report "has shown the kinship of its ideology with totalitarian fascism."[78]

In addition to the indignation which the report evoked in Christian circles, some prominent Hindu leaders also came forward to repudiate it. Dr. Hare Krishna Mahatab, governor of Bombay, expressed his sorrow over the controversy which the report had stirred up all over India, and intimated that the caste Hindus, not the Christian missionaries, were the ones who had exploited the tribal people and other backward classes.[79] Nine distinguished non-Christian leaders issued a statement in November 1956 which paid tribute "to the high standards of integrity and public service generally maintained by Christian missionaries in their work."[80] While the statement did not specifically mention the Niyogi report, it took note of the recent "indiscriminate and extravagant attacks on missionaries."

Dr. A. Krishnaswami, a member of Parliament and one of the signers of this statement, was given a special assignment by a subcommission of the United Nations Commission on Human Rights. Serving as special rapporteur, he prepared a draft report entitled "Study of Discrimination in the Matter of Religious Rights and Practices." In his discussion of the question of foreign missionaries, Dr. Krishnaswami pointed out that in India responsible men of differing political persuasions had criticized the Niyogi committee, "not only for erring in its presentation of facts, but also for over-

[75] Thomas, *op. cit.*, p. 395.　　[76] *Ibid.*, p. 396.
[77] *Loc. cit.*　　　　　　　　　[78] *Ibid.*, p. 397.
[79] Pothacamury, *op. cit.*, p. 20.
[80] *N.C.C. Review*, 1957, vol. 77, pp. 40-41.

stepping the bounds of propriety and national interest in attempting to reverse the general trend in favor of a broad-based freedom."[81]

The Niyogi report has been discussed in considerable detail. It does not represent the majority viewpoint. But it is important because, more clearly than any other public document, it illustrates certain forces at work even outside the Hindu communalist groups, forces which challenge the democratic secular state in present-day India.

The Issue for the Secular State

It is worth noting the fact that in approaching this particular problem there are no precedents or analogous situations in the older western democracies which can be studied. This, incidentally, is not true of most of the problems dealt with in this book. The legislatures and courts of secular states such as France or the United States, for example, have had to define the status of the predominant religion, the rights of religious minorities, the jurisdiction of ecclesiastical law, the place of religious instruction in public schools, etc. In dealing with these problems modern India can and does profit from the political experience of the West. But in determining the policy toward foreign Christian missions working within her borders, India (and the other newly independent states of Asia and Africa) must face problems which have never arisen in the western world.

The secular state does not operate from any theological position; it has no creed and no religious preferences, and its policies in every area of governmental activity should reflect none. Applying this idea to the question of foreign missionaries, the secular state cannot deny entry visas to missionaries on the basis of: hostility to Christianity, the desire to maintain the religious status quo, the idea that conversion from one religion to another is wrong, etc. The truly secular state has no view at all regarding the relative merits of Hinduism and Christianity, or regarding the desirability or undesirability of conversion from one religion to another. Obviously, what is suggested here is an ideal which has never been completely attained by any state. It is quite clear that, in India, religious considerations have had some influence on the shaping of policy regarding foreign missionaries.

It is far easier to discern religious bias in the statements of Dr. Katju

[81] A. Krishnaswami, "Study of Discrimination in the Matter of Religious Rights and Practices." United Nations document E/CN.4/Sub.2/L.123, November 15, 1957, pp. 59-60.

than it is to set out the positive *secular* considerations on which a sound missionary policy ought to be based. On what basis should the government of India decide whether the number of missionaries in the country should be closer to five thousand or one thousand? There is obviously no formula; but even rough guidelines are not evident. One point, however, is clear. The secular state in the liberal democratic tradition should strive to preserve the spirit as well as the letter of the constitutional guarantee of freedom of religion.

The issue of religious liberty (the spirit, not the letter) is relevant not at the point of the missionary himself, but at the point of the Indian Christian churches and their interests. Most missionaries from the West now go to India only at the invitation of the Indian church, to perform specialized tasks which that church feels need to be done. If the Indian church invites a missionary and the government refuses to allow him to enter the country, this decision undoubtedly affects the work of the church and of the Indian Christians who constitute its membership.

The controversy over the foreign missionary question has tended to obscure the fact that there is an area of basic agreement in the objectives of the government, the Indian Christian churches, and the missionary societies themselves. All three would like to see the Indian churches self-sufficient in leadership and resources. Given substantial agreement on this fundamental objective, it should be possible to move together in a spirit of cooperation, the state formulating its policies on the basis of consultation with responsible leaders of the Indian churches. It has been the lack of such consultation which on occasion has distressed the Indian Christian community. Despite certain problems, the government's policy regarding the missionaries has, on the whole, been a liberal one. The very presence, fourteen years after independence, of over 4,000 foreign Christian missionaries in a country which is over 85 per cent Hindu attests to this fact.

CHAPTER 8

PROBLEMS OF REGULATION AND REFORM

Apart from questions concerning the propagation of religion, which have been considered in the two preceding chapters, there are important areas of religious practice which the state has had to regulate. Regulation in the interest of public health and safety and the maintenance of law and order became firmly established in the British period and continue today. While it is sometimes claimed that such regulations infringe on freedom of religion, this is not a serious problem in present-day India. In a later section we shall discuss the historical role of the state in the reform of religious practices; in this connection there are acute problems in India, not only of religious liberty but of the limits of the secular state's activities in religious reform.

Public Safety and the Regulation of Religion

The Indian Constitution recognizes that certain forms of religious practice may be physically or morally harmful to the individual or society. Hence article 25(1) provides: "*subject to public order, morality and health* and to all the other provisions of this Part, all persons are equally entitled to freedom of conscience and the right to profess, practice and propagate religion." [Italics added] Anti-social practices sanctioned by religion are not thereby shielded from state interference.

It should be noted that the right of the state to legislate in matters of social and religious custom was first asserted only in the British period. Hindu kings had no legislative authority; their function was to uphold and enforce existing laws and customs. The coming of Islam to India strengthened this conception of a state without legislative power. The Muslim kings could not change Islamic laws based on the divinely revealed Koran, and so with few exceptions allowed their Hindu subjects to be governed by their own customs without state interference. K. M. Panikkar made the following categorical assertion: " 'Til the East India Company, through the agitation of Rammohan Roy, took up the question of *sati*, there was no instance of an exercise of state authority for the purpose of prohibiting anti-social customs."[1] In order to see our subject in proper historical perspective, we must now examine the nineteenth-century legislation which abolished certain customs despite their association with religion.

The suppression of anti-social religious practices

The Sanskrit word *sati* originally meant a chaste and virtuous woman, but by a curious development came to mean the self-immolation of a widow on the funeral pyre of her husband. The custom appears to have prevailed in India from very early times, and detailed descriptions of a case of *sati* were recorded by Greek writers in the fourth century B.C. In the epic *Mahabharata* the story is told of king Pandu's two wives, who, after his death, engaged in an agonizing dispute over which should have the privilege of being burned on their husband's funeral pyre. *Sati*, although highly praised by the ancient Hindu law-givers as a meritorious act, was never made a religious obligation. But the promised rewards for such an act were glorious indeed: "Dying with her husband she sanctifies her maternal and paternal ancestors; and the ancestry of him to whom she gave her virginity. Such a wife, adoring her husband in celestial felicity with him, greatest, most admired, with him shall enjoy the delights of heaven while fourteen Indras reign."[2]

Strong social pressure was frequently brought to bear on widows to make this sacrifice. In some cases the male members of the husband's family, anxious to secure for themselves the spiritual merits which would accrue upon the performance of *sati*, drugged the widow or used physical force to drag her to the pyre. *Sati* was not practiced in every part of India; it was more prevalent in Bengal and Rajputana than elsewhere. Nevertheless, in the early nineteenth century, more than five hundred cases of *sati* were reported in the districts around Calcutta every year.

The basic policy of the British government was one of strict laissez

[1] K. M. Panikkar, *Hindu Society at Cross Roads*, Asia Publishing House, Bombay, 1955, p. 41. Actually, the British abolished infanticide earlier, in 1802.
[2] Quoted in Edward Thompson, *Suttee: A Historical and Philosophical Inquiry into the Hindu Rite of Widow-Burning*, George Allen and Unwin Ltd., London, 1928, p. 50.

faire in all religious and social matters. This was the prevailing attitude, even with regard to *sati*. In 1789 the collector of Shahabad wrote to the governor-general regarding this practice: "The rites and superstitions of the Hindu religion should be allowed with the most unqualified tolerance, but a practice at which human nature shudders I cannot permit without particular instructions." His superior informed him, however, that as regards *sati* his action must be "confined to dissuasion and must not extend to coercive measures or to any exertion of official power."[3]

What was it that brought about the reversal of this policy forty years later? Several important factors converged at the right time. The Christian missionaries, convinced that *sati* should be abolished, were unsuccessful in their attempts to persuade the government in India to take such bold action. Thereupon, they launched a determined campaign to arouse and inform public opinion in England, which would in turn influence Parliament. Many pamphlets were written, and an association called the Society for Promoting the Abolition of Human Sacrifices in India was formed.[4] In India the Hindu reformer Raja Rammohan Roy led a forceful attack against *sati* by pamphlet and petition and gradually gathered a group of influential progressive Hindus around him. In his pamphlets he examined all of the relevant Shastras (Hindu scriptures) to prove that *sati* was not strongly recommended in the oldest texts. Public opinion had thus been prepared in both England and India when Lord William Bentinck was appointed governor-general.

Upon his appointment, Bentinck was instructed to consider measures for the immediate or gradual abolition of *sati*. After careful study of the problem he decided on immediate abolition, although Raja Rammohan had urged a more cautious approach. Regulation XVII, passed in December 1829, declared *sati* illegal and punishable by the courts. This regulation applied only to the Bengal presidency, but a year later similar measures were passed by the governments of Bombay and Madras. The Madras measure declared that the governor-in-council was enacting the regulation "without intending to depart from one of the first and most important principles of the

[3] R. C. Majumdar, H. C. Raychaudhuri, and K. Datta, *An Advanced History of India*, Macmillan and Company, London, 1950, p. 824.
[4] Kenneth Ingham, *Reformers in India 1793-1833*, Cambridge University Press, Cambridge, pp. 44-54.

system of British government in India, that all classes of the people be secure in the observance of their religious usages."[5]

Infanticide was practiced with religious motives among certain groups of Hindus: sometimes children were thrown into the sacred river in fulfillment of religious vows. A childless woman, for example, might vow that if the gods granted her more than one child, she would offer one to Mother Ganges. Although this practice was not as widely prevalent as *sati*, it was equally inhuman, and the intervention of the government was demanded. Bengal Regulation VI of 1802 declared such an act of infanticide to be murder.

The *thags* (term from which the English word "thug" was derived) were organized bands of criminals who travelled in disguise and murdered their victims by strangulation. Although the members of these secret bands were recruited from both the Muslims and the Hindus, they regarded themselves as devotees of the Hindu goddess Kali. The origin of *thagi* was explained as the result of a great battle between the goddess and an all-devouring demon. From every drop of the demon's blood a new demon was created, so Kali finally formed two men and gave them a strip of cloth. They strangled the demons with the cloth, and were then commanded by the goddess to go forth and overcome men by the same method.[6] Governor-General Bentinck appointed special officers to crush the secret bands and passed a series of acts to deal with this situation. During 1831-1837, more than three thousand *thags* were apprehended, and *thagi* was rapidly suppressed.

Sati, infanticide, and *thagi* were special problems which called for vigorous state interference—not regulation, but total suppression. In other areas, however, the state has been compelled to regulate the normal and lawful day-to-day religious activities of both Hindus and Muslims. The state has also had to legislate to prevent the eruption of public disturbances caused by the wounding of religious feelings. We must now examine these areas of state regulation.

The preservation of public order

There are two basic reasons for the extensive governmental regulation of religious festivals and pilgrimages in India. First, both Hinduism and Islam lack the centralized organization and authority

[5] The Madras *Sati* Regulation (Regulation I of 1830).
[6] Percival Griffiths, *The British Impact on India*, MacDonald and Company Ltd., London, 1952, p. 206.

necessary to provide for the orderly conduct of such religious activities. Second, in both Hinduism and Islam great importance is attached to religious functions which take place in the out-of-doors, especially in the form of *melas* and processions.

The Kumbha Mela is a religious fair of vast proportions which takes place every twelve years at the confluence of the rivers Ganges and Jamuna at Allahabad. Millions of Hindu pilgrims from all over India converge on the holy place to participate in the *mela*. The fair is a major administrative responsibility for the government, and it cannot well be otherwise. There is simply no other agency equipped to deal with the enormous problems of public health and safety created by the religious function.

The Kumbha Mela was last celebrated in 1954, and a few details concerning the arrangements will indicate the magnitude of the problem and of the government's responsibilities. The district magistrate of Allahabad was required to present the *mela* budget (specifying the needs of the various departments of the government in connection with the fair) by October 1952. Three-and-a-half months before the fair began a special officer-in-charge was sent, at the request of the district magistrate, to direct the arrangements for the health and safety of the pilgrims. The officer-in-charge had the powers of an additional district magistrate, and below him were seven area magistrates. Directly responsible to him was an officer of the tahsildar grade who was appointed manager of the *mela*, with his eight subordinates. The staff included one senior superintendent of police, one superintendent of police, and ten gazetted officers, besides an assistant commandant of the provincial armed constabulary. There were ninety-eight non-gazetted officers (circle inspectors, reserve inspectors, etc.). Eight police stations were set up, with a fire station attached to each, and twenty-seven police outposts. The total strength of the police force deputed to the *mela* was 2,882; there were also 250 watchmen.

An additional 550 policemen were deputed to the cholera inoculation barriers; the order requiring inoculation of all pilgrims was later cancelled, however. The director of the medical and health service set up eight hospitals and eight first-aid posts. There were seventeen medical officers, three lady doctors, twenty nurses, and the necessary number of ward boys, cooks, and stretcher bearers. In charge of the sanitary arrangements were forty medical officers of health, nine chief sanitary inspectors, thirty-three sanitary inspectors, and 926 provincial armed constabulary men. Over 6,000 sweepers were employed. The government sanctioned more than 1,700,000 rupees (over $360,000) for medical and public health arrangements. In order to accommodate the millions of pilgrims, a vast area had to be provided with drinking water, lighting, and latrines. The public works department constructed six pontoon bridges and a number of new roads.[7]

To help defray the expense of such elaborate arrangements, a pilgrim tax has for many years been levied in various centers of pilgrimage throughout India. This tax generally took the form of a terminal tax levied on railway passengers to pilgrim centers. The Taxation Inquiry Commission recommended the extension of this tax to all pilgrim centers of relative importance. "A demand has been put forward on behalf of local bodies and supported by state governments that pilgrim taxes should be extended to places of pilgrimage generally and in particular to all such centers of pilgrimage as are called upon to provide various civic amenities to large visiting populations. We support the proposal." The government of India accepted this recommendation in 1955, and legislation was adopted to implement it.[8]

The role of government in the regulation of this kind of religious activity is international in the case of the Muslim Haj (pilgrimage to Mecca). Before independence there was a portfolio of Haj in the central government, but even now official responsibilities are extensive. Medical teams of doctors and compounders are sent to Saudi Arabia by the government of India every year during the Haj season to give medical assistance to Indian pilgrims. In 1955 the government granted exemption to deck class Haj pilgrims from the necessity of obtaining income-tax clearance certificates before departure. Pilgrim passes are issued in order to obviate the necessity of obtaining international passports. In 1959, the Reserve Bank of India announced that arrangements had been made for the issue of special Haj notes in denominations of 10 and 100 rupees, which could be spent by pilgrims in Saudi Arabia.[9] About 15,000 Indian Muslims undertake the Haj pilgrimage every year.

[7] *Report of the Committee appointed by the Uttar Pradesh Government to Inquire into the Mishap which occurred in the Kumbha Mela at Prayaga on the 3rd. February 1954*, Superintendent, Printing and Stationary, U.P., Allahabad, 1954, pp. 38-41.

[8] See the news article and editorial in *The Hindu*, July 17, 1955.

[9] *Foreign Affairs Record*, New Delhi, 1955, vol. 1, p. 4; and *The Hindu Weekly Review*, May 11, 1959.

Extensive governmental regulation is necessitated by the important part played by outdoor religious processions in both Hinduism and Islam. The use of public streets for such purposes inevitably creates certain practical difficulties which must be dealt with by the police and other authorities. This problem would exist even if all the inhabitants of a given city were Hindus or if all were Muslims. But it has been intensified a hundredfold by the sometimes uneasy coexistence of the two communities in many parts of India. The playing of music by Hindu processions passing by mosques at the time of prayer has led to countless bloody riots. The killing of cows as sacrifice during the Muslim *Bakr-Id* festival has been another fruitful source of Hindu-Muslim conflict. When Hindu and Muslim festivals happened to fall on the same day, it has been almost taken for granted that communal clashes would occur in some of the cities of north India.[10]

One incident which took place in 1946 illustrates the kind of potential law-and-order problems with which local authorities have frequently had to deal. A Muslim procession at Banaras during the Muharram festival had to pass under a peepal tree which belonged to a nearby Hindu temple. A low branch of the tree obstructed the passing of the *tazias* (wood and paper representations of the tombs of the martyrs Hasan and Hussain) borne by the procession. Because the peepal tree is regarded by Hindus as holy, the Muslims were not permitted to cut down the projecting bough. The Hindus accused the leaders of the procession of having built the *tazias* bigger than usual. As the Muslims refused to take the *tazias* through in a slanting position, the procession was held up for three hours and the discussion became heated. With a communal clash imminent, a resourceful police officer ordered the road under the tree to be dug to a depth of one foot so that the *tazias* could pass in an upright position.[11] Such incidents have decreased greatly since the partition, but are still far from unknown.

Indian law has long provided for regulatory measures to prevent breaches of the peace resulting from religious processions. Sections 30 and 30A of the Police Act provide for the licensing and regulation of processions; the exact course the procession is to take must

[10] Clifford Manshardt, *The Hindu-Muslim Problem in India*, George Allen and Unwin Ltd., London, 1936, pp. 40-46.
[11] *Notes on Islam*, 1946, vol. 1, pp. 63-64.

be approved in advance, and it is accompanied by policemen to prevent any disturbances. Under section 144 of the Code of Criminal Procedure a magistrate can prohibit processions and meetings altogether, and such an order is always promulgated during times of communal tension.

Chapter 15 of the Indian Penal Code, "Of Offenses relating to Religion," deals with a variety of acts which would disrupt public order. The authors of the code, enacted in 1860, commented with regard to India: "There is perhaps no country in which the government has so much to apprehend from religious excitement among the people."[12] Section 295 punishes the destruction, damage, or defilement of any place of worship or any object held sacred by any class of persons with intent to insult their religion. Section 295A, considered in some detail in chapter 6 of this book, punishes the use of spoken or written words with malicious intent to outrage the religious feelings of any class of persons. Section 296 punishes the deliberate disturbance of public worship; section 297, trespass on a sacred place with the intent to wound religious feelings; section 298, the utterance of words with that intent.

A very important aspect of the state's role in the preservation of public order is the settlement of religious disputes in courts of law. There is a vast amount of litigation involving religious institutions which every year occupies the attention of the courts. Lawsuits are frequently filed in the district courts to determine the control of places of worship where there are conflicting claims made by two communities (for example, Hindus and Jains), or two factions of the same religious organization (Christian churches have been involved in numerous disputes of this nature). Sometimes the right to build a place of worship in a particular locality is challenged in the courts, especially if it is to be a mosque in a Hindu area or a temple in a Muslim area. The courts have had to decide the validity of orders issued by government officials under the Hindu religious endowment acts. To some extent the large amount of litigation involving religious institutions can be attributed to a factor mentioned above, namely, the lack of hierarchical ecclesiastical authority which characterizes both Hinduism and Islam. But there are obviously many other contributing factors.

[12] Quoted in R. Ranchhoddas and D. K. Thakore, *The Law of Crimes*, Bombay Law Reporter Office, Bombay, 1948, p. 671.

Restrictions on political involvement

It will be convenient at this point to mention the unsuccessful attempts which have been made to restrict the political role of religious organizations and places of worship, although the object was not related to the public safety. In 1960 both houses of Parliament rejected Communist-sponsored bills seeking to restrict "the use of the Catholic Church for political purposes and the participation of ecclesiastical personnel of the Catholic Church in political activity." Catholic bishops had issued circulars at the time of the Andhra elections of 1955 and the crucial Kerala elections of 1959, warning that Catholics who supported the Communist Party faced excommunication. In early 1960 the Roman Catholic bishop of Trivandrum, Kerala, ordered the excommunication of all Catholics who were members of the Communist or Revolutionary Socialist parties. In a pastoral letter to churches in his diocese the bishop directed priests to deny the sacraments to anyone who had openly supported or was known to have voted for candidates of these parties in the state elections.

Moving the bill in the Lok Sabha, T. Nagi Reddi, a Communist from Andhra Pradesh, declared that such threats of excommunication constituted a dangerous interference in the political life of the nation. "Religious incursions in politics must be put an end to if the secular democracy in our country is to be strengthened."[13] Article 25(2)(a) of the Constitution, he pointed out, permitted restrictions to be imposed on political activities which might be associated with religious practice. The bill provided that any person using the Catholic Church or church premises or resources for political activity should be warned by the appropriate government and his name, together with the warning, published in the official gazette. "Political activity" was defined, very broadly, as any activity for or against any government or political party or group.

The Communists and the Hindu communal parties, deadly enemies on most issues, found themselves in complete agreement on these bills. Some Congressmen supported the principle behind the legislation but objected to the discrimination involved in singling out the Catholic Church. Furthermore, the bills were widely interpreted in Congress circles as a kind of reprisal against the Kerala Catholics

[13] *The Hindu Weekly Review*, April 11, 1960.

for their significant part in the "liberation movement" and the Communists' defeat at the polls in 1959. Some opponents of the bill took the position that, as Indian citizens, the Catholic clergy had as much right to take part in politics as anyone else. B. N. Datar, minister in the ministry of home affairs, firmly declined to accept the bill moved in the Lok Sabha. He cited judicial pronouncements which supported the right of the Catholic clergy to tell their congregations not to support any party which was opposed to their spiritual concepts.[14] The bills were rejected by overwhelming majorities in both houses.

It should be noted that the Representation of the People Act does contain a provision which would appear to have some relevance to this situation, although it refers to the undue influence of individuals over individuals, not to the general pronouncements of ecclesiastical authorities. The act states that any person who "(i) threatens any candidate, or any elector, or any person in whom a candidate or an elector is interested, with injury of any kind including social ostracism and excommunication or expulsion from any caste or community; or (ii) induces or attempts to induce a candidate or an elector to believe that he, or any person in whom he is interested, will become or will be rendered an object of divine displeasure or spiritual censure, shall be deemed to interfere with the free exercise of the electoral right of such candidate or elector within the meaning of this clause."[15]

In February 1961 a nonofficial resolution asking the government to bring forward legislation to prevent the use of places of religious worship and pilgrimage for political propaganda and agitation was moved in the Lok Sabha by another Communist member, S. V. Parukekar. As his speech indicated, the mover of the resolution was mainly concerned with the political activities conducted from Catholic churches. However, the resolution made no specific mention of the churches, and in the inconclusive debate much attention was given to the extensive use made of Sikh *gurdwaras* as bases for the Punjabi Suba agitation.[16] Opposing any such regulation of the *gurdwaras*, the Chief Khalsa Diwan adopted a resolution declaring that

[14] *Ibid.*, April 25, 1960.
[15] Representation of the People Act (43 of 1951), as amended by Act 27 of 1956, section 123(2)(2).
[16] This question is discussed in the section on the Sikhs in chapter 14, "A Report on the Minorities."

the protection of religious rights could sometimes be interpreted as political activity. "We feel, therefore, that it is only the followers of that religion or worshippers of a particular place of pilgrimage and worship who have the sole right to prescribe do's and dont's for their holy places. Once it is conceded that government can interfere in such matters, there may be no end to such or even more drastic interference depending upon the sweet will of the party in power or its dogmas."[17] Thus far, all legislative attempts to restrict the use of religious organizations or places of worship for political activities have failed.

The State as Religious Reformer

Another area of the modern Indian state's legislative activity which is of interest here is more than simple regulation; it can only be described as religious reform, the reform of Hinduism by the secular state. This area of state intervention raises acute problems of both freedom of religion and the proper limits of the state's role in religious reform. In order to understand the implications of the state's assumption of this role some historical examples from the West will be useful. We shall then deal with the general problem in the light of Indian conditions.

The historical perspective

In the examples cited, no personal value judgment is implied by the use of the word *reform*. A reform is a change in the existing state of things which is regarded as an improvement by those who initiate it. In some cases the reforming state was motivated largely by genuine religious concern; in others political considerations were primary, although the religious aspect was also present. In some cases the reforms were carried out by the state in a spirit of cooperation with the church; in other cases, in a spirit of hostility.

Tsarist Russia presents a picture of the most comprehensive reform and regulation of religion by the state. Upon the death in 1700 of Patriarch Adrian, head of the Russian Orthodox Church, Tsar Peter I (Peter the Great) did not appoint a successor. In 1721 he finally abolished the patriarchate altogether and vested the powers

[17] Resolution of the Chief Khalsa Diwan, Amritsar, adopted on February 9, 1961. Legislation regulating the administration of *gurdwaras* is discussed in some detail in chapter 14, "A Report on the Minorities."

of that office in a commission known as the Holy Synod. The synod was composed of bishops, abbots, and other clergy appointed and removable by the Tsar, and headed by a procurator-general, an army officer also chosen by the Tsar.

The synod's powers of regulation covered practically the entire field of church doctrine, ritual, education, administration, and discipline, and a sincere effort was made to reform the church.[18] But the state's own objectives also were openly promoted, and the clergy were required to inform against those who in confession disclosed any trace of disloyalty to the state. Whatever gains the church may have made through valid reforms imposed by the state, the price was ecclesiastical and spiritual freedom. A summary extract from a 1905 petition sent by the Metropolitan of St. Petersburg to the Tsar stated: "All the religious duties of members of the Orthodox Church were strictly regulated (by the synod). . . . It was laid down exactly how one should comport oneself in church . . . what attitude one should take before the sacred picture, how one should spend festival days, go to confession, and see that the members of the Orthodox Church remained loyal to their faith. . . . These efforts to subject to police prescription the facts and phenomena of spiritual life . . . undoubtedly brought into the ecclesiastical sphere the mortifying breath of dry bureaucratism."[19] The religious reforms carried out by the state became an instrument of Tsarist autocracy and led to a stifling uniformity in spiritual matters.

The Protestant Reformation of the sixteenth century provides many examples of the state in the role of religious reformer. The German princes who sided with Martin Luther were motivated by mixed religious and political considerations. The complex political situation of the day involved the Holy Roman Empire, the Pope, and the numerous German princes, some of whom found it expedient to support Luther in his struggle against both Empire and Pope. But religious concerns were also of great importance, for the church was widely regarded as corrupt, and Luther's teachings had made a great impact upon the people.

As regards religion, the states of Saxony in 1527 were in the utmost confusion, due to the uneven acceptance of Lutheranism and the

[18] M. Searle Bates, *Religious Liberty: An Inquiry*, International Missionary Council, New York, 1945, p. 240.
[19] Quoted in Bates, *op. cit.*, p. 242.

lack of a central authority. Diverse forms of the liturgy were in use; the bishops had remained Catholics, and so the churches were without episcopal leadership. Under these circumstances the prince stepped into the breach (Luther viewed him in the role of an emergency bishop), and in 1527 appointed committees of clergy and laity to visit the churches in order to standardize their worship and organization in accordance with Lutheran teaching. The committee was referred to by the prince as "our authorized visitors" as if they were state officials, and Professor Bainton noted: "From this expression may be dated the beginning of the state church."[20] Thus, Luther supplied the ideas for reform but the princes assumed responsibility for their implementation.

The state played an even more active role in the Reformation in the Scandinavian countries, and the motivation was largely secular. The Swedish king, Gustavus Vasa, wanted to secure the vast wealth of the church for his impoverished treasury, and so quickly threw his support to the Lutheran cause. In England also, the Reformation proceeded by royal decree and act of Parliament. Under Henry VIII, the Act of Supremacy (1554) declared that the king was to be "the only supreme head in earth of the Church of England." In the reign of the same monarch the monasteries were suppressed and the English Bible installed in the churches. Under Edward VI the Book of Common Prayer was published, and in the reign of Queen Elizabeth Parliament enacted the Thirty-nine Articles, the first doctrinal statement of the church. The same pattern of religious reform by the state was followed in the turbulent seventeenth century, as in the case of the abolition of the episcopacy by the Parliamentary Party.

Leaving aside these periods of religious and political upheaval, what has been the role of the state in religious reform in normal times? In the first half of the nineteenth century, a remarkable series of ecclesiastical reforms was promoted by the British prime minister, Sir Robert Peel. These reforms were of such far-reaching effect that they have been described as "the Second Reformation." The spiritual and moral life of the Church of England was at low ebb. The laity and those outside the church clearly saw the need for reform, but most of the bishops and clergy were blind to the urgent necessity of

[20] Roland H. Bainton, *The Reformation of the Sixteenth Century*, Beacon Press, Boston, 1952, p. 71.

extensive changes in church administration.[21] In 1835 Sir Robert Peel appointed a commission to investigate the need for church reform, and the recommendations made in its report were soon acted upon by Parliament.

Legislation was enacted to reduce the huge incomes of some of the bishops (the bishop of Winchester formerly received £50,000; this was reduced to £8,000) and to use the surplus saved to raise the incomes of the poorer dioceses. New dioceses were created, and the boundaries of others altered. A permanent body with the title of Ecclesiastical Commissioners was created and given the responsibility of administering church property. The tithe was formerly paid to the church in kind, but a new law substituted a money payment assessed on a seven-year average. The Pluralities Act of 1838 attempted to eliminate the prevailing practice whereby a clergyman could hold several benefices and draw large incomes from them while leaving their care to underpaid curates. These and other reforms designed to remove abuses were almost entirely the result of the state's intervention.

Twentieth-century reforms of the Church of England have followed a different pattern, however. The initiative has come from the church, and the reforms have been carried out either by the church on its own authority or by Parliament at its request. Under the Enabling Act, measures of reform have been adopted by the church assembly and then sent to Parliament for enactment. By the latter method measures have been passed dealing with the creation of new dioceses, the management of cathedrals, the reorganization of parishes, the selection of clergymen for particular parishes, the elimination of simony, the power of a bishop to remove a parish minister, etc. However, in one very important area of reform, the revision of the Prayer Book, the measures were rejected by Parliament in 1927 and 1928.[22]

In chapter 1 we defined the secular state in terms of three principles: freedom of religion, equal citizenship, and separation of religion and state. Ordinarily, religious reforms will not be carried out by the secular state, simply because religious matters are not within its proper area of concern. That is, there are certain inherent limita-

[21] Cyril Garbett, *Church and State in England*, Hodder and Stoughton, London, 1950, p. 173.
[22] *Ibid.*, pp. 175-179.

tions on the functions of a secular state. In the words of Jefferson, endorsed by the American Supreme Court, there is a "wall of separation" between church and state. The basic assumption must be that the secular state will have nothing to do with religious affairs; any departure from this principle must be justified on reasonable secular grounds. The only valid reason for state interference in religion is for the protection of the interests of the public.

Whenever the state touches religion, whether to reform it or for any other reason, there are two special dangers to the secular state: (1) that the state will violate freedom of religion, (2) that the state will seek to promote religion. But even in cases where these two dangers do not appear to be serious, state interference in religion is permissible only if it can be justified on valid secular grounds. Religious reform per se is not a function of the secular state.

In several of these historical examples, the religious reforms imposed by the state were accompanied by serious infringements of freedom of religion. The state's reforms of the Russian Orthodox Church thus resulted in the almost total loss of ecclesiastical independence and spiritual freedom. Whatever the merits of the Protestant Reformation, it was surely imposed by German princes and Scandinavian kings with scant concern for their subjects' consciences. The nineteenth-century reforms of the Church of England, salutary as they may have been, were opposed by many of the bishops and other clergy.

In general, reforms of religion are a means of promoting religion. A religious body which has become careless or corrupt in its worship, discipline, or temporal affairs tends to lose public confidence, esteem, and support. Obviously, reforms which eliminate serious defects will enhance the prestige of a religion, strengthen its competitive position vis-à-vis other religions, and contribute to its advancement. The normal expectation, therefore, is that a religious body will initiate internal reforms and carry them out on its own authority.

It is significant that in all these historical examples the state was reforming an *officially established state church*. That is, the state was legally and morally committed to promote the interests of one particular religion; reform was a means of doing this, and so the state assumed the role of religious reformer. In the German states, Catholicism was the official religion until some of the princes sided with Luther. But the method by which Luther's reforms were carried out, i.e., by state-appointed commissions, ensured the emergence of a new official religion, the Lutheran state church. In England, the numerous reforms of religion undertaken by the state in the nineteenth century were a part of the state-church system by which the government was responsible for strengthening, supporting, and promoting the Church of England. Historically, the state's role as religious reformer has been closely tied to the state-church system. It has not been a function of states based on the principle of separation of church and state.

The problem for the modern Indian state

There is very little recognition in present-day India of the limitations placed on the state's legislative powers by the conception of the secular state. The question is frequently asked: If the government can regulate in great detail vast areas of social and economic life, why can't it regulate religion in the same way? It is widely assumed that legislation is the solution to most problems, and there is very little awareness of the reasons for excluding religion from its scope. In the West, the religious liberty of the individual and the freedom of the church from domination (as well as the freedom of the state from ecclesiastical interference) were achieved after centuries of struggle. In India, happily, such a struggle was never necessary; but this fact has also resulted in the Hindu's willingness to entrust much of his religion to the state. As the government is now controlled by members of his own faith and not by foreigners, he has no hesitation in making the state the instrument of far-reaching religious reform.

There is thus very little fear among Indians that freedom of religion might be endangered by the intervention of the state. And completely absent from discussions of religious reform by the state is the consideration that such reforms are a means of promoting Hindu religion, which might also undermine the secular state.

The tendency to look to the state is strengthened by the characteristic lack of organization of Hindu religion. It is composed of a large number of castes, sects, and subsects, most of which do not even have an effective organization of their own, to say nothing of Hinduism as a whole. The question which arises then is this: If Hinduism is in need of reform, who is going to reform it? Lacking the effective organizational means to reform itself, Hinduism (represented by progressive Hindus) turns to the state.

An interesting situation which developed in Ceylon in 1949 illustrates this tendency. A committee composed of seven Hindu members of Parliament was appointed to inquire into the need for legislation regulating the financial affairs of Hindu temples and prohibiting animal sacrifices in them. Several of the leaders of the Hindu community who presented their opinions to the committee spoke with the utmost frankness of Hinduism's organizational deficiencies and of the need for state intervention if reforms were to be effected. One gentleman stated: "The absence of recognized and authoritative Hindu 'Church' organization consisting of men of acknowledged authority is a great obstacle. This is a historical defect in the evolution of Hinduism as a religion, but of course it is also an advantage in that perfect freedom of conscience is assured. The Christians have their church, the Buddhists their Sangha, and so on, commanding unquestioned obedience to tenets religious and social."[23] The consequence of this situation, according to another Hindu gentleman, was that "we are compelled to solicit state aid in the form of legislation to put our house in order, only because we are unable to organize ourselves as some other religionists have done."[24]

"State aid in the form of legislation"—this is a phrase well worth pondering. Should the secular state, which is prohibited from granting financial aid to religion, extend aid in the form of special legislation for the reform of a particular religion? Historically, separation of church and state has meant that the coercive power of the modern legislating state, with all of its machinery of enforcement, cannot be placed at the disposal of any religion on request.

There is nothing sinister in the tendency to make the state the instrument for the reform of Hinduism. It is the natural outcome of the factors which we have noted. There is no religious discrimination in this approach; the Hindu is perfectly willing to help in providing legislation to reform other religions as well. If there is a Hindu Religious Endowments Act, there is also a Muslim Waqf Act, and a Sikh Gurdwaras Act. In general, however, the minorities have understandably been reluctant to extend the scope of state control over their religious affairs beyond what is absolutely necessary.[25] The

[23] *Report of the Special Committee on Hindu Temporalities, Etc.*, Government Press, Colombo, 1951, p. 216.

[24] *Ibid.*, p. 430.

[25] With respect to the role of the state in the election of the unique ecclesiastical body which controls Sikh *Gurdwaras*, see chapter 14.

Christian churches have their own ecclesiastical hierarchies, canon laws, constitutions, and traditions of autonomy in matters of doctrine, discipline, and administration of property. Any regulation of their affairs by the Indian state comparable to the above-mentioned legislation would surely be regarded as an unwarranted interference in their corporate religious freedom.[26]

While there is nothing discriminatory in the trend to legislate religious reform, since the same means are available to the minorities, Hinduism (professed by 85 per cent of the population) naturally receives the greatest attention. Hindu legislators become zealous reformers when dealing with their own religion, with the result that elaborate governmental machinery has been set up in some states to regulate the affairs of Hindu temples. The powers of state control over these institutions are enormous, but, in the hands of sincere and devout Hindu administrators, have been used to enhance the prestige of Hindu religion. In the process, what has evolved resembles nothing so much as an official ecclesiastical department committed to the advancement of a state religion.

In the opinion of the present writer, the proper approach of the secular state in the matter of religious reform is as follows. Religious reform per se is not a valid function of the secular state; it is not the business of the secular state to concern itself with religious matters. Furthermore, any such interference is likely to violate religious liberty, lead to the state promotion of religion, or both. Religious reform should never be the motive behind state legislation. Valid reforms of religion by the secular state are the *incidental* results of the state's protection of the public in cases where religious practices clearly tend to injure human beings physically or morally, where religious institutions grossly misuse offerings and endowments made by the public, or where social institutions connected with religion violate basic human rights.

If the dedication of Hindu women as *devadasis* leads to the practice of temple prostitution, and if the state prohibits such dedication in order to protect the morals and welfare of women, then a reform in Hinduism is effected as a by-product of the state's action. If the caste system, which is supported by religious sanction, restricts and hampers the individual, and the state seeks to liberate him by abolishing certain aspects of caste, this naturally, although

[26] See chapter 9 for a discussion of the effect of the Bombay Public Trusts Act (1950) on the Christian churches.

incidentally, effects a most fundamental reform of Hinduism. The secular state can only be neutral with regard to any religion, but it has a positive duty to protect the interests of the citizen. If in so doing the state incidentally reforms religion, there can be no objection.

This distinction between the basic objective and the by-product of legislation might appear to be academic and of no practical significance, but such is not the case. In the first place, measures of religious reform have been enacted which have no bearing at all on the public welfare (for example, the abolition of animal sacrifices in Hindu temples). Secondly, the failure to observe this distinction has enabled the state to penetrate deeply into the internal affairs of religious institutions, far beyond what is necessary to protect the interests of the public (for example, the regulation of Hindu religious endowments).

As was pointed out in chapter 4, the Indian Constitution grants to the state sweeping powers to regulate and reform religious and social institutions. Article 25(2) empowers the state to regulate or restrict any economic, financial, political, or other secular activity which may be associated with religion. The state can interfere with religious practice in order to provide for social welfare and reform and to throw open Hindu temples to Harijans. Under article 26, a religious denomination has the fundamental right to own and acquire property, but its right to administer it must be exercised "in accordance with law."

The complete abolition of Hindu and Muslim law, and their replacement by a uniform civil code, is directed elsewhere in the Constitution (article 44, one of the Directive Principles of State Policy). This will amount to a revolutionary reform of both Hinduism and Islam, for it will strip these two great faiths of the distinctive socio-legal institutions which have made them total ways of life. The secularization of law, which has already taken place in the West, is essential to the emergence of a modern Indian state. But in the process of this radical reform, traditional religion may be reduced to a matter of private belief and worship.[27]

In the light of this historical, theoretical, and constitutional background, we must consider in the following chapter the most important area of religious reform by the state in present-day India.

[27] See chapters 10 and 11.

CHAPTER 9

THE REFORM OF HINDU TEMPLES

THERE was little doubt regarding the need for reform in the institutions of Hindu worship when Indian independence was achieved in 1947. In many of the temples, primitive practices such as animal sacrifices had found a place alongside of the performance of Sanskrit rituals. Temple prostitution, while it had declined greatly since the end of the nineteenth century, still flourished in some places. In most parts of India, temple officers and priests forbade the entry of the ceremonially unclean untouchables, who represent a large minority within the Hindu fold.

The administration of temple property was notoriously corrupt in many places; managers frequently embezzled temple funds, leased or sold temple lands to relatives and friends for a pittance. The traditional rituals and ceremonies were neglected, and many of the magnificent ancient temples were in a deplorable state of disrepair. The Hindu public's support of temple worship was at a low ebb. For the educated Hindu, the temple was more often a source of embarrassment than of pride. As one Hindu gentleman put it, "Hinduism desperately needed to be made respectable."[1]

This chapter considers the legislation which has sought to reform the Hindu temples. While reform movements in some of these areas have a considerable history, it is only since 1947 that most of the reform legislation has been enacted.

REFORM OF RELIGIOUS AND CASTE PRACTICES

Animal sacrifices and temple prostitution

In 1950 legislation was enacted which bore the following title: "An act to prohibit the sacrifice of animals and birds in or in the precincts of Hindu temples in the state of Madras." The debate in the

[1] Statement made in an interview with the author, February 1961.

235

legislative assembly revealed the very considerable extent of the practice in various parts of the state. Shakti worship in Malabar (now a part of Kerala) involved a large number of sacrifices to gods and goddesses. One member referred to a temple in Dharapuram where every Tuesday thousands of kids were sacrificed and their blood poured in the deity Muni's cupped hands held in a drinking position. In another temple a man dressed like the goddess Kali received the blood of sacrificed kids in a silver cup and drank it in the presence of the worshippers. In one village in Koilkuntla taluq over three hundred buffaloes were sacrificed in one day. Special sacrifices were made to propitiate the deities during times of drought, famine, or epidemic.[2]

Among those who participated in the debate, there was complete unanimity as to the desirability of the measure but disagreement regarding the basis for its justification. One member attempted to interpret the legislation as a law-and-order measure, claiming that "hundreds and thousands" of riots and murders would be prevented, as disputes frequently arose among the villagers over whose animal was to be sacrificed first! This far-fetched argument apparently impressed no one in the assembly. Some attempt was made by the law minister to describe the object of the bill as the prevention of a public nuisance, but it was pointed out that ample legislation already existed to deal with any act which could be so described. A number of members stated that they supported the bill because they wished to end the revolting and gruesome scenes of animal slaughter. But it was obvious that no one was compelled to witness such scenes.

The secular rationalizations were not altogether convincing. After all, what the assembly was doing was legislating a reform in Hindu religion. Animal sacrifice was a religious practice of which the members disapproved. As D. V. Ramaswami described it: "Under the pretext of gaining some merit in the eyes of God, and for the selfish purpose of rising in the estimation of the deity, this practice of sacrificing animals and birds is resorted to." It was pointed out that such sacrifices were practiced only by those who were at the "lowest rungs of the ladder of Hindu ceremonials." The practice conflicted with the Hindu precept of *ahimsa* according to which the killing of any creature is repugnant in the eyes of God himself. Some

[2] *Madras Legislative Assembly Debates,* 1950, vol. 4, p. 122.

speakers referred to animal sacrifice as a "heinous sin" and quoted Gandhi's statement that this practice in the name of God was a "remnant of barbarism." The legislators conveniently overlooked the fact that animal sacrifices are prescribed by the highest scriptural authority of Hinduism, the Vedas.[3]

This reform of Hinduism had certain nationalistic as well as religious implications. In the West, the dominant impression of Hindu life still perhaps followed the lines of Katherine Mayo's *Mother India.* It was necessary to eradicate whatever primitive and barbarous practices tended to confirm this view. The international prestige of Hinduism and India would be raised by such legislation. V. I. Muniswamy Pillai referred to the Temple Entry Act and the bill under discussion and declared: "Taking into account how the world views the religion of the Hindus, I think it is high time that these small blemishes that are a blot on the Hindu religion should be removed. . . . It will go a long way to show to the world how sacred our religion is and how pure its worship." T. Vishwanatham asserted: "I do not like any outsider, whether in this country or outside India, to point his finger of scorn and say: 'Here are Hindus who kill animals in the name of religion.'"[4]

There was practically no concern expressed over the possibility that such legislation might interfere with freedom of religion, although no one could doubt that this issue was involved. One worshipper offers flowers and fruit to the image, another presents a slaughtered fowl because he believes it is more pleasing to the deity. What right has the state to forbid the latter act of worship when it does not endanger public order, morality, or health? D. S. Ramachandra Rao touched on this problem while pointing out the inherent limitations of religious reforms effected by the state. Legislation could not change the worshipper's conception of God. "If they attribute to (the) godhead principles of cruelty demanding a particular kind of sacrifice, we cannot possibly make them immediately give up their method of appeasing that cruelty. They will begin to feel that we have deprived them of a great religious consolation."[5]

[3] Gandhi had a unique way of handling scriptural authority when it sanctioned a practice of which he disapproved. On the subject of animal sacrifices he said: "There is no *smriti* which countenances these sacrifices. If there is, it is not a *smriti.*" Mahadev Desai, *The Epic of Travancore,* Navajivan Karyalaya, Ahmedabad, 1937, p. 50.

[4] *Madras Legislative Assembly Debates,* 1950, vol. 4, pp. 113, 629.

[5] *Ibid.,* pp. 135-136.

The Madras Animal and Bird Sacrifices Abolition Act of 1950 is an example of religious reform per se, not the incidental result of the state's pursuit of a valid secular object. It constitutes an infringement of religious liberty and is clearly an attempt to promote and advance the interests of the Hindu religion. The slaughter of goats and fowls in connection with worship is undoubtedly a primitive practice, and it is bound to decline with the rise in the general educational level and the impact of modern life. But the enforcement of such a reform by the state is contrary to our basic conception of the secular state.

In addition to animal sacrifice arose the question of legislation abolishing *devadasi* dedication. In many Hindu temples it was a long established practice to dedicate young girls to the deities as *devadasis* (literally, "servants of God"). The *devadasis* danced and sang before the images in the temples and in religious processions. Despite the religious origin of the practice, in time it degenerated to such an extent that most of the *devadasis* became temple prostitutes.

The dedication of girls to temples was first abolished in the progressive Indian state of Mysore in 1909. In Madras, similar legislation was introduced in the legislative assembly in 1927. In the statement of objects and reasons of the bill the framers explained their secular and religious motives: "It is necessary that the sanction of our temple authorities to such a practice of dedication which breeds immorality, promiscuity and irresponsibility in both men and women, be done away with in the interest of the individual and the nation at large; and thus the public be disabused of the notion that our religion encourages immorality in either man or woman and that the services of these women in any way form an essential part of the worship in temples."[6] The measure was completely justified on secular grounds alone; the state could certainly abolish such a practice in the interests of public order, health, and morality just as it had abolished *sati*. However, the framers declared also that one of their objects was to reform Hindu religion and raise it in public esteem.

Several attempts were made to produce effective legislation on this subject in Madras, but the Devadasis (Prevention of Dedication) Bill

[6] Quoted in P. Ramanatha Iyer and P. R. Narayana Iyer, *The Madras Hindu Religious and Charitable Endowments Act*, Madras Law Journal Press, Madras, 1953, p. 43.

was not passed until 1947. In the debate preceding its passage there were few objections raised to the bill. One member declared that the *devadasis* performed legitimate functions in temple worship, that the number who became immoral was not great, and that, therefore, legislation was not necessary. Most members, however, had no doubts about the necessity for an effective law. The question was dealt with as a matter of social reform, and Muslims as well as Hindu members of the assembly spoke in support of the bill.[7]

Madras Act 31 of 1947 not only prohibits the ceremony of dedication but also the acts commonly performed by *devadasis*, such as temple dancing. "Dancing by a woman, with or without *kumbha-harathy* (the ceremony of *devadasi* dedication) in the precincts of any temple or other religious institution, or in any procession of a Hindu deity, idol or object of worship . . . or at any festival or ceremony . . . is hereby declared unlawful."[8] The act has been well enforced throughout the state, and it has effectively protected the individual and the public from the evils associated with *devadasi* dedication. In the process the law has also effected a significant and welcome reform in Hindu temple worship.

Temple entry rights for Harijans

The temple entry movement was first started in 1919 in the princely state of Travancore, when a member of the assembly made a representation to the maharaja's government urging that steps be taken to effect this reform. The government, however, refused to interfere on the plea that such action would be a breach of religious neutrality. Several other unsuccessful attempts were made in the following decade, both in Travancore and in the province of Bombay.

Considerable impetus was given to the movement by a conference of Hindu leaders in 1932 which resulted in the founding of the All India Anti-Untouchability League. A bill introduced in the legislative assembly of Delhi in 1933 did not provide for positive interference with social or religious institutions, but merely sought to remove the official recognition of untouchability by the courts and the executive. The courts on occasion granted injunctions to prevent the entry of Harijans into temples from which they were excluded by long established custom. The bill would have eliminated such in-

[7] *Madras Legislative Assembly Debates,* 1947, vol. 7, pp. 643-660.
[8] Madras Devadasis (Prevention of Dedication) Act, 1947, section 3(3).

junctions, but even this mild reform measure was bitterly opposed by the orthodox Hindus, and the bill was withdrawn.

During this entire period Gandhi waged his vigorous campaign against untouchability in all forms. A major breakthrough, as far as temple entry is concerned, came with the 1936 proclamation of the maharaja of Travancore, which is here quoted in full: "Profoundly convinced of the truth and validity of our religion, believing that it is based on divine guidance and on all-comprehending toleration, knowing that in its practice it has throughout the centuries adapted itself to the need of the changing times, solicitous that none of our Hindu subjects should, by reason of birth, caste or community, be denied the consolation and solace of the Hindu Faith, we have decided and hereby declare, ordain and command that, subject to such rules and conditions as may be laid down and imposed by us for preserving their proper atmosphere and maintaining their rituals and observances, there should henceforth be no restriction placed on any Hindu by birth or religion on entering or worshipping at temples controlled by us and our government."[9] The proclamation was acclaimed by many prominent leaders, including Brahmans and members of the Hindu Mahasabha, as a courageous and far-reaching reform. Srimati Rameswari Nehru declared that the opening of the temples to Harijans "will revitalize our religion and put new life and strength into it."

The background of the maharaja's proclamation was a situation in which members of the untouchable castes were becoming increasingly restive and were openly talking of abandoning Hinduism in favor of a religion in which they would be treated as equals. Christian and Muslim missionaries saw their opportunity and vigorously presented the claims of their respective faiths. Gandhi rejected the idea that the proclamation was simply a device to prevent mass conversions to Christianity or Islam. His own motivation, as he explained it, was the desire to purge Hinduism of something that was morally wrong, without regard to possible consequences. The eradication of untouchability was a moral end in itself, and Gandhi denied that he was attempting to strengthen Hinduism in relation to other religions.

[9] Desai, *op. cit.*, p. 5. Compare the first phrases of the maharaja's proclamation ("Profoundly convinced of the truth and validity of our religion") with those in the paragraph on religious liberty in Queen Victoria's proclamation of 1858 ("Firmly relying ourselves on the truth of Christianity").

"I ask you to take me at my word," he declared, "when I say that I am wholly indifferent whether Hindu religion is strengthened or weakened or perishes; that is to say, I have so much faith in the correctness of the position I have taken up that, if ... (it) results in weakening Hinduism, I cannot help it and I must not care."[10]

Following the temple entry proclamation in Travancore, several legislative attempts to attain the same objective were made in the province of Madras. A bill was passed in 1939 which permitted the trustees to throw open a temple to Harijans if public opinion favored such a step, even though custom and usage might be opposed to it. On the basis of this permissive legislation a number of temples were opened to Harijans in various parts of the province. The logical culmination of this movement was reached in Madras in 1947 when new legislation compelled the throwing open of all temples in the state to all Hindus irrespective of caste or sect.[11] The Central Proinces, Bihar, Bombay, and other provinces rapidly followed suit. In 1955 the Indian Parliament enacted the Untouchability (Offenses) Act. One of the provisions of this important piece of legislation makes it an offense punishable with six months' imprisonment to prevent any person on the ground of untouchability from entering or worshipping in a Hindu temple.

Harijan temple entry legislation is specifically provided for in the Constitution of India. After the general statement of the right to freedom of religion, article 25(2) asserts: "Nothing in this article shall affect the operation of any existing law or prevent the state from making any law ... (b) providing for social welfare and reform or the throwing open of Hindu religious institutions of a public character to all classes and sections of Hindus." The temple entry provision was tacked on to the social reform clause by an amendment moved by K. M. Munshi, and approved by the Constituent Assembly.

While the social reform and temple entry provisions are linked together by the Constitution, they represent two fundamentally different categories of legislation. Laws attempting to remove the disabilities imposed by untouchability with regard to access to shops, public restaurants, hotels, etc., are properly described as measures of "social welfare and reform." Although the exclusion of Harijans

[10] *Ibid.*, pp. 36-39, 115.
[11] The Madras Temple Entry Authorization Act (Act V of 1947).

from temples is but another manifestation of untouchability, the fact that it involves the practices of religious institutions gives the problem a new dimension, and it becomes primarily a matter of "religious reform." As such, temple entry laws must be scrutinized in the light of the twofold danger to the secular state: that such legislation will either violate religious liberty or promote the interests of religion.

The most orthodox Hindus certainly regard Harijan temple entry legislation as an undue interference in their religious affairs. Their position is that the *Agamas* explicitly lay down rules as to the places inside a temple from which persons of the different castes should offer worship. These authoritative scriptures clearly state that the Panchamas (Harijans) are not permitted to worship from inside a temple. Their place is in the outer courtyard, and it is for their benefit that the god or goddess is taken in procession during the annual festival. It is thus clearly the religious duty of the trustees to exclude Harijans from the temples, and for the state to interfere in the performance of this duty, is, according to them, a flagrant violation of religious liberty.

In a decision handed down in 1958 the Supreme Court came to grips with this problem. The case involved a denominational temple belonging to the Gowda Saraswath Brahmans, which claimed not to be subject to the Madras Temple Entry Authorization Act. The trustees held that as a religious denomination they had the right to manage their own affairs in matters of religion under article 26(b) of the Constitution, and that it was a matter of religion as to who were entitled to take part in worship in a temple. After examining the regulations contained in the *Agamas*, the court agreed: "Thus, under the ceremonial law pertaining to temples, who are entitled to enter into them for worship and where they are entitled to stand and worship and how the worship is to be conducted are all matters of religion."[12]

Having reached this logical conclusion, however, the Supreme Court was confronted with an apparent conflict between two provisions of the Constitution. Under article 26(b) a denominational temple could exclude those who do not belong to that particular denomination, but under article 25(2)(b) a law throwing the temple open to all classes and sections of Hindus was valid. Finally the

[12] *Sri Venkataramana Devaru* v. *State of Mysore*, Supreme Court Judgments 1958, p. 390.

court approved a compromise arrangement by which only Gowda Saraswath Brahmans could attend certain traditional ceremonies restricted to the members of that community, but which permitted other Hindus, including Harijans, to participate at all other times. The case is significant in that the court took the right of corporate freedom of religion seriously, contrary to the general trend in the legislatures; its significance is limited, however, because there are so few *denominational* temples to claim this right.

Temple entry legislation, as we have seen, raises important problems of religious freedom; it also raises the question as to whether it is a means for the promotion of Hinduism by the state. Gandhi rejected the strengthening of Hinduism as an acceptable motive for the fight against untouchability. Harijans should be permitted to enter temples, but not out of fear that they will become Muslims or Christians if not granted equality. Other Hindu leaders, however, have not hesitated to state publicly that temple entry legislation is necessary to prevent conversions. The very survival of Hinduism, according to some leaders, depends on the eradication of untouchability, especially in temple worship.

It is not suggested here that the fear of conversions to Christianity or Islam is the principal motive behind temple entry legislation. The day of the mass movements of Harijans to Christianity is past, and since the partition, conversions to Islam in India are few. Most Hindu legislators regard temple entry laws as simply measures of social reform, motivated by humanitarian considerations and concern for social justice. They fail to appreciate the predominant religious aspect in this area of reform. There is also a general desire, not necessarily related to the conversion question, to remove from Hinduism the glaring defects which have given it a bad reputation in the modern world. Few would dispute the fact that reform is needed, but the conception of secularism imposes certain limitations on the functions of the state. Not everything that needs to be done should be done by the state.

Reform of Temple Administration

The demand for effective state supervision of Hindu temple administration is intensified by the fact that some of the institutions possess vast wealth in the form of money, jewels, and especially income-producing agricultural lands. In many cases this land, or the revenue derived from it, was dedicated to the temple deity hundreds of years ago by devout Hindu rajas. It should be noted, however, that temple lands have not been exempted from a number of state land reform measures enacted since independence.[13]

We have noted in chapter 3 that the regulation and even direct administration of Hindu temples had long been regarded as an important function of the state, under both Hindu and Muslim rulers. The British East India Company assumed this traditional governmental role as early as 1810 but abandoned it around the middle of the century under pressure from Christian circles in both India and England.[14]

In the absence of proper supervision, the administration of the temples suffered considerably at the hands of unscrupulous trustees. Repeated requests by prominent Hindu leaders for legislation finally led the Imperial Legislature to pass Act 20 of 1863. This act set up local committees to exercise supervision over temples, but the committees were so limited in both jurisdiction and powers of enforcement that it proved to be an ineffective measure.

Numerous abortive amending bills were introduced during the following fifty years which would have given the government a larger role in the supervision of these institutions. The British, however, were acutely aware of the dangers involved when the state assumes the role of religious reformer, and sought to avoid any action which might be interpreted as either interfering with or favoring Hindu religion. Constant representations from temple managers on

[13] The object of such legislation has been to transfer the ownership of agricultural land to those who actually work it. In Orissa, the High Court upheld the compulsory acquisition by the state, with the payment of compensation, of lands which had been dedicated to a Hindu deity. *Chintamoni* v. *State of Orissa*, A.I.R. 1958 Orissa, p. 18. In Mysore, the Religious and Charitable Inams Abolition Act of 1955 empowered the government to resume lands which had been assigned by the maharaja to religious institutions; as compensation the state now makes an annual payment to the institutions. A number of the state legislatures are presently in the process of fixing ceilings on land holdings. Uttar Pradesh, Madhya Pradesh, Orissa, Assam, and West Bengal have agreed to exempt temple lands from these ceilings. In some of the other states, especially in south India where some of the wealthiest temples are found, a maximum has been fixed for temple land holdings, although higher than that for individual landowners. See *Message of India,* New Delhi, vol. 2, June 1960, and *The Hindu,* June 8, 1961.

[14] See, for example, the chapter on "Government Support of Idolatry," in William Campbell, *British India in its Relation to the Decline of Hinduism and the Progress of Christianity,* John Snow, London, 1839.

one hand and Christian missionaries on the other achieved their common purpose, and the government declined a more active role in temple supervision.

In 1919, however, constitutional changes in both the central and provincial legislatures made them more democratic and representative of the people, and so the stage was set for reforms which would emanate more clearly from the Indian representatives than from the British government of India. In 1920 central legislation was enacted to facilitate the obtaining of information regarding religious and charitable trusts. After much debate and some technical legal difficulties, the legislature of Madras province passed the Madras Religious Endowments Act of 1927. Under this act the government appointed a board of commissioners headed by a president to supervise the administration of Hindu endowments.[15] After independence, legislation imposing stricter supervision was demanded, and as a result the Madras Hindu Religious and Charitable Endowments Act, 1951, was passed.

The Madras legislation

The most basic structural change introduced by the act was the creation of a new department of government headed by a commissioner for Hindu religious and charitable endowments. The task of supervising temples and *maths* thus passed from a regulatory commission to an executive department directly under a cabinet minister. The administrative functions were decentralized and exercised by deputy commissioners (three were appointed in 1951) with approximately equal territorial jurisdictions. Under each deputy commissioner were a number of assistant commissioners in charge of territorial divisions of his area. Each assistant commissioner was assisted by a committee of five members drawn from the nonofficial public.

The powers of the commissioner under the act of 1951 were extensive indeed. The general provisions were stated in section 20: "Subject to the provisions of this act, the administration of all religious endowments shall be subject to the general superintendence and control of the commissioner; . . . the power to pass any orders

[15] Ramanatha Iyer and Narayana Iyer, *op. cit.*, pp. 31-41. See also Bijan Kumar Mukherjea, *The Hindu Law of Religious and Charitable Trust*, Eastern Law House Ltd., Calcutta, 1952, pp. 49-51.

which may be deemed necessary to ensure that endowments are properly administered and that their income is duly appropriated for the purpose for which they were founded or exist." The commissioner and his subordinates were given the right to enter the premises of any religious institution in order to discharge their duties. The trustees of temples had to submit detailed reports and accounts and had to obtain the sanction of the commissioner before any sale or mortgage of immovable temple property could be effected. The act stipulated the purposes for which surplus temple funds could be spent, and particular expenditures in accordance with these purposes had to be sanctioned by the deputy commissioner.

The commissioner or deputy commissioner had power in certain cases to suspend or dismiss trustees of religious institutions and to appoint others in their place. The commissioner was empowered to fix the fees which were to be paid to the religious functionaries in the temple worship. The commissioner, if convinced that a particular institution was being mismanaged, by notification could take over the administration of a temple or *math* entirely, and vest it in an executive officer appointed by him. The trustees' annual budget had to be approved by the commissioner, and an annual audit made of their accounts.

The salaries, allowances, and other remuneration of the commissioner and other public servants in the Hindu Religious and Charitable Endowments (Administration) Department were to be paid by the government. The religious institutions, however, "in respect of the services rendered by the government and their officers," were required to pay to the government an annual contribution (not exceeding 5 per cent of their income) as might be prescribed. The commissioner and every other officer appointed to carry out the purposes of the act had to be persons professing the Hindu religion, and would cease to hold office if they should cease to profess that religion.

This brief outline of the 1951 Madras legislation is sufficient to indicate the enormous powers of control over religious institutions which were vested in the department. It is no exaggeration to assert that the commissioner for Hindu religious endowments, a public servant of the secular state, today exercises far greater authority over Hindu religion in Madras state than the archbishop of Canterbury does over the Church of England. The contention that the commissioner is concerned only with financial and administrative affairs, and not with religious matters, will not stand close scrutiny; it is based on a sharp distinction between *secular* and *religious* which in this context is simply untenable. When a deputy commissioner sanctions the expenditure of surplus temple funds for the establishment of orphanages rather than for the propagation of the religious tenets of the institution, he is dealing as much with religion as he is with finances. Behind this preference lies a whole set of religious assumptions which are in effect being imposed on the temple trustees.

The Madras act and similar legislation in other states are based on article 25(2)(a) of the Constitution. After the statement of the right to freedom of religion, it is provided that nothing in this article shall prevent the state from making any law regulating or restricting any economic, financial, political, or other secular activity which may be associated with religious practice. Article 26 recognizes the right of a religious denomination to establish and maintain institutions, to manage its own affairs *in matters of religion*, to own and acquire property and to administer it *in accordance with law*. The right of a religious denomination to manage its own affairs in matters of religion is thus a fundamental right which no legislature can take away, but the administration of its property can be regulated by laws imposed by the legislature.

The language of article 26 is closely patterned after that of the 1937 Constitution of Eire, with the notable addition, however, of the above two italicized phrases. In a secular state in the West, a church has the right to manage its own affairs in all respects—in doctrine, discipline, and administration of property; this broad conception of corporate religious freedom is not recognized by the Constitution of India. The western guarantee presupposes the existence of well-organized churches with a tradition of self-government; the Indian provision presupposes largely unorganized religious institutions over which the state has traditionally exercised considerable regulation and control.

The Madras act of 1951 was quickly challenged in the courts, and some of the decisions which have been handed down are notable affirmations of the right of corporate religious freedom against state interference. However, the powers of regulation left to the state are still extensive. The courts have struck down many of the main provisions of the act in so far as they relate to *maths*, monastic organizations over which the *mathadhipatis* (superiors or abbots) have traditionally exercised far greater spiritual and administrative authority than have trustees over temples.

Parts of the act have also been declared unconstitutional as applied to denominational temples, places of worship founded primarily for the use of particular sects or castes (for example, a temple belonging to the Gowda Saraswath Brahmans, in *Devaraja* v. *State of Madras*, 1953). Both *maths* and, to a lesser extent, denominational temples have a significant tradition of autonomy which the courts have respected. However, the great majority of the Hindu religious institutions do not fall into either of these categories, but are temples belonging to the general Hindu public.

In the well-known Shirur Math case, 1954, the Supreme Court pointed out that the religious tenets of a Hindu sect might prescribe the performance of very elaborate rituals in the worship of an idol and that "all these would be regarded as parts of religion and the mere fact that they involve expenditure of money or employment of priests and servants or the use of marketable commodities would not make them secular activities partaking of a commercial or economic character; all of them are religious practices and should be regarded as matters of religion within the meaning of article 26(b)."[16] The court recognized the unique status of the *mathadhipati* or superior as both the manager of the temporalities of the *math* and the spiritual head of a fraternity devoted to the teaching of a certain set of religious doctrines. He should not be brought down to the level of "a servant under a state department."

The Supreme Court declared invalid the provisions of the act by which: the commissioner or his subordinates had unrestricted right of entry into a *math*; the superior would have to be "guided" by the commissioner in the expenditure of surplus income; the commissioner could require the superior to appoint a manager for administration of the secular affairs of the institution and, in case of default, make the appointment himself; the religious institution would have to pay up to 5 per cent of its annual income to the government in respect of the "services rendered by the government."

While the court regarded these provisions as too drastic an interference in the administration of the *math*, other very drastic pro-

---

[16] *Commissioner, Hindu Religious Endowments* v. *Sri Lakshmindra Thirtha Swamiar of Sri Shirur Mutt*, A.I.R. 1954 Supreme Court, p. 290.

visions were approved. For example, the judgment declared that a religious denomination had "complete autonomy" under article 26 (b) to decide what rites and ceremonies were essential to its tenets but added: "Of course, the scale of expenses to be incurred in connection with these religious observances would be a matter of administration of property belonging to the religious denomination and can be controlled by secular authorities in accordance with any law laid down by a competent legislature." The court added only that the right of administration could not be taken from the hands of a religious denomination altogether and vested in some other authority. The court upheld the commissioner's power to make any additions to or alterations in the religious institution's budget.

Following the adverse decision in the Shirur Math case, the Madras legislature amended the Hindu Religious and Charitable Endowments Act. But the 1954 amendments effected merely verbal changes in some of the provisions, and the extent of state control was actually increased in certain amended sections. The commissioner, for example, was empowered to *direct* the utilization of surplus funds for particular religious, educational, or charitable purposes, whereas previously the initiative lay with the superior who had to obtain the commissioner's approval. The Madras High Court, in *Suhindra* v. *Hindu Religious Endowments Commissioner*, 1956, quickly struck down a number of the same sections which had been held invalid before. The petitioners in the case were the superiors of the Shirur *math* and eight other *maths.*

The 1959 version of the endowments law

The Madras Hindu Religious and Charitable Endowments Bill of 1959 was the next move in the legislature's struggle with the judiciary. In the drafting of this bill a more serious attempt was made to meet the objections of the courts, but without surrendering the commissioner's extensive powers of control over the temples. In the debate in both houses of the state legislature, members of the opposition pointed to the incongruity of claiming to be a secular state and at the same time interfering in such a drastic manner in the internal affairs of religious institutions.

Some legislators indeed declared that the government was steadily moving in the direction of the "nationalization of temples."[17] As if to

[17] *The Hindu*, September 9, 17 and 18, 1959.

confirm further the existence of this trend, some supporters of the measure had already suggested that temple executive officers and other temple employees be classified as government servants and that land rent owed to the temples be collected through the revenue department.[18] An editorial in *The Hindu* charged that the bill as drafted "sought to tighten further the hold of government over the temples and other religious institutions in the state, under the guise of better management and regulation, so that these stood virtually nationalized, functioning as a department of government and subject to all the vicissitudes of party politics in a secular parliamentary democracy. Devout Hindus were naturally concerned at the inroads of the state into matters religious that the bill sought to perpetuate."[19] Despite this fact, the editorial continued, the joint select committee which reported on the bill in the state legislature had failed to tone down the powers of the commissioner and had in some respects even increased them. The writer emphasized the view that the scope of legislation in such matters should be "strictly limited to the immediate ends in view, namely, the prevention of gross abuse of funds." Despite all objections, the bill was passed with few amendments.

The 1959 act exempted *maths* from certain controls; for example: "Nothing in this section shall prevent the trustee of a math . . . from utilizing the surplus . . . in such manner as he deems fit" (section 36). It is also stated (section 107) that the act is not to affect any rights of a religious denomination conferred by article 26 of the Constitution, so that denominational temples will not be subjected to as rigid control. The entry of the commissioner or his subordinates into a religious institution is regulated so as to remove the objections expressed in previous court judgments. But the whole system of control over temples belonging to the general Hindu public, with vast powers vested in the commissioner, has remained intact. As has been mentioned, these temples constitute the great majority of the Hindu religious institutions.

The Madras legislation has produced some very serious problems of religious freedom. The provisions which are most frequently criticized relate to the commissioner's control over surplus temple funds and his power to divert endowments to purposes different from those of the donors when in his opinion the original objects can

[18] *Ibid.*, April 29, 1959.
[19] *Ibid.*, September 5, 1959.

no longer be realized (the *cy pres* doctrine). Such powers were extremely broad under the 1951 and 1954 acts, but have been restricted somewhat under the 1959 version. Even now a deputy commissioner may direct that a particular endowment be appropriated to any one or all of a number of purposes, some of which are distinctly religious (e.g. the propagation of the institution's religious tenets, the establishment of schools for the training of temple priests, etc.), while others are of a philanthropic or educational nature (homes for the destitute, leper asylums, school and colleges in which Hinduism will also be taught, promotion of fine arts and architecture). It is for the official of the secular state, we emphasize, to choose from among these numerous valid purposes.[20]

The complaint has been that the commissioner has frequently used temple funds for social, educational, or philanthropic purposes to the neglect of distinctively religious objects. Funds from the famous temple at Tirupathi (regulated by special legislation) have been used to establish a university, schools, orphanages, hospitals, etc. Throughout south India, Tirupathi has become the symbol and the model of the new Hinduism which transforms the offerings of individualistic piety and devotion to God into social institutions, dedicated to the service of man. Hinduism is being infused with a modern outlook and a new sense of social responsibility. This is a religious reformation of a fundamental nature. But as the agency of this reform is to a large extent the state, it should not be surprising if devout Hindus object to the liberties being taken with their religion.

Another editorial complained: "Existing state legislation governing Hindu endowments has erred on the side of stretching the doctrine of *cy pres* to such an extent that surplus resources of temples could be diverted to a variety of purposes, far removed from the intentions of the original donors. Such diversion could have little justification when, as against a few religious institutions with a surplus, there are thousands of others that have not the wherewithal for even the conduct of the daily *pujas*, or still worse, stand desolate or in ruins."[21] The Hindu Mahasabha passed a resolution at its thirtieth annual session in 1952 asserting that Hindu endowment

[20] Section 66 of the 1959 act.
[21] *The Hindu,* January 24, 1961. *Puja* is the general term used for Hindu worship or the ceremonies connected with it.

funds should not be diverted to "profane, secular, non-Hindu and non-religious purposes, however laudable such purposes might be." The resolution condemned the Madras government especially and called on all Hindus to take effective measures "for protecting the religious freedom of Hindus against encroachments by a secular and anti-Hindu government."

The Madras legislature has granted the power and the department of Hindu religious endowments has created the machinery for the extremely detailed regulation of Hindu institutions. As we have seen, the resulting interference with religious freedom has been considerable. The courts have invalidated some of the objectionable provisions of this legislation, but the basic powers of control remain. It is but natural that concern should be expressed over the future course of events in this area. An editorial in *The Hindu Weekly Review* commented on this question as follows: "We have fortunately a minister of endowments in this state who has the faith and courage to defend traditional religious values and temper the impact of the rather sweeping provisions of the Madras act by its sympathetic enforcement. But . . . other political groups with less faith or with atheism as their creed may be swept into power in future, both here and in other states of India."[22] The machinery for the complete domination of temples by the state already exists, and could be utilized to that end with little difficulty.

While there is convincing evidence that important aspects of religious freedom are in jeopardy, the secular state is also compromised by the official promotion of Hinduism which has resulted. The department of Hindu religious endowments has provided a kind of ecclesiastical structure which Hinduism previously lacked. Essentially, the department has become the central authority which historic Hinduism never developed. Within this structure, long-range plans are being made which will raise the prestige of Hinduism enormously. The new emphasis on social welfare institutions has already been mentioned. Hinduism, at least within the state, is being welded into some semblance of unity through the efforts of the department. Surplus funds from the wealthier temples are being diverted to aid the poorer institutions, and temple worship is being revived as old temples are restored.

[22] *The Hindu Weekly Review*, March 14, 1960.

There is abundant evidence to indicate that the department charged with supervising the secular affairs of temples interprets its functions as being the general furtherance and promotion of the Hindu religion. A glance at the 1958-1959 administration report of the department reveals the following items: (1) Drive for the renovation and repair of temples—"A fillip was also given to the drive by giving government grants of Rs. 300,000 to the needy and important institutions numbering sixty-seven." (2) Drive toward "improvement of religious atmosphere of temples to make them serve as living centers of religious culture." (3) "Religious propagandists were recommended and religious discourses were arranged on ordinary and special occasions." (4) "Festival programs were arranged to be printed and pamphlets distributed to the worshippers. Important festivals were arranged to be published in newspapers." (5) "Publication of religious books . . . under auspices of religious institutions were encouraged." (6) Devotional songs of eminent musicians "were encouraged to be recorded and gramaphone plates of such songs made available to be broadcast through amplifiers in temples." (7) A forty-five-day refresher course in the *Agamas* was provided for temple priests. (8) A monthly journal was published in Tamil by the department; along with administrative matters there are articles on the activities of temples, the importance of rituals and worship, the significance of certain festivals, and the history of saints.[23]

In Andhra Pradesh, formerly a part of Madras, the minister of Hindu religious endowments has urged publicly that the teachings of the Vedas and Shastras be more widely disseminated and that steps be taken to popularize the Hindu religion. One deputy commissioner remarked that the department wanted "good propagandists to propagate and inculcate *bhakti* (religious devotion) in the people."[24] It is unnecessary to multiply such illustrations; it is quite evident that many of the officials involved have no clear idea of the distinction between the *regulation* and the *promotion* of Hindu religious institutions.

Alternative approaches to the problem

The theoretical basis of Hindu religious endowments legislation is perfectly sound. The principle is simply that all endowments

[23] *Administration Report of the Hindu Religious and Charitable Endowments (Administration) Department*, Government of Madras, Madras, 1960, pp. 22-25.
[24] *The Hindu*, May 31, 1955.

should be used according to the real intent and will of the grantor. This is a principle recognized by all modern democratic states, and all have procedures by which trusts for educational, charitable, or religious purposes can be established. All modern states exercise certain regulatory powers in order to see that the purpose of endowments are carried out; this is nothing more than another way in which the state protects the interests of the public. In India some of the temples and *maths* have been endowed with extensive properties by rajas and other people of wealth, and such endowments are still being made. The Indian state does have an obligation to supervise the administration of religious endowments, or endowments for any legitimate purpose.

Thus, the state certainly has a valid *negative* function—to prevent the misappropriation of endowment funds by establishing procedures for effective supervision. The question is how deeply involved the state should become in the *positive* function of furthering the objects of religious endowments. The intent of the grantors was, in general terms, to promote and advance the cause of Hindu religion. The secular state must provide the necessary conditions by which the grantors' intent can be fulfilled, yet must not itself become involved in promoting and advancing Hindu religion. The greater the powers which the state assumes in actively carrying out the intent of the grantors, the more directly the state becomes engaged in furthering Hindu religion. This is what has happened in the activities of the Madras department of Hindu religious endowments, and it has happened by such a natural development that very few people seem to sense the problem which is thus created.

The only solution, unpalatable as it would be to the vested interests of bureaucracy, is that the functions of the state in relation to Hindu religious endowments be cut back to a minimum, with the emphasis on financial supervision to prevent misappropriation of funds. The annual audit of the accounts of religious institutions should be the most important aspect of governmental regulation. It is only by a drastic reduction in the state's enormous powers of control over religious institutions that full religious freedom and separation of state and religion can be secured in India.

There can be no disagreement with the proposition that the best answer would be the development of an organization by which Hindu worshippers and trustees could manage their own temple affairs effectively. A workable regional organization, neither highly centralized nor with complete autonomy for the local temple authorities, would seem to be desirable. If such an organization could administer temple property with a minimum of state interference, this would surely be better than having a governmental department do it all.

In the past there has not been much evidence to make one believe that such a development is possible. Present legislation assumes that conditions will remain static, and that, therefore, government will have to continue its present extensive responsibilities in temple administration. But the Indian situation is anything but static. A massive attack on the problem of illiteracy has been undertaken. Universal adult suffrage and elections are educating the people in one aspect of the democratic process. The new emphasis on village self-government (*panchayat raj*) is developing a sense of civic responsibility in local affairs. There is a marked proliferation of voluntary associations of all kinds in cities and towns, and this trend is beginning to reach the villages as well. In short, conditions are developing which will be more favorable to the growth of responsible self-governing religious associations. *But*, is voluntary responsibility in temple affairs likely to develop in an atmosphere of omnipresent state control? Even if it should develop, history records few examples of the state's willing surrender of power, even when changing circumstances make its imposition unnecessary.

Extensive consideration has been given to the Madras legislation because it has gone farthest in controlling the administration of Hindu endowments. Less comprehensive regulation exists in Orissa, Mysore, Bombay, Bihar, and other states, although the extent of state control is by no means negligible. The Supreme Court, in *Sri Jagannath* v. *State of Orissa*, 1954, struck down a provision by which the commissioner could frame a scheme for the administration of the property of a *math*, with no provision for an appeal against his order to the court. An amendment to the Orissa act providing for such an appeal was sufficient to validate the section (*Sadasib Prakash* v. *State of Orissa*, 1956). But other far-reaching powers of state control were upheld in the first case.

Special mention should be made of the Bombay Public Trusts Act of 1950, for in several important respects it represents a much sounder approach to the question of religious endowments than the Madras legislation.[25] In the first place, it deals with all religious and charitable trusts on the same basis, whether managed by Hindus, Jains, Buddhists, Parsis, Christians, or Muslims. This is obviously an approach more in keeping with the secularity of the state, since whatever restrictions are imposed or benefits conferred will affect all religious denominations equally. In particular, this avoids the situation whereby the religion of the majority becomes closely identified with government through a kind of ecclesiastical department, as in Madras. Secondly, the powers of the charity commissioner to interfere in the internal administration of religious institutions are considerably less than those of his counterpart in Madras. This is the inevitable consequence of dealing with all religions on an equal basis, since the exercise of great regulatory powers in the affairs of the minorities would obviously create major problems. The great emphasis is placed on the registration of public trusts, the keeping of regular accounts, and the annual audit.

In *Ratilal* v. *State of Bombay*, 1954, the Supreme Court voided two provisions of the act which were not in keeping with its otherwise sound approach. Section 44 laid down that the charity commissioner could be appointed to act as trustee of a public trust by a court. The Supreme Court pointed out that if the charity commissioner were appointed as the superior of a *math*, the result would be disastrous and would constitute a flagrant violation of corporate religious freedom. Such a possibility was never contemplated by the legislature, and it was simply a case of poor drafting. More serious, however, was the very broad interpretation given to the *cy pres* doctrine in the act. In striking down this provision, the Supreme Court declared: "To divert the trust property or funds for purposes which the charity commissioner or the court considers expedient or proper, although the original objects of the founder can still be carried out, is to our minds an unwarrantable encroachment on the freedom of religious institutions in regard to the management of their religious affairs."[26]

The petitioners in this case were the manager of a Jain public temple and the trustees of the Parsi Panchayat Funds and Properties in Bombay. The Christian minority in the state, and especially the Roman Catholics, strenuously objected to the act on the ground that the administration of their properties was already well regulated by

[25] See K. S. Gupte, *The Bombay Public Trusts Act, 1950, with Rules*, Western India Law Printing Press, Poona, 1956, p. xix.
[26] *Ratilal* v. *State of Bombay*, A.I.R. 1954, S.C., p. 394.

ecclesiastical authorities and canon law. "Canon law lays down precise, definite and comprehensive regulations on various points connected with the acquisition, possession and administration of ecclesiastical goods by various moral and juridical persons in the church."[27] State interference was therefore unwarranted by circumstances, and the fee charged for the administration of these unnecessary regulatory powers (2 per cent of the endowment income) constituted a heavy burden upon the church.

There is certainly significance in the contention of the Christian churches that their property is well administered and that such state regulation is unnecessary. There would seem to be need for no more financial supervision of church property than that which is exercised in the United States, which is practically nil. Certainly it is true that if Hindu religious institutions were as well organized and administered as these churches, there would be little need for the Bombay Public Trusts Act at all. The approach of dealing with the property of all religious institutions on the same basis thus produces difficulties when the organizational differences among the institutions are so great. But in the long run, this general approach will prove to be sound in the building of a secular state.

The central government enters the picture

Thus far we have considered only state legislation; in 1959 attention began to turn to the possibility of central legislation regarding Hindu endowments. Prime Minister Nehru announced that consideration was being given to legislation which would prevent the misuse of funds belonging to the many temples and *maths* all over the country. In March 1960 the government of India appointed a Hindu Religious Endowments Commission, the chairman of which was Dr. C. P. Ramaswami Aiyer, a respected elder statesman. The terms of reference of the commission were broad; it was to examine the whole subject of the administration of Hindu religious endowments and recommend measures for its improvement. The commission prepared and circulated a comprehensive questionnaire on the subject and toured the country to hear and discuss the views of religious leaders, associations, and officials concerned with the problems of Hindu endowments.

[27] *Report of the Meetings of the Working and Standing Committees of the Catholic Bishops' Conference of India, 1952*, Good Shepherd Convent Press, Bangalore, 1952, p. 172.

Within a month of the appointment of the commission, however, the law minister introduced the Religious Trusts Bill of 1960 in the Lok Sabha. Despite its title, the bill would apply only to Hindu trusts. It would provide for the appointment of a commissioner of religious trusts by each state government, and would grant him extensive regulatory powers over Hindu endowments. Opposition to the bill was chiefly based on the fact that the government had not waited for the commission report; the decision was later made not to proceed with the bill.

In a sharply critical analysis of this hastily introduced legislation, Mahant Dig Vijai Nath, chief priest of the Gorakhnath temple in Gorakhpur and working president of the Hindu Mahasabha, assailed the trend toward state control of everything despite continuous authentic reports of inefficiency, corruption, and waste of public funds in government offices. "In the opinion of our present government, *Officialization* is the panacea for all the evils of the country, whether social or religious or economic or cultural." The mahant pictured the proposed commissioner as the archbishop of the state, with absolute ruling power over all property-owning Hindu institutions but with no necessary knowledge of the Hindu scriptures or faith in the temple rites and ceremonies.[28]

The genius and continuity of Hinduism, he went on, has been directly related to the autonomy of its institutions. "This autonomy or freedom of self-development of the religious institutions and non-interference of all political powers with their special activities and distinctive modes of development has been the most powerful factor in the maintenance of the truly spiritual character of Hindu religion and in saving religion from becoming a department or an instrument of the rising and falling states. It is for this reason that Hinduism has never been secularized and its fate has never been linked up with the fates of the governing powers of the country." The mahant emphasized that all reforms and improvements must come from within the religious institutions. He proposed the establishment of all India organizations of the various Hindu sects, with powers to regulate the institutions within their respective jurisdictions. Unfortunately, such an attractive alternative to state control appears to be totally impracticable under present circumstances.

[28] Mahant Dig Vijai Nath, *What the Religious Trusts Bill means to the Hindus,* Shri Lakshmi Printing Press, Delhi, 1960.

After more than two years of intensive work, the Hindu Religious Endowments Commission submitted its report (May 31, 1962). One of the commission's important conclusions was that "there is no insuperable difficulty or complication in enacting a uniform type of legislation dealing with the religious endowments of all communities in India."[29] This, however, was put forth as a consideration for the formulation of long-range policy. With reference to the immediate needs of Hindu institutions, the commission recommended that suitable legislation be speedily enacted in those states (Assam, Punjab, West Bengal and Uttar Pradesh) which at present have no provision at all for governmental supervision of temples.[30]

The tone of the report is one of balanced moderation, and the recommendations are cautious. The commission made several references to the considerable volume of opinion opposed to the state's interference in day-to-day temple administration, and was apparently itself impressed by the force of these arguments.[31] Deeply concerned over the low educational level of the Hindu "clergy," the commission recommended that each state establish institutes for the systematic instruction of temple priests in Sanskrit, Hindu scriptures, and rituals. Also recommended was the creation of four Hindu theological colleges, in which religion would be studied along with the humanities as in colleges of divinity in the West.[32] The important reforms of Hinduism proposed by the commission will be difficult to implement, however, since the chief responsibility for the regulation of temple administration will continue to rest with the state governments.

Regulation of the activities of sadhus

It is interesting to note the non-governmental approach to religious reform in the related problem of the Hindu *sadhu*—the saffron-robed holy man who, having renounced the world, wanders about living on food provided by devout householders and sometimes imparting religious teachings to those whom he meets. The number of *sadhus* in India runs into the hundreds of thousands and is said to be increasing. While some are attached to long-established monastic orders, large numbers are subject to no discipline at all.

---

[29] *Report of the Hindu Religious Endowments Commission*, Ministry of Law, New Delhi, 1962, pp. 31, 172-173.
[30] *Ibid.*, p. 172.   [31] *Ibid.*, pp. 100, 123-124.   [32] *Ibid.*, pp. 74, 174, 178.

Nehru has on occasion severely denounced the numerous *sadhus* who simply wander around the country begging and stealing.

In 1956 a private bill dealing with this problem was introduced in Parliament by Mr. Radha Raman. In the objects and reasons of the Sadhus Registration Bill it was stated: "In the guise of saintly order, most of them (the *sadhus*) indulge in vices, begging and other anti-social acts, which is undesirable and which, if not checked, will help the crime incidence to increase unabated." The bill required that every *sadhu* report to the local district magistrate for a license and have his name written in an all-India register. Anyone attempting to function as a *sadhu* without a license would be punished with two years' imprisonment. The general idea behind the bill was that registration would enable the government to keep some kind of check on the activities of these wandering ascetics, although it is not clear exactly how this measure would achieve the desired object. A few months before this bill was introduced, however, the Bharat Sadhu Samaj (India Sadhu's Association) was formed. The possible enactment of unfriendly legislation gave added impetus to the acceptance of the Samaj by the *sadhus*; it represented the organizational means by which they could attempt to put their own house in order without state interference. The Samaj formed a solid opposition to the bill, and in response to this pressure and to other criticism the bill was withdrawn.[33]

Although the Bharat Sadhu Samaj is a non-governmental organization, officials acting in their private capacity have played a large role in its formation and the development of its program. In fact, the union minister of planning, labor, and employment, Gulzari Lal Nanda, was chiefly responsible for the creation of the organization, and continued to serve as chairman of its central advisory committee. Both the president and the vice president of India addressed the members of the Samaj when the cornerstone of their new building (costing 500,000 rupees) was laid in 1959. The close personal link with the central government, especially through G. L. Nanda, has undoubtedly been of great help in extending the influence and raising the general prestige of the organization.[34] Critics, however, especially in the ranks of the Hindu Mahasabha, scornfully refer to the members of the Bharat Sadhu Samaj as "Congress *sadhus*."

[33] Gyananand, "Bharat Sadhu Samaj," *Message of India*, 1959, vol. 1, p. 177. This publication is the official organ of the Bharat Sadhu Samaj.
[34] But no government grants of money are made to this association.

One of the main functions of the Samaj is to restore the dignity of the ascetic orders by eliminating the undesirable elements. Referring to the saffron-clad impostors who have been exploiting the orthodox and devout Hindu public, one statement promised: "A list of *sadhus* and *sannyasis* is being compiled which will eliminate these bad elements and save the common man from their mischiefs and misdoings."[35] The constitution adopted in 1960 mentions the following among the objects of the organization: the promotion of the spiritual progress of society, the raising of moral standards, the development of appreciation for the cultural heritage of India, the promotion of sanitation in places of worship and pilgrimage, and the safeguarding of the administration of temples and *maths*. In addition to these religious objects, the following is listed separately: "To cooperate in the constructive activities associated with the economic and social development programs of the country, in ways suited to the position of *sadhus*; and (1) To find and develop avenues of voluntary service for the citizens of India in order (a) to promote national self-sufficiency and build up the economic strength of the country, (b) to promote the social welfare of the community and to mitigate the hardships of its less privileged sections; (2) to mobilize the spare time, energy and other resources of the people and direct them into various fields of social and other economic activities."[36]

Planning Minister Nanda's idea of using *sadhus* to carry the message of the Five Year Plans to the villages, reflected in this quotation, has evoked much merriment among the cartoonists of the Indian press. However, the revolutionary nature of the religious changes which are being attempted must not be overlooked. The individualistic *sadhu* who has renounced the world in order to follow the path leading to spiritual liberation for himself is now being charged with responsibility for promoting the economic welfare of society. "As far as I know, our scriptures do not enjoin indifference toward this world," President Rajendra Prasad told a conference of the Bharat Sadhu Samaj. "People like you who have taken to the sacrificial way of life should come forward to guide the people in worldly matters as well."[37] The development of a "social gospel" among this segment

[35] See the pamphlet by Swami Harinarayananand, *Role of Sadhus in India*, Bharat Sadhu Samaj, New Delhi, 1959.

[36] *Bharat Sadhu Samaj Constitution*, 1960, article 2.

[37] Address delivered at the annual conference of the Bharat Sadhu Samaj, Ahmedabad, 1958.

of the Hindu "clergy" would involve a radical transformation of traditional values and practices.

In the context of this chapter, the chief point to be made is that religious reform need not proceed by legislation and state interference, as is so often presupposed in present-day India. The Bharat Sadhu Samaj was clearly formed with official inspiration and encouragement, but this does not detract from its significance or value as an approach to the problem of religious reform. Once established, it can chart its own course. Given the competent leadership which the Samaj now seems to have, and the inherent vitality of Hindu religion, there is reason to believe that substantial progress can be made in bringing the ascetic orders into line with the requirements of the changing times.

A government ecclesiastical department could probably perform *part* of this task faster and more efficiently. But this approach would entail the loss of the more creative impulses within Hindu religion. The Sarvodaya movement of Gandhi and Vinoba Bhave, surely one of the most creative developments in modern Hinduism, could not possibly have emerged from an official ecclesiastical department.[38] Such creative ideas do emerge from religious groups which enjoy the freedom to think and to experiment.

There are a number of devout Hindu intellectuals having no connection with the vested interests in temples, who are deeply convinced that a strict separation of state and religion is necessary for the expression of the essential genius of Hinduism. Hinduism's lack of ecclesiastical organization, they claim, is closely related to its spiritual greatness. If the state imposes organization and regulation, this cannot help but detract from spontaneous religious creativity. While the abuses within Hinduism are deplored, these Hindu leaders would prefer to promote reform from within, at the cost of slower progress, or even to tolerate the abuses, rather than sacrifice the freedom which they regard as essential to the real spiritual life of Hinduism.

---

[38] *Sarvodaya* (literally, "the welfare of all") is the Gandhian term for the ideal society built upon cooperative effort and moral law, as opposed to the emphasis on the state and coercion. One expression of Sarvodaya is Vinoba Bhave's *bhoodan* (land-gift) movement of land reform through the landlords' voluntary sharing with the landless.

PART FOUR

STATE VERSUS RELIGIOUS REGULATION

OF SOCIETY

CHAPTER 10

RELIGION, LAW, AND SECULARISM

Traditional Hinduism and Islam were far more than "religions" in the usual meaning of the word. Historically, both came very close to being total ways of life in the most literal sense; they prescribed detailed regulations for virtually every act of human existence, the great events which mark the life cycle and the day-to-day routine. All-pervasive religion regulated not only general social relationships but the whole area of what we now call criminal and civil law. In the Hindu or Muslim state the king had no legislative powers. The function of the state was to enforce the law but not to make it, since the law was already complete, enshrined in the sacred texts and in immemorial custom. Despite static conceptions of divinely ordained law, it did change by imperceptible degrees in response to new situations. Changes in practice generally came first, and these were later rationalized by the interpretations of the doctors of the law or the writers of commentaries. But the state had no direct role in this process.

Since the early nineteenth century, the impact of the West has produced drastic changes in the countries where Hinduism and Islam are professed. The rise of Asian nationalism in some ways intensified the processes of modernization begun by the European imperialist powers. The new independent states now seek to forge themselves into modern sovereign states after the western pattern. While religion in many cases served as a useful ally of Asian nationalism, its role must now be circumscribed if these modern states are to emerge. And nowhere is the tension more evident than in the area of law, where the authority of traditional religion and the modern sovereign state lay claim to the same territory. The outcome is not in doubt; one side represents the static past and the other the dynamic present and future. The secularization of law is thus an important facet of the modernization of the state. The consequent

restriction of religion to the area of private faith and worship constitutes a religious reformation of the first magnitude, although imposed
by the state.

India is the historic meeting-place of these two great civilizations,
Hinduism and Islam. Hindu and Muslim law continue to regulate
important civil matters such as marriage, divorce, adoption, guardianship, and inheritance. The existence of *two* major religious communities and systems of religious law within the state, and the
consequent minority problem, inevitably produces complications in
the process of modernization. A further complication is that India
is committed to becoming not only a modern sovereign state but a
secular state in the liberal democratic tradition. Some of the drastic,
even ruthless, methods which have been elsewhere adopted to achieve
the former objective (as in the case of Turkey) are thus denied to it.
India must strive to attain the same ends within the procedural
framework of parliamentary democracy. While the idea of the
secular state certainly implies secular law, it also contains a conception of freedom of religion which for many present-day Hindus and
Muslims has a direct bearing on the continuance of their respective
religious laws. In order to understand this problem, it must be
examined in historical perspective, both in relation to the West and
in India itself.

The Problem in Historical Perspective

The secularization of law in the West

The Christian church began very early to develop its own legal
system. In the beginning the bishops acted as arbitrators of disputes
with no power beyond their spiritual authority to enforce decisions.
Under Constantine, however, these decisions came to be regarded
as binding. Canon law (church law) continued to evolve as a legal
system following the collapse of the Roman Empire and reached its
peak of influence during the Middle Ages.[1] Canon law drew its
substance from a variety of sources: the scriptures, the traditions of
the church fathers, papal decretals, the legislation of church councils,
the customs of the clergy, and also secular legal sources such as

[1] H. D. Hazeltine, Ecclesiastical Courts," *Encyclopedia of the Social Sciences,*
1937, vol. 3, p. 309. Cf. Rene A. Wormser, *The Law,* Simon and Shuster, New York,
1949, p. 189.

Roman law, Germanic law, and feudal custom.[2] This great variety of sources, plus the accumulated legal work of centuries, produced an enormous mass of unintegrated material. The first comprehensive codification was made around the year 1140 by Gratian, a Benedictine monk of Bologna. His *Decretum* served as the foundation for the later *Corpus juris canonici*, the officially approved body of canon law of the medieval church.

The scope of the canon law was impressive indeed, as was the jurisdiction of the ecclesiastical courts (bishops' courts and papal courts) which enforced it. In the beginning the church had limited its jurisdiction to ecclesiastical matters. "In course of time, however, the church went beyond the purely ecclesiastical sphere and entered the domain of lay jurisdiction in criminal cases; and as an important aspect of its rise to a position of dominance in the medieval world it ultimately acquired a jurisdiction which was truly criminal in character and so extensive in scope that it materially curtailed the criminal jurisdiction of medieval territorial states."[3] The church claimed jurisdiction over all offenses of the clergy; but with regard to the laity certain distinctions were made. In cases of heresy, schism, apostasy, and simony, that is, offenses directed against the faith, the church claimed jurisdiction even though these were punished by the secular tribunals. Offenses such as perjury, blasphemy, sacrilege, sorcery, usury, adultery, and fornication were in a different category—here the church could exact the punishments recognized by secular law only if the state did not prosecute.[4]

In the twelfth and thirteenth centuries the ecclesiastical courts exercised an equally impressive civil jurisdiction. Marriage was a sacrament of the church, and as such all questions of engagements to marry, dower, status, legitimation, and divorce came under its jurisdiction. The foundation of benefices, tithes, wills, and contracts confirmed by oath also were dealt with according to canon law. The basis for ecclesiastical courts' jurisdiction in all of these matters was the religious aspect involved. The taking of an oath to confirm a contract was a religious act. In matters affecting last wills and testaments, it must be remembered that the chief wealth was in land, which under the feudal system could not be left by will. Hence a will

[2] H. D. Hazeltine, "Canon Law," *Encyclopedia of the Social Sciences*, 1937, vol. 2, p. 182.
[3] *Loc. cit.*   [4] *Ibid.*, p. 183.

could only deal with personal property. The church courts customarily allotted one-third of the deceased man's personal property to the priests, so that their prayers would help his soul to leave purgatory at an early date.[5]

The stability of the substantive canon law and the enlightened civil procedure of the church courts often combined to make the ecclesiastical legal system more popular than the secular one. The struggle for civil jurisdiction between the two systems was a feature of the larger church-state conflict in all the countries of Europe. As the states became stronger they centralized and improved their system of courts and enlarged their civil jurisdiction, although they generally recognized the church's jurisdiction over marriage. Hazeltine noted: "From the end of the fifteenth century the growth of temporal justice, at the expense of spiritual justice, was ever more marked: one by one many of the subject matters of the civil jurisdiction of the church were absorbed by the civil courts of temporal powers."[6]

Although the power of the ecclesiastical courts declined, canon law exerted a powerful influence on the development of secular law, especially in the laws of possession, contract, and marriage. In the conflict between canon law and Roman law the latter eventually won out, "but not until canon law had made such deep inroads into the legal systems of Europe, including England, that it remains as one of the most important ancestors of our own legal system."[7] Many of the principles of medieval canon law thus continue to be operative, although now embodied in the secular laws of many states.

After the Reformation of the sixteenth century, the general tendency in both Catholic and Protestant states was to limit the jurisdiction of the church courts to ecclesiastical discipline and related matters. But this was by no means a rapid or uniform process. In medieval England ecclesiastical courts punished numerous offenses such as adultery, procuration, incontinency, incest, defamation, sorcery, witchcraft, swearing, drunkenness, and profaning the Sabbath. This wide criminal jurisdiction continued in full force until abolished by Parliament in 1641, only to be restored twenty years later.[8] Unnatural offenses and bigamy, however, were made felonies by the

---

[5] John Maxcy Zane, *The Story of Law*, Ives Washburn, New York, 1927, p. 219.
[6] Hazeltine, "Canon Law," *op. cit.*, p. 184.
[7] Wormser, *op. cit.*, p. 189.
[8] H. D. Hazeltine, "Ecclesiastical Courts," *op. cit.*, p. 311.

beginning of the seventeenth century, and other offenses mentioned above gradually passed to the jurisdiction of the lay courts. Jurisdiction in cases of perjury, defamation, and brawling by laymen in church was not removed from the ecclesiastical courts until the nineteenth century, 1860 in the case of the last offense. With regard to civil law, it was not until 1857 that Parliament removed the jurisdiction in divorce and testamentary cases from the church courts and vested it in the Probate, Divorce, and Admiralty Division of the High Court of Justice.[9]

At the present time, the state courts in European countries generally have exclusive jurisdiction in criminal cases. Theoretically the Church of England courts still have jurisdiction with respect to certain kinds of immorality, but in practice this is exercised only in cases involving the clergy. Significant power is still present, however, for "the duly rendered sentences of the ecclesiastical courts are enforced by the state, even to the extent of imprisoning those who disobey its lawfully issued judgments."[10] Throughout Europe the state courts generally have exclusive jurisdiction in civil cases, and the only discipline exercised by the ecclesiastical courts over the laity is penitential. In Spain, Portugal, and Peru, however, the courts of the Roman Catholic church still have competence within certain limits in cases of marriage and divorce, and the decisions are enforced by the state.

In considering the development of India's legal system, it is necessary to remember this often uneven progress of the secularization of law in the West. India is a few paces behind the western world in the evolution of its law, but it is on the same path which the West itself has trodden.[11]

The early legal system of British India

The seventeenth-century official of the British East India Company had come to a country in which two ancient and very different systems of law prevailed, each rooted in a religion which claimed the totality of life for its proper jurisdiction. Law was an integral part of both Hinduism and Islam.

[9] *Ibid.,* pp. 311-312.
[10] Leo Pfeffer, *Church, State and Freedom,* Beacon Press, Boston, 1953, p. 47.
[11] William A. Robson, *Civilization and the Growth of Law,* Macmillan Company, New York, 1935, p. 51.

Hindu law is of great antiquity and is derived from several sources: (1) *Shruti*, that is, the divinely inspired Vedas, some of which date back to the middle of the second millennium B.C.; (2) the *Dharmashastras*, or law codes, the oldest and most influential of which is the Code of Manu written sometime between 200 B.C. and 100 A.D.; and (3) custom.[12] The central conception of Hindu law is *dharma*, and it is important to grasp the essentials of this conception. S. V. Gupte wrote: "The law of the Dharmashastras is a mixture of morality, religion and law. The distinction drawn by modern jurists between positive law and moral law is not observed in Hindu jurisprudence. According to Hindu conception, law in the modern sense was only a branch of *dharma*, a term of the widest significance. The term *dharma* includes religious, moral, social and legal duties and can only be defined as the whole duty of man; positive law was therefore regarded as only a branch of *dharma*."[13] Indicative of the broad meaning of *dharma* is the fact that it is impossible adequately to translate it by a single English word, although duty, virtue, religious creed, religion, justice, and law have all been used.[14]

Muslim law (*shari'ah*) is derived from four sources: (1) the Koran; (2) *hadith*, the teachings of the prophet Mohammed preserved by tradition and handed down by authorized persons; (3) *ijma*, the consensus of those learned in Islamic law; and (4) *qiyas*, deduction by analogy from the first three sources when they do not apply to a particular case.[15] The comprehensive scope of this law was such that virtually every aspect of life was brought under the regulation of the faith. Writing of the integrating power of Islam among the Arabs of an earlier period, W. C. Smith comments: "The center of this unifying force was religious law, which regulated within its powerful and precise sweep everything from prayer rites to property rights."[16]

[12] Ludwik Sternbach, "Law," *India, Pakistan, Ceylon,* ed. W. Norman Brown, Cornell University Press, Ithaca, N.Y., 1951, pp. 119-120.

[13] S. V. Gupte, *Hindu Law in British India*, N. M. Tripathi Ltd., Bombay, 1947, p. 3.

[14] D. Mackenzie Brown, *The White Umbrella: Indian Political Thought from Manu to Gandhi*, University of California Press, Berkeley, 1953, pp. 15-17. See also P. V. Kane, *History of Dharmashastra*, Bhandarkar Oriental Research Institute, Poona (4 vols., 1930-1946), vol. 2, p. 2.

[15] Sternbach, *op. cit.*, p. 123.

[16] Wilfred Cantwell Smith, *Islam in Modern History*, Princeton University Press, Princeton, 1957, p. 29.

Islamic law, more than any other agency, effectively integrated the ethnically diverse peoples which later embraced the faith.[17]

India at the beginning of the seventeenth century had none of the essential factors which would have been conducive to the secularization of law such as took place in the West. Effective political unification was lacking. There was no law available based on non-religious sources like the secular laws of Europe (based on Roman or Germanic law, or feudal custom). Not only was all law religious law but there were *two* widely differing systems of religious law. Both of these systems sought to regulate every detail of life with a thoroughness never approached by Christian canon law. Custom, the one possible source of secular law, was generally absorbed by religion.

Christianity from the beginning recognized two distinct spheres of life, each with its own functions, powers, and institutions: the temporal and the spiritual, the state and the church. In Europe there were two systems of law and courts, secular and ecclesiastical. Because of this theoretical and institutional duality there could be and was conflict between the two. In general, Hinduism and Islam did not recognize this duality, so there was little conflict. Without the conflict there could be no triumph of the secular.

Upon their arrival in India, the British found both of these ancient systems of law in at least partial operation. However, during the first century of the East India Company's exercise of judicial powers (1661 to 1765) the courts applied only the law of England, only in the small settlements of Madras, Bombay, and Calcutta, and for the most part only to European British subjects. In 1765 the company obtained from the puppet Mughal emperor at Delhi the *diwani* (vice regency) with governmental powers over Bengal, Bihar, and Orissa. After an unsuccessful experiment of delegating the administration of the land revenue and civil justice to two Indian officers, in 1772 the company decided to "stand forth as *Diwan*" and discharge these functions directly through its own officers. Warren Hastings thereupon proceeded to establish a new system of courts of justice.[18]

In the provinces of the Mughal Empire civil law was administered by the *diwan*, but the function of maintaining law and order and

[17] H. A. R. Gibb, *Mohammedanism*, New American Library, New York, 1955, p. 17.
[18] George C. Rankin, *Background to Indian Law*, Cambridge University Press, Cambridge, 1946, pp. 1-3. M. P. Jain, *Outlines of Indian Legal History*, Delhi University Press, Delhi, 1952, pp. 60-61.

enforcing the criminal law was exercised by another officer, the *nizam*. These latter powers also were obtained by the company, and the courts set up by Hastings in 1772 were based on this well-established division of jurisdiction. In each district there was created a *Diwani Adalat* to apply civil law and a *Nizamat Adalat* with criminal jurisdiction. Superior courts were established to hear appeals from these district courts.[19]

The criminal law enforced by the *Nizamat Adalat* was the Muslim law, which the British regarded as defective. The principle of *kisas* or retaliation was applied to wilful killing, and gave to a murdered person's next of kin the right to demand the criminal's death. If the next of kin did not demand it, the death penalty could not be exacted by the public or the state, and *diya* or blood-money was simply paid to the victim's family. Two male eye-witnesses were necessary to establish a charge of murder, but if the defendant were a Muslim, the testimony of non-Muslims would be invalid. Cutting off the criminal's hands was the prescribed penalty for theft, but, as Rankin points out, "the savagery of the penalty was compensated by difficulty in getting a conviction."[20]

At first the company permitted Muslim law officers, *kazis* or *muftis,* to sit as judges in the criminal courts, and the British collectors exercised only a general supervisory control over them. From 1790, however, the company directly assumed criminal jurisdiction, and the Muslim criminal law was continued as part of the public law of the land as it had been under Muslim rulers.[21] This law applied to Hindus as well as to Muslims in Bengal, in Madras, and later on in other parts of India.[22] British officials became the judges, but the Muslim *kazis* continued to serve the courts as authorized exponents of the law, although the judges were able to circumvent their opinions. Gradually a substantial body of secular criminal law was developed through numerous regulations passed by the government in order to supplement and amend the Muslim criminal law. Regula-

[19] Jain, *op. cit.*, pp. 57-66.
[20] Rankin, *op. cit.*, p. 165.
[21] *Ibid.*, p. 164.
[22] In Bombay the situation was quite different, for at the time of annexation by the British, large territories in western India had not been under Mughal rule. Here both the civil and criminal law which was to be applied depended on the religion of the individual involved, Hindu or Muslim. Christians and Parsis came under the English law. Criminal law was thus a personal law in Bombay until 1827, when a uniform criminal code was enacted.

tion 6 of 1832 finally marked the end of the Muslim criminal law as a system of general law applicable to all persons.[23]

The revolutionary legal principle introduced by the British during this period was that of equality before the law. This western conception was diametrically opposed to the basic assumptions of both Hindu and Muslim law. Hindu law assumed the hierarchical caste system, and the ancient codes prescribed different penalties for the same crime, varying with the respective castes of the offender and the person against whom the offense had been committed. Muslim law assumed a basic distinction between the Muslim and the *Kafir* (infidel), as illustrated above. The radically new principle of the equality of all before the law was to lay a solid foundation for the establishment of a common citizenship in a secular state.

The *Diwani Adalats* established by Warren Hastings in 1772, as we have noted, were to apply civil law. In contrast with the decision by which Muslim criminal law became the law of the land, applicable to Hindus as well as to Muslims, Hastings' plan provided that "in all suits regarding marriage, inheritance, the laws of the Koran with respect to Mohammedans, and those of the Shastras with respect to Gentus (Hindus) shall be invariably adhered to."[24] Thus, Hindu law and Muslim law were treated equally, although the granting of this status to the former was bitterly resented by high-ranking Muslims as completely improper in a territory under the (nominal) dominion of the Mughal Emperor.[25] Nevertheless, Hastings' plan prevailed, and soon Brahman pandits were appointed to expound the Hindu law in courts presided over by English officers of the company, just as the *kazis* interpreted and applied the Muslim law.

The judges, administrators who knew very little English law, were completely ignorant of the laws contained in Sanskrit, Persian, and Arabic texts, and thus had to rely heavily on the opinions of the Indian law officers. The judges disliked being in the position of dependence, and there was also reason to believe that the Indian law officers were often open to corruption and bribery. Even if the law officers were thoroughly honest, the legal texts represented such a mass of unintegrated and sometimes conflicting provisions that

[23] Rankin, *op. cit.*, pp. 180-181.
[24] Courtenay Ilbert, *The Government of India*, Clarendon Press, London, 1898, pp. 389-390.
[25] Rankin, *op. cit.*, pp. 4-5.

decisions were bound to be arbitrary. The one remedy for this tangled situation was the preparation of digests of Hindu and Muslim laws, translated into English.

Hastings therefore obtained the services of ten learned pandits who prepared a Code of Hindu Law in Sanskrit, based on the most authoritative texts (1775). This was later translated into Persian and then English. As to Muslim law, Hastings also had an English translation made of the Arabic *Hidaya*. Later, under Governor-General Cornwallis, English translations of the Muslim laws of intestate succession and inheritance (1792) and the Hindu Ordinances of Manu (1794) were made by Sir William Jones. Jones began the preparation of a Digest of Hindu Law but died before its completion; the work was finally finished by his pandit Jaganath. Later scholars continued this work of codification and translation. However, it was not until 1864 that the government discontinued the services of the pandits and *kazis* in the courts of civil justice.[26]

This, then, was the essence of Hastings' plan—the application of Hindu law to Hindus, Muslim law to Muslims, in all matters regarding "inheritance, marriage and caste and other religious usages and institutions." An act of 1781 added to this list cases of succession, contract and dealing between party and party. This system of personal law (as opposed to territorial law) was not without defects. It entirely ignored the fact that the Hindus were and are divided into numerous sects and subsects with differing laws and customs, and that different schools of Hindu law prevail in various parts of India. Similarly, there are two major divisions in Islam, the Shi'as and the Sunnis, as well as local variations in Muslim law and custom. Nevertheless, Hastings' basic plan, although modified in details, has continued in operation to the present time. As M. P. Jain states: "To a very great extent this scheme holds the field today after a period

[26] Jain, *op. cit.*, pp. 490-495. This decision created great resentment among the Muslims, who claimed that according to their usage the presence of *kazis* appointed by the government was required at the celebration of marriages and the performance of certain other rites and ceremonies. Responding to these pressures, the government of India in 1880 enacted the Kazis Act, which empowered the provincial governments to appoint *kazis* for these ceremonial functions. The act did not confer any judicial or administrative powers on the *kazis*, nor did it render their presence necessary at the performance of any ceremony, nor did it prevent any person from discharging the functions of a *kazi*. This act is still in force, and has been extended to certain places in the states of Bombay (now Maharashtra and Gujarat), West Bengal, Uttar Pradesh, Punjab, Madhya Pradesh, and Assam.

of one hundred and eighty years. Today the Hindu law governs the Hindus in topics of marriage, adoption, joint family, debts, partition, inheritance and succession."[27]

It seems clear that the system evolved during the British period tended to rigidify Hindu personal law and to prevent its normal development in accordance with changing social custom. The pandits who served as law officers until 1864 were basically religious teachers, not lawyers, and were given no training for their official work. They tended to rely heavily on the most ancient texts and often neglected the role of usage and custom in Hindu law.

But the same was frequently true of the British judges; Mayne stated that, far from reading modern European legal principles into Hindu law, "My belief is that their influence was exerted in the opposite direction, and that it rather showed itself in the pedantic maintenance of doctrines whose letter was still existing but whose spirit was dying away."[28] Referring to the great influence of the eleventh-century *Mitakshara* in the courts of south India, the same author commented: "The consequence was a state of arrested progress in which no voices were heard unless they came from the tomb."[29] Furthermore, the British were most reluctant to modify Hindu or Muslim law by legislation, fearful of alienating their Indian subjects over religious questions. Thus the Second Law Commission reported in 1855 that it was not advisable to attempt to codify the personal laws: "The Hindu law and the Mohammedan law derive their authority respectively from the Hindu and Mohammedan religion. It follows that as a British legislature cannot make Mohammedan or Hindu religion so neither can it make Mohammedan or Hindu law."[30]

Codification and legislation under the British

Nineteenth-century England was profoundly influenced by Jeremy Bentham, who advocated many legal reforms, but especially the codification of law. India became the testing-ground for the Benthamite principle of codification. In 1833 Lord Macaulay urged upon

[27] *Ibid.*, p. 490.
[28] John D. Mayne, *Hindu Law and Usage*, Higginbothams, Madras, 1900, pp. 42-43.
[29] *Ibid.*, p. 44. See also Justice Gajendragadkar, *The Hindu Code Bill*, Karnatak University, Dharwar, 1951, pp. 10-13.
[30] Quoted in Rankin, *op. cit.*, p. 158.

Parliament India's great need for a code or codes of law. "We do not mean that all the people of India should live under the same law: far from it. We know how desirable that object is but we also know that it is unattainable. . . . But whether we assimilate those systems or not, let us ascertain them, let us digest them. . . . Our principle is simply this—uniformity where you can have it—diversity where you must have it—but in all cases certainty."[31] The Charter Act of that year provided for a legislature with jurisdiction over the whole of India (previously regulations were passed only at the provincial level), and the appointment of a Law Commission in India. The proper instrumentality for carrying out the codification of law had now been created.

Under Macaulay's leadership the Law Commission drafted a penal code based on the English criminal law and submitted it to the government in 1837, but nothing was done by the legislature. In 1858, however, when government was assumed by the crown, in rapid-fire succession the codes were enacted: the Code of Civil Procedure (1859), the Penal Code (1860), and the Code of Criminal Procedure (1861). The Indian Succession Act (1865), based on English law, applied to all those who did not come under either the Hindu or the Muslim inheritance and succession laws—Europeans, Jews, Christians, Armenians, Eurasians, and Parsis. The Indian Contract Act (1872) moved into an area formerly reserved to personal law, and was made applicable to all Hindus, Muslims, and others. In the same year the Indian Evidence Act was passed, and a decade later the codes relating to trusts, transfer of property, and easements.[32]

Although the process of codification seemed to be moving apace, it did not touch the important areas of personal law. Indeed, the Fourth Law Commission reported in 1879 that since this law was mingled with religion for the great mass of the people, no further codification was advisable. Isolated acts had been passed, however, which modified the personal laws. The Caste Disabilities Removal Act of 1850 (also known as the Freedom of Religion Act) set aside the provisions in both the Hindu and the Muslim law by which conversion to another religion meant forfeiture of inheritance rights. The Hindu Widows' Remarriage Act (1856) legalized the remarriage of a Hindu widow.

[31] *Ibid.*, pp. 136-137.
[32] Jain, *op. cit.*, pp. 452-485.

In the twentieth century further legislation was passed, much of which sought to improve the social status of Hindu women, such as the Hindu Women's Rights to Property Act (1937) and the Hindu Married Women's Right to Separate Residence and Maintenance Act (1946).[33] It must be remembered that these last measures, unlike the former ones, were passed by a legislature in which the large majority of the members were Indians. Thus, despite the general reluctance of the British rulers to legislate in this field, these and other acts did modify the Hindu personal law; the changes in Muslim law were exceedingly few.[34]

The Problem in Present-Day India

Important areas of civil law, including marriage, divorce, inheritance, succession, thus remain under the religious personal laws. On a given point relating to inheritance, for example, three entirely different laws are applied by the courts to a Hindu, a Muslim, and a Christian. India is committed by its Constitution to the elimination of this system of personal laws. Thus, in the Directive Principles of State Policy, article 44, we find: "The state shall endeavor to secure for the citizens a uniform civil code throughout the territory of India." In this part of the chapter we shall discuss the steps which have been taken toward this objective and the issues which these steps have created for the secular state.

The Special Marriage Act and the Hindu Code Bill

The most important developments since independence concern the codification of Hindu law as a necessary step before Hindu, Muslim, and other personal laws can yield to a uniform code. At the same time a different, more direct approach is being made to a uniform civil code, based on legislation passed in the nineteenth century. We shall first consider this direct approach.

The Special Marriage Act of 1872 provided for a civil marriage before a registrar between persons neither of whom professed the Hindu, Buddhist, Sikh, Jain, Muslim, Jewish, Parsi, or Christian religion. The marriage could be solemnized in any form, provided that each party said to the other in the presence of the registrar and

[33] Gajendragadkar, *op. cit.*, pp. 22-23.
[34] None of the changes in Muslim law dealt with questions of social reform as did the Hindu law legislation.

witnesses, "I (A) take thee (B) to be my lawful wife (or husband)." Before the marriage could be solemnized, both the bridegroom and the bride had to make declarations in the prescribed form that they did not profess any of the religions mentioned above. The basic object of the act was to make legal provision for marriages celebrated in repudiation of personal laws. Inter-caste marriages among Hindus or marriages across religious lines (for example, a Hindu with a Muslim) were not permitted by personal laws. All who wished to marry under the Special Marriage Act were therefore compelled to renounce their religion in order to escape the restrictive provisions of their personal laws.[35]

The Special Marriage Act of 1954 seeks the same objects as the old act but does not require any denial of faith by the individual in order to come under its provisions. Furthermore, in the case of a valid marriage already contracted according to personal law, it is possible for the parties to apply for the registration of their marriage under the act so that its provisions become applicable to them. Among these provisions are: liberalized grounds for divorce, the automatic severance from a joint family of a Hindu who marries under the act, and a new legal basis for succession to property—the Indian Succession Act (based on English law) rather than the Hindu law of succession or other personal law. In the debate in the Lok Sabha, the law minister, C. C. Biswas, pointed out that when two people of different religions married, it would not be possible to apply the personal law of either party. It was therefore necessary to make some other provision in matters such as succession.[36]

The Special Marriage Act of 1954 is thus, in a sense, a uniform civil code in embryo. Prime Minister Nehru described it as a first step toward bringing about uniformity in social observances. Those who voluntarily decided to come under the provisions of the act became a kind of community to which all Indians could belong without giving up their religion in any way. In regard to certain important functions such as marriage and succession, they gave up their personal law but not their religion.[37]

[35] Mayne, *op. cit.*, pp. 74-75. Act 30 of 1923 amended this act so that certain of its provisions could be secured by those *professing* the Hindu, Buddhist, Sikh, or Jain religions.

[36] *Times of India*, September 16, 1954.

[37] *Loc. cit.* The act was strongly criticized by orthodox Hindus and Muslims alike for the effect which it would have on personal laws. Indicative of the type

Although the Special Marriage Act is a direct step toward a uniform civil code, it is of course a voluntary and permissive piece of legislation which people may or may not accept. The number of Indian citizens who come under its provisions represents an extremely small percentage of the total population. In seeking to achieve the secularization of civil law, the major effort must therefore be directed at the modification of the personal laws themselves in the direction of uniformity. This brings us to the subject of the Hindu Code Bill and the bills which succeeded it.

During most of the British period the government rejected proposals that Hindu personal law be codified. Hindu law was thus far from uniform throughout India. Baroda had a Hindu Code different from that of the rest of India. In Kerala and Mysore the Hindu law with regard to women's property rights differed from that found in other areas. Two principal schools of Hindu law existed: (1) the Dayabhaga school, which prevailed in Bengal and Assam, and (2) the Mitakshara school, with four main subdivisions, throughout the rest of India. The two schools differed in the matter of joint family property, and succession and inheritance laws, and the differences were by no means trivial. As one authority put it: "Anyone who compares the Dayabhaga with the Mitakshara will observe that the two works differ in very vital points, and that they do so from the conscious application of completely different principles."[38] Clearly, the most pressing need was to introduce greater uniformity in the sphere of Hindu law itself before reaching out toward a uniform civil law for all communities.

The history of the Hindu Code Bill is a checkered one. In 1941 the government of India appointed a Hindu Law Committee with

---

of criticism was the statement of M. Mohammed Ismail, president of the Indian Union Muslim League, who appealed to all Muslims to observe April 29, 1955, as "Shariat Law Preservation Day." He urged that they send telegrams to the president and prime minister requesting that steps be taken to exempt Muslims from the operation of the Special Marriage Act. Mr. Ismail commented: "The spokesman of the government (Mr. Nehru) . . . stated that the enacting of the Special Marriage Act was only the beginning of the process of replacing the Muslim Shariat and other personal laws by uniform civil code. This is really a serious and grave matter. Muslims hold religion as the most valuable thing in life and their whole life is governed by their religion. Shariat or Personal Law is a vital part of their religion and they cannot conceive of the possibility of the abrogation of Shariat Law on any account." *The Hindu*, April 27, 1955.

[38] Mayne, *op. cit.*, pp. 54-55.

Sir B. N. Rau as chairman. The Rau committee, as it came to be known, recommended the codification of Hindu law in gradual stages, beginning with the laws of intestate succession and marriage. Drafts of these bills produced by the committee were introduced in the central legislature in 1943 but were eventually allowed to lapse because of opposition from the orthodox Hindus. However, the committee was reappointed, toured the country extensively taking evidence from representative individuals and associations, and after three years of hard work submitted its report with the draft Hindu Code Bill. The bill was introduced in the old central assembly in 1947 just before the partition of India, but the tremendous upheavals which accompanied the latter event made it necessary to shelve the measure for the time being.[39]

The bill was finally reported out by the select committee of the Constituent Assembly (Legislative) in 1948, after which it was debated at length on the floor, with no little use of the filibuster and other delaying tactics by some orthodox Hindu members. Despite the able leadership of the law minister, Dr. B. R. Ambedkar, the bill failed to reach the final stages of enactment, and in September 1951 it was dropped by the government. In announcing this decision, Prime Minister Nehru pleaded shortness of time as the reason, although a news article suggested that "there was no doubt that government have responded, though only partially, to the pressure of public opinion against the bill."[40] Others believed that the real reason was simply the approaching general elections. The dropping of the bill was the occasion for Dr. Ambedkar's resignation from the cabinet, and also for Swami Satyananda Saraswathi's giving up his ten-day-old fast. The swami had undertaken his fast outside the Parliament chamber to protest against the Hindu Code Bill.[41]

In the general elections campaign of 1951-1952, however, Nehru took a strong stand on the issue and repeatedly declared that he would never disown the Hindu Code Bill. In his statements he frequently emphasized the progressive social attitudes behind the provisions of the bill. "Thus, the Hindu Code Bill, which has given rise to so much argument, became a symbol of the conflict between progress and reaction in the social domain. I do not refer to any partic-

---

[39] Renuka Ray, "The Background of the Hindu Code Bill," *Pacific Affairs,* 1952, vol. 25, pp. 273-275.
[40] *The Hindu,* September 20, 1951.　　[41] *Ibid.,* September 27, 1951.

ular clause of the bill . . . but rather to the spirit underlying that bill. This was a spirit of liberation and of freeing our people and, more especially, our womenfolk, from outworn customs and shackles that bound them."[42] Shortly after the election of the new Parliament, the main parts of the code were introduced as separate bills and were finally passed in rapid succession by heavy majorities. In 1955 and 1956 the following received legislative approval: the Hindu Marriage Bill, the Hindu Succession Bill, the Hindu Minority and Guardianship Bill, and the Hindu Adoptions and Maintenance Bill. Having noted the background and the tortuous course of these measures through the legislative process, we may now turn our attention to their implications for the secular state.

Hindu marriage, divorce, adoption and succession

The debate on this legislation which took place both in Parliament and from public platforms was not centered in the issue of the secular state. Although the question of the effect on Hindu religion was generally present to a certain extent, the problems which engaged the attention of most participants in the debate were of a social nature. They were more concerned with the probable effect on the Hindu social structure of such provisions as divorce, inter-caste marriages, women's inheritance rights, and provisions affecting the joint family system. Codification of Hindu law was not the central issue; it was the progressive social provisions which sought to modify (some said "destroy") the traditional Hindu social pattern. Thus *The Hindu* complained editorially: "The object with which the Hindu Code Committee was first set to work was to codify and simplify the personal law of the Hindus, not to amend it in conformity with the promptings of social reform."[43] Although we are here concerned only with the aspects which touched upon the secular state, the discussion should not be interpreted as implying that these were the most prominent aspects of the debate.

One of the anomalous situations created by the debate in Parliament was the role assumed by the law minister who piloted the bills. An official of the secular state, he became an interpreter of Hindu religion, quoting and expounding the ancient Sanskrit scriptures in

[42] Speech of October 18, 1951, *Presidential Address to the Indian National Congress*, pp. 9-10.
[43] *The Hindu*, December 10, 1954.

defense of his bills. In a speech on the Hindu Marriage Bill, H. V. Pataskar explained the Hindu concept of *dharma* and contrasted it with the elements of dogma in Christianity and Islam. He urged that the objections raised by opponents of the bill were based on a rigid interpretation of the Sanskrit texts, and this was attributable to the influence of these other religions which stressed their sacred scriptures as the final authority.[44] The law minister quoted from the Bhagavad Gita, the *Arthashastra*, the *Manu Smriti*, and the *Narada Smriti* in order to support the provision for divorce in the bill.

Other members of Parliament were quick to take the minister to task for this approach. Acharya Kripalani pointed out that the search for religious authority for legislation was not in keeping with the secular state. "We call our state a secular state. A secular state goes neither by scripture nor by custom. It must work on sociological and political grounds." V. Muniswamy decried the fact that both proponents and opponents of the bill based their arguments on the Vedas. He chided: "I am submitting with all respect to the honorable minister of law that the trouble started only with him. I should submit that there was no necessity to bring in quotations from the Vedas to introduce the bill."[45] Once the law minister had chosen this approach, all the opponents of the bill very readily followed suit. Mr. Muniswamy quoted a Tamil proverb: "A man gave half an anna for a beggar to dance and then had to give one anna to stop the dance because it was so awkward."

Furthermore, if the arguments in support of legislation are based on ancient scriptures, one must logically accept the authority in its entirety. Muniswamy pointed out that isolated verses in the Bhagavad Gita might be used, but the basic framework was totally opposed to progressive legislation. "In the very first chapter of the Gita you will find Arjuna telling Krishna, 'If I start fighting against my friends, then there will be inter-caste marriages, therefore I will not fight.' . . . If you want to quote the Gita, therefore, you must be prepared to accept the caste system."[46]

Delivering the presidential address at the All India Convention on the Hindu Code in April 1955, Dr. Radhabinod Pal emphasized the

[44] *Lok Sabha Debates*, 1955, part 2, vol. 4, cols. 6476-6477.
[45] *Ibid.*, col. 7343.
[46] *Ibid.*, col. 7347.

same point. "If the legislature is thinking of reverting to the Vedic age in respect of the Hindu law then I believe many other changes will have to be introduced and I do not think the particular change proposed in the code will be at all justifiable."[47] Muniswamy's attitude toward those who dreaded any alteration of ancient principles was humorously expressed: "Some of the people say, do not touch the Vedas, do not touch the principles of the Vedas, and so on. I should like to tell them that I quite approve of what they say, and I would tell them, keep the Vedas untouched not only now but forever. Then only we shall be able to make any progress."[48]

The Hindu Marriage Bill contained three provisions which represented revolutionary departures from the principles of traditional Hindu law: inter-caste marriage, monogamy, and divorce. Inter-caste marriages had already been legalized by the Hindu Marriages Validating Act of 1949, and this position was reaffirmed in the new legislation. Hindu bigamous marriages had already been prohibited by state legislation in Bombay (1946) and Madras (1949), and the new bill sought to extend the principle to the whole country.

The provisions in the Hindu Marriage Bill for divorce elicited a lively debate in Parliament over whether Hindu marriage is a sacrament. N. C. Chatterjee, then leader of the Hindu Mahasabha, quoted many modern authorities on Hindu law to show that in the Hindu conception, marriage is regarded as one of the ten *sanskaras* or sacraments, necessary for the regeneration of men of the three highest castes, and the only sacrament for women and Shudras. According to this conception "marriage is not a mere contract; it is a part of the life of the soul." Chatterjee made a fervent appeal to the Parliament: "Manu himself says that Vedic marriage is a *sanskara*. That is a solemn injunction. It is an inviolable union, an indissoluble union; it is an interminable union; it is an eternal fellowship. . . . In all humility . . . I appeal to all sections of the House, don't tamper with the Hindu sacramental marriage and introduce divorce into it."[49] Divorce was an institution completely foreign to the thinking of the ancient Hindu law-givers, Manu and Yajnavalkya, who were "God-given, God-intoxicated men, inspired by . . . intense devotion to eternal values."[50]

[47] *The Hindu*, April 11, 1955.
[48] *Lok Sabha Debates*, 1955, part 2, vol. 4, col. 7347.
[49] *Ibid.*, col. 6855.   [50] *Ibid.*, col. 6536.

To these assertions the law minister replied, rather ineffectually, that the Sanskrit *sanskara* was not the exact equivalent of the English word "sacrament" as generally understood by Christians. Prime Minister Nehru, on the other hand, readily admitted that Hindu marriage was sacramental, a sacrament being something which had religious significance, a religious ceremony. Nehru then went on to neutralize Mr. Chatterjee's argument by insisting that not only marriage but all forms of human relationship should have an element of sacrament; more so in the case of the intimate relationship of husband and wife. But is it a sacrament "to tie up people to bite each other and to hate each other?"[51] The bill was passed.

During the debate on the Hindu Adoptions and Maintenance Bill, a much-disputed point involved the provision for the adoption of daughters as well as sons. The law minister, Pataskar, declared: "It is as a result of wrong readings of some of the original Sanskrit texts that we have regarded the adoption of a daughter as something which is irreligious."[52] He then quoted from the texts *Dattaka Mimansa* and *Sanskar Kausthuba* in order to establish his point, and asserted that although not commonly practiced among Hindus, the adoption of daughters was not inconsistent with any religious belief.

N. C. Chatterjee and other conservative Hindus, however, maintained that adoption among Hindus was based on a spiritual concept, namely, the necessity of having a son to offer *pindas* (oblations) after the father's death, a function which could not possibly be performed by a daughter. Another member of Parliament, Mr. Barman, stated: "My objection is that after all this law of adopting a son as it obtains now under the Hindu shastras has been introduced into Hindu customs because of some religious beliefs, and in *Dayabhaga* it is said: '*Putrarthey kriatey Bharjya, Putra Pinda Prayojaka.*' That is, a man requires a son, a man marries because he requires a son, a son is required because of the religious performances, the oblations that the son can offer for the salvation of the father after his death. That is the religious foundation for adoption according to Hindu law and Hindu shastras, and it is for that reason that if a man has got a son, he cannot adopt another, and even if he had got no son, he cannot accept a girl."[53] Although Pataskar was

---

[51] *The Hindu*, May 7, 1955.
[52] *Lok Sabha Debates*, 1956, part 2, vol. 10, col. 2854.
[53] *Ibid.*, cols. 2979-2980.

again accused of trying to destroy the Hindu religion by this bill, he insisted that the *Dattaka Mimansa* was an authoritative Hindu text, and that the adoption of daughters was valid.[54] What would have happened had no text been available to the law minister of a secular state can only be left to conjecture. The bill was passed.

The Hindu Succession Bill introduced another significant innovation, namely, the granting to the daughter of rights as a simultaneous heir along with the son, widow, etc. Under the old Hindu family system a daughter never received a part of the father's estate, the assumption being that she was either already a member of another family (if married) or soon would be. The Muslim law of succession, on the other hand, did grant such rights to daughters. In the debate in Parliament on the Hindu Succession Bill, several members claimed to see in the measure a wholesale engrafting of a principle "more Mohammedan than the Mohammedan Law." It was an attempt to impose certain aspects of the *shari'ah* (Muslim law) on Hindus.[55] Despite such protests, the bill was passed.

The points raised over divorce and the Hindu sacramental marriage, the adoption of daughters, and the granting of succession rights to daughters, have been cited in order to illustrate the numerous religious implications of personal law. The critics who stressed the view that the Hindu law derives not only its authority but its content from the religious tenets of Hinduism are in fact supported by the unbroken tradition of Hindu legal scholarship. The constant effort of orthodox scholars has been to emphasize the spiritual and cosmic basis of the regulations of the law. The following definition of Dharmashastra, found in a book published in 1952, illustrates the point: "Dharmashastra is a comprehensive code to regulate human conduct in accordance with the unalterable scheme of Creation, and to enable everyone to fulfill the purpose of his birth. The whole life of man, considered both as an individual and as a member of groups (small and large) as well as man's relations to his fellow men, to the rest of animated creation, to superhuman beings, to the cosmos generally and ultimately to God come within the purview of Dharmashastra."[56]

[54] *Ibid.*, col. 2991.
[55] *The Hindu*, May 7, 1955.
[56] K. V. Rangaswami Aiyangar, *Some Aspects of the Hindu View of Life*, 1952, p. 62.

J. D. M. Derrett, however, suggested that in the context of civil law, Hindu jurisprudence in some cases deliberately utilized religious doctrines in order to justify rules which on purely secular grounds were found to be sound and desirable. Furthermore, historically, Hindu law achieved an authority quite independent of its formal religious basis. The Buddhists ridiculed the alleged authority of the Vedas but apparently followed the regulations of the Hindu law regarding civil disputes and other matters. "Thus, while the authority which justified the application of the law was admittedly religious, the rules themselves could and in fact did persist by virtue of their own merit and not merely by reason of a superstitious sanction attaching to their alleged source."[57] If this interpretation of Hindu law were to gain broader acceptance in present-day India, it would surely make the task of reform less painful to the religious-minded.

Interpretations of Hindu law legislation

N. C. Chatterjee frequently complained that, despite the fact that Nehru's government prided itself on its secularism, the legislation modifying Hindu law which it was sponsoring was *communal* in nature.[58] Chatterjee held that it was contrary to the fundamental rights of the Indian Constitution for the state to discriminate by law against a particular religion or community. "Again, why is this attempt to change the personal laws confined to Hindu society alone? Is not this communal legislation repugnant to the clear directive principles of the Constitution that there should be a uniform civil code for all the citizens of India?"[59]

Acharya Kripalani, a leader of the Praja Socialist Party and very far from being a Hindu communalist, took the same position. In the debate on the Hindu Marriage Bill he declared: "If we are a democratic state, I submit we must make laws not for one community alone. Today the Hindu community is not as much prepared for divorce as the Muslim community is for monogamy. . . . Will our government introduce a bill for monogamy for the Muslim community? Will my dear law minister apply the part about monogamy to every community in India? . . . I tell you this is the

[57] J. D. M. Derrett, "Religion and Law in Hindu Jurisprudence," *All India Reporter,* 1954, vol. 41, p. 80.
[58] Speech in Delhi under the auspices of the All India Convention on the Hindu Code, April 15, 1955.
[59] *Ibid.*

democratic way; the other is the communal way. It is not the Mahasabhites who alone are communal; it is the government also that is communal, whatever it may say."[60]

Chatterjee charged that the Congress government professed to hate communalism, but was in fact anxious to enact communal legislation to moralize only one community.[61] Dr. Gokul Chand Narang, one of the speakers at the All India Convention on the Hindu Code, 1955, declared that if Parliament were to launch a program of reasonable social reform applicable to all communities in India, he would have no objection, "but to pass a measure affecting the Hindus alone with votes which will include the votes of non-Hindus, is anything but fair and just."

Evidence is not lacking that many orthodox Hindu leaders regarded the legislation as a deliberate frontal attack on Hindu religion. V. G. Deshpande of the Hindu Mahasabha told Parliament that the various measures constituted a "big conspiracy to encroach upon the personal laws of the Hindus" and a direct attack on Hinduism.[62] Nandlal Sharma of the Ram Rajya Parishad declared that the present government, by changing Hindu law, was perpetrating something so terrible that it had not been attempted even by the Mughal Emperor Aurangzib or the British. He was surprised to hear people who did not believe in the Hindu shastras quoting scripture—"It is like the devil quoting scriptures when it suits him."[63]

Contending that divorce provisions violated the ideal of the Hindu sacramental marriage, Chatterjee declared: "Imbued with western ideas some people in power are seeking to change the basic concepts of Hindu *dharma* by making laws which are repugnant to the basic principles of Hinduism."[64] He noted that all this is being done in the name of secularism. "But what is this secularism? Secularism is not the negation or the destruction of religion." Dealing with the prohibition of bigamous marriage, Chatterjee pointed out that the act would encourage the conversion of Hindus to Islam. Any Hindu who wanted to marry more than one wife could simply embrace

[60] *Lok Sabha Debates*, 1955, part 2, vol. 4, col. 7376.
[61] *Presidential Address to All India Hindu Mahasabha*, 30th session, 1952, New Delhi, p. 14.
[62] *The Hindu*, December 10, 1954.
[63] *Ibid.*, May 4, 1955.
[64] Speech in New Delhi under the auspices of the All India Convention on the Hindu Code, April 15, 1955.

Islam and automatically come under a different personal law which still permitted polygamy. Chatterjee asked: "Is it the intention of the Parliament of India or the government of this country to facilitate and encourage the conversion of Hindus to non-Hindu faiths? This bill, if enacted, will, therefore, accentuate the evils of conversion and disrupt Hindu society."[65]

Most of the critics of the various bills which codified Hindu law could see only these negative aspects—that the legislation would in one way or another prove detrimental to the interests of Hindu religion. They tended to see in the legislation the violation of freedom of religion. Acharya Kripalani, however, perceived an entirely different interpretation of the same facts—the secular state was giving special advantages to the majority religion and community. "If they (members of the legislature) single out the Hindu community for their reforming zeal, they cannot escape the charge of being communalists in the sense that they favor the Hindu community and are indifferent to the good of the Muslim community or the Catholic community in the matter of divorce. Do we want some one community to be in advance of other communities in India, simply because it happens to be in the majority? The charge levelled against Hindu communalists is that they want their community to be in a more advantageous position than other communities."[66] Kripalani's conclusion was inescapable: "Whether the marriage bill favors the Hindu community or places it at a disadvantage, both ways, it becomes a communal measure." If monogamy and divorce are good and desirable features of a marriage law, why favor the Hindus and withhold monogamy from the Muslims and divorce from the Catholics? If, on the other hand, these reforms are not so good and desirable, why punish the Hindus alone?

As we have seen in chapter 4, legislation which prohibits the practice of polygamy among Hindus has been upheld as constitutional by the courts. In *State of Bombay* v. *Narasu Appa*, 1952, the Bombay High Court declared that polygamy could not be regarded as an integral part of Hindu religion. While Hinduism recognizes the necessity of a son to perform certain religious ceremonies after the father's death, Hinduism also provides the possibility of adoption if no son is born to him. The religious necessity of

[65] Speech at the All India Convention on the Hindu Code, April 10, 1955.
[66] *The Hindu*, May 21, 1955.

polygamy is therefore eliminated. The court held, furthermore, that such legislation (in this case enacted in Bombay state) did not discriminate against the Hindus and that it was not contrary to the principle of equality before the law. The constitutional position of the Hindu Marriage Act of 1955 is therefore not in question.

If we are thinking only of the *principles* involved, there can be little doubt but that the critics of this legislation are right. The enactment of civil laws for one community only is discriminatory, it does represent a communal approach, it does undermine the basic principle of equality before the law, it does place the state in a position where it is either persecuting Hinduism or promoting it, depending on one's point of view. Looking at the total picture quite objectively, it is true that the principles of secularism are not being adhered to. But several other comments are in order.

First, it must be remembered that the critics who represent the Hindu Mahasabha, the Jana Sangh, the Ram Rajya Parishad, and other communalist Hindu parties cannot be credited with any real concern for the maintenance of the secular state in India. Leaders of these parties who argued very cogently that the bills discussed above are opposed to the secular state, on other occasions argued that secularism is a curse and that India must become a Hindu state. Motivated largely by a deep-seated distrust of any efforts to change ancient Hindu social usages, these critics are quite willing to buttress their position with any arguments that are handy, including the secular state. Although they are calling for a uniform civil code rather than a codified Hindu law, it is certain that their opposition will be no less vociferous if and when a uniform civil code bill is introduced. The sacramental Hindu marriage and other Hindu socio-religious institutions are not likely to fare better under a uniform civil code than under the measures which have been enacted. Regardless of motives, however, we cannot dismiss arguments which are perfectly valid.

Second, many of the criticisms of the Hindu Code Bill and the bills which succeeded it are in reality criticisms of the whole structure of religious personal law inherited from the British. The communal nature of such personal law, the denial of equality before the law, the different provisions found in the various systems of personal law—these are not innovations introduced by the Hindu Code Bill, but an inherent part of the legal system which goes back to Warren

Hastings' plan of 1772. Nehru's government cannot be blamed for a situation which it did not create but only inherited.

Third, it is clear that a uniform code is the answer to the whole problem. Why has it not been enacted? When asked this question the law minister, Mr. Pataskar, replied that even these bills would apply to 85 per cent of the people, and would thus constitute a big step toward uniformity.[67] The codification of Hindu law was regarded as a preparatory step toward the fulfillment of article 44 of the Constitution. The following exchange with a member of Parliament brought out Nehru's approach. Commenting on the proposal of some that a uniform civil code be enacted, the prime minister declared:

> Well, I should like a civil code which applies to everybody, but . . .
> Mr. More: What hinders?
> Mr. Nehru: Wisdom hinders.
> Mr. More: Not wisdom but reaction hinders.
> Mr. Nehru: The honorable member is perfectly entitled to his view on the subject. If he or anybody else brings forward a Civil Code Bill, it will have my extreme sympathy. But I confess I do not think that at the present moment the time is ripe in India for me to try to push it through. I want to prepare the ground for it and this kind of thing is one method of preparing the ground.[68]

Nehru commented that arguments in favor of a uniform civil code immediately might appear very progressive and advanced, but might prevent the nation from taking even one step in that direction.

Undoubtedly, much of Nehru's hesitation over a uniform civil code derives from his concern that nothing be done which would have an unsettling effect upon the minorities, especially the Muslims. The *shari'ah* (Muslim law) occupies an even more central place within Islamic religion than Hindu law does within Hinduism. As we have noted, Indian Muslims would be likely to regard any alteration at all of their personal law as a grave violation of freedom of religion.[69] With clear memories of the tragic fratricidal Hindu-Muslim conflicts of the recent past, Nehru is understandably cautious. The situation is indeed paradoxical: in order to build up the confidence of religious minorities in the non-communal secular nature of the Indian

[67] *Ibid.*, May 4, 1955.   [68] *Times of India*, September 16, 1954.
[69] For an analysis of this important problem facing the Indian Muslims see chapter 14, "A Report on the Minorities."

state, Nehru is constrained to sacrifice for the time being other significant principles of the secular state such as a uniform civil code. But the day of such a uniform code is coming, and Indian Muslims, like their Hindu and Christian fellow-citizens, and as their coreligionists in other countries have done, should prepare themselves for these inevitable changes.

In conclusion, what can be said of India as a secular state with respect to its civil laws? The right objective of a uniform civil code is being aimed at, and considerable progress has been made through the codification of Hindu law; but serious difficulties remain. India's problem is by no means unique. Thus the state of Israel, despite the European origin of most of its leaders, has a system of rabbinical courts which control all cases of marriage, divorce, and guardianship. According to Pfeffer, the perpetuation of this system of religious courts which existed under Turkish and British rule "has resulted in the continuation of laws that are grotesquely anachronistic and out of place in a modern, democratic republic with a distinctly western orientation."[70]

India's progress must be measured in terms of its starting-point, in terms of what has been done with the situation which was inherited in 1947. In this connection it is not inappropriate to compare the courses of action taken in India and Pakistan. In March 1957 an Indian Christian weekly, *The Guardian* of Madras, made some interesting comments in this regard. The editor referred to two news items which had appeared in the general press during that week. In Pakistan the government had just announced the appointment of a commission under the provisions of the 1956 Constitution to make recommendations "as to the measures for bringing existing law into conformity with the Injunctions of Islam" (article 198). In India the Allahabad High Court had just upheld the Hindu Marriage Act, although one of the petitioners contended that bigamy was an integral part of the Hindu religion. *The Guardian*'s comment was: "While Pakistan is reforming secular law to conform to traditional religion, India is legislating to change traditional practices to be brought into keeping with a modern, progressive outlook."[71]

[70] Leo Pfeffer, *Church, State, and Freedom*, Beacon Press, Boston, 1953, p. 59.
[71] *The Guardian*, Madras, 1957, vol. 35, p. 122. The 1956 Constitution of Pakistan was abrogated, however, following the imposition of military rule in 1958. In 1961 the military government of President Ayub Khan promulgated the Muslim Family Laws Ordinance which, among other things, makes polygamy all but impossible.

CHAPTER 11

CASTE AND THE SECULAR STATE

◇⫘⫘◇

Jawaharlal Nehru, in discussing his conception of the secular state, once wrote: "a caste-ridden society is not properly secular."[1] This chapter investigates government policies toward caste in the light of the secular state. The subject is one of some complexity and can only be dealt with after considering the historical relationships of the caste system to Hindu religion and to the state.

Changing Relationships: Caste and Religion

Is caste to be regarded as an integral part of Hindu religion, or is it simply the social structure which happened to develop in India, ultimately not dissimilar from rigid class systems elsewhere? On one hand, Hutton wrote that "the social habits of caste are inextricably tied up with religion";[2] on the other, is the assertion of Panikkar that the social institutions of the Hindus "are unconnected with their religion and based wholly on law and custom and are therefore secular."[3] It is a matter of considerable importance whether caste is "inextricably tied up" or "unconnected" with Hindu religion. If the latter interpretation is correct, government policies regarding caste have no real relevance to the conception of the secular state. We shall first attempt to define the relationship between caste and traditional Hindu religion, and then move on to consider this relationship under the impact of modern reformist influences.

Caste and traditional Hindu religion

A number of points can be made in support of the view which emphasizes the close association of caste and Hindu religion. In one

[1] *Circular to the Pradesh Congress Committees*, New Delhi, All India Congress Committee, 1954.
[2] J. H. Hutton, *Caste in India: Its Nature, Function, and Origins*, Oxford University Press, Bombay, 1951.
[3] K. M. Panikkar, *Hindu Society at Cross Roads*, Asia Publishing House, Bombay, 1955, p. 3.

of the later Rigvedic hymns, the *Purushasukta*, it is stated that the four original classes emanated from the sacrifice of the Primeval Being. The Brahmans, Kshatriyas, Vaishyas, and Shudras are said to have come respectively from the mouth, the arms, the thighs, and the feet of the Creator. This explanation is repeated with slight variations in most of the later works; in some of them, according to Ghurye, "not only is the origin of the classes interpreted theologically, but also a divine justification is sought to be given to their functions and status."[4] Another writer suggested that the Rigvedic reference was only a poetic image portraying the organic nature of society, but which later came to be interpreted quite differently. "In later ages the Hindu lawgivers, epic poets, and authors of popular religious works persistently maintained this theocratic ideal so that ... people looked on the fourfold caste system as a divine institution to which they should conform if they would save their souls."[5]

Dharma (frequently translated as religion, duty, or law) is the central conception of Hindu religious thought, and has traditionally been closely associated with caste duty. Max Weber wrote that Hinduism did not possess a universally valid ethic, for the religious and moral code (*dharma*) of each caste was different. Each status group had a *dharma* corresponding to its position on the caste scale. There is thus nothing in Hindu thought comparable to the western conception of natural law. Weber noted: "The conception of an 'original sin' was quite impossible in this world order, for no 'absolute sin' could exist. There could only be a ritual offense against the particular *dharma* of the caste."[6] *Dharma* depends, then, upon the caste into which the individual is born. A nineteenth-century observer wrote: "With many Hindus the highest form of religious observance is the complete fulfillment of the claims of caste; and most of them conceive of sin as a breach of caste discipline rather than of moral law."[7]

The Bhagavad Gita, one of the most important of the Hindu sacred scriptures, stresses the supreme merit of performing one's

---

[4] G. S. Ghurye, *Caste and Class in India,* Popular Book Depot, Bombay, 1957, p. 44.

[5] D. S. Sarma, "The Nature and History of Hinduism," *The Religion of the Hindus,* ed. Kenneth W. Morgan, Ronald Press Company, New York, 1953, p. 17.

[6] Max Weber, *The Religion of India: The Sociology of Hinduism and Buddhism,* Free Press, Glencoe, Illinois, 1958, p. 144.

[7] M. A. Sherring, *Hindu Tribes and Castes,* Calcutta, 1881, vol. 3, p. 276.

particular caste duties. "One's own duty (i.e. *dharma* or caste rules), though defective, is better than another's duty well performed." Other scriptures assert that perfection can be attained only by one who fulfills his caste obligations without deviation. The laws of Manu (second century B.C.), according to Dandekar, lay down that "obedience to caste rules is the very essence of *dharma*."[8]

Another important Hindu conception which undergirds the caste system is *karma*. This conception is accepted by almost all Hindus, heterodox as well as orthodox, despite wide divergences on other beliefs. The doctrine of *karma* occupies a central place in Hindu ethical theory. Based on belief in the transmigration of souls, the doctrine of *karma* asserts that every single ethically relevant act produces inevitable consequences which constitute the individual's fate in the next existence.[9] The caste into which the individual is reborn is an important aspect of this ethically-determined fate. Wrong-doing in this life leads to low birth in the next.[10]

The doctrine of *karma* thus justifies caste inequalities as being part of the divine order of the universe. Weber referred to it as "the unique Hindu theodicy of the existing social, that is to say, caste system."[11] The doctrine enabled the orthodox Hindu to regard an untouchable's miserable lot as nothing but his just punishment for sins committed in a previous existence. There was hope for the untouchable, for right action in this life might result in his rebirth in a high caste.[12]

There appears, then, to be considerable evidence to support the thesis that caste is so integral a part of Hinduism that "a Hindu without a caste is almost a contradiction in terms."[13] In terms of traditional Hinduism this statement is for the most part accurate.[14] But it does not take into account the many new developments which have vigorously challenged traditional Hindu society in the past one

[8] R. N. Dandekar, "The Role of Man in Hinduism," *The Religion of the Hindus*, p. 146.

[9] Max Weber regarded the belief in the transmigration of souls and the doctrine of *karma* as the only "dogmatic" doctrines of Hinduism. *Op. cit.*, p. 118.

[10] L. S. S. O'Malley, *Indian Caste Customs*, Cambridge University Press, Cambridge, 1932, p. 18.

[11] Weber, *op. cit.*, p. 118.

[12] *Ibid.*, p. 122.

[13] O'Malley, *op. cit.*, p. 19.

[14] Even so, seventeenth-century Jesuit missionaries found it possible to interpret caste as a social custom without religious significance, and fully observed caste distinctions in dealing with their converts.

hundred and fifty years. In particular, it ignores the work of the Hindu social and religious reformers, many of whom made a deliberate effort to separate caste from Hindu religion.

Caste, religion, and reform

The renascence of Hinduism began with the work of Raja Rammohan Roy in the early part of the nineteenth century, largely as a result of the confrontation of traditional Hinduism with Christianity and western social values.[15] The sectarian movements which emerged were primarily concerned with religious reform, but could not ignore Hindu social institutions which were in open conflict with the new ideas of freedom and equality. The reformers held that religion was not responsible for social injustices, but that the objectionable practices were the excrescences of which Hindu society must be purged.

The Paramahansa Sabha, organized in Bombay in 1840, was committed to the abolition of caste, but it soon failed due to intense opposition. Two decades later Keshab Chandra Sen and his followers were openly celebrating inter-caste marriages.[16] Swami Dayananda Saraswati, founder of the Arya Samaj, raised his voice against caste restrictions and urged that personal merit, not birth, should determine social status. Intelligence and knowledge should entitle a man to be called a Brahman regardless of his caste background. Swami Vivekananda, the first internationally-known apologist of Hinduism, declared in 1893 that while caste had once performed a useful function, it now was only "filling the atmosphere of India with its stench."[17]

Twentieth-century leaders of the Hindu renascence, according to Roland W. Scott, were motivated in their opposition to caste practices by both social idealism and religious self-preservation. A new sense of responsibility for the depressed castes made their uplift an end in itself. But the possibility of their conversion to Christianity or Islam was also a powerful consideration.[18] Gandhi asserted that unless

[15] See J. N. Farquhar, *Modern Religious Movements in India*, Macmillan Company, New York, 1915, and D. S. Sarma, *The Renaissance of Hinduism*, Benares Hindu University, Benares, 1944.

[16] R. C. Majumdar, H. C. Raychaudhuri, and K. Datta, *An Advanced History of India*, Macmillan Company, London, 1950, p. 878.

[17] Swami Vivekananda, *The Complete Works of Swami Vivekananda*, Prabuddha Bharota Office, Almora, 1922, vol. 5, p. 19.

[18] Roland W. Scott, *Social Ethics in Modern Hinduism*, YMCA Publishing House, Calcutta, 1953, p. 161.

untouchability were destroyed it would destroy Hinduism. Any religion was doomed to perish if it could not eradicate "invidious and iniquitous distinctions between man and man."

Dr. B. R. Ambedkar, leader of the depressed classes, insisted that caste, based on the authority of the Vedas and Shastras, was a part of Hindu religion. "To ask people to give up caste is to ask them to go contrary to their fundamental religious notions."[19] This analysis led him to the position that the only hope for the untouchables was to embrace any religion or religions which promised equality of status. Within the mainstream of Hindu reform, such a solution was obviously unacceptable. The religious reformers had to continue their efforts on two fronts: first, the interpretation of caste in more egalitarian terms than those found in the traditional conception, and, second, the interpretation of religion in terms which would facilitate its dissociation from the traditional caste system.

Both Gandhi and Radhakrishnan produced idealized conceptions of caste.[20] Gandhi's theory, however, simply demonstrated to one writer that caste could not readily be dissociated from religion. O'Malley noted: "Hindu reformers who condemn untouchability also maintain that a caste system, though not perhaps in its present form, is essential to Hinduism."[21] By 1936, however, Gandhi's position had shifted significantly, and he was able to declare that caste had nothing to do with religion but was simply a custom, the origin of which was unknown.

The new interpretation of Hindu religion necessitated a radical departure from the traditional understanding of *dharma*. This was no longer defined in terms of caste regulations, but in terms of the free individual's search for truth and morality. Gandhi asserted repeatedly that true morality meant not obedience to rules but finding out the true path for oneself and following it. A metaphysical foundation for the new Hindu social ethic was supplied by the conception of the ultimate unity of all beings in the Absolute. If all individual souls are part of the same ultimate Reality, all are equal. Radhakrishnan could thus construct a new social ethic which emphasized

[19] B. R. Ambedkar, *Annihilation of Caste*, Bharat Bhushan Publishing Press, Bombay, 1937, pp. 37-39.
[20] See especially S. Radhakrishnan, *Eastern Religions and Western Thought*, Oxford University Press, London, 1939, pp. 366-373.
[21] O'Malley, *op. cit.*, pp. 175-177.

the principle of equality on the basis of ancient Hindu metaphysical thought.[22]

Scott rightly observed that "it is possible to understand the dissociation of religion from caste only as a rational procedure in the development of new religious and social attitudes."[23] In the traditional Hindu society, religion and caste were bound together by the strongest ties of mythology, metaphysics, ethics, and ritual. It was only a radically reformulated Hindu religion, which frankly accepted modern democratic values, which could be separated from social institutions based on inflexible inequality.

The history of Hindu religious reform should suffice to indicate clearly that caste is not "inextricably tied up" with Hindu religion. There are obviously many educated Hindus to whom religious values are of great importance, although quite unrelated to rigid social patterns. It must be remembered, however, that the reformulated Hinduism of Gandhi and Radhakrishnan is still far from being the religion of the masses. In terms of popular religion, Dr. M. N. Srinivas wrote in 1956: "If and when caste disappears, Hinduism will also disappear."[24]

Regardless of future developments, it is surely true that, in general, the present connection between caste and religion is a fairly strong one. This relationship cannot be ignored by the secular state in its program of social legislation. We shall deal with this problem in a later section of the chapter. But first we must consider the historical relationships which have obtained between caste and political authority.

Changing Relationships: Caste and the State

Caste and the Hindu state

The ancient Hindu literature refers repeatedly to the king's special responsibilities toward the priestly caste. The laws of Manu regard the Brahman as by right the chief of this whole creation. As such he may take a Shudra's property for the purpose of sacrifice without fear of the slightest punishment. The king shall never execute a Brahman "though convicted of all possible crimes," for banishment (with all his property intact) is the maximum penalty which can be

[22] S. Radhakrishnan, *Religion and Society*, George Allen and Unwin Ltd., London, 1947, p. 42.

[23] Scott, *op. cit.*, p. 158.

[24] M. N. Srinivas, "A Note on Sanskritization and Westernization," *Far Eastern Quarterly*, 1956, vol. 15, p. 495.

inflicted upon a member of that caste. "No greater crime is known on earth than slaying a Brahman; and the king, therefore, must not even form in his mind an idea of killing a priest."[25]

The Brahman's superior legal status and other special prerogatives were established by the laws of Manu (second century B.C.), and have in some cases been recognized and maintained in modern times. Lands owned by Brahmans were assessed at considerably lower rates than those levied upon others, and the ancient law exempting Brahmans from capital punishment was rather widely respected.[26] A British writer noted in 1834: "The Brahmans of Travancore, as in most other parts of India, have taken care to be exempted as much as possible from punishment; at least, their sentence is far more lenient than that passed on the other castes for the same crimes."[27]

In addition to the special protection of Brahmans, the traditional Hindu state was charged with the general enforcement of caste regulations. One ancient text states: "Let the king, paying attention to all the laws of countries, castes and families, make the four *varna* (castes) fulfill their particular duties. Let him punish those who stray."[28] To a large extent each caste was permitted to govern itself and to enforce its own regulations, but ultimately the political authority had extensive jurisdiction over caste. There is abundant evidence that the king actually exercised considerable authority in caste matters, issuing marriage regulations for castes, and promoting or demoting subcastes in the social hierarchy.[29]

The 1911 census report stated that the maharaja of Cochin (a Kshatriya) exercised final authority over the caste matters of the Nambudri Brahmans, and that final expulsion from any caste required his sanction.[30] The maharaja of Kashmir established a *Dharma Sabha*, a council of persons learned in Hindu law, which met in his temple at Srinagar and delivered judgments not only in religious but also in caste matters, and could deprive people of their castes.[31] In the larger states of Rajputana the civil courts performed this function, and their powers even extended to the excommunication of

---

[25] Quoted in Hutton, *op. cit.*, p. 93.   [26] Ghurye, *op. cit.*, pp. 14-15.
[27] James Forbes, *Oriental Memoirs*, R. Bentley, London, 1834, vol. 1, p. 256. Quoted in Ghurye, *loc. cit.*
[28] Quoted in Hutton, *op. cit.*, p. 93. See also D. Mackenzie Brown, *The White Umbrella: Indian Political Thought from Manu to Gandhi*, University of California Press, Berkeley, 1953, p. 21.
[29] O'Malley, *op. cit.*, p. 56.   [30] Hutton, *op. cit.*, p. 94.
[31] O'Malley, *op. cit.*, pp. 67-68.

Brahmans. Authority over caste matters, in one form or another, was exercised by the Hindu governments of Indore, Gwalior, Baroda, the Simla Hill States, Bastar, Jashpur, Manipur, and many other Indian states. Early in the twentieth century, however, the maharajas of most of the larger states allowed their jurisdiction in caste matters to lapse.

The untouchables suffered under state-imposed disabilities in many of the Hindu kingdoms until fairly recent times. In Travancore the members of certain untouchable castes were slaves and could be dealt with precisely as any other form of property. It was not until 1855 that the maharaja issued a proclamation liberating all state slaves and forbidding the law courts to recognize the private owner-ship of slaves. The untouchables were forbidden by law to wear shoes or carry umbrellas, and their women could not wear any clothing above the waist. Only in 1859 was this latter privilege granted by royal proclamation, but even then it was specified that the untoucha-ble women should not dress "like women of high castes."[32]

Until 1911 the state of Jaipur maintained separate courts of law for untouchables, and members of the unclean sweeper caste were required to wear crow's feathers on their turbans. The low caste people were admitted to the regular courts, but had to transmit papers to the judge through other hands. Many of the hereditary Indian princes enforced untouchability in their territories, and in some states the untouchables were not permitted to enter the same schools with caste children until after India became independent.

Nepal is the only remaining Hindu kingdom in the world. Until recently the penal code of Nepal was based on the Shastras, and social, religious, and criminal offenses were dealt with by identical procedures. Brahmans were immune from capital punishment, and the crime of killing a cow could bring the death penalty. In the latter part of the nineteenth century the judge of the Chief Court of Nepal remarked: "Below (i.e. in the plains of India) let any man and woman commit what sin they will, there is no punishment pro-vided, no expiatory rite enjoined. Hence Hinduism is destroyed; the distinctions of caste are obliterated. Here, on the contrary, all those distinctions are religiously preserved by the public courts of justice, which punish according to caste and never destroy the life of a

[32] *Ibid.*, p. 148.

Brahman. Below, the Shastras are things to talk of; here they are acted up to."[33]

In 1956 the coronation of King Mahendra took place in Kathmandu, the capital of Nepal. The Hindu monarch is regarded by the Nepalese as an incarnation of Lord Vishnu the Preserver. Despite his divinity, a most important part of the coronation ceremony came when Mahendra prostrated himself at the feet of the priests. The Brahmans then sprinkled him with clarified butter from a golden jar, curds from a silver pot, milk from a copper bowl, and water from an earthen vessel. By this act of obeisance the Kshatriya ruler "acknowledged the superior ranking of the Brahmans and symbolically guaranteed their age-old privileges; in Nepal no Brahman may be executed, not even by the king."[34] Only after this and other rites did the priests cry out: "O people! This man is your king! He is the king of us Brahmans!"

Caste and the British government of India

Early British policy regarding caste was largely an inheritance from the Muslim rulers whom the East India Company displaced. The Muslims looked down upon the Hindus as idolatrous heathens, and were at first inclined to allow them to settle caste questions as they pleased. Nevertheless, during the eighteenth century the Mughal government in Bengal asserted its right to sanction readmission to caste, and with the Mughal downfall this traditional prerogative of government passed to the British. Hutton pointed to this fact as a striking illustration of the time-honored principle that "the secular power is the final arbiter of caste."[35]

The instructions drafted in 1769 for British revenue officers in Bengal included the following: "When any man has naturally forfeited his caste, you are to observe that he cannot be restored to it without the sanction of government; which was a political supremacy reserved to themselves by the Mohammedans."[36] In the same year, however, this power over restoration to caste was waived by the British government.

For some time a Caste Cutcherry (court), with fairly extensive

[33] Brian Houghton Hodgson, *Miscellaneous Essays Relating to Indian Subjects*, Trübner and Company, London, 1880, vol. 2, p. 241.
[34] E. Thomas Gilliard, "Coronation in Katmandu," *National Geographic Magazine*, 1957, vol. 112, p. 150.
[35] Hutton, *op. cit.*, p. 96.   [36] Quoted in O'Malley, *op. cit.*, p. 60.

jurisdiction over caste disputes, was maintained by the government in Calcutta. The British governor, Warren Hastings, was nominally the president of the court, although its proceedings and decisions were actually in the hands of Hastings' Hindu agent. The cutcherry was soon abolished, however, and, apart from isolated instances involving individual officers, the British government thereafter declined to interfere in caste questions except when the civil courts had to decide cases of Hindu law.

The legal system of British India produced drastic changes in the traditional working of the caste system. The establishment of British courts restricted the judicial powers of caste panchayats, for offenses such as assault, adultery, and rape were now dealt with by courts administering a uniform criminal law. The British government, by refusing to recognize the caste as an agency empowered to administer justice, deprived it of one of its most significant functions as a community. Closely related was another change, one of revolutionary significance, namely, the introduction of the principle of equality before the law. The British refused to accept the proposition that the seriousness of a crime was affected by the respective castes of the offender and the one against whom it was committed.[37]

In certain areas of civil law, however, caste continued to be a significant factor. As the Hindu law relating to marriage, succession, adoption, etc., was based on the Shastras and regarded as an important part of Hindu religion, it was maintained intact and applied in the ordinary courts. As the Hindu law based many of its regulations on caste distinctions, these too had to be recognized and enforced by the British courts. The question of marriage was especially important, and caste panchayats were stripped of their power to regulate it. In 1876 the High Court of Bombay ruled: "Courts of law will not recognize the authority of a caste to declare a marriage void, or to give permission to a woman to remarry."[38]

Inter-caste marriages being strictly prohibited by the Shastras, some of the early court decisions even held invalid marriages between Brahmans belonging to different subcastes. Later decisions, however, took a more liberal position. It was not until the enactment of the Special Marriage Act of 1872 that inter-caste marriages became legal,

[37] M. N. Srinivas, "Caste in Modern India," *Journal of Asian Studies*, 1957, vol. 16, p. 530.
[38] Quoted in Ghurye, *op.cit.*, p. 186.

provided that both parties solemnly renounced their caste and religion. The 1923 amendment to the act deleted this requirement but added other handships. The parties to the marriage had to forfeit certain rights of adoption and succession under Hindu law. Amazing as this might seem, it is nevertheless true that inter-caste marriages without such penalties did not become possible until after India's attainment of independence.

Of the multitudinous divisions of Hindu society, the untouchable castes naturally gained most from the British policy of legal equality for all Indian subjects. One of the government's administrative measures concerned the admission of untouchable children in schools. In 1858 the Bombay government resolved that all government schools would be open to all classes of its subjects without distinction.[39] In 1923 the government resolved that no grants would be paid to any aided school to which untouchable children were denied admission. As in any situation in which social mores are involved, implementation lagged behind official policy to a considerable degree. The significant point, however, is that at a relatively early date these policies, so important in the evolution of India as a secular state, were debated and affirmed.

But it was not enough to secure the untouchables' legal rights; centuries of social and economic oppression had left these castes in circumstances which called for more positive measures of aid. In 1878 Chatfield, the director of public instruction in Bombay, initiated the policy of allowing the children of these castes in primary schools special concessions in fees. This policy was gradually adopted in other parts of India, and fee concessions and scholarships were also extended to secondary school and college students.[40]

In the years following World War I, attempts were made to ensure adequate representation for the untouchables in both legislative bodies and government services. The Government of India Act of 1919 provided for special representation through mixed electorates. In Bombay Presidency, for example, the Hindu population was divided into three political tiers: Brahmans and other high castes, Marathas and other intermediate castes, and the backward castes including untouchables. The same classification was used in recruiting for government posts. A 1923 resolution of the government of Bombay finance department prohibited recruitment to the lower

[39] *Ibid.*, p. 189.   [40] *Ibid.*, p. 190.

302

services from the higher castes until the representation of the intermediate and backward classes came up to a certain level. During this
same period the government of Madras worked out an elaborate
communal rule for appointments: out of twelve posts, five had to
go to non-Brahman Hindus, two to Brahmans, two to Muslims, two
to Anglo-Indians and Christians, and one to a member of the
Depressed Classes.

The principle of communal reservation was extended still further
in proposals for constitutional reform a decade later. At the first
session of the Round Table Conference held in London (1930-1931),
Dr. B. R. Ambedkar, leader of the Depressed Classes, insisted on
separate electorates for his group.[41] He regarded the untouchables as
a minority group quite distinct from the caste Hindus, and entitled
to the same constitutional safeguards claimed by the Muslims and
other minorities. In 1932 the British prime minister, Ramsay Mac-
Donald, announced the government's constitutional proposals. These
included the Communal Award, under which the depressed classes
were granted the separate electorates sought by Ambedkar.

Gandhi, who was then in prison, was dismayed at the news of the
award. A separate electorate for the depressed classes would be
"harmful for them and for Hinduism," for it would "simply vivisect
and disrupt" the Hindu community.[42] If the untouchables were
treated as a separate political group, a constitutional wall would be
erected between them and the caste Hindus, and the moral evil of
untouchability would be harder to eradicate. Gandhi's fervent crusade
against untouchability, begun in the early 1920's, was imperiled by
the award. He announced a "fast unto death" unless Ambedkar and
the caste Hindus could reach an agreement eliminating the separate
electorates. Under the emotional and political pressures of the fast,
negotiations were begun. Ambedkar finally gave up the separate
electorates, but his price was high; the number of seats reserved for
his community in the legislature was increased from 71 to 148. This
agreement was known as the Poona Pact and was later incorporated
in the Government of India Act of 1935.[43]

[41] "Depressed Classes" is another term for the untouchable castes. In the Government of India Act of 1935 and in the Constitution of 1950 the term "Scheduled
Castes" is used to denote in general the same groups. "Harijans" (children of God)
was Gandhi's term for the untouchables, and is also widely used in present-day
India, both in common parlance and in official documents.
[42] *The Indian Review*, March 11, 1932, quoted in Scott, *op. cit.*, pp. 155-156.
[43] William Roy Smith, *Nationalism and Reform in India*, Yale University Press,
New Haven, 1938, pp. 410-416.

Indian writers have charged that the British policy of giving preference to the low castes was a deliberate attempt to divide the Hindu community even more completely, as part of the technique of "divide and rule." Srinivas wrote that the policy of the British government "was in accordance with its humanitarian sentiments, but it also had the effect of making the lower castes look up to the British for protection."[44] Another British practice which frequently came under fire was that of recording caste in the decennial census. At each recurring census the authorities received innumerable petitions from different castes requesting the government to recognize their claims to higher rank. The practice of recording caste clearly provided a new field for caste conflict and tended to perpetuate caste consciousness. The British census commissioner eliminated the return of caste in the 1941 census schedule, but more because of the questionable accuracy of such returns than because of their harmful social consequences.

The broad significance of the British impact must not be obscured by differences over details. Essentially, the foundation was laid for the building of a modern sovereign state. The state expanded its jurisdiction at the expense of the traditional caste regime by drastically reducing the powers of the caste panchayats. Within the enlarged scope of the state's jurisdiction, the basic assumptions of the old caste regime were rejected *in toto*. Equality before the law and equal citizenship constituted the basic premises of the new Indian state which was emerging. Furthermore, caste regulations based on sacred texts and immemorial custom were no longer permitted to hold unchallenged sway over Hindu social life. With the British came the revolutionary principle that it was within the province of the state to regulate and *change* society by legislation. It was only the prudent caution of a European ruler in dealing with Hindu religio-social matters which accounted for the relatively small amount of such legislation.

Problems of Present-Day Policy

The basic lines of present policy were drawn during the British period, but independence brought with it greatly increased opportunities for social reform through legislation. These opportunities were eagerly seized. In this part of the chapter it is our task to

[44] M. N. Srinivas, "Caste in Modern India," p. 532.

examine present policies in the light of the conception of the secular state.

Non-recognition of caste

The Indian secular state disregards the individual's caste in the same way that it disregards his religion in defining the rights and duties of citizenship. Discussing the concept of the secular state in its Indian context, Percival Spear wrote: "It represents the substitution of the idea of the individual with equal rights and duties as the unit of society and a society of such equal units, for the idea of groups of unequal individuals with varying rights and duties arranged in an ascending order of magnitude. An egalitarian society of individuals has become the official basis of society instead of a hierarchy of under- and over-privileged groups."[45] Equality before the law is the positive expression of this principle. As stated in article 14 of the Indian Constitution: "The state shall not deny to any person equality before the law or the equal protection of the laws within the territory of India." As has already been pointed out, untouchability involved a legal status recognized by some of the princely Indian states right up to the time of independence. In addition to the private social discrimination involved in the practice of untouchability, certain disabilities were directly imposed and enforced by the state. Article 17 declares that untouchability is abolished and its practice in any form forbidden.

The basic constitutional guarantee of non-discrimination is found in article 15(1): "The state shall not discriminate against any citizen on grounds only of religion, race, caste, sex, place of birth or any of them." Chapter 4, "The Constitutional Framework," examined in detail the three areas in which this principle is applied: public employment, admission to state educational institutions, and representation in legislatures. In 1951 the Supreme Court, in two key cases, declared unconstitutional a Madras government order under which qualified Brahman applicants for a government job and admission to an educational institution, respectively, were rejected on the basis of caste and community quotas.[46]

In the area of civil law, the principle of non-recognition of caste

[45] Percival Spear, "Christian Higher Education in India," *International Review of Missions*, 1951, vol. 40, p. 87.
[46] *Venkataramana* v. *State of Madras*, A.I.R. 1951 S.C., p. 229; and *State of Madras* v. *Sm. Champakam Dorairajan*, A.I.R. 1951 S.C., p. 226.

was applied in the Hindu Marriages Validating Act of 1949. This legislation validated without qualification, for the first time in the history of Hindu law, all inter-caste marriages. The state thus refused to recognize caste status as in any way affecting the individual's right to enter into the civil contract of marriage. This position was re-affirmed in the Hindu Marriage Act of 1955.

The non-recognition of caste was impressively illustrated in the realm of practical politics when in 1960 Damodaram Sanjivayya, a Harijan, assumed office as the chief minister of Andhra Pradesh. The Harijans represent only 15 per cent of the state's population, but other factors operated in his favor. The choice of Mr. Sanjivayya came after weeks of maneuvering by the sharply divided factions of the state Congress Party. He emerged as the only experienced cabinet minister who was acceptable to all sides.

Legislation to protect the individual

It is not enough for the state to refuse to discriminate among its citizens on the basis of caste; it must also use its coercive power to protect the citizen from the social disabilities imposed by other citizens. This has necessitated a massive campaign against certain social practices associated with untouchability. "The government of independent India," wrote A. M. Rosenthal, "was the first in the country's history that declared total war on untouchability."[47]

On November 29, 1948, the Constituent Assembly of India approved the constitutional provision abolishing untouchability, amidst cries of "Mahatma Gandhi ki Jai!" (Victory to Mahatma Gandhi!).[48] Article 17 not only abolishes the legal status of untouchability but goes on to declare: "The enforcement of any disability arising out of 'Untouchability' shall be an offense punishable in accordance with law." Similarly, article 15(2) prohibits restrictions not only with regard to the use of facilities maintained wholly or partly out of state funds but also with regard to access to shops, public restaurants, hotels, etc. The Constitution goes beyond the sphere of government and prohibits discriminatory acts by individuals against other individuals.[49]

[47] A. M. Rosenthal, "India Spurs Fight to End Caste Bias," *New York Times,* February 23, 1958.

[48] *Constituent Assembly Debates,* 1948, vol. 7, pp. 665-669.

[49] Om Prakash Aggarawala, *Fundamental Rights and Constitutional Remedies,* Metropolitan Book Co., Delhi, 1953, vol. 1, p. 212.

The language of the Constitution clearly indicated the need for legislation by the Indian Parliament to enforce these provisions. Even before the Constitution came into force, however, a number of the state legislatures sought to protect the Harijans from various forms of discrimination by individuals. An example of such legislation is the United Provinces Removal of Social Disabilities Act of 1947. Similarly titled laws were enacted in West Bengal, Bombay, Madras, and other states. The United Provinces act makes it a criminal offense to prevent any person merely on the ground that he belongs to a Scheduled Caste from having access to or using streams, wells, or other sources of water, public roads and sanitary conveniences, public conveyances, places of public entertainment, educational institutions, hospitals, etc. It is also a criminal offense to refuse any professional service to a Harijan, or to annoy him when exercising any lawful right.

In an interesting case the Allahabad High Court upheld the conviction under this act of two *dhobis* (washermen) who had refused to wash the clothes of Chamars, an untouchable caste.[50] In a similar case in West Bengal, a barber had refused to cut the hair of individuals belonging to a caste of cobblers and leather workers. He was thereupon charged with having committed a criminal offense under the Hindu Social Disabilities Removal Act of 1948. On a reference to the Calcutta High Court, it was held that the act did not prevent the petitioner from carrying on the profession of a barber, as he alleged, but really enlarged the scope of his business by compelling him to serve all alike. The court held that whatever restrictions were imposed by the act were reasonable ones which in no way deprived the petitioner of his constitutional rights.[51] A number of the state legislatures have also enacted laws specifically concerned with the right of Harijans to enter Hindu temples. One example of such legislation is the Madras Temple Entry Authorization Act of 1947. This problem has been considered in some detail in chapter 9.

Thus far we have considered the role of state legislation in the campaign to eradicate untouchability. The Untouchability (Offenses) Act of 1955, enacted by Parliament, covers much the same ground. Penalties are provided for preventing an individual, on the ground of untouchability, from equal access to roads, wells, shops, hotels,

[50] *State of U.P.* v. *Banwari*, 1951, A.I.R. 1951 Allahabad, p. 615.
[51] *Banamali Das* v. *Pakhu Bhandari*, A.I.R. 1951 Calcutta, p. 167.

public hospitals, educational institutions, employment in any trade or profession, etc. The act prescribes penalties for refusing to sell goods or render services to a Harijan because of his caste, or for preventing a Harijan from entering and worshipping in a Hindu temple or taking water from a sacred tank.

It is widely recognized by Indian officials that legislation alone is not likely to be effective in eradicating untouchability. Extensive educational campaigns have therefore been launched by central and state governments. "Harijan Days" and "Harijan Weeks" are observed in almost all the states in an effort to focus public attention on the problem.[52] Legislation and education combined, however, can claim but limited success, and in India's villages caste orthodoxy is still largely unchallenged. Recent reports of the commissioner for Scheduled Castes and Scheduled Tribes tell of thousands of villages in which a Harijan still dare not draw water from a public well, carry an umbrella, or ride a bicycle.

One of the reasons for the persistence of untouchability, despite such vigorous frontal attacks against it, is the close connection between caste and traditional Hindu religion. "Much of the propaganda against untouchability is wasted," declared one Harijan leader. "The voice of reason doesn't carry because most Hindus still feel that it is their religious duty to shun the Harijan. For generations this teaching has been drilled into them by mothers and grandmothers."[53] The orthodox Hindu is strongly inclined to the opinion that the government's all-out attack on untouchability constitutes an interference with his own freedom of religion. His interpretation of the state's policy will resemble the following. The present government is for the most part a godless one, having rejected the counsel and commands of the Hindu Shastras. The secularizing state seeks to impose its own social pattern in place of the divinely ordained pattern of the caste system. The state attacks caste and hence Hindu religion (for the two are inextricably tied together) while regimenting the individual in religio-social matters.

Legislation permitting inter-caste marriages, the high-caste orthodox Hindu might continue, runs directly counter to the Shastras and undermines caste and hence Hinduism. The state coerces the ortho-

[52] *Report of the Commissioner for Scheduled Castes and Scheduled Tribes, 1958-1959*, Government of India Press, New Delhi, 1959, pp. 37-42.
[53] Elie Abel, "India's Untouchables—Still the 'Black Sin,' " *New York Times Magazine*, March 1, 1959.

dox man's conscience when it compels him to send his children to a school attended by untouchables. The state offends his religious scruples when it compels him to use water from a well polluted by those who are ceremonially unclean. In short, the present government's entire policy of breaking down the distinctions between *varna* and *avarna* (caste and outcaste), confounding the hierarchy of caste functioning in accordance with the law of *karma*, constitutes an attack upon the Hindu religion.

The government's interpretation of its policy is naturally quite different. While the historical connection between caste and Hindu religion is generally recognized, this aspect of the present problem is minimized. Untouchability and caste discrimination in general is looked upon as a purely social problem. Certain caste practices clearly restrict and injure the individual citizen. The function of the state is to protect the individual; it is therefore necessary for the state to restrict caste. The state uses its coercive power to punish those who, on the ground of caste, would prevent the individual from exercising his lawful rights.

The liberal democratic secular state is above all concerned with the welfare of the individual, and religion cannot be allowed to protect practices which clearly injure the individual, whether these be human sacrifices, *sati*, temple prostitution, or untouchability. There is no necessity for the state to deny the patent fact that the practice of untouchability is regarded by many Hindus as a religious duty. Whether religion, social custom, or both, if it clearly harms the individual in visible and tangible ways, the secular state has every right to abolish it.

Are there, then, no aspects of the caste system which are protected from state interference by the principle of religious freedom? There are, chiefly in family and intra-caste matters. The orthodox Hindu who abhors inter-caste dining and inter-caste marriages as a matter of religious conviction will certainly never be compelled by the secular state to participate in such practices in his home. Caste associations will continue to enjoy full freedom to carry on their activities to advance their respective communities. But as soon as an individual or a caste seeks to impose disabilities on other individuals or castes, or prevent them from exercising their lawful rights, state intervention is justified.

But the orthodox Hindu statement is correct on one important point. The ultimate objective of the present government goes far beyond the protection of the individual from caste-imposed disabilities. Nehru's government is committed to a fundamental reconstruction of Indian society along egalitarian lines. Its hostility is aimed not only at untouchability but at the caste system in its entirety. Nehru wrote in 1945: "In the context of society today, the caste system and much that goes with it are wholly incompatible, reactionary, restrictive, and barriers to progress. There can be no equality in status and opportunity within its framework, nor can there be political democracy, and much less, economic democracy. Between these two conceptions conflict is inherent, and only one of them can survive."[54]

Several currents of thought coalesced in the condemnation of caste—liberalism, democracy, socialism, and others. Increasingly, the implications of socialism for Indian society were emphasized. Thus, in 1951 Nehru could interpret the Constitution in the following terms: "After all, the whole purpose of the Constitution, as proclaimed in the directive principles, is to move towards what I may call a *casteless and classless society*. It may not have been said precisely in that way; but that is, I take it, its purpose, and anything that perpetuates the present social and economic inequalities is bad."[55] The Indian National Congress in 1955 adopted as its objective the attainment in India of a "socialistic pattern of society." "Casteless and classless society" has become a popular catch-phrase in present-day India.

The state is attacking untouchability and other overt expressions of caste which are clearly detrimental to the individual. But what can the state do about caste as a social system based on endogamous units outside of which normal social relations are very limited? In 1962 the Kerala state government sanctioned a plan for the grant of financial assistance to inter-caste married couples, in cases in which one spouse is a member of a Scheduled Caste. This novel method of attacking untouchability, by promoting such marriages, will surely create other problems.[56] The most important step which has been taken thus far is the attempt to bring about greater equality through

[54] Jawaharlal Nehru, *The Discovery of India*, John Day Company, New York, 1946, p. 254.
[55] *Parliamentary Debates*, 1951, part 2, vol. 12, col. 9831. (Italics added.)
[56] *The Hindu Weekly Review*, July 23 and 30, 1962.

the special political, educational, and economic rights which have been accorded the former untouchable castes.

Special aid to Harijans

As we have seen, the state refuses to recognize caste in dealing with the individual, and also uses its coercive power to protect the individual by preventing certain harmful caste practices. The first principle indicates a largely passive role for the state; the second indicates an active but negative role. We now come to the third main principle; here we see the state assuming an active and positive role.

The special rights and privileges extended to the Harijans consist of: (1) reserved seats in legislatures, (2) reserved posts in government service, and (3) special educational and economic aid. The Constitution (articles 330, 332, and 334) provides for the reservation of seats for the Scheduled Castes and Tribes in both central and state legislatures. The reservation of seats is proportionate as far as possible to their population in the states. This system was to last only for a period of ten years from the inauguration of the Constitution (1950), but was extended for another ten years by the eighth amendment. At present the Lok Sabha reserves seventy-six of its 500 seats for members of the Scheduled Castes and Tribes. These groups constitute about one-seventh of the total population of India, and their representation is roughly the same. There are also three members of these groups in the Lok Sabha who have been elected to unreserved seats by the free choice of the voters.

The same article which guarantees equality of opportunity for all citizens in the field of public employment also contains a provision for the reservation of posts. Article 16(4) is as follows: "Nothing in this article shall prevent the state from making any provision for the reservation of appointments or posts in favor of any backward class of citizens which, in the opinion of the state, is not adequately represented in the services under the state."[57] In 1950 the government decided to reserve 12½ per cent of the civil service jobs for Harijans when the recruitment is on an all-India basis.

[57] This is a statement of the principle in negative terms. Article 335, however, is a positive directive: "The claims of the members of the Scheduled Castes and the Scheduled Tribes shall be taken into consideration, consistently with the maintenance of efficiency of administration, in the making of appointments to services and posts in connection with the affairs of the Union or of a state."

Special adjustments in qualifications have been made in an effort to fill the quota of posts reserved for Harijans. The age limit for their recruitment has been raised, their examination fees have been drastically reduced, and appointing officers have been given considerable discretion to waive requirements in the case of Harijan applicants. Government employing authorities must submit annual reports on the number of Harijans appointed, and cases of default are taken up by the commissioner for the Scheduled Castes and Scheduled Tribes.[58] A number of the state governments have also established quotas for Harijans. Despite such efforts, the Harijans' representation in government services has increased very slowly, mainly because of the lack of suitable candidates.

In May 1961 the Supreme Court settled by a majority judgment of three to two an important point of interpretation concerning article 16(4) of the Constitution. The question was whether the phrase "reservation of appointments or posts" enabled the state to fix Scheduled Caste quotas for promotions as well as for initial appointments. The court decided that it did. The case involved a railway employee belonging to a Scheduled Caste. He was rejected for a promotion earlier when judged solely on the basis of merit. On the strength of the Railway Board's circular providing for communal reservation in promotion, however, he was advanced to the new post. It is inevitable that both efficiency and morale in the public services will suffer under a system in which caste, not merit, determines to such a large extent the possibilities of advancement.[59]

Statutory devices such as reserved seats in the legislatures or posts in the civil service are of but limited usefulness. What the Harijans most need is to be strengthened educationally and economically so that they can stand on their own feet. The Indian Constitution recognizes this fact, and article 46 affirms: "The state shall promote with special care the educational and economic interests of the weaker sections of the people, and, in particular, of the Scheduled Castes and the Scheduled Tribes." Active steps have been taken by the central and state governments in the implementation of this constitutional directive. The states have established Harijan welfare departments which administer numerous and varied programs, supported in part by sizable grants from the government of India.

[58] *India: A Reference Annual 1957*, Publications Division, Government of India, Delhi, 1957, pp. 157-159.
[59] *The Hindu*, April 30 and May 3, 4, and 5, 1961.

Educational concessions available to Harijan children include free tuition, stipends, scholarships, books, stationery, and in some cases, clothing and midday meals. Special schools and hostels for Harijans have been built. In addition, the central government's program of college scholarships for qualified Harijan students has produced startling results. In 1954-1955, the number of students who received such scholarships was about 10,000; by 1958-1959 the figure had risen to over 32,000.[60] The Harijan welfare departments have undertaken various projects of economic aid: the provision of free reclaimed wasteland, irrigation facilities, house sites, wells, sanitary amenities, and the establishment of an extensive system of credit cooperatives which facilitate the purchase of livestock, fertilizer, tools, seed, etc.

We have briefly surveyed the special rights and privileges which are being extended to the members of those castes which have suffered the greatest disabilities in the past. It is abundantly clear that this third main principle is in logical contradiction with the first principle—that the state deals with the individual only as a citizen and not on the basis of caste. The first principle is completely sound and an essential of the secular state. It is also obviously the more fundamental of the two principles in the structure of the Indian Constitution. The third principle therefore comes under suspicion and must be examined more closely.

The provision for reserved seats in the legislatures expires in 1970 (unless extended by another constitutional amendment, as was done in 1960) and hence need not be commented upon at length. As has already been pointed out in a slightly different context, the device is generally detrimental to the development of secularism. As a purely temporary measure toward the solution of a practical problem, however, it is not without merit, and it has probably served its purpose well in the past twelve years. The provision for reservation of posts in the government services, similarly, is not in strict keeping with the democratic concept of citizenship, but, as a practical measure, has value. The number of civil service jobs reserved for Harijans is roughly in proportion to their strength in the total population. The arrangement is an equitable one, although it is recognized that it does not coincide with the ideal of the secular state. In these areas,

[60] *Report of the Commissioner for Scheduled Castes, 1958-1959*, pp. 56-57.

the state resorts to protective discrimination in favor of those who are unable to compete with other sections of the population.

In *State of Madras* v. *Sm. Champakam Dorairajan*, 1951, the Supreme Court relied on the non-discrimination principle found in article 29(2) in invalidating a government order which established communal quotas for admission to state educational institutions. This decision undermined the legal basis for the system of reservation of seats in such institutions for the Scheduled Castes and Tribes and necessitated a constitutional amendment. The amendment took the form of article 15(4): "Nothing in this article or in clause (2) of article 29 shall prevent the state from making any special provision for the advancement of any socially and educationally backward classes of citizens or for the Scheduled Castes and the Scheduled Tribes."

In defending his proposed amendment in Parliament in 1951, Prime Minister Nehru remarked that it meant essentially giving up a strict interpretation of equality in favor of the gradual elimination of the inequalities to which the backward classes had been subjected. Nehru conceded that for the state to deal with people as castes or communities did go against certain explicit or implied provisions of the Constitution. Nevertheless, the fact was that certain communities were socially, educationally, and economically backward, and something had to be done for them. In attempting to give them special opportunities, the government had come up against court decisions which interpreted strictly the constitutional provisions regarding equality and non-discrimination. In raising the backward classes equality was the ultimate goal, but the paradox was that "in trying to attain equality we come up against certain principles of equality laid down in the Constitution."[61] Nehru declared that, while aiming ultimately at a casteless society in which individuals would not think in terms of group loyalties but of the country at large, the government still could not ignore the present divisions in Indian social life.

The crucial point in Nehru's argument was the assertion that a close relationship exists between economic backwardness and membership in a Scheduled Caste. The government's assumption that there is a high correlation between caste status and economic cir-

[61] *Jawaharlal Nehru's Speeches, 1949-1953*, Publications Division, Government of India, New Delhi, 1954, p. 518.

cumstances has drawn heavy fire from the critics. One editorial in *The Hindu* stated the case very well: "Our governments proclaim their fidelity to secularism and their hostility to casteism. Their policies for uplifting the backward are, however, fundamentally vitiated by identifying backwardness with caste and sub-caste. The result is that casteism flourishes, while no attempt is made to find out who are really backward and to give them a helping hand irrespective of whether they belong to this or that caste or sect or other socio-religious group. Poverty, ignorance, ill-health are to be found in every community; and the recognition of the citizen's fundamental rights involves the acceptance by our governments of their obligation to remedy the condition of every citizen who is handicapped and not to assume without question that a man must be well off because he belongs to a particular community or that another must be badly off because he belongs to a community which the government have chosen to describe as backward."[62]

This same criticism has been voiced in the Lok Sabha from time to time.[63] There are well-to-do Harijans, and there are poverty-stricken Brahmans.[64] One paper complained of the undemocratic anomalies which exist when "many continue to receive benefits by virtue of their birth in a Harijan caste irrespective of their economic status, while others in real distress are deprived of state help because of their traditionally high caste."[65]

Closely related to this point is the criticism that the special aid to Harijans tends to perpetuate the caste system by establishing new vested interests. The Harijan is not encouraged to forget his untouchable caste background for it is precisely because of it that he receives special benefits from the state. For him to surrender his membership in one of the Scheduled Castes would mean the loss of his children's free tuition in school, his opportunity of acquiring free land, etc.

The inherent contradiction between the Indian government's objective of a casteless society and its policy of granting special aid on the basis of caste was clearly revealed in a parliamentary debate

---

[62] *The Hindu*, August 7, 1955.

[63] See, for example, the comments of Pandit S. C. Mishra, *Lok Sabha Debates*, 1955, part 2, vol. 3, col. 5377.

[64] The poor Brahman, in fact, is one of the frequently encountered characters in popular Indian literature.

[65] *The Guardian*, 1954, vol. 32, p. 90.

in April 1955. A private member's bill entitled the Caste Distinctions Removal Bill was introduced by Fulsinghji B. Dabhi. The basic object of the measure was to remove caste distinctions among Hindus for official and public purposes. This would appear to be completely in line with the government's goal of a casteless society. However, the bill was immediately attacked by Dr. Monomohan Das, parliamentary secretary for education (and a Scheduled Castes member), on the ground that if the recognition of caste distinctions for official purposes were withdrawn, the Scheduled Castes would immediately be deprived of their special rights and privileges. How could Scheduled Castes be recognized, another M. P. asked, if caste distinctions were removed in official matters? He regarded the bill as positively "mischievous."[66]

In April 1960 the government of India sent a circular to the state governments asking them not to include any reference to caste or sect in registers or forms used for purposes of the public services and judicial proceedings. In September of the same year a similar circular requested the deletion of such references to caste or sect in application forms for admission to schools, colleges, and universities. In both circulars an exception was made with respect to the Scheduled Castes and Tribes, in order to give effect to the reservations which have been made for these sections of the population. General reaction to these steps was very favorable; they were interpreted as attempts further to implement the principle of the secular state. However, backward-classes associations in various parts of the country immediately protested the government circulars. Their prospects for special aid and reservations, like those of the Scheduled Castes, depend entirely on the continued official recognition of caste. There is a profound contradiction between the objective of a casteless society and the method of elevating the backward on a caste basis.[67]

Backward classes to the fore

Despite such criticisms, some individuals in official circles are urging not only the continuation but the *extension* of this system. The Backward Classes Commission was appointed to determine the criteria by which any section of the people, in addition to the

[66] *Lok Sabha Debates*, 1955, part 2, vol. 3, cols. 5324-5386.
[67] *The Hindu Weekly Review*, April 25, 1960; *The Hindu*, September 28 and 29, 1960.

Scheduled Castes and Tribes, could be treated as socially and educationally backward. In its report of 1955, a majority of the commission's members felt that the position held by an individual in the social hierarchy based on caste determined the extent and degree of backwardness. The commission therefore listed 2,399 additional castes which it regarded as backward and recommended that these be made eligible for benefits similar to those granted to the Scheduled Castes and Tribes.

The report of the commission is a curious document indeed. The chairman, Kaka Kalelkar, in his forwarding letter to President Rajendra Prasad upon the submission of the report, repudiated the fundamental conclusions of his commission. He wrote that, almost at the end of the committee's labors, he realized that the remedies suggested were worse than the evils they sought to combat. "I could not stem the current of opinion within the commission itself and ultimately decided, though reluctantly, to side with the majority with whom I had cooperated throughout in formulating remedies on caste basis. It is [sic] only when the report was being finalized that I started thinking anew and found that backwardness could be tackled on a basis or a number of bases other than that of caste."[68] Kalelkar was driven to this conclusion by observing how Indian Christian and Muslim converts, whose respective religions reject caste, were nevertheless trying to revive their former caste identities with the hope of obtaining government aid. He was also impressed by the anomalies created when extremely poor and illiterate members of the upper castes were denied state aid on the basis of caste.

Kalelkar's belated enlightenment (the commission had been at work for two years) found eloquent expression in his letter. He decided that the whole line of investigation pursued by the commission was "repugnant to the spirit of democracy," since in democracy it is the individual, not the family or the caste, which is the unit. He recommended that the state regard as backward and entitled to special educational and economic aid all persons whose total family income is less than 800 rupees per year, regardless of their caste or community. Kalelkar opposed the reservation of posts for the backward classes in the government services, which was recommended by the commission.

[68] *Report of the Backward Classes Commission*, Government of India Press, Delhi, 1956, vol. 1, p. vi.

The government of India issued a memorandum in which it took issue with the findings and recommendations of the commission and warned that such an approach would serve to perpetuate existing caste distinctions. While statements made by the union home minister seemed to support the idea of adopting economic criteria for backwardness, no clear-cut policy has yet been announced by the central government.[69] Grants and scholarships for members of the backward classes are granted by the government of India on the basis of recommendations made by the states which maintain their own lists of these classes.

In several of the states the lists of Scheduled Castes and Tribes and backward classes now represent a majority of the total population of the state. In Andhra Pradesh 55 per cent of the posts in the government services are reserved for these groups, and the reservation extends to promotions as well as initial appointments.[70] But the ultimate extension of this principle was reached in Mysore state. In the 1956 case of *Kesava Iyengar* v. *State of Mysore* the High Court upheld a government order by which all communities other than Brahmans were classified as backward, and seven out of ten government jobs were reserved for them. According to a 1959 Mysore government order, in addition to the reservation for the Scheduled Castes and Tribes, 57 per cent of government posts and of seats in technical institutions were reserved for 165 castes and communities listed as "Other Backward Classes." A system of rotation was followed in allotting seats in colleges and making appointments to the public services. If no eligible candidate from a caste were found for a particular opening, candidates were considered from the next caste in turn.[71] In 1960, however, the Mysore High Court found that this policy violated article 15(4) of the Constitution.[27] It was therefore necessary to make a fresh approach to the whole problem.

In January 1960 the Mysore Backward Classes Committee was appointed, with Dr. R. Nagan Gowda as chairman, for the purpose of determining the criteria for the classification of the backward

[69] See law minister A. K. Sen's answer in the Rajya Sabha to complaints that the central government had not implemented the recommendations of the Backward Classes Commission. *The Statesman*, February 22, 1961.

[70] *The Hindu*, May 8, 1961.

[71] L. M. Shrikant, *Report of the Commissioner for Scheduled Castes and Scheduled Tribes, 1958-1959*, Government of India Press, Delhi, 1959, p. 12.

[72] *S. H. Partha and others* v. *State of Mysore and others*, Mysore Law Journal 1960, p. 159.

classes in the state. In its interim report submitted a month later, the committee recommended that "backward classes should be listed only on the basis of their caste or community and their backwardness judged on the basis of the percentage of literacy in the community and their representation in government service."[73]

The whole approach, however, has created vested interests in backwardness, and the attempt to reverse the process met with the opposition which was expected. The Lingayats, formerly listed as a backward community, were deprived of this valuable label by the committee's interim report, while a rival community, the Vokkaligas, retained it. The controversial report was attacked from public platform and on the floor of the legislative assembly, and charges of communal bias were freely made. Lingayat associations throughout the state passed resolutions denouncing the discrimination against their community and demanding that they be reinstated as "backward."[74] The final report of the Nagan Gowda committee recommended that the backward communities be divided into "backward" and "more backward" classes, and reaffirmed the earlier decision to classify the Lingayats as a forward community. But the state government finally gave in under extreme pressure and the Lingayats retained their legal status as a backward class. [75]

Since the committee had encountered considerable difficulty in gathering statistics about the numerous castes and communities in the state, it recommended in its final report that the state government request the government of India to have caste recorded in the census. This was done by the British until the 1941 census, and, as has been noted, the practice was condemned by Indian nationalists as a calculated effort to perpetuate the divisions in Hindu society.[76]

On July 31, 1962 the Mysore government issued an order providing

[73] *Mysore Backward Classes Committee: Interim Report*, Government Press, Bangalore, 1960, p. 3.
[74] *The Hindu*, June 10, 1961.
[75] *Mysore Backward Classes Committee: Final Report*, Government Press, Bangalore, 1961, p. 20. See the note of dissent by M. S. Patil on the classification of the Lingayat community, pp. 33-38. The Lingayats, the largest single community in the state, constitute 15.6 per cent of the population. Their representation in high political office is by no means insignificant; in 1961 the chief minister and three other members of the cabinet were Lingayats. Regarding the cabinet decision to classify the Lingayats as one of the backward classes, contrary to the committee report, see *Deccan Herald*, Bangalore, June 29, 1961.
[76] *Final Report*, p. 26.

for reservation of 68 per cent of the seats in medical and engineering colleges for backward classes and Scheduled Castes and Tribes. The order listed 81 "backward classes" and 135 "more backward classes." In striking down the order two months later, the Supreme Court declared that it was "a fraud on the Constitution." The judgment held that the classification of backward classes on the sole basis of caste was not permitted by article 15(4). Furthermore, the reservation was clearly excessive, as it reduced the field of general competition to a mere 32 per cent of the seats. The special provision, in other words, had so weakened the fundamental rule (equality of opportunity) as to rob it of most of its significance.[77]

It is obvious that this approach of the state governments to the problem of educational and economic backwardness is based on fundamentally unsound premises which must inevitably tend to undermine the secular state. Let us for a moment consider how the problem of economic need is handled in a modern democratic country. In any program of state aid to the underprivileged, the ascertainment of the existence and extent of need is a major administrative problem. Many thousands of welfare workers are engaged exclusively in the task of investigating applications for state aid. Each application is filed by an individual, and his case is dealt with strictly on the basis of actual proved need.

India has taken a gigantic administrative shortcut. By identifying certain castes as underprivileged, the state has reduced its problem to the relatively simple one of verifying a given applicant's membership in one of these castes. This procedure is not followed by any modern state, even where a high correlation exists between economic need and membership in certain religious or ethnic groups.

Such a correlation does exist, for example, in the case of the Negroes in the United States. But the fact that an individual belongs to this group does not entitle him to state aid. This would be patently unfair, for some Negroes are professional people with high incomes, and there are many white tenant farmers in some areas of the country whose standard of living is not much above that of bare subsistence. But apart from the basic unfairness of such a system, it would meet with strong objections from the Negro community itself, which would resent the official label of social or economic backwardness.

[77] *The Hindu*, September 30, 1962.

Equality before the law and equal protection of the laws can only mean that the state deals with the individual as a citizen and not as a member of a group. If the state is concerned about the problem of economic backwardness, it must seek to help individuals who are economically backward. India's administrative shortcut is proving a very costly one, for the price being paid is the perpetuation of caste and the general weakening of the foundations of the secular state.

As an example of a sounder approach, in 1955 the government of Madras announced its intention to exempt all poor children from the payment of school fees in elementary and secondary schools. A pupil was to be considered poor if the annual gross income from all sources of the parent or guardian did not exceed 1,200 rupees (about $255).[78] It was not possible, however, to implement the new policy immediately in the higher classes. At the end of 1960, free education was available to all children in the state up to the fifth standard and to poor children up to the eighth standard. Beyond this, free education was available only to children belonging to the Scheduled Castes and the backward classes. In February 1961 the Madras government resolved to extend free education up to the eleventh standard to all poor children.[79]

Bombay state was the first to extend this principle to all levels of primary and secondary education. An editorial in the *Times of India* pointed out: "By offering free education at all levels to those whose parents' annual income is below 900 rupees, the Bombay government has taken a first major step toward destroying the old basis of classification and establishing a rational system in which financial disabilities rather than caste considerations are the decisive factors."[80] Similar steps in the field of education are being taken in Andhra Pradesh, Mysore, and other states. This sound approach, although more difficult to administer, is likely to gain increasing acceptance throughout India.

As India becomes a welfare state in fact as well as in theory, many of the present anomalies and injustices will automatically disappear. Before too many years will have passed, free elementary and secondary education will be available throughout India. With the extension of welfare services to all citizens, caste discrimination by the state

[78] *The Hindu*, June 17, 1955. [79] *Ibid.*, March 1, 1961.
[80] *Times of India*, April 17, 1959.

will cease. The reservation of government jobs, however, is a different matter. This system cannot be absorbed in a larger scheme of things. The only way to end the reservation of posts for caste groups is by the painful process of withdrawing such reservations. And it can be taken for a certainty that the vested caste interests will oppose this necessary democratic decision tooth and nail, whether it comes ten years or fifty years from now.

The problem of Harijan converts

The objections to the caste approach to backwardness are reinforced when one considers the uncertainties and injustices which have at times characterized official policies toward Scheduled Caste converts to other religions. Before the Constitution came into force, the special benefits available to Christians of Harijan background varied widely from one state to another. For example, in 1946 the government of Bombay extended the same educational concessions provided for the Scheduled Castes to Christian converts, on the ground that they continued under the same social and economic disabilities after conversion.[81] In the United Provinces some aid was available for the converts when classified as backward, rural Christians, while Hindu children of the same social background but enrolled as Scheduled Caste members received stipends many times greater.[82] The government of Madhya Pradesh issued orders in 1947 that even individuals classified as members of *backward classes* should cease to be eligible for educational concessions upon their conversion (from Hinduism) to another religion.[83]

The Constitution of 1950 should have resulted in a clear, uniform policy of equal treatment. Indeed, article 15(1) declares that the state shall not discriminate against any citizen on grounds only of religion, caste, etc. However, the interpretation of other articles produced almost the opposite effect. Article 341(1) gives the president the authority to specify by public notification the castes "which shall for the purposes of this Constitution be deemed to be Scheduled Castes." In accordance with this provision the Constitution (Scheduled Castes) Order was promulgated in August 1950. The order

[81] *National Christian Council Review*, 1946, vol. 66, p. 86.
[82] *Ibid.*, 1949, vol. 69, p. 322.
[83] L. M. Shrikant, *Report of the Commissioner for Scheduled Castes and Scheduled Tribes for the Period Ending 31st December, 1951*, Government of India Press, New Delhi, 1952, p. 56.

stated that "no person who professes a religion different from Hindu-ism shall be deemed to be a member of a Scheduled Caste." The order went on, however, to include in the list of Scheduled Castes several castes which profess Sikhism.[84]

As soon as this order was published, a number of the state governments withdrew whatever educational and economic benefits they had been extending to Christians of Scheduled Caste background. Representations were made to the president and prime minister, who explained that the order applied only to the Scheduled Castes' reserved seats in the legislatures, not to other forms of special aid. But the fact remained that in many cases this aid had been withdrawn. A memorandum drawn up by the Christian members of Parliament stated in part: "A great source of distress to the Christian community has been the refusal, by almost all the state governments, to give to Harijan converts to Christianity the educational, social and economic assistance which is being given to Hindu Harijans. We realize that the Scheduled Caste Christians are not to be included in the provision for the reservation of seats in the legislatures which has been judged necessary for the Hindu and Sikh Harijans for a time. But the case for economic assistance is based on other grounds. It used to be given to Scheduled Caste Christians even when they were politically merged with the other Christians. They live in the same economic and social conditions as Hindu Harijans and need the protection of government as much as the others."[85]

By dint of innumerable resolutions, representations, and deputations to state governments, considerable progress has been made since 1951 in securing comparable educational and economic assistance for Christians of Harijan background. The governments of Andhra Pradesh in 1956, and Madras and Kerala in 1957 recognized their claims for educational concessions.[86] In some of the states, converts from the Scheduled Castes are classified as backward classes and given state aid on the same basis as castes included in this category. In some cases this is considerably less than the aid extended to the Scheduled Castes; significant inequalities continue to exist. It is

[84] The order was amended in 1956. It now excludes persons professing "a religion different from the Hindu or the Sikh religion."

[85] *N.C.C. Review*, 1951, vol. 71, p. 105.

[86] *Catholic Bishops' Conference of India: Report of the Meetings of the Standing Committee, 1958*, St. Mary's Industrial School Press, Bangalore, 1959, pp. 15-16.

still true, despite improvement in the situation, that it is economically far more advantageous to be a Hindu Harijan than a Christian of Harijan background.[87] The situation in some places represents a significant economic inducement to reconversion to Hinduism, and such cases are not unknown.

In previous chapters we mentioned the mass conversions of Scheduled Castes members to Buddhism, which began under the leadership of the late Dr. Ambedkar in 1956. The new converts to a religion which originated in India experienced precisely the same difficulties encountered by those who embraced Christianity. The Bombay government passed an order annulling the educational and other concessions which were formerly extended to them. A delegation of eight members of the Scheduled Castes' Federation, who were also members of Parliament, met with Prime Minister Nehru in 1957 in order to plead the case of those converts to Buddhism who consequently lost their special privileges. The neo-Buddhists began a vigorous agitation for the restoration of these privileges. In May 1960 the bilingual state of Bombay was divided, and the chief minister of the new state of Maharashtra promised that the neo-Buddhists would be made eligible for all the concessions and facilities available to the Scheduled Castes. This promise was fulfilled under the watchful eye of R. V. Bhandare, prominent neo-Buddhist and leader of the opposition in the Maharashtra legislative assembly.[88]

In Maharashtra, the neo-Buddhists now enjoy an impressive list of privileges. They are granted exemption from payment of all fees in educational institutions regardless of the family income, receive the same scholarships provided for the Scheduled Castes, and are admitted to seats reserved for these castes in educational institutions. They are eligible for the grant of government waste lands for cultivation and housing purposes, and for financial help to start trades and businesses. However, the success of the neo-Buddhists' political agitation in Maharashtra underlines the injustice of the whole approach. Christian converts in the same state or Buddhist converts in other states, less effective politically, still have not received many of these benefits.

Neo-Buddhists in Uttar Pradesh and the Punjab are still attempting to secure the restoration of their old concessions as mem-

[87] See, for example, the memorandum submitted by the Andhra Provincial Harijans and Christians Association. *N.C.C. Review*, 1958, vol. 77, p. 100.
[88] *The Hindu*, October 1, 1960.

bers of Scheduled Castes. In 1961 the Lok Sabha rejected by a vote of 74 to 23 a non-official resolution seeking the extension of educational and economic provisions made for Scheduled Castes under the Constitution to the neo-Buddhist converts. Supporters of the resolution contended that the constitutional safeguards were provided because of the backwardness of certain sections of the population and should not be taken away simply because those people changed their religion. Those who opposed the resolution claimed that this would import the stigma of untouchability into other religions. The government opposed the resolution, claiming that in so doing the spirit as well as the letter of the Constitution was being followed.[89]

The basis for exclusion of Christians and Buddhists from Scheduled Caste aid is that theoretically their respective faiths do not recognize caste and hence upon conversion untouchability ceases. In point of fact, caste consciousness is rather firmly entrenched among many Christian groups, especially in south India, and is the source of many problems for the churches.[90] But the most significant point is that conversion has not usually led to much improvement in economic status. The converts frequently continue to be treated as untouchables by high-caste Hindus. Even if real equality does exist within the Christian fold, this group is after all a small minority whose members are frequently dependent on high-caste employers.

It is impossible to escape the conclusion that religious discrimination is at the bottom of *some* of the present policies. The Hindu Harijans are looked upon as a group which remained loyal to Hinduism despite the terrible disabilities which they suffered. They resisted the temptation to seek social equality and economic uplift through conversion to another religion. The present state aid represents Hindu society's long-overdue reward for their faithfulness. But the reward would lose much of its significance if granted equally to those who have abandoned their ancestral faith. The present discrimination in the treatment of Hindu and non-Hindu can operate as a powerful deterrent for any Harijan who is contemplating conversion. "Economic inducements," rightly condemned if offered by foreign missionaries seeking converts, are now being

[89] *The Hindu*, April 29, 1961.
[90] See the special number on "Caste in Church and Nation," *Religion and Society*, Bangalore, 1958, vol. 5, no. 3.

extended by some state governments in such a way as to perpetuate the religious status quo.

It is likely that such considerations play a part in the thinking of some legislators and administrators. For the most part, however, the politicians and officials are simply unable to get away from the whole approach of state aid on the basis of caste and are unwittingly drawn into the problems of religious discrimination discussed above. The fundamental point is *not* that Christian and Buddhist converts from the Scheduled Castes should be given equal privileges with Hindu Harijans. This would simply rectify a few of the numerous injustices of the present system. The ultimate solution of the larger problem can only come with the complete abandonment of the policy of dealing with economic need on the basis of the irrelevant factor of caste. Only in this way can the ideal of the secular state be approximated.

Caste in Indian politics

The chief concern of this chapter has been with government policy toward caste. It is clear that at some fundamental points this policy has been defective, has tended to strengthen caste consciousness and correspondingly weaken the secular state. But various other factors, for which government policy cannot be held responsible, tend to produce the same result. The basic fact, of course, is that Hindu social life, for the vast majority, is still based on caste divisions. Caste loyalties are still second only to family loyalties in the thinking of the Hindu masses. When an individual moves into the area of politics, it is ridiculous to imagine that the basic assumptions of his social existence can be left behind. When the masses move into the area of active political participation through adult suffrage, caste loyalties and prejudices go with them.

The democratic process enshrined in the Indian Constitution has given caste a new lease on life. Caste solidarity makes for bloc-voting. The objective of the politician, then, is to secure a majority of votes by a careful manipulation of appeals to caste loyalties. To maintain the support of an effective combination of such caste interests is in many parts of India the crux of the political process. In the selection of candidates, the formation of ministries, and the composition of patronage-dispensing committees and boards, the factor of caste is omnipresent. Democratic elections have injected new vigor into the life of caste associations and have encouraged the proliferation of such organizations. Their political role is already a very important one in certain parts of the country. By and large, the Congress Party has been as guilty as any other in playing this kind of politics, despite frequent resolutions condemning the evils of casteism and calling for the emotional integration of the nation. Jayaprakash Narayan was hardly exaggerating when he declared in 1960 that under the present system of elections, "caste has become the strongest party in India."[91]

An excellent recent study of caste associations considered in some detail the political role of the *Vanniya Kula Kshatriya Sangham* in Madras state.[92] The Vanniyars are primarily a caste of agricultural laborers and cultivating owners, but as early as the 1871 census they had petitioned to be classified as Kshatriyas (the second highest caste, traditionally composed of rulers and warriors). By dint of several books on the "history" of the caste, the imitation of high caste social customs (child marriage, vegetarianism, prohibition of widow remarriage), and constant pressure on the census authorities, their Kshatriya status was fully recognized in 1931. The formal organization of the caste association took place at about the same time. The Vanniyars were fairly well prepared for a vigorous political role when independence was achieved; they had a well-established organization, leaders who understood pressure group techniques, and a past history of effectiveness in dealing with the government.

Failing to secure guarantees of adequate representation in civil service appointments and in Congress Party nominations, the *Vanniya Kula Kshatriya Sangham* decided in 1951 to test its own electoral strength. A state-wide caste association conference formed a political party called the Tamilnad Toilers Party under the leadership of N. A. Manikkavelu Naicker and S. S. Ramaswami Padayachi. The party soon split over local rivalries, however, and the Vanniyars of two districts rallied to the new Commonweal Party formed by Naicker. During the elections, the caste organization was effectively utilized at the village level to assure solid Vanniyar voting for one or the other party. The Commonweal Party captured 6 seats and

---

[91] *Deccan Herald*, October 31, 1960.
[92] Lloyd I. Rudolph and Susanne Hoeber Rudolph, "The Political Role of India's Caste Associations," *Pacific Affairs*, 1960, vol. 33, pp. 5-22.

the Tamilnad Toilers 19 in the state legislative assembly, giving the Vanniyars 13 per cent of the seats (they numbered only 10 per cent of the population). Because of the Congress Party's failure to win a majority, Naicker and later Padayachi were given cabinet posts in exchange for legislative support. With two ministers in the eight-man cabinet, both Vanniyar parties were dissolved and their members joined the Congress. Similar tactics have been employed by caste associations in other states.[93]

Selig S. Harrison's important study sought to establish "the crucial importance of caste manipulation as a source of Andhra Communist strength."[94] Neither ideologies nor economic interests were as important as caste alignments in the 1951 election contest between the Congress and the Communists. A single subcaste, the Kamma landlords, has provided the leadership of the Andhra Communist Party since its founding. In the elections, the Communists were able to appeal effectively to their Kamma brethren, warning them of the Congress dominated by the Reddis (a rival landlord caste). "The victorious Communist in 1951 drew on the numbers of the landless laborers and protest votes of erstwhile Congress supporters, but powerful Kamma backers gave him in a substantial number of cases even more decisive support—identification with village-level authority."[95] However bewildering the whole process of elections might be to the villager, the appeal to his caste loyalty was something he could understand and respond to.

These illustrations of the importance of caste in Indian voting behavior, however, should not lead one to too broad a generalization. Caste is undoubtedly a highly significant factor in elections, but it is usually one factor among many, and one which is sometimes cancelled out. Thus, in a constituency where one caste is numerically very strong, all parties will generally put up candidates belonging to that caste. This indeed demonstrates the importance of the caste

[93] The authors of this study argue that the caste association, which has characteristics of both the natural and the voluntary group (one must be born in the caste and also "join" the association), may serve a useful purpose in the development of democratic political life. "Ironically, it is the caste association which links the mass electorate to the new democratic political processes and makes them comprehensible in traditional terms to a population still largely politically illiterate." *Ibid.*, p. 22. However, in other and more obvious ways the caste association clearly tends to undermine the values of secular democracy, as the authors recognize.
[94] Selig S. Harrison, "Caste and the Andhra Communists," *American Political Science Review*, 1956, vol. 50, p. 378.
[95] *Ibid.*, p. 395.

factor, but also its limitations, since the candidates are then forced to appeal to the voters on the basis of other considerations. In many constituencies the candidates, to secure a majority of votes, must appeal to five or six caste groups. The very multiplicity of castes in some situations tends to reduce their importance, and the more significant considerations may be economic interests, the personalities of the candidates, or purely local issues.

In the reporting and analysis of political developments, the Indian press generally deals with the caste factor in a very matter-of-fact tone. Consider, for example, the following account which appeared in a weekly news magazine of the Bihar chief minister's visit to New Delhi to seek advice on the selection of his cabinet. "The caste groups constituted a challenge to the High Command. The Bhumihars had considered themselves to be the ruling community in the state so far and in order to avoid creating in them an impression of having been dethroned it was necessary to give them representation in the new ministry. But they wanted 'adequate' representation. And if they were recognized as a caste group, the Rajputs too wanted representation on caste basis, and on par. How could the Kayasthas be ignored when their claims were backed by 'high quarters?' What are described as backward communities and classes claimed privileged positions and their present representation was not to be disturbed."[96] The article went on to describe the negotiations and the settlement which was reached, and commented that, despite its efforts to curb casteism and groupism, the Congress High Command ultimately had to recognize and deal with the powerfully entrenched caste interests.

This kind of politics is obviously very different from that required by the conception of a secular state. What is the solution? In the long run, education, economic development, and nationalism will push caste into the background and ultimately eliminate it. The forces of modernization will prevail in the end, but caste is likely to remain powerful for another generation.

[96] *Link*, February 19, 1961, pp. 15-16.

A NOTE TO PART FOUR

RELIGION AND SOCIETY: DISENGAGEMENT AND NEW RELATIONSHIPS

IN THESE two chapters dealing with law and caste we have noted the continuing process by which the state in India is expanding its jurisdiction at the expense of traditional Hindu religion. Religion has been largely stripped of its authority as the regulator of society. Hindu personal law based on the ancient Shastras has been drastically modified by legislative acts, and will shortly be discarded altogether in favor of a uniform civil code. Caste regulations supported by religious texts have been repudiated in favor of a Constitution and laws which embody egalitarian principles. These developments are of revolutionary significance for the state, religion, and society. From the point of view of the state, they mark the emergence of a modern sovereign state exercising the full panoply of powers of its western model. The consequences for Hindu religion and society need to be examined carefully.

As long as social institutions were totally integrated by Hinduism, the demand for social change was equivalent to an attack upon religion. The protest against social injustice could only be made by relatively small religious reform movements which were usually later accommodated within Hinduism as new sects, by individual religious reformers, or by westernized social reformers who approached the problem from a basically secular point of view. Since the middle of the nineteenth century, the state has become the principal instrumentality for social reform. Individual Hindus, whether motivated by religious or secular considerations, quickly grasped its significance as the only agency capable of bringing about some of the desired changes. The important point is that Hindu religion, apart from the sectarian movements or individual reformers like Gandhi, had no prophetic role to play. It was impossible for Hindu religion to stand apart and criticize the gross social injustices perpetrated by institutions of its own creation, or with which it was at least intimately associated. Far from being the critic of society, to a large extent religion *was* society.

The power to regulate society has now shifted decisively from religion to the state. The entire field of law must be brought within the state's jurisdiction. Apart from the egalitarian basis of the political structure, legislation is steadily being enacted to further a program of social reform. The welfare state is increasingly assuming responsibilities formerly borne by the joint family and caste. Nevertheless, the state in India recognizes certain definite limits to its own jurisdiction. It is not totalitarian in its objectives. The liberal and democratic principles on which the state is based assert the pre-eminent value of freedom in individual and social life. In the new situation which is emerging, society is for the most part free from the totalitarianism of both religion and state, although ultimate authority over it is now firmly held by the latter.

If society is being liberated from the strangle-hold of static Hindu orthodoxy, it is also true that this very process liberates Hindu religion from the dead past. While this forcible liberation is painful to the orthodox, it opens up new areas of creativity for a reformulated Hinduism. Hinduism is now called upon to face a new situation. As one element in a free pluralist society, Hindu religion must now attempt to relate its ethical and spiritual resources to a vast array of new problems.

The role of Hinduism is being reduced approximately to that of religion in western society: private faith and worship, and corporate religious life expressed through voluntary organizations. Hinduism must now face the problem which Christianity has had to face since the impact of the Industrial Revolution began to be felt. The problem is simply whether religion is or can be made relevant to the needs of modern society. Having been stripped of its traditional regulatory functions within society, must Hindu religion now be concerned solely with individual faith and morality, or does it have a broader social relevance for the twentieth century? This is surely one of the great challenges which faces Hinduism at the present time.

In the West, Christianity has to a limited extent met this challenge (1) through the development of a social ethic which relates theology to social, economic, political, and international problems, and (2) through the working of organizations which seek to influence the makers of public policy to pay heed to the imperatives of the social ethic. The church is frequently ineffective but rarely *silent* on the great issues of the day; its role as the conscience of society may be denied by many, but it cannot be totally ignored.

There are indeed some notable interpreters of the new Hindu social ethic. Gandhi's *satyagraha* contributed a philosophy and technique of effective political action in the nationalist movement, and its successful use in the continuing struggle for racial equality in parts of the United States illustrates its potency. Vinoba Bhave's reinterpretation of Hindu religious values produced his remarkable movement of non-coercive land reforms by *bhoodan* (land-gift). The entire Sarvodaya movement, of which this is a part, is evidence of the vitality of Hinduism in meeting the challenge.

However, there is no connection at all between this movement and what goes on in the temples and in the festivals which express the real religious life of the Hindu masses. Sarvodaya, as a social philosophy, may well fail to exercise any significant influence on the development of Hindu religion as a whole. The lack of organization in Hinduism, to which reference has already been made, makes it difficult to introduce any substantial changes except through an outside agency—the state. The same organizational deficiencies militate against the assumption of an effective prophetic role as proclaimer of a social gospel, as critic of government and society. Hinduism is not lacking in individual prophetic voices, but its corporate influence as one factor within a pluralist society is all but nonexistent. This would indeed be a radically new role for Hindu religion, and the opportunities for creative experimentation are clearly present. Hinduism can relate itself meaningfully to society under the new circumstances, but it must do so by a completely different process than that of the past.

PART FIVE

THE SECULAR STATE

AND CULTURE

CHAPTER 12

EDUCATION AND RELIGION

IN INDIA as in the West, education was for many centuries closely associated with religion. William Meston was quite correct when he asserted that "the Indian mind finds it hard to think of an education worthy of the name which is dissociated from religion. The schools of the past owed their distinctive features to what was taught in the precincts of Hindu temple and Mohammedan mosque."[1] One may therefore expect that education will be one of the most crucial areas in which India's commitment to secularism will have to be defined. This has indeed been the case in other secular states such as France and the United States, where controversy-begetting problems continue to appear in one form or another. We must first examine the historical background of educational policy in India.

THE PATTERN OF EDUCATION IN BRITISH INDIA

In the late eighteenth and early nineteenth century, diverse factors contributed to the evolution of the East India Company's educational policy. Among these factors were: the role of the former Mughal rulers which had presumably been inherited by the British, the significant educational work carried on by Christian missionaries, and the open disagreement among the British themselves over the relative merits of oriental and western learning.

Early policy decisions

At the beginning of the British period, elementary education consisting of the three R's, and religious teaching was imparted in Hindu *pathsalas* and Muslim *maktabs*. Higher education was confined to the study of classical Sanskrit, Persian, and Arabic texts and was thus also oriented toward religion.[2] The East India Company was at

[1] William Meston, *Indian Educational Policy: Its Principles and Problems*, Christian Literature Society for India, Madras, 1936, p. 419.
[2] R. C. Majumdar, H. C. Raychaudhuri, and K. Datta, *An Advanced History*

first completely unconcerned with education, but it could not long evade the traditional duty of an Indian ruler to patronize the classical learning of the country.[3]

Accordingly, Warren Hastings encouraged the revival of Indian learning by founding in 1781 a school of Islamic studies known as the Calcutta *Madrasa*. Three years later Sir William Jones founded the Asiatic Society of Bengal in order to promote classical studies. In 1792 the Banaras Sanskrit College was established by the government with the object of preserving and cultivating the literature, laws, and religion of the Hindus. Customary stipends were also paid to Brahmans and Muslim scholars at various centers.

Christian missionaries took the lead, however, in establishing many elementary and secondary schools in Madras and Bengal. A Baptist missionary, William Carey, came to Calcutta in 1793 and began establishing schools as soon as his command of the Bengali language would permit. By the early nineteenth century a large number of missionary societies of different denominations were at work in India, and they all founded educational institutions. The mission schools, and later colleges, provided education on western lines and to a large extent through the English language. Some government grants were made to the missionary societies for their educational work, but these were usually quite small.[4]

The missionaries undoubtedly assumed that the diffusion of true knowledge on almost any subject would help to prepare the way for the acceptance of Christianity. Thus, as Ingham points out, "the introduction of history and geography, taught in the light of western

of India, Macmillan Company, London, 1950, p. 816. Despite the fundamentally religious orientation of traditional Indian education, a valuable experiment was undertaken by the emperor Akbar. According to Husain, "Akbar, perhaps for the first time in the history of India, opened a large number of government schools in which Hindu and Muslim children were taught together through the medium of Persian." This system of common education for all citizens necessarily included a purely secular syllabus. Among the subjects taught were Persian literature, ethics, logic, arithmetic, geometry, physics, medicine, political science, and history. This experiment was short-lived, however, for the objective of Hindu-Muslim cultural understanding was violently rejected by later Mughal emperors, especially Aurangzib. See S. Abid Husain, *The National Culture of India*, Jaico Publishing House, Bombay, 1956, p. 71.

[3] W. H. Moreland and Atul Chandra Chatterjee, *A Short History of India*, Longmans Green, London, 1957, p. 343.

[4] Kenneth Ingham, *Reformers in India 1793-1833*, University Press, Cambridge, 1956, pp. 59-60.

knowledge, made possible an attack upon the cosmography of the Hindus and so helped to weaken the faith of the students in their traditional superstitions."[5] Along with this indirect approach, there was of course the direct instruction in Christian doctrine which was compulsory for all students. Regardless of their precise motivation, the missionaries' educational contributions were remarkable, and more than one modern Hindu writer would be willing to call them "noble bands of workers to whom India owes the beginning of English education."[6]

William Carey's example was followed by Raja Rammohan Roy and other liberal-minded Hindus, and several English schools were established by them in Calcutta. When the company's charter was renewed in 1813, Parliament directed that 100,000 rupees be set apart each year for the "improvement of literature and the encouragement of the learned natives of India, and for the introduction and promotion of a knowledge of the sciences among the inhabitants of the British territories in India."[7] Parliament's directive thus envisaged financial aid to both oriental and English education. But it was not until 1823 that sufficient surplus revenue was available, and in that year a Committee of Public Instruction was appointed in Bengal.

The first decision of the new committee was to continue the cautious policy of leaving undisturbed the cultural traditions of Indian society. The committee decided to establish a Sanskrit College in Calcutta. The Hindu reformer, Raja Rammohan Roy, vigorously and eloquently protested this decision in an historic petition to the governor-general. The proposed Sanskrit College, he wrote, could only be expected "to load the minds of youth with grammatical niceties and metaphysical distinctions of little or no practical use to the possessors or to society. The pupils will there acquire what was known two thousand years ago with the addition of vain and empty subtleties since then produced."[8] Rammohan Roy expressed the hope that the sum of money set aside for education might be used to employ European gentlemen of talent to instruct the Indians in

[5] *Ibid.*, p. 67.
[6] Majumdar, *op. cit.*, p. 816.
[7] *Ibid.*, p. 817.
[8] William Theodore de Bary, ed., *Sources of Indian Tradition*, Columbia University Press, New York, 1958, p. 593.

mathematics, natural philosophy, chemistry, anatomy, and other useful sciences.

The Sanskrit College was, however, established. Yet the arguments and example of both liberal Hindus and Christian missionaries in support of western education were not without effect. The Committee of Public Instruction became divided into two camps: the "Orientalists," who favored the policy then prevailing, and the "Anglicists," who urged the adoption of liberal education on western lines through the medium of English.

The appointment of Thomas Babington Macaulay in 1834 as president of the committee turned the tide in favor of the Anglicists. Declaring that "a single shelf of a good European library was worth the whole native literature of India and Arabia," Macaulay was able to convince the governor-general of the rightness of his position.[9] In 1835 the decision was made: the existing oriental institutions were to continue, but with sharply reduced grants; henceforth the available public funds were to be spent in importing "a knowledge of English literature and science."

The British policy of religious neutrality in India had been declared some years before this historic decision.[10] What were the religious implications of the government's new educational policy? Macaulay dealt with this problem in his famous "Minute on Education" quoted above. The Orientalists had argued that the study of Sanskrit and Arabic should receive special encouragement because these were the languages in which the sacred books of Hinduism and Islam were written. Macaulay noted: "Assuredly it is the duty of the British government in India to be not only tolerant, but neutral on all religious questions." But, he went on to argue, from an educational point of view one could not justify the teaching of a barren, sterile body of learning simply because of its close connection with religion. He ridiculed the Orientalists by exclaiming, "We are to teach false history, false astronomy, false medicine, because we find them in company with a false religion."[11]

Macaulay went on to suggest that the principle of religious neutrality must be applied to the government's policies toward Hinduism as well as toward Christianity. "We abstain, and I trust shall

[9] *Ibid.*, p. 597.
[10] Discussed in detail in chapter 3.
[11] de Bary, *op. cit.*, p. 600.

always abstain, from giving any public encouragement to those who are engaged in the work of converting natives to Christianity. And while we act thus, can we reasonably and decently bribe men out of the revenues of the state to waste their youth in learning how they are to purify themselves after touching an ass, or what text of the Vedas they are to repeat to expiate the crime of killing a goat?"[12]

While Macaulay's basic position was that English education was intrinsically superior, and would be vastly more productive of an improved social and material life for India, he was well aware of the secularizing effect it would have. "No Hindu who has received an English education ever remains sincerely attached to his religion," he wrote in 1836. "It is my firm belief that if our plans of education are followed up, there will not be a single idolater among the respectable classes in Bengal thirty years hence. And this will be effected without any effort to proselytise; without the smallest interference in their religious liberty; merely by the natural operation of knowledge and reflection."[13] Indeed, Macaulay and Bentinck, the governor-general, shared with many others the belief that a purely secular western education would ultimately result in the Christianization of India.[14] This was regarded, however, as the inevitable by-product—not the basic object—of English education. History has proved Macaulay mostly right as regards the secularization and westernization of the Indian elite, but wrong on the question of its religious conversion.[15]

The principle of religious neutrality was explicitly applied to the government's new educational policy almost immediately. Before leaving India in 1835, Lord William Bentinck was honored in a farewell address presented by some of the missionaries. In his reply Bentinck asserted: "The fundamental principle of British rule, the compact to which the government stands solemnly pledged, is strict neutrality. To this important maxim, policy as well as good faith have enjoined upon me the most scrupulous observance. The same maxim is peculiarly applicable to general education. In all schools and colleges supported by government, this principle cannot

---

[12] *Loc. cit.*

[13] James Johnston, *Our Educational Policy in India*, John Maclaren and Son, Edinburgh, 1880, p. 36.

[14] Arthur Mayhew, *Christianity and the Government of India*, Faber and Gwyer Ltd., London, 1929, pp. 165-166.

[15] de Bary, *op. cit.*, p. 589.

be too strongly enforced. All interference and injudicious tampering with the religious belief of the students, all mingling of direct or indirect teaching of Christianity with the system of instruction ought to be positively forbidden."[16] This policy was so rigorously applied that, up to 1854, the Bible was even excluded from the libraries of government schools. Furthermore, the teachers were strictly forbidden to give any explanation of the Bible or Christianity, even if asked by the pupils.[17]

Thus, strange as it might at first appear, India became one of the very first countries in the world to develop a system of secular public schools. In a book published in 1872, Arthur Howell commented on "that most remarkable feature in Indian education, the religious neutrality of the government."[18] Whether this policy was a wise one or not was a complex question; Howell was chiefly concerned at this point with its uniqueness: "But it is, I believe, absolutely without precedent or parallel elsewhere, besides being entirely opposed to the traditional idea of education current in the East. In Europe, it is almost an axiom that the connection of any state system of education with religion is not the mere result of tradition; 'it is an indissoluble union, the bonds of which are principles inseparable from the nature of education.' This is admitted almost universally."[19] Howell then went on to describe the close connection between religion and education in Europe. He pointed out that in Germany, for example, religion had always been a standard subject in the elementary schools, and that the teacher's religion had to correspond to that of the majority of his pupils. The American system, "while repudiating all doctrinal or dogmatic teaching, provides everywhere for the regular daily reading of the Bible and for prayer."[20]

The dispatch of 1854

The dispatch of Sir Charles Wood, dated July 19, 1854, laid the foundations of present-day India's educational system. This "Magna

[16] Quoted in Arthur Howell, *Education in British India*, Superintendent of Government Printing, Calcutta, 1872, p. 34.

[17] Mayhew, *op. cit.*, p. 178, and Eugene Stock, *The History of the Church Missionary Society*, Church Missionary Society, London, 1899, vol. 2, p. 240.

[18] Howell, *loc. cit.*

[19] Howell's quotation is from J. K. Shuttleworth, *Public Education*, p. 290.

[20] Howell, *op. cit.*, p. 35. It was not until 1962 that the United States Supreme Court declared that it was unconstitutional for the state of New York to prescribe a short non-sectarian prayer for use in the public schools.

Charta of Indian education," as it has been called, provided for a coordinated system of elementary, secondary, and higher educational institutions. The policy of religious neutrality was reaffirmed. Religious instruction in government institutions was forbidden, for as these "were founded for the benefit of the whole population of India . . . the education conveyed in them should be exclusively secular."[21]

It should be noted that this principle was under constant fire from several quarters, Indian as well as European. One of the most outspoken of the Christian missionaries, Dr. Alexander Duff, made the following comment before a committee of the House of Lords in 1853: "While we rejoice that true literature and science are to be substituted in place of what is demonstrably false, we cannot but lament that no provision whatever has been made for substituting the only true religion—Christianity—in place of the false religion which our literature and science will inevitably demolish."[22] Indians, on the other hand, found the exclusion from the curriculum of their respective religions equally distasteful, so that complaints of "godless education" were heard on all sides.

A new feature of educational policy introduced by the dispatch was the system of government grants-in-aid to private institutions. It was recognized that the government alone was financially unable to undertake the whole educational task. Government schools and colleges would therefore provide the educational models, and the grants-in-aid the stimulus to encourage voluntary effort. Aided private schools had to comply with official regulations and were subject to government inspection.

These aided schools might be conducted by Hindus, Muslims, Christian missionaries, or others, and the managers were at liberty to provide whatever religious instruction they desired without government interference. The inspectors of the education departments were strictly required to take "no notice whatsoever . . . of the religious doctrines that may be taught in any school."[23] An educationally sound private institution would be equally entitled to gov-

[21] *Selections from Educational Records*, Bureau of Education, Calcutta, 1920, vol. 1, pp. 388-389.
[22] *Report of the University Education Commission*, Government of India Press, Simla, 1950, vol. 1, p. 288.
[23] Bhagwan Dayal, *The Development of Modern Indian Education*, Orient Longmans, Bombay, 1955, p. 455.

ernment aid whether it taught the religion of the Bible, the Shastras, or the Koran.

While this principle of strict impartiality was clearly enunciated and faithfully adhered to, the immediate effect of the grant-in-aid system cannot be overlooked. The various religious communities were unequally prepared for this new educational opportunity. The Christian missionary schools were in a position to take immediate advantage of it. In fact, at that time the missionary institutions contained four times as many pupils as the government schools. Ingham states that in 1854 the latter had only 12,000 students, while the number of mission school pupils had exceeded this figure a generation earlier.[24] Schools under Hindu or Muslim auspices, by contrast, were few.

It is undeniable that the system of government grants to missionary schools contributed to the propagation of Christianity. When a new elementary school was opened in a village, the Indian Christian who was placed in charge of it was expected to be an evangelist as well as a teacher. Bishop Stephen Neill frankly stated the facts: "The church in south India has been largely built up by the work of the village teacher-catechist, by far the greater part of whose salary has been met from government grants."[25] The educational work in itself was undoubtedly of great value, and this was what the government was supporting. But in the earlier period, the missionary school was often more important as a base for Christian evangelism.

The policy of excluding religious instruction from the curriculum of government schools was challenged and reaffirmed from time to time. In 1858, on the occasion of the transfer of the government of India from the company to the British crown, the Church Missionary Society presented a memorial to Queen Victoria. The queen was urged to declare that since the adoption of the Christian religion would be of "incalculable benefit" to the people of India, the government's policy henceforth would be to use any legitimate measures for bringing that religion to their attention. In particular, the memorialists suggested that the queen's declaration should include the announcement "that the Bible will be introduced into the system of education in all the government schools and colleges, as the only

[24] Ingham, *op. cit.*, p. 66.
[25] Stephen Neill, *East and West Review*, April 1954, p. 35.

standard of moral rectitude, and the source of those Christian principles upon which your Majesty's government is to be conducted."[26]
Victoria's proclamation of that same year, however, emphatically reaffirmed the principle of religious neutrality, to the disappointment
of the missionaries.

But the exclusion of religious teaching from government schools
was also criticized on other grounds. Many British writers, regardless of their personal religious beliefs, were convinced that India's
moral welfare could not be furthered without regular *religious* instruction—in Hinduism, Islam, Christianity, or whatever religion
the pupils might profess. Arthur Howell wrote that "it seems a
tremendous experiment for the state to undertake . . . the direct
training of whole generations above their own creed, and above that
sense of relation to another world upon which they base all their
moral obligations."[27] James Johnston, zealous Christian though he
was, readily admitted the useful role of Hinduism and Islam in
upholding public and private morality.[28] The whole moral fabric of
society seemed to be imperiled by an educational system which attempted to teach morality apart from religion.

The Commission of 1882

The report of the Indian Education Commission explicitly recognized the limitations and inadequacies of an educational system
which excluded religious teaching. Religious feeling in India was
so inflammable, however, and sectarianism so prevalent, that no
departure from existing policy could be recommended. The religious
neutrality of the state forbade the teaching of one faith, and the
alternative of providing instruction in the several religions of the
country involved insuperable practical difficulties. However, the commission recommended the preparation of a textbook on morality based
on the principles of "natural religion." In a vigorous note of dissent,
K. T. Telang, an Indian member of the commission, rejected this
proposal.[29]

[26] Julius Richter, *A History of Missions in India*, Oliphant, Anderson and Ferrier, Edinburgh, 1908, pp. 207-208.
[27] Howell, *op. cit.*, p. 35.
[28] Johnston, *op. cit.*, pp. 9-10.
[29] *Report of the Indian Education Commission: Appointed by the Resolution of the Government of India dated 3rd February 1882*, Superintendent of Government Printing, Calcutta, 1883, p. 614.

The government of India also rejected it in a resolution passed in 1884. "It is doubtful whether such a moral textbook as is proposed could be introduced without raising a variety of burning questions; and strongly as it may be urged that a purely secular education is imperfect, it does not appear probable that a textbook of morality, sufficiently vague and colorless, to be accepted by Christians, Mohammedans and Hindus would do much, especially in the stage of collegiate education, to remedy the defects or supply the shortcomings of such an education."[30]

The commission felt that the emphasis in the educational system should be shifted from the maintenance of government schools to the aiding of privately managed institutions. Hence it recommended the "progressive devolution of primary, secondary and collegiate education upon private enterprise and continuous withdrawal of government from competition therewith." Government institutions were to be gradually transferred to responsible local bodies composed chiefly of Indians. The commission explicitly excluded missionary societies from this new role, recording its unanimous opinion that "departmental institutions of the higher order should not be transferred to missionary management." The missionaries themselves, both those on the commission and those who appeared as witnesses, were in unanimous accord on this point.[31]

Rather inconsistently, however, the commission envisaged the imparting of religious instruction in the institutions to be taken over by local Indian committees, and listed "the encouragement to religious instruction" as one of the advantages to be gained from government withdrawal.[32] In effect, then, the new policy would have resulted in greatly increased activity in the teaching of Hinduism and Islam, the religions professed by the vast majority of the pupils. The question is an academic one, however, since the new policy was never implemented and was later officially abandoned.[33] The number of both government and aided educational institutions increased steadily during the early decades of the twentieth century.

[30] Government of India Resolution No. 10/309, dated October 2, 1884.
[31] James Johnston, *Abstract and Analysis of the Report of the Indian Education Commission*, Hamilton, Adams and Company, London, 1884, p. 76.
[32] *Report of the Indian Education Commission*, p. 460.
[33] Dayal, *op. cit.*, p. 259.

Grants-in-aid and religious instruction

It might be well at this point to consider some of the implications of the grant-in-aid system, so important in Indian education from 1854 to the present. As has been pointed out, the grants-in-aid were given to all sound educational institutions in support of the secular instruction imparted, regardless of the particular religion which was also taught. This strict impartiality satisfied the requirements of the British policy of religious neutrality. But did the system meet the standard set by the conception of separation of church and state, or the secular state, as defined in our first chapter?

This interesting question was debated by American Baptist missionaries in India as early as 1893, but no clear-cut answer was found. In 1919 the problem was taken up again at the Telugu Baptist Mission Conference. The findings of the conference were contained in a statement which frankly acknowledged certain inconsistencies in the application of Baptist principles at home and abroad. "After making all due allowance for the difference in the two systems as followed in America and in India, free schools under public management against privately managed schools under grants-in-aid, it may still be difficult to explain how a religious body like the Baptists, who believe in liberty of conscience and in the entire separation of church and state, can make the study of the Bible compulsory in its mission schools, and how it can accept state aid for maintaining those schools."[34]

The pressure was intensified when the Northern Baptist Convention, meeting at Buffalo, New York, in June 1920, adopted a resolution calling for an amendment to the United States Constitution. The proposed amendment provided for a more perfect application of the principle of complete separation of church and state, especially as it applied to the use of state funds for support of schools and other institutions under ecclesiastical management. In January 1922 the representatives of the various American Baptist missions in India gave further consideration to the question. The joint conference affirmed its agreement with the proposed constitutional amendment. It expressed the hope that India would in time develop a universal system of government schools and disavowed any intention

[34] *Report of the Joint Conference of Representatives of the American Baptist Missions in British India on Policy Regarding Government Grants-in-aid*, Baptist Mission Press, Calcutta, 1922, p. 12.

of perpetuating its system of mission schools through grants-in-aid beyond the transitional period.

The key resolution of the joint conference, however, was as follows: "That we recognize that the acceptance of grants-in-aid is not in perfect accord with the historic Baptist principle of the separation of church and state as applied in a resolution of the Northern Baptist Convention adopted at Buffalo on June 29, 1920. We maintain, however, that the subject of the acceptance of grants-in-aid from the government in India cannot be properly dealt with by the same arguments as would apply to the discussion of the relation of church and state in America."[35] The sharply divided conference passed the resolution by a vote of six to five.

Closely related to the question of grants-in-aid to educational institutions managed by religious groups is the problem of compulsory religious instruction for the pupils in such institutions. The Indian Education Commission of 1882 had recommended the adoption of a "conscience clause" by which, under certain circumstances, pupils could be excused from religious instruction. This recommendation, however, was not implemented by the government of India.

Henry Whitehead, the Anglican bishop of Madras, devoted a chapter to the question of a conscience clause in a book published in 1924. He took note of the dilemma which confronted some of the British free church missions working in India (very similar to that of the American Baptists mentioned above). He observed: "It is perhaps a little difficult for those Christian churches, that have in times past vigorously protested in England against any grants being given to schools in which denominational teaching was made compulsory, to reconcile their principles in England with their acceptance of grants for missionary schools in India."[36] But the bishop himself claimed to see no infringement of the principle of religious neutrality, since the grants were given to the institutions of all religious bodies alike with strict impartiality.

He did concede, however, that the position of the Indian nationalists who were agitating for a conscience clause was "quite intelligible." If a conscience clause was considered fair and just in England, why not in India? "Why, it is asked, should Hindus and

[35] *Ibid.*, p. 3
[36] Henry Whitehead, *Indian Problems in Religion, Education and Politics,* Constable and Company, London, 1924, p. 189.

346

Mohammedans contribute out of their taxes towards the maintenance of schools which are established in order to propagate a religion that they dislike? If Christians of one denomination may reasonably object to contributing through their taxes to the support of schools in which the doctrines of another Christian denomination are taught, is it not reasonable for Hindus and Mohammedans to object to contributing through their taxes to the support of schools and colleges in which Christianity is compulsorily taught?"[37] Whitehead stated the case for the opposing viewpoint much more convincingly than his own.

The essence of his rebuttal was that the government would have to increase its budget for education by 30 per cent if the missionary schools and colleges were closed. It would be a serious blow if the government had to provide direct instruction for the many thousands of Hindus and Muslims then being educated in mission institutions. Yet the latter might well be closed if a conscience clause were introduced, for their basic purpose was religious; the supporters of missionary work in Great Britain would never subscribe a penny to provide a cheap secular education for Hindus and Muslims.[38] Hardly a statement of high principle!

During the British period the government of India never enacted a conscience clause; various provincial governments did, however. In 1920 the United Provinces forbade making religious instruction in Christian schools compulsory. Each student was given the right to be excused from the classes in religion on the request of his parent or guardian. Similar regulations were subsequently introduced in various other parts of India.[39]

Having surveyed the main lines of development of educational policy in relation to religion in the British period, we shall now turn our attention to the policies of independent India. To a great extent the problems are the same, and the solutions being found are also generally similar, with certain notable exceptions.

Religious Instruction in Government Schools

The dominant pattern regarding religious instruction which emerged from the British period was twofold: no such teaching in

[37] *Ibid.*, p. 191.
[38] *Ibid.*, p. 192.
[39] *National Christian Council Review*, 1947, vol. 67, p. 474.

government schools and instruction in one religion only (that of the management) in private aided schools. A third possibility, however, was explored in several private institutions patterned after the British "public schools." Aitchison College in Lahore, for example, regarded the necessity for religious instruction as "axiomatic." Accordingly, a temple, *gurdwara*, and mosque were maintained in the college compound for the use of the Hindu, Sikh, and Muslim students. Services of worship were conducted every morning and evening by a pandit, bhai, and moulvi, and attendance was required unless parents expressed a desire to the contrary. Regular classes in religion were conducted by three senior Indian masters, who instructed the pupils in their respective scriptures, history, beliefs, prayers, and observances.[40]

This arrangement of having the institution provide instruction in the pupils' respective creeds was also quite compatible with the principle of religious neutrality, as some interpreted it. With the attainment of independence, this and other possibilities were actively considered by those in authority. Despite the history of the past century, there was no foregone conclusion as to how the question of religious instruction in government schools would be answered.

Proposals for religious instruction

One of the most significant statements was made in January 1948 by the late Maulana Abul Kalam Azad, minister for education in the government of India, and a devout Muslim. Addressing the Central Advisory Board of Education, Azad declared that India's difficulties, unlike those of Europe and America, were not due to materialism and rationalism but rather to religious fanaticism. But the solution to this problem did not lie in a purely secular curriculum for government schools, for if this path were followed people would naturally try to provide religious education for their children through private sources.

But what could be expected of these private teachers of religion? Azad asserted that most of them were literate but not educated, and to them "religion means nothing but bigotry." The conclusion to which the minister of education was led by this line of reasoning was as follows: "If we want to safeguard the intellectual life of our

[40] *The Indian Public School: An Outline of the Aims of Members of the Indian Public Schools Conference,* Oxford University Press, Bombay, 1942, pp. 74-77.

country against this danger, it becomes all the more necessary for us not to leave the imparting of early religious education to private sources. We should rather take it under our direct care and supervision. No doubt, a foreign government had to keep itself away from religious education. But a national government cannot divest itself of undertaking this responsibility."[41]

Prime Minister Nehru, however, strongly disagreed with this proposal. The Constituent Assembly also disagreed, and so article 28(1) of the Constitution of 1950 simply declares: "No religious instruction shall be provided in any educational institution wholly maintained out of state funds." But this statement in the Constitution has by no means laid the matter to rest. On the contrary, a constant flood of misgivings and protests, emanating from official as well as private circles, has questioned the desirability of the present policy.

The late John Matthai, vice-chancellor of Bombay University, referred in a convocation address to the inadequacy of general secular education and noted: "Religion has a place in the formation of right motives which is of greater importance than is recognized in this age of the cult of the intellect."[42] S. R. Das, chief justice of India until 1959, declared in a public address that "education which does not bring any spiritual enlightenment is not education at all." While noting the restriction imposed by article 28 of the Constitution, Das stated, nevertheless, that education with a spiritual orientation was a vital necessity, and that religious instruction should commence early in life.[43]

C. Rajagopalachari, India's last governor-general, declared in 1957 that there should be no divorce between school and religion in the early training of the child. He asserted that even the present secular government could be persuaded to change its mind if enough people demanded that religion be taught in the schools.[44] Rukmini Devi Arundale, in her contribution to a symposium on education published by the government of India, complained: "India's basis and root are in religion, yet we do not allow religious education.

[41] *Speeches of Maulana Azad 1947-55*, Publications Division, Government of India, Delhi, 1956, p. 25.
[42] *The Hindu Weekly Review*, September 10, 1956.
[43] *Educational India*, December 1958.
[44] *Christian Century*, 1957, vol. 74, p. 368.

Just because the religious spirit has deteriorated we decide to give up the whole basis of our civilization."[45]

Dr. Sampurnanand, then chief minister of Uttar Pradesh, presented a Hindu religious and philosophical view of education in the same publication. He expounded the following thesis: "The highest object of a man's life should then be *moksha* and his life so molded as to be an embodiment of *dharma*. . . . This being the purpose of human life, the purpose of education itself is clearly defined. A system of education will be judged by the extent to which it equips a man to achieve this object."[46] Sampurnanand went on to suggest the best metaphysical basis for religion, society, and therefore education: "The whole universe is one organism, we are all indissolubly connected with one another as cells in the body of the Universal Being. Like the blood-stream which gives nourishment equally to all parts of the body, we are all bathed in, and derive sustenance from, the Super-Prana, the Divine Spirit."[47] The chief minister saw a bright future for Indian education if it could surmount the obstacles of "a false emphasis on secularism" and "spurious intellectualism." India would have to break free from the leading strings of the West, ignore the accusation of revivalism, and devote herself to the remolding of the whole educational system on the basis of *dharma*.

The growing demand for religious instruction in independent India was not at all reflected in the 1953 report of the Secondary Education Commission. The commission dealt with this subject in a very brief section; it referred to the nature of the secular state, the relevant provisions of the Constitution, and the limitations of the classroom approach to moral and religious teaching. The commission cited with approval the practice followed in some schools of holding a daily assembly of all teachers and pupils, when a "general non-denominational prayer" is offered. But apart from this, religious instruction would have to be organized on a private basis.[48]

[45] Rukmini Devi Arundale, chapter in *The Future of Education in India*, Publications Division, Government of India, Delhi, 1956, p. 48.
[46] Dr. Sampurnanand, chapter in *ibid.*, p. 73.
[47] *Ibid.*, p. 74.
[48] *Report of the Secondary Education Commission*, Government of India, Delhi, 1953, p. 134.

The Radhakrishnan report

The University Education Commission, on the other hand, went into the subject of religious instruction in great detail. The chairman of this ten-man commission was Dr. S. Radhakrishnan, and chapter 8 of the report ("Religious Education") clearly bears the imprint of his philosophical and religious convictions. The basic line of reasoning developed in the chapter may be analyzed as follows: (1) dogmatic religion leads to conflict; (2) religious conflict leads to the secular state; (3) the secular state bans only dogmatic religious instruction in state schools; (4) the state can and should provide for the teaching of universal religion. These four steps of the argument should be considered in greater detail.

First, dogmatic religion leads to conflict. The existence of differing dogmatic creeds has in the past tended to produce intolerance. "Other religions may teach the same doctrines, even use the same words, but still we were taught that the one Voice came from Heaven and the other from the opposite region."[49] Divisive creeds and group loyalties thus encouraged social disharmony and the spirit of strife.

Second, religious conflict leads to the secular state. The report presents an extremely negative interpretation of the origin of the secular state. "The abuse of religion has led to the secular conception of the state."[50] It is specifically stated that the difficulties through which India had passed in recent years (Hindu-Muslim and other communal conflicts) led to the adoption of the principle of the secular state, as found in the American and Australian Constitutions. Most interpreters of the principle in those countries, however, would regard it as a great achievement for the protection of the individual's freedom of conscience. The commission seemed almost to regard the secular state as a necessary evil.

Third, the intention of the secular state "is not to ban all religious education but to ban dogmatic or sectarian religious instruction in state schools."[51] Since this is the only kind of religion which creates conflict and necessitates the secular state, the teaching of dogmatic religion alone is prohibited by the Indian Constitution. "To prescribe

[49] *The Report of the University Education Commission*, Government of India Press, Simla, 1950, p. 294.
[50] *Loc. cit.*
[51] *Loc. cit.*

dogmatic religions in a community of many different faiths is to revive the religious controversies of the past. To turn the students over to theologians of different denominations for instruction in the conflicting systems of salvation is to undermine that fellowship of learning which defines a college or a university."[52]

Fourth, the state can and should provide for the teaching of universal religion. The idea of universal religion is held to be one of the central features of "the Indian view of religion." There is no constitutional problem, for "the adoption of the Indian outlook on religion is not inconsistent with the principles of our Constitution."[53] This view of religion regards the various historic faiths as simply diverse expressions of the hunger of the human heart for the Infinite. The report urges a syncretistic approach: "A religion worthy of the all-embracing God must harmonize all faiths in one universal synthesis." This would necessitate at the very least a new interpretation of historical uniqueness, for "if religion concerns itself with peculiar historical events, there is not much meeting ground among followers of different religions who adopt different historical events as their religious bases."[54]

The report rejects the view that moral instruction can take the place of religion in the educational curriculum. Furthermore, "if we exclude spiritual training in our institutions we would be untrue to our whole historical development."[55] Near the end of the chapter the question of the secular state is once more raised but quickly disposed of: "The absolute religious neutrality of the state can be preserved if in state institutions, what is good and great in every religion is presented, and what is more essential, the unity of all religions."[56]

The report makes four recommendations. The first is that all educational institutions begin each day with a few minutes of silent meditation. Second, that the lives of great religious leaders like Gautama the Buddha, Confucius, Socrates, Jesus, Ramanuja, Mohammed, Gandhi, etc., should be studied in the first year of the

[52] *Ibid.*, p. 296.   [53] *Ibid.*, p. 295.   [54] *Ibid.*, p. 298.
[55] *Ibid.*, p. 299. Note also the earlier statement: "We do not accept a purely scientific naturalism as the philosophy of the state. That would be to violate our nature, our *svabhava,* our characteristic genius, our *svadharma.* Though we have no state religion, we cannot forget that a deeply religious strain has run throughout our history like a golden thread." *Ibid.*, pp. 294-295.
[56] *Ibid.*, p. 302.

degree course. Third, that selections "of a universalist character" from the scriptures of all religions be studied in the next year. "We should not prescribe books which feel an obligation to prove that their religion is true and often that it alone is true."[57] Finally, that various problems of the philosophy of religion be considered in the third year.

In a previous chapter we have discussed the limitations of a syncretistic view of religion as the theoretical basis for the secular state.[58] These limitations are equally relevant to the question of religious instruction in state schools. The commission rejects the teaching of the dogmas of individual sectarian religions as opposed to "the critical methods of inquiry followed in other disciplines of the curriculum."[59] Rather, what is to be taught is "the unity of all religions." Yet this too is a religious *dogma* explicitly rejected by most Indian Muslims and Christians. Will this dogma be propagated among non-Hindu students in the university under the guise of "the Indian view of religion"? And will the critical methods of inquiry in the classroom be permitted to challenge this dogma? Or will this quasi-official universal religion be regarded as The Truth (as it apparently was by the commission) and not a matter for inquiry? And finally, what of the student whose parents are atheists or agnostics? Serious problems of freedom of conscience are involved.

The unity of all religions is one dogma. The identity of the soul with the absolute is another and is discussed in Rev. J. D. M. Stuart's critique of the report: "The impossibility of a religion existing without dogma is admirably illustrated by the commission's own proposals. Probably the most important of these is the provision of a daily period for meditation. And how is this described?—in terms of *self-realization*. 'We will find the Supreme, the only Supreme, which it is possible for us to know, when we are taught to look within.' To the orthodox Christian or Muslim this is based on a dogma, which they cannot fail to recognize, because it is a dogma which they both alike reject, namely the identity of the soul with *Brahma*. (No one presumably claims that this belief is rationally verifiable?) And to this extent the state is being asked to foster, not

---

[57] *Loc. cit.*
[58] See chapter 5, "The Theoretical Undergirding."
[59] *Report*, p. 296.

353

a truly universal religion, but a form of neo-Hinduism, based on a single, but essentially dogmatic, article of faith."[60] Stuart went on to criticize the report's misinterpretation of various passages from the Bible, which had been quoted in support of the above doctrine.

The four recommendations made by the commission are in themselves unobjectionable. A few moments of silent meditation each day could not possibly harm anyone. No one would deny that a balanced university curriculum might very well include the study of the great men of religious history, the various religious books, and the philosophy of religion. What is disturbing is the fact that these subjects are all to be taught from a particular point of view, determined by the doctrinal assumptions of neo-Hinduism. This being the case, scholarly objectivity as well as religious neutrality are bound to suffer. The Koran, like the Rig Veda, will be made to teach that "the Real is one; sages call it by various names," for the commission has already announced that "this is the teaching of Islam when taken in its profoundest sense."

The limitations of universal religion have often been pointed out. Writing in 1937, A. N. Basu asserted that if one were to seek the common denominator of all the sects of Hinduism alone, the result would be "like the chemical properties of hydrogen, tasteless, colorless and odorless, in a word absolutely ineffective."[61] He conceded that it might be argued that in their essence all religions are the same, but this is only true of religions in their philosophical, not their theological, aspects.

In an article published in 1959, C. Rajagopalachari emphatically affirmed the view (also held by the commission, as noted above) that morality could not be effectively taught apart from religion. Rajagopalachari's article was significantly entitled "Religion, our Only Real Policeman." But what kind of religion will be effective in this role? The idea of universal religion is rejected, for "myths and icons are indispensable for expressing as much as we can express of the ineffable." Therefore Harischandra, Rama, Krishna, Sita, Hanuman, etc., and even Ravana, all have a rightful place in "the glorious galaxy that Hindus have inherited."

[60] J. D. M. Stuart, "Religious Education: Some Comments on Chapter VIII of the Report of the University Education Commission," *N.C.C. Review*, 1950, vol. 70, p. 321. In Hindu thought *Brahma* is the soul of the universe.
[61] A. N. Basu, *Education in Modern India: A Brief Review*, Orient Book Company, Calcutta, 1947, p. 170.

The chief weakness of universal religion is simply that it has no emotional appeal. Rajagopalachari's conclusion: "No religion appeals to the heart as well as the religion one has been brought up in, with all its great images and myths and traditional history. It is therefore necessary that we should all be strengthened *each in his own religion*" [italics added]. The writer pointed out that Gandhi's central theme was to combine equal respect for all religions with wholehearted adherence to one's own faith. It should be possible for a government which reveres Gandhi to evolve a system of religious instruction which avoids conflict without falling into "the error of avoiding trouble by a formless artificial synthesis that has no holy tradition or myth or ancient ritual to support it."[62]

The University Education Commission submitted its report in 1949. The next official body to review the question in detail was the Committee on Religious and Moral Instruction, appointed by the government of India in 1959. The chairman of the four-member committee was Sri Prakasa, governor of Bombay, and the membership of the committee included one Muslim and one Christian. The terms of reference of the committee were to examine the desirability and feasibility of providing for "the teaching of moral and spiritual values" in educational institutions and to define the content of such instruction.

After discussing the problems of student indiscipline, anti-social activities, and the general absence of wholesome ideals in campus life, the committee concluded that the teaching of moral and spiritual values in educational institutions was definitely needed, and within certain limits was quite feasible. The content of the recommended instruction would include the following: "A comparative and sympathetic study of the lives and teachings of great religious leaders and at later stages, their ethical systems and philosophies. The inculcation of good manners, social service and true patriotism should be continuously stressed at all times."[63]

While the Committee on Religious and Moral Instruction was strongly influenced by the specific curriculum recommendations made by the Radhakrishnan commission, it did not attempt to base

[62] C. Rajagopalachari, "Religion, our Only Real Policeman," *Swarajya*, January 3, 1959.
[63] *Report of the Committee on Religious and Moral Instruction*, Government of India Press, New Delhi, 1960, p. 16.

these on a Vedantic "Indian view of religion." In this sense its report marked a definite advance over that of the earlier commission. The recommendations are simply founded on the sound observation that religious diversity is one of the most important features of Indian life and that every educated citizen should understand the basic principles and values of religions other than his own. The objective is to promote the spirit of tolerance through the understanding of differences, not to prove the unity of all religions by syncretistic harmonization. Of course, it could be expected that many Hindu teachers would take the latter approach in actually presenting this material in the classroom.

Religion in basic education

Another area in which significant differences over religious issues have arisen is that of basic education. This is the system of elementary education first proposed by Gandhi in 1937 (frequently referred to as "the Wardha Scheme") and adopted by the government since independence.[64] Sectarian religious instruction was deliberately omitted from the plan, for which Gandhi was roundly criticized.[65] Although he too was deeply convinced personally that all religions are true, he did not propose the teaching of a syncretistic universal religion but only basic morality. Gandhi wrote: "Fundamental principles of ethics are common to all religions. These should be regarded as adequate religious instruction so far as the schools under the Wardha scheme are concerned."[66]

Gandhi's decision to exclude the formal teaching of religion was approved by the Central Advisory Board of Education in 1939 and has been reaffirmed since then. Shrimali points out, however, that "the Wardha Scheme aims at developing tolerance and mutual respect for all religions."[67] Accordingly, the syllabus included stories of the ancient Indian, Chinese, Christian, and Islamic religions and civilizations. The University Education Commission Report, however, quotes with approval the following sentence from the revised syl-

[64] S. N. Mukerji, Education in India—Today and Tomorrow, Acharya Book Depot, Baroda, 1950, pp. 16-23.
[65] For a discussion of these criticisms, see K. L. Shrimali, The Wardha Scheme: The Gandhian Plan of Education for Rural India, Vidya Bhavan Society, Udaipur, 1949, pp. 212-231.
[66] Harijan, July 16, 1938, quoted in M. K. Gandhi, Basic Education, Navajivan Publishing House, Ahmedabad, 1951, p. 70.
[67] Shrimali, op. cit., p. 225.

labus used in training teachers for basic schools: "Reverential study of the different religions of the world showing how in essentials they meet in perfect harmony the Religion of Man."[68] By a subtle twist the teaching of respect for all religions becomes the propagation of religious syncretism.

But the most important religious question with respect to basic education has arisen over the practice of common worship. It was reported in 1955 that as a matter of general practice all students in basic training schools were expected to take part in common daily worship, which included "the reading of the scriptures of various religions and prayers addressed to God under various names."[69] In response to this situation the executive committee of the Church of South India Synod issued a statement for the guidance of members of that church.

Basic education sought to develop a sense of community among pupils and teachers, and this was approved of by the church, in addition to the religious orientation given to education. But the executive committee dissented vigorously from the theological implications which it found in the practice of common worship. "As Christians we do not and cannot believe that the knowledge of God, and true community based upon that knowledge, can be achieved by adding together or pooling all men's beliefs about God. On the contrary, we believe that God had provided the final and sufficient revelation of Himself in Jesus Christ."[70]

Holding that it was "impossible" for Christians to accept this form of common worship, the statement went on to raise the issue of religious liberty. "In taking this stand we are entitled to appeal to the Constitution of India which defines the Republic as a secular state in which the differing beliefs of the religions concerning God and man are to be acknowledged and respected, and the power of the state is not to be used to enforce one view as against others. If the present practice of requiring attendance at common worship is continued, it will be a breach of the clear provisions of the Constitution."[71] The statement recognized that the Christians who took this unpopular position and refused to participate might well become

[68] *Report of the University Education Commission*, p. 302.
[69] "Common Worship in Basic Training Schools," *N.C.C. Review*, 1955, vol. 75, p. 288.
[70] *Loc. cit.*
[71] *Ibid.*, p. 289.

the objects of misunderstanding and resentment, but it pointed out that it has often been thus, "from the days when the first Christians had to suffer wrath rather than take part in the officially sponsored religious rites of the Roman Empire." On the other hand, some Christian groups quickly responded positively and introduced basic education, including the provision for common worship, in their mission schools.[72]

What general conclusions may be drawn from this discussion? During the British period the problem was handled very simply by providing for *no* religious instruction. In the preceding pages we have discussed a number of other proposals and experiments. In the opinion of the author, however, they all create more problems of religious liberty for the secular state than they solve for the religious-minded.

In March 1958 Dr. K. L. Shrimali, the present minister for education, announced that it had been suggested to the states that schools and colleges hold a daily assembly of all teachers and pupils for a universal prayer or a brief period of silent meditation.[73] This is certainly unobjectionable. But any more elaborate form of common worship creates substantial problems relating to freedom of conscience. Comparative religion and philosophy of religion are certainly valid subjects of study for inclusion in a university curriculum. But they should be taught with some measure of scholarly objectivity, without attempting to prove that all religions are saying essentially the same thing as Hinduism, but in slightly different words. Formulators of present-day Indian educational policy, in short, might profitably reconsider Bentinck's speech of 1835 in which he sternly warned against "all interference and injudicious tampering with the religious belief of the students."

State Control of Private Schools

We now come to the second broad problem area, which chiefly concerns government control over state-aided private schools managed by religious bodies.

[72] See Lloyd Lorbeer, "Basic Education in Christian Schools," *N.C.C. Review*, 1955, vol. 75, pp. 427-428.
[73] *The Hindu Weekly Review*, March 17, 1958.

New aspects of religious instruction

By 1947 a conscience clause similar to that described earlier in the chapter had been included in the educational codes of many provinces. Most of these conscience clauses provided for "opting out" —that is, each pupil was expected to attend the religious and moral instruction classes given in the institution unless his parent or guardian requested in writing that he be excused from them. In Madras, for example, the announcement of religious instruction in a Christian secondary school included the following: "Attendance at these classes is voluntary, and other arrangements are made for engaging—during these periods—pupils not being eighteen years of age, whose parents have conscientious objections to the instruction provided in these classes. Such objections should be stated in writing and addressed to the principal."[74]

The "opting out" procedure provided by this form of conscience clause generally tended to discourage requests for exemption. Whether due to this procedure or simply because of a tolerant willingness to learn about another religion, the fact is that relatively few Hindu parents withdrew their children from such instruction. Indeed, it was reported in 1948 that only one out of 1,000 students at Madras Christian College had asked to be excused, and he later withdrew his request.[75]

The conscience clause adopted in Travancore, on the other hand, provided for "opting in"—that is, religious instruction could not be imparted to anyone without the written consent of the parent. Under this regulation there were many who declined to receive religious instruction in mission schools.[76] This was the form of conscience clause which was incorporated in the Constitution of India. Article 28(3) states: "No person attending any educational institution recognized by the State or receiving aid out of state funds shall be required to take part in any religious instruction that may be imparted in such institution or to attend any religious worship that may be conducted in such institution or in any premises at-

[74] Rev. D. Chellappa, "Religious Teaching in Schools," *N.C.C. Review*, 1948, vol. 68, p. 385.
[75] Robert Root, "The Christian Prospect in India," *Christian Century*, 1948, vol. 65, p. 708.
[76] Chellappa, *op. cit.*, p. 386.

tached thereto unless such person or, if such person is a minor, his guardian has given his consent thereto." When this provision appeared (in a slightly different form) in the draft Constitution, a conference under the auspices of the National Christian Council passed a resolution calling for the substitution of the "opting out" procedure.[77] The Constituent Assembly, however, retained the "opting in" wording.

In 1947 the government of Madras amended its educational rules to include the regulation that religious instruction should not constitute an attack on any other faith, and that "staffs, pupils and buildings of any school or college shall not be utilized for proselytization purposes" (Rule 9-A). The word "proselytization" remained undefined and gave rise to considerable controversy.[78] A public meeting that assembled under the auspices of the South India Christian Association condemned this part of the amendment as "a serious infringement of the fundamental rights of every citizen in a free India to preach and propagate his faith" and appealed to the government to cancel it.[79]

Another aspect of the problem was the demand, frequently voiced in Hindu circles as national independence drew near, that Christian educational institutions be required to provide instruction in other religions for their non-Christian pupils. The General Synod of the Methodist Church in India, Burma, and Ceylon, meeting in February 1946, passed the following resolution: "The Synod declares that no recognition of, or aid to, our schools by the state should result in acceptance of the state's dictation of religious policy. The Synod recognizes the right of parents to claim exemption for their children from attendance at Christian worship and instruction on conscientious grounds, but it cannot accept the proposal which has been made requiring the teaching of other religions in our schools."[80]

No such regulations have been issued by the state governments, but since independence difficult situations have arisen over the demand made by students for permission to conduct non-Christian worship. At St. Columba's College in Hazaribagh some Hindu

---

[77] "Minutes of the Joint Conference of the Central Board of Christian Higher Education and the Committee on High Schools," *N.C.C. Review*, 1948, vol. 68, pp. 417-418.

[78] Chellappa, *op. cit.*, p. 385.

[79] *The Guardian*, 1947, vol. 25, p. 331.

[80] Chellappa, *op. cit.*, pp. 386-387. See also *The Guardian*, 1946, vol. 24, p. 152.

students demanded that they be allowed to install an image of Saraswati in the college premises and to organize and celebrate Saraswati *puja* there. The request was refused. Several years later, when a similar request was turned down by the authorities of St. Paul's College in Calcutta, a student filed a writ petition in the Calcutta High Court. In a 1957 judgment dismissing the petition, the judge examined the question in relation to articles 25, 29(2), and 30 of the Constitution and upheld the right of Christian institutions to exclude non-Christian worship.[81]

While certain problems remain, the official policies evolved with respect to religious instruction in private schools have generally been fair and reasonable. Independent India has sought to protect the individual's freedom of conscience, yet with due regard for the rights of others to teach their faith.

State control of private school administration

The system under which government grants-in-aid are given to educational institutions conducted by religious bodies is inconsistent with a strict interpretation of the secular state. The system involves the indirect subsidization of religion by the state and thus violates a basic principle of secularism.

It is important to examine the *raison d'être* of educational institutions administered by religious groups. Clearly, their establishment does not come about because of a deep conviction that such institutions will be able to teach the facts of literature, geography, or mathematics better than state schools. Rather, such schools are started with a primarily religious objective—to secure the opportunity for direct religious instruction and to develop a religious atmosphere and viewpoint even for the study of literature, geography, and mathematics. In other words, a religious body establishes and maintains schools in order to create a total environment which will be favorable to the promotion of its particular religious values.

On the other hand, the state which aids these institutions (this is true at least of India) is motivated primarily by secular considerations. As far as the state is concerned, the teaching of literature, geography, and mathematics to the child is an end in itself. The grant-in-aid system is a method of partially discharging the state's recognized responsibility for the education of the population, within

[81] *Sanjib Kumar* v. *St. Paul's College*, A.I.R. 1957 Calcutta, p. 524.

the stringent limits of its financial resources. The partnership with private agencies maximizes the educational result. But the state cannot ignore the concomitant religious effects which its actions produce. The state, inevitably, also contributes to the realization of the religious aims of the private agency.

The basic incompatibility of the secular state with state aid to church-operated schools is sensed most acutely when the latter have *compulsory* religious instruction. But even when this form of coercion in spiritual matters does not exist (this is the case under the present Constitution of India), the problem for the secular state still remains. For the private agency is still using state funds to promote, propagate, and enhance the prestige of its particular religious values. For this reason, the first amendment of the United States Constitution, as interpreted by the Supreme Court, prohibits state financial aid to church schools. One observer wrote in 1948: "There is irony in the fact that while almost all Protestants in America object to any kind of government subsidy for religion, Protestant mission schools in India, including American schools, depend heavily on grants from the government—which, quite naturally, expects to have something to say about the operation of the schools."[82]

The last part of this quotation introduces the other problem connected with the grant-in-aid system. State aid to religion is almost invariably a two-edged sword; the state frequently interferes with religion by the same action which promotes it. Stated differently, state interference is the price of state aid.

Despite the negative tone of these comments on the theory of the grant-in-aid system, it would be unfair to ignore the great practical benefits in the field of education which have been made possible by that system. In India the grant-in-aid system has over a century behind it. During this century, thousands of schools were established by religious bodies at great expense, with the understanding that the state would grant them financial aid without interfering with their distinctive religious purposes. On the whole this partnership between the state and private agencies has worked well. Christian mission or church schools, which still constitute in many areas the majority of aided institutions, have often been highly praised by prominent non-Christians for their significant educational contribution.

[82] Root, *op. cit.*, p. 708.

Since independence, however, the basis of the partnership between the state and private agencies has been undergoing radical changes. Some of the state governments have adopted measures which severely limit the authority of private agencies over their own institutions. The tightening of state control is explicitly based on the principle that where state funds are expended, state control is justified and must be expected. As there are no a priori limits to such control, official policy in some states seems to be moving steadily in the direction of nationalization of private aided schools.

The record of *some* private schools in the country has undoubtedly been bad: poor teaching, lack of discipline, abuses in the appointment and payment of teachers, embezzlement of school funds by unscrupulous managers. Increasing governmental regulation of private institutions is in part a response to this record of mismanagement by a minority of their number. But other factors contribute to the trend toward greater state control. There is a strong underlying assumption in all of present-day Indian life that state control makes for greater efficiency. Along with this goes the bureaucratic demand for standardization. Furthermore, the present political leadership is committed to the goal of a socialist society, with the consequent emphasis on the public sector at the expense of the private sector.

Certain methods of state control over private educational institutions have long been exercised, and their validity has not been questioned. For example, no one disputes the government's powers of inspection, granting of recognition, auditing of accounts where public funds are involved, and prescription of the qualifications of teachers. But the present tendency is to go beyond these accepted methods of control and to assume new powers in the internal management of private aided institutions. In Bihar and Assam (and formerly in Uttar Pradesh), for example, every board of managers must include three members appointed by the government. Christian organizations operating schools have expressed the fear that their distinctive religious purposes "may be thwarted by the inclusion in the managing body of men and women who may not be in sympathy with the ideals and purposes of these institutions."[83]

In the former Bombay state (now Maharashtra and Gujarat) and other states, the appointment of headmasters must be by seniority.

[83] *N.C.C. Review*, 1953, vol. 73, p. 240.

In a report to the 1958 Catholic Bishops' Conference of India, it was pointed out that this rule could prove most embarrassing for a Catholic school, for the senior master might well be a non-Catholic.[84] In Bihar, teachers in aided schools may be appointed only from an approved list drawn up by state authorities. In Madras and Andhra Pradesh, teachers may not be transferred except with the consent and approval of the educational department, and in several states no teacher may be dismissed without the consent of this department.

A 1950 Madras act permits aided institutions which are found to be poorly managed to be taken under the temporary control of the government (buildings, playgrounds, equipment, and staff). The government will then either manage them directly or transfer their management to different bodies of the same or similar denomination. After a period not exceeding two years, the future management will be finally decided. The trend toward increased state control became most evident in the Andhra Educational Institutions Act of 1956. This legislation empowers the state government to withdraw permission granted to private agencies to operate educational institutions and to take over the management of properties after paying "reasonable compensation" to the owners. This was a step in the government's announced policy of bringing all schools under unified control and of raising their level of efficiency. The government decided to implement the legislation first by taking over all aided elementary schools in Nellore district, and would eventually extend the plan to secondary schools.[85]

Many of the private educational institutions are managed by Christian agencies, and the question must be raised as to whether the increasing state control reflects an anti-Christian bias on the part of governments manned mostly by members of the majority community. A 1958 Roman Catholic report stated: "Since complaints have been made of the steady encroachment of educational departments in the states on what ought to be the exclusive province of the private school, it is necessary to remember that such steps are not inspired by any prejudice against our schools, but (are) merely the result of the present climate in the country which is less favorable to

[84] *Catholic Bishops' Conference of India: Report of the Meetings of the Standing Committee, 1958*, St. Mary's Industrial School Press, Bangalore, 1959, p. 61.
[85] *Christian Century*, 1956, vol. 73, p. 1432.

private enterprise and would rather encourage the public sector. That the encroachments are serious can hardly be denied; but except in Kerala and certain districts of M. P., they are not proof of anti-Catholic prejudice, and all private schools are similarly affected."[86] Most Christian leaders in the field of education would concur in this analysis of the problem.

The Kerala Education Bill

The Kerala Education Bill, introduced by the Communist government of that state in 1957, deserves special attention. The ideological and political struggle between Catholicism and Communism was indeed one aspect of the twenty-eight months of Communist rule. But the controversy over control of private education had a considerable history, in which the conflict chiefly involved religious and caste communities in the state. In 1945-1946 the Travancore government unsuccessfully attempted to put into operation its long declared intention of taking over primary education in its entirety, to the exclusion of private agencies. In 1950-1951 an acute controversy in the Travancore-Cochin state developed over the government's plan to increase the salaries of private school teachers, with the accompanying requirements that 80 per cent of the school fees be remitted to the government, and that teachers be appointed only from an approved list published by the state.[87] This crisis was resolved by a compromise. Rules later adopted also required that the headmaster of a school be appointed by seniority.

Underlying much of the conflict was the fact of the dominant position long occupied by Christian agencies in the field of education. Christian enterprise in Kerala was largely responsible for producing the highest literacy rate in India, twice as high as that of neighboring states. Control of a large segment of the state's education inevitably meant considerable social and political influence in a Hindu-majority area, and this influence was utilized effectively. The political pressure exerted by the Catholic hierarchy in its controversies with the government produced much resentment among Hindu leaders.

Thus, the tendency toward increased state control of private schools, and even nationalization, was evident long before the

---

[86] *Catholic Bishops' Conference of India, 1958*, p. 58.
[87] The Indian states of Travancore and Cochin were merged after independence, and formed the largest part of the state of Kerala after the 1956 states reorganization.

Communists came to power. Their opposition to the church as a "reactionary vested interest" was reinforced by communal rivalries of long standing. The "totalitarian approach" incorporated in the Kerala Education Act was made the focal point of the struggle against the Communist government, but this was not the most important issue, even for the Catholics.

Christians, a majority of whom are Roman Catholics, constitute 22 per cent of Kerala's population of 15 million. Out of about 11,000 schools in the state, 7,000 are under private management. The proportion of privately managed schools was even higher before independence. Of these 7,000 private institutions, about 3,000 are operated by Christian agencies (again, mostly Catholic) and another 3,000 by a Hindu caste organization, the Nair Service Society. While state grants to these private schools were once small, they increased steadily until the teacher's *entire salary* was being paid by the state. Impartial opinion recognized the existence of fairly widespread abuses in the appointment and remuneration of staff. In some cases teachers were compelled to make monthly "donations" to the school in order to retain their jobs. Teachers in many private institutions had no provident fund benefits and no security of service, being subject to arbitrary dismissal at any time.

The Communist ministry's Kerala Education Bill received the enthusiastic support of most of the private school teachers for its provisions accorded to them most of the rights and privileges enjoyed by teachers in government schools. Many Hindus welcomed the measure as a blow against the power of the Catholic Church. But a substantial body of opinion, both in Kerala and elsewhere, regarded the legislation as a necessary attempt to achieve educational reform and social justice, although some of the provisions of the bill were unduly restrictive of the rights of management.

The key provisions of the bill, as introduced in 1957, were as follows: all teachers' salaries to be paid directly by the government, and all fees collected by the management to be remitted to the government; appointment of teachers only from a state register prepared by the government; the extension to teachers in aided schools of provident fund, pension, and insurance at state expense; power granted to the government to take over the management of any school for five years if the manager neglects to perform his duty; power to take over any category of aided schools if this step is regarded as necessary in order to standardize general education or improve the level of literacy. Private agencies were compelled to agree to these regulations as a condition for the receipt of state aid.

The agitation against the bill was based on the assertion that it represented an attempt to "communize" education, that its provisions were an unprecedented interference with the rights of managers. However, a pro-Communist account is quite correct in pointing out that the bill was hardly more radical than the Andhra Educational Institutions Act of 1956.[88] A later modification of the bill permitted the management of an aided institution the option to operate it as a recognized school without government grants. An institution might thus be exempted from the drastic state regulation provided for by the bill.

The bill was passed with some changes by the state assembly in September 1957 and sent to the president for his approval; in an unusual move it was referred to the Supreme Court for an advisory opinion. The court held that clauses 14 and 15 of the bill, which empowered the government to take over entirely the management of aided schools, were unconstitutional. However, it rejected the view that the bill as a whole constituted an attack on the right of minorities in Kerala to establish and administer schools of their choice, as guaranteed by article 30(1) of the Constitution. There was nothing in the bill which discriminated against minorities; if any private school solicits state aid, it must be willing to submit to reasonable regulations. The court held that, with the exception of clauses 14 and 15, the conditions laid down in the bill were reasonable, although they constituted "serious inroads on the right of administration and appear perilously near violating that right."[89] The bill was revised in the light of this judgment, passed by the Kerala legislature, and received the president's assent in February 1959.

The Nair Service Society and the Christian churches had already united in a massive campaign of opposition to the legislation. Private schools were closed by managers in protest against the Communist regime, and violent clashes occurred in many places. Virtually all of the non-Communist political and religious organizations in the state combined to fight the Communist ministry and finally

[88] H. D. Malaviya, Kerala: *A Report to the Nation*, People's Publishing House, New Delhi, 1958, pp. 31, 33.
[89] *In re Kerala Education Bill, 1957*, A.I.R. 1958 S.C., p. 956.

succeeded in securing the intervention of the central government and the proclamation of president's rule in the state on July 31, 1959.

Probably the most fundamental Christian objection to the Kerala Education Act was that it took away the freedom of the management to appoint the kind of teachers needed to maintain the distinctive orientation and atmosphere of a Christian school.[90] In late 1960 the Kerala assembly (by this time controlled by a non-Communist majority) debated and passed an amendment to the education act. The controversial section 11 of the act had provided that appointment of teachers should be made by the Public Service Commission with due regard to the principle of communal reservation. According to the 1960 amendment, the managers were given the power to appoint teachers from among persons who possessed the prescribed qualifications. But the element of state control would come at the earlier stage of selection of candidates for training in private teachers' colleges; 80 per cent of these candidates would be chosen by the Public Service Commission on the basis of communal reservation.[91] The communal reservation (45 per cent of the seats for the backward communities, the rest according to a communal population ratio) would effectively control the composition of the candidates qualified for appointment as teachers. Regulation by the state in this instance may have changed its form, but it had not decreased.

Trends and countertrends

The U. P. Intermediate Education (Amendment) Act of 1958 contains at least one provision of questionable constitutionality. Clause 14 of the Kerala Education Bill, held invalid by the Supreme Court, empowered the government to take over the management of aided schools. The U. P. act, however, grants power to the government under certain circumstances to take over not only aided institutions but also government-recognized institutions not receiving aid. According to the U. P. legislation, the selection of a principal or headmaster is vested in a three-member committee, one member of which is chosen by the institution's committee of management from a panel of names prepared by the director of education. Thus one member out of three might well be of a

[90] C. P. Mathew, "Churches in Kerala and the New Education Act," *N.C.C. Review*, 1959, vol. 79, pp. 271-272.
[91] *The Hindu*, December 30, 1960.

different religion than the management of a minority educational institution. The selected candidate must be approved by the regional deputy director of education. In the appointment of teachers, candidates are also selected by a committee, but the final authority rests in the hands of the district inspector of schools.

One of the regulations made under the act does attempt to relax the official control in the appointment of principals, headmasters, or teachers in schools managed by minorities. "In the case of institutions run by religious and linguistic minorities, especially for the benefit of their children, the approving authority will not normally interfere with the selection made by the selection committee provided the person so selected fulfills the conditions of minimum qualifications prescribed for the post and is otherwise eligible."[92] The interpretation of the phrase "especially for the benefit of their children" would appear to offer a sizable loophole, since in most Christian schools the Christians are far outnumbered by the Hindu and Muslim pupils.

It is evident that the system of state-aided private schools, a basic part of the pattern of Indian education since 1854, is undergoing radical changes. State control of the internal administration of these institutions is constantly being tightened, and the distinction between private and government schools is rapidly becoming blurred. Perceiving the handwriting on the wall, some religious agencies are voluntarily turning their schools over to the government. When the distinctive religious and educational purposes for which these institutions were founded are no longer being served, they reason, it is better to let the state shoulder the whole responsibility. In December 1960 the government of Ceylon assumed control of about 2,500 aided private schools throughout the island, despite the intense opposition of the Roman Catholic Church. It is not unlikely that the nationalization of schools in Ceylon will give added impetus to the trend in the same direction already evident in some parts of India.

However, the trend is by no means a uniform one. In 1959 Dr. K. L. Shrimali, union minister of education, declared that the central government intended to do everything possible to keep secondary education in the hands of private management. "Even if the government gives 99 per cent grants to voluntary educational institutions, I find no reason why secondary education should not be left to the super-

[92] No. AI-5365/XV-1692-58, chapter 2, regulation 18.

vision of private management."[93] In April 1961 Dr. Shrimali told the Lok Sabha that it was the government's policy to encourage private educational institutions; he praised the contribution made by these schools to the cause of Indian education.[94]

In Mysore state the education minister, Anna Rao Ganamukhi, gave assurances that there was no intention to take over aided primary and secondary schools. Furthermore, in April 1961 he announced that the government's policy was to encourage private enterprise in regard to the opening of *new* high schools by giving them substantial grants. He explained that the government could thus save money which was needed to start new primary schools in the state. Replying to a question in the assembly whether the standard of teaching in aided schools had not declined, the minister stated that, on the contrary, the standard had deteriorated in government schools. A nonofficial resolution urging an increased scale of grant-in-aid for aided secondary schools (these constitute the majority of the secondary schools in Mysore) received unanimous support from all sections of the state legislative council.[95]

There are, thus, trends in opposite directions, toward the nationalization of privately managed schools in some states and toward the extension of the system of aided schools in others. There are two important factors which restrain the zeal of those who would like to press for nationalization: constitutional and financial considerations. Since many of the institutions are managed by religious minority communities, especially Christian agencies, article 30(1) and the Supreme Court judgment on the Kerala Education Bill are serious obstacles. This decision showed that the state could constitutionally go very far indeed in controlling the internal administration of educational institutions managed by religious minorities, but it could not take them over entirely. There would be no constitutional difficulty in taking over private schools not managed by minorities, except that the government would have to pay compensation for the assets of the institutions in the shape of buildings and equipment. This would necessitate a heavy outlay of money which the states are not in a position to make. Thus, even in Kerala where almost the entire expenditure of aided schools is met from govern-

[93] *The Mail*, November 18, 1959.
[94] *The Hindu*, April 6, 1961.
[95] *Ibid.*, April 5, 1961.

ment funds, the additional outlay for compensation would be difficult to make. The state governments cannot easily abandon the system of grants-in-aid to privately managed schools, even where there is a strong desire to do so.

The privately managed schools have indeed made a great contribution to the cause of Indian education. Their continued existence will help to strengthen certain liberal democratic values. In a day when the state's powers are growing, they help to counterbalance the tendency toward too much regimentation. All autonomous cultural institutions have an important role in preserving a free society. However, the negative aspects of the situation must not be overlooked. At a time when India desperately needs to strengthen the emotional integration of the most heterogeneous population in the world, a large segment of education is controlled by various religious agencies each of which is committed to its own set of values. These need not be and, in most cases, are not narrow or communalist values. Nevertheless, the religious agencies represent units which are less than the whole Indian nation. In the very nature of things, the state must assume the major burden in the educational task of consolidating national unity. The powerful role of the American public school in molding one nation out of many diverse groups is directly relevant to India's present situation. As the financial resources of government increase, the state will assume a much larger proportion of the responsibility for elementary and secondary education.

CHAPTER 13

HINDUISM AND INDIAN CULTURE

WHAT IS CULTURE? A valuable study cited 164 definitions of culture taken from the writings of anthropologists, sociologists, psychologists, and philosophers.[1] A number of the definitions stress the idea that culture is a collective name for the material, social, religious, and artistic achievements of human groups, including traditions, customs, and behavior patterns, all of which are unified by common beliefs and values. Values provide the essential part of a culture and give it its distinctive quality and tone.

What is the relation of religion to culture? It is religion which most explicitly articulates the distinctive values of a culture. If we think in terms of a traditional, pre-industrial culture, the role of religion is a basic one, for it effectively formulates, interprets, and transmits the values which permeate the entire culture. In a modern secularized society such a relationship does not exist; but this is a recent phenomenon in terms of the sweep of history.

"Throughout the greater part of mankind's history, in all ages and states of society, religion has been the great unifying force in culture," wrote Christopher Dawson. "It has been the guardian of tradition, the preserver of the moral law, the educator and the teacher of wisdom. . . . In all ages the first creative works of a culture are due to a religious inspiration and dedicated to a religious end. The temples of the gods are the most enduring works of man. Religion stands at the threshold of all the great literatures of the world."[2] This relationship between religion and culture was emphasized by S. Radhakrishnan when he wrote that it is after all the norms, beliefs, and values which determine the social frame-

[1] A. L. Kroeber and Clyde Kluckhohn, *Culture: A Critical Review of Concepts and Definitions*, Harvard University Printing Office, Cambridge, Massachusetts, 1952, p. 149.
[2] Christopher Dawson, *Religion and Culture*, Meridian Books, Inc., New York, 1948, pp. 49-50.

work of a historic culture. The very names Hindu India, Buddhist Asia, Western Christendom, or Islamic society suggest the fundamental role of spiritual traditions in the shaping of each society.[3]

All that has been said in general about the important role of religion in culture applies a fortiori to India. Social organization, law, customs, traditions, architecture, sculpture, literature, music, and dance have all been shaped, or at least powerfully influenced, by religion. In the entire field of classical Indian art, what we would regard as secular art did not exist.[4] Given the intimate relationship between Indian culture and religion, what is the relevance of this fact to India as a secular state? In India the state is deeply involved in problems of culture, to a far greater extent than are the democratic states of the West. Decisions regarding cultural problems have to be made, and many of these problems have serious religious implications. It is impossible for the secular state to avoid these sensitive areas by declining to deal with questions of culture. Three factors make this involvement necessary.

First, as a newly independent state, India has had to make and is making some very basic decisions. The necessity for formulating policies in certain areas of culture has been thrust upon the state. The question of a national language was probably the most important, and the Constituent Assembly had to deal with this knotty problem. As we shall see, the religious implications of the Hindi-Urdu question are important. The ministry of education has had to decide the lines of future development of the Banaras Hindu University and the Aligarh Muslim University. What is to be the role of these state-administered institutions in relation to their respective religious and cultural traditions? Directors of public instruction in the state governments have had to decide matters of school curriculum. Are the mythological stories of the *Ramayana* a part of the Indian culture which every child should be taught? These and similar questions were there, and had to be dealt with whether the state welcomed them or not.

[3] S. Radhakrishnan, *East and West: Some Reflections*, George Allen and Unwin Ltd., London, 1955, p. 17. Note also the statement of Harold E. Fey: "Religion is the main instrument for the expression of values. It is the carrier of ethics, the molder of personal and social behavior. It supplies the ethos, the prevalent tone or sentiment, of a culture." "Religion and Culture in Japan," *Christian Century*, 1958, vol. 75, p. 405.
[4] Benjamin Rowland, *The Art and Architecture of India*, Penguin Books, Baltimore, 1956, p. 7.

Second, Indian nationalism was nurtured by memories of India's glorious past, of the lofty ancient culture which flourished at a time when Europe was still in the stone age. Cultural decline in India, it was asserted, was connected with political subjugation, and the imposition of an alien western culture. With the attainment of independence, the natural demand was made that the state reject the cultural vestiges of foreign rule and set about restoring the past greatness of Indian culture. In its extreme revivalist form this demand has been decisively rejected. Nevertheless, nationalist sentiment still compels the state to do its part in promoting the renascence of Indian culture.

Third, the state has had to become the chief patron of the arts, largely because it eliminated the old patrons. During the long period of alien domination, the maharajas of the princely states and the *zamindars*, who held vast tracts of land, did much to maintain the country's cultural traditions. With the integration of the Indian states and the abolition of the *zamindari* system, the government felt constrained to shoulder the responsibility for the promotion of cultural activities. As stated in a government publication, "now that the princes and the former landed interests are no longer able to sustain them, the central government has assumed direct patronage of art and culture."[5] In a later section the activities of the ministry of scientific research and cultural affairs and of the three national academies which seek to encourage the various arts will be discussed.

INTERPRETATIONS OF INDIAN CULTURE

It is clear, in the light of these three factors, that the state's involvement in the problems of culture is fairly deep, and that it is likely to continue for a long time to come. It is therefore necessary that the state have a basic theory of culture. The most fundamental question, which, Vishnu-like, has manifested itself in many forms, concerns the definition of Indian culture. Two divergent conceptions are struggling for supremacy.

Indian culture as Hindu culture

One view simply equates Indian culture with Hinduism and Hindu culture; all non-Hindu aspects which have been assimilated

[5] *India: A Reference Annual, 1956*, Publications Division, Government of India, Delhi, 1956, p. 309.

are regarded as contaminating influences. The Hindu communal political parties are the most vocal exponents of this view.[6]

In an interesting speech a Hindu Mahasabha leader attempted to list the cultural changes which Indian Muslims would have to undergo in order to become acceptable nationals of the Indian (Hindu) state of the future. First, they would have to accept the *Ramayana* and *Mahabharata* as their epics and reject the Arabic and Persian classics. They would have to regard Ramachandra, Shivaji, and the Hindu gods Rama and Krishna as their heroes, and condemn various Muslim historical figures as foreign invaders or traitors. The Muslims would also need to discard their Arabic names (Abdulla, Mohammed, Ibrahim) in favor of Hindu names such as Ram, Krishna, Hari, etc. If the Muslims of India would accept the Hindu manner of dress, personal laws, and customs from birth to death, they could then retain their own religion! "We would not much mind their following any path for their personal salvation."[7] The conception is clear; the extent to which cultural manifestations diverge from the Hindu norm is the measure of their un-Indian nature. Indian culture is identical with Hindu culture.

One of the most interesting phenomena of recent Indian history is the way in which Hindu communalism and Muslim communalism (represented by the Muslim League), poles apart on most questions, were in agreement on the interpretation of Indian culture. According to M. A. Jinnah, India consisted of two nations, Hindu and Muslim, each with its own religion, history, traditions, and culture. Hindu communalism, while vehemently opposed to the partition of India, propounded precisely the same view of Indian culture which was used to justify the demand for partition.[8]

The Hindu communal parties are not the only spokesmen for the view which equates Indian culture with Hindu culture. Many influential Indian leaders have expressed similar ideas, although usually without the bitter anti-Muslim sentiments which characterize the communalists. P. V. Rajamannar, chief justice of the Madras High Court, delivered an address in August 1955 which merits careful attention. He pointed out that the political inde-

---

[6] *Presidential Address by Sri N. C. Chatterjee, M. P., President All India Hindu Mahasabha*, New Delhi, 1952, p. 17.

[7] V. G. Deshpande, *Why Hindu Rashtra?* All India Hindu Mahasabha, New Delhi, 1949, p. 10.

[8] *Ibid.*, p. 4.

pendence achieved by India in 1947 would have no real meaning without cultural advancement. So far as Indian culture ("by which I mean Hindu culture") was concerned, its essential characteristic was that it was thoroughly infused with religion. From the earliest historical times India had a culture which was essentially religious. Mr. Rajamannar declared that the religious basis could be seen in every festival, social institution, and custom (including the practice of giving to their children the names of gods and goddesses), and in all of art and music.[9] While these facts are perfectly true, the conception of Indian culture which emerges allows no room for the recognition of Muslim or western contributions. As Rajamannar frankly stated, by Indian culture he meant Hindu culture.

The Indian Muslim and Christian minorities have become increasingly sensitive to what they regard as the anti-national cultural exclusivism of some segments of the majority community. K. G. Saiyidain, joint educational adviser to the government of India and a Muslim, decried the tendency of some to interpret normative Indian culture in terms of the pre-Islamic past. "The people in the dock are really those who advocate or indulge in dreams of an exclusive cultural revivalism which would intolerantly reject the great gifts which, say, the civilization of Islam or the civilization of the West has brought to India and who hanker after an ancient and *exclusive* 'Hindu' way of life which is gone beyond recall."[10] A group of Protestant Christians expressed their concern over the widespread identification of Indian culture with Hinduism. "There has been a tendency to regard Indian culture as synonymous with the religious practices of the majority community. Consciously or unconsciously, those who wield authority seek to impose these outward forms of the religion of the majority on others."[11] The statement urged the necessity of distinguishing between those aspects of Indian culture which are the possession of all and those aspects which are intimately associated with Hindu religion.

In an editorial entitled "What Is Indian Culture?" the *Times of India* noted that the RSS (Rashtriya Swayamsevak Sangh) had declared that its aim was the revival of India's ancient culture. But the

[9] *The Hindu*, August 17, 1955.
[10] K. G. Saiyidain, *Education, Culture and the Social Order*, Asia Publishing House, Bombay, 1952, p. 126.
[11] *The Secular State in India: A Christian Point of View*, Y.M.C.A. Publishing House, Calcutta, 1954, p. 6.

precise components of that culture which the RSS wanted to resurrect were not explained in any detail. "So far as we can gather from its slogans and shibboleths its aim is the revival of militant Hinduism reaching not so much into an enlightened future but groping back to a past lost in the mists of mythology and time."[12] The writer saw the greatest danger lurking precisely in this extreme vagueness, for "Indian culture then becomes a thing clothed in the airy fancies of its progenitors." He deprecated the RSS's talk of Indian culture as if it were a "special exalted cult."

Indian culture as composite culture

Leaders of the various religious minorities are, of course, firmly committed to the view that Indian culture is a composite thing, to which many different religions and traditions have contributed. K. G. Saiyidain, quoted above, regarded Indian culture as a fusion of many different strands, including the Dravidian, the Aryan-Hindu (with its Buddhist variation), the Muslim (with its Turkish, Persian, and Mughal variations), and the western culture brought by the British. Regarding the contributions of the Muslim culture, he stated that they were "so many and so varied and they are so securely woven into the total pattern of Indian culture that they cannot be disentangled and removed without weakening and impoverishing the whole pattern."[13] The genius of India has been its ability to welcome and to assimilate within its culture elements of value from many different sources. On the foundation of this confluence of cultures India should strive to build "a broad-based cultural synthesis." In similar vein, two Christians wrote of the pressing need to reintegrate India's national culture, although with due regard for its multi-patterned character.[14]

Although spokesmen for the minorities have stressed this view of a composite Indian culture, some of its strongest statements have come from Hindu national leaders. Gandhi refused to narrow his cultural heritage as an Indian. "Indian culture," he wrote, "is neither

---

[12] *Times of India*, August 13, 1949.
[13] Saiyidain, *op. cit.*, p. 108. See also *Speeches of Maulana Azad 1947-1955*, Publications Division, Government of India, Delhi, 1956, pp. 225-229; and S. Abid Husain, *The National Culture of India*, Jaico Publishing House, Bombay, 1956, pp. xxiii-xxiv.
[14] P. D. Devanandan and M. M. Thomas, *India's Quest for Democracy*, Y.M.C.A. Publishing House, Calcutta, 1955, p. 64.

Hindu, Islamic nor any other, wholly. It is a fusion of all."[15] Prime Minister Jawaharlal Nehru gave one of the clearest expositions of the composite nature of Indian culture in his book *The Discovery of India*. He wrote that it is entirely misleading to equate Indian culture with Hindu culture. An Indian Buddhist or Jain has roots only in the thought and culture of India, yet neither is a Hindu by faith. Nehru agreed that in ancient times, the Hindu religion, philosophy and way of life were largely synonymous with Indian culture; but later, cultural influences from outside the subcontinent became extremely important. During the Mughal period, India's culture was profoundly influenced by Islam, yet remained distinctively Indian. Especially in northern India, music, painting, architecture, food, clothes, language and traditions were affected by the impact of Islam, and a composite culture emerged which was neither Hindu nor Muslim. Nehru wrote that "some inner urge toward synthesis" has been the dominant impulse which has characterized India's long cultural development.[16]

Our task is now to evaluate these two opposing views of Indian culture adhered to in present-day India. Hindu culture or composite culture—which view comes closer to the truth? If forced to choose between them, one would immediately select the latter. Indian culture is a complex pattern, a composite culture into which have gone many diverse elements, foreign as well as indigenous. To *equate* Indian culture with Hindu culture is factually wrong. However, a second statement must follow immediately, namely, that despite the composite nature of Indian culture, Hinduism remains by far the most powerful and pervasive element in that culture. Those who lay great stress on the composite nature of Indian culture frequently minimize this basic fact. Caught up in their enthusiasm for the idea of cultural synthesis, and with the best of motives (usually the desire to strengthen communal harmony and national unity), they seem to suggest that the cultural fusion is of a kind which might have resulted from blending together *equal quantities* of the principal ingredients. This, of course, is simply not the case.

Hinduism has indeed provided the essential genius of Indian culture; this cannot be denied. Significant cultural synthesis has not

[15] Jawaharlal Nehru, *The Discovery of India*, John Day Company, New York, 1946, p. 366.
[16] *Ibid.*, pp. 64-65, 266-267.

taken place everywhere; with the exception of Christianity in the small state of Kerala, there is much less non-Hindu cultural influence in south India than in the north. Thus, while not denying the reality and importance of the composite culture, we must be prepared to deal with an Indian culture largely rooted in Hinduism. Those who equate Indian culture with Hindu culture can produce considerable evidence in support of their position, although that part of empirical Indian culture which they ignore or reject makes their equation factually wrong; the use to which their argument is put is frequently disruptive and anti-national.

THE ROLE OF THE STATE

How does this discussion bear upon the problem of India as a secular state? If Indian culture were in actuality a complete fusion of several contributing cultures of relatively equal influence, the problem would be less difficult, for it would be impossible to single out one religion as the fundamental basis of the culture. Hence there would be no temptation to seek the renascence of national culture through the promotion of any one religion. But this is not the case in India. Although Indian culture is composite, Hinduism is clearly the most potent factor within that culture. The state is charged with responsibility for the promotion of Indian culture, but as a secular state must not promote Hinduism. The state, then, must actively encourage the valuable cultural contributions of all religious traditions. In a sense the state becomes a catalytic agent in the process of cultural synthesis which has been going on for centuries.

The chief responsibility for the formation of the Indian government's policies regarding culture rests with the Ministry of Scientific Research and Cultural Affairs. This ministry was created only in 1958; while scientific research had previously been attached to other ministries (natural resources, education), cultural affairs received this status for the first time. Professor Humayun Kabir has headed this ministry since its inception, and it is surely indicative of Nehru's deep convictions about the secular state that a Muslim should be in charge of cultural affairs.[17]

[17] The same, of course, was true of the late Maulana Azad's position as union minister of education. Culture and education are obviously sensitive areas in which the natural tendency would be for official policy to be strongly influenced by the religion of the majority.

Some of the recent activities of the ministry are as follows: the sanctioning of grants to cultural and literary organizations, making grants to individuals engaged in literary activities, the establishment of an institute of Indology, the publication of rare manuscripts, the writing of a three-volume history of the Indian freedom movement, the establishment of open-air theatres at Delhi and the state capitals, the interstate exchange of cultural troupes, the sponsoring of the Rabindranath Tagore centenary celebrations in 1961, the reorganization and development of museums and libraries, and excavations carried out by the department of archaeology.[18]

The ministry of cultural affairs also makes grants to the three national academies established by the government in 1953 and 1954. The Sangeet Natak Akademi (Academy of Dance, Drama, and Music) seeks to promote through these arts "the cultural unity of the country."[19] This institution coordinates the activities of regional organizations, promotes research, sponsors festivals, and awards prizes for outstanding achievement in dance, drama, and music. The Sahitya Akademi (National Academy of Letters) seeks to coordinate literary activities in all the Indian languages. The Lalit Kala Akademi (National Academy of Art and Architecture) encourages and promotes study in painting, sculpture, architecture, and applied arts.

The ministry also sponsors various activities aimed at promoting cultural relations with foreign countries. Financial assistance is granted to cultural societies abroad which seek to strengthen ties with India (for example, the Indo-Iranian Cultural Association in Teheran). Cultural agreements have been concluded with numerous foreign countries, and delegations of musicians, dancers, poets, and scholars are exchanged. Exhibitions of Indian art are sent abroad, and the work of foreign artists is displayed in the major cities of India. The Indian Council for Cultural Relations is specifically concerned with relations with foreign countries, and administers some of the above-mentioned programs. The council was established by the government of India as an autonomous body; however, its president is Professor Kabir and it is maintained by grants sanctioned by the ministry of cultural affairs. The present (1962) secretary of

[18] See *Report 1960-1961, Ministry of Scientific Research and Cultural Affairs*, Government of India Press, New Delhi, 1961.

[19] *India: A Reference Annual, 1956*, p. 309.

the Indian Council for Cultural Relations is Inam Rahman, a Muslim.

How does the ministry of cultural affairs deal with the problem of religion and culture? In general it encourages and promotes those aspects of Indian culture which can be appreciated for their secular aesthetic values alone, quite apart from whatever religious associations, past or present, they might have. However, there is no thorough-going attempt made to separate the relatively non-religious from the relatively religious aspects of Indian culture.

The position taken by Professor Kabir is that as long as the cultural contributions of all the religious traditions are recognized and encouraged, there is no conflict with the principle of the secular state. Thus, grants have been made by the ministry for the translation of various Hindu, Buddhist, and Zoroastrian scriptures and of Maulana Azad's Urdu commentary on the Koran. While laying the foundation-stone of the new building of the Vedic Shamshodan Mandal, an institute devoted to research in the Vedas, Kabir stressed the need for research in all the religious scriptures in India. He commended the institute for also undertaking a comparative study of the Avesta—the religious scriptures of the Parsis.[20]

This position, of course, is quite in keeping with the traditional role of the Indian state as the patron of all creeds and cultures. The scriptures are a part of Indian literature, but their primary significance is overwhelmingly religious. In aiding all religions the state is *fair,* but is it secular? We have already noted the persistent tendency in present-day India to define secularism simply in terms of non-discrimination in the promotion of religion. To most Indians, *secular* means non-communal or non-sectarian, but it does not mean non-religious. For most, the basis of the secular state is not a "wall of separation" between state and religion, but rather the "no-preference doctrine" which requires only that no special privileges be granted to any one religion. As defined in this book, the secular state includes the principle that the functions of the state must be non-religious.

It is therefore necessary to make some distinctions in choosing the elements of Indian culture which the secular state can promote. *Bharata natyam,* one of the schools of the south Indian classical

[20] *The Hindu,* January 11, 1961.

dance, was developed in the temples as an integral part of Hindu worship. But the performance of *bharata natyam* today is generally regarded as art, not religion, and is universally appreciated as a valuable form of artistic expression in its own right. There is absolutely no reason why the secular state should not encourage and promote such elements of culture. But the translation of religious scriptures is obviously in a different category. The valuable cultural contributions associated with all the religious traditions of India should be encouraged by the state, provided that these are distinguishable from religion itself.

As has already been noted, in the actual promotion of cultural activities, the ministry of cultural affairs operates chiefly through various quasi-autonomous bodies (the three national academies, the Indian Council for Cultural Relations) and through non-governmental cultural organizations to which grants are made. The only alternative to this approach would be to administer all cultural programs through a government department; the effect of bureaucracy on artistic creativity need hardly be commented upon. But the subsidization of private cultural organizations also produces problems.

The Ramakrishna Mission Institute of Culture in Calcutta is one such organization which has received large grants both from the ministry of cultural affairs and from the West Bengal government. Recently a magnificent building was constructed to house the institute, and a very high percentage of the cost was met by government grants. The program of the institute is excellent and includes lectures on a wide variety of social, economic, political, religious, and philosophical subjects, delivered by scholars representing all possible points of view. International seminars and symposia, facilities for research, the preparation and publication of the multi-volume work *The Cultural Heritage of India,* Sanskrit and Hindi classes, etc., are also important aspects of the institute's work. The intellectual atmosphere is cosmopolitan and free.[21]

However valuable the program of the institute, the stated principles which underlie it cannot but raise serious questions. The Ramakrishna Mission is, after all, a religious organization interested in propagating a definite point of view, namely, the philosophical and religious affirmations of Vedanta. The first aim of the institute

[21] *Bulletin of the Ramakrishna Mission Institute of Culture,* 1961, vol. 12, pp. 68-72.

is "to present a proper interpretation and appraisal of Indian culture."[22] The basic idea of Indian culture, we are told, is summarized by the word "religion," and the result of India's religious quest was the discovery of the spiritual oneness of all things in the universe and the divinity of man. In other words, what is really important in Indian culture is religion, not all religion nor even all Hindu religion, but Hindu religion which is based on metaphysical monism. If this is the "proper interpretation" of Indian culture, many will find it a highly selective one.

We have already referred to India's cultural relations with foreign countries. This is a significant factor in reinforcing the policy of promoting impartially the cultural contributions of all religious traditions. In a religiously pluralist society, there are built-in checks to restrain the tendency of the state to become identified with one religion. In the case of India, the minorities play an important role in the building of the secular state. In a religiously pluralist international society, similar checks are operative.

Hostility or even indifference to the cultural heritages associated with Buddhism or Islam within India would make friendship with other Asian countries difficult. The Indian Council for Cultural Relations publishes a quarterly journal, *The Indo-Asian Culture*, which attempts to strengthen the ties with predominantly Muslim and Buddhist countries. The Indian approach to the Muslim world is evidenced even more clearly in the council's publication of a quarterly journal in Arabic, *Thaqafat'ul-Hind*. The complete neglect of the Islamic heritage at home would make flourishing cultural *and political* relations with the numerous Muslim countries of Asia and Africa virtually impossible. The question of culture in India has international implications which cannot be ignored.

With these general remarks on the role of the state in the promotion of Indian culture, we must now turn to a consideration of the policies which have been adopted in specific areas of culture.

CULTURAL POLICY IN PRACTICE

Official policies must deal with both ancient and contemporary Indian culture. In the case of ancient culture the aim is to preserve the cultural heritage of the past and to increase people's understand-

[22] Swami Nityaswarupananda, *The Threefold Cord: Statement of the Principles Underlying the Aims of the Institute*, Ramakrishna Mission Institute of Culture, Calcutta, 1959, p. 1.

ing and appreciation of it. With regard to contemporary Indian culture, the government must seek to give recognition and encouragement to the valuable elements of popular culture, and to promote the best creative effort in the various artistic media. There are numerous problems for the secular state in both these areas of culture, past and present.

Ancient Indian culture

One of the questions of government policy involves those Hindu temples which are not only places of worship but important centers of ancient Indian sculpture and architecture. Are these valuable achievements of historic Indian culture to be neglected simply because of their present association with religious worship? An editorial in *The Hindu* of Madras warned of the dire consequences which would result from continued neglect of the temples. "Unless prompt steps are taken to restore and preserve them, all the architectural and sculptural wealth embodied in them and the traditions they stand for may be lost to us and to posterity." The temples are "rich treasure houses of art" and "the repositories of our ancient culture."[23] Both the government and the general public were urged to contribute toward the repair of these historic shrines. The Madras government selected sixty-two temples for renovation and made grants totaling 400,000 rupees for this purpose.[24] Other states have made similar grants.

It is very doubtful that there is any clear distinction in the minds of most people between the religious and the cultural aspects of the Hindu temples which the government is helping to restore. The preservation of Indian sculpture and architecture by the state must inevitably entail the improvement of a place of Hindu worship and to that extent the promotion of Hindu religion. Whatever problem this situation poses for the secular state is not a matter of serious concern for legislators, administrators, or the general public.

It seems obvious that, if private efforts are inadequate, the state does have a valid function to perform in the preservation of ancient temples which represent sculptural and architectural achievements

[23] *The Hindu*, January 24, 1961.
[24] *The Hindu Weekly Review*, March 21, 1960; *The Hindu*, January 24, 1961; *Administration Report of the Hindu Religious and Charitable Endowments (Administration) Department, 1957-1958*, Government of Madras, Madras, 1960, pp. 11-12.

of outstanding significance.[25] These are cultural attainments of the past of which all Indians ought to be proud, and the use of state funds to preserve them is justified. But, if public funds are used to protect these "repositories of ancient culture," they must surely be open to people of all creeds.

The ancestors of the Indian Muslim or Christian also contributed to the building of ancient Indian civilization. But how can one expect their descendants to feel pride in these cultural achievements when they are refused admission to the temples? In a number of the temples throughout India, a non-Hindu is not even allowed into the outer courtyard. Harijans, formerly excluded as ceremonially unclean, by law must now be admitted. But no matter how sincerely the non-Hindu might wish to understand and appreciate his cultural heritage, he will be turned away from many temples. If public funds are used for the preservation of Indian culture, temple authorities must also discard the exclusivist and sectarian approach to that culture. If the temples are to continue to be regarded as centers of *Hindu* culture only, then there is no justification for the use of state funds. "Public funds for public purposes" is an axiom of the democratic state.

It is interesting to note that legislation enacted by Parliament in 1958 made specific provision for the practice objected to in the previous paragraph. The Ancient Monuments and Archaeological Sites and Remains Act provides for the acquisition by the central government of a "protected monument" deemed to be of national importance. Where such a monument or any part thereof is used for any form of religious worship, "the collector shall make due provision for the protection of such monument or part thereof, from pollution or desecration—(a) by prohibiting the entry therein, except in accordance with the conditions prescribed with the concurrence of the persons, if any, in religious charge of the said monument or part thereof, of any person not entitled so to enter by the religious usages of the community by which the monument or part thereof is used."[26]

As a result of this provision there can be "national" monuments open only to Hindus, and others open only to Muslims.

[25] The qualification contained in the last part of this sentence is important, and would exclude a majority of the temples.
[26] Section 16(2).

Respect for existing religious practices is understandable, but this never hindered the state from legislating and enforcing Harijan temple entry measures. Is it not highly incongruous to have a provision protecting a national monument from the "pollution or desecration" caused by the mere presence of people who happen to belong to a different religion? In the light of this provision, section 18 of the act has a very hollow ring to it: "Subject to any rules made under this act, the public shall have a right of access to any protected monument."

Nehru wrote that the ancient past of India belonged to all of the Indian people, Hindus, Muslims, Christians, and others, because their forefathers had helped to build it. Subsequent conversion to another religion could not deprive them of this heritage, any more than the Greeks, after their conversion to Christianity, could have ceased to feel proud of the achievements of their ancestors. "If all the people of India had been converted to Islam or Christianity, her cultural heritage would still have remained to inspire them and give them that poise and dignity which a long record of civilized existence with all its mental struggles with the problem of life gives a people."[27] The past of India, with all its greatness, is a common heritage of all Indians, and in no sense a monopoly of the Hindus. Nehru vividly expressed this idea in an address delivered in 1948 at the Aligarh Muslim University. "You are Muslims and I am a Hindu," he declared. "We may adhere to different religious faiths or to none; but that does not take away from that cultural inheritance that is yours as well as mine."[28] Yet the sound approach expressed in Nehru's words has not always been adopted.

A few months after the attainment of independence, Deputy Prime Minister Sardar Patel vowed not to rest until the Somnath temple in Gujarat, partially destroyed by Muslim invaders in the eleventh century, was reconstructed. There can be no doubt that for many Hindus this project represented not the restoration of an example of ancient architecture, but something of religious and communal significance. It symbolized the repudiation of almost a thousand years of Muslim domination in India, and the reassertion of Hindu supremacy. A campaign was begun to raise funds for this project. In the state of Uttar Pradesh, a system of indirect taxation was devised

[27] Nehru, *op. cit.*, p. 343.
[28] *The Hindu*, January 25, 1948.

to pay for the restoration of the temple. A Muslim writer noted bitterly: "And so indirectly all Hindus and non-Hindus, monotheists, polytheists and atheists have been paying this religious levy in the twentieth century to the government of the secular state of India, for the rebuilding of an ancient Hindu shrine."[29]

In May 1951 elaborate Hindu ceremonies, with the chanting of Vedic hymns by Brahman priests, hailed the partial restoration of the temple. Dr. Rajendra Prasad, president of India, took a prominent part in the function by installing the *jyotilingam* image in the temple. An Indian Christian writer noted with irony: "President Rajendra Prasad took occasion to speak some words of religious tolerance when he consecrated the idol in the renovated temple of Somnath."[30] It seems clear that the whole inspiration of this project, with which high government officials (but not Nehru) were so closely identified, was very far indeed from the approach which is expected of the secular state. The plea that the deputy prime minister and the president were acting as individuals in their private capacities is not adequate justification for such activities; the influence and prestige of high office inevitably becomes associated with whatever they do in public.

The failure to distinguish between Indian culture and Hindu religion is illustrated by the large stone image of reclining Vishnu located at the entrance to the headquarters of the inspector-general of police in Bangalore. The piece was excavated a few years ago, and is a fine example of Indian sculpture. However, it is not understood in these terms, but as a religious object. Thus, the visitor finds that Vaishnavite sect marks have been placed on the forehead of the statue, fresh garlands of flowers are regularly placed around its neck, and some government servants entering the building to go to their offices can be seen in an attitude of reverence with palms together as they approach it.

If temples represent ancient Indian architecture and sculpture, the great literature of the past is found in the Sanskrit classics. Regarding the importance of Sanskrit, many would agree with K. M. Panikkar: "The basis of our cultural unity is Sanskrit. It is the literature that is embodied in that great language that provides us all over India with

[29] Prem Nath Bazaz, *The History of Struggle for Freedom in Kashmir*, Kashmir Publishing Company, New Delhi, 1954, p. 360.
[30] P. Oomman Philip in *Christian Century*, 1951, vol. 68, p. 831.

the background of our culture. It is to the classics of that language that our traditions are to be traced. Without the continued cultivation of Sanskrit by the intelligentsia of the country, the cultural unity of India will suffer."[31] In 1959 the government of India established a Central Sanskrit Board to advise the government on matters of policy pertaining to the propagation and development of Sanskrit in the country.

The Sanskrit epics, the *Ramayana* and the *Mahabharata*, have played a powerful role in the evolution of Indian culture. It is impossible for any Indian to understand his heritage without a knowledge of these great works. Practically every Indian school child reads some passages from them, usually in translations in the regional language. While some parts of these epics are essentially non-religious, and simply very interesting narrative, other parts have strongly religious content. Is it possible to teach these works without promoting or propagating Hinduism? Yes, if they are approached in the right way.

Prime Minister Nehru once described the *Ramayana* as "a great epic of our race, which has molded the thoughts and emotions of uncounted generations of people in India during the past ages." For Nehru, it stood as one of the great treasures of Indian culture. C. Rajagopalachari, a former governor-general of India, however, emphasized a different aspect. In a series of radio talks over the state-operated All India Radio, he dealt with the *Ramayana,* at least in part, as a religious book. After considering the views of various writers regarding the status to be attributed to the hero Rama, Rajagopalachari made his personal comment that "to try to undo the work of ages and undeify Rama in India would be as futile as positively mischievous."[32] The *Ramayana* is both a literary classic and a source book of Hindu religion, and either aspect can be emphasized by its interpreter.

The inclusion of Hindu mythological material in some of the readers prescribed for school children has occasioned complaints by members of the minority communities. As an example of such material, the Basic Hindi Reader for the fifth class, edited by the

[31] K. M. Panikkar, *The State and the Citizen*, Asia Publishing House, Bombay, 1956, p. 90.
[32] *The Guardian*, 1954, vol. 32, p. 227.

director of education, U. P., contains the following: "Indians regard the river Ganges as sacred. It is said that emerging from the feet of Lord Vishnu, the Ganges came to the thick hair of Lord Shiva and from there to the Himalayas. Lord Brahma, much pleased by king Bhagirathi's austerities, sent Ganges to the earth to bring salvation to living creatures. The Ganges is believed to wash away all sins (literally, to be the destroyer of sins)."[33] The reading then went on to describe the beauty of the Ganges and the worship which takes place on its banks at the famous pilgrimage centers. Quite apart from the mythological account of the origin of the Ganges, the references to belief in its sacredness ("*Indians* regard the Ganges as sacred") and power to wash away sins will be disturbing to Muslim and Christian parents.

Other stories found in the Hindi readers recounted the race of the gods around the earth which was won by Lord Ganesh (the elephant-headed god) entitling him to priority of worship, the miracles of Lord Krishna as a small boy, and various tales from the *Ramayana* and the *Mahabharata*. The quantity of mythological material is not large, being limited to one story in each of the readers examined. Some recognition is also given to Muslim culture; for example, the same reader which related the miracles of Krishna contained a description of the celebration of *Id*, although the emphasis was on the social and not the religious aspect of this Muslim festival.[34] Maulana Syed Abul Hasan Ali Nadvi dealt at some length with the question of mythology in the textbooks in an address entitled "Education or Cultural Aggression in Free India?" After examining a number of examples the Maulana concluded: "It is evident this is a preaching of purely Hindu beliefs, which is hardly proper or permissible to be incorporated in textbooks meant for children pursuing different faiths and creeds."[35] The problem certainly merits further inquiry, and a committee of the U. P. legislative assembly was appointed to consider it.

[33] *Basic Hindi Reader: Fifth Book,* ed. by Director of Education, Government of Uttar Pradesh, Lucknow, 1960, p. 3. (Translated for the author.)
[34] *Basic Hindi Reader: Part Two*, ed. by Director of Education, Government of Uttar Pradesh, Lucknow, 1960, pp. 55-56 and 60-61. (Translated for the author.)
[35] Maulana Syed Abul Hasan Ali Nadvi, *Education or Cultural Aggression in Free India?* English translation by Obaidur Rahman, Anjuman-I-Taaleemaat-I-Deen, Lucknow, 1960, p. 12.

The Buddha Jayanti celebrations

Another aspect of the state's concern with ancient Indian culture was reflected in the Buddha Jayanti celebrations of 1956. The full-moon day of May 1956 marked the 2,500th anniversary of the traditional date of the Buddha's death. The government of India decided to celebrate the event as one of great cultural significance for the country. A high-powered committee was appointed, with Vice-President S. Radhakrishnan as chairman and the chief ministers of several states as members. Public funds were appropriated for the celebrations, which included public meetings, exhibitions of Buddhist art, the visits of foreign Buddhist scholars, the publication of forty volumes of the Tripitakas (Buddhist scriptures) in Pali and Sanskrit, the issue of special postal stamps, and the erection of a monument in New Delhi to commemorate the event.[36] In addition to the cultural program, roads and rest houses were constructed at important Buddhist centers for the convenience of the many pilgrims who visited India during that year.

Some people in India sensed that this kind of activity, in the name of ancient Indian culture, was somehow inappropriate for a secular state. An article which appeared in the periodical *Thought* suggested that there was a great confusion of ideals in present-day India. Among other points the writer noted: "We speak of secularism but yield to a riot of official enthusiasm over the 2,500th anniversary of the *Mahaparinirvana* of the Buddha."[37]

Some penetrating questions were asked in the twenty-four page booklet entitled *Is the Republic of India Secular?* by Srimad Acharya Swami Neminath Maharaj. The writer's approach was that of an orthodox Hindu religious leader who regarded Buddhism as a historical revolt against Hinduism. The author pointed out the Buddha's rejection of Vedic ritual and ceremonialism and the refutation of Buddhism by such great Hindu teachers as Shankara. The swami categorically denied the claim that the Buddha should be regarded as the ninth *avatar* (incarnation) of the god Vishnu. As a rebel against Hinduism, the Buddha could have no honorable place within that religious system. The author compared the Buddha with Rama, who lived many centuries earlier, and who, he claimed,

---

[36] *India: A Reference Annual*, 1956, pp. 315-316.
[37] S. D., "Ideals of the Republic," *Thought*, vol. 9, January 26, 1957, p. 3.

was greater than the Buddha in every way, and then asked: "Is India going to celebrate the one hundredth century of Ram?" Another important question was the following: "Is a secular government justified in expending huge sums of public taxpayers' money over a religious function like the Buddha Jayanti celebration?"[38] The swami charged that in India secularism apparently meant a policy of respect to all religions, coupled with active encouragement and support to Buddhism in particular.

The 2,500th anniversary of the Buddha's *parinirvana* was undoubtedly a religious event of great importance for the Buddhist world. Celebrations in the Buddhist countries of South and Southeast Asia were of a decidedly religious nature. In Rangoon the Sixth Great Buddhist Council was held from 1954 to 1956, and monks from all parts of Buddhist Asia participated. While for the Buddhist countries the significance of the event was primarily religious, for India it *could* be primarily cultural. Buddhism was one of the important vehicles by which Indian culture—languages, art, architecture, sculpture, customs—was spread to parts of East and especially Southeast Asia. The government of India saw the opportunity to strengthen ties with these countries by generous participation in the Buddha Jayanti celebrations. The Buddha's position as a great and honored figure of Indian history, and the location in India of the most sacred Buddhist places of pilgrimage, made India a natural focal point of interest for the Buddhist world.

The government could afford to display a lively interest in a religion which was professed by such a tiny minority within India.[39] It could not do anything comparable in the case of a Hindu religious event, regardless of its cultural significance, without fostering the suspicion that it was promoting the majority religion. To answer the swami's first question, it is highly doubtful that the government would celebrate the passing of a hundred centuries since Rama, even if the year could be agreed upon.

[38] Srimad Acharya Swami Neminath Maharaj, *Is the Republic of India Secular?*, D. L. Dardiya, Raphael Art Press, Calcutta, 1956, p. 2.

[39] At the same time, extravagant praise from visiting Buddhist dignitaries must also cause some embarrassment to the leaders of the secular state. In December 1960 Mrs. Bandaranaike, the prime minister of Ceylon, expressed her astonishment at the progress which had been made in the provision of facilities for pilgrims at Sarnath and Bodh Gaya. "This tremendous progress," she is reported to have said, "is due to an ardent desire of the Indian government to propagate the causes of Buddhism." *The Mail*, December 29, 1960.

But the relation of Buddhism to Hinduism is still being debated by scholars. While the swami regarded the Buddha as a rebel and enemy of Hinduism, Dr. S. Radhakrishnan has long contended that he was a Hindu reformer whose fundamental principles had their roots in the Upanishads. According to Radhakrishnan, the Buddha believed in the Brahman of the Upanishads, only he called it *Dharma*.[40] Radhakrishnan's emphasis on the reaffiliation of Buddhism to Hinduism was expressed in an address delivered in connection with the same Buddha Jayanti celebrations. "The Buddha did not feel that he was announcing a new religion. He was born, grew up, and died a Hindu. . . . For us, in this country, the Buddha is an outstanding representative of our religious tradition. . . . While the teaching of the Buddha assumed distinctive forms in the other countries of the world in conformity with their own traditions, here, in the home of the Buddha, it has entered into and become an integral part of our culture."[41] If Buddhism is really a part of Hinduism, as Radhakrishnan holds, then the large-scale Buddha Jayanti celebrations might well be criticized as the promotion of Hinduism by a professedly secular state.

Buddhists, however, almost unanimously reject Radhakrishnan's interpretation, and while Hindus are naturally more favorably disposed toward it, government policies in India still distinguish sharply between Hindus and Buddhists. Thus, as we have seen, when several hundred thousand Harijans followed Dr. B. R. Ambedkar in embracing the Buddhist faith in 1956, the educational and other concessions which as Hindu Harijans they had received from the state governments were quickly withdrawn.[42] Hindus may be encouraged to appreciate Buddhism, but if they become converts to it they will likely encounter difficulties.

The central government regards Buddhism in India as a cultural phenomenon worthy of encouragement and makes a small annual grant to the Maha Bodhi Society. But Buddhism in India today is far more than a museum piece; it is a vital missionary faith which is attracting a considerable number of Hindus. The mass movement

[40] D. S. Sarma, *Studies in the Renaissance of Hinduism*, Banaras Hindu University, Banaras, 1944, pp. 615-618.

[41] S. Radhakrishnan, *Occasional Speeches and Writings 1952-1959*, Publications Division, Government of India, 1960, pp. 341, 345.

[42] The concessions were restored to the Buddhist converts, in the state of Maharashtra only, after several years and considerable political agitation.

among the Mahars continues, and Buddhism bids fair to stage a significant come-back in the land of its birth. According to the Maha Bodhi Society, "The revival of Buddhism in India is in many ways one of the most remarkable phenomena of this century. . . . More and more people are becoming convinced that the revival of Buddhism, and the revival of Buddhism alone, can lift India to the heights of prosperity and peace which were hers during the reign of the illustrious Ashoka."[43] In the light of recent developments, it is clear that whatever future encouragement the government gives to Buddhism on the cultural level will have a direct effect on the religious situation in the country.

We have thus far considered the role of the state in the preservation of ancient Indian culture, and in the promotion of popular appreciation of it. It is obvious that the university has a special responsibility with respect to these same functions. The university acts as a bridge linking the culture of the past with that of the present. One important aspect of the cultural situation in India should be noted, namely, that the traditions of Hinduism and Islam, the two strongest elements in the composition of Indian culture, are represented separately in two central universities, the Banaras Hindu University and the Aligarh Muslim University. It is to be hoped that the cultural synthesis among Hindu, Muslim, Christian, and other traditions is continuing in all the universities in India and in all other walks of life, as it has for centuries. But, in addition, there is real merit in an arrangement whereby the individual traditions can be developed in centers of instruction and research. From the viewpoint of the secular state, to have such institutions managed and financed by non-governmental agencies would of course be preferable. But it seems necessary for the present to work within the framework of the existing system.

It is especially important that minority cultural traditions be given opportunities for development in institutions of their own, in an atmosphere free from minority complexes. The special importance of the Aligarh Muslim University as a center of Muslim culture has been recognized by the government of India, and large sums have been spent on the expansion and development of the institution. The Aligarh Muslim University Inquiry Committee, instigated by

[43] D. Valisinha, *Buddhism in India*, Maha Bodhi Society of India, Calcutta, n.d., p. 9.

the central government, stressed this aspect of Aligarh's role in its report submitted in 1961: "It should develop and emphasize the study of what we may describe as the contribution of the Muslim community to the complex pattern of our national culture, and in fact to the worldwide culture of humanity. That Islam has made very substantial and notable contributions to this heritage both historically as well as currently in our own age, is a patent truth which no one with any pretensions to the study of the history of civilization will dare to deny. It is this living tradition, this dynamic force, which we should like to preserve and cherish in this university."[44] The committee recommended the building of strong departments for the study of languages associated with Muslim culture (Arabic, Persian, and Urdu) and the development of a strong history department which would pay special attention to the contributions of Islam to Indian polity, thought, and art. The approach taken by the committee is a sound one, and necessary for the maintenance of the composite nature of Indian culture.

Contemporary Indian culture

In a previous section we touched upon the work of the three national academies which seek to promote the best creative effort in the fields of dance, drama, and music (the Sangeet Natak Akademi), literature (the Sahitya Akademi), and art and architecture (the Lalit Kala Akademi). While there are the problems inherent in a situation in which a state organization must attempt to judge the quality of creative artistic achievement, these are not problems for the secular state. In general it can be said that a sincere effort has been made to give due recognition to the cultural contributions of the non-Hindu traditions, and to the composite culture which has resulted. This is especially clear in the field of north Indian music, which evolved during Mughal times through the imperceptible fusion of Persian and Hindu elements. This composite tradition is proudly continued, and a high percentage of the most prominent Indian musicians today are Muslims.[45]

[44] *Report of the Aligarh Muslim University Inquiry Committee*, Aligarh Muslim University Press, Aligarh, 1961, p. 142. Compare this approach with that taken by a Jana Sangh publication: "Obviously there is no place for a Muslim University in Hindustan. Aligarh Muslim University will continue to be suspect as long as it indulges in its dubious aim as the repository of Muslim culture in India." *Organizer*, vol. 14, February 6, 1961, p. 3.

[45] Uma Vasudev, "Indian Music Today," *Times of India Annual, 1961*, Times of India, Bombay, 1961, pp. 53-60.

The state-operated All India Radio is of obvious importance in the promotion of Indian music and adheres to the sound policy stated above. One special problem is that a large number of the AIR stations broadcast daily programs of "devotional songs." These are Hindu religious songs, frequently in the form of prayers addressed to particular Hindu deities. They are appreciated chiefly for their religious content. Thus, a letter to the editor of *Swarajya* expressed gratitude to the AIR station in Vijayawada for broadcasting a variety of devotional songs daily at 6:40 A.M. "It is doing a yeoman service, especially now when people are caring more about money than religion and God."[46]

It is highly doubtful that such programs of devotional songs can be justified on any secular ground. The literal message of the songs is of course highly religious, but this is not the most important test. It is rather the general understanding and interpretation of the significance of the music which should be the determining factor. A program of Negro spirituals or Gregorian chants would be almost totally religious in terms of the words which are sung. Nevertheless, a western audience will in most cases appreciate the musical form for its own sake without entering into the religious experience conveyed by the words. It is quite clear that the Hindu devotional songs are neither sung nor listened to in this spirit. They are a means of promoting devotion to the Hindu religion and, however popular they may be with the radio audience, this is not a function of the secular state. Some AIR stations, Bangalore for example, go one step further and broadcast the recitation of Sanskrit religious verses (*mantras*) in the early morning. This is totally opposed to the principles of secularism.

In India the state is concerned with promoting not only the work of professional artists, musicians, and dancers but also the valuable elements of popular culture. Thus, Republic Day celebrations in New Delhi annually include elaborate programs of folk dance and music from all parts of India. One of the great needs of present-day India is for the development of social festivals which can become expressions of a truly *national* culture. Thanksgiving in America is celebrated as a national festival in which Protestants, Roman Catholics, and Jews join together. Christmas has largely become such a festival in western countries. When the president of the United

---

[46] *Swarajya*, vol. 3, November 22, 1958.

States each year switches on the lights to the Christmas tree on the White House lawn, virtually no one regards it as an identification of Christianity with the state. Christmas has largely become a secularized general festival; many non-Christians participate with no sense of being outsiders. It is still, of course, a religious festival for those who wish to make it so; but for the rest it is a secular social event which stimulates a feeling of goodwill.

Festivals are a valuable medium for the development of cultural unity and the emotional integration of a nation. They provide opportunities for the expression of national art, drama, and music and help to break down the social exclusivism of groups and classes. Dr. P. D. Devanandan noted some of the more or less secularized festivals of religious origin in western countries and then raised the question of certain Hindu festivals which are more occasions of popular rejoicing than purely religious observances. "Of course these festivals have a Hindu religious background, but the question is whether they can be 'secularized' without giving offense to Hindu religious sentiment and made acceptable to all people in our country as public festivals in which everyone can participate."[47] *Divali* and *Holi* are two festivals which in large part have already taken on the nature of non-religious social and national occasions. Many other regional and local festivals offer similar opportunities. The need for such a development is obviously great. At the same time, any active measures taken by the state to encourage this development are likely to be misinterpreted by both the Hindus and the minorities.[48]

As far as the minorities are concerned, they are already very much disturbed over the tendency to identify the religious culture of the Hindus with the nation. Few corner-stones of state or local government buildings are laid without the performance of Sanskritic ritual by Brahman priests. Ministers of the central and state governments have sometimes performed *puja* (worship) and used various religious symbols (for example, a swastika mark made with vermilion) in the inauguration ceremonies of government projects.

[47] P. D. Devanandan, "Christian Participation in Hindu National Festivals," *N.C.C. Review*, 1957, vol. 77, p. 312.

[48] The most that the government of India has done thus far in the matter of Hindu festivals is to introduce a new calendar standardizing the dates for the observance of the numerous religious and seasonal festivals throughout the country. The new calendar went into effect on March 22, 1957, and is used by the central and state governments in setting public holidays.

A photograph which appeared in the newspapers showed the president of India seated cross-legged amidst the various utensils required for Hindu ceremonies; the caption read: "President Rajendra Prasad performing the religious ceremony on the occasion of the laying of the foundation-stone of the Goshala of Kasturba Samarak Trust at Koba."[49] The emblem of Madras state contains a *gopuram* (tower of a Hindu temple), which, while illustrating one important feature of south Indian culture, is likely to suggest to the Muslim or Christian the identification of the state with Hinduism.

The official language of India

Undoubtedly the most fundamental single decision regarding culture made since 1947 was the adoption of Hindi in the Devanagari script as the official language of the Indian Republic. We must here attempt to understand the background and the significance of this decision. A different but closely related question involves the status of Urdu as one of the languages recognized by the Constitution. The religious and cultural implications of this question are of great significance for the secular state. Because of its intimate connection with the life of the Muslim minority, this latter question is considered separately in another chapter.[50]

Religion and language are two areas of culture which are interrelated at many points. As one writer expressed it: "If we were to single out the one sociological factor that has had the deepest influence on the history of language and has in turn been most deeply influenced by language, religion would probably be that factor."[51] Most languages in existence have as their earliest written document a religious text. One of the most dramatic illustrations of the intimate relationship between language and religion is found in the history of Hebrew. Hebrew was replaced by Aramaic as the spoken language of Palestine before the time of Nehemiah, and for twenty-three centuries was a dead language. "For all this length of time, until within living memory," Toynbee noted, "Hebrew survived only as the language of the liturgy of the Jewish church and of the scholarship that concerned itself with the Jewish law."[52] Hebrew has now

[49] *The Mail*, December 25, 1960.

[50] See chapter 14, "A Report on the Minorities."

[51] Mario Pei, *The Story of Language*, J. B. Lippincott Company, Philadelphia, 1949, p. 196.

[52] Arnold J. Toynbee, *A Study of History*, Oxford University Press, New York, abridged ed., 1947, p. 511.

been brought out of the synagogue to become the vibrant living language of the new state of Israel.

In order to understand the significance of the adoption of Hindi as the official language, it is necessary to review the background of the Hindi-Urdu controversy. When the Muslim invaders came to India, they found a Sanskrit-derived language called Hindi (the language of Hind or India) being spoken throughout a large area in northern and central India. As Persian was the court language of the conquerors, Hindi absorbed many Persian words. The word "Urdu" came into use during the Mughal period and referred to this same language, written in the Perso-Arabic script. Many Muslims, who generally favored this script, continued to call the language Hindi.

In time Urdu developed into a literary language with a beautiful style of poetic expression. Its script related Urdu to the sources of Islamic culture, and increasing use was made of Persian and Arabic loan words. In the development of literary Hindi, on the other hand, stress was placed on the native Devanagari script and a more highly Sanskritized vocabulary. Thus Urdu and Hindi developed along different lines as literary languages. However, the spoken language of the masses, both Hindus and Muslims, did not change much. It remained essentially one language, called Hindustani by many writers.

Because of the preeminent position of Persian, Urdu did not come into use in government offices and courts until after the collapse of the Mughal Empire. By the early nineteenth century, Urdu was the court language throughout northern India. The Hindi-Urdu controversy erupted in the 1870's, when Hindu agitations demanded the displacement of Urdu by Hindi in the courts and offices of the British government. Although government orders were passed to give effect to this change in Bihar, and later in Uttar Pradesh, the battle for Hindi was unsuccessful. But the communal antagonisms which were stirred up by the Hindi-Urdu controversy continued.[53] The formation of Muslim and later Hindu communal political parties in the twentieth century added further fuel to the fire. The Muslim League became the champion of Urdu, and the Hindu Mahasabha of Hindi. The controversy increased in intensity in the

[53] Ram Gopal, *Indian Muslims: A Political History (1858-1947)*, Asia Publishing House, Bombay, 1959, pp. 39-43.

1930's and 1940's as the question of a national language for an independent India became each year a less academic one.[54]

The issue was usually argued in terms of the written languages, Hindi and Urdu. However, both Gandhi and Nehru took the position that the spoken language, Hindustani, should be recognized as the national language and that for official purposes it could be written in either script. This became the official position of the Congress Party. Hindustani was regarded as the product of the fusion of the Hindu and Islamic cultures, the expression of composite Indian culture. Just a few days before independence, Gandhi wrote: "The Congress must stand firm like a rock. It dare not give way on the question of the *lingua franca* of India. It cannot be Persianized Urdu or Sanskritized Hindi. It must be a beautiful blend of the two simple forms written in either script. Let us not turn away from the Urdu script."[55]

In 1949 the Congress and the Constituent Assembly decided otherwise. In the meetings of the party and of the assembly drafting committee the pressure for Hindi in the Devanagari script was overwhelming. Coming in the wake of partition and unprecedented Hindu-Muslim violence, the decision was strongly influenced by communal sentiment. Mohammed Hifzur Rahman expressed his sense of bewilderment in the Constituent Assembly. "Today I am confused and confounded because until yesterday the whole Congress was unanimous regarding the solution of the language problem. There was no dissenting voice. All said with one voice 'Hindustani shall be the national language of our country, which shall be written in both the scripts, Hindi and Urdu.' But today they want to change it." Maulana Azad was bitterly disappointed when the Congress rejected Hindustani, and he later resigned from the drafting committee. He protested that "from one end to another narrow-mindedness reigned supreme."[56] Article 343(1) of the Constitution states: "The official language of the Union shall be Hindi in Devanagari script."

With the partition of India, the majority of the Muslim popula-

[54] Suniti Kumar Chatterji, *Indo-Aryan and Hindi*, Gujarat Vernacular Society, Ahmedabad, 1942, pp. 198-235; Z. A. Ahmed, ed., *National Language for India: A Symposium*, Kitabistan, Allahabad, 1941.
[55] *Harijan*, August 10, 1947.
[56] *Constituent Assembly Debates*, vol. 9, pp. 1339, 1456-1457.

tion, and the majority of those who claimed Urdu as their language, became citizens of the new dominion, Pakistan. Although the decision to adopt Devanagari as the sole script for the official language of India was undoubtedly made with communal bias in the minds of some, this particular decision was sound from a practical and administrative point of view. The use of two scripts would undoubtedly have further confounded an already difficult linguistic situation. The Devanagari script is used not only for Hindi but in slightly varying forms for Gujarati, Bengali, Assamese, Marathi, and other important languages, and is thus known throughout north and central India. The adoption of the Devanagari script for the official language does not represent a denial of what the secular state's cultural policy should be. In a decision of this type, the most important considerations should be practical ones, and the number of people who already know the script should rank first. Maulana Azad himself recognized the force of this argument, and had agreed to the adoption of the Devanagari script. So much for the question of script.

But the question of vocabulary represented another problem. The significance of the name "Hindustani," and the reason for Gandhi's desire to have it recognized as the official language, was that it was a living spoken language which expressed the cultural synthesis which had already taken place in north India. The natural process by which a Sanskrit-derived language had assimilated Persian and Arabic expressions over a period of hundreds of years was recognized in the name "Hindustani." As Maulana Azad explained to the Constituent Assembly, "by adopting the name of Hindustani, the Congress had recognized that natural law by which languages evolve."[57] The use of the term "Hindi" suggests a different kind of development, with emphasis on the literary language which has drawn heavily upon Sanskrit.

While the Constitution is completely clear as to script, the directive for the development of Hindi vocabulary is somewhat ambiguous. Article 351 states: "It shall be the duty of the Union to promote the spread of the Hindi language, to develop it so that it may serve as a medium of expression for all the elements of the composite culture of India and to secure its enrichment by assimilating without inter-

[57] *Ibid.*, p. 1455.

fering with its genius, the forms, style and expressions used in Hindustani and in the other languages of India specified in the Eighth Schedule, and by drawing, wherever necessary or desirable, for its vocabulary, primarily on Sanskrit and secondarily on other languages." The article upholds the concept of "the composite culture of India" by allowing for the assimilation of "expressions used in Hindustani" (presumably including the latter's Persian and Arabic loan words), but concludes that Hindi's vocabulary should be expanded by drawing "primarily on Sanskrit."

The Official Language Commission, appointed in 1955, was directed to make recommendations regarding the progressive use of Hindi for official purposes, the restrictions on the use of English for these purposes, and the time schedule for this gradual replacement. The commission report, submitted in 1956, included a brief section on article 351 and reaffirmed the need to develop the Hindi language as a medium of expression for all the elements of the composite culture of India. The commission took cognizance of the frequently voiced criticism that well-known words of Persian origin were being rejected in favor of awkward and artificial creations from the Sanskrit. "Thus, for instance, in the Delhi-Punjab area, people complain of Hindi becoming unintelligible on account of an undue admixture of what they regard as highly Sanskritized and 'jaw-breaking' new vocables being imported into the literary language." However, the commission also noted that in the non-Hindi areas, the Sanskrit-derived words were more likely to be intelligible than Urdu or Persian expressions.[58]

The Official Language Commission held that a shorter and simpler Urdu word should be preferred to a longer and more difficult Sanskrit word, and vice versa. When both words are equally simple, both could be embodied in the Hindi vocabulary as synonyms. "No harm is done if the Hindi language were to develop, so to say, in two different styles, one with a bias for Sanskrit and the other with a bias for Urdu in such border-line cases." However, primary attention should be given to the development of the language of daily use, not the high-flown literary medium which would tend to be either highly Sanskritized or highly Arabicized.[59]

[58] *Report of the Official Language Commission*, Government of India Press, New Delhi, 1957, p. 235.
[59] *Ibid.*, p. 236.

In practice, these generally sound recommendations have frequently been ignored. The commission itself recommended a rapid transition from English to Hindi for official purposes and thus indirectly encouraged the Hindi extremists who are intent on "purifying" the language of all foreign influences (Persian, Arabic, and English) and establishing its predominance throughout the country. These efforts have produced a stilted and often incomprehensible language. The following description is only slightly exaggerated: "The New Hindi, as I call it, is rapidly becoming not a language but a language burlesque. The frantic efforts of self-styled purists and self-appointed lexicographers to manufacture new words and phrases have made the new Hindi an object of ridicule even in the Hindi states. Unfortunately, this language burlesque has received the blessings even of the central government. Railway sign boards, the names of government offices, notices in the Lok Sabha are now identified by a string of polysyllabic resurrections from a dust-bin of dead words or by a tortured combination of weird expressions fresh from the manufacturers of the new Hindi vocabulary. The new Hindi has made even those who were formerly regarded as literate in Hindi virtually illiterate."[60]

All of this is unfortunate from the viewpoint of language as a means of communication. But the departure from one of the key principles of the secular state is no less serious. The state should promote authentic and valuable aspects of Indian culture impartially, irrespective of the religious tradition with which they are associated. The partial repudiation of the Muslim contribution to a composite language is a serious lapse from secularism.

[60] Minute of dissent by Mr. Frank Anthony in *Report of the Committee of Parliament on Official Language*, Government of India Press, New Delhi, 1959, p. 93.

PART SIX

MAJORITY-MINORITY RELATIONS

CHAPTER 14

A REPORT ON THE MINORITIES

RELIGIOUS minorities have played a significant role in the evolution of the secular state in the West. In India also, the minorities have made an important contribution, although this has often been a somewhat negative one. The constant pressure of Muslim opinion both within and outside of the Indian nationalist movement during the 1920's and 1930's made it abundantly clear that the free India of the future could not be a Hindu state. In addition to their distinctive cultural contributions, religious minorities are the natural guardians of the secular state, for their position would certainly be endangered by any significant departure from the principle of secularism.

Dr. K. N. Katju, formerly home minister in the central government, declared in 1953 that "without a Hindu majority, India could not have adopted a secular constitution."[1] His point was that the religious tolerance fostered by Hinduism's catholic outlook was the foundation of the secular state. While Hindu tolerance is surely an important factor, due recognition must also be given to the role of the minorities who feared, and not always without reason, the imposition of a Hindu Raj and therefore struggled to reinforce the religious neutrality of the state.

In seeking to understand the position of the minorities in present-day India, it is important to note the constitutional safeguards which have been set up for their protection. We must also recognize the assumptions underlying these safeguards.

PROTECTION OF THE RIGHTS OF MINORITIES

There are two broad approaches to the protection of minorities; the state might aim to secure (1) the equality of the individual citizen, or (2) the protection of the socio-religious group. The first

[1] *Times of India*, June 11, 1953.

approach has been the more important one in western Europe and America; the second, in eastern Europe and the Middle East. The first approach promotes the identification of the individual with the total political community by guaranteeing him equal rights of citizenship without regard to his religion. The second approach guarantees the separate status and rights of the socio-religious group, thus insulating it from the encroachment of the majority. The choice, in short, must be between the integration of the individual and the insulation of the group.

The most extreme example of the insulation of religious minorities · was found in the treatment of the non-Muslim communities in Turkey under the Sultans. The bishop of the Eastern Orthodox minority in a given place functioned as the political head as well as the spiritual leader of his community. He represented his community before the Ottoman authorities, and had charge of its collective interests, specifically its schools and other institutions. The ecclesiastical hierarchy ruled the community in matters of marriage, divorce, inheritance, etc., by applying the laws of the church. Thus, the fusion of temporal and spiritual functions most characteristic of Islam was in a sense extended to other socio-religious groups.[2] The protection of religious minorities was effected by isolating them from the majority through separate social, legal, and political institutions. The equality of the individual was never dreamed of, but minority groups in isolation from the majority were tolerated.

Even today, the basic idea of minorities protection through separation is embodied in Lebanon's political institutions. Each of the main communities (Christians—Maronite, Greek Orthodox, Greek Catholic, Armenian; Muslims—Sunni, Shi'a, Druze) is represented in Parliament in proportion to its numerical strength. The principle of communal representation is followed in filling cabinet posts, other political offices, and even administrative positions. The system, achieving a static kind of justice for all communities, nevertheless produces certain major problems, the "excessive crystallization of communal prerogatives" and the "usurpation of power by socio-religious groups." According to Professor Rondot, while the Leban-

[2] The most remarkable recent confirmation of this pattern came in 1960 when Archbishop Makarios, leader of the Greek community on Cyprus, where the Greeks are the majority and the Turks the minority group, became the president of the newly independent state.

ese solution "achieves perfect mutual tolerance and reduces confessional clashes to a minimum, it does not seem to open an easy path toward the complete modernization of the state."[3]

The problem in India is to develop a common citizenship on individualistic lines among a people whose legal and political institutions have for many centuries been based on socio-religious groups. As we have noted in earlier chapters, equality before the law provided the foundation for a common citizenship in nineteenth-century British India. Separate electorates, however, were an expression of the other approach to minorities protection, and contributed greatly to the political separateness of the various religious communities. After independence and partition, the future of communal representation for the minorities became one of the vital constitutional questions which had to be settled.

The Objectives Resolution adopted by the Constituent Assembly in 1947 declared its solemn resolve to draw up a constitution which would guarantee to all the people of India social, economic, and political justice and equality of status, of opportunity, and before the law. The resolution further stated that "adequate safeguards shall be provided for minorities."

The abolition of separate electorates was a foregone conclusion, as they were widely held to be a major factor in the separatist tendencies which had resulted in partition. This decision was made by the Constituent Assembly at an early date, and became article 325 of the Constitution: "There shall be one general electoral roll for every territorial constituency . . . and no person shall be ineligible for inclusion in any such roll or claim to be included in any special electoral roll for any such constituency on grounds only of religion, race, caste, sex or any of them." However, at its August 1947 session the Constituent Assembly accepted certain political safeguards which had been recommended by the Advisory Committee on Minorities and Fundamental Rights. The chairman of this committee was Sardar Vallabhbhai Patel.

The safeguards, which were later embodied in the draft Constitution, were in accordance with the general position which the Indian National Congress had maintained for twenty years. All elections to the central and provincial legislatures were to be held

[3] Pierre Rondot, "The Minorities in the Arab Orient Today," *Middle Eastern Affairs*, 1959, vol. 10, p. 226.

on the basis of joint electorates with reservation of seats for certain minorities on the basis of their population. This reservation was to be for a period of ten years, at the end of which the position was to be reconsidered. There was to be no weightage for minorities, but members of these communities were to have the right to contest general as well as reserved seats. The minorities for whom seats were to be reserved were the Muslims, Scheduled Castes, and Indian Christians.[4]

The Sikhs also demanded political safeguards. The Shiromani Akali Dal sought separate electorates and weightage for that community in the East Punjab legislature. A subcommittee of the advisory committee rejected these demands as both unnecessary so far as the political strength of the Sikhs was concerned and bad in principle and probable outcome. "The demands of the Dal are, in principle, precisely those which the Muslim League demanded for the Muslims and which led to the tragic consequences with which the country is all too familiar." The subcommittee concluded that to accede to these demands would lead, "by an inevitable extension of similar privileges to other communities, to a disrupting of the whole conception of the secular state which is to be the basis of our new Constitution."[5]

The Advisory Committee on Minorities and Fundamental Rights had recommended communal reservation of seats in its 1947 report, but with certain misgivings. It was regarded as a concession to the communal approach to politics. Nevertheless, the committee had recommended this "in order that minorities may not feel apprehensive about the effect of a system of unrestricted joint electorates on the quantum of their representation in the legislature."[6] Nehru later attempted to explain the reasons for the advisory committee's recommendation of communal reservation: "Reason number one was that we felt that we could not remove that without the goodwill of the minorities concerned. It was for them to take the lead or to say that they did not want it. For a majority to force that down their throats would not be fair to the various assurances that we had given in the past, and otherwise, too, it did not look the right thing to do.

---

[4] *Constituent Assembly Debates*, vol. 8, appendix A, pp. 310-311.
[5] *Ibid.*, pp. 313-315.
[6] *Ibid.*, p. 310.

Secondly, because in our heart of hearts we were not sure about ourselves nor about our own people as to how they would function when all these reservations were removed, we agreed to that reservation, but always there was this doubt in our minds, namely, whether we had not shown weakness in dealing with a thing that was wrong."[7]

By the end of 1948, several spokesmen for the minorities on the advisory committee had come forward with the proposal that the question of reservation of seats be reexamined. Dr. H. C. Mookerjee, a Christian, and Mr. Rajamul Husain, a Muslim, gave notices of resolutions seeking to recommend to the Constituent Assembly that there should be no communal reservation. The Indian Christian community had some tradition of progressive nationalist leadership. Dr. S. K. Datta and Mr. K. T. Paul represented their community at the London Round Table Conferences (1930-1932) and, alone among the spokesmen for the various minorities, opposed the principle of separate electorates.[8] Dr. H. C. Mookerjee continued this nationalist tradition, and on May 11, 1949, the advisory committee passed the following resolution moved by him: "That the system of reservation for minorities other than Scheduled Castes in legislatures be abolished."[9]

Defending this new resolution before the Constituent Assembly, Nehru declared that it was psychologically a good move for the nation and for the world, for "it shows that we are really sincere about this business of having a secular democracy."[10] Under the Constitution as ratified, there was reservation of seats for Scheduled Castes and Anglo-Indians only, for a period of ten years.

It is interesting to compare India's approach to minorities protection in the political sphere with that adopted in Pakistan. In undivided India, the Muslim League regarded separate electorates as the only adequate political safeguard for the minorities. The Congress preference for joint electorates was interpreted by the League as an expression of Hindu determination to secure even more complete domination over the Muslims. With partition, the Hindus living in Pakistan suddenly became a minority. But the

[7] *Constituent Assembly Debates*, vol. 8, pp. 329-330.
[8] *The Guardian*, 1947, vol. 25, p. 394.
[9] *Constituent Assembly Debates*, vol. 8, pp. 310-311.   [10] *Ibid.*, p. 332.

dramatic exchange of majority-minority positions between the two communities did not alter their respective stands on this issue![11]

The Hindu leader of the Pakistan National Congress declared in the Constituent Assembly: "In my dictionary there is no such word as 'majority' or 'minority.' I do not consider myself as a member of the minority community or this or that community; I consider myself as one of the seven crores (70,000,000) of Pakistanis. I do not want any special rights. I do not want any privileges. I do not want reservation of seats in the legislature."[12] The Hindu political leaders felt that their effectiveness would be severely limited as long as they were relegated to the role of spokesmen for a minority interest. Joint electorates, on the other hand, would open up opportunities for a broader participation in national life.

The Muslim majority, however, insisted on the continuance and extension of the principle of separate electorates. Muslim League leaders argued that the Hindus did not really know how best to protect their own interests. Professor Keith Callard also noted: "Undoubtedly the orthodox religious tradition that Muslims and non-Muslims may live at peace within a single state but can never be merged into one community has a bearing on the majority attitude."[13] At any rate, the first Constituent Assembly decided on separate electorates for Muslims, Caste Hindus, Scheduled Castes, Christians, Buddhists, and Parsis. Because of sharp disagreements, and against the background of a generally confused political picture, the second Constituent Assembly deferred a final decision on the question. The 1956 Constitution of the Islamic Republic of Pakistan simply gave Parliament the power to determine whether joint or separate electorates should be adopted (article 145).

By the rejection of the principle of communal representation in the legislatures, in the form both of separate electorates and of reserved seats, the Constitution of India has committed itself to the alternative approach to the protection of minorities. Members of minority groups are protected by the same fundamental rights which are guaranteed to all citizens and upheld by courts of law armed with powers of judicial review. The approach is to secure the equality of the individual citizen.

[11] See the excellent chapter on "The Minorities" in Keith Callard, *Pakistan: A Political Study*, George Allen and Unwin Ltd., London, 1957.
[12] *Constituent Assembly of Pakistan Debates*, 1954, vol. 16, p. 292.
[13] Callard, *op. cit.*, pp. 242-243.

It is now necessary to consider how these general principles have been implemented with respect to specific minority communities in present-day India. Our discussion will explore the problems relating to the Muslims, the Christians, and the Sikhs, the three largest minority communities, representing, respectively, 9.9 per cent, 2.3 per cent, and 1.7 per cent of the total population. Other minority groups such as the Jains, the Buddhists, the Parsis, and the Jews are much smaller and do not present nearly as broad a range of problems as the three largest groups.

The Muslims: Radical Reorientation

The status of the Muslim minority is fundamental in any consideration of India as a secular state. Chester Bowles recognized this important relationship when he wrote that one of Prime Minister Nehru's greatest achievements was "the creation of a secular state in which the forty-five million Muslims who chose not to go to Pakistan may live peacefully and worship as they please."[14] The treatment meted out to religious minorities is the best gauge of any state's commitment to secularism; in the case of the Muslim minority in India, however, this test is absolutely crucial.

It is not necessary to review here the tragic events of 1947-1948, the communal massacres and population exchanges which followed the partition of the Punjab. In 1949-1950 Bengal became the scene of a new wave of Hindu-Muslim violence, and again refugees moved across the border in both directions. With talk of war hanging over them, the prime ministers of India and Pakistan, Jawaharlal Nehru and Liaquat Ali Khan, signed the Delhi Pact in April 1950. This pact affirmed the rights of minorities in their respective states, including "complete equality of citizenship irrespective of religion." The agreement made it clear that the minorities were expected to be loyal to the state of which they were citizens, and should look only to their own government for redress of grievances, not to that of the other state.[15] The pact succeeded in dispelling the war scare, although reports of the mistreatment of minorities on both sides continued.

The first three years of independence were very unsettled, and

[14] Chester Bowles, *Ambassador's Report*, Harper and Brothers, New York, 1954, p. 104.
[15] *New York Times*, April 9, 1950. The entire text of the pact is given here.

much happened that was obviously beyond the control of the government. It is only since the end of 1950, then, that a relatively stable pattern of relationships involving the Muslim minority has been able to emerge throughout India.

The Muslim minority has had to make some difficult emotional adjustments. The Indian Muslim has had to learn to regard his co-religionist in Lahore, whom he supported in the demand for Pakistan, as a foreigner. The Hindu neighbor, with whom he has never had any social intercourse, is a fellow-citizen with whom he must take up arms, if need be, against the Pakistanis. Even this radical psychological reorientation, if achieved, may not be enough to ensure him the good will of the majority. For any heightening of tensions between India and Pakistan, whether over border incidents, Kashmir, or other disputes, almost automatically produces new hardships for the Indian Muslim.[16]

The government of India has sincerely sought to deal justly with the Muslim citizens, and in many respects the effort has been successful. The ideal of the secular state has made some impact upon the thinking of educated Hindus, and the Indian National Congress has of course long been committed to it. However many failures there might be in its realization, the recognition of this particular ideal is in itself significant.

Furthermore, the secular state does not exist simply as an abstract ideal, for the Muslims have seen it come to life in the actions of their national leaders. Gandhi's fast of January 1948, for example, was ended only after Hindu and Sikh leaders pledged to redress the wrongs done to the Muslims of Delhi. At the time of the fast, 117 mosques in the city were occupied by non-Muslims, and some of them had been converted into temples.

Similarly, in 1950 Nehru dealt with the Bengal crisis in several speeches in Parliament. Referring to the proposal made by some speakers that the minority problem be solved by the exchange of population (Hindus to India, Muslims to East Pakistan), Nehru declared: "Such proposals shame us in the eyes of the world. They show that we are narrow, petty-minded, parochial bigots who talk

[16] Wilfred Cantwell Smith, *Islam in Modern History*, Princeton University Press, Princeton, 1957, p. 269. Smith's chapter on "India: Islamic Involvement" contains an illuminating discussion of the psychological problems faced by the Indian Muslim community.

of democracy and secularism but who, in fact, are totally incapable of even thinking in terms of the world or of this great country. They put us in a position in which we have to say to people who are our own fellow-citizens, 'We must push you out, because you belong to a faith different from ours.' This is a proposition which, if it is followed, will mean the ruin of India and the annihilation of all that we stand for and have stood for."[17] Nehru declared that he would fight this proposal with all the strength at his command, for "we shall not let India be slaughtered at the altar of bigotry."

But practical political considerations as well as the ideal of secularism support the government's determination to treat the Muslim minority justly. India's position in the Kashmir dispute is highly relevant to this question. One of Pakistan's arguments is that because the majority (77 per cent) of the people of Kashmir profess Islam, they must, inevitably, become part of Pakistan, an Islamic state. India rejects this thesis, claiming that in accordance with her secularism religion is absolutely irrelevant to citizenship, and points with considerable effectiveness to her large Muslim minority in support of this claim. Any major disruption of Indian Muslim life therefore weakens India's position in the United Nations on the Kashmir issue.[18]

Another political consideration which strengthens the government's policy of treating fairly the Muslim minority involves India's role as leader of the Asian-Arab bloc in the United Nations and as spokesman for many of these countries in other situations. In 1952 the secretary-general of the Arab League thanked India for her support of Muslim nations struggling for their political independence, and recognized India's leadership of the bloc. To Pakistan's

[17] *Jawaharlal Nehru's Speeches, 1949-1953*, Publications Division, Government of India, Delhi, 1954, pp. 309-310.

[18] We have already indicated, however, that in terms of general communal relations within India, as distinct from government policy, disputes with Pakistan produce difficulties for the Indian Muslim. In 1951 Dr. Zakir Hussain, then vice-chancellor of the Aligarth Muslim University (now vice-president of India) and other prominent Muslims submitted a memorandum to Dr. Frank P. Graham supporting India's stand on the Kashmir issue. The memorandum also asserted that "Pakistan's policy in general and her attitude towards Kashmir in particular tend to create conditions in this country which in the long run can bring to us only suffering and destruction." *Notes on Islam*, Calcutta, 1951, vol. 4, pp. 103-104. Other Indian Muslims, however, strongly criticized this part of the memorandum for the lack of confidence in India's treatment of minorities which it seemed to imply, and protested that the future of the Muslims in India should not have been linked with the Kashmir dispute, or Pakistan's policies. *Ibid.*, p. 126.

413

surprise, the Muslim states refused to support her automatically on the Kashmir issue but preferred a position of neutrality. These evidences of India's successful diplomacy in the Muslim world might easily be reversed if her largest minority were subjected to a policy of harsh treatment.[19]

There is thus much at stake, ideologically and practically, in India's handling of the minority problem. How much of her professed secularism has been implemented? There is no simple answer to this question; the government of India's policies are generally sound, but important subjects come under the regulation of the state governments, and ultimately all policies have to be administered on the local level. The state governments can frequently afford to ignore Nehru's most eloquent pleas or agitated reprimands on this as on other subjects—such are the limitations of the central government in India's federal system. And Hindu administrators can, and in some cases do, manage to misplace applications bearing Muslim names.

One of the most distressing aspects of the situation is the continued eruption of large-scale Hindu-Muslim violence from time to time. Regardless of which side starts the riot (this is often impossible to determine objectively), the Muslims are generally the relative losers in terms of lives lost and property destroyed. The serious communal riots in Jabalpur and other cities and towns of Madhya Pradesh in February 1961 resulted in the loss of fifty-five lives, mostly Muslims. Muslim leaders charge that police and administrators, frequently under the influence of communally-minded politicians, allow the disturbances to go unchecked for some time, since the minority group will in most cases bear the brunt of the violence. In a number of such disturbances, local Hindu communalist newspapers have played a major role in fanning the flames of anti-Muslim sentiment.

[19] Werner Levi, *Free India in Asia*, University of Minnesota Press, Minneapolis, 1952, pp. 64-68. King Saud of Saudi Arabia went to India in 1955 on a seventeen-day state visit. Speaking at a banquet given in his honor by the Indo-Arab Society, the king said: "I desire now at the conclusion of my visit to India to say to my Muslim brethren all over the world with great satisfaction that the fate of the Indian Muslims is in safe hands. Not only was I reassured of that by the wise president of the Republic and your leader Mr. Nehru, and many other responsible Hindu leaders, but this assurance has been corroborated by all Muslim leaders whom I met." *Hindustan Times*, December 11, 1955. Less than a year later, Nehru paid a brief visit to King Saud, and was publicly addressed as "Rasul-al-Salam" (apostle of peace), to the unconcealed annoyance of the Pakistani press.

Communal violence is a big problem in India, and if this problem is not solved it could render meaningless the careful work which has gone into the establishment of a secular state. There is nothing so basic as the protection of the life and property of the minorities from physical violence. It is not always possible for a local administrator to foresee and hence prevent the eruption of communal disturbances. But with the vast resources of state power available, it should be possible to bring any law-and-order situation under firm control within a matter of hours. In too many cases there has been a certain indecisiveness and reluctance to make use of the full force available.

The problem has a broader context. In India, unfortunately, mob violence—whether over communal or linguistic matters, workers' wages or students' examinations—has frequently achieved its ends. Partly a legacy of the struggle for independence, there is a general feeling that people have almost a right to create a little public disturbance over something they feel strongly about. Furthermore, police firing to disperse a violent mob will automatically produce political repercussions in the state legislative assembly. The administrators and the police know it, and the leaders of the mob know it too. This accounts for much of the paralysis which seems to strike the local administration in time of emergency.

A National Integration Committee, with Mrs. Indira Gandhi as chairman, was appointed by the Congress president in early 1961 to consider the whole problem of how to accelerate the emotional integration of India's diverse linguistic, religious, and caste communities. The subcommittee which dealt with the law-and-order question made several of the points considered in the above analysis. "Insistent complaints by members of Parliament and the press that firing was resorted to without discretion by the police is apparently responsible for the hesitancy on the part of the police to take strong action." The final report of the committee stated: "Where the administration is efficient, rioting, loot and arson do not take place; where there is a breach of peace, the responsibility for it should be fixed and appropriate action taken. . . . Constant vigilance should be exercised by higher officials to see that communal and sectarian tendencies do not develop in the lower staff." The committee recommended that the provisions of the Preventive Detention Act be resorted to when the communal situation deteriorates or disturbances threaten to erupt, and that collective fines be imposed on the community which has attacked another.[20] The report will be of some use, but on the whole is not a very impressive effort. The preservation of law and order is still the most fundamental function of the state, and more serious attention will have to be given to this basic problem.

Muslims in government

At the top level of India's government are a number of highly respected and trusted Muslims who have served their country with great devotion. An eminent nationalist leader and scholar, Dr. Zakir Hussain, served as governor of Bihar before his election in 1962 to the vice-presidency of India, succeeding Dr. S. Radhakrishnan who became president. Maulana Abul Kalam Azad, a former president of the Indian National Congress, was union minister for education and scientific research until his death in 1958. Rafi Ahmed Kidwai was a distinguished member of the central government cabinet until his death in 1954. Dr. Syed Mahmud served for a number of years as a minister in the ministry of external affairs. The present union minister for scientific research and cultural affairs is Professor Humayun Kabir. India's negotiations with Pakistan on the canal-water dispute were handled by Mr. Hafiz Mohammed Ibrahim, union minister of irrigation and power.

A casual glance through the pages of *India: A Reference Annual*, published by the government of India, will reveal a substantial number of Muslim names on the lists of judges, civil service commissioners, ambassadors, etc. For a number of years Major General E. Habibullah occupied a key post as commandant of India's National Defense Academy. One of the most outstanding appointments in the ambassadorial category was that of Mohammed Ali Currim Chagla to Washington in September 1958. The *New York Times*, frequently critical of Nehru, hailed the appointment of this dis-

---

[20] *The Hindu*, May 19, 1961; *Report of the National Integration Committee*, All India Congress Committee, New Delhi, n.d. (1961), p. 11. An editorial criticized the committee severely for all but ignoring the tremendous harm done by vicious propaganda in inciting communal violence. "Much of the serious disturbances with which state governments have had to deal could have been averted if at an earlier stage they had been vigilant and energetic enough to take action against the inciters and promoters of communal hatred." *The Hindu*, May 26, 1961. Section 153A of the Penal Code gives the state adequate power to deal with such persons.

tinguished Muslim as "one more blow in his battle for a truly secular state."[21]

It is with reference to the lower levels of government jobs that bitter charges of discrimination are made by the minority. An All India Muslim Convention, held at Aligarh in 1953, expressed grave dissatisfaction with the central government's policies toward their community. One of the resolutions adopted called upon the government of India to fix a certain percentage of reserved posts for Muslims in the government services.[22] In 1955 Mohammed Ismail, president of the All India Muslim League, declared that the number of Muslims being recruited to the various services was dwindling "in a fearful manner." He pointed out that in the most recent list of candidates selected for the Administrative and Foreign Services, not a single Muslim name appeared. Similarly, among several hundred candidates selected in the Madras area for clerical jobs in the post and telegraph department, there was only one Muslim.[23] Speeches at the Indian Muslim Convention held in New Delhi in June 1961 emphasized similar facts, although the resolutions of the convention did not call for reservation of posts.[24]

It would be entirely erroneous to assume that communal discrimination is the chief explanation for this regrettable situation. The public service commissions, both central and state, have developed as sound a system of recruitment as could be desired. The competitive examination is the heart of the system, and it has never been contended that there is discrimination in the administration of the examinations. In the commission's interview with the candidate there is, of course, the opportunity for communal bias to affect the evaluation. However, most of the commissioners must be counted as

[21] New York Times, September 5, 1958.
[22] Notes on Islam, 1953, vol. 6, p. 149. The president of the convention was later detained under the Preventive Detention Act, and the chairman of the reception committee was arrested on charges of delivering highly provocative and communal speeches. The latter was prosecuted under sections 153A and 124A of the Indian Penal Code—causing disaffection toward the government and promoting enmity among the different classes. See Times of India, February 15, 25 and 26, 1954.
[23] The Hindu, April 19, 1955.
[24] Resolutions adopted at Indian Muslim Convention, New Delhi, June 10-11, 1961, pp. 7-8. Before independence, Muslims were guaranteed 25 per cent of the civil posts under the central government. This policy was adopted in 1934. See Ram Gopal, Indian Muslims: A Political History (1858-1947), Asia Publishing House, 1959, pp. 239, 263.

fair-minded men and include in their number members of the minority communities. The author's own conclusion, after speaking with a number of people closely connected with the working of the Union Public Service Commission, is that there is exceedingly little communal discrimination at that level. In some of the state commissions there is possibly more.

On the other hand, in Mysore state the Muslims representing 10 per cent of the population hold 13 per cent of the class I, II, and III posts in government service. In south India the principle of communal reservation (for caste as well as religious communities) has a long history, and has resulted in a static kind of justice. Communal reservation, except for the Scheduled Castes and Tribes and other backward classes, is now unconstitutional, but in Mysore state the Muslims have been classified as backward.

The educational gap between the Hindus and the Muslims has always been wide and continues to be reflected in the results of civil service examinations. For some time after partition, a substantial number of young Muslims found government jobs in Pakistan after graduation from Indian universities. Also, the sense of frustration which gripped many Indian Muslims in the first few years of independence prevented many from even applying for government posts. This failure to try, based on the assumption that they are bound to be discriminated against, is still a significant problem.

These factors have undoubtedly contributed heavily to the present situation, but communal discrimination—Hindu against Muslim—has also been at work, especially in the lower posts filled by department heads and by district and municipal boards. In May 1958 Nehru began a personal campaign of vehement exhortation to the majority community to abandon discriminatory practices against the Muslims. A resolution adopted by the top-level working committee of the Congress Party urged that the minority communities should be given full opportunities to enter the public services.[25] There could be no doubt but that communal discrimination as well as caste preference and personal influence, all played and continue to play some part in appointments.

How have the Muslims fared without the political safeguard of separate electorates? Nehru was greatly concerned over this question

[25] *New York Times*, May 18, 1958.

as the first general elections approached. In September 1951 he wrote to the state election committees of the Congress party: "It is not only a matter of honor for us, but something of great practical importance, that we put up representatives of the minority communities in adequate numbers. Separate electorates and reservation have been given up and this has increased our responsibility in this respect. If we fail to discharge this responsibility, critics will be entitled to say that joint electorates have failed and that we cannot adequately protect the interests of the minorities."[26] Certain aspects of the election results were most encouraging. In one large constituency where there were hardly a hundred Muslim voters, the Congress had put up a Muslim candidate, who was opposed by the president of the Hindu Mahasabha. Nehru saw in the victory of the Congress Muslim candidate a growing political consciousness among the people, opposed to the narrow attitudes of communalism.[27]

The numerical representation of the Muslims in the legislatures, however, has generally been poor. The Indian Muslim community represents about 9.9 per cent of the total population; after the 1951-1952 elections Muslims held about 4 per cent of the seats in the Lok Sabha (22 out of 500 seats). In the 1962 elections 20 Muslim candidates were elected to the Lok Sabha, and 3 others were given nominated seats. Muslim representation in the Rajya Sabha has been very close to the population ratio. But it is the situation in the Lok Sabha, with its superior powers and prestige, which is of decisive importance for the Muslims or any minority.

As in the case of the public services, there are legitimate reasons which partly explain the inadequate Muslim representation. Most of the Indian Muslims with political experience were members of the Muslim League, and many opted for Pakistan in 1947.[28] Those who remained were discredited by their past associations and found but limited opportunities within the Congress party, the organization which has dominated Indian politics since independence.

[26] *The Hindu*, September 27, 1951.
[27] *Ibid.*, October 11, 1952.
[28] Note the bitter words of Abul Hayat: "Despite all the heroic talk of Islamic culture and Muslim salvation, what actually happened was that as soon as Pakistan came into being, the so-called leaders of Indian Muslims heroically installed themselves into positions of power and affluence, deserting the rank and file of their poor coreligionists to fend for themselves in India. Without doubt, it was a good strategy, but decidedly it was not good political morality." "Role of Muslims in India," *Vigil*, 1951, vol. 2, p. 13.

With the exception of those (like Abul Kalam Azad) who had been identified with the Congress long before independence, then, the older generation of Muslim politicians has found it difficult to function in the new situation.

In 1960 and 1961, however, there were some signs of a revival of the Muslim League in various parts of India. The League organization continued after 1948 only in south India. Partly as a result of the new respectability which it acquired through participation with the Congress and other groups in the anti-Communist United Front in Kerala, and probably more because of Muslim frustrations, fears, and grievances, the League began once more to give vent to its own aggressive brand of communalism. In municipal elections in Bombay, Ahmedabad, Bhopal, and other places, the League proved that its appeal to Muslim solidarity could still be effective.[29] Partly in an effort to combat this trend, in June 1961 Maulana Hifzur Rahman of the Jamiat Ulama-e-Hind organized the Indian Muslim Convention to give expression to the community's grievances within a framework of nationalist commitment. The convention appealed to all Muslims to "stand shoulder to shoulder with their non-Muslim brethren inside secular political and social organizations."[30] In the 1962 general elections the Muslim League won two seats in the Lok Sabha.

Crisis for Islamic law

Sooner or later the government of India will have to face the problem of legislating a uniform civil code. This is a responsibility imposed by the Directive Principles of State Policy (article 44) of the Constitution, and is recognized by India's present leadership as essential to the development of a modern, progressive secular state. The task of codifying Hindu personal law has been completed, but as yet the Muslim *shari'ah* has remained untouched by the Indian Parliament.[31] The future decision to tackle this delicate problem, and it is inevitable, will probably create a major area of tension between the government and the Muslim minority.

In 1931 the working committee of the Congress, in an effort to reach a solution to the communal problem, resolved: "Personal

[29] *The Statesman*, February 24, 1961; *The Hindu*, April 3, 1961.
[30] *Resolutions adopted at Indian Muslim Convention*, New Delhi, June 10-11, 1961, p. 3.
[31] See chapter 10, "Religion, Law, and Secularism."

laws shall be protected by specific provisions to be embodied in the constitution."[32] Independence and partition changed many things, however. In 1948 the Constituent Assembly rejected the amendments proposed by Muslim members to exempt the *shari'ah* from the directive principle regarding a uniform civil code.[33] The Assembly declined to accept the Muslim contention that their personal law was an inseparable part of Islamic religion.

The Special Marriage Act of 1954 does permit Muslims as well as Hindus, Christians, and others, under certain circumstances, to marry without conforming to the regulations of their respective personal laws. Opposing the application of this act to Muslims, Mohammed Ismail declared: "Muslims hold religion as the most valuable thing in life and their whole life is governed by their religion. *Shari'ah* or personal law is a vital part of their religion and they cannot conceive of the possibility of the abrogation of *shari'ah* law on any account."[34] This view cannot be dismissed as either historically unfounded or presently unrepresentative of Indian Muslim opinion. The conception of a social community organized according to the Law is in fact part of the essence of historic Islam.

The Koranic distinction between *Dar-ul-Islam* and *Dar-ul-harb*[35] is still in the background of the thinking of most of the orthodox *ulamas* in India. Various interpretations of a third possibility are being expounded, some with considerable ingenuity, to rationalize the situation in which the Indian Muslims find themselves. They are living in a country which is neither ruled by Muslims nor hostile to Islam. But one point is repeatedly made: the final and conclusive proof that India is not *Dar-ul-harb* is that the Muslims are still governed by their sacred *shari'ah*. The Law represents the one link between the Indian Muslims and the classical Islam which was a state as well as a religion. The secularization of law by the Turks, according to most Indian *ulamas*, was un-Islamic. But the Turks or their leaders at least made this decision for themselves, as a Muslim community. In India the Muslims are in a minority, and any at-

---

[32] Sadiq Ali, *Congress and the Problem of Minorities*, Allahabad Law Journal Press, 1947, p. 122.

[33] *Constituent Assembly Debates*, vol. 7, pp. 540-552.

[34] *The Hindu*, April 27, 1955.

[35] *Dar-ul-Islam*: "The Abode of Islam," a country where the law of Islam is in full force. *Dar-ul-harb*: "The Abode of War," a country belonging to infidels which has not been brought under the rule of Islam.

tempt by the government to secularize personal law would violate their freedom of religion and, paradoxically, constitute a serious departure from the secular state as they understand it.

The minority status of the Indian Muslims offers opportunities for great creativity, but it may also result in a pitiable stagnation. In the area of social reform no legislation has been enacted to promote the social progress of the Muslims since independence. During the same period vast strides have been made toward the social reform of the Hindu community. It may be readily admitted that the Hindus needed social reform legislation far more than the Muslims did. But the Muslims have no cause for complacency. Legislation prohibiting the dowry system, passed in 1961, excludes from its scope those to whom Muslim law is applied. In many parts of India the dowry system is as onerous a burden to the Muslims as to the Hindus. Although the practice of polygamy is declining due to economic pressures, it is still perfectly legal for Indian Muslims; for Hindus the practice was prohibited in 1955. The law still permits a Muslim to divorce his wife by telling her "I divorce thee" three times.

The continuation of such medieval social practices will mean that Indian Muslims will lag far behind their coreligionists elsewhere, not only in Turkey or the United Arab Republic, but in Pakistan as well. Even in Pakistan, where in 1955 a former president, Major General Iskander Mirza, and a former prime minister, Mohammad Ali, took additional spouses, far-reaching changes have been made. Overruling the traditionalist *ulamas*, the military government of President Ayub Khan in 1961 promulgated the Muslim Family Laws Ordinance which raises the marriageable age for girls from fourteen to sixteen, makes polygamy all but impossible (the consent of both the present wife and an arbitration council must be obtained), and also makes divorce difficult.

It is unfortunately possible that Indian Muslims may remain, as a community, an isolated static unit in what is at present one of the most dynamic countries in the world. Inevitably, the community will act as a drag on the progress of the rest of the country. The secularization of law is absolutely essential to the evolution of a modern sovereign state; the present system is an anachronism. The Hindus, Christians, Sikhs, Parsis, and other communities are, on the whole, prepared for the enactment of a uniform civil code. The Muslims are not.

The problem of the isolation of the Indian Muslim community is of course much larger than the question of personal law, but this is of special significance in that it directly involves the community's interpretation of Islam. This particular question is difficult, not because the main lines of the solution are unclear, but because of reluctance to follow them. Legislation has already largely reduced Hinduism to a religion of private faith and worship finding corporate expression solely through voluntary organizations. Its role as the regulator of society is a thing of the past. It is inevitable that the same process must take place in Indian Islam, although the initiative cannot come from the state. The new individualistic Islam will have to use the words of tradition, but with a radically transformed content. For example: "Wherever there is a believing Muslim, there is *Dar-ul-Islam*."[36]

The initiative for the modification and eventual abolition of Muslim personal law in favor of a uniform civil code must come from within the community itself. The government of India cannot force this reform down unwilling throats, no matter how essential to the progress of the country. In a sense the present situation is analogous to pre-independence days when the British were reluctant to interfere with the socio-religious customs of either the Hindus or the Muslims. But at the present time it is very difficult to see where this needed Muslim leadership is to come from. The Jamiat Ulama-e-Hind, which has served the community and the secular state with distinction in other respects, could be expected to oppose this measure tooth and nail.

The future of Urdu

Another burning issue for the Indian Muslim community is the question of language, in particular the future of Urdu. S. Abid Husain, in his book *The National Culture of India*, discusses discrimination against minorities in the political, economic, and cultural fields. He points out, however, that in the first two fields the discrimination is not universal and furthermore is strongly condemned by many leaders in civic affairs and government. With regard to the

[36] Statement made by Professor M. Mujeeb, vice-chancellor of the Jamia Millia Islamia, New Delhi, in an interview with the author in November 1960.

third field he writes: "But cultural intolerance is so widespread and strongly rooted that few of our leaders have the inclination or the courage to raise their voices against it. The reason why this intolerance, which is against all Indian tradition, has affected so many people, is that it appears in the guise of patriotism. Many people sincerely believe that in order to establish a strong and lasting unity on an all India level (or regional level) it is necessary that in the whole of the Indian Union (or in the whole of the regional unit) there should be one culture and one language, and that obviously the language and culture of the majority, which uniformity can only be achieved by blotting out of existence, or at least keeping down to a subordinate position, the languages and the cultural traditions of the minorities."[37] It is significant that Husain regards cultural problems as the most critical in the entire range of majority-minority relations, and many other Muslims would agree with him.

While acts of discrimination against Muslims in the political and economic sphere are naturally resented, those which concern their culture and language strike most deeply. A survey of resolutions passed by Muslim conferences and organizations since independence will clearly indicate that there has been much greater anxiety over the place of Urdu than over administrative discrimination. The majority community and the state governments have at times been most insensitive and even irresponsible in their handling of this issue.

In a previous chapter the question of India's official language was considered.[38] This is part of the critical problem of the interpretation of Indian culture as a composite culture or as equated with Hinduism —a matter of great concern to the leaders of the Muslim minority. India's Constituent Assembly decided that Hindi written in the Devanagari script would be the official language. This decision, although bitterly opposed by Indian Muslim leaders at the time, is no longer an issue. Hindi is the official language of the Republic of India. The present conflict is over the place to be accorded to Urdu as one of the fourteen Indian languages recognized by the Constitution.[39]

Urdu fared badly in India during the first decade of independence.

[37] S. Abid Husain, *The National Culture of India*, Jaico Publishing House, Bombay, 1956, pp. xxiii-xxiv.
[38] See chapter 13, "Hinduism and Indian Culture."
[39] Constitution of India, Eighth Schedule.

Throughout large areas of northern and central India (in the states of Uttar Pradesh, Bihar, Madhya Pradesh, Rajasthan) Urdu was virtually eliminated as a medium of instruction in schools. In Madhya Bharat, a state later merged with Madhya Pradesh, legislation enacted in 1949 made it an offense for a government servant to use any language other than Hindi in the Devanagari script. The Punjab government took steps to ban the use of Urdu in administration and public educational institutions. In May 1948 the U.P. government issued new regulations which stated that children would be educated through the medium of Hindi exclusively. According to the new syllabus, a child whose mother tongue was Urdu would have no opportunity to study his own language except as an optional subject when he reached the sixth standard.[40]

In 1949 an important resolution was adopted at the Provincial Education Ministers' Conference and approved by the government of India. It stated that the medium of instruction in primary education must be the mother tongue of the child, and, where this was different from the regional or state language, "arrangements must be made for instruction in the mother tongue by appointing at least one teacher, provided there are not less than forty pupils speaking the language in the whole school or ten such pupils in a class."[41] The "forty-ten plan" was endorsed by the state governments, but in a rather calculated way implementation lagged far behind in states with sizable Urdu-speaking minorities.

In Uttar Pradesh, a special officer for compulsory education issued an order completely contrary to the principle of instruction in the mother tongue which resulted in the expulsion of Urdu as a medium of instruction in primary schools controlled by municipal and district boards. In 1951 Dr. Zakir Hussain presented to the U.P. education minister over 10,000 applications of parents in the city of Lucknow alone who requested that their children be educated through Urdu. Assurances were given that the "forty-ten plan" would be implemented, but no action was taken. As a test case, an application was signed in 1952 by ninety parents in one ward of Lucknow, requesting that since Urdu was the mother tongue of their children, instruction be provided for them through this medium.

[40] *Notes on Islam*, 1948, vol. 2, p. 75.
[41] *Report of the Commissioner for Linguistic Minorities (First Report)*, Government of India Press, New Delhi, 1959, p. 53.

The application was submitted to the minister of education, U.P., and to the superintendent of education of the municipal board, Lucknow, but no reply to the application was made nor were arrangements made for Urdu instruction.[42]

Many resolutions were adopted by various Muslim organizations urging that Urdu be accorded the status of a regional language in U.P. and also in Bihar.[43] In 1954 the All India Anjuman Taraqqi-e-Urdu, an association for the promotion of the Urdu language, presented to the president of India a memorandum praying that under article 347 of the Constitution he direct that Urdu be recognized as one of the regional languages of U.P. for certain purposes: (1) the use of Urdu as medium of primary education for children whose mother tongue is Urdu; (2) the entertainment of applications written in Urdu by courts and government offices; (3) the publication of important laws, rules and notifications in Urdu, etc. Over 2,050,000 adult citizens of the state, representing all creeds, signed the petition; the number of non-adult members of the families of signatories was over 2,200,000. In 1956 a similar memorandum requesting the recognition of Urdu as one of the regional languages of Bihar, signed by 915,000 adults, was presented to the president. But no action was taken on these representations.

The treatment meted out to Urdu undoubtedly helped to create a sense of insecurity and apprehension in the minds of many Indian Muslims. Their cultural rights had indeed been guaranteed by the Constitution, for article 29(1) states: "Any section of the citizens residing in the territory of India or any part thereof having a distinct language, script or culture of its own shall have the right to conserve the same." But in practice this guarantee meant very little. Precisely *how* could the Indian Muslims conserve their culture if their mother tongue was banished from the primary school attended by their children? Indeed, Professor W. C. Smith's comment, written in 1956, is as follows: "The [Indian Muslim] community is in danger of being deprived of its language, than which only religious faith is a deeper possession. Nine years of gradual adjustment in other fields have brought no improvement in this, and little prospect of improvement."[44]

[42] Representation of the Anjuman Taraqqi-e-Urdu to the President of India, February 15, 1954.
[43] For example, see the resolutions adopted by the Jamiat Ulama-e-Hind in April 1951. *Notes on Islam*, 1951, vol. 4, p. 74.
[44] Smith, *op. cit.*, pp. 266-267.

However, even in 1956 other events were taking shape which indirectly were to produce an important change in the whole context of the Urdu question. Up to this point, the question was inevitably considered as essentially a communal problem. Despite all the efforts of the Urdu protagonists to refute this partly inaccurate identification, the demand for the recognition of Urdu was popularly regarded as a demand of the Muslim minority. The demand was made against the background of the long history of the bitter Hindi-Urdu controversy with its strongly communal character.

In 1955 the States Reorganization Commission submitted its report in which it recommended the redrawing of state boundaries largely on a linguistic basis. The commission recognized that no possible scheme of states reorganization could totally solve the problem of linguistic minorities. It therefore made a number of important proposals, including a constitutional amendment, for the protection of the legitimate interests of the many linguistic minorities which would remain after the reorganization. In 1956 the government of India issued a memorandum on "Safeguards for Linguistic Minorities" in which it was stated that most of the commission's recommendations were being accepted.[45]

In the same year the Constitution (Seventh Amendment) Act inserted articles 350A and 350B as proposed in the commission report. Article 350A states: "It shall be the endeavor of every state and of every local authority within the state to provide adequate facilities for instruction in the mother tongue at the primary stage of education to children belonging to linguistic minority groups, and the president may issue such directions to any state as he considers necessary or proper for securing the provision of such facilities." Article 350B provides for the appointment of a special officer for linguistic minorities whose duty it is to investigate all matters relating to the safeguards provided for linguistic minorities under the Constitution. The Commissioner for Linguistic Minorities, B. Malik, was appointed by the president in 1957, and submitted his first annual report the following year.

The states reorganization which was effected on November 1, 1956, had no direct bearing on the Urdu question, but it brought in its train a series of events which greatly aided the cause of Urdu. These developments have placed the Urdu question in the broader context of an all India problem of diverse linguistic minorities. The

[45] *Commissioner for Linguistic Minorities (First Report)*, p. 48.

problems of the Urdu-speaking population in U.P. are considered on the same basis as the problems of Bengalis in Assam, Tamils in Andhra Pradesh, or Gujaratis in Maharashtra. This is in itself a great gain. The Constitution now lays upon state and local officials the positive obligation to provide for primary education through the mother tongue, and empowers the central government (through the president) to intervene in order to secure these facilities. The reports of the commissioner for linguistic minorities thus far submitted have provided valuable information on the Urdu question, publicized the grievances of this linguistic minority, and put the state governments in a position in which they must be prepared to defend their linguistic policies openly.

In early 1958 the Anjuman Taraqqi-e-Urdu submitted another representation to the president, reiterating the demand for the official recognition of Urdu in U.P. and Bihar and extending the demand for its recognition in Delhi and the Punjab. The petition concluded with these words: "We hope that . . . the legitimate demands of the Urdu-speaking public will be realized very soon and the biggest linguistic minority in the country accorded its full rights." In May 1958 Nehru expressed his fear that the country was sliding back into communalism, as evidenced partly by the treatment accorded to Urdu. In response to his exhortations, the Congress Working Committee adopted a resolution specifying the facilities which should be provided for the Urdu-speaking population of the country.

Two months later a press note was issued by the ministry of home affairs stating the government of India's official position on the Urdu question. This was essentially an elaboration of the Congress working committee resolution. The note stated that in the areas where the Urdu language is prevalent, all children whose mother tongue is declared by the parent or guardian to be Urdu should receive instruction through the medium of that language, arrangements should be made for the training of teachers in Urdu, facilities for instruction in Urdu should also be provided in secondary schools, documents in Urdu should be accepted by all courts and offices without the necessity of translation or transliteration, and important laws and regulations should be issued in the Urdu language also. The note admitted that while the central government's policy regarding Urdu had been repeatedly stated and was clear, "there appears to be some justification for the complaint that it has not always been

428

fully implemented."[46] The difficulty, of course, although the note did not mention this basic point, was that these policies had to be implemented by the states, not the central government. The U.P. government shortly thereafter issued a press communiqué which revealed considerable touchiness on the subject of Urdu. The U.P. government stated categorically that it accepted the central government's position in full, and tried to make out that this had been its own policy "from the very beginning." The government was very anxious to refute the interpretation that the government of India's statement constituted a severe criticism of its policies, which in fact it did.[47]

The over-all position of Urdu in India has improved substantially since 1956, and there is good reason to believe that it will improve further. The basic demands have been conceded by official policy, and it is now a matter of constant prodding to expedite their implementation. In 1959 the U.P. government finally issued orders that documents written in Urdu script should be accepted for registration without requiring the executants to file a Hindi translation of it.[48] Instruction through Urdu medium is now being given in some schools, although not nearly to the extent required. As a literary medium Urdu still manages to do well; in terms of the number of newspapers and periodicals published, among the Indian languages it is surpassed only by Hindi and Bengali.

Cultural values or economic progress?

The Indian Muslims whose mother tongue is Urdu (over half of the community) must have the right to preserve their own language. However, with the firm recognition and secure establishment of this right, a second question must be raised, namely, whether it is in the best interests of the community to emphasize its linguistic separateness. This is a question which Indian Muslims must answer for themselves, and they must be free to choose their own course. The attempt of some of the state governments to impose their own answer to this question upon the Muslim community is what has been ob-

[46] *Ibid.*, p. 139.

[47] *Commissioner for Linguistic Minorities (Second Report)*, pp. 144-145.

[48] This fact alone refutes the U.P. government's claim in 1958 that it had all along been following the same policy as that indicated in the central government's statement on Urdu. Circular issued by J. P. Singh, inspector general of registration, U.P., dated August 31, 1959.

jected to in the above discussion. But it is possible for the Muslims themselves to adopt a policy which will be ultimately self-defeating.

For most Muslims in West Bengal, Kerala, and certain other states, Urdu is a second language if known at all. With regard to the Bengali Muslims, it is instructive to recall East Pakistan's prolonged struggle to secure equal constitutional recognition of Bengali along with Urdu as official languages of Pakistan. But for those Indian Muslims whose mother tongue is Urdu, there are inevitable disadvantages involved in clinging too tenaciously to their language.

First, to be a linguistic as well as a religious minority naturally reinforces differences and makes emotional and psychological integration with the rest of the nation more difficult. The isolation of the Muslim community is obviously made much more acute when Muslim children associate only with members of their own community in the Urdu-medium primary and secondary schools. In the states of Madras, Mysore, and other parts of south India, there used to be government schools exclusively for Muslim children. While Hindu, Christian, and other denominational schools were managed by private agencies and received state grants, the government directly operated a separate system of schools for Muslims. "Government Muslim schools" no longer exist. There are, however, Urdu-medium schools in which there will not be found a single non-Muslim pupil. The old communal separatism has been continued under a linguistic label. While twenty-five years ago there were many non-Muslims in north India who willingly sent their children to Urdu-medium primary and secondary schools, this is obviously no longer the case. The emphasis on Urdu will inevitably tend to segregate the Muslims educationally and hence socially.

Second, it is a patent fact that, in terms of preparation for business, the professions, politics, etc., the student whose education has been in other than the major language of the region will be at a disadvantage. This of course applies to all linguistic minorities. However, the Madrasi Telugu who is educated through his mother tongue can always leave Tamil Nad and return to his (or his ancestors') homeland in Andhra Pradesh. But the Urdu-speaking Indian is in a minority *everywhere*. Even in Kashmir with its Muslim majority, the dominant language is not Urdu but Kashmiri. The simple truth is that in the near future, no one will be able to hold any job requiring the skills of literacy in the states of U.P., Bihar, Madhya

Pradesh, or Rajasthan without a good knowledge of Hindi written in the Devanagari script. The process of eliminating English has already gone quite far. Pupils in Urdu-medium schools may study Hindi as a second language, but they must nevertheless later compete in Hindi with those who have been taught in Hindi-medium schools. The practical aspects of the problem are important. Too great a preoccupation with Urdu may be a luxury few Muslims can afford. Too fervent a devotion to Urdu culture may diminish the chances of earning a decent living.

Some of these problems were highlighted in the discussions at the Maharashtra Muslim *Talimi* (Education) Conference held at Miraj in October 1960. Inaugurating the conference, Y. B. Chavan, chief minister of Maharashtra, declared that he was prepared to accept the importance or Urdu, but appealed to the 2,000 delegates to pay sufficient attention to Marathi, the regional language and the language of administration, and to be partners in every activity of the state. A good knowledge of Marathi would go far in promoting the emotional integration of all sections of the state's population.

The conference had before it the Kazi Scheme, which proposed Marathi as the medium of instruction for primary and secondary education, with Urdu as a second language. From a purely pragmatic point of view, Marathi was absolutely necessary for the Muslims' educational and economic progress; Urdu, as the language which embodied their cultural heritage, would also be studied. The conference, however, rejected the Kazi Scheme and passed a resolution demanding Urdu as the medium of instruction for both primary and secondary education. The adopted resolution represented the victory of sectarian sentiment over realism. Five-sixths of the Muslims are scattered throughout the villages of Maharashtra and are economically backward. In the absence of a sufficient number of secondary schools in the rural areas, the insistence on Urdu as the medium of instruction at that level would simply mean that most Muslim children will have no secondary education. With its limited resources the government will inevitably have to give priority to establishing schools which can serve the vast majority of the population in any given area.[49] The Muslim leadership is not yet prepared to face some of the hard facts of life.

[49] *The Hindu*, October 24 and 30, 1960.

The Christians: Integration Without Syncretism

Like the Muslim, the Christian in India bears a stigma imprinted by history. It is the foreign origin of both Islam and Christianity, their past associations with foreign rulers, and their present international ties which lead some Hindus to doubt the "Indian-ness" of those who profess these faiths.

The cultural tensions involving the Christian community derive from a widespread feeling in India that Christianity is a western religion. In point of fact, Christianity entered India before most of Europe embraced this faith. According to tradition it was brought to the Malabar coast by St. Thomas in 52 A.D. The tradition is unconfirmable, but by the fourth or fifth century a community of Nestorian (Syrian) Christians was well established there.

This fact has frequently been emphasized by Prime Minister Nehru, who has spoken of Christianity as "an old and honored religion of the land." At the St. Thomas' Day celebration in New Delhi in 1955 President Rajendra Prasad declared: "Remember, St. Thomas came to India when many of the countries of Europe had not yet become Christian, and so those Indians who trace their Christianity to him have a longer history and a higher ancestry than that of Christians of many of the European countries. And it is really a matter of pride to us that it so happened."[50]

This, of course, does not dispose of the problem of Christianity's association with the West. Syrian Christians represent a minority of the total Christian community, and they are found in substantial numbers only in the state of Kerala. Roman Catholicism was brought to western India by the Portuguese early in the sixteenth century, and Protestant missions began their work in south India in the following century. The nineteenth century was the period of greatest Christian missionary expansion in India as in many other parts of the world. This movement coincided with the territorial expansion of western imperialism. Of these two facts there is no doubt; but the relationship between them is not easily defined.

While colonial administrator and Christian missionary frequently aided each other, sometimes their interests were diametrically opposed. For a long time Indian converts to Christianity were discriminated against in recruitment to the armed services; nervous

[50] *Times of India*, December 19, 1955.

officials feared the charge of partiality toward the small Christian minority. But our point here is not to investigate this complex historical problem, but simply to record the fact that, in the minds of many Hindus, Christianity and Christians are associated with the support of western imperialist rule.

It must also be stated that, with some notable exceptions, Christians tended to remain aloof from the Indian nationalist movement. A sense of identification with their British coreligionists is far from the complete explanation, although undoubtedly this was one important factor. The Christian, like the Muslim, found it difficult to join wholeheartedly in a political movement which used such Hindu symbols as *Bande Mataram* or Gandhi's *Ram rajya*.[51] Some Indian Christians, however, such as K. T. Paul and S. K. Datta, made a significant contribution to the nationalist movement by opposing separate electorates for the minorities.

Since independence, the controversy over foreign missionaries has frequently generated the communalist charge that Indian converts to Christianity tend to be disloyal to India. V. D. Savarkar of the Hindu Mahasabha advised Hindus to resist conversion on the ground that a change of religion amounted to a change of nationality.[52] A. Shrinivas Rao of the same organization contended that the loyalty of Hindus to India was not suspect because they regarded India "not only as their fatherland but also as holy land and the birthplace of their religion." Muslims and Christians, on the other hand, regarded other countries as their holy lands.[53]

We have already noted that Pakistan's policies toward India have a considerable effect on the position of the Indian Muslim minority. In a similar way, but to a far lesser degree, the foreign policies of the United States and the United Kingdom have a bearing on the position of the Indian Christian minority. Thus, the Niyogi report saw a direct and sinister relationship between the objectives of the Indian churches and American foreign policy objectives in the cold war. Feelings of resentment toward western imperialism and United States policy found expression in hostility toward Indian Christians. The loyalty which Indian Roman Catholics extend to

[51] E. Stanley Jones, "Opportunities for the Church Facing Indian Nationalism," *National Christian Council Review*, 1946, vol. 66, p. 99.
[52] *Times of India*, January 2, 1954.
[53] *Ibid.*, September 28, 1955.

the Vatican was interpreted as an objectionable form of "extra-territoriality."[54] But these were extreme views which did not at all reflect the attitudes of the general Hindu public.

Some Christian leaders in India are making a serious effort to clothe their faith in Indian cultural forms. To a large extent, the architecture, music, liturgy, and theology of the churches still bear the mark of their western origin. Yet many Indian Christians do not sense the need to adopt indigenous forms to give expression to their faith. The Rt. Rev. D. Chellappa, a bishop of the Church of South India, recounted the following incident: "Recently, an Indian re-vivalist went to conduct a retreat at an *ashram*, and he sniffed at the beautiful Dravidian Christian temple there, obviously Dravidian, yet looking natural in its setting, and yet equally obviously Christian, with a large cross surmounting the *gopuram*, and devoid of idols and of all heathen symbolism. But all that the revivalist brother could do was to roundly accuse the brethren of trying to please the Hindus and not the Lord Jesus."[55] Rigidity of this kind has undoubtedly been an important factor in perpetuating the idea of Christianity's foreignness.

The relationship of the Indian church to Hindu culture is somewhat paradoxical. On one hand there is a deliberate attempt to adapt certain aspects of Hindu religious culture (e.g. the Dravidian temple mentioned above) for use in distinctively Christian worship. The argument behind such attempts is that the use of Hindu architectural forms for Christian worship will make Christianity less foreign, more "Indian." On the other hand, Christian leaders strenuously object to the Hindu's tendency to equate Indian culture with Hinduism. The Christian viewpoint is that Indian culture is a composite of many diverse traditions—Hindu, Buddhist, Jain, Islamic, Christian, European, etc. Christian leaders are in the peculiar position of holding that: (1) Indian culture is a composite, of which their religious tradition is one component, and (2) their religious tradition would become more "Indian" by coming closer to the Hindu pattern in some respects. The first proposition explicitly rejects the notion, seemingly accepted in the second, that what is distinctively Hindu is normative for Indian culture.

[54] See chapter 7, "The Question of Foreign Missionaries."
[55] D. Chellappa, "Towards an Indian Church," *N.C.C. Review*, 1958, vol. 77, p. 84.

One of the factors which has operated to keep the Christians somewhat isolated from the majority community is theological. The Indian church is fearful of the all-embracing religious syncretism of neo-Hinduism, which would all too readily accept Christ on its own terms. This fear is largely responsible for the lack of meaningful dialogue on a serious religious level between Hindu and Christian in India, and for the failure of the church to produce an authentic Indian theology. Convinced that there are elements of absolute uniqueness in their own faith, Indian Christians are unhappy about attempts to define the "Indian view of religion" as the belief that all religions are equally true. The logical inference is that Indian Christians profess un-Indian beliefs. Such attempts to promote religious universalism can thus lead to a new kind of exclusivism.

Christians and the government

The policies of both central and state governments toward the Christian minority have usually been fair. Over half of the Indian Christians are Roman Catholics, and several significant gestures of good will and acceptance have been made toward that community. Official recognition of the international ties of Roman Catholicism was accorded when an Indian ambassador, Dirajlal Desai, was sent to the Vatican. In the words of Archbishop Thomas Pothacamury: "Proof of India's recognition of the unique position of the Catholic Church and of her supranational and universal character was accorded when diplomatic relations were established, on August 15, 1948, between our young Republic and the Vatican."[56]

In 1953 the archbishop of Bombay was elevated to the cardinalate, the first Indian to be so honored. At a reception attended by 70,000 persons—Catholics and non-Catholics alike—high government officials not only paid tribute to Cardinal Gracias but also expressed pleasure at the recognition which was being given to India. Mr. Mangaldas Pakvasa, acting governor of Bombay, declared that the whole country shared the Catholic community's joy and pride.[57]

A few Christians have risen to high political office. Two Protestants have served as members of the central cabinet, Rajkumari Amrit Kaur, a former minister of health, and the late Dr. John Matthai, who

---

[56] Thomas Pothacamury, *The Church in Independent India*, Maryknoll Publications, Maryknoll, N.Y., n.d. (1958?), p. 10.
[57] *Times of India*, February 17, 1953.

was minister of finance. The late Raja Sir Maharaj Singh was governor of Bombay from 1948 to 1952. An active layman, in 1944 he was president of the Indian Christian Association, and later became a member of the central committee of the World Council of Churches. The late Dr. H. C. Mookerjee, also a Protestant, served with distinction as governor of West Bengal. Dr. Mookerjee had been vice-president of the Constituent Assembly and a leading spokesman for the Christian minority. In 1957 A. J. John, a devout Catholic and former chief minister of Travancore-Cochin, was appointed governor of Madras. There are a number of Christians who hold important posts in state government cabinets.

After the 1951-1952 elections an editorial in the *National Christian Council Review* reported that many Christians had been elected to Parliament and the state legislatures and that "the confidence that the Christian community reposed in the majority community by rejecting the idea of separate electorates was not misplaced."[58] Nevertheless, the percentage of seats held by Christians had declined somewhat with the abandonment of reservation of seats. After the 1962 elections there were about ten Christians in the Lok Sabha.

The National Christian Council has to some extent served as the spokesman for Protestant Christians in matters relating to governmental policy. But this organization is chiefly concerned with securing a greater degree of cooperation in the religious work of the numerous churches and missions which comprise its membership. Furthermore, it has been very careful to avoid any kind of political action which might be interpreted as a manifestation of Christian communalism. Hence a National Christian Council statement of 1956 asserted: "In a country where communalism is the bane of politics, the Christian community should not organize itself as a Christian political party or association to fight for Christian interests in the state."[59] This view is almost unanimously held in Protestant Christian circles.

The Roman Catholic Church, on the other hand, has not hesitated to intervene directly in politics when its interests have been affected. The church's greatest source of political power lies in the clergy's influence over Catholic voters. The one state in which the Catholic

[58] *Ibid.*, 1952, vol. 72, p. 376.
[59] "The Call to Share in the Life of the Nation," *N.C.C. Review*, 1956, vol. 76, p. 485.

population is large enough to make the Church's political influence a major factor is Kerala, where Catholics represent about 15 per cent of the population. In 1954 the archbishop of Varapuzha issued a circular concerning the coming state elections which were being contested by the Communists, the Praja Socialists, and the Congress. The archbishop declared that there were moral aspects involved in the use of the vote and warned Catholic voters against "this grave sin" of voting for the opponents of the Congress.[60] In 1959 the Catholic clergy assumed an important role in the successful agitation against the Communist government which had been elected two years before.

Hindu-Christian tensions

A number of serious problems involving the Indian Christian community, such as the right to propagate religion, the missionary controversy, government aid to Christian Harijans, and state control of Christian schools, have been considered in other chapters. Mention should be made here, however, of some of the acts of violence which have resulted from Hindu-Christian tensions. In October 1955 a Catholic church in Vardhaman Nagar, Bihar, was attacked by a group of local Hindu Mahasabha leaders. Interrupting the celebration of the mass, the Hindu extremists beat up the priest and members of the congregation and desecrated the place of worship. The responsible persons were arrested and sentenced to prison terms.[61]

Another incident which greatly disturbed the Indian Christians was the almost total destruction in August 1957 of the Gass Memorial Center, an institution maintained by the American Evangelical Mission at Raipur, Madhya Pradesh. The center included a library, hostel, auditorium, and other facilities which were used by educated young people and college students of all communities. The difficulties started when the superintendent of the center pointed out to the organizers of an Independence Day program the regulations which forbade the representation of idol worship on the stage. Nevertheless, the program was allowed to be presented as originally planned, with one tableau depicting prayer before a Hindu image. But the local newspaper *Mahakoshal* found the superintendent's attitude to be

[60] Jupiter, "The Catholics and the Congress: A Socialist Viewpoint," *Thought*, February 20, 1954, p. 4.
[61] Pothacamury, *op. cit.*, p. 26.

disrespectful of Hindu religion and culture, and a series of inflammatory articles, coupled with the activities of the Hindi Sahitya Mandal, soon produced a tense situation. On August 26 a mob attacked the center, gutted and looted the buildings, and left little remaining except the walls and roof. In attempting to bring the mob under control, the police resorted to firing, and one boy was killed.

The government of Madhya Pradesh instituted a judicial inquiry into the events and appointed Justice G. P. Bhutt of the High Court to undertake the investigation.[62] The Bhutt report exonerated the management of the center of the charges of disrespect to Hindu religious sentiments. But Christian leaders found it a disappointing document in that it did not attempt to determine definite responsibility for the outrage, beyond concluding that undoubtedly "some persons acting secretly had incited the students."[63] While the report made it clear that the Raipur daily newspaper had played an important role in inciting the agitation, it failed to recommend any measures to deal with it.[64] Such anti-Christian disturbances have been few in the years since independence.

All religious minorities have a vital interest in the maintenance of the secular state; discrimination by the state on the basis of religion can only mean difficulties for them. But among India's three largest minorities, only the Christians (and only Protestant Christians) have a real tradition of church-state separation behind them. Both the Muslims and the Sikhs have strongly theocratic elements in their traditions, and secularism does not have much inherent appeal, apart from their minority status. But some of the most creative thinking regarding the nature of the secular state in India today is being done by Christians, in the consultations of the National Christian Council and in the publications of the Christian Institute for the Study of Religion and Society, Bangalore. The historical creativity of religious minorities in this area is being re-enacted in present-day India.

The Sikhs: Religio-political Conflicts

Guru Nanak, the first of the ten Gurus (spiritual teachers) of the Sikhs, was born near Lahore in 1469. Although of Hindu back-

[62] *Report on the Disturbances which took place at Raipur,* Government of Madhya Pradesh, Nagpur, 1958.
[63] *Ibid.,* p. 29.
[64] "The Bhutt Report and After," *N.C.C. Review,* 1958, vol. 78, pp. 202-204.

ground, Nanak rejected both caste and image worship, and his religious teachings combined elements of monotheistic Islam with devotional Hinduism. According to Khushwant Singh, "the Sikhs were the most outstanding example of Hindu renaissance produced by Islam—an edifice built as it were with Hindu bricks and Muslim mortar."[65] Under the leadership of successive Gurus, Sikhism underwent a remarkable transformation from a religious sect with ascetic and pacifist ideals into a militant theocracy.

The distinctiveness of the community was emphasized by the early development of Gurmukhi—a new alphabet which was used for the sacred writings of the Sikhs. Punjabi was the spoken language of the area, but written in the Gurmukhi script it became a new language of religion, distinct from both the Arabic-Persian characters associated with Islam and the Devanagari script of Sanskrit and Hinduism.[66] Even the name of the script, Gurmukhi, has religious significance: in the Sikh scriptures, *gurmukh* means one who obeys the commands of the Guru. Thus one who used the script was reminded of his duty to the Guru. Gurmukhi also helped to break the domination of the Brahman priestly caste which had monopolized Sanskrit learning.[67]

With the steady growth of the new religious community through conversions, the Sikh genius for organization soon became evident. Under the third Guru, the territory inhabited by his followers was divided into twenty-two dioceses; devout Sikhs were appointed as his political and religious vicegerents. The fifth Guru, Arjun, compiled the Sikh canon, the *Adi Granth*, and these scriptures provided a code of both sacred and secular law. He declared it the duty of every Sikh to give one-tenth of his income to the communal treasury and appointed collectors for each of the twenty-two dioceses. This system of fixed dues was reputedly more efficient than the taxation system of the Mughal Empire. Sikhism became a state, a theocracy in which the Guru was the true king. Rejecting the asceticism of the early Gurus, Arjun adopted the elegance and magnificence of a temporal monarch's court.

[65] Khushwant Singh, *The Sikhs*, George Allen and Unwin Ltd., London, 1953, p. 19.
[66] John Clark Archer, *The Sikhs*, Princeton University Press, Princeton, 1946, pp. 138-139.
[67] Gokul Chand Narang, *Transformation of Sikhism*, New Book Society, Lahore, 1946, p. 46.

His son, Har Gobind, on the day of his accession to the exalted office of Guru, was presented with the two swords of *Miri* and *Piri*, representing temporal and spiritual authority. All of the powers of state and religion were inseparably blended in the person of the Guru. As the Sikh challenge to Mughal sovereignty met with violent repression (Guru Arjun was martyred in 1606), the Sikhs built up their own army to defend their domains.

Under the last of the ten Gurus, Gobind Singh, the Sikhs underwent the final stage in their transformation into a militant religio-political community. On the Hindu New Year's Day in 1699, Gobind Singh formed a new fraternity which he called the Khalsa ("the pure"). He instituted the five outward signs of the brotherhood (hair and beard unshorn, a comb, steel bangle on the right wrist, a pair of shorts, a sword worn at all times), and the use of the name "Singh" (lion) by all the members of the Khalsa. He succeeded in welding the Sikhs into an effective fighting force, although their victories over the Mughals were few during this period. Although Guru Gobind Singh had four sons, he declared that the line of Gurus would come to an end with his death. He provided that religious and temporal decisions would thereafter be made by the majority of an elected representative assembly. A decision made by the representatives of the Khalsa became a *gurumata* (order of the Guru). Thus, with the last of the Gurus, the Sikh theocracy exchanged a monarchical form for a democratic one.

During the eighteenth century the political and military fortunes of the Sikhs fluctuated greatly. A confederacy of twelve military governors, functioning in different parts of the Punjab, was consolidated into a powerful Sikh kingdom under Maharaja Ranjit Singh. Abolishing the political aspects of the *gurumata* assemblies, Ranjit Singh sought to secularize government and even appointed Hindu and Muslim advisers. One writer has described Ranjit Singh, with some exaggeration, as the "founder of the first secular state in India."[68] A decade after his death in 1839 the Punjab was annexed by the British. The Sikhs became noted for their loyalty to the British crown, especially after their help in quelling the mutiny of 1857. This loyalty declined rapidly under the pressures of the religio-political conflicts which began during the period of the first World War.

[68] Teja Singh, *Sikhism: Its Ideals and Institutions*, Orient Longmans, Bombay, 1951, pp. 97-98.

This historical sketch has emphasized some of the unique elements in the Sikh tradition which have a bearing on the problems of this minority in present-day India. In particular, we have noted the persistent tendency of this religious community to express itself in institutionalized political life. This is only partially explained as a defensive reaction to Mughal oppression; other sectarian offshoots from Hinduism expressed themselves in devotional religion and were accorded the tolerance of Islam. Regardless of possible explanations of its origin, the Sikh tradition of organized and militant political action is very much a part of Punjab politics today.

Several problems have confronted the Sikhs since independence. Underlying many of their cultural, religious, and political tensions is the deep-seated fear of the Sikh leaders that their community is destined to be absorbed by Hinduism. The question of the relationship between Hinduism and Sikhism has always been problematical. Guru Arjun indeed attempted to express the distinctiveness of Sikhism in the most categorical terms:

> I have broken with the Hindu and the Muslim,
> I will not worship with the Hindu, nor like the Muslim go
>   to Mecca.
> I shall serve Him and no other.
> I will not pray to idols nor say the Muslim prayer.
> I shall put my heart at the feet of the one Supreme Being,
> For we are neither Hindus nor Mussulmans.[69]

Nevertheless, there has always been a marked tendency for Sikhism to gravitate toward Hindu beliefs and practices. Some of the Sikhs, called Sahajdharis, refused to conform to the five outward symbols prescribed by Guru Gobind Singh. The clean-shaven Sahajdhari is all but indistinguishable from a Hindu.

Even among the orthodox Sikhs of the Khalsa, some regard Sikhism as a Hindu sect. Needless to say, many Hindus so regard it. In 1924 Gandhi wrote in his periodical *Young India* that the Sikhs, far from being non-Hindus, were "a part of the Hindu community, the *Granth Sahib* is filled with the Hindu spirit and the Hindu legends, and millions of Hindus believe in Guru Nanak."[70] Gandhi expressed the hope that the separatist tendencies of the Sikhs would

[69] Khushwant Singh, *op. cit.*, p. 27.
[70] Quoted in Archer, *op. cit.*, pp. 301-302.

decline. Two years later, however, after a tour of the Punjab in which he observed Sikh solidarity and group consciousness, Gandhi promised that he would never again refer to them as Hindus.

The revivalist Akali movement (discussed below) and other factors in the pre-independence period helped to maintain the Sikh identity distinct from Hinduism. But the present trend is to abandon the distinctive forms and symbols of Sikhism—to have the hair cut and the beard removed, to discard the turban, the steel bangle, and the dagger. These forms and symbols are of the utmost importance to the orthodox, for it is chiefly the external appearance of the Sikh which distinguishes him from the Hindu. One Sikh writer noted with alarm, "The process of relapsing back into Hinduism is gathering speed. . . . If the process continues at the present pace, within a short period of history (fifty years at the most) we may witness the remarkable phenomenon of a religious community which achieved the semblance of nationhood disappear in the quicksands of Hinduism."[71]

Many of the younger Sikhs today regard the symbols of their community as anachronistic, and are unconcerned about the preservation of the Sikh group identity. Others are driven by deep psychological needs to assert and strengthen the distinctiveness of Sikh traditions. Outside observers might tend to feel that the latter group over-emphasizes the matter of Sikh outward forms and symbols. In point of fact, many educated Indian Muslim and Christian men are outwardly indistinguishable from Hindus. Nevertheless, these other minority communities maintain their distinctive beliefs, worship, festivals, and customs. Sikhism, in its purely religious aspects, has distinctive institutions such as its *gurdwaras* (shrines), forms of congregational worship, etc. In the West, certain groups among the Quakers, the Mennonites, the Jews, and others have been able to preserve their religious heritage while modifying or abandoning elements of distinctiveness in dress.

While the emphasis on the outward symbols might be questioned, the underlying fear of absorption by Hinduism is understandable and not without grounds. Muslims and Christians to some extent share this fear, although they are larger minorities and are sustained by much longer traditions and by the knowledge that elsewhere in the world their coreligionists are powerful majorities. The Sikhs,

[71] Khushwant Singh, *op. cit.*, p. 180.

however, representing 1.7 per cent of the Indian population, can look for sustenance only to their own five centuries of history, enacted in one corner of India. The agitation for a separate Sikh state in the Punjab is in part a desperate attempt to preserve by political means the solidarity of a community in real danger of losing its identity.

The politics of gurdwara control

Conflict between the Sikh community and the government over control of the *gurdwaras* (Sikh shrines) began in 1914, was settled in 1925, but has reappeared since independence. In the earlier period, the problem centered in the mismanagement of the *gurdwara* property and the corruption of Sikh worship by the *mahants* or priests. Some of the shrines had been heavily endowed, and the income from landed estates as well as the offerings of devout worshippers brought in large sums of money. In some cases the *mahants*, who were supposed to be ascetics, were living in conspicuous luxury and immorality. Most of the priests were of the sect of Udasis, Sahajdhari Sikhs who had never accepted Guru Gobind Singh's forms of orthodox Sikhism. Their natural affinity to Hinduism led some of them to introduce elements of Hindu ritual and even images in the *gurdwara* worship, and in some cases Hindus and Sikhs worshipped together. The danger of absorption by Hinduism was thus increased even by the Sikhs' own priests.

The Akalis, a zealous reform group, made little headway before World War I. Their determination to regain control of the *gurdwaras* for the orthodox Sikh community was frustrated by the British legal and political structure. The latter had introduced the conception of a freehold estate, and in some cases the priests acquired a prescriptive right to the *gurdwara* property, and had the titles registered in their own names. Civil suits to effect the removal of particular priests involved tremendous expense and were frequently unsuccessful after years of litigation.[72]

In 1920 the Akalis adopted, under Gandhi's inspiration, a policy of direct action by non-violent means. A large band of Sikhs would simply occupy a *gurdwara* and compel the intimidated priest to re-

[72] William Roy Smith, *Nationalism and Reform in India*, Yale University Press, New Haven, 1938, p. 323. See also Sat Sri Akal, *The Gurdwara Reform Movement and the Sikh Awakening*, Desh Sewak Book Agency, Jullundar, 1922.

sign. At first the *mahants* gave in, and with the sanction of the government a considerable number of shrines came under the management of the Shiromani Gurdwara Prabandhak Committee (Committee of Shrine Management), formed by the Sikhs for this purpose. Government policy changed, however, and Akali "disturbers of the peace" soon felt the strong arm of the law come down heavily upon them. Many fervent Akalis whose only concern was the honest administration of their shrines were convicted of criminal trespass and robbery, and thrown into prison. The movement for *gurdwara* liberation thus became as much a struggle against the Punjab government as against the priests.

In 1921 the priests at Nankana (the birthplace of Guru Nanak) allowed a band of 130 Sikhs to enter the shrine, had the gates closed behind them, and then had a force of Muslim mercenaries shoot them down in cold blood. The Nankana massacre and several other crises produced powerful demands that the government abandon its simple role as upholder of law and order and enact legislation which would enable the Sikhs to regain control of their own places of worship. The Sikh Gurdwaras and Shrines Management Act of 1922 provided for certain controls over the *mahants* but also recognized their vested interests, and hundreds of Sikhs were killed and thousands wounded in attempting to occupy by non-violent means the shrines guarded by police.

The government's attitude of neutrality toward the shrine question was decisively reversed with the enactment of the Sikh Gurdwaras and Shrines Act of 1925. Under this act, the hereditary tenure of the priests was abolished (they received financial compensation), and an elaborate machinery was set up to ensure that the property and income of the *gurdwaras* would be used for valid religious purposes. Control of the institutions was placed in the hands of the Shiromani Gurdwara Prabandhak Committee, a board elected for a five-year term with the vote of every adult Sikh, man and woman. The Sikh community enjoyed the right of universal adult franchise in *gurdwara* elections long before the Constitution of India established this principle. The act also provided that the rituals and ceremonies in the *gurdwaras* should be conducted in strict accordance with the sacred scriptures of Sikhism.

Control of the 168-member Shiromani Gurdwara Prabandhak Committee is of the utmost importance in Sikh politics, and has been the constant goal of rival factions among the Akalis. The SGPC administers the huge income of several hundred *gurdwaras* and their endowments, and has great patronage with thousands of posts to be filled—of priests, missionaries, managers, and servants. In this unique institution we see again the characteristic Sikh blending of religious and political concerns. "So far as their religious affairs and organization are concerned," Gokul Chand Narang noted, "the Sikhs have established, so to say, an *imperium in imperio*. It has enabled their central board to employ hundreds of preachers who are not mere reciters of sacred texts but are virtually their political agents, not only propagating the Sikh religious views but also consolidating the community and watching their social and political interests."[73]

The elections to this unusual ecclesiastical institution, the SGPC, are conducted entirely by the state's electoral machinery. Most of the members of the SGPC are elected from single-member constituencies which have been demarcated in most parts of the Punjab. There are fifteen double-member constituencies; one of the members elected from each must be a Sikh representative of the Scheduled Castes. This is the same device used to ensure the election of Hindu members of these castes to central and state legislatures. Some SGPC members are also selected by nomination, and a few others are co-opted. Certain regulations of the Representation of the People Act, which governs the conduct of general elections, have also been applied to *gurdwara* elections.[74]

Several Sikh parties contest these elections: the dominant Shiromani Akali Dal led by Master Tara Singh,[75] the Chief Khalsa Diwan, and the Khalsa Dal composed of "Congress Sikhs." As the SGPC undeniably represents political power in the Punjab, even Sikh Communists sponsored by the Desh Bhagat Board stand for election to this religious body! *Gurdwara* election campaigns are

[73] Narang, *op. cit.*, p. 328.
[74] Harbans Singh, "The SGPC: Symbol of Sikhs' Struggle for Religious Reformation," *The Spokesman*, vol. 7, January 1957, pp. 19-20.
[75] The Akali Dal has also been the strongest Sikh group on the broader political scene, holding four seats in the Lok Sabha and a sizable number in the former PEPSU and East Punjab assemblies after the first general elections (1952). In accordance with the 1956 pact with the Congress, the Akali Dal withdrew from active politics, and a number of its members contested the second general elections on the Congress ticket. Early in 1959 the Akali Dal revoked the pact, and announced its intention of contesting the 1962 elections on its own ticket. It won 3 seats in the Lok Sabha and 19 seats in the Punjab assembly.

445

conducted much like regular political campaigns except that the candidates direct their propaganda only to Sikhs. The *gurdwaras* themselves have not infrequently been used for campaign propaganda, especially by the party or faction which at the time happens to control the SGPC. According to many leaders of the Sikh community, *gurdwara* elections have all the evils of political contests, including bribery and other corrupt practices.

Master Tara Singh, leader of the Akali Dal, has long dominated *gurdwara* politics, and since independence he has precipitated several crises with the Punjab government over control of the shrines. The Sikh Gurdwaras Act of 1925 has been frequently amended by the Punjab legislature. In 1953 and 1954 it was amended several times without the approval of the SGPC, contrary to the usual practice, and the Punjab government was charged with unwarranted interference in the management of the *gurdwaras*.[76] Master Tara Singh declared in 1955 that the Punjab Congress and the Punjab legislative assembly were dominated by Hindus who wished "to finish" the Sikhs. It was therefore necessary to create a state in the Punjab in which the Sikhs would have effective political power and be assured of the means necessary to protect their *gurdwaras*. "The greater the interference in our religion by the government with its political power, the greater the need of political power to protect our religion from this satanic interference."[77] This is one interesting facet of the Punjabi Suba agitation, discussed in some detail in the next section of this chapter. It should be noted in passing that Tara Singh's demand on this occasion was clearly for a *Sikh state*, not a Punjabi-speaking state.

To the surprise of virtually everyone, Master Tara Singh was defeated in the 1958 elections for the presidency of the SGPC. He charged that there had been a conspiracy by the Sikh ministers in the Punjab (Congress) government to get rid of him so that they could seize control of the *gurdwaras*. The Sikh Gurdwaras (Amendment) Act of 1959 produced further bitter controversy between Master Tara Singh and the government. The amendment temporarily increased the number of nominated members of the SGPC, and added others indirectly elected by an electorate which included

[76] Sardar Bhagat Singh, "Gurdwara Legislation," *The Spokesman*, vol. 9, Baisakhi number, 1959, p. 24.
[77] *The Hindu*, August 14, 1955.

non-Sikhs. However, all members of the SGPC and of the electoral college were Sikhs.[78] Master Tara Singh denounced the legislation as a violation of freedom of religion and as a further attempt on the part of the Punjab Congress to gain control of the Sikh shrines.

In April 1959, Tara Singh informed Prime Minister Nehru of his decision to undertake a fast unto death in order to "stir the conscience" of the nation and draw the country's attention to the sinister activities of the Punjab government. The proposed fast was abandoned after talks with Nehru resulted in the setting up of a committee to consider any complaints of government interference in *gurdwara* management. In the campaign preceding the January 1960 election of the SGPC, the Akali Dal leader charged that the Congress government aimed at setting up a Hindu raj in the country, and he demanded the immediate formation of a Punjabi Suba (Punjabi-speaking state). Master Tara Singh's overwhelming success in these elections was soon followed by the launching of a powerful Punjabi Suba agitation.

The *gurdwaras* appear to be hopelessly enmeshed in Punjab politics. As long as he is in control, Master Tara Singh has no compunction about using them for anti-Congress propaganda, for he regards it as his duty to warn the Khalsa of the dangers which threaten its very existence. The 1960-1961 Punjabi Suba agitation was almost entirely directed from the Sikh shrines. The deep involvement of the *gurdwaras* in politics is probably inevitable as long as the present system of SGPC elections is continued. The Punjab chief minister, Sardar Pratap Singh Kairon, suggested in 1959 that members of all political parties might be debarred from membership in that body, and hastened to add that this would apply to the Akali Dal as well as to the Congress. Such an amendment would be a step in the right direction.

The whole system of *gurdwara* regulation set up by the act of 1925 is decidedly an anomaly in the context of India as a secular state. Government and religion are tied together in so many ways that in-

[78] In a case which arose under this act, the Supreme Court held that it did not violate article 26(b) of the Constitution (the right of a religious denomination to manage its own affairs in matters of religion). The court held that the electoral law was not a matter of religion and the inclusion of non-Sikhs in the primary electorate was too remote an infringement of freedom of religion. Elections to the SGPC were for the purpose of administration of property, which according to article 26(d) must be in accordance with law. *Sardar Sarup Singh* v. *State of Punjab,* A.I.R. 1959 S.C., p. 860.

dividual and corporate religious freedom, and the religious neutrality of the state, must inevitably be compromised to some extent. Master Tara Singh did well to ask why the Punjab assembly with a Hindu majority should have the right to amend the Sikh Gurdwaras Act. An editorial note in *Thought* stated that "it is amazing that non-Sikhs should have been deemed entitled to legislate or pronounce on a matter so markedly religious as the administration of Sikh shrines."[79] While there is something of a convention that a measure affecting a particular religious community should be passed only when it is supported by a majority of the legislators belonging to that community, every member of the assembly has a constitutional right to vote freely on every bill. Such awkward situations are inevitable so long as the state is made the chief instrumentality for carrying out religious reforms.

While the present system of centralized *gurdwara* regulation through the SGPC has produced some beneficial results, an important question must be raised regarding the lines of future development of Sikhism as a religion. Is the present dependence on the state's electoral and legal machinery to be a permanent feature of Sikhism's ecclesiastical structure, or will it develop organizational strength in the *gurdwara* congregations which would be the natural units for representation in the central committee? Quite apart from the anomaly of having the secular state provide the apparatus for the election of a religious denomination's highest ecclesiastical body, such dependence on the state perpetuates Sikhism's organizational weakness. Services rendered by the state to religion are often at the price of restrictions on religious liberty; even the lesser price of debilitating dependence is not negligible.

Punjabi Suba or Sikh State?

It has long been an article of faith with the Shiromani Akali Dal that Sikh religion cannot be divorced from politics. In the 1960 *gurdwara* election campaign Master Tara Singh made this point repeatedly and emphatically. And it must be said that from a purely historical point of view, there is much support for his assertion. With few exceptions (for example, certain aspects of Maharaja Ranjit Singh's rule) religion and politics in Sikh history have been of a piece. As stated in a recent monograph, "there is no ultimate di-

[79] *Thought*, vol. 11, January 10, 1959, p. 3.

chotomy in the true Sikh doctrine between this world and the next, the secular and the religious, the political and the spiritual."[80] The writer then went on to discuss the "theo-political status" of the Golden Temple in Amritsar and other *gurdwaras* from which the Akalis have directed the Punjabi Suba agitation.

More moderate Sikh opinion recognizes the close historical connection between religion and politics but asserts that the Gurus never decreed that the expression of the faith was to be static and changeless without regard to circumstances. In the light of India's attempt to build a modern secular state, Sikhism must make a conscious effort to separate religion from politics, for the ultimate security of the Sikhs and other minorities lies in the successful establishment of secularism.

According to some Sikh leaders, the Punjabi Suba agitation illustrates the harmful effects of the Akalis' mixing of religion and politics. The demand for a unilingual Punjabi state, justifiable on the same linguistic grounds which were recognized in the formation of other states, has been turned into a communal Sikh demand by the Akali Dal's handling of the issue. As asserted in an editorial in *The Spokesman*: "By making Sikh shrines as operational bases for the Punjabi Suba agitation, they have thrown a religious cloak on an otherwise just political demand."[81]

Whatever the objective merits of the present Punjabi Suba demand, it is made against a historical background of communal separatism. In 1946 the Akali Dal submitted a memorandum to the British government in which it asserted that Pakistan should not be conceded to the Muslims without at the same time conceding the claim for an independent sovereign Sikh state. Many such pronouncements were made by Akali leaders during the year preceding independence. The idea of an independent Sikh state was rejected, but after the upheaval of the partition, certain sections of the community began to talk in terms of a separate homeland for the Sikhs within the Indian Union. "However, as this demand was described

[80] Anonymous, *The Golden Temple: Its Theo-Political Status*, Caxton Press Private Ltd., New Delhi, 1960, p. 3.
[81] "Misuse of Sikh Shrines," *The Spokesman*, vol. 10, July 4, 1960, p. 3. Note also the following general comment relating to the use of *gurdwaras* in politics: "We have been advocating that for Sikhs religion and politics are not separate things. We have tried to nourish them together. But the result has been disastrous." *Ibid.*, vol. 10, January 4, 1960, p. 16.

by some as communal," narrates a Sikh Youth Federation publication, "the Sikhs switched over to the secular demand for a Punjabi-speaking state, which was consistent with the principles canvassed by the Indian National Congress since 1928."[82] That the "switch-over" involved a change in basic objectives, however, is hard to believe, for the proposed state would have a Sikh majority.

The question of the formation of a Punjabi-speaking state soon became a bitter Hindu-Sikh communal controversy. The Arya Samaj led the forces of Hindu communalism against the Akali Dal. Large sections of the Hindu population were persuaded to repudiate Punjabi as their mother-tongue and, in the 1951 census, declared that their language was Hindi. The Sikhs, on the other hand, insisted not only on the Punjabi language as the basis for the proposed state, but Punjabi written exclusively in the Gurmukhi script. To most Hindus, this was an arrogant attempt to impose upon them the script of Sikh religion and culture. Hindus frequently preferred the Devanagari script, and many Punjabis of both communities were accustomed to writing their language in the Persian script. Before partition, Urdu was the language of administration and the chief literary medium for all communities, and paradoxically, much of the Hindi-Punjabi controversy is still being waged on both sides through the medium of Urdu.[83]

The States Reorganization Commission, which submitted its report in 1955, rejected the Akali Dal's arguments for a Punjabi-speaking state, although it recommended the demarcation of almost all the other states on a linguistic basis. The commission pointed out that the Punjabi and Hindi languages as spoken in the Punjab were closely akin to each other and both were well understood by virtually all the people of the state. If the Punjabi-speaking areas were formed into a separate state, facilities would still have to be provided for the large minorities which would demand Hindi as the medium of instruction for their children. There was simply no way to avoid bi-lingualism in the Punjab. The commission noted that opinion on the proposal was divided almost entirely on a Hindu-Sikh communal basis and concluded that "the minimum measure of agree-

[82] *The Demand for the Punjabi Suba*, The Sikh Youth Federation, Calcutta, 1960, p. 4.
[83] The Urdu daily *Partap*, a pro-Hindu communalist paper with a large circulation, published a series of articles in early 1961 urging all Punjab Hindus to register their mother tongue as Hindi in the coming census.

ment necessary for making a change in the present setup does not exist so far as the proposal for the Punjabi-speaking state is concerned."[84]

The commission not only rejected this proposal but also recommended that PEPSU (in which the Sikhs were the largest community) be merged with the Punjab. The Akalis thereupon launched a determined agitation to secure their demands. Master Tara Singh vehemently proclaimed that the religion, language, script, culture, and very existence of the Sikhs were in grave peril. Arya Samajist elements were working with fanatical zeal to wipe out the Sikh identity by forcing their absorption into Hinduism. The community was in danger, and could be secure only in a state in which it held effective political power.

Negotiations between the Akali leaders and the central government led to the 1956 Regional Formula. PEPSU and Punjab were merged, and the compact state was divided into Hindi-speaking and Punjabi-speaking regions. While there was to be a single legislature for the state, the legislators and ministers from each of the two areas were to constitute regional committees with special powers to advise the state government and the legislative assembly on certain subjects. This unworkable arrangement was never fully implemented by the Punjab government, and broke down amidst conflicting interpretations of the extent of the regional committees' powers. Charges of bad faith were hurled at each other by the Akali Dal and the Punjab government.

Master Tara Singh's spectacular victory in the 1960 SGPC elections (136 out of 140 seats) launched the second major Punjabi Suba agitation. Tara Singh was soon imprisoned under the Preventive Detention Act, and many thousands of Sikh volunteers courted arrest by defying the government's ban on the shouting of the slogan "Punjabi Suba Zindabad" (Long live Punjabi Suba).

The line of reasoning which appealed to many Sikhs is well illustrated by the following quotation from a pamphlet. "India claims to be a secular state. At present Hindus are in the majority in every state of the Union. The unilingual principle has been applied to all states except the Punjab. The Punjab is the only state where application of the unilingual principle may reduce Hindus to a minority

[84] *Report of the States Reorganization Commission,* Government of India Press, New Delhi, 1955, p. 146.

community. If the principle is not made applicable in [the] case of Punjab, the unavoidable inference would be that this is done to see that Hindus do not lose their majority status in any state."[85] Nehru countered with the argument that the government had never accepted the idea that language was to be the *sole* determining factor in states reorganization.

The prime minister declared emphatically at the 1961 Bhavnagar Congress session that there was no discrimination against the Sikhs in the government's opposition to the partition of the Punjab on a linguistic basis. "The Punjab itself is, broadly speaking, a Punjabi Suba and Punjabi is the dominant language there. It is true that some parts of the Punjab have Hindi, but essentially Punjabi is the dominant language and it should be encouraged in every way."[86] Considerable importance was attached to Nehru's assurance to the Sikhs, and Sant Fateh Singh, second-in-command in the Punjabi Suba movement, thereupon gave up his fast unto death (on the twenty-third day of the fast) so that further talks with the government could be arranged. Nehru's declaration enabled the Akali leaders to call off the agitation with a minimal loss of face. At the same time, however, Nehru reiterated his position that any division of the state would be very harmful to the Punjab, to the Sikhs as well as to the Hindus, and to the whole of India. The Punjab government released over 5,000 Akali prisoners as soon as the agitation was called off in January 1961.

The Akali truce with New Delhi was short-lived, however, and seven months later Master Tara Singh himself vowed to fast unto death in the cause of a Punjabi-speaking state. The Sikhs as a community were suffering intolerable discrimination, he declared, and the only solution was a Punjabi Suba. His fast ended after forty-eight days, again with some conciliatory gestures from New Delhi. Since Tara Singh had charged that the entire Sikh community was being discriminated against, the government appointed a distinguished three-man commission to investigate the charge. The commission consisted of the chairman, S. R. Das, retired chief justice of India, Dr. C. P. Ramaswami Aiyer, and M. C. Chagla. But Master

[85] Balbir Singh Mann, *The Punjabi Suba Morcha: A Plea for Sympathy*, Ashok Fine Art Press, Delhi, n.d., p. 15.
[86] *The Hindu*, January 9, 1961.

Tara Singh then attacked the personnel and terms of reference of the commission and refused to cooperate with it.

In its report submitted in January 1962 the commission cited with approval the following points made in a memorandum prepared by the Nationalist Sikhs. Both in the Punjab legislature and in Parliament the Sikhs enjoyed political representation commensurate with their historical and social importance. Though they constituted only 34 per cent of the population of the Punjab, their representation in the Punjab cabinet had always been 40 to 50 per cent. The chief minister of the Punjab was a Sikh. Since independence there had always been a Sikh in the central cabinet. There was a Sikh governor of a state, several Sikh ambassadors, and in various other high positions the community was well represented. The Das commission concluded that on the basis of the evidence before it, "no case of discrimination against the Sikhs in the Punjab has been made out."[87]

A careful study of the Akali case for a Punjabi-speaking state leaves the outside observer with the strong feeling that, despite all protestations to the contrary, the basic objective of the movement is still a Sikh state. In private interviews with scores of Akali leaders, the professed concern for language is easily dropped, and there is considerable frankness in admitting their determination to secure a state in which the *Panth* (Sikh community) would be in control.

While opportunism accounts for much that goes on in Sikh politics, as in any kind of politics, this much is clear. There is a genuine and well-founded fear that the Sikhs may lose their identity as a community by the natural process of lapsing back into an all-absorbing Hinduism. The charge that this is taking place as the result of a deliberate policy of the government is made with much less sincerity, and has no real foundation in fact. Nevertheless, many Sikhs see the creation of their own state as the only possible means of checking the forces which threaten to dissolve the distinctive solidarity of the *Panth*. But is political power ever capable of preserving the real vitality of religious values?

[87] *The Hindu Weekly Review,* February 19, 1962.

CHAPTER 15

THE CHALLENGE OF HINDU COMMUNALISM

FREQUENT references have been made to the Hindus, the Muslims, the Christians, and the Sikhs as religious "communities." While the term "communal" is sometimes used simply as the neutral adjectival form (as in "communal representation"), it is generally associated with a narrow, selfish, divisive, and aggressive attitude on the part of a religious group. The term "communalism," as it is used in India today, refers to the functioning of religious communities, or organizations which claim to represent them, in a way which is considered detrimental to the interests of other groups or of the nation as a whole.[1] The term usually implies some kind of political involvement; the numerous associations concerned solely with the religious and cultural affairs of particular sections of the population are not regarded as manifestations of communalism.

This chapter deals with the challenge of Hindu communalism to the secular state. By definition, all forms of communalism—Hindu, Muslim, Christian, Sikh—are contrary to the principles of the secular state. Muslim communalism, in the form of Muslim League separatism, was responsible for the partition of the country in 1947, and the communalism of any minority in independent India is naturally a matter of serious concern.[2] In the present context, however, the only force capable of becoming a real threat to Indian secularism is that communalism which attempts to function in the name of the majority community.

THE ORIGIN AND DEVELOPMENT OF HINDU COMMUNALISM

The Hindu communal groups which will be discussed in this chapter—the Hindu Mahasabha, the Rashtriya Swayamsevak Sangh,

[1] The term is sometimes applied also to the similar functioning of caste groups, although the term "casteism" has come into common use in the past few years and there is a tendency to distinguish it from "communalism." Thus, Congress politicians frequently decry "communalism, casteism and linguism" as the three threats to India's unity.
[2] See chapter 14, "A Report on the Minorities."

the Ram Rajya Parishad, and the Jana Sangh—have their roots in the traditions of late nineteenth-century Hindu nationalism. Swami Dayananda Saraswati, founder of the Arya Samaj, worked not only for religious reform but for the creation of a spirit of Hindu unity and militant opposition to anti-Hindu influence. His unceasing efforts to eradicate caste and idol-worship and to restore Hinduism to the purity of Vedic times were accompanied by aggressive denunciations of Islam, Christianity, and the West. Despite the non-Vedic origin of the Hindu belief in the sanctity of the cow, he espoused the cause of cow protection, and it became a symbol of Hindu resurgence. Dayananda attributed India's sufferings and troubles to the "meat-eating and wine-drinking foreigners, the slaughterers of kine."[3] He sought to rouse the Hindu community into active resistance to the alien influences which threatened it.

Tilak and the Extremists, who blended Hinduism with nationalism, provided much of the direct inspiration for the Hindu communal parties.[4] Tilak developed the Ganapati and Shivaji festivals as means of strengthening Hindu solidarity vis-à-vis the community's enemies, the British and the Muslims, and his anti-cow slaughter agitation continued Dayananda's work. In 1906 Tilak secured for one of his young admirers a scholarship for study in England, and V. D. Savarkar later became a powerful leader of the Hindu Mahasabha.[5] Tilak, Savarkar, and other leaders of militant Hinduism came from the Chitpavan Brahman community of Maharashtra.

The difference between Indian nationalism and Hindu communalism was not always clear. Nationalism inevitably drew part of its inspiration from India's ancient cultural traditions, and these were mainly Hindu. India was the only home of the Hindus, and whatever patriotic demands were made in the name of the majority would naturally appear to be expressions of Indian nationalism.[6] The separatist implications were not as readily discernible as in the case of Muslim communalism.

The Muslim League was founded in 1906, significantly, during the period of Extremist ascendancy in the Congress. The Hindu Mahasabha, in turn, developed largely as a reaction to the Muslim

[3] Valentine Chirol, *Indian Unrest*, Macmillan and Company, London, 1910, p. 110.
[4] See the section on nationalism in chapter 3, "The Historical Foundation."
[5] Dhananjay Keer, *Savarkar and His Times*, A. V. Keer, Bombay, 1950, pp. 3, 19-20, 25.
[6] Jawaharlal Nehru, *Recent Essays and Writings: on the Future of India, Communalism and other Subjects*, Kitabistan, Allahabad, 1934, pp. 48-49.

communalism of the League. According to some accounts, the origins of the Hindu Mahasabha can be traced to the Punjab Hindu Conference held in Lahore in 1907.[7] However, for more than a decade the organization remained in obscurity and did not function on an all India basis. The Congress had drawn into its ranks the best leaders of Hindu society; the Congress dominated nationalist politics and thus left little scope for the Hindu communalists.

Communally minded Hindus within the Congress, however, were gradually alienated by the Congress leadership's "appeasement" of the Muslims. By the Lucknow Pact the Congress accepted the League's principle of separate electorates. Under Gandhi's leadership the Congress participated in the Muslim Khilafat movement which agitated for the restoration of the Sultan of Turkey—the Caliph of Islam—to his prewar status. Serious Hindu-Muslim riots in the 1920's added to the general communal tension. Increasingly the feeling developed in some sections of the Congress that Gandhi was completely ignoring Hindu interests in his ill-conceived attempts to secure the cooperation of the Muslim minority, and that his compromises only led to larger Muslim demands.[8]

Still, the open break with the Congress did not come immediately. The first important session of the Hindu Mahasabha was held in 1923, and the following year it met at Belgaum while the Congress session was being held there. A number of prominent Congress leaders attended the Mahasabha meeting, including the Ali brothers, Dr. Mahmood, M. Hasrat Mohani, Maulana Abul Kalam Azad and other Muslims. Pandit Madan Mohan Malaviya, who presided, declared that every Hindu should support the Congress. The aim of the Mahasabha was to supplement and strengthen the Congress by dealing with those non-political questions—social, cultural, and religious—which were outside its area of concern. In the 1925 session this position was reiterated by the president, Lala Lajpat Rai, who insisted: "The Hindu Sabhas should make no encroachment on the province of the Congress, except so far as purely communal questions

[7] Bhai Parmanand, in "Foreword" to Indra Prakash, *A Review of the History and the Work of the Hindu Mahasabha and Hindu Sanghatan Movement*, Akhil Bharatiya Hindu Mahasabha, New Delhi, 1952.

[8] Richard D. Lambert, "Hindu Communal Groups in Indian Politics," in Richard L. Park and Irene Tinker, eds., *Leadership and Political Institutions in India*, Princeton University Press, Princeton, 1959, p. 214.

are concerned." Many members of the Hindu Mahasabha continued to be Congressmen.

Within the next few years, however, the two organizations parted ways. The Hindu Mahasabha decided to put up its own candidates in elections and in 1933 came out in open opposition to the Congress. The intensely anti-Muslim sentiment of the Mahasabha had by this time profoundly affected its nationalism; it preferred to compromise with the British rather than with the Muslims. In the Ajmer session Bhai Parmanand, the president, declared: "I feel an impulse in me that the Hindus will willingly cooperate with Great Britain if their status and responsible position as the premier community in India is recognized in the political institutions of new India."[9]

Violent Hindu-Muslim upheavals led to the formation of the Rashtriya Swayamsevak Sangh (RSS) in Nagpur in 1925. The RSS, the Hindustan National Guard, and the Hindu Rashtra Dal provided disciplined troops to fight the Hindu cause in the communal riots which flared up in many parts of north and central India during this period. The emphasis on the militarization of the Hindu community became characteristic of the communalist groups.

A key word in the vocabulary of Hindu communalism during the 1920's and 1930's was *Sanghatan*—unification, integration, consolidation.[10] The Hindu community, fragmented by sect, caste, and language, had to be consolidated into an organic nation with a clear political self-consciousness. The Hindu Mahasabha provided the leadership of the Hindu Sanghatan movement. Sanghatan was necessary if the Hindus were to meet successfully the external threats to their national existence, and Sanghatan necessitated the uprooting of those Hindu traditions which perpetuated their weakness. Thus, the communal groups on one hand idealized and exalted the ancient Hindu religion and culture and looked to the past for the true values which were lacking in modern life. On the other hand they produced social reformers, who, like Swami Dayananda before them, rejected outright certain basic aspects of the traditional Hindu way of life.

[9] The material in this and the preceding paragraph is largely drawn from Asoka Mehta and Achyut Patwardhan, *The Communal Triangle*, Kitabistan, Allahabad, 1942, pp. 186-189.

[10] Bhai Parmananda, *Hindu Sanghatan,* Central Hindu Yuvak Sabha, Lahore, 1936, p. 226.

The Sanghatanists recognized that caste inequality, and especially untouchability, not only kept the Hindus divided but encouraged mass conversions to Islam and Christianity.

This blending of revivalism and reformism was frequently not understood, and the Hindu Mahasabha was regarded by many as the party of Hindu orthodoxy. Yet V. D. Savarkar, president of the Mahasabha from 1937 to 1942, had long been associated with such reforms as temple entry for untouchables, inter-caste dining, and even inter-caste marriage. Other prominent Hindu Sanghatan leaders, however, rejected this position, and the followers of Tilak always opposed social reform. One present-day Hindu communal party, the Ram Rajya Parishad, is very orthodox in its views on caste. But social reform is a logical implication of Sanghatan, and this element has always been present to some extent in the Hindu communalist tradition.

During this same period the reclaiming of those who had left the Hindu fold became an important part of the Sanghatan program. The *shuddhi* (literally, "purification") movement was started to reconvert Hindus who had been forcibly converted to Islam, but as almost all Muslims and Christians were the descendants of converts from Hinduism, they were all regarded as potential candidates for the *shuddhi* ceremony. Both the Arya Samaj and the Hindu Mahasabha were very active in this movement, which had important political implications in view of the system of separate electorates.

One of the most influential works in the development of Hindu communalist ideology was the treatise on *Hindutva,* by V. D. Savarkar, first published in 1923. The main contributions of this small book were two: a definition of the word "Hindu," and the conception of "Hindutva." In attempting to answer the question "Who is a Hindu?" numerous writers had emphasized various aspects of Hindu religious faith and practice—belief in the Vedas, the caste system, etc. But these definitions invariably failed to find a universally acceptable common denominator, and were also deficient in that they neglected the cultural, historical, and national aspects implied in the word "Hindu." Savarkar's definition: "A Hindu means a person who regards this land of Bharat Varsha, from the Indus to the seas as his Fatherland as well as his Holy Land, that is, the cradle land of his religion." The definition was broad enough to include the adherents of all the creeds and sects of Indian origin—the Jains, the Sikhs, the Arya Samajists, etc. The reference to Fatherland identified the Hindus as a racial and national unit.

This last aspect was further developed in the conception of Hindutva, or "Hinduness." Hinduism, a system of religious beliefs and practices, is only one part of Hindutva. "Hindutva embraces all the departments of thought and activity of the whole Being of our Hindu race."[11] Hindutva refers to a people united by a common country, blood, history, religion, culture, and language. The Hindus are vastly more than a religious community; they are a nation. "Hindu Rashtra" (Hindu nation), a basic conception in the ideology of Hindu communalism, was first systematically formulated by V. D. Savarkar.

Savarkar agreed that it was necessary to cultivate a sense of attachment to the greater whole, whereby Hindus, Muslims, Parsis, Christians, and Jews would think of themselves first as Indians. But this national consciousness would have to be built upon the solidarity of the majority. "So with the Hindus, they being the people whose past, present and future are most closely bound with the soil of Hindustan as *Pitrabhu* (Fatherland), as *Punyabhu* (Holy land), they constitute the foundation, the bedrock, the reserved forces of the Indian state. Therefore, even from the point of Indian Nationality, must ye, O Hindus, consolidate and strengthen Hindu Nationality."[12]

Savarkar discussed the Muslims in a tone of moderation in *Hindutva*, but the growing communal tensions of the following two decades were reflected in the aggressive attitude which he increasingly displayed toward them in his speeches and writings. The separatist implications of his concept of Hindu Rashtra became clearer. The Hindus were a nation; the Muslims were but a community. In his presidential address to the Hindu Mahasabha in 1937, however, he elevated the Muslims to the status of a nation also. "India cannot be assumed today to be a unitarian and homogeneous nation, but on the contrary there are two nations in the main; the Hindus and the Muslims." And again: "There are two antagonistic nations living side by side in India."[13] M. A. Jinnah could have

---

[11] V. D. Savarkar, *Hindutva*, V. G. Ketkar, Poona, 1942, p. 4.
[12] *Ibid.*, p. 116.
[13] V. D. Savarkar, *Hindu Rashtra Darshan*, L. G. Khare, Bombay, 1949, p. 26.

constructed his two-nation theory, which led to the demand for Pakistan, on the basis of Savarkar's speech!

In the pre-independence period, the Hindu Mahasabha did not stand for the creation of a Hindu state in the sense of a formal constitutional recognition of Hinduism. In the same speech quoted above Savarkar declared: "Let the Indian state be purely Indian. Let it not recognize any invidious distinctions whatsoever as regards the franchise, public services, offices, taxation on the grounds of religion and race. Let no cognizance be taken whatsoever of (a) man's being Hindu or Mohammedan, Christian or Jew."[14] The Mahasabha leader complained that it was the Congress which had departed from secular national principles by agreeing to separate electorates, reservation of government posts, and other arrangements which brought religion into public life.

Hindu communal leaders regarded the Congress as singularly inept in its handling of the "Muslim problem." Merely because Hindu members of the Congress found it easy to forget their Hindu background and merge with others in a common Indian nationality, they imagined that the Muslims would do likewise. This was the basic error. Despite innumerable compromises and special concessions to the Muslim League, the Congress had not been able to secure its cooperation in the nationalist cause. Rather, each new concession was interpreted as a further sign of weakness, and the Muslims demanded more and more. The demand for Pakistan came in 1940, and in the years following the Hindu Mahasabha leveled a steady stream of fire at the Congress for its weakness in dealing with this "fantastic proposal to vivisect the Motherland." Popular support for the Mahasabha increased considerably, although the Congress again swamped the Mahasabha in the elections of 1946.

THE HINDU MAHASABHA: IDEOLOGY SINCE 1947

In this and the following two sections of the chapter we shall consider the ideological bases and programs of the major Hindu communal groups. This discussion will be followed by a consideration of the political fortunes of these groups since 1947. The Hindu Mahasabha has attempted to broaden its ideological base since independence by incorporating a wide range of policy issues in its

[14] *Ibid.*, p. 18.

manifestos. While its general orientation on economic policy is decidedly conservative, its statements regarding specific problems are vague, eclectic, and self-contradictory. It is clear that the only matters about which the Mahasabha has real convictions are religious and communal questions and relations with Pakistan.

The Mahasabha stands for the reestablishment of Akhand Bharat (undivided India), since the 1947 partition agreement constituted an act of betrayal by the Congress. While more recent statements stress that the reunion of India and Pakistan will be sought "by all constitutional means," Professor V. G. Deshpande declared in 1949 that the Mahasabha would not shrink from waging war with Pakistan to achieve this if other methods failed.[15] As long as Pakistan remains a separate state, it should be dealt with on the basis of strict reciprocity; the Mahasabha "will not hesitate to force" Indian Muslims to migrate to Pakistan in order to maintain parity in migration.

The Mahasabha holds that "the misconceived notion of secular democracy cannot inspire the masses" and that only the ideals of Hindu Rashtra are capable of doing this.[16] In the face of the fissiparous tendencies of provincialism and linguism, according to the Mahasabha, "the real uniting link among the people of this vast country is Hinduism, which has been systematically ignored and thrown into the background by the present rulers."[17] The party pledged itself to fight against "anti-Hinduism carried on by the Congress in the name of secularism."[18]

The Mahasabha "stands for establishing Hindu Raj in Bharat, with a form of government in accordance with Hindu conceptions of policy and economy." This would require fundamental amendments of the Constitution "so that it may be in consonance with the tradition and culture of the land and make Bharat a truly democratic Hindu state."[19] If the United Kingdom can be a Christian state, Israel a Jewish state, and Pakistan a Muslim state, the Mahasabha argues, why should Hindustan not be a Hindu state? The exact nature of such a Hindu state, however, has never been explained.

[15] V. G. Deshpande, *Why Hindu Rashtra?*, Akhil Bharat Hindu Mahasabha, New Delhi, 1949, p. 15.
[16] Election Manifestos of 1951 and 1957.
[17] Resolution of the Working Committee of the Mahasabha. *All India Hindu Mahasabha Bulletin*, no. 1, September 1960, p. 13.
[18] *Ibid.*, p. 20.
[19] Election Manifesto of 1951.

What will be the position of non-Hindus? Hindus alone are the nationals of India, and non-Hindus can be classified only as Indian citizens. The non-Hindus shall be entitled to equal rights and privileges under normal conditions; in the event of war or other emergency, however, the government would have powers to distinguish between Hindu and non-Hindu citizens.[20] The 1951 election manifesto accused the Congress of "continuing its game of Muslim appeasement and thereby creating fifth columnists and enemies inside our body politic." The 1957 manifesto was somewhat more moderate in that it did not refer to the Muslims directly but, after guaranteeing equal rights of citizenship to all, added: "This equality would not be allowed to be exploited by anti-Indian fifth columnists, with sympathies outside India, to carry on their activities without hindrance."

Conversions from Hinduism to other religions must be stopped, since a change in religion is equivalent to a change in nationality, according to Mahasabha ideology. Those who are already adherents of Islam and Christianity must be "naturalized"—presumably subjected to some degree of Hinduization. Their reconversion to Hinduism would be the ultimate solution, and the Mahasabha has continued to place great emphasis on the *shuddhi* movement. The 1957 election manifesto, in discussing the services rendered by the Mahasabha, claimed that "more than 5,000 Christians were converted to Hinduism during the last five years." The party has consistently demanded a ban on foreign missionaries in India, as Christian converts weaken the security of the country. In his presidential address of 1959, Professor Ram Singh declared that "every Christian or every Muslim in India is a disruptive force."

Some of the other important items in the Mahasabha platform are: a total ban on cow slaughter, the repeal of the Hindu Marriage Act and other "anti-Hindu legislation," the complete integration of *all* of Kashmir with the Indian Republic, a stern policy toward Pakistan, India's withdrawal from the Commonwealth, and an intensive program of compulsory military training. The principle of the militarization of the Hindu nation has long been an important part of the Hindu communalist tradition ("Hinduize all politics" and "militarize Hindudom").

[20] *Mahasabha and its Ideals*, Akhil Bharat Hindu Mahasabha, New Delhi, p. 7.

An interesting sidelight on Mahasabha ideology is its glorification of the orthodox Hindu Kingdom of Nepal. Tilak, Savarkar, Bhai Parmanand, and other Hindu leaders proudly looked upon Nepal as the only remnant of Hindu greatness and glory. In Savarkar's presidential addresses to the Hindu Mahasabha he stressed the admiration felt by all Hindus for the sturdy Himalayan state which was the sole remaining independent Hindu Kingdom. When the late King Tribhubana visited New Delhi, the Hindu Mahasabha address of welcome to him declared: "The noble ideals of Hinduism find their best expression in the life of Your Highness, and we who cherish the best traditions of Hindutva, look up to you as the greatest exponent and foremost upholder of our ancient culture. . . . We look up to Your Highness—the only independent Hindu ruler of the world—as the Defender of our faith in these critical times. . . . As a true Hindu Your Highness stands before us as the most accredited cultural representative of our ancient Dharma." Writing in 1950, a Mahasabha leader regarded the government of Nepal not as autocratic and backward, but as a glorious rule "in strict conformity with the tenets of the Hindu Shastras and in accordance with the ancient customs of its inhabitants."[21]

After disastrous defeats in the general elections of 1951-1952 and 1957, leaders of the Hindu Mahasabha began to give some thought to a revision of the party's ideology, especially with regard to economic policy. Responding to the general swing toward socialism, marked ever since the Congress in 1955 adopted a socialistic pattern of society as its objective, the Mahasabha suddenly discovered "Hindu socialism." Less than a year before the 1962 general elections, V. G. Deshpande announced this discovery in his inaugural address to the forty-sixth session of the Mahasabha. He declared that the system of caste and village organization was based on the socialist principle of "from everyone according to his capacity and to everyone according to his need." There was no feudalism in the Hindu system; landlordism had been introduced in India (as one might have expected!) by the Muslim rulers. Shivaji introduced revolutionary land reforms, and was in fact the founder of Hindu socialism.

According to Deshpande, Hindu socialism was non-Marxist, nationalistic, based on India's spiritual heritage, and would preserve

[21] "A Wayfarer" (Indra Prakash), *Nepal Today*, The Hindu Outlook, New Delhi, 1950, pp. 2, 56-57.

human dignity and individual freedom. In an interesting modification of the socialist classless society, the speaker declared that the present classes based on economic exploitation would have to go, and their place might be taken by divisions based upon spiritual, intellectual, and ethical values analogous to the Hindu *varnas* (castes).[22] The substitution of caste for class is hardly what Nehru has in mind! The 1962 manifesto of the party, however, simply affirmed that national economic policy "must be framed in such a way as to avoid on the one hand the evils of Capitalism, and to secure on the other hand all benefits of Socialism." But the Mahasabha's basic conservatism was revealed in its opposition to land reform legislation.

The Ram Rajya Parishad is a party of regional significance only. Its strength is concentrated chiefly in Rajasthan, where it has enjoyed the support of the landed interests. In attempting to ascertain the principles of the Parishad, one must read through much of its 1951 manifesto before discovering that the organization is a political party. This document is replete with Sanskrit quotation, moral exhortations, metaphysical subtleties, and even arguments for the existence of God. The key to the name of the party, however (Ram Rajya—Rama's Kingdom or Divine Kingdom), is this: "in the blessed days of Lord Rama's reign, every citizen was contented, happy, gifted with learning, and religious-minded." The vision of the Parishad is to restore these conditions to present-day India, since the ruling party has failed so dismally. "Secular Materialism does not possess the power to bring into existence the state of eternal Bliss."

The present Constitution of India is criticized as a slavish patchwork imitation of western systems of government—"None of its clauses bears the mark of our culture." It will, therefore, have to be replaced entirely. Under the new Constitution there shall be full freedom to practice and preach religion in a proper manner. Apparently referring to the jurisdiction of personal law, it is promised that "there shall be a State Department of Religious Affairs to administer justice which shall be based on the recognized religious books, and in consultation with the religious heads with full impartiality, and keeping in view the interests of the Nation and the Society." Under the new Constitution the people will be ruled by Dharma; as the government itself shall be "based on religious

[22] *The Hindu*, April 24, 1961.

doctrines," it will be in a position to foster social service as a part of religious duty.

The orthodox orientation of the Parishad is indicated by its treatment of the caste system. While the Hindu Mahasabha, the RSS, and the Jana Sangh reject caste in varying degrees, and untouchability strongly, the Parishad is concerned with helping the untouchables to maintain their hereditary occupations, although under improved conditions. "They shall be given high posts in the management of the sanitary departments and the leather and hides trade shall be mostly placed in their hands." In this way fullest attention will be given to their "economic prosperity and spiritual salvation." However, any responsible post in the government will be open to them on the strength of individual merit.

The RSS: Militant Hindu Society in Embryo

Unlike the Hindu Mahasabha and the Ram Rajya Parishad, the Rashtriya Swayamsevak Sangh (National Volunteer Corps) has never functioned as a political party.[23] Founded by Dr. Keshav Hedgewar in 1925, the RSS has concentrated its efforts on the development of a tightly disciplined corps of well indoctrinated, physically fit, devoted *swayamsevaks* (volunteers)—Hindu youth who represent the Sanghatan ideal of Hindu society in miniature. Convinced that political power cannot effect the necessary revitalization of the Hindus, the RSS has sought to create a model society which will eventually expand to include the entire "Hindu nation." By an intensive program of ideological discussions, Sangh rituals, military discipline, calisthenics, and drill, the volunteers are prepared for their role as the vanguard of the new Hindu nation. While rejecting politics as the means to attain its particular objectives, the RSS has nevertheless in the past supported the political work of the Hindu Mahasabha, and now is closely linked with the Jana Sangh.

The structure of the RSS is hierarchical, and at the apex is the Sar Sanghchalak, the Leader, who exercises autocratic control over the entire organization. The founder, Dr. Hedgewar, occupied this position until his death in 1940, when the successor whom he had

---

[23] See J. A. Curran, Jr., *Militant Hinduism in Indian Politics: A Study of the RSS*, Institute of Pacific Relations, New York, 1951. See also Govind Sahai, *RSS: Ideology, Technique and Propaganda*, Naya Hindustan Press, Delhi, 1956.

designated, M. R. Golwalkar, became the Sar Sanghchalak. Golwalkar is reverently referred to as "Guruji," and he has many of the marks of the traditional Hindu guru. "Golwalkar's bearded countenance, religious learning, ascetic habits, magnetic personality, oratorical skill, and aura of mysticism place him in the category of charismatic leader."[24]

The clearest exposition of the RSS ideology is found in the small book published by Golwalkar in 1939, *We or Our Nationhood Defined*. The influence of Savarkar's *Hindutva* on this work is very evident. Golwalkar defined "nation" as a people united by a common country, race, religion, culture, and language; he then proceeded to show that in every respect the Hindus were a nation. Muslims, Christians, and other minorities were outside of the nation. The fundamental error of the Congress leaders was their concept of territorial nationality by which they regarded all Indians as part of the nation, ignoring the profound differences in religion and culture.

In his preface, Golwalkar claimed that he was dealing with the concept of nation, a cultural unit, not with the state, a political unit. Nevertheless, the idea of a Hindu state is clearly implied in his discussion of the Hindu Nation. With respect to the minorities, for example, he wrote: "The non-Hindu peoples in Hindustan must either adopt the Hindu culture and language, must learn to respect and hold in reverence Hindu religion, must entertain no idea but those of glorification of the Hindu race and culture, i.e., they must not only give up their attitude of intolerance and ungratefulness towards this land and its age-long traditions but must also cultivate the positive attitude of love and devotion instead—in a word they must cease to be foreigners, or may stay in the country, wholly subordinated to the Hindu nation, claiming nothing, deserving no privileges, far less any preferential treatment—not even citizen's rights."[25] Golwalkar's idea of the best solution to the minorities problem is contained in one word—assimilation. Just as immigrants of diverse nationalities were naturally assimilated in the populations of the United States of America, England, or France, so Indian Muslims and Christians would have to shed their foreign ways and become

[24] Lambert, *op. cit.*, p. 217.
[25] M. S. Golwalkar, *We or Our Nationhood Defined*, 4th ed., Bharat Prakashan, Nagpur, 1947, pp. 55-56.

merged with the Hindu Nation. Concerning the use of this particular analogy no comment is necessary!

Golwalkar's exaltation of Hindu race, religion, and culture was
matched only by his contempt for Islam and the West—"The Race
evolved a culture, which despite the degenerating contact with the
debased 'civilizations' of the Mussalmans and the Europeans, for
the last ten centuries, is still the noblest in the world." Immediately
following these highly uncomplimentary references to other civilizations, and with no apparent consciousness of incongruity, Golwalkar
wrote of "the spirit of broad catholicism, generosity, toleration,
truth, sacrifice and love for all life, which characterizes the average
Hindu mind."[26]

Golwalkar rejected the proposition that religion is an individual
question and should have no place in public and political life. He
traced this notion to the experience of Europe and asserted that it
"is based upon a misconception of religion, and has its origin in
those who have, as a people, no religion worth the name." The
western conception of religion is both individualistic and dogmatic,
and a secular political life was found to be the only way to maintain
peace among conflicting sects. Hinduism, on the other hand, en-
compasses the whole of life, and politics cannot be artificially
separated from it. "We cannot give up religion in our national life
. . . as it would mean that we have turned faithless to our Race-
Spirit, to the ideal and mission for which we have lived for ages."[27]

It is likely that the ideas expounded in his book represent the
real ideology of Golwalkar and the RSS. The fourth edition of the
book was published in 1947, and it is still used in RSS centers as
the authoritative statement of the Sangh creed.[28] However, following
the central government's banning of the RSS in 1948, Golwalkar
issued several statements which attempted to present its ideology in
quite different terms. For example: "The RSS does not advocate a
Hindu Raj to the exclusion of non-Hindu citizens of the country."

[26] *Ibid.*, p. 49. In 1949 the RSS accused the Jamiat-ul-Ulama of leading the
Muslims in U.P. and Delhi in an "unholy advocacy" of a Hindu-Muslim cultural
synthesis. "U.P. at the Cross-Roads," *Organizer*, December 14, 1949, p. 15.
[27] Golwalkar, *op. cit.*, p. 30.
[28] Golwalkar explicitly reaffirmed the Hindu Rashtra concept in an address delivered in 1960. *Speech Delivered by Parama Poojaneeya Sri Guruji to the Elite
of Bangalore on November 30, 1960*, Rashtriya Swayamsevak Sangh, Bangalore,
1961, pp. 14-15.

Golwalkar also demonstrated great dexterity in dealing with the concept of the secular state. "To a Hindu, the state is and has always been a secular fact. It was only a departure from the Hindu way of life that brought about, for the first time, a non-secular theocratic concept of state under Ashoka."[29] The Buddhist Ashoka and later Muslim rulers founded theocratic states, but Shivaji restored the Hindu tradition of the secular state in which people of different creeds could hold high posts in government. While it is not impossible to reconcile this statement with the one quoted two paragraphs above, given the many facets of the term "secular state," the differences are striking. In the first statement the secular state is the unfortunate but inevitable result of western dogmatism and unspirituality; in the second it is the remarkable achievement of Hindu catholicity.[30]

Nehru once remarked that Hindu communalism was the Indian version of fascism, and, in the case of the RSS, it is not difficult to perceive certain similarities. The leader principle, the stress on militarism, the doctrine of racial-cultural superiority, ultra-nationalism infused with religious idealism, the use of symbols of past greatness, the emphasis on national solidarity, the exclusion of religious or ethnic minorities from the nation-concept—all of these features of the RSS are highly reminiscent of fascist movements in Europe. Fascism, however, is associated with a concept of state-worship, the state as the all-absorbing reality in which the individual loses himself and in so doing finds ultimate meaning. This conception has no counterpart in RSS ideology; in fact, the Sangh explicitly rejects the notion that its objectives could be attained through the power of the state. Its aim is the regeneration of Hindu society, which must come from within. However, it is impossible to say how the RSS would respond if political power ever came within reach, either directly or through the Jana Sangh. The implementation of certain aspects of its ideology (the policy toward Muslims and other minorities, for example) presupposes extensive use of the machinery of the state.

[29] Press statement of November 2, 1948. *Justice on Trial: A collection of the Historic Letters between Sri Guruji and the Government, 1948-1949*, Jupiter Press, Bangalore, 1959, p. 77.

[30] For an interesting account of discussions with an RSS worker which touched on the major ideological principles of the organization, see Richard L. Park, " 'Angularities' and the Secular State: an Interview with India's RSS," *Radical Humanist*, vol. 25, January 15 and February 5, 1961.

THE JANA SANGH: REVISIONIST COMMUNALISM

The communal nature of the Hindu Mahasabha has never been in doubt. Its membership is open only to Hindus (those who profess a religion of Indian origin), and it stands for Hindu Rashtra and the creation of a Hindu state. Mahasabha leaders have plainly declared that theirs is a *communal* party (open to only one community); they reject the term "communalist," however, with its more decidedly negative connotations.

The relationship of the Bharatiya Jana Sangh to Hindu communalism is more difficult to define. The founder, Dr. Syama Prasad Mookerjee, was deeply influenced in his early political career by Dr. Hedgewar (founder of the RSS) and by V. D. Savarkar, and he succeeded the latter as president of the Hindu Mahasabha in 1943.[31] Mookerjee served in his independent capacity as a member of Nehru's cabinet from 1947 to 1950, resigning in protest over the government's policy on the Bengal border disturbances. There were personal rivalries with other Mahasabha leaders, and the Mahasabha was still associated in the popular mind with the assassination of Gandhi. But Mookerjee broke openly with the party over the issue of its membership, being convinced that the Mahasabha had no political future functioning solely as a Hindu organization. He therefore founded the Jana Sangh in 1951.

All Jana Sangh accounts of the founding of the party lay great stress on this matter of membership; a fundamental principle was involved. Mookerjee, wrote one Jana Sangh M. P., "severed his relations with the Hindu Mahasabha because of that party's unpreparedness to admit into its fold all Indian citizens irrespective of creed or sect." The Jana Sangh's open membership policy is therefore the result of deep conviction, according to party spokesmen. "The decision to keep the party's doors open to all citizens irrespective of religion or sect is not prompted by any considerations of political expediency, as some critics would have one believe. The Jana Sangh holds that the state, by its very nature, is a secular body, and therefore it should not align itself with any particular religion or sect. The party is opposed to politics being linked with religion, and also feels that religious institutions should confine their activities to

[31] Balraj Madhok, *Dr. Syama Prasad Mookerjee,* Deepak Prakashan, New Delhi, 1954, pp. 7-8, 16.

their particular fields. In the partition of the country, we have already had a grim experience of the consequences of mingling religion with politics."[32] It would be difficult to find a member of the Hindu Mahasabha who would make a statement of this kind. However, there was another significant factor behind the founding of the Jana Sangh which should be mentioned here.

As we have noted above, the RSS has never entered the electoral field as a political party; it has concentrated on building up a corps of young men thoroughly disciplined and committed to its communalist ideology. The eighteen-month ban on RSS operations (1948-1949) imposed by the Congress government, however, clearly indicated the importance of political power. According to Mookerjee's biographer (himself a leading Jana Sangh figure), the RSS leaders began to feel the need of a party which would "reflect the ideas and ideals of the RSS in the political sphere" and hence command their willing allegiance.[33] Mookerjee was well aware of this feeling, and the Jana Sangh was founded with at least the tacit understanding that RSS support would be forthcoming. Nehru went so far as to describe the Jana Sangh as the "illegitimate child of the RSS."[34] Since 1951 the ties between the two organizations have been greatly strengthened. The expressed political philosophy of the Jana Sangh must be evaluated in the light of these facts.

Jana Sangh manifestos and speeches contain ideas which run directly counter to the Hindu Rashtra ideology of Savarkar and Golwalkar. The party "looks upon all Indians irrespective of their caste and creed who owe allegiance to India as their motherland and cherish her age-old culture as one nation."[35] In his 1958 presidential address, Devaprasad Ghosh expounded a view of nationhood which was completely incompatible with the Hindu nation theory. He pointed out that India with her vast area and diversity of races, religions, and languages is not really comparable to the nation-states of Europe such as France or Germany; India is more comparable to Europe itself. The idea of nationhood for India as a whole has developed, especially during the past century and a half, as a result of common subjection to foreign rule. The underlying unity of

---

[32] Atal Bihari Vajpayee, "The Bharatiya Jana Sangh," an article included in Marathi souvenir of a state Jana Sangh meeting held at Nasik, November 4-6, 1960.
[33] Madhok, *op. cit.*, p. 53.
[34] *The Hindu*, January 6, 1952.
[35] *Bharatiya Jana Sangh: A Brief Introduction*, Delhi, 1957, p. 2.

India must be strengthened, but attempts to "steam-roller the rich diversity of India's life and culture into a flat and drab uniform pattern" are doomed to failure. Devaprasad Ghosh then went on to speak with appreciation of the educational and humanitarian work done by the Christian community in India.

In his presidential address of 1960, Pitamber Das flatly rejected a related tenet of Hindu communalism. "A change of religion surely does not mean a change of our ancestors or a change of nationality," he declared. "The wrong-founded old notions in this regard must be shed and a healthy outlook developed." On the other hand, the 1957 election manifesto of the Jana Sangh asserted that the party would promote national unity, "nationalizing all non-Hindus by inculcating in them the ideal of Bharatiya Culture." What this procedure of "nationalization" means has never been explained in detail. It would presumably include a uniform system of education through which cultural ideas could be imparted, but it could obviously mean a great deal more.

The Jana Sangh, like the Hindu Mahasabha, has frequently accused Nehru and the Congress of a policy of "Muslim appeasement," which they see as a continuation of the pre-1947 concessions to the Muslim League. "What passes as secularism today, however, is only an euphemism for the policy of Muslim appeasement. It is neither nationalism nor secularism but only a compromise with communalism which demands a high price even for its lip-loyalty to this country."[36] Any deliberate effort to give representation to the Muslims in appointments to high government posts, according to the Jana Sangh, represents an anti-national approach. There should be equal rights and opportunities for all citizens; the Jana Sangh "does not recognize majorities or minorities based on religion." It is difficult to quarrel with the Jana Sangh position in theory, although from the viewpoint of building up the confidence of the minorities in the secular state, some special consideration is sound in practice.

The Jana Sangh's position on a number of issues is similar to that of the Hindu Mahasabha: legislation banning cow slaughter, repeal of the Hindu Marriage Act and other "anti-Hindu" measures, implementation of the Niyogi report calling for a ban on foreign missionaries, Akhand Bharat (undivided India), total integration of Kashmir in the Indian Republic, compulsory military training, and

[36] *Manifesto and Program of the Bharatiya Jana Sangh,* December 1958.

471

a tough policy toward Pakistan. But the party has given no support to the *shuddhi* movement, and it has gone on record as being strongly opposed not only to untouchability but to "casteism."

The Jana Sangh has developed a more convincing concern for a wide range of national and international issues than the Mahasabha. It stands for a unitary state which it will somehow combine with the decentralization of political power, a general policy of economic decentralization but with nationalized basic industries, profit-sharing plans to enlist the willing cooperation of labor, the abandonment of joint cooperative farming schemes. In foreign policy the Jana Sangh has strongly criticized Nehru's tendency to minimize the seriousness of communist aggression in Hungary, Tibet, and the Indian border areas.

Is it correct to regard the Jana Sangh as a Hindu communal party? The party can offer evidence to support its negative reply to this question. First, membership is open to citizens of all religions, and a few Muslims and Christians have joined the party. The late Dr. V. K. John, founder-president of the Madras State Jana Sangh, was a "true Christian who fully believed in the divinity of Christ."[37] A Muslim is the president of the West Bengal party organization. Second, the ideology of the party is not based on the Hindu Rashtra theory which has played such a prominent role in the history of Hindu communalism. This theory was fully discussed at the time of the founding of the Jana Sangh, and the term "Bharatiya" (Indian) was deliberately chosen instead of "Hindu."[38] Third, the Jana Sangh does not appear to be obsessed with communal questions, but has evidenced a wholesome concern about a wide range of national problems.

On the other hand, the charge of Hindu communalism cannot be dismissed as simply an example of malicious Congress propaganda. Addressing a press conference in 1961, Deendayal Upadhyaya, general secretary of the Jana Sangh, declared that the party would have no truck with Communists or communalists in the 1962 general elections. In the latter category he included the Akali Dal, Muslim League, and Dravida Munnetra Kazhagam. Asked about the Mahasabha, he replied, "No, we do not consider the Hindu

[37] V. Rajagopalachari, "Dr. V. K. John," *Tamil Nad Jana Sangh: First Conference Souvenir, October 8-9, 1960.*
[38] Madhok, *op. cit.*, pp. 56-57.

Mahasabha a communal party."[39] Upadhyaya's own identification of Hinduism with Indian nationalism ruled out the possibility of attaching such a label as "communal" to the Mahasabha. The late Dr. S. P. Mookerjee's connections with the Hindu Mahasabha were extremely close. But more important for the present are the intimate Jana Sangh ties with the RSS, which has provided many of its younger leaders and workers. In the long run the liberal elements in the Jana Sangh (and they *are* there) are likely to be overpowered by the vigorous young men whose political indoctrination in illiberal and communalist thinking has been very thorough.

POLITICAL FORTUNES SINCE INDEPENDENCE

The partition of India in 1947 was accompanied by communal upheavals and violence on an unprecedented scale. The Hindu communal groups, especially the RSS, sent organized bands of volunteers to help the Hindu refugees in border areas, to defend Hindus from the attacks of Muslim bands, and to launch attacks on the Muslims when the circumstances seemed favorable. General public support of the communalists naturally increased in view of their role as active defenders of Hindu interests.

The assassination of Gandhi on January 30, 1948, by a fanatical Hindu communalist who had past associations with both the Hindu Mahasabha and the RSS, and who was known as a trusted lieutenant of V. D. Savarkar, produced a violent revulsion in public opinion. The Mahasabha suspended political activity; Golwalkar and other RSS leaders were arrested, and the organization was banned. The government was unable to prove direct complicity of these organizations in the crime, but they were judged guilty at the bar of public opinion.

Speaking in the Constituent Assembly on April 3, 1948, Nehru declared that "the alliance of religion and politics in the shape of communalism is a most dangerous alliance, and it yields the most abnormal kind of illegitimate brood."[40] The Assembly then passed the following resolution: "Whereas it is essential for the proper functioning of democracy and the growth of national unity and solidarity that communalism should be eliminated from Indian life,

[39] *Organizer*, January 9, 1961, p. 13.
[40] Jawaharlal Nehru, *Independence and After*, John Day Company, New York, 1948, p. 47.

473

this Assembly is of the opinion that no communal organization which by its constitution or by the exercise of discretionary power vested in any of its officers or organs, admits to or excludes from its membership persons on grounds of religion, race and caste, or any of them, should be permitted to engage in any activities other than those essential for the bona fide religious, cultural, social and educational needs of the community, and that all steps, legislative and administrative, necessary to prevent such activities should be taken." The resolution was of some significance in giving a lead to the country regarding the problem of communalism, but no legislative or administrative steps were ever taken to implement it.

On May 28, 1949, the Hindu Mahasabha resumed political activity. The ban on the RSS was lifted three months later, on the assurance of Golwalkar that the Sangh would not participate in politics. Another condition was that the constitution of the RSS be put down in writing, and this was done. Following his release, Golwalkar was greeted by huge crowds and enthusiastic ovations wherever he went. The government's case against the RSS was not a strong one; many of the charges made—that the RSS was undemocratic in its internal organization, that many of the key leaders belonged to one particular community (Maharashtrian Brahmans), that its life membership pledge smacked of a secret society, etc.—were irrelevant and certainly no justification for banning the organization.[41] Regarding the really important charges that the RSS was inspiring communal hatred and indulging in systematic violence, the government's evidence was apparently insufficient. To some extent, Golwalkar's enthusiastic receptions reflected the opinion that the government had treated him unfairly.

The Hindu communal parties have generally fared poorly in election contests. In 1951-1952 the Hindu Mahasabha won only 4 seats in the Lok Sabha, and the Jana Sangh and Ram Rajya Parishad each captured 3 seats. Their representation in the state assemblies, although better, was still unimpressive. However, considering the fact that the Jana Sangh was formed only a few months before the elections began, its showing was a fairly creditable one. The Jana Sangh was the only communal party to gain the necessary 3 per cent of the popular vote to retain its status as a national party

[41] See the collection of letters in *Justice on Trial* noted above.

along with the Congress, the Praja Socialist Party, and the Communist Party.

As a result of the 1957 elections the Hindu Mahasabha's representation in the Lok Sabha was reduced from 4 to 2, and the Ram Rajya Parishad lost all 3 of its seats. The decline of the Hindu Mahasabha, long the vociferous spokesman for Hindu interests, was dramatized by the defeat of three of its former presidents, Dr. N. B. Khare, V. G. Deshpande, and N. C. Chatterjee. (Mr. Chatterjee later severed his connections with the Mahasabha to join the Swatantra Party of C. Rajagopalachari.) The Jana Sangh, however, increased its strength in the Lok Sabha from 3 to 4 seats and in the state assemblies from 34 to 46 seats.

Since 1957 the Jana Sangh has achieved some notable successes in municipal corporation elections in Delhi, Lucknow, Kanpur, Agra, Banaras, and Allahabad. A truly spectacular victory came in April 1961 when the Jana Sangh candidate, Professor Balraj Madhok, defeated his Congress opponent in the New Delhi by-election to the Lok Sabha. As the seat of the government of India, New Delhi obviously holds a special position, and the Jana Sangh's electoral success in that well-educated constituency brought great prestige to the party.

In the 1962 general elections, the Ram Rajya Parishad won 2 seats and the Hindu Mahasabha 1 seat in the Lok Sabha, and in the Madhya Pradesh assembly these two parties took 10 and 6 seats, respectively. The Jana Sangh, however, made major advances and more than doubled its strength in both the Lok Sabha and the state assemblies (14 and 115 seats, respectively). Even more significant was the distribution of seats in the state legislatures. In the Uttar Pradesh and Madhya Pradesh assemblies the Jana Sangh became the second largest party (48 seats to the Congress' 248 in U.P., 41 seats to the Congress' 142 in M.P.). It is obvious that in Madhya Pradesh where Hindu communalist forces have long been active, the Jana Sangh, Ram Rajya Parishad, and Hindu Mahasabha, together controlling 57 votes in the state assembly, will constitute an important political factor.

The Jana Sangh also met with serious electoral defeats in the unseating of two of its important leaders in the Lok Sabha, A. B. Vajpayee who was leader of the Jana Sangh parliamentary group and an able orator, and A. Rama Rao, president of the party. The Jana

Sangh's measure of success at the polls in the 1962 elections was also clouded by the superior performance of the Swatantra Party, a party which had come on the political scene barely three years before. The Swatantra Party captured 22 seats in the Lok Sabha and 167 seats in the state assemblies, compared with the Jana Sangh's 14 and 115. This new party of economic conservatism became the main opposition party in Bihar, Rajasthan, and Gujarat. Led by a respected elder statesman and former governor-general of India, C. Rajagopalachari, the Swatantra Party has siphoned off much of the support which the forces of economic conservatism, traditional allies of the communal parties, might well have given to the Jana Sangh.

The Jana Sangh has not done badly in the decade of its existence; it has survived the death of its founder, strengthened its organizational base and leadership through RSS support, and in challenging the Congress Goliath has shown itself capable of winning votes. It has something to say on the whole range of issues facing the nation. But the Jana Sangh has no leaders of national stature, and it has not succeeded in convincing most educated people that it is not a communal party. In fact, there are tensions within the party over its relations with the RSS. Charges of direct RSS interference in Jana Sangh organizational matters have frequently been made. At the ninth annual session held at Lucknow in 1960, a committee was appointed to inquire into the grievances of anti-RSS units of the Jana Sangh.[42] It is obvious that friction over this question could become very damaging to party unity, as well as draw public attention to its ties with the openly communal RSS.

It is interesting to compare the Hindu communal groups with the nineteenth-century "nativist" movement in the United States. The nativists' defense of American culture, traditions, and institutions (they were "100 per cent pro-Americanism") took the form of intense opposition to European Catholic immigrants and to Catholicism in general. Many of their charges against Catholics are paralleled by anti-Muslim pronouncements in present-day India: Catholics owed their first religious and political loyalty to Rome; their authoritarian and theocratic traditions were opposed to the democratic

[42] In February 1961 a former organizer of the RSS, Sanwaldass, undertook a fast in front of the central office of the Jana Sangh in Delhi, protesting the interference of the RSS, "a totalitarian body," in Jana Sangh affairs. He charged that a number of changes in the leadership of Jana Sangh units had been made as a result of RSS pressure. *Link*, February 5, 1961, p. 11.

institutions of the country; their culture was incompatible with that of the majority, etc. The sequel to the story of nativism, however, is that one century later the American people elected a Roman Catholic president. While there are still vestiges of nativism in the United States, on the whole the country has outgrown it.

It is an undoubted fact that popular support of the Hindu communal groups has varied in direct proportion to the prevalence of Hindu-Muslim tension and conflict, and since independence, in direct proportion also to tensions between India and Pakistan. This being the case, there is a strong tendency for these groups to magnify every Hindu-Muslim communal incident, to exploit every Indo-Pakistani difference. The communalist groups have a vested interest in conflict, both internal and international, and there is a natural temptation to create it if it does not appear spontaneously.

In June and July of 1960 Assam was rocked by a series of riots directed against the Bengali-speaking minority in the state. While the general press of the country described the serious disturbances as a conflict of linguistic groups, the Jana Sangh-related *Organizer* found the Muslims to have played a large part in the tragedy. In a long article on "The Terrible Role of Muslims in the Genocide of Bengalis in Assam" ("By an Eye-witness"), much was made of alleged behind-the-scenes machinations on the part of the two Muslim ministers in the Assam cabinet. The article charged that much of the looting of Hindu Bengali houses and shops was carried out by Muslim gangs, and clearly hinted that the government of Pakistan had also been involved in engineering the riots. The article is replete with unsubstantiated charges, insinuations, and innuendoes, and was obviously calculated to inflame communal feelings.[43]

The Hindu communalists eagerly seize upon any incidents which illustrate Muslim communalism. Unfortunately, certain Muslim leaders are foolish enough to provide them with broad targets from time to time. Mohammed Ismail, president of the Indian Union Muslim League, has contributed substantially to the Hindu communalist cause by the propagation of his own aggressive brand of communalism. The spectre of a revived Muslim League is undoubtedly very useful to the RSS and Jana Sangh.[44]

[43] *Organizer*, August 8, 1960, pp. 5-6, 11-12.
[44] *Ibid.*, September 26, 1960, pp. 1-2.

As we have noted above, the assassination of Mahatma Gandhi led to vigorous repression of the Hindu communal groups by the government. The Jabalpur Hindu-Muslim riots of February 1961, in which fifty-five persons were killed, produced a somewhat similar reaction, although not nearly as intense. In December 1960 a seven-member committee had been appointed by the Congress parliamentary party to study the growth of communal organizations and to suggest ways to promote national integration. Following the Jabalpur riots, the committee decided (one member dissenting) to recommend to the party that organizations bearing communal denominations should be banned from contesting elections. A few days later, however, the general opinion expressed in the Congress parliamentary party meeting was not in favor of such a ban.[45]

Many Congressmen felt that their own party should be blamed for having indirectly encouraged communalism by entering into an alliance with the Muslim League in Kerala in order to fight the Communists. Others were more impressed with the legal and constitutional difficulties. The law minister, A. K. Sen, gave a legal opinion that a permanent ban on communal parties contesting the elections could not be imposed without infringing the fundamental rights guaranteed by the Constitution. However, he added that an amendment of section 123 of the Representation of the People Act could be made to permit the withdrawal of recognition of communal parties.

Even as it stands, section 123(3) of this act, in effect, prohibits a communal party from conducting its election campaign on a communal basis. The act lists as one of the prohibited corrupt practices the following: "The systematic appeal by a candidate or his agent or by any other person, to vote or refrain from voting on grounds of caste, race, community, or religion or the use of, or appeal to, religious symbols . . . for the furtherance of the prospects of that candidate's election."[46] The Supreme Court upheld the application of this law where it was found that a candidate had made a systematic appeal to Chamar voters to vote for him on the basis of his caste.[47]

The objections to legislation banning communal parties from contesting elections were weighty. The timing of this proposal, less

---

[45] *The Hindu*, April 3, 18 and 19, 1961.
[46] Representation of the People Act (43 of 1951), as amended by Act 27 of 1956.
[47] *Jamuna Prasad* v. *Lachhi Ram*, A.I.R. 1954 S.C., p. 686.

than a year before the 1962 elections, understandably led opposition party leaders to believe that the Congress intended to use the power of the state to eliminate competition. Fundamental rights would surely suffer if such a ban were imposed. It is unlikely that a ban would affect the most powerful Hindu communal party, since the Jana Sangh is constitutionally and in practice open to persons of all communities. In June 1961 the decision was made by the union government to drop the idea of a total statutory ban on communal parties. Plans were made, however, to amend both the Representation of the People Act and the Indian Penal Code in order to deal with communalist activities more severely.[48]

COMMUNALISM IN THE CONGRESS

It would be a great error to assume that the forces of Hindu communalism find expression only in the Hindu Mahasabha, RSS, and Jana Sangh. Almost from its inception, the Congress has contained elements sympathetic to the communalist viewpoint, and we have already noted the close association of the Hindu Mahasabha with the Congress during the period 1924-1926. Some Hindu Mahasabites retained their Congress membership well into the 1930's. Article V(c) of the Congress constitution stated: "No person who is a member of any elected Congress committee can be a member of a communal organization, the object or program of which involves political activities which in the opinion of the working committee are anti-national and in conflict with those of the Congress." It was only in 1938 that the working committee declared that for the purposes of this article, the Hindu Mahasabha and the Muslim League were to be regarded as communal organizations.[49]

V. D. Savarkar declared in 1940 that hundreds of Hindu Congressmen had congratulated him on the stand taken by the Mahasabha on various issues in opposition to the Congress. Why did they then remain in the Congress? Because a place on the Congress ticket guaranteed them election to the legislatures; Congress membership assured them of some post or profit.[50] There is no reason to believe that the situation is totally different today.

[48] *The Statesman*, June 24, 1961.
[49] Proceedings of the Working Committee, December 11-16, 1938.
[50] Savarkar, *Hindu Rashtra Darshan*, pp. 182-183.

The communalist sentiment within the Congress has come to the surface over such issues as the Hindu Code Bill, proposals to ban cow slaughter, the question of foreign Christian missionaries, and the treatment of the Muslim minority. Many of the Hindi enthusiasts are not without some communalist sympathies. Purushottamdas Tandon, Pandit Thakur Dass Bhargava, and Govind Seth Das have been the most outspoken advocates of Hindu causes. While the late deputy prime minister, Sardar Vallabhbhai Patel, took vigorous action against the RSS, he did not hesitate to press for some recognition of Hinduism in India's national life and vowed not to rest until the Somnath temple (destroyed by Muslim invaders in the eleventh century) was restored. One of the arguments urged in Mahasabha circles against the resumption of political activity in 1949 was that it was not necessary since Sardar Patel was pursuing a strong Hindu policy.[51]

At the time of the Nasik Congress of September 1950, Nehru noted a certain "flabbiness" among some sections of the Indian National Congress in their attitude toward communalism. Injustice was being done to minorities in Pakistan, and there was a considerable reaction in India in favor of retaliatory measures against Muslims. Some Congressmen were affected by the pressure of public opinion and, in Nehru's words, were bringing out the theory that "democracy means that whatever the people feel regarding any matter is to be accepted, and that is the crux of democracy. If injustice is done to minorities in Pakistan, is it a valid reason to adopt a similar attitude here?"[52] Nehru's answer, of course, was an emphatic negative. He warned against the "indirect infection of communalism among Congressmen" by which they were being unconsciously influenced by the communal spirit.

Purushottamdas Tandon, who had been supported by Sardar Patel, was president of the Congress at this time, and there was considerable tension between him and Nehru on the communal issue. The overwhelming support given to Nehru in the presidential elections at the Nasik Congress, although with reluctance on the part of some, was hailed as a significant victory for the secular state. The *New York Times* in a leading article said: "In effect, the decision made at Nasik was that India will continue along the Gandhi-Nehru line

[51] Deshpande, *op. cit.*, p. 1.
[52] *The Hindu*, September 22, 1950.

toward a secular welfare state, not toward an orthodox Hindu oligarchy."[53]

Nehru's leadership of the Congress has not been challenged since then. But it would be foolish indeed to assume that his deep convictions regarding the secular state are shared by all his fellow Congressmen. Probably the majority at the present time does fully accept the secular state, only a tiny minority (secretly) rejects it, but a substantial minority merely acquiesces in the present policy and would be willing to go in a different direction. Nehru declared that from his own inquiries it appeared that local Congress leaders made no attempt at all to calm the communal frenzy which seized Jabalpur and other cities and towns of Madhya Pradesh during the riots of February 1961. They simply sat in their houses like "purdah ladies" while the situation deteriorated. This lack of positive conviction about secularism, and the willingness to stand by passively in the presence of communalist disruption are serious defects. The Congress parliamentary party resolved in April 1961: "Those Congressmen who by their acts or inaction in an emergency support directly or indirectly communalistic activities are not worthy of remaining in the Congress."[54]

It is difficult to think of any potential successor to Nehru who is likely to take an equally strong stand on the question of secularism. One cannot rule out the possibility of a Congress drift to the right after Nehru, allowing the latent Hindu communalist sentiment to become a significant political force.

Apart from the Hindu-minded elements within the organization, the Congress is involved in communalism in two other ways. First, it has on occasion made electoral alliances, or come to a similar kind of understanding, with communal political parties representing the minority communities. While spurning any association with the Hindu Mahasabha or Jana Sangh, and in fact opposing these groups as bitterly as it opposes the Communists, the Congress has made special arrangements with Sikh and Muslim communal parties which have clothed them with a certain respectability. In 1956 the Shiromani Akali Dal, the strongest Sikh political organization, came to an agreement with the Congress on several disputed matters, and directed its members to join the Congress for their political activities.

[53] *New York Times*, September 22, 1950.
[54] *The Hindu*, April 15 and 24, 1961.

The Akali Dal was to limit its work to serving the educational, cultural, and economic interests of the community. Many of the Akalis contested the 1957 elections on Congress tickets.[55]

Twenty-eight months of Communist rule in Kerala were brought to an end on July 31, 1959, by the intervention of the central government. A United Front—the Congress, the Praja Socialist Party, and the Muslim League—successfully fought the 1960 midterm election to restore democratic government to the state. While the alliance was forged chiefly by the PSP, the Congress also agreed to work with the Muslim League, the party which had been the instrument of what Gandhi called "the vivisection of India." After the election, however, the Congress preferred not to be reminded of its political opportunism and refused to include a Muslim League member in the cabinet, although the PSP was willing.

In the Congress discussion of the role of communal parties in Indian political life, following the Jabalpur riots, the Kerala alliance was an obvious embarrassment. The Congress president, N. Sanjiva Reddy, denied that there had been an alliance with the League. As he explained it, the Congress simply declined to contest ten seats which it had no chance of winning. The League contested these seats.[56] Reddy made a categorical declaration that the Congress would on no account enter into any electoral alliance or understanding with communal or socially reactionary parties in the 1962 elections. This stand was quickly endorsed by the Congress parliamentary party, which declared that it was essential that communalism be combated on all fronts.[57] Meanwhile, the coalition in Kerala continued, and state Congress, PSP, and Muslim League leaders were anxious to hold it together. Hindu communal leaders bitterly complained that Congress recognition and "encouragement" of the Muslim League in Kerala was responsible for its emergence in the municipal politics of Ahmedabad, Bombay, Bhopal, and other cities where it had been all but defunct.

The other way in which the Congress is involved in communalism

[55] *The Spokesman,* vol. 9, nos. 1 and 2, 1959, p. 26.

[56] This is hardly an accurate account. During the election campaign many Congressmen, including central ministers and the Congress president himself, addressed public meetings from the same platforms with Muslim League leaders, urging support for the candidates of the United Front. This was quickly pointed out by the president of the Indian Union Muslim League. *The Hindu,* April 18, 1961.

[57] *Ibid.,* April 9 and 15, 1961.

(and here we take the term to include "casteism") is in its day-to-day political activities. Caste and religious groups represent political power—in the final analysis, so many votes. The strong social cohesion of such groups makes their votes "deliverable" by their recognized leaders. The refusal to recognize the actual importance of communal loyalties in politics as well as in social life involves risks which the Congress (like the PSP, the Communists, and other parties) is frequently not prepared to take. The religion or caste of a candidate must be "right" for a particular constituency. In the make-up of state cabinets, representation must be given to various caste and religious groups. In chapter II we cited the example of the chief minister of Bihar, who had to seek the advice of the High Command in dealing with the pressing demands of the Bhumihars, the Rajputs, the Kayasthas, and the backward classes for "adequate representation" in his cabinet. Despite its frequent condemnation of casteism, the High Command ultimately had to recognize the powerfully entrenched caste groups and negotiate with them.[58] Communalism in this sense is one of the basic facts of Indian political life. As one study noted: "Even those who want to build a secular non-communal state and society are forced to engineer with communal group-interests. This is unavoidable, in the present state of social transition."[59]

THE CONTROVERSY OVER COW SLAUGHTER

It is appropriate to consider here the problems arising out of attempts to prevent cow slaughter by legal enactments. The relevance of this subject to our discussion of Hindu communalism is twofold. First, since the late nineteenth century the protection of the cow has been a symbol of Hindu resurgence, and the Hindu communal groups discussed in this chapter have all agitated for laws banning cow slaughter. Second, as we shall see, such legislation has been enacted by Congress governments in a number of states, indicating the strength of Hindu communal sentiment within that party. As a matter of fact, the breach between Nehru and many of his fellow Congressmen on this issue has been a wide one.

[58] *Link*, February 19, 1961, pp. 15-16.
[59] P. D. Devanandan and M. M. Thomas, eds., *Christian Participation in Nation-Building*, National Christian Council of India and the Christian Institute for the Study of Religion and Society, Bangalore, 1960, p. 43.

The Hindu belief in the sanctity of the cow can claim absolutely no Vedic authority, but the much later *Mahabharata* (completed about the fourth century A.D.) states that he who kills a cow lives as many years in hell as there are hairs on the cow's body.[60] A modern Hindu's devotion to the cow was illustrated by Gandhi's description of himself as "a worshipper of the cow whom I regard with the same veneration as I regard my mother."[61] In the same statement, however, Gandhi contended for the full freedom of Muslims to slaughter cows, as he regarded recognition of this right as "indispensable for communal harmony."[62]

As the Constituent Assembly began its work of drafting a constitution for independent India, Seth Ramakrishna Dalmia, an orthodox Hindu industrialist of great wealth, launched a nation-wide propaganda campaign for the inclusion of a clause forbidding cow slaughter. As a result of the pressure which was brought to bear on the assembly, a committee was appointed to consider the question of having a ban on cow slaughter included in the fundamental rights. This idea was rejected, and the draft Constitution made no reference at all to the protection of cows.

During the debate on the draft Constitution, Thakur Dass Bhargava, a member of the Congress, proposed the inclusion of such a provision as one of the Directive Principles of State Policy.[63] Some speakers who favored the proposed article made passing allusions to the religious sentiment associated with the cow. Thakur Dass Bhargava pointed out that the ancient sages and rishis regarded the cow as "very sacred," and that Lord Krishna served cows with great devotion. Dr. Raghu Vira declared that in ancient thought the entire universe was one and the cow was the symbol of the oneness of life; the killing of a Brahman and the killing of a cow

[60] See W. Norman Brown, "The Sanctity of the Cow in Hinduism," *Journal of the Madras University*, vol. 28, January 1957, p. 37. Concerning the many references to cattle in the Vedas, Professor Brown wrote: "Yet in all this richness of reference to cattle there is never, I believe, a hint that the animal as a species or the cow for its own sake was held sacred and inviolable" (p. 31). See also Mukandi Lal, *The Cow Cult in India*, pamphlet 3, The Radical Humanist, Calcutta, n.d.

[61] *Harijan*, April 27, 1940.

[62] It is interesting to note, however, that some of the Mughal emperors issued edicts to prevent cow slaughter, a policy well calculated to win the loyalty of their Hindu subjects. See Angelo Moses, "Cow Protection in Mughal India," *Modern Review*, 1948, vol. 80, pp. 402-403.

[63] *Constituent Assembly Debates*, vol. 7, pp. 568-581.

were on a par. However, a very determined effort was made to defend the proposed article on economic grounds; India being an agricultural country, it was necessary to protect its "cattle-wealth."

Strictly from the viewpoint of agricultural economics, it would be impossible to justify a total ban on cow slaughter.[64] India has one-fourth of the cattle population of the whole world; at least one-fourth of India's cows are uneconomic, and many are diseased. The production of fodder in the country is sufficient to maintain no more than three-fourths of the present cattle population. Because of these facts, other members of the Constituent Assembly called for the abandonment of economic arguments and for the frank acknowledgment of the religious sentiment behind the proposed amendment. Syed Muhammad Sa'adulla of the Muslim League declared that he would have no objection to it if the proponents of the article would come out openly and declare that the cow should be protected because it was part of their Hindu religion.

The government realized that there was powerful public support behind the proposal and ultimately gave in as a concession to Hindu sentiment. Dr. B. R. Ambedkar, the law minister, did not reject the amendment as he did hundreds of others. Article 48 of the final Constitution is as follows: "The state shall endeavor to organize agriculture and animal husbandry on modern and scientific lines and shall, in particular, take steps for preserving and improving the breeds, and prohibiting the slaughter, of cows and calves and other milch and draught cattle."

The directive principles of state policy, including article 48, cannot be enforced in courts of law, but are to serve only as guiding principles in the formulation of public policy. A number of unsuccessful attempts have been made in the Indian Parliament to secure legislation which would implement article 48 on an all India basis. Bills have been introduced by Nand Lal Sharma, U. N. Trivedi, Jhulan Sinha, and Seth Govind Das. In the debate on the Useful Cattle Preservation Bill of 1951, K. M. Munshi, then minister for food and agriculture, declared that respect for the cow was a unifying sentiment for the Hindus and that there was "no higher Dharma" than her protection.[65] In the 1955 debate on Seth Govind

[64] See J. Bali, "The Cow in India: A Story of Perverse Sentiment and Abiding Shame," *Caravan*, April 1961, pp. 13-14.
[65] *Parliamentary Debates*, 1951, vol. 8, cols. 3519-3521.

Das' Indian Cattle Preservation Bill, Nehru asserted that it was a matter for the state governments, not Parliament, to consider. Responding to cries of "shame, shame!" by Hindu Mahasabha and Ram Rajya Parishad M.P.'s, Nehru declared that he was prepared to stake his prime ministership on this issue. The house rejected the bill by a vote of 95 to 12; two Congressmen, Purushottamdas Tandon and Thakur Dass Bhargava, ignored the hastily issued Congress whip and voted for the measure.[66]

The Expert Committee on the Prevention of Slaughter of Cattle in India, appointed by the central government, submitted its report in 1955. After considering the subject in some detail, the committee concluded that "a total ban on slaughter of all cattle would not be in the best interests of the country."[67] Thus it would seem that the government of India's position on this issue is quite strong. But the constant pressures upon it for the protection of the cow have not been without effect. An earlier committee had recommended the establishment of Gosadans in which useless cattle could be housed cheaply and allowed to die a natural death. Accordingly, a plan for the establishment of 160 Gosadans was included in the First Five Year Plan and a sum of Rs. 9,715,000 was included in the budget for this purpose![68] The expert committee, however, rejected this tremendously costly solution to the problem of useless cattle.

Nehru's success in staving off legislation on cow protection in the Indian Parliament has not at all been paralleled by developments in the state assemblies. In the key state of Uttar Pradesh, a Gosamvardhan Inquiry Committee was appointed by the government. The chairman was Pandit Sita Ram, and among the twenty-one members of the committee were three Muslims. In its 1955 report, the committee asserted that the problem of the cow should receive as high priority as national defense, and that this problem ("the

[66] *The Hindu*, April 11, 1955.

[67] *Report of the Expert Committee on the Prevention of Slaughter of Cattle in India*, Government of India Press, New Delhi, 1955, p. 63.

[68] *Ibid.*, p. 62. *The Second Five Year Plan* reported that out of the 160 Gosadans for which provisions had been made in the First Plan, only 22 had been established (p. 283). The Second Plan set a target of only 60 Gosadans, but even this was not met. "The relatively slow progress of the scheme was due to the lack of suitable sites, transport difficulties and absence of necessary legislative sanction in some states." *Second Five Year Plan Progress Report 1958-1959*, Government of India Press, Delhi, 1960, p. 44. There is no reference to Gosadans in *Third Five Year Plan: A Draft Outline*, Planning Commission, Government of India, New Delhi, 1960, pp. 168-169 dealing with animal husbandry.

biggest that confronts the nation") would have to be solved despite "the heavy expenditure involved in this undertaking, totally unproductive though it might appear for years to come." The committee unanimously recommended that the slaughter of the cow and her progeny be totally banned.[69]

The U.P. government accepted the recommendation of the committee, and the decision to ban cow slaughter was announced amidst the cheers of all sections of the assembled two houses of the state legislature. Although Nehru had declared that this was a matter for the states to decide for themselves, he did not hesitate to criticize the U.P. decision as "a wrong step." The chief minister of the state, Dr. Sampurnanand, made it clear that the U.P. government had no intention of dropping the bill, despite the prime minister's disapproval.[70] The U.P. bill was passed, and similar legislation imposing a total ban on cow slaughter has been enacted in Bihar, Madhya Pradesh, and Rajasthan. All of these governments, of course, have been controlled by the Congress party.

In *M. H. Quareshi* v. *State of Bihar*, 1958, the Supreme Court considered the constitutionality of Bihar, Uttar Pradesh, and C.P. and Berar (Madhya Pradesh) legislation banning cow slaughter. The petitioners in the case were Muslims engaged in the butchers' trade and related occupations such as the sale of hides, tannery, glue making, etc. They complained that the laws in question violated their freedom of religion guaranteed under article 25 of the Constitution, since it was customary for Muslims to sacrifice cows on *Bakr-Id* day. The court, upon examination of the relevant verses in the Koran and *Hidaya*, found that it was optional for a Muslim to sacrifice a goat for one person or a cow or camel for seven persons. As it was not obligatory that a cow be sacrificed, according to the tenets of Islam, there was no infringement of religious freedom in the total ban on cow slaughter.

The petitioners contended that the impugned laws, if enforced, would compel them at once to close down their business and would, in effect, amount to a complete denial of their right to carry on their occupation, trade or business as guaranteed by article 19(1)(g) of the Constitution. The court held that the laws regulated and re-

[69] *Report of the Gosamvardhan Inquiry Committee*, Superintendent, Printing and Stationery, U.P., Allahabad, 1955, pp. 74-76.
[70] *The Hindu*, February 12, 1955, and April 6, 1955.

stricted these occupations, but did not deprive the petitioners of the right to practice them. Thus, butchers could still slaughter certain classes of bulls, bullocks, and buffaloes, as well as sheep and goats.

The court recognized the religious element involved in the legislation banning cow slaughter. "There can be no gainsaying the fact that the Hindus in general hold the cow in great reverence and the idea of the slaughter of cows for food is repugnant to their notions and this sentiment has in the past even led to communal riots. It is also a fact that after the recent partition of the country this agitation against the slaughter of cows has been further intensified." Furthermore, the court asserted that these facts could not be excluded from its consideration of the case. "While we agree that the constitutional question before us cannot be decided on grounds of mere sentiment, however passionate it may be, we, nevertheless, think that it has to be taken into consideration, though only as one of many elements, in arriving at a judicial verdict as to the reasonableness of the restrictions."[71] However, there was more than a hint of criticism in the court's passing allusion to the situation in which "the Hindu sentiment for the divinity and sanctity attributed to the cow has to be propped up by legislative compulsion."

The Supreme Court held that a total ban on the slaughter of cows of all ages and calves of cows and she-buffaloes was quite reasonable and valid and was in consonance with the directive principles laid down in article 48 of the Constitution. A total ban on the slaughter of *useful* she-buffaloes, breeding bulls, or working bullocks was also held to be reasonable, but not a total ban on their slaughter after they had ceased to be capable of yielding milk or breeding or working as draught animals. Why was not the same criterion of *usefulness* applied to the question of the slaughter of cows? The Court's attempt to justify the discrimination is indeed a curious bit of reasoning which never faced this question frankly.[72]

Nehru's outspoken opposition to anti-cow slaughter legislation has

[71] M. H. Quareshi v. State of Bihar, S.C.J. 1958, p. 992.
[72] The court declared: "As already stated, the she-buffalo and the breeding bulls and working bullocks (both cattle and buffaloes) for their value, present and future, do not run the same amount of danger as a dry cow does. Regulation of slaughter of animals above a specified age may not be quite adequate protection for the cow but may be quite sufficient for the breeding bulls and working bullocks and the she-buffaloes. These considerations induce us to make an exception even in favor of the old and decrepit cows." *Ibid.*, p. 1006.

often attracted the wrath of orthodox Hindu elements. In 1958 Nehru told an assembly of students at Allahabad that he looks up to the cow as he does to the horse. Pandit Sita Ram, chairman of the U.P. committee referred to above and Nehru's opponent in two general elections, took serious exception to this statement which struck him as something akin to blasphemy. He threatened to prosecute the prime minister under section 295A of the Criminal Procedure Code for speaking "with deliberate and malicious intention of outraging the religious feelings of the Hindus." Nehru was not prosecuted, but the incident illustrates the intensity of feeling aroused by devotion to the cow.[73]

What is the significance of these legal bans on cow slaughter? Assuming that economic considerations have had relatively little to do with their enactment, they must be viewed primarily as attempts to impose the taboos of one religion upon all citizens. They are certainly contrary to the spirit of the secular state. The cow protection legislation is undoubtedly the result of Hindu communalism; the coercive power of the state is pressed into the service of Hindu religion, to the detriment or at least inconvenience of beef-eating Muslims and Christians.

The anti-cow slaughter agitations have illustrated the intensity of a certain form of communalist sentiment, not only in the Hindu parties where it would be expected but in the Congress as well. For some, cow protection is the symbol of Hindu dominance, and could well lead to more serious inroads on the secular state. For most, however, it appears to be an isolated objective, which, when attained, leads to nothing in particular. The anti-secular implications of the laws are significant, but should not be exaggerated.

[73] *Manchester Guardian Weekly*, November 3, 1958.

PART SEVEN

PROBLEMS AND PROSPECTS

CHAPTER 16

THE BUILDING OF A SECULAR STATE

THIS concluding chapter will attempt to weigh the numerous factors of strength and weakness in the secular state in India. As one surveys the total scene, it is evident that the factors which support secularism are by no means negligible. Those who would dismiss the secular state as a superficial attempt by a handful of westernized leaders to impose a concept foreign to India's history have not considered all of the facts.

The secular state is built on substantial historical foundations. The Hindu state of ancient, medieval, or modern times was not a narrowly sectarian state in any sense; patronage was frequently extended simultaneously to various sects and religions. The British policy of religious neutrality was the direct antecedent of the secular state, and the legal and administrative institutions introduced by the foreign rulers pointed the way to the development of a common citizenship. India's present system of secular public schools has over a century of history. The mainstream of Indian nationalism, which led to independence in 1947, had a decidedly secular orientation throughout most of its history.

The religion of the majority in India is Hinduism, a faith which on the whole is favorable to the development of the secular state. The Hindu view of history is that ultimately it is unreal; a Hindu theocracy, if it should ever be attempted, could claim no support from the ultimate religious and metaphysical values of Hinduism. Hinduism has a strong tradition of freedom of conscience and tolerance of religious diversity. Religious liberty is based not on considerations of political expediency but on the conviction of the ultimate oneness of the religious quest, however numerous the different paths which might be followed. Furthermore, Hinduism lacks the ecclesiastical organization and centralized authority which would be essential for any kind of theocratic challenge to the secular state.

The existence of sizable and influential religious minorities is another factor which strengthens secularism. The minorities are the natural custodians of the secular state. The Muslims and the Sikhs have little in their respective traditions which lends positive support to this concept of the state; they will strengthen Indian secularism chiefly by guarding the rights of their respective communities. Protestant Christians, however, can speak not only as a minority but as a religious group with a significant tradition of church-state separation.

Indo-Pakistan relations have a bearing on the secular state in India in various ways, both negative and positive. Tensions between the two countries may unfortunately produce increased difficulties for the Indian Muslim. But there is another aspect of the situation which impresses itself on thinking people in India. The fact is that India cannot become a Hindu state, either constitutionally or in practice, without justifying the creation of Pakistan and at the same time imitating that country's policies. While Pakistan has never accepted India's claim that it is a secular state, the adoption of Hinduism as the state religion would confirm the Pakistani interpretation of the last twenty years' history of the subcontinent. And no Indian nationalist would want this to happen.

The Constitution of India is a basic law which, without using the term, clearly erects the structure of a secular state. The Constitution undoubtedly contains certain anomalies in this regard, some of them inevitable. However, as long as the provisions relating to religion retain their present form, it is difficult to envisage any fundamental rejection of secularism. In interpreting this Constitution the Supreme Court, through its power of judicial review of legislation, has proved to be another great bulwark against any tendency of the state to restrict freedom of religion.

The political party in power, the Indian National Congress, has behind it a long tradition of non-communal nationalism and has on the whole been faithful to the ideal of the secular state since independence. It is the party to which the religious minorities (with the exception of the Sikhs) have instinctively looked for the protection of their interests; there is at least a clear ideal which can be appealed to. There are elements of religious revivalism within the Congress, but these are weak, very weak as compared with those in the major parties of neighboring countries (the Sri Lanka Freedom Party in Ceylon, the Union Party in Burma).

The political parties in India which directly challenge the secular state can claim but a microscopic amount of popular support. The Jana Sangh is the only Hindu party which appears to have the potentiality for an important role on the national political scene. But its total strength at present is represented by 14 seats out of 500 in the Lok Sabha. Outside of the communal parties there has been no movement of any significance to make India a Hindu state.

It is impossible to think of the secular state in India apart from the tremendous influence which Prime Minister Jawaharlal Nehru has exercised in implementing this principle. Nehru has indeed been the great champion of Indian secularism, and it is likely that the impact of his convictions will be felt by the body politic long after he passes from the scene. For India to reject the secular state, it will have to repudiate both Gandhi and Nehru.

The forces of westernization and modernization at work in India are all on the side of the secular state. Industrialization, urbanization, the break-up of the joint family system, greatly increased literacy, and opportunities for higher education—all tend to promote the general secularization of both private and public life. The indifference to religion which characterizes the contemporary western outlook has already made a powerful impact on certain sections of Indian society, and the process is a continuing one. Whether good or bad in terms of the individual, this process tends to strengthen the secular state.

There are, to be sure, some very serious problems facing secularism—problems of ill-defined objectives, of faulty policies, of failure in implementation.

Major Problems for the Secular State

Undoubtedly the most serious problem is that of communalism, using the term now in its broadest sense. It is the tenacious loyalty to caste and community which tends to undermine the secular state at every turn. Communal loyalties easily lead to communal rivalries, and this tendency is greatly accentuated by an underdeveloped economy in which there is never enough of anything to go around.

495

Communal rivalries are endemic in India, and easily erupt into violent conflict.

The most urgent requirement in present-day India is the development at the state and local levels of government of both the *will* and the *means* to put down communal violence quickly and sternly. The fact is that communal agitators and irresponsible communally-motivated newspapers are apparently still able to indulge in their anti-social activities with impunity, despite the Preventive Detention Act, the Press Act, and the whole armory of other state powers. Let it be said plainly: the secular state will be reduced to a hollow mockery if the state cannot protect the life and property of the citizen, whether he be of a minority or the majority religion, from communal violence.

The prevention of communal violence is the negative function of the state in dealing with the problem of communalism. There is still no state responsibility so fundamental as the preservation of law and order. But the development in India of a truly secular state involves much more, the emotional integration of the nation by which the individual's consciousness of caste or community will be subordinated to his Indian citizenship. In this area also, unfortunately, government policies are not likely to achieve the desired results.

The greatest harm has been done by the attempts of both central and state governments to define economic, social, and educational need in terms of caste groups and to extend aid on that basis. Scholarships, economic aid, reserved posts in government, and reserved seats in colleges are extended not only to the Scheduled Castes and Tribes but to the hundreds of "Other Backward Classes." This approach has served only to perpetuate and accentuate caste consciousness and has resulted in grave injustices in the many cases in which there is no correlation between caste status and economic need.

The second major problem for the secular state is the extensive state interference in Hindu religious institutions. The close supervision or even outright administration of temples and *maths* was one of the traditional functions of the Hindu state. In independent India there is a clear trend for the state to revert to its former role in temple administration. The trend is justified by pointing to the need for reforms in financial administration which the state alone is equipped to bring about. The state has thus become the principal agency of Hindu religious reform. In present-day India there is a strong tendency for the state to do for Hinduism whatever it cannot do for itself because of organizational deficiencies.

In the case of temple administration, there is also a decided tendency for the state to become closely identified with Hinduism through state Hindu religious endowments departments. The distinction between the negative function of regulating temple administration to prevent abuses, which the government is empowered to perform, and the positive promotion of Hindu religion, is either not understood or ignored.

If the state deals with the religion of a minority, there are definite political checks which will tend to limit the extent of the interference. When Hindu legislators and administrators deal with their own religion, that of the majority, there are no such checks. State interference in Hindu temples has been limited somewhat by the judiciary's interpretation of article 26 of the Constitution, but it is still very extensive. What is almost totally lacking is the consideration that the concept of the secular state itself imposes certain definite limitations on the functions of government. Not everything that needs to be done should be done by the state.

With the submission of the report of the C.P. Ramaswami Aiyer commission, it is likely that official involvement in the reform of Hindu religious institutions will increase not only on the state level but possibly through other agencies created by central legislation. This trend constitutes an important problem for the secular state, one of the essential components of which is the separation of state and religion.

The third major problem is the position of religious personal law in the legal structure of present-day India. That a Hindu, a Muslim, and a Christian, all citizens of the same country, should be governed by different inheritance laws is an anachronism indeed in modern India and diametrically opposed to the fundamental principles of secularism. The Constitution declares that the state must strive for a uniform civil code, and important progress has been made by legislation unifying the Hindu law. In enacting this legislation the Indian Parliament took great liberties with the Hindu legal tradition by introducing provisions for divorce, inheritance by daughters, and other revolutionary ideas.

The seemingly innocuous directive principle that "the state shall endeavor to secure for the citizens a uniform civil code throughout the territory of India" is far-reaching in its implications. Paradoxically, the secular state, in order to establish its sovereignty and confirm its secularity, is required to undertake the most basic possible reform of religion. It is called upon by the Constitution to strip Hinduism and Islam of the socio-legal institutions which have distinguished them as total ways of life, to reduce these two great religious systems to their core of private faith, worship, and practice.

The modification of Hindu law, while painful to the orthodox, has been accepted; after all, the vast majority of the legislators were Hindus. But the next step must inevitably deal with the *shari'ah* in one way or another, and the sovereign Parliament must decide what to do with the Holy Law of the Muslim minority. The conception of the secular state both presupposes a uniform civil law, and requires that the religious beliefs of a minority be respected. Probably over 90 per cent of the Indian Muslims feel that their law is of the very essence of Islam. This is the dilemma which must one day be faced.

The fourth and last major problem facing the secular state is one of basic definition. What is the meaning of the term "secular state" in the Indian context? This might at first appear to be a point of academic significance only, but its practical implications are immediate and profound. The most basic question is simply whether the secular state means (1) a state which aids all religions impartially, or (2) a state which is separate from religion. If the latter, then the ideal will be for the state to aid no religion, to assume no religious functions.

This is an old and familiar problem in the United States, and the Supreme Court still vacillates between the "no-preference" doctrine and the "wall of separation" doctrine. The tax exemption granted to all religious institutions illustrates the first doctrine; the absolute prohibition of the appropriation of public funds to support religious institutions illustrates the second. The Constitution of India prohibits only special taxes for the support of "any particular religion" but would presumably permit a general tax for the support of all religions. This expression of the "no-preference" doctrine must be contrasted with the "wall of separation" prohibition of all forms of religious instruction in state schools.

In India there is a strong inclination to support the "no-preference" doctrine. It is in keeping with some of the traditions of the Hindu state and is closely allied to the neo-Hindu emphasis that all religions are true. There is a real danger that the "no-preference" doctrine may be used to justify state promotion of a syncretistic "Universal Religion of Man" which is nevertheless based on Hindu assumptions. This tendency was clearly revealed in the Radhakrishnan report on university education.

There is much at stake in the ultimate decision whether the secular state in India will be a non-sectarian state or a non-religious state. In *McCollum* v. *Board of Education* the United States Supreme Court interpreted separation of church and state as follows: "Separation is a requirement to abstain from fusing functions of government and of religious sects, not merely to treat them all equally. . . . Separation means separation, not something less." This interpretation is still a matter of debate in the United States, and other court decisions have taken the opposite view. The acceptance of this position and its application to India is not based on the "authority" of the American Supreme Court. But after considering in the preceding chapters all of the problems involved, my own conviction is that this interpretation of the secular state provides the clearest and the simplest answers to the questions which India must deal with.

Is India a Secular State?

We have considered both the strong points and the weaknesses of secularism in India, and must now come to some kind of general conclusion. It is well to remind ourselves that the *completely* secular state does not exist. Even the classic example, the United States, illustrates the reluctance to separate state and religion completely. Presidents and governors issue proclamations urging the citizens to attend their respective places of worship, sessions of federal and state legislatures are opened with prayer, Bible readings and the Lord's Prayer are still used in many tax-supported schools, and every coin bears the motto "In God we trust." While Indian secularism is deficient in several respects when judged by the American standard, in other respects (including all of the points mentioned above) the Indian practice is a closer approximation to the theory of the secular state.

Is India a secular state? My answer is a qualified "Yes." It is meaningful to speak of India as a secular state, despite the existence of the problems which have been discussed. India is a secular state in the same sense in which one can say that India is a democracy. Despite various undemocratic features of Indian politics and government, parliamentary democracy *is* functioning, and with considerable vigor. Similarly, the secular state; the ideal is clearly embodied in the Constitution, and it is being implemented in substantial measure. The question must be answered in terms of a dynamic state which has inherited some difficult problems and is struggling hard to overcome them along generally sound lines.

While there is room for cautious optimism, it would obviously be foolish to think that secularism is so firmly established in India that its future is assured. A war with Pakistan, the flare-up of widespread Hindu-Muslim riots, a more compromising attitude toward communalism on the part of Nehru's successor—any of these possible developments might strengthen the Hindu parties sufficiently to make their challenge to secularism a serious one, if combined with the break-up of the Congress monolith. Nor can we discount a possible upsurge of the latent communal sentiment within certain sections of the Congress itself. The forces of Hindu communalism are biding their time, and it is not unlikely that the future will bring circumstances more congenial to their growth. The secular state is one aspect of India's total democratic experiment, the success of which depends on continued stable leadership, steady progress in economic development, population control, and various other factors. There is obviously much that could go wrong.

The poor showing made by the Hindu communal parties, and the overwhelming success of the Congress in three general elections, cannot be interpreted as the deliberate espousal by the huge electorate of the principles of secularism. Many millions are still voting for the Congress as the party of Mahatma Gandhi, and as the late M. N. Roy wrote: "It is neither a philosopher nor a moralist who has become the idol of the Indian people. The masses pay their homage to a Mahatma—a source of revealed religion and agency of supernatural power."

It must be recognized that the de-emphasis of religion in public life necessitated by the adoption of a secular constitution has created a real problem; what is required is the development of a sense of loyalty to abstract ideals. The full force of this difficulty has not yet been felt, due to the deep personal devotion which the masses feel toward their prime minister. The Hindu communal parties affirm that "the misconceived notion of secular democracy cannot inspire the masses." The argument of this book is that the notion is well conceived and indeed vital to India's national development; but it cannot be denied that it lacks emotional appeal.

It is far too early to dismiss the possibility of a future Hindu State in India. However, it must be said that, on the basis of the evidence now before us, the possibility does not appear a strong one. The secular state has far more than an even chance of survival in India.

INDEX

Police Act, 222
Politiques, 13
polygamy, *see* monogamy
pongyis, 49-50. *See also* Sangha
Poona Pact, 303
Pothacamury, Thomas, ix, 207, 435, 437
Praja Socialist Party, ix, 286
Prasad, Rajendra, 143, 387, 397, 432
Prevention of Excommunication Act, 110-11
Prevention of Hindu Bigamous Marriage Act, 107-08, 115
Preventive Detention Act, 415, 417, 451, 496
princely states, 94; Mysore, 94-98, 109, 177; Travancore, 94, 96-98, 109, 130, 240-41, 298-99, 359, 365; Cochin, 96, 130, 298, 365; Surguja, 98, 178-79; Raigarh, 177-78; Patna, 178; Udaipur, 179-80; Kashmir, 298; Jaipur, 299
processions, religious, 222-23
propagation of religion; constitutional right to propagate, 102-03, 181-84; in educational institutions, 132-33, 342, 345-61; general Hindu attitude, 163-68; within Hinduism, 163-65; objections to conversion, 165-66, 168-69; Hindu universalist approach, 168-69; Hindu communalist position, 169-72; and *shuddhi* movement, 169-71; Indian Christian stand, 172-75; humanist liberal position, 175-76; anti-conversion laws, 177-81, 184-86; and Hindu personal law, 186-87; and maintenance of public order, 188-92. *See also* conscience clause, conversions, educational policy, missionaries, proselytization
proselytization, 23, 165, 201, 208, 210-11, 360
protective discrimination, 117, 125, 314
public order, 103-04; and propagation of religion, 174-75, 188-92; suppression of anti-social practices, 216-17; and *sati*, 217-19; and infanticide, 219; and *thagi*, 219; regulation of festivals, 219-23; and *devadasi* dedication, 238-39
Public Safety Act, 180-81
Public Trusts Act, 233, 255-57
Punjab disturbances, 8
Punjabi Suba agitation, x, 225, 446-53
Punyabhu, 459
Purcell, Victor, 42
purohita, 58-59, 94
Purushasukta, 293

Qiyas, 270

Radhakrishnan report, 150, 351-56, 499

Radhakrishnan, S., ix, 416; on the meaning of history, 26; on separate electorates, 93; on Hindu tolerance, 146-50; and University Education Commission, 150, 351; interpretation of caste, 296-97; on relation of religion and culture, 372-73; on relation of Buddhism to Hinduism, 390, 392. *See also* Radhakrishnan report
Radha Raman, 260
Radhaswami sect, 28
Radical Humanism, 157
Raghu Vira, Dr., 484
Rahman, Inam, 381
Rai Singh, 64
rajadharma, 61
Rajagopalachari, C.; on state promotion of religion, 151; on conversion, 165; on religious instruction, 349; rejection of universal religion, 354-55; on Rama as deity, 388; and Swatantra Party, 475-76
Rajagopalachari, V., 472
Rajamannar, P. V., 375-76
Rajamul Husain, 409
Rajgarh State Conversion Act, 177
Rama (Hindu deity), 31, 60, 354, 375, 388, 391, 464
Ramakrishna Mission, 28, 112, 382-83
Ramakrishna Mission Institute of Culture, 382-83
Ramanathan, Ponnambalam, 50
Rama Rao, A., 475
Ramaswami, D. V., 236
Ramaswami Aiyer, C. P., ix, 257, 259, 452
Ramaswamy Naicker, E. V., 157
Ramayana, 64, 373, 375, 388-89
Ram Gopal, 398, 417
Ramji Lal Modi v. *State of U.P.*, 190
Ram Rajya, 92, 433
Ram Rajya Parishad, 287, 289, 455, 464-65, 474-75, 486
Ram Singh, 462
Ramachandra Rao, D. S., 237
Rammohan Roy, 69, 217-18, 295, 337-38
Ramzan, 75
Ranade, M. G., 89
Ranchhoddas, R., 223
Rangaswami Aiyangar, K. V., 285
Rangila Rasul, 189
Ranjit Singh, 440
Rankin, George C., 271-72, 275
Rashtriya Swayamsevak Sangh (RSS), ix; on Hinduism and Indian nationalism, 172; on revival of Indian culture, 376-77; origin of, 454-57; organization of, 465-66; ideology of, 466-68; and fascism,